EXAMINATION OF WITNESSES
IN CRIMINAL CASES

SIXTH EDITION

EARL J. LEVY, Q.C.

CARSWELL®

ISBN 978-0-7798-3624-6

A cataloguing record for this publication is available from Library and Archives Canada.

Composition: Computer Composition of Canada Inc.

Printed in Canada by Thomson Reuters.

THOMSON REUTERS

CARSWELL, A DIVISION OF THOMSON REUTERS CANADA LIMITED

One Corporate Plaza	Customer Relations
2075 Kennedy Road	Toronto 1-416-609-3800
Toronto, Ontario	Elsewhere in Canada/U.S. 1-800-387-5164
M1T 3V4	Fax: 1-416-298-5082
	www.carswell.com
	E-mail www.carswell.com/email

To Michele,

my loving wife and

best friend,

and to my granddaughter Ella

who entered the world after my last dedication

to her brother Griffin.

Foreword

Our profession owes an enormous debt of gratitude to the many contributions which Earl Levy has made to the administration of criminal justice and the development of ethical and effective advocacy. However, none of these achievements has been greater than the labour of love which Mr. Levy has nurtured for almost 25 years.

Francis Wellman only managed four editions of his classic treatise, *The Art of Cross-Examination*. As Mr. Levy's text, *Examination of Witnesses in Criminal Cases* enters its 6th edition, it has not only become a Canadian classic, but it offers practical guidance and mentorship for counsel throughout the common law world.

Louis Nizer observed that "in cross-examination, as in fishing, nothing is more ungainly than a fisherman pulled into the water by his catch." Earl Levy, with patience and clarity, teaches us not only how to best ensure that the fish is irretrievably caught but also provides an invaluable guide to navigating the rapids and surviving the undercurrents.

The latest edition continues the tradition of ensuring a current and comprehensive analysis of the case law and its application to the myriad of practical challenges which both examiner and cross-examiner must meet. Charles Dickens said that "lawyers hold that there are two kinds of particularly bad witnesses: a reluctant witness and a too willing witness." Earl Levy expands that list of demanding witnesses and provides prudent and practical instruction as to the approach which may win the day yet is unfailing in his commitment to professionalism and civility

The text again meets the challenge of combining Mr. Levy's extensive experience as a defence counsel in criminal cases and the experiences of other counsel by the strategic use of actual proceedings to both illustrate his themes and to provide guidance to even the experienced practitioner.

As Justice Doherty observed in a previous foreword: "in advocacy, as in most things, experience is the best teacher. The experiences Mr. Levy assembles and shares with the reader provide a first rate education."

In his Introduction, Mr. Levy concedes that many great advocates "possess qualities which cannot really be taught in any book: common sense, good judgment and an understanding of human nature." Earl Levy has not only done a masterful job in providing comprehensive strategies to effectively examine virtually every class of witness, but he has done so in a manner which so clearly exhibits his common sense, his good judgment and his understanding of human nature.

Brian H. Greenspan
May 2011

Acknowledgments

This is the sixth edition of *Examination of Witnesses in Criminal Cases*, the first being published by Carswell in 1987. Any success this book has achieved is due to a number of individuals. They include those eminent members of the bench and bar who have taken the time to write the Forewords in each of the editions, those counsel who have contributed to its content and those who have written positive reviews.

I am also grateful to the members of the profession who promoted this work by word of mouth and to counsel both from the defence and Crown sides who have written or spoken to me personally about how these pages have helped them in their trial work. On one occasion this book received a high compliment from a surprising source which I must confess gave me a great sense of satisfaction and special feelings of confidence that *Examination of Witnesses in Criminal Cases* was proving to be a very helpful teaching aid. I refer to an article several years ago in one of the Toronto newspapers which noted that after a somewhat complicated fraud trial was concluded in Milton, Ontario, involving a number of accused who were represented by counsel, the trial Judge, after acquitting an unrepresented accused complimented him on his advocacy skills. The successful accused responded that his ability to represent himself was as a result of reading this work.

Finally, I wish to recognize my secretary of 40 years, Linda Barber, who has, with great patience, effort and skill, put up with my work habits, particularly with respect to this book.

Table of Contents

Table of Cases

Introduction

This book is not just about teaching the art of examining witnesses in criminal cases. It is also about strategy, insight and other practical considerations that are part of any criminal trial. Importantly, it includes a number of chapters devoted to evidentiary topics that often become issues in criminal cases. A good grasp of the evidentiary rules as well as the law that relates to the relevant criminal statutes will better enable counsel to determine at times which witnesses to call or not call to testify, what questions counsel will or will not ask or be able to ask of a witness, and when counsel can properly object to questions posed by an opponent, or respond to an objection by an opponent without being rebuffed by the trial Judge. In addition, such knowledge of the law can have an influence on counsel's trial throughout.

Also, there are some pretty good cartoons throughout.

I am keenly aware that books which have been written on advocacy have a defence-orientated view. This is not difficult to understand since these books most often have been written by defence counsel and the readership market is largely from the defence bar. Of course many techniques and some strategies written about apply equally for the prosecutors. I have, however, made an effort to keep the Crown attorneys in mind while writing this book. If I have failed to do the job adequately, it is no doubt due to the fact that I have never been a prosecutor and am not completely sensitive to that side of the courtroom. I have been encouraged however by the comments of a number of Crown attorneys who have found the book quite helpful.

My original idea was to pepper this book with transcripts of Canadian examples of examinations to illustrate the points I wanted to make. It soon became clear to me that this idea would be difficult to implement, although not impossible. Many fine counsel in this country, perhaps out of a sense of humility, do not tend to keep transcripts of their own or feel embarrassed to have their work advertised. A number of examples I have used had been reproduced earlier for teaching purposes and as a result were preserved. Other examples are ones that I was personally aware of and bothered counsel to dredge up for me, for which I am personally grateful. Some were taken from reported case, texts and papers including examples of examinations by some of the renowned English barristers of the past. Some examples are my own.

Another point struck me in reading a number of other advocacy books for my research. Frequently, lengthy examples of examinations which usually required some time to explain were included in these books. As a result, I found my own interest and attention fading at times and I was concerned about the same thing happening to readers of this book. For this reason, although there are some excellent lengthy examinations available from appeal transcripts by counsel in this country, they are not reproduced here (with a few exceptions).

There are some memorable examples of examinations available which I felt did not fall within the scope of this book. A well-done, entertaining examination or one displaying the ingenuity of the questioner can be quite different than a well-done examination reflecting an identifiable technique that can be taught. The former style, although enjoyable, cannot be taught and, if someone has that innate ability, he or she should use it for all that it is worth.

As far as tactics and the techniques of persuasion and strategy are concerned, a not inconsiderable amount of what I have written comes from decades of experience at the defence bar. However, I have no illusions regarding what this book can accomplish for anyone who is desirous of becoming a better counsel. It will not automatically turn anyone into a Charles Dubin, G. Arthur Martin, David Humphrey, Arthur Maloney or J.J. Robinette, who were the role models for many of us growing up doing criminal trial work in Ontario. Those who have walked the mountaintops of our profession across this country no doubt have done their fair share of reading about what others have had to say regarding advocacy, but they also possess qualities which cannot really be taught in any book: common sense, good judgment and an understanding of human nature.

While counsel can often make a good impression in obtaining an acquittal in a winnable case, they can most distinguish themselves in my view when they shine in a very difficult or losing case. I am mindful of a quote by Lee Gruenwald in the book *The Expert*, a quote I am certain that will resonate with experienced counsel. "Life in court isn't a matter of always holding good cards, but of playing a poor hand well. You don't get to be a brilliant and respected lawyer by trying only sure things."[1] I hope that my book helps counsel in "playing a poor hand well" because then I will feel confident that he or she will have developed into an accomplished advocate in the best traditions of the bar.

---

1 Penguin Books.

1

The Roles of Defence and Prosecution Counsel

The ethical behaviour of lawyers as advocates has to a large extent been defined by the various provincial codes of conduct as well as the Canadian Bar Association Code and by those who have written articles and texts on the subject. The role and duty of a defence advocate has been most succinctly expressed in the English case of *Rondel v. Worsley*[1] this way:

> Every counsel has a duty to his client fearlessly to raise every issue, advance every argument, and ask every question, however distasteful, which he thinks will help his client's case. As an officer of the court concerned in the administration of justice, he has an overriding duty to the court, to the standards of his profession, and to the public, which may and often does lead to a conflict with his client's wishes or with what the client thinks are his personal interests. Counsel must not mislead the court, he must not lend himself to casting aspersions on the other party or witnesses for which there is no sufficient basis in the information in his possession, he must not withhold authorities or documents which may tell against his client, but which the law or the standards of his profession require him to produce. By so acting he may well incur the displeasure or worse of his client so that if the case is lost, his client would or might seek legal redress if that were open to him.

Throughout this book there are examples which bring into focus the duties of the Crown and defence. Perhaps the most oft-quoted statement generally describing the role of the prosecutor is from Justice Rand in *R. v. Boucher*[2]:

---

1 [1967] 3 All E.R. 993 at 998 (U.K. H.L.), per Lord Reid. See also C.B.A. Code, Chapter ix, Commentary 1 and Ontario Rule 10, Commentary 2 which basically echo Lord Reid's pronouncement. See also *Tuckiar v. R.* (1934), 52 C.L.R. 335 (Aus. H.C.).

2 (1954), (sub nom. *Boucher v. R.*) [1955] S.C.R. 16 at 24 (S.C.C.).

Role of Defence Counsel

"He's a brilliant attorney, but he can't stand to lose a case."

The New Yorker Book of Lawyer Cartoons. New Yorker Magazine Eds. (Illus.). Alfred A. Knopf Inc., 1997. © 1993 by New Yorker Magazine, Inc.

"It cannot be over-emphasized that the *purpose of a criminal prosecution is not to obtain a conviction;* it is to lay before a jury what the Crown considers to be credible evidence relevant to what is alleged to be a crime. Counsel have a duty to see that all available legal proof of the facts is presented: it should be done firmly and pressed to its legitimate strength, *but it must also be done fairly. The role of prosecutor excludes any notion of winning or losing;* his function is a matter of public duty than which in civil life there can be none charged with greater personal responsibility. It is to be efficiently performed with an ingrained sense of the *dignity*, the seriousness and the justness of judicial proceedings."

In *Boucher*, Taschereau J. added the following comments which were cited with approval by Lamer C.J.C. in *R. v. Swietlinski*, [1994] 3 S.C.R. 481, 92 C.C.C. (3d) 449 (S.C.C.), at pp. 494–95 [S.C.R.]:

> "[TRANSLATION] *The position held by counsel for the Crown is not that of a lawyer in civil litigation.* His functions are quasi-judicial. His duty is not so much to obtain a conviction as to assist the judge and jury in ensuring that the fullest possible justice is done. His conduct before the court must always be characterized by *moderation and impartiality.* He will have properly performed his duty and will be beyond all reproach if, *eschewing any appeal to passion,* and *employing a dignified manner suited to his function, he presents the evidence to the jury without going beyond what it discloses."*

In *R. v. Chamandy* (1934), 61 C.C.C. 224 (Ont. C.A.) at 227, Ridell J. made it clear that a criminal prosecution is not a trial between individuals where the Crown is trying to convict and the accused endeavoring to be acquitted. It is an investigation that should be conducted without animus on the part of the prosecution, with the single view of determining the truth.

The above sentiment has been repeated in various codes of conduct across the country and in the Canadian Bar Association Code[3] which states that the prosecutor is not to seek a conviction, but to "present to the trial Court all available credible evidence relevant to the alleged crime" and make disclosure to the defence of all relevant facts and known witnesses, whether tending to show guilt or innocence.

Justice Rand's pronouncement in *R. v. Boucher*[4] does not mean that the Crown should not be a strong advocate. The Crown should "vigorously pursue a legitimate result to the best of its ability".[5] In this regard it is instructive to read the judgment by Esson J.A. in *R. v. Chambers* quoting the British Columbia Court of Appeal decision in *Moore-Stewart v. Law Society (British Columbia),*[6] summing up the duty of Crown counsel:

> He may prosecute with earnestness and vigor—indeed, he should do so. But, while he may strike hard blows, he is not at liberty to strike foul ones": Sir Robert Megarry, "A second Miscellany-at-Law" (Stevens, 1973, p. 36). The question whether any given blow was foul, or merely hard, is often one about

---

3 Chapter ix, Commentary 9; see also *Berger v. United States*, 55 S.Ct. 629 at 635 (1935), per Justice Sutherland; *Donnelly v. De Christoforo*, 416 U.S. 637 at 648-649 (1974), where Justice Douglas stated that the prosecutor's function is "not to tack as many skins of victims as possible to the wall" but to give those accused of crime a fair trial.

4 *Supra.*

5 *R. v. Fosty* (1991), (sub nom. *R. v. Gruenke*) 67 C.C.C. (3d) 289 (S.C.C.), per L'Heureux-Dubé J.

6 (1988), 54 D.L.R. (4th) 482 at 501 (B.C. C.A.).

which reasonable people can reasonably differ. The question arises in the context of an adversarial system of trial which expects of counsel that he will strike blows. The system will not work if appellate courts are too ready to find any given blow to have been foul.

It is also important to keep in mind that the question for us is not whether foul blows were dealt; it is whether in the end the right to a fair trial was unfairly prejudiced. In any trial of the length and complexity of this one, it is virtually certain that there will be some foul blows. The collective common sense of a jury is likely to be effective in identifying a foul blow as such and in discounting it. Furthermore, it must be kept in mind that questions or arguments which at first blush seem to have been foul blows may, when regard is had to context, be seen as innocuous or even apropriate.

The difference in the roles of the defence counsel and prosecutors has been explained by Justice White of the United States Supreme Court thusly:[7]

> Law enforcement officers have the obligtion to convict the guilty and to make sure they do not convict the innocent. They must be dedicated to making the criminal trial a procedure for the ascertainment of the true facts surrounding the commission of the crime . . . But defence counsel has no comparable obligation to ascertain or present the truth. Our system assigns to him a different mission. He must be and is interested in preventing the conviction of the innocent, but . . . we also insist that he defend his client whether he is innocent or guilty. The State has the obligation to present evidence. Defence counsel need present nothing, even if he knows what the truth is. He need not furnish any witnesses to the police, or reveal any confidences of his client, or furnish any other information to help the prosecution's case. If he can confuse a witness, even a truthful one, or make him appear at a disadvantage, unsure or indecisive, that will be his normal course. Our interest is not convicting the innocent permits counsel to put the State to its proof, to put the State's case in the worst possible light, regardless of what he thinks or knows to be the truth. Undoubt- edly there are some limits which defense counsel must observe but more often than not, defense counsel will examine a prosecution witness, and impeach him if he can, even if he thinks the witness is telling the truth, just as he will attempt to destroy a witness who is lying. In this repsect, as part of our modified adversary system, and as part of the duty imposed on the most honourable defense counsel, we countenance or require conduct which in many instances has little, if any, relation to the search for truth.

One cannot, in my opinion, argue with the legitimacy of the above views expressed by Justice White. They go to the very heart of our criminal

---

7   *U.S. v. Wade*, 388 U.S. 218 at 256-258 (U.S. Tex. 1967). In *Lawyers and Ethics, Professional Responsibility and Discipline* (Carswell), p. 6-17, the author, Gavin Mackenzie notes that the Crown and defence "play dramatically different roles in the process. One example of the difference is that although defence counsel may make witnesses look like they are testifying inaccurately or untruthfully when they know they are not, prosecutors may not do so."

justice system. It follows that it is not totally correct to say, as is so often quoted, that a trial is a "search for the truth". In reality a trial is more a search for proof than truth, at least from the defence perspective, otherwise adverse comments could be made if the accused did not testify on his/her behalf and there would not be a *Charter of Rights and Freedoms* with exclusionary rules.

How far then can counsel go in discrediting an opposing witness or the opponent's case having been advised by the client that he or she is guilty? Professor Monroe Freedman offers an interesting viewpoint:[8]

Searching For The Truth

"We find the defendant guilty, his lawyer tricky, the expert witnesses arrogant and dogmatic, the judge out of touch with reality and the whole system slanted toward flashy, clever argumentation rather than finding the truth."

National Law Journal. © New York Law Publishing Co.

---

8 M. Freedman, "Professional Responsibility of the Criminal Defence Lawyer. The Three Hardest Questions", 64 Mich.L.Rev. 1469 at 1474-1475 (1966).

The same policy that supports the obligation of confidentiality precludes the attorney from prejudicing his client's interest in any other way because of knowledge gained in his professional capacity. When a lawyer fails to cross-examine only because his client, placing confidence in his lawyer, has been candid with him, the basis for such confidence and candor collapses. Our legal system cannot tolerate such a result. . . . The client's confidences must "upon all occasions be inviolable," to afford the "greater mischiefs" that would probably result if a client could not feel free to "repose [confidence] in the attorney to whom he resorts for legal advice and assistance." Destroy that confidence, and "a man would not venture to consult any skillful person, or would only dare to tell his counsel half his case."

The C.B.A. Code and the Ontario rule[9] state that an admission of guilt "may impose strict limitations on the conduct of the defence" and "will impose a limit upon the extent to which the lawyer may attack the evidence for the prosecution." In this regard the commentary to the Ontario rule states that counsel cannot set up an affirmative case inconsistent with the client's guilty admission, such as calling an alibi to show the witness had not committed the offence. It also seems safe to opine that while a witness could be cross-examined as to the accuracy of an eye witness identification, by stressing such areas as vantage point, time, ability to see, state of mind, etc., counsel could not go further and suggest that another was responsible for the crime instead or that the witness is mistaken.[10] Counsel may suggest alternative explanations even when they know the prosecution's evidence is true.[11]

See Chapter, "Further Limitations and Obligations in Examining Witnesses" for examples that relate to the Roles of Defence and Crown Counsel.

CIVILITY

It seems that much has been written and said more recently about civility in the courtroom — or is it more accurate to say the lack of civility? Counsel should not only be civil to the trial judge but be civil with his or her fellow counsel on the opposite side and with witnesses. Civility has been defined "as a range of behaviours including courtesy, dignity, acting in good faith and respect." Civility does not mean that as an advocate for your client's defence that you should be fawning before the trial Judge, solicitous or overly nice to your opponent or witness. Those who lack civility in the courtroom misinterpret what "adversarial" means in the lexicon of

---

9   Chapter ix, Commentary 11; Ontario rule 10, Commentary 11.
10 See comment by Joseph Sedgwick (1969) L.S.U.C. Lectures 319.
11 Harry I. Subins, "The Criminal Lawyer's Different Mission on the Right to Present a False Case," (1987-88) Georgetown Journal of Legal Ethics.

our justice system. One can be adversarial without being overly combative, rude and annoying.

The criminal courtroom is a place of very serious business where an individual's liberty is often at stake. It is a place that demands respect. The respect that counsel show for each other, the trial judge and witnesses translates into respect for our justice system and impacts positively on the public opinion as to the workings of our court; not so when there is a lack of civility.[12] We are officers of the Court.

Counsel who have earned the reputation of being less than civil gain an unfavourable reputation amongst trial judges and the bar. This kind of reputation can spread even beyond the legal profession. No reasonable client wants an advocate who is known for his or her lack of professionalism.

12 See *R. v. Felderhoff* (2003), 180 C.C.C. (3d) 498 (Ont. C.A.).

2

Crown Disclosure

R. v. Stinchcombe

The Supreme Court of Canada's decision in *R. v. Stinchcombe*[1] has had a significant effect on the disclosure required to be given by the Crown to the defence. As a result, defence counsel will have a greater insight into the case against an accused client than ever before and will have a solid foundation for preparing their examinations of witnesses. In addition, counsel's approach to the conduct of the defence will change in certain respects; for example, if counsel is satisfied that the disclosure is accurate he/she may wish to hear from fewer witnesses at the preliminary hearing stage. When a witness had not refreshed his/her memory from their statement before testifying at the preliminary hearing, it was held that a judge at that stage did not have the power to order production of that statement,[2] but with full disclosure now being required, which could include photocopies of the police officer's notebooks, this scenario should rarely, if ever, present itself.

As a result of the decision in *Stinchcombe* the Crown has an ongoing duty to make timely disclosure of all relevant material in its possession or control, unless the information is clearly irrelevant, is privileged, or protected by a Court order or statutory provision that it not be disclosed. The duty to disclose includes material which may only have marginal relevance.[3] Relevant information is that which could reasonably be used by the defence in meeting the case for the Crown, advancing a defence, or otherwise helping to make a decision which may affect the conduct of the defence, as for example, deciding whether to call evidence or conduct further investiga-

---

1 [1991] 3 S.C.R. 326.
2 *Patterson v. R.* (1970), 2 C.C.C. (2d) 227 (S.C.C.); *Cohen v. R.* (1976), 32 C.C.C. (2d) 446 (Que. C.A.). At trial, it was held in *R. v. Savion* (1980), 52 C.C.C. (2d) 276 (Ont. C.A.), that the trial judge had a discretion to order disclosure of statements to ensure full answer and defence. See also *R. v. Dorion* (1985), 19 C.C.C. (3d) 350 at 363 (N.S. C.A.).
3 *R. v. McCormack*, 2009 CarswellOnt 7019 (Ont. S.C.J.).

tion;[4] or is relevant to sentence. Because relevance may be elusive as circumstances change there will be times when the Crown may not be aware of the defence that may be raised, the Crown should err on the side of inclusion unless the information is clearly irrelevant.[5] The Crown is obligated to disclose any information in its possession that is relevant to the credibility or reliability of any proposed witness;[6] for example, any inconsistent statements or recantations, particulars relating to any promise of immunity or assistance to a witness with respect to a pending charge, bail or sentence or any other benefit etc., and any information relating to any mental disorder the witness suffers from that impacts on the reliability of the witness testimony.[7]

The materials are in possession of the Crown when it is in physical possession of that material as well as those materials collected or gathered by a police agency in the course of an investigation and are in physical possession of that police agency.[8]

Following *Stinchcombe*, the Attorney General of Ontario convened a Committee, chaired by the Honourable G. Arthur Martin, with committee members representing the defence bar, Crown Attorneys, Crown Law Office and police forces. This Committee produced a 523-page report with respect to charge screening, disclosure and resolution discussions[9] and concluded amongst other things, that the *Stinchcombe* case is authority for the following propositions:

1. The fruits of the investigation which are in the possession of the Crown are not the property of the Crown for use in securing a conviction, but, rather, are the property of the public to ensure that justice is done.

2. The general principle is that all relevant information must be disclosed, whether or not the Crown intends to introduce it in evidence. The Crown must disclose all relevant information, whether it is inculpatory or exculpatory, and must produce all information which may assist the accused. If the information is of no use, then it is irrelevant and will be excluded by Crown counsel in the exercise of the Crown's discretion, which is reviewable by the trial judge. The Court does not have the power to order disclosure at the preliminary hearing stage. See *R. v.*

---

4   *R. v. McQuaid* (1998), (sub nom. *R. v. Dixon*), [1998] 1 S.C.R. 244 (S.C.C.) at para. 23; *R. v. Egger*, [1993] 2 S.C.R. 451 (S.C.C.).

5   *R. v. Chaplin* (1994), 96 C.C.C. (3d) 225 (S.C.C.); *R. v. Dixon, supra*, at para. 21.

6   *R. v. T. (L.A.)* (1993), 84 C.C.C. (3d) 90 (Ont. C.A.) at 94.

7   See *R. v. Hawke* re mental illness affecting competency (1975), 7 O.R. (2d) 145 (C.A.).

8   *R. v. T. (L.A.), supra*, at 94; *R. v. Styles* (2003), 2003 CarswellOnt 6647 (Ont. S.C.J.) at para. 14; *R. v. Arsenault* (1994), 93 C.C.C. (3d) 111 (N.B. C.A.).

9   See Report of the Attorney General's Advisory Committee on Charge Screening, Disclosure and Resolution Discussions, published by the Ontario Ministry of the Attorney General, 1993.

Hynes (2001), [2001] S.C.J. No. 80, 2001 CarswellNfld 316, 2001 CarswellNfld 317 (S.C.C.).

3. Apart from practical advantages, the overriding concern is that failure to disclose impedes the ability to make full answer and defence, which is now enshrined in s. 7 of the Charter. In order to show that the failure to make proper disclosure amounted to a denial of full answer and defence the accused will have to show that there was a reasonable possibility such failure affected the outcome of the trial or the overall fairness of the trial. If that occurs, an even otherwise valid guilty plea can be withdrawn, where the failure to disclose affected the accused's decision to admit guilt.[10]

4. All statements obtained from persons who have provided relevant information to the authorities should be produced even though the Crown does not propose to call them. When statements are not in existence, other information, such as investigator's notes, must be produced; if there are no notes, then, in addition to the name, address, and occupation of the witness, all information in the possession of the prosecution, relating to any relevant evidence that the person could give, should be disclosed.

5. Crown counsel has a discretion, reviewable by the trial judge, with respect to the relevance of information. Although the Crown must err on the side of inclusion, it need not produce what is clearly irrelevant.

6. Crown counsel has a discretion, reviewable by the trial judge, to delay production of information in order to protect the identity of informers, the safety of witnesses of persons who have supplied information to the authorities, or to protect those persons from harassment. The Crown also has a discretion to delay disclosure in order to complete an investigation, but delays in disclosure on this ground should be rare. The absolute withholding of evidence relevant to the defence can only be justified, however, on the basis of the existence of a legal privilege which excludes the evidence from disclosure.[11]

7. The trial judge, on a review, should be guided by the principle that

---

10 See *R. v. Taillefer* (2003), 179 C.C.C. (3d) 353 (S.C.C.).

11 See also *R. v. Leipert*, [1997] 1 S.C.R. 281, and *Re Application to proceed in camera* (*sub nom. Named Person v. Vancouver Sun*) (2007), 224 C.C.C. (3d) 1 (S.C.C.) re evidence that would tend to disclose the identity of a confidential informant; see *R. v. Lam* (2000), 148 C.C.C. (3d) 379 (B.C. C.A.); *R. v. Blair*, 2000 CarswellOnt 2924 (C.A.) re observation posts; *R. v. Meuckon* (1990), 57 C.C.C. (3d) 193 (B.C. C.A.) and section 38, *Canada Evidence Act* re matters affecting national security, matters affecting defence or international relations; for safety of witnesses see *Stinchcombe, supra*, at para 22; also *R. v. Newsome* (1996), 199 A.R. 309 (Alta. Q.B.); *R. v. Richards* (1997), 115 C.C.C. (3d) 377, (Ont. C.A.); *R. v. Antinello* (1995), 97 C.C.C. (3d) 126, (Alta. C.A.); *R. c. Bernier*, (*sub nom. R. v. Bernier*) 229 C.C.C. (3d) 364 (Que. C.A.), leave to appeal refused [2008] 1 S.C.R. vi (note).

information ought not to be withheld if there is a reasonable possibility[12] that the withholding of information will impair the accused's right to make full answer and defence, unless the non-disclosure is justified by the law of privilege. The trial judge, in some circumstances, may conclude that the existing law of privilege does not constitute a reasonable limit on the accused's right to make full answer and defence, and, thus, require disclosure in spite of the law of privilege.

8. The denial of disclosure cannot be justified on the ground that the material disclosed will enable the defence to tailor its evidence, for example, to conform with a prior statement to the police. There is nothing wrong with a witness refreshing his or her memory from a previous statement. The witness may even change his or her evidence as a result. The cross-examiner may be deprived of a substantial advantage, but fairness to the witness may require that a trap not be laid, by allowing the witness to testify without the benefit of seeing contradictory writings. The principle has been accepted that the search for truth is advanced rather than retarded by disclosure of all relevant material.

9. The obligation of the Crown to make disclosure where an accused is represented by counsel is triggered by a request by or on behalf of the accused.

10. In the rare case in which the accused is unrepresented by counsel, Crown counsel should advise the accused of his or her right to disclosure, and a plea should not be taken unless the trial judge is satisfied that this has been done.

11. Disclosure should be made before the accused is called upon to elect the mode of trial or to plead. These are crucial decisions which the accused must make, which may affect his or her rights, and it will be of great assistance to know, before making these decisions, the strengths and weaknesses of the Crown's case. Provided the request for disclosure has been timely, it should be complied with so as to enable the accused, before plea or election, to consider the information disclosed.[13]

12. The Crown's obligation to disclose is a continuing one, and disclosure must be made with respect to additional information when it is received.

13. Disputes over disclosure will arise infrequently when it is made clear that Crown counsel is under a general duty to disclose *all* relevant information. The tradition in Canada of Crown counsel in carrying out their role as ministers of justice has generally been very high. Having regard to this fact, and to the obligation on defence counsel as officers of the Court to act responsibly, disputes with respect to disclosure will

---

12 See *R. v. Taillefer* (2003), 179 C.C.C. (3d) 353 (S.C.C.).

13 In *R. v. Girimonte* (1997), 121 C.C.C. (3d) 33 (Ont. C.A.) the Court held that the accused will not be called upon to elect or to plead if he/she has not received sufficient disclosure to make an informed decision.

usually be resolved without the intervention of the trial judge. But, when they cannot be resolved by counsel, the trial judge must resolve them. At trial, a *voir dire* can be a useful method of exploring and resolving outstanding disclosure issues.

14. Defence counsel has a duty to bring any non-disclosure to the attention of the trial judge as soon as he or she becomes aware of it.[14]

15. The administration of justice will also benefit from early disclosure. There is compelling evidence that much time would be saved, and delays reduced by reason of guilty pleas, withdrawal of charges, and the shortening or waiver of preliminary hearings, by early disclosure.

The Commission on Proceedings Involving Guy Paul Morin (wrongfully convicted of murder) made recommendations with respect to in-custody informers. See Chapter, "Jailhouse Informants and Analogous Witnesses" for details.

Crown's Continuing Disclosure Obligation

Initial disclosure should be provided before the client has to elect mode of trial or enter his plea but new information must be disclosed when it has been received.[15] When the Crown is aware of new information it should be provided to the defence in sufficient time to prepare cross-examination and to arrange to call any conflicting evidence that is available. Without more, disclosure alone will not necessarily make the evidence inadmissible.[16] This is so where the accused is unable to show that the delay of disclosure was prejudicial to making full answer and defence[17] or where circumstances changed during trial.[18] The Crown's obligation to disclose however can depend on the circumstances, such as when it arises during the trial.[19]

For the Crown to say the police have failed to provide relevant disclosure is no excuse.[20] Any improper delay in providing disclosure will count against the Crown, whether delay is inadvertent or deliberate.[21]

The Crown is, however, entitled to withhold disclosure where it is for the purpose of protecting informer privilege, public interest immunity or

---

14 See *R. v. O'Connor* (1994), 89 C.C.C. (3d) 109 (B.C. C.A.). See also *R. v. McQuaid* (1998), (sub nom. *R. v. Dixon*), [1998] 1 S.C.R. 244 (S.C.C.).

15 *R. v. tinchcombe, supra*, at para. 28; *R. v. Girimonte, supra*, at 42.

16 *R. v. Buric* (1996), 106 C.C.C. (3d) 97 (Ont. C.A.), affirmed [1997] 1 S.C.R. 535.

17 *R. v. Crumly* (1995), 58 B.C.A.C. 289 (C.A.).

18 *R. v. Wilson* (1994), 87 C.C.C. (3d) 115 (Ont. C.A.); *R. v. Horan* (2008), 237 C.C.C. (3d) 514 (Ont. C.A.) at para 26.

19 *R. v. Crumly, supra.*

20 *R. v. V. (W.J.)* (1992), 72 C.C.C. (3d) 97 (Nfld. C.A.) at para. 78.

21 *R. v. Girimonte* (1997), 121 C.C.C. (3d) 33 (Ont. C.A.) at para. 42.

falls within section 37 of the *Canada Evidence Act*.[22] Also the Crown may withhold disclosure where privacy interest concerns or legislation that mandate the proper procedures are to be followed.[23]

Disclosure may be delayed to protect security of individuals when relevant to protect them from injury or harassment;[24] but disclosure eventually is to be made in time for the accused to properly defend the charges he or she faces.[25]

The Crown is obligated to disclose any new relevant information during the appeal process[26] and beyond.[27]

McNeil Disclosure

The practice memo, [2009] No. 1 from the Ontario Ministry of the Attorney-General, Criminal Law Division, is helpful in not only dissecting the Supreme Court's decision in *R. v. McNeil*[28] relating to the disclosure by the Crown of police misconduct evidence but is a heads-up as to how the Ontario Crowns will respond to a defence request for the aforementioned disclosure. It would not be surprising if the reaction by Crowns across the country would be somewhat similar. The following part of the above-mentioned Crown practice memo which relates to the *McNeil* disclosure is reproduced here without objection from the Ontario Ministry of the Attorney-General.

(A) Disclosure of Police Misconduct Materials

In *Attorney General of Ontario (3ʳᵈ Party Record Holder) v. McNeil*, [2009] S.C.J. No. 3, the Supreme Court of Canada discussed disclosure obligations with respect to files relating to police misconduct.

The *McNeil* decision imposes an obligation on the police to provide to the Crown two types of information: (a) findings or allegations of police misconduct that relate to the subject-matter of the offence for which the accused is charged; and (b) findings/allegations of serious misconduct that could reasonably bear on the case against the accused.

---

22 *R. v. Stinchcombe, supra,* at 339; *R. v. Chaplin* (1994), 96 C.C.C. (3d) 225 (S.C.C.) at para. 21; *R. v. Egger,* [1993] 2 S.C.R. 451, at para. 19.

23 For example, third party records pursuant to section 278 of the *Criminal Code* or *R. v. O'Connor* (1995), [1995] 4 S.C.R. 411.

24 *Stinchcombe, supra,* at para. 16.

25 *R. v. Valdirez-Ahumada,* 1992 CarswellBC 1507 (B.C. S.C.).

26 *R. v. Grant* (2002), 170 C.C.C. (3d) 222 (Ont. C.A.).

27 *R. v. Trotta* (2004), 23 C.R. (6th) 261 (Ont. C.A.).

28 (2009), 238 C.C.C. (3d) 353 (S.C.C.). See paras. 13, 35, 39, 42, 49, 53, 56, 59.

(B) The Stinchcombe (or First Party) Disclosure Package

In *R. v. Stinchcombe*, [1991] 3 S.C.R. 326, the Court held that the Crown's obligation at trial is to make timely disclosure to an accused of all relevant information in the Crown's possession. In the trial context, relevant information refers to any information that there is a reasonable possibility it may assist the accused in any aspect of the exercise of the right to make full answer and defence.

Records pertaining to findings or allegations of police misconduct that relate to the subject-matter of the offence are so interrelated to the investigation of the accused as to be properly considered part of the fruits of the investigations against the accused. Therefore, this material should be disclosed as part of the main *Stinchcombe* disclosure package, whether or not the misconduct (actual or alleged) is "serious" in nature.

(C) The McNeil Package

The second type of records, serious police misconduct that is not related to the incident, was previously dealt with by way of *O'Connor* applications for third party records. However, the Supreme Court of Canada in *McNeil* has determined that these records should be reviewed by the Crown to determine if there is any material that could reasonably impact the case against the accused. The Supreme Court speaks of the disclosure of these records as being required to bridge the gap between disclosure and *O'Connor* applications. This disclosure is not intended to provide defence counsel with all of the information he or she might need to raise the misconduct at trial, but rather, Crown counsel should provide enough information so that the defence can either raise the issue at trial or make an informed decision as to whether to bring an *O'Connor* application to obtain the rest of the records.

Information regarding findings or allegations of serious police misconduct that do not relate to the incident at hand provided by the police in a separate, sealed *McNeil* package, should be reviewed by Crown counsel to see if there is information there that could reasonably impact the case against the accused.

(i) Contents

The police should provide to the Crown the following records in a sealed package:

(a) Any convictions or findings of guilt under *the Canadian Criminal Code* or *Controlled Drugs and Substances Act*;[29]
(b) Any outstanding charges under the *Criminal Code* or the *Controlled Drugs and Substances Act*;
(c) Any conviction or finding of guilt under any other federal or provincial statutes;[30]
(d) Any finding of guilt for misconduct after a hearing under the *Police Services Act* or its predecessor Act;
(e) Any current charge of misconduct under the *Police Services Act* for which a Notice of Hearing has been issued.

The package should contain the date of the conviction or allegation, the charge, and any findings. In addition, a synopsis should be enclosed, or if a synopsis does not exist, a brief description of the offence should be provided.

The *McNeil* package will not include records of misconduct that do not come within one of these five types of misconduct. For example, misconduct findings exclusive to the employer-employee relationship, such as finding pertaining to trade union activities; political activities; improper dress; and leaving work without an excuse will not be part of any package provided to the Crown.

(ii)   Screening the *McNeil* Package

Crown counsel must review these *McNeil* materials but recognize that the standard of relevance at this stage is the *Stinchcombe* standard ("likely relevant" or to state in the negative "not clearly irrelevant"). This analysis is two-fold as the Crown should look to the role the officer played with respect to the current case before the Court and the nature of the misconduct, and then determine whether the nature of the misconduct is relevant in light of the role the officer played. For example, if the officer did *not* handle exhibits or deal with an accused and his/her role was limited to crowd control in the current matter, what relevance exists in relation to a prior finding of misconduct ten years ago?

Crown counsel should consider any submissions provided in writing from the subject police officer in relation to the disclosure of the documents.

---

29   The police are not required to disclose: findings of guilt for which a pardon has been granted; findings of guilt that have resulted in an absolute or conditional discharge, where the requirements of section 6(1) of the *Criminal Record Act* have been met (more than one year has elapsed since the offender was discharged absolutely; or more than three years have elapsed since the offender was discharged on the conditions prescribed in a probation order). Youth records should be dealt with in accordance with the records provisions of the *Youth Criminal Justice Act*.

30   As per the Ferguson report and approved of in *McNeil*.

However, the decision about whether or not the law requires the disclosure of the information rests with the Crown.[31]

(iii) Disclosing the *McNeil* Package

After vetting about identifiers etc., Crown counsel should provide to the defence materials deemed to be likely relevant. Crown counsel should disclose these materials, only to the defence counsel, in a sealed envelope. There should be an accompanying notice to defence counsel setting out that there is an implied undertaking in the acceptance of the package that the materials are only for use with respect to the current matter before the Court and are not to be provided to anyone else or used for any other purpose. The letter should also advise defence counsel of any limitation on the gathering, by the police service, of *McNeil* package materials, such as no search for POA convictions or no records kept before 1998, etc. A draft notice setting out the implied undertaking and other suggested conditions is attached as an Appendix to this memorandum, and may be reproduced or modified for use as necessary.

Unrepresented accused should not be provided with a copy of the *McNeil* package and will instead have to review the materials on-site in the Crown Attorney Office. Accused persons should not be permitted to photocopy or take away any portion of these records.[32]

A copy of the cover letter, outlining exactly what *McNeil* materials were disclosed to the defence, will be forwarded to the officer who compiled the original *McNeil* package in accordance with local disclosure protocols arranged between the Crown Attorney Office and the local police service. This will enable the compiling officer to advise any officer impacted by this disclosure, and will enable the police to track what has been disclosed in relation to each case an officer is involved in, if so desired.

(iv) Duty to inquire

Crown counsel have a duty to inquire/seek out more information beyond that which is included in the *McNeil* and *Stinchcombe* packages when they are put on notice of the existence of relevant information and where it is reasonably feasible to do so.

---

31 Any such admissions from the police are not subject to disclosure; they are privileged, and should be retained with the Crown copy of the *McNeil* package.
32 Such a practice conforms to the Martin Report.

(v)   When *McNeil* Materials should go in first party *Stinchcombe* disclosure package

When reviewing the *McNeil* package, Crown counsel should bear in mind that there may be records pertaining to findings of serious misconduct that reach a level of relevance such that they would be properly part of the Crown's first party disclosure obligations and for which the Crown may be required to inquire into and provide the underlying materials. Examples include previous findings related to perjury or to drug offences where the investigation relates to drugs.

However, most of the material in the *McNeil* package that relates to serious police misconduct will be material that the Crown needs only to review to determine whether it is relevant for the purpose of facilitating an *O'Connor* style, third party records application.

(vi)   *McNeil* materials that are NOT disclosed

Materials that are not disclosed are to be retained in a sealed envelope within the Crown copy of the brief. Given the ongoing disclosure obligation of the Crown, Crown counsel should maintain an on-going awareness of the issues within the trial, and whether relevance is triggered at a later date within the process. At any time Crown counsel makes any further disclosure of these materials, he or she should include a *McNeil* cover letter, and should provide the compiling officer with a copy of the cover letter.

Burden of Proof

The onus shifts on the basis of whether the material that is subject to the disclosure request is inside the police investigative file or outside the investigative file. If inside, it is presumptively relevant and the onus is on the Crown to justify non disclosure if outside, the onus shifts to the defence to establish a basis for believing that the disclosure requested exists and is relevant.[33]

Remedies

In *R. v. O'Connor*[34] the British Columbia Court of Appeal held that although it is not only desirable that orders relating to disclosure be made

---

33 *R. v. Chaplin* (1994), 96 C.C.C. (3d) 225 (S.C.C.); *R. v. Girimonte* (1997), 121 C.C.C. (3d) 33 (Ont. C.A.).

34 (1994), 89 C.C.C. (3d) 109 (B.C. C.A.). See also *R. v. McQuaid* (1998), (sub nom. *R. v. Dixon*), [1998] 1 S.C.R. 244 (S.C.C.).

by the trial Judge, some rulings are necessary before a trial Judge is appointed and there is no impediment for a Judge other than a trial Judge to make such a pre-trial disclosure order when the necessity arises. There is no appeal under the *Criminal Code* from a pre-trial disclosure order. Even if the Crown has legitimate concerns about a pre-trial disclosure order, he or she is bound by that order until it is varied by a Judge.

Where the existence of the material is disputed by the Crown and the Crown has alleged it has fulfilled its obligation to disclose it cannot be required to justify the non-disclosure of material, the existence of which it is unaware or denies. The defence must then establish a "basis" which could allow a Judge to conclude there is further material "which is potentially relevant in making full answer and defence. The defence may establish "a basis" by oral submissions" without the necessity of a *voir dire*. But where the Judge cannot resolve the matter on the basis of submissions by counsel, *viva voce* evidence and a *voir dire* may be required.[35]

"In situations where the existence of certain information has been identified then the Crown must justify non-disclosure by demonstrating either that the information sought is beyond its control or that it is clearly irrelevant or prejudicial. The trial Judge must afford the Crown an opportunity to call evidence to justify such allegation of non-disclosure." See also *Stinchcombe* at p. 341.

(A) *Late Disclosure*

When Crown disclosure is late thereby constituting a violation of the accused's *Charter* rights, a stay of proceedings was held on appeal to be inappropriate where the trial Judge could have granted an adjournment of sufficient length to permit the defence to review the late disclosure.[36] Not only is there cause for an adjournment but it may be appropriate to request that a previously examined witness be recalled to cross-examine that witness on the new evidence.[37]

In *R. v. T. (L.A.)*,[38] where there was late disclosure of a key witness's statement, it was held that a mistrial should have been declared as it could

---

35 *R. v. Chaplin, supra; R. v. Dixon, supra.*

36 *R. v. Douglas* (1991), 5 O.R. (3d) 29 (C.A.), affirmed (1993), [1993] 1 S.C.R. 893. See *R. v. Caccamo* (1975, 29 C.R.N.S. 78 (S.C.C.); *R. v. Rowbotham (No. 2)* (1977), 2 C.R. (3d) 222 (Ont. Co. Ct.), affirmed (1977), 2 C.R. (3d) 222 at 236 (Ont. H.C.).

37 *R. v. Pizzardi* (1994), 17 O.R. (3d) 623 (C.A.), affirmed [1994] 3 S.C.R. 1018.

38 (1993), 84 C.C.C. (3d) 90, 14 O.R. (3d) 378 (Ont. C.A.). In *R. v. Johnson* (1994), 89 C.C.C. (3d) 90 (B.C. C.A.), it was held that failure to make proper disclosure before electing the mode of trial could be remedied by the Crown agreeing to re-election. See also *R. v. Denbigh* (1990), 4 C.R.R. (2d) 141 (B.C. S.C.); See also *R. v. Bailey (No. 2)* (July 13, 1990), Doc. Vancouver CC890780 (B.C. S.C.), summarized at 10 W.C.B. (2d) 192.

not be said "with certainty that the appellant was not prejudiced." In this case, it was the defence's position that if it had received timely disclosure it might not have re-elected to be tried by Judge alone, the accused's decision to testify may have been affected and counsel would have conducted the cross-examination of the two material Crown witnesses differently. However, there can be situations where late disclosure could lead to a stay of proceedings such as late disclosure of evidence which could exculpate the accused.[39]

Where there is late disclosure by the Crown the remedy may be an adjournment or a mistrial depending on the circumstances. The accused need only show on a balance of probabilities that a realistic opportunity to garner evidence or make decisions about the defence was lost.[40]

In *R. v. Armitage*,[41] a witness was called by the Crown at the preliminary hearing but not the trial. This witness was called by the defence at trial and cross-examined by the Crown on a prior inconsistent statement which the Crown had not disclosed to the defence. A mistrial was declared because it was likely the defence would not have called the witness if it had known of this prior inconsistent statement.

In *R. v. O'Connor*,[42] it was held that a violation of the accused's right to disclosure under section 7 of the *Charter* will be made only where it has had an adverse effect on his or her right to make full answer and defence. This entails a material non-disclosure and the Court must make an enquiry into this aspect. There would not be a permanent or irremediable damage to the accused's right to full answer and defence if that right was protected by an appropriate adjournment, by recalling the witnesses who had already testified for further cross-examination if this was necessary or by declaring a mistrial if the former two remedies were not sufficient. The evidence must disclose more than a mere risk to the right to make full answer and defence.[43]

The Crown cannot refuse to provide the accused with copies of videotapes unless paid for by the defence. Providing adequate opportunity for

---

39   *R. v. Denbigh, ibid.*

40   *R. v. Antinello* (1995), 97 C.C.C. (3d) 126 (Alta. C.A.); *R. v. Dixon, supra*. The Court in *Dixon* discusses what remedies are available under section 24(1) of the *Charter of Rights and Freedoms* after there has been an impairment to full answer and defence.

41   (February 12, 1988), Hutchison Co. Ct. J. (B.C. Prov. Ct.), summarized at 6 W.C.B. (2d) 137. It is no argument for the Crown to support non-disclosure by claiming it would lose the tactical advantage of surprising defence witnesses on cross-examination. See *R. v. Parks* (1988), 33 C.R.R. 1 (Ont. H.C.). See also *R. v. Barembruch* (1997), 119 C.C.C. (3d) 185 (B.C. C.A.); *R. v. Creamer* (1995), 97 C.C.C. (3d) 108 (B.C. C.A.).

42   (1994), 89 C.C.C. (3d) 109 (B.C. C.A.). See also *R. v. Johnson* (1994), 93 C.C.C. (3d) 211 (Nfld. C.A.).

43   *R. v. Carosella* (1995), 26 O.R. (3d) 209 (Ont. C.A.). See also *R. v. Pizzardi* (1994) (C.A.), affirmed [1994] 3 S.C.R. 1018 (S.C.C.).

counsel and client to view the tapes does not fulfil the Crown's disclosure obligation.[44]

Failure to disclose can result in costs being awarded against the Crown where such failure results in a denial of full answer and defence. *R. v. Logan* (2002), 59 O.R. (3d) 575 (Ont. C.A.). See also *R. v. Robinson* (1999), 142 C.C.C. (3d) 303 (Alta. C.A.).

A stay of proceedings would only be granted in exceptional cases where the accused's right to make full answer and defence cannot be remedied or where irreparable prejudice could be caused to the integrity of the judicial system if the prosecution were continued.[45]

(B) Lost or Destroyed Disclosure

Lost or destroyed disclosure may occur "through inadvertence, negligence, human error, administrative record purging deficiencies in recording equipment, acts of nature (e.g. fire), deliberate destruction, deliberate non-creation with intent to avoid having to disclose."[46] Examples of such evidence can be: transcripts, recordings, videotapes, police notes, police notes deliberately not made, forensic evidence, erased tapes, contents of police files, physical evidence, including documents, etc. It is not unusual to receive disclosure of police officers' handwritten notes which are indecipherable. This is not disclosure in the intended sense. It is non-disclosure. Counsel should immediately contact the Crown's office for a typed version of these notes or at least a better handwritten copy of the notes. Do not wait until it is too close to your trial or preliminary hearing date to request this disclosure as these dates may be upon you before this disclosure is prepared and in your hands. In such an instance you will not likely receive a sympathetic ear from the trial Judge if you seek an adjournment on the basis of lack of disclosure.

In *R. v. La*[47] the Supreme Court held that all evidence that is reasonably capable of affecting the accused's ability to defend himself must be presented by the prosecution. The Crown has an obligation to explain the

---

44 *R. v. Blencowe* (1997), 35 O.R. (3d) 536 (Ont. Gen. Div.). For Crown's duty to provide defence with programmes to retrieve files from hard drive and paying reasonable expenses to learn how to use programmes, see *R. v. Cassidy* (2004), 182 C.C.C. (3d) 294 (Ont. C.A.). *R. v. Piaskowski* (2007), 2007 CarswellMan 105 (Man. Q.B.) at paras. 21, 43.

45 *R. c. Taillefer* (2003), *(sub nom. R. v. Taillefer)* 179 C.C.C. (3d) 353 (S.C.C.); see also *R. v. La* (1997), 116 C.C.C. (3d) 97 (S.C.C.); *R. v. Regan*, [2002] 1 S.C.R. 297 *Canada (Minister of Citizenship & Immigration) v. Tobiass*, [1997] 3 S.C.R. 391.

46 2009 National Criminal Law Program, Vol 2. By Lucie Joncas of DesRosiers, Jocas and Massicotte, Montreal, Quebec.

47 *Supra.* See also *R. v. Bero* (2000), 151 C.C.C. (3d) 545 (Ont. C.A.); *R. v. Carosella*, [1997] 1 S.C.R. 80 at 106; *R. v. McQuaid* (1998), (sub nom. *R. v. Dixon*), [1998] 1 S.C.R. 244 (S.C.C.) at 22.

missing evidence. It is no excuse for the Crown or police to argue that the item was no longer considered necessary for the prosecution.[48] If the accused's section 7 constitutional right to full answer and defence is breached a remedy can be sought under section 24(1) of the *Charter*.

Remedies for lost or destroyed evidence are available such as a Court order at trial for production which could call for an adjournment, perhaps an order for costs where there has been a "marked and unacceptable departure from the reasonable standards expected of the prosecution,"[49] the right to examine or re-examine a witness, or reducing the charges where the missing evidence may have prejudiced the outcome of particular charge,[50] or prevented the testimony of witnesses.[51] A stay of proceedings or a mistrial will only be granted in exceptional cases where an accused's right to make full answer and defence cannot be remedied or there would be irreparable prejudice caused to the integrity of the judicial process if the prosecution was continued.[52]

In determining whether lost or destroyed evidence has impacted on the accused's right to make full answer and defence, the Court must first be satisfied on the balance of probabilities that the evidence had existed and would have been subject to an order for disclosure or a production order. The Court would then evaluate the reason for the loss or destruction. If the explanation is satisfactory, the accused must show prejudice to their defence that calls for a remedy.[53]

Electronic Disclosure

Electronic disclosure has become more prevalent especially in the bigger cases where it entails acres of pages. There are counsel who for one reason or another are not competent to operate a computer and use software to retrieve data on disks. In *R. v. Oszenaris*[54] the Newfoundland and Labrador Court of Appeal held that it is "not sufficient for defence counsel to merely raise in general terms as to whether her degree of computer literacy might be up to the task of adequately examining the electronic disclosure package." The Court went on to say that in today's world it is not reasonable

---

48   *R. v. La, supra; R. v. Carosella, supra; R. v. Bero, supra.*

49   *Ontario v. 974649 Ontario Inc.* (2001), (sub nom. *R. v. 974649 Ontario Inc.*) 159 C.C.C. (3d) 321 (S.C.C.) at para. 80.

50   *Ibid.*

51   *Ontario v. 974649 Ontario Inc., (sub nom. R. v. 974649 Ontario Inc.),* [2001] 3 S.C.R. 575.

52   *R. c. Taillefer, supra; R. v. La, supra; R. v. Sheng* (2010), 254 C.C.C. (3d) 153 (Ont. C.A.).

53   *Ibid.*

54   (2008), 236 C.C.C. (3d) 476 (N.L. C.A.) at para. 20, leave to appeal refused 2009 CarswellNfld 89, 2009 CarswellNfld 90 (S.C.C.).

to expect that counsel will be in a position to utilize a computer for the management of large volumes of material. In *R. v. Anderson*[55] the Court held that the day has come when counsel who wish to act in cases involving voluminous amounts of data should have as a "core competency requirement the ability to operate a computer and use software to retrieve data stored on disks and other media."

There is no doubt those defence counsel who would be happy to read the annotation to *R. v. Oszenaris* by Professor Tim Quigley[56] who offered that some latitude must be given to lawyers who are not at that level of computer expertise, otherwise it would be unfair to a defence counsel and the rights of an accused who has retained that counsel; we are not at that stage where we can say with confidence that all lawyers are adept at using electronic disclosure. I would add to the words of Professor Quigley that defence counsel practising on his or her own is at a disadvantage as opposed to counsel from a larger firm which has the financial ability to have on staff or is able to hire the expertise required.

In *R. v. Dunn*[57] Boswell J. set out the principles relevant to adequate electronic disclosure as follows:

i)   The Crown's obligation to effect meaningful disclosure flows from the constitutional right of the accused to make full answer and defence

ii) electronic disclosure is meaningful disclosure if it is reasonably accessible

iii) reasonable accessibility is a matter to be assessed contextually on a case by case basis, but certainly to be accessible disclosure must be reasonably organized and searchable.

The cases where electronic disclosure has been challenged have to be read as they are fact specific when it comes to whether or not the disclosure has been adequate. The application for better disclosure is brought pursuant to section 7 of the *Charter* with a remedy sought under section 24(1) of the *Charter*. Some of the factors to be considered in determining whether the disclosure is reasonably accessible are.[58]

- Whether the Crown or police have made arrangements for defence counsel and/or the accused to receive any hardware, software, and/ or technical training necessary to access the disclosure;
- Whether the materials can be legibly printed to assist counsel in communicating with his or her client;

---

55   2009 CarswellSask 814 (Sask. Q.B.) at para. 19.
56   University of Saskatchewan College of Law.
57   (2009), 251 C.C.C. (3d) 384 (Ont. S.C.J.).
58   Law at LAO, Criminal Law, Spring Edition, 2010 Vol. 10 No. 1.

- Whether the electronic disclosure allows for reasonable access to handwritten officers' notes;
- Whether the cost of accessing the material is prohibitively expensive (including whether legal aid will pay for printing costs);
- Whether the electronic disclosure excludes encrypted information in the partial possession or control of the Crown;
- Whether the electronic disclosure is technically flawed;
- Whether an accused person can access the disclosure materials via inspection at a separate location;
- Whether an in-custody accused can adequately access the disclosure;
- Whether an accused person is represented by counsel;
- Whether language or translation issues justify a particular form of disclosure; and
- The technical sophistication of the accused and/or counsel.

Defence Counsel's Responsibility

There is a positive duty on defence counsel "to be duly diligent in pursuing disclosure. To do nothing in the face of knowledge that relevant information has not been disclosed will, at a minimum, often justify a finding of lack of due diligence, and may, in certain cases, support an inference that counsel made a strategic decision not to pursue disclosure ... Counsel should have brought (the missing document) to the attention of the trial Judge at the earliest opportunity."[59]

While *Stinchcombe* states that the obligation for the Crown to provide disclosure where an accused is represented by counsel is triggered by a request by or on behalf of the accused, the Crown often supplies disclosure in a non-complex, non-lengthy case within the first month or so of the accused being charged without even a request by the defence. In some parts of the country it may be that defence counsel have been lulled into not seeking disclosure expecting that it will be coming, and after some time when disclosure has not been forthcoming it will only be then when counsel makes a disclosure demand. It is best to send out a letter to the Crown requesting disclosure as soon as you are retained in order to protect a possible section 11(b) *Charter* motion later down the road. Just remember not to sit back on that one letter seeking disclosure. It will not be helpful if there is a contest later.

---

59 *R. v. Dixon, supra.*

Undertaking By Defence Not To Use Disclosure Except for Full Answer and Defence

In *P. (D.) v. Wagg*,[60] the Ontario Court of Appeal found that it was not necessary in that case to decide whether there was an implied undertaking rule applicable to Crown disclosure, although there would seem to be compelling reasons for recognizing such a rule. In *R. v. Schertzer*,[61] the Crown sought a signed undertaking from defence counsel not to use Crown disclosure for a collateral purpose beyond the need to make full answer and defence. The Court, in *Schertzer*, reviewing the authorities held that "[i]t is highly likely that defence counsel... implicitly undertakes not to use the disclosure for a collateral purpose." In this case, there was a concern about risks to the privacy, safety and security interest of potential witnesses and third parties, and on this basis and a close review of the Crown materials, the Court made an order that defence counsel enter into an express undertaking not to use the disclosure materials or the information contained therein beyond the need to make full answer and defence, before the materials need be released by the Crown to the defence.

Crown Cross-Examining Accused on Disclosure

The propriety of the Crown cross-examining an accused that she reviewed the disclosure and implying that she tailored her evidence as a result must be considered on a case by case basis — on the one hand the accused's right to disclosure could turn into a trap, on the other hand the accused may open the door for such cross-examination by raising disclosure. Doherty J. suggests that questions to the accused regarding disclosure are appropriate in some circumstances but they are always potentially dangerous and the proposed line of questioning should be vetted by the trial Judge.[62]

---

60 (2004), 184 C.C.C. (3d) 321 (Ont. C.A.).

61 *Per* Justice Ewaschuk, Ont. S.C.J., September 1, 2004.

62 *R. v. Cavan* (1999), 139 C.C.C. (3d) 449 (Ont. C.A.), leave to appeal refused (2000), 254 N.R. 396 (note) (S.C.C.), leave to appeal refused (2000), 254 N.R. 396 (note) (S.C.C.). In *R. v. White* (1999), 132 C.C.C. (3d) 373 (Ont. C.A.), the Court ruled that it was improper for the Crown to suggest that the accused's evidence should be viewed as suspect because he had received full disclosure and had not been cross-examined before trial and, therefore, one could infer the accused tailored his evidence to fit the disclosure. Otherwise, fundamental rights would be turned into a trap for accused persons.

3

Client and Witness Interviews

How does counsel begin the interview with his or her client? A debated ethical issue has been whether counsel is entitled to advise the client as to what the law is pertaining to the case before counsel has received the client's version of the events. Those who say no would argue that to allow this approach would encourage the client to fabricate his or her evidence so as to come within a legal defence. A counter argument is "that to require a client to commit a version of events without the benefit of legal advice and without understanding what is in the client's interest is to prejudge the client as a perjurer.[1] The Canadian Bar Association Code does not prevent counsel advising the client on the law before inquiring about the client's version. However, it is clear that counsel cannot induce a client to fabricate testimony.[2] Indeed, counsel doing so could find themselves facing charges of suborning perjury and obstructing justice. An example which I would suggest crosses the ethical line is from the movie *Anatomy of a Murder*. In that film actor Jimmy Stewart plays the role of an attorney defending a soldier who is charged with murder. Counsel commences the interview by telling the accused there are four different ways to defend murder and the accused wants to know what they are. Counsel describes them, one of which is the defence of insanity. The accused, bright but obviously not crazy, warms to the idea and counsel departs the interview suggesting to the accused that he try to figure out just how crazy he is.

Counsel is permitted to direct a witness to the relevant issues, probing him to refresh his memory of relevant facts and preparing him for cross-examination.[3]

Experienced counsel know and young lawyers should be aware not to fall in love with the client's first version of events that the client has given

---

1 G. Mackenzie, *Lawyers and Ethics: Professional Responsibility and Discipline* (Toronto, Carswell, 1993), p. 59-76.
2 Canadian Bar Association Code of Professional Conduct, Chapter ix, Commentary 2(e) as well as certain provincial Codes of Conduct.
3 *Lawyers and Ethics: Professional Responsibility and Discipline, supra,* at pp. 4-23-4-24.4.

them, especially before they see disclosure. The clients may be honestly mistaken about the details of some of those events or are simply untruthful. Their memories may have faded or they confabulate or rationalize. Don't be swayed by demeanour. Practised liars can be convincing. During your interviews play the devil's advocate by asking questions about the reasonableness of the client's version of events and how it stacks up against the prosecution's case. Look for weaknesses just as the prosecutor will so that you will be better able to determine the strength of your client's defence or perhaps even recommend a negotiated plea of guilty.

See also Chapter, "Preparation for Cross-Examination – The Client and Witnesses."

In preparing the witness to testify, whether the witness is the accused or otherwise, it is worthwhile to first assess his or her personality so that any damaging personal traits that may surface on the witness stand can be addressed. Does their body or verbal language convey the wrong message, such as rapid eye blinking at significant moments in their story; or when they start a number of sentences with—"to be perfectly honest". Is the witness the nervous type? Is he quick to lose his temper? Will the witness become timid if pressed? Is the witness argumentative? Does the witness speak in a hesitant manner or in a way which sounds unconvincing? Is the witness responsive or evasive? Does the witness tend to give gratuitous answers? Are there weaknesses in the witness's testimony that must be defended or at least met? Such witnesses require pre-trial counselling. This is not to say that the witness is to be coached about what to say but counsel can prepare the witness on how to handle the anticipated cross-examination.

The client should be dressed appropriately out of respect for the Court and to show that he recognizes the seriousness of the process and the charges he faces. There are basic rules for any witness. A witness should be polite and respectful but not obsequious. If a witness loses his temper he may say things without thinking carefully and come to wish he had remained calm. Losing one's temper may leave the impression the witness is losing the exchange with counsel. The jury will not be sympathetic toward a combative, argumentative witness. An evasive or halting witness will not sound credible. A witness who exaggerates will be found out and will be damaged. A witness should display conviction in his or her testimony but should also be candid in admitting any limitations. The witness should not speak in absolutes if called for as to do so may open themselves to a strong challenge. If a witness is unable to recall, is not completely sure of the answer to a question or can only give an approximation or can only say she doesn't know, then she should be encouraged to do so. But to seek refuge in these responses too often may appear disingenuous.

Exactitude of language can be very important in a courtroom, which the ordinary witness may not appreciate. In everyday conversation many people speak loosely and much does not depend on what they say and they don't expect to be challenged. If witnesses are not careful with their language in a courtroom, under oath, their credibility will be attacked. Often people speak of matters they know of only through hearsay but speak as if they have first-hand knowledge. The witnesses should be questioned closely about their source of knowledge. To guess or speculate may produce answers which would contradict other witnesses on the same side or offend human experience.

A witness should not go out of her way to support the side that called her in the face of contrary facts or she will display a bias which will damage her credibility. A witness should not volunteer information. Volunteering answers may indicate a bias and may give the cross-examiner an opening for penetrating questions. Answer only the question posed. Advise the witness that if she leaves anything out in her answer and it is important, you will bring it out in re-examination.

A witness should be advised to listen carefully to the questions and answer clearly and responsively. If the witness asks counsel to repeat the question too often the witness may appear evasive, or that he or she is looking for more time to answer the question because of uncertainty, or is attempting to fabricate a response.

Do not let the cross-examiner try to speed up the witnesses' responses so that she may become careless in her answers. If the client does not like the question she should be advised that you will object to it if it is improper.

It has been said that the eyes are a reflection of the soul. A witness should look at the jury periodically, particularly when answering important questions to show that he is not afraid to let his judges look him in the eye.

Defence counsel should advise any client who will be testifying that the client's demeanour on the witness stand will be extremely important and inform him or her of the fact that the trial Judge may charge herself or the jury with respect to the accused's demeanour. Sincerity should be the hallmark of any witness's testimony and the accused more than anyone should be made aware of that fact. Be alert in your client interviews at what points in the story your client becomes emotional. You may wish to push that button during the client's testimony at trial to lend impact and credibility to his or her evidence. See "Demeanour When Testifying" in Chapter, "Observation and Recollection."

Clients should be counselled to conduct themselves appropriately in the prisoner's dock or sitting next to counsel, if there is any concern in this regard. For example, they should not make faces or noises when hearing evidence they do not like. Such actions may be viewed as contrived dramatics. Conversely, you can explain in your final submissions that if any of the jurors thought it strange or incriminating because your client did not show any upset at hearing inculpatory evidence, that this was not the first time your client has heard that evidence—there was the preliminary hearing as well as disclosure and so the defence was not caught by surprise at trial.

Other examples of client conduct to be avoided in the courtroom would be laughing inappropriately, speaking out, or exhibiting a posture in the prisoner's dock which does not recognize the seriousness of the proceedings and reflects a perceived unpleasing aspect of the client's personality.

It is important that the witness should be advised of all the issues in the case and how his or her testimony will bear on those issues. If the witness does not understand what is at stake he or she may give in too easily to the cross-examiner on a point which doesn't seem important to the witness but is in fact significant to the case.

The client should be told that, in direct examination, leading questions cannot be asked but that the cross-examiner can put leading questions to the witness. The meaning of leading questions should be explained,[4] i.e., questions which suggest or tend to suggest the answer or questions which assume facts not yet established. The witness should be advised to be alert to leading questions and to their exact import as the cross-examiner will be attempting to lead the witness to say certain things which really do not reflect the client's position. Leading questions are discussed later in this chapter.

However, the client should be aware that you will object if the cross-examiner badgers her or exceeds the bounds of what is allowed. Examples of unfair questions could arise from misquoting earlier testimony, questions involving a matter of law rather than fact, asking for an opinion from a non-expert on a question with respect to matters beyond the witness's knowledge or asking irrelevant and embarrassing or unfair questions. If there is no objection the witness should answer the question without loss of temper and fairly so that he maintains his or her credibility. It should further be explained to the witness that after cross-examination is completed there is the right to re-examine. The client will then have the opportunity to explain or enlarge on some of his/her answers arising out of questions during cross-examination which he/she did not have the opportunity to do before.

Sometimes the client, on being asked questions in cross-examination, will look toward the counsel who called him or her to testify. This action could result from nervousness but it is dangerous as it can be interpreted by some jurors as a mute cry for assistance. An alert cross-examiner, attempting to damage the witness's credibility, will ask the witness not to constantly look at counsel before answering questions. The witness should therefore be warned against any such habit.

---

4   See Chapter, "General Techniques of Cross-Examination," heading "Open-ended Questions."

Accused's Trial Conduct

"Sounds like it musta took a lotta guts tellin off the whole jury that way. What'd they say?"

Trial Diplomacy Journal's Cartoon Album. David M. Freedman, Ed. © 1980 Court Practice Journal, Inc.

The client should be made aware of anticipated questions that opposing counsel may pose in an attempt to negate his/her evidence-in-chief. Counsel should review with the witness any evidence that could impeach him/her, such as prior statements, other witness's testimony or exhibits. A witness is less likely to be nervous when he/she is aware of all the potential weaknesses of his/her testimony and knows how best to respond to them when they are exposed. Counsel should put himself in the shoes of his/her opponent and ask the witness those searching questions a well-prepared cross-examiner would ask. If this is not done then the witness could be caught off-guard in cross-examination and fumble through his/her answers with the result that his/her credibility and/or reliability is seriously damaged. But if forewarned, the witness, in the calm atmosphere of counsel's office, may think of answers which could satisfactorily explain seeming inconsistencies or may even readily admit his/her error which counsel would bring out in-chief with an astute touch to diminish any possible negative impact during the cross-examination.

Anticipating the opponent's cross-examination can be overdone if it means that the direct examination will lose its force and focus and will cause confusion where the witness is making an explanation when he/she has not yet been attacked. In most cases it would be best if the witness were prepared to answer these tough questions in cross-examination or where the answers will have more impact. In this way the direct examination is not taken up by making excuses. An exception would be where, by not asking the question, the jurors could feel that counsel was trying to mislead or give them a false impression by not bringing out certain testimony himself. Professor Hegland[5] makes this point:

> The line between presenting a convincing direct [examination] and antic-ipating attacks is essentially this: would a perceptive person, listening to the direct examination have any questions concerning its credibility? If so, answer those questions at a point, judged to be most favourable by the defence, during examtnation-in-chief. Your opponent may not raise them in cross-examination. The jury almost always does.

In addition to explaining the meaning of leading questions counsel should also explain some of the basic rules of evidence, such as the rule against the admissibility of hearsay testimony. (Discussed later in this chap-ter and in more detail in a separate chapter). So instructed, the witness may be helped to not be nervous or become frustrated and confused (by objec-tions from opposing counsel or from interference by the trial judge) while giving evidence.

Professor Robert Keeton[6] gives the following advice to counsel about the nervous witness:

> Adequate preparation of the witness is a most important factor. Fear of the unknown causes nervousness. Knowledge of what is to come induces confi-dence and composure. A thorough interview before the witness is called to testify is one effective method of reducing the chances that the witness will become nervous and confused as he testifies.
>
> In addition to advance preparation of the witness, you should, as you proceed with your direct examination, bear in mind the interest in keeping the witness composed and at ease. It is your duty to avoid rushing the witness, to make your questions clear and direct, and by all means to refrain from showing displeasure if the witness misunderstands or gets excited or confused. In short,

5   K.F. Hegland, *Trial and Practice Skills in a Nutshell* (St. Paul: West Publishing Co., 1978), p. 16.
6   R.E. Keeton, *Trial Tactics and Methods* (Toronto: Little, Brown, 1973), p. 28.

you should yourself be composed during the direct examination. The response of your witness is likely to reflect your state of composure or nervousness.

If, before testifying, a witness is aware of the procedures used in a courtroom, that knowledge may help to reduce apprehension and nervousness. If the witness is very nervous counsel should take the witness to the courtroom beforehand and explain to the witness what will happen there. It should be explained that, if a Judge gives an order excluding witnesses from the courtroom, witnesses must leave the Court, remain nearby waiting to be called and will not, therefore, hear the evidence given by witnesses called ahead of them.

Taking the witness or client to the scene, when possible, may help the witness to recall more facts which could be helpful and give him or her more confidence about their evidence when he or she testifies many months after the event.

You of course want the witness to appear as impartial as possible. You might therefore suggest to the witness that after he or she has testified, to leave the courthouse so as to negate any possible impressions of having an interest in the verdict. This suggestion would not apply to someone who is closely related or to someone who is obviously a close friend of the client as the trier of fact would no doubt expect this kind of witness to be concerned about the outcome of the case.

For some witnesses a dress rehearsal could be very helpful provided there is not any memorizing of the questions and answers. Although the witness should be advised of the questions that will be posed, a memorized script will give the appearance of contrived testimony and the witness may become confused if he or she has to depart from the script.

After the witness has been given the benefit of the above advice, counsel should also advise the witness that there was nothing improper about these discussions. Coaching witnesses is improper but it is not the same as preparing them for the witness stand. If opposing counsel asks whether the non-accused witness has discussed the matter with counsel then the witness should readily admit the discussion. This question is sometimes asked as a trap. Some witnesses feel that by admitting that the interview took place that they will be admitting to a form of collusion and, as a result, may deny ever having discussed the matter with counsel. If the witness makes a false denial, the cross-examiner will disbelieve him because he knows that such a denial does not accord with reality and the result will be further cross-examination on the issue. As a result, the examiner-in-chief is put in an embarrassing position because he knows that the witness has lied and, as an officer of the Court, he should advise the Court of this fact.

It is also not unusual for a witness to discuss the case with the accused or others. There is really no objection to this so long as there was no attempt to influence the witness's testimony. If asked, the witness should admit to any such discussions. It would be hard to believe, for example, that a husband did not discuss the case with his wife. In most cases it would be better if the accused left any discussions about the case with potential witnesses to counsel in order to avoid any appearances, inferences or accusations that the witness was improperly influenced.

Human nature is such that it can be difficult to convict someone who has an appealing appearance and disposition. The client should therefore appear as attractive as possible in Court. Grooming and dress are very important. No flashy jewellery or clothes, or strong scents should be worn or used. Trial consultants will even tell you that the colour of your client's clothes will convey a message—for example, dark blue is the most powerful colour, followed by grey, tan and brown. Most jurors take Court proceedings very seriously. Your client should be dressed to reflect this formal atmosphere. The client's clothing should represent an image consistent with his or her defence if possible. "Dress is a medium of communication that conveys information about who a person is and is not. Observers use clothing to categorize people on variables such as social status, occupation, ethnicity, sex role identification, honesty, believability and perceived credibility."[7] An example of how not to dress was seen in California in the way the accused, Hollywood Madam Heidi Fleiss, clothed herself for her Court appearances—for example, a wrap-around dress barely covering her chest and at times falling open to show a patch of thigh which was accompanied by high-heeled pumps and sunglasses. No doubt her choice of dress helped to secure her appearances in the National Enquirer and on nightly T.V. news magazines, but at the end of the day who was going to believe she was not a procurer of sex for money as alleged. On the other hand in the first trial of the young Menendez brothers who were accused of murdering their parents, a hung jury resulted, notwithstanding overwhelming evidence. The young accused wore dark suits for their arraignment showing respect for the proceedings. But once the trial began, they started wearing crew-neck sweaters and long-sleeved plaid shirts in an attempt to present themselves as the boys-next-door.[8]

Many accused have been convicted, not on evidence that was available prior to arrest, but on evidence from the accused's own mouth given after arrest. Certain individuals will discourse with accused persons about their charges in order to learn incriminating evidence or to twist innocent conversation into incriminating evidence for their own gain. Examples of such

---

7 Margaret C. Roberts, *Trial Psychology* (Toronto, Butterworth Legal Publishers, 1987).

8 How far an accused can go in creating an impression is no doubt open to debate. If the client was being deceptive, as for example, wearing a wedding ring when not married, then there would be those who would argue this tactic is unethical.

Bad Advice on the Clothes

"Yes. I'd just like to say that during this trial my wardrobe has been provided by Ross and Tompkins on the Kensington Mall."

Trial Diplomacy Journal's Cartoon Album. David M. Freedman, Ed. © 1980 Court Practice Journal, Inc.

people are a prison inmate who is seeking to gain favour with the prosecution or an undercover officer who is placed in jail pretending to be an inmate in order to gather more evidence from the accused's own mouth. If the client is on bail, others on the street may pass on conversations with the accused, even though innocent, which could come back in a twisted form to haunt the accused in the courtroom. The client's telephone, automobile or room conversations may be electronically intercepted. Counsel's advice to clients should be that, in the event anyone wishes to speak to them about the case, they should say they have been instructed by their counsel not to discuss the matter and if anyone wishes to discuss the case it can be pursued with counsel.

Do You Believe I Am Innocent?

There are accused who feel that it is important to have a counsel who believes in their innocence because only then will you try your best on their behalf. This client may feel that if you don't believe he or she is innocent, it would be best to seek out one who does. Even if you choose to answer the question you would no doubt decline if you have not received full disclosure, explored your case in detail and if there is a preliminary inquiry to be held, heard the evidence under oath. If the time comes when you feel your client wants a response and if you do not believe in his or her innocence or are unsure, I would suggest an answer along the following lines: "Mr. or Ms. Client, I am unable to tell you at this point whether I believe in your innocence. I do not know enough about the case as yet, my job is not to believe or disbelieve you, I am not your Judge and jury, Mr. Client. My job as your advocate is to put forth the best defence I can on your behalf. My job is to do that even if I was to believe in your guilt." You might wish to go on and say – "What I cannot put forth is evidence which I know (not that I suspect) to be false as that would be committing a fraud on the Court. If you were to tell me that you committed the crime for which you are charged I cannot call you to the witness stand to testify under oath because I know you will not be telling the truth when you deny your guilt. The law presumes you to be innocent and I can rely on the weaknesses of the Crown's case and argue at the end of the day for your acquittal because the Crown has been unable to prove you guilty beyond a reasonable doubt. And even if you do not take the stand to testify neither the prosecutor nor the Judge are allowed to say anything to the jury that you did not, because that is your right in our justice system." If you don't feel an approach along these lines will satisfy the client then I can only leave you to your own devices.

At some point you should advise the client as to the obstacles they must meet in the evidence. By doing so the client may more readily appreciate their difficulty in achieving a not guilty verdict and instruct you accordingly. A client may feel by your probing questions you may not believe in his innocence. I would suggest you tell the client you are asking questions that the prosecutor is certain to ask and it is best to be prepared for that eventuality. It is best to know as much about the weaknesses of the defence as you can and to assess your client's credibility and reliability to help you decide the advisability of calling him as a witness. Also, at some point you may have to advise the client about his chances of being successful at trial or whether or not seeking a resolution is the better course, if the client is prepared to admit guilt.

I'm Not Guilty But I Will Plead Guilty to Take the Deal

There often comes the time when the client says that even though he is innocent, he will take the deal offered by the Crown and plead guilty. I explain to my client that I will not plead a man guilty who claims he is innocent. Be aware that later it is not unusual for a client to suffer buyer's remorse and appeal his sentence with new counsel and may say to the Court that he told his trial lawyer he was innocent but the lawyer convinced him to take the deal. Explain to the client that when he pleads guilty that the facts supporting the plea will be read out in open Court by the Crown and he will be asked by the Judge if the facts read out are true. If he says no or waffles, the Judge will no doubt strike the plea of guilty and the trial would proceed on the basis of a not guilty plea. If the client still maintains his innocence but wants to plead guilty, you may wish to advise him to seek other counsel. If the client then chooses to plead guilty, for your own protection, have him acknowledge in writing that the choice to plead was his and he was doing so because he was in fact guilty.

The Well-Counselled Client

"*Franklin can't discuss that—he's under constant electronic surveillance.*"

Trial Diplomacy Journal's Cartoon Album. David M. Freedman, Ed. © 1980 Court Practice Journal, Inc.

Should Your Client Give a Statement to the Police?

During your career you will often be told by clients that the police want to speak to them and the clients want to know whether they should provide a statement. No charges have yet been brought. It is surprising to learn how many individuals wrongly feel they have to speak to the police, even if they are charged. The client may feel by not being co-operative they will look guilty in the eyes of the police. There are also some clients who feel by talking to the police, they can convince them not to lay a charge when they hear the client's side of the story. In most cases this is wishful thinking if the client is the target, unless the client has a sound alibi. There are those clients who feel they cannot go through a trial for medical or other reasons such as the embarrassment and hurt to his family or for business reasons. They are hoping that by providing what they feel is an exculpatory statement they will not have to face a trial. Again, this is wishful thinking.

You should first determine what the police have exactly said to the client; whether it appears that he/she is a suspect or a potential witness only. You can of course ask the officer but you may receive a vague answer. But at some early point, depending on whether your client is charged or not, you will want to know whether your client's co-operation will assist in obtaining immunity or a reduction in charges if he/she provides a statement, or is your client not going to provide a statement, or is your client going to co-operate for no ulterior motive, but as a good citizen.

In most cases the client has very little to gain by speaking to the police when it appears he/she may be a suspect, unless of course an immunity deal can be reached or some satisfactory negotiated plea of guilty can be arranged with, at times, the client becoming a Crown witness. But often there is no question of negotiation because it's not that type of case. The police may say they want to ask your client questions but you know your client is going to be charged in any event. It serves the client no useful purpose in this circumstance to speak to the police. The best approach for you is to call the relevant police officer and advise him/her that your client, on advice of counsel does not wish to be questioned by the police and then discuss surrender and bail if he/she is to be charged.

Clients most often convict themselves through their own mouths either by a statement they gave to the police, through intercepted communications or by what they have told others, or by talking to the police. If the police have spoken to the client near or at the end of their investigation then they usually have your client in their sights as a prime suspect. They have questioned pretty well everyone else who can provide information so that when they come to question your client they know all the best questions to pose given that they have significant knowledge of the circumstances. Even if the client was to give seemingly exculpatory answers, they may turn out at trial to be incriminating when placed against objective or otherwise credible evidence. Your client may not have intended to lie but because of the passage of time or a faulty memory or other reasons may be confused about certain facts and give incorrect answers which could come back to haunt him or her in the courtroom. Even if you are thinking in the rare circumstances of advising your client to provide a statement you will have to make a judgment as to whether your client is credible otherwise he will be achieving nothing but trouble for himself by co-operating. This is where you play the role of the Crown Attorney with your questions to your client.

If a client answers some questions but refuses to answer others, this will appear incriminating in a courtroom; perhaps even more so if the statement is on video and the client's demeanour looks inculpatory.

It is not unheard of for counsel to tell the police that the client will answer questions but only if they are forwarded first in writing. If the matter comes to trial this can give the Crown the opportunity to suggest to the Court that the accused wanted time to fashion his/her answers in the best possible light. Very few Crowns would accede to this request in any event.

In the last analysis, if you feel your client is a suspect and is in danger of being charged an exculpatory statement is not going to exonerate him/her in the eyes of the prosecution as the statement will be seen as self-serving. If the Crown does not feel your client's statement will help the prosecution's case the Crown in all likelihood will not introduce it into evidence and of course you will be unable to do so except in the rare circumstances discussed in other parts of this book.

If for any reason your client wishes to provide a statement on the basis that the Crown is offering some form of leniency you should seek from the Crown an acknowledgment in writing that the statement is an induced one and whatever the client says during the interview, or any evidence obtained as a result of the interview would not be used in any proceedings brought by the Crown. Your client should obtain this acknowledgment from the Crown rather than the police as it is the Crown who has the last say and may not abide by what the police have offered. The client won't be able to take his statement back.

Your advice to the client as to whether or not he/she should provide a statement to the police is one of the most important decisions that you will make as a defence counsel. It is a decision that you will be called on by the client to make for him before the client is charged and at times after the charge. In the latter case your advice is more easily given because at this stage your client is usually seeking to make a deal for whatever reason, (mostly because the evidence against him or her is overwhelming) or will be pleading not guilty and giving a statement will not assist him unless it describes a helpful alibi.

However, prior to being charged, your advice can result in significant consequences for the client and you want not only to protect his or her interests foremost, but also to protect your reputation if the client is charged because you advised him or her to speak to the police and incriminated themselves. If the client chooses to speak to the police, obtain in writing that it was ultimately their decision, after you have explained the potential consequences. You should have a knowledgeable student with the client if he provides a statement to the police. It is best for counsel not to be present to prevent becoming a witness in case there is any dispute during the questioning although with video-taping, this problem seems obviated.

There is a different scenario. Your client has already been arrested or you advise him to surrender to the police because there is a warrant for his arrest. You advise the client not to say anything to the police. In the recent Supreme Court decision of *R. v. McCrimmon*,[9] it was held that while the suspect has a right to speak to a lawyer and to be informed of that right, they don't have the right to counsel being present when they are interrogated. The police will not assault or threaten your client or offer inducements to influence a confession that would be inadmissible. However, provided the police don't conduct themselves in a way that would shock the conscience of the community, the courts will not criticize the police in obtaining a confession.[10] Your advice to the client is that they must maintain their resolve notwithstanding persistent questioning by the police even though the client maintains he does not wish to say anything, and that trickery by the police to obtain a confession will be part of the officer's investigative technique.

Heather A. McArthur[11] offers sage advice as follows when advising detained clients not only what their rights are, but how to exercise those rights and how the police will attempt to undermine those rights:

- The client has the right to remain silent and should refuse to say anything.
- The refusal to answer questions by the police and remaining silent **cannot** be used at trial. The judge (or jury) will **never** hear that the client refused to answer questions.
- Although the client has the right not to say anything, the police are entitled to interrogate the client against their will.
- The police are allowed to ignore assertions of the right to silence.
- The police will use many different tactics to try to get the client to talk. They will often start out by saying that they just have to get some "basic information" for the "forms." Let the client know that this is a common trick to get them to start talking and to lower their defences. Tell the client not to respond to these questions or simply repeat that they have nothing to say.
- The police can keep the client in the interrogation room for many, many hours against their will. Give examples, i.e., "I once had a client who

---

9   (2010), 259 C.C.C. (3d) 515 (S.C.C.).

10 How far the police can go in questioning a detained accused is quite far. See *R. v. Oickle* (2000), 147 C.C.C. (3d) 321 (S.C.C.); *R. v. Sinclair* (2010), 259 C.C.C. (3d) 443 (S.C.C.); *R. v. Singh* (2007), 225 C.C.C. (3d) 103 (S.C.C.).

11 C.S. McArthur Barristers, The Six-Minute Defence Lawyer, April 2, 2011.

was interrogated for over eight hours before the police gave up." Tell the client to be prepared for an endurance contest.
- The police are allowed to ignore requests to speak with counsel again. This is likely the *only* opportunity that the client will have to speak with counsel.
- The client does not have to participate in any line up or polygraph or provide bodily samples. If the police ask the client to participate in anything along these lines, ask to speak to counsel again. But keep in mind that an overzealous officer may still refuse another call to counsel. Do not participate in any of the above.
- The police are allowed to lie about the evidence. For example, they may assert falsely that they have fingerprints, DNA or eyewitnesses which implicate the client.
- The client, however, is not allowed to lie to the police. Any lies told during an interrogation may be used as evidence of guilt at the trial. (Or may form the basis for an obstruction of justice charge.)
- Anything that the client says to the police can be used in evidence against them. It does not have to be a "formal" statement. Any utterances at all may be used against them. On the flip side of that, if the client gives an exculpatory story, it is often inadmissible.
- The police will likely say that this is the client's only opportunity to give their side of the story. That is false. The client will have an opportunity to provide information to the prosecution, police or the Court at a later time.
- It is important to wait until disclosure comes and can be reviewed with counsel before divulging anything.
- The client can always provide their side of the story to the police or the prosecution through counsel after counsel has had an opportunity to review the disclosure and discuss the matter with the client.

KNOWING THE RULES OF EVIDENCE

It is vital that counsel be completely aware of the rules of evidence in a criminal trial. There is no more important place for that knowledge than during an examination-in-chief. If opposing counsel is continually objecting to leading questions or other irregularities it could be upsetting and confusing to the witness and may detract from a jury's understanding of the case due to the breaks in testimony to argue the objections. Objections may be distracting to younger and inexperienced counsel by throwing them off stride. The result is that the questioner will not only lose prestige with the jurors but will also impair his or her concentration when presenting the facts of the case.

One basic rule of evidence is that, subject to what will be said later, counsel cannot lead his or her own witness. A leading question is one that suggests the desired answer to the witness. Where the questioner wishes to elicit from the witness a description of a hat that the witness observed, the witness should not be asked: "Was Mr. Jones wearing a white straw hat?" The witness should be guided through a series of questions of this nature: "Did Mr. Jones have anything on his head? What was it? What was the hat made of? What colour was the hat?" A question is also leading if it assumes a fact in dispute which has not been given in evidence so that the witness has ostensibly to admit the fact in order to answer the question. Professor Morton[12] gives the following example of both types of leading questions in this way:

(a) A question which suggests the answer—'You saw Smith running from the scene of the crime, didn't you?'

(b) A question which takes for granted certain facts which the witness has not sworn to—if the witness has said nothing about Smith fleeing, the question 'What happened after Smith fled?' would be leading.

Leading questions can weaken the credibility of the witness, particularly when the trial is before a judge without a jury. The impression could be left that counsel is fearful of permitting the witness to say too much by giving the evidence himself or herself.

There are exceptions to the rule that leading questions may not be asked.[13] Such questions may be asked about undisputed matters that are introductory or preliminary, such as the witness's name, age, occupation, residence, etc.;[14] where the question would assist a defective memory after all attempts have been exhausted, particularly in a complicated area;[15] where the witness does not understand the question because of the complicated nature of the subject-matter;[16] to bring the witness's attention to persons or things;[17] where a witness who is having difficulty remembering, is a child or is ill or has difficulty with the language of the trial, or lacks education;[18] and to contradict another witness about what was said on a particular occasion,[19] for example:

---

12 J.D. Morton, *Evidence in Criminal Cases: A Basic Guide* (Toronto: Butterworth, 1961), pp. 53-54.

13 In *R. v. Coffin* (1956), 114 C.C.C. 1 at 22 (S.C.C.), Justice Kellock stated: "but while, as a general rule, a party may not either in direct or re-examination put leading questions, the Court has a discretion not open to review, to relax it whenever it is considered necessary in the interest of justice..."

14 *Maves v. Grand Trunk Railways* (1913), 5 W.W.R. 212 at 219 (Alta. C.A.); R. Cross, *Cross on Evidence*, 3rd ed. (London: Butterworth and Co., 1967), p. 189.

15 *Ibid.*

16 *Ibid.*

17 *Ibid.*

18 *Ibid.*; 3 Wigmore on Evidence (Chadbourn rev., 1970), §778.

19 *Ibid.*

Q: Mr Jones, were you present during the discussion regarding a suit between Mr. Black and Mr. Green on the evening of November 10th at Mr. Black's home?

A: Yes I was.

Q: Mr. Green has testified that Mr. Black said he could have the suit as a gift. Was that in fact said by Mr. Black?

A: I never heard that.

Q: What in fact did you hear, if anything, regarding a suit?

A: Mr. Black told Mr. Green that the suit had great sentimental value to Mr. Black and he did not wish to part with it.

The above example is not only a proper use of leading questions with respect to contradicting another witness about what was said on a prior

"Objection, Your Honor . . . counsel
for the defense is leading the witness!"

© Unknown.

occasion, but also with respect to bringing the witness's attention to a certain thing, namely, the suit.

In addition to the aforementioned, counsel may lead on any relevant matters with the consent of the opposite side which normally occurs with respect to preliminary matters not in dispute.

If the answer to a leading question is given before objection such answers are not inadmissible but the answer will normally carry very little weight, particularly on a critical issue.[20] *R. v. Rose*[21] is a case in which the Crown breached a number of rules relating to the examination of witnesses. The following relates to leading questions. A number of Crown counsel's questions were clearly suggestive of the answers to his own witness.

Q. All right and do you recall when — when and how you first met Mr. Rose?

A. No.

Q. And what's your connection with Mr. Rose?

A. What do you mean, connection?

Q. Well, what do you do with Mr. Rose?

A. I talk to him.

Q. What else do you do with him?

A. That's about it.

Q. *Does he supply you with crack cocaine?*

A. Sometimes.

Q. *Now, my information is that the police had set up surveillance on yourself and on the 19th of August you got into a motor vehicle with Mr. Rose. The 21st of August you got into a motor vehicle with Mr. Rose.*

. . .

Q. Mr. Beaudry, I started advising you that my information is that the police were conducting surveillance and on the following dates they saw you get into a motor vehicle which Mr. Rose was driving and those dates were August 19, August 21, September 4, and September 5. Did you, in fact, meet Mr. Rose on those dates?

A. If it's right there, I guess so. I don't mark it in a book, you know, it's just —

Q. You didn't mark it. *How many times have you purchased crack cocaine from Mr. Rose?* You don't have to give me an exact number, give your best estimate or you can give me a range.

A. Three, four times.

Q. Three or four times, and do you recall when those three or four times would have been?

A. No.

Q. Now, on the 6th of September — or the 5th of September, you were in an automobile with Mr. Rose and the police stopped that automobile?

A. Yeah.

---

20 *Moor v. Moor*, [1954] 2 All E.R. 458 (C.A.); *Connor v. Brant* (1914), 31 O.L.R. 215 at 280 (Ont. C.A.); *Calgary Grain Co. v. Nordness*, [1917] 2 W.W.R. 713 at 714 (Alta. C.A.); Archbold, *Pleadings, Evidence and Practice in Criminal Cases*, 42nd ed. S.G. Mitchell and P.J. Richardson (eds.) (London: Sweet & Maxwell, 1985), p. 393, §4-292; *R. v. Williams* (1982), 66 C.C.C. (2d) 234 (Ont. C.A.).

21 (2001), 153 C.C.C. (3d) 225 (Ont. C.A.). This case recognized that the Court has some latitude in allowing leading questions of one's own witness but not so when the evidence is crucial.

Q. You remember that?

A. Yeah. I don't remember the date, but I remember when they stopped us.

Q. And there were police cars in front and back of Mr. Rose's car?

A. Something like that.

Q. And do you recall what kind of automobile Mr. Rose was driving or drives?

A. A black car.

Q. You don't know the make?

A. No.

Q. The license number? Has it been — *all the times that you've purchased crack cocaine from Mr. Rose, has he been in the same motor vehicle?*

A. Yeah.

Q. And that's the black car you just indicated?

A. Black car, yeah.

Q. *Now, when the — on the 5th of September when the police officers stopped the motor vehicle, you were in Mr. Rose's automobile, were you not?*

A. Yeah.

Q. *Mr. Rose was in the automobile?*

A. Yeah.

Q. Correct, and who was driving the automobile?

A. Mr. Rose.

Q. Mr. Rose, and you were in which seat, *the front passenger seat?*

A. Yeah. The front seat.

Q. Was there anyone else in the car?

A. No.

Q. All right, and what was the purpose for being in that automobile on that date and time, why were you there?

A. To tell you the truth, I don't even know because it happened so fast. I didn't have time to say nothing or nothing, you know.

Q. *Well, were you going to purchase crack cocaine from Mr. Rose on that date?*

A. I guess I would have tried.

Q. Did you have the money with you?

A. Yeah. Of course, it was my rent money, but. . .

Q. *Well, I — is it fair to say that every time you had gotten into Mr. Rose's automobile in the past you purchased crack cocaine from him?*

A. Maybe two out of three.

Q. Two out of three. Did you have any crack cocaine with you at that time when you got into Mr. Rose's car on the 5th of September?

A. No.

Q. You had money with you though?

A. Yeah.

Q. *Would you agree with me that it's — it seems that you were there to buy crack cocaine from him?*

A. I could have.

Q. Other than meeting Mr. Rose to buy crack cocaine from him, have you and Mr. Rose ever done anything else together? Do you go to the movies together, go to see friends together?

A. No, we just went for coffee.

Q. *Coffee and when you go for coffee does that end up — is that when you have a conversation about whether —*
A. Sometimes.
Q. *— he has crack cocaine?*
A. Sometimes no. All depends.
Q. How often would you have gone for coffee with Mr. Rose?
A. I don't know. Four times, three times.
Q. *Okay, as many times as you've bought crack cocaine from him?*
A. Maybe a little bit less.
Q. Now, when the police stopped the automobile they found some crack cocaine in the automobile?
A. That's what they claim.

In explaining hearsay testimony to the client or any other witness it is sufficient to advise that they cannot tell the Court what other people have told them for the purpose of proving the *truth* of what was said to them because those other people are not before the Court to be cross-examined under oath. Counsel may elaborate that there are numerous exceptions to this rule but to go through them with the witness (unless they are relevant) will cause confusion. Counsel will explain to the witness that if it becomes necessary for him or her to ask whether the witness spoke to a particular person, counsel probably won't be able to ask him what the other person said (with some exceptions, as in the example set out above) but counsel will ask: "As a result of what Mr. Smith told you, what did you do?"

For a detailed discussion of hearsay, see the later Chapter, "The Hearsay Horror."

THE WITNESS'S STATEMENT

It is always important to interview a witness as soon as possible after an event occurs when recollections are clearest. If the witness is first asked to recall the event a considerable time later, he or she is open to attack on a memory that may not be complete and accurate due to the passage of time. This is particularly so when there are alibi witnesses who will be called upon to remember a particular time of a particular day in a particular month and there is nothing special to help them identify that time period. See Chapter on Alibi for witness statements supporting alibi.

When possible a signed statement should be obtained from the witness so that he or she is able to refresh their memory from that statement many months or even years later when called upon to testify. More often than not memories will fail or will at least become hazy with the effluxion of time, but if the witness later refreshes his memory from his signed statement there will be no doubt in his mind about what occurred months and perhaps years earlier. In addition, a signed statement becomes useful if the witness proves hostile during examination-in-chief.[22] Also, if the cross-examiner accuses the witness impliedly or overtly of recent fabrication, a signed statement by the witness at an early stage can be presented to the witness to rebut that allegation of recent fabrication. Further, if the Crown decides to call a witness who gave the defence a signed statement, or vice versa, the cross-examiner will have potential ammunition to damage the witness's credibility if the witness's evidence conflicts with what is in the statement.

When possible, a sworn statement should be obtained from important witnesses or those witnesses whom counsel feels might change their testimony. This is the best way to impress upon witnesses the importance of what they are saying and to hold the witnesses in line for fear of facing a perjury charge if their testimony changes from that which is in the sworn statement. As a result of the Supreme Court of Canada's decision in *R. v. B. (K.G.)*,[23] a prior sworn statement may be used as evidence of the truth of the deponent's words even though not adopted at trial if there are additional guarantees of the statement's trustworthiness.

For the prosecution, however, a sworn statement can be a double-edged sword. A Crown witness who gives a sworn statement is often an accomplice or a police informant. If the defence were to argue forcefully that the accomplice lied because he/she received a favour, such as a lighter sentence, the Crown would be able to counter with the argument that there would be no reason for the witness to continue with the lie under oath since he/she had already received his/her reward and there was therefore nothing more to gain. But with the sworn statement, defence counsel would be able to argue forcefully that the witness knows he cannot change his original story because he could be charged with perjury, a danger of which he was warned at the time of swearing the statement. Even if the statement was not sworn, there is still the defence countering argument that if the witness were to later exonerate the accused the witness could face charges of mischief and obstructing justice.

If a sworn statement is not taken, consideration should be given to having the witness write out his/her statement in his/her own handwriting. If the statement is not in the witness's own handwriting, the witness should initial each page and initial corrections. It is a good idea to make intentional errors on each page of the statement since the witness will notice errors and correct them. If these precautions are taken the witness will have a difficult time in Court if he says that he did not appreciate what he was signing.

If the witness is prepared to give an interview but there is a concern that the potential witness is not prepared to sign a statement then it is imperative that counsel have an assistant from his or her office witness any

---

22 "The Hostile Witness" is discussed in a later chapter.
23 (1993), 79 C.C.C. (3d) 257 (S.C.C.). This case is discussed in Chapter, "Prior Inconsistent Statements."

utterance and ensure that the utterance is reduced to writing. In this way if the witness, called by the interviewer, testifies differently from his/her oral utterance there is someone available, if necessary, to testify on an application to declare the witness hostile. If this witness is called by the opposite side and testifies differently than his oral utterance, he can be asked whether or not he told counsel and the assistant something different on a prior occasion and if the witness denies this, the assistant can be called to contradict him. Another way to confirm the witness's original version is to tape-record the interview.

In order to make the witness's statement more complete and accurate there may be occasions when it is advisable to go with the witness to the scene of the incident about which she is to testify to refresh her memory so that she can better explain what happened.

In my experience in Toronto the police normally do not give witnesses a copy of any statement they have signed unless pursued by the witness. The reason may be that the police do not wish the witness to show the statement to others, particularly the accused or the accused's counsel at a very early stage. Defence counsel should seriously consider not giving a witness a copy of her statement unless it is requested, as the statement may find its way into the hands of the prosecution, allowing the Crown to prepare a better cross-examination. Another reason not to give the witness her statement is that if the witness later proves hostile she will have the benefit of recalling the details of what she had previously said, thereby enabling her to thwart cross-examination designed to challenge her credibility. A witness may be friendly one day but for any number of reasons unwilling or hostile the next day.

However, when a favourable defence witness is called to testify by the side who took her statement then the witness should be given a copy of her statement to refresh her memory shortly before testifying. Of course, in this circumstance the Crown will be entitled to see the statement if he elicits from the witness that the witness refreshed her memory from the statement within a reasonable time before testifying.

During the interview the witness (including the client) should be questioned closely to ensure there are no exaggerations and his/her evidence does not come from hearsay sources. In this way counsel will not become disappointed should the witness take the stand and (either in-chief or in cross-examination) it is discovered for the first time that what the witness was telling counsel in his office really came from a third party or was exaggerated. Some witnesses may exaggerate only slightly, but if those exaggerations are detected by opposing counsel then they can be highlighted to the point where the witness's credibility will be damaged. "After all, if a witness exaggerates about a minor detail, how much would she exaggerate about a more significant matter?" opposing counsel might well submit.

In most cases it is wise to interview witnesses and take their statements separately from each other. If the witnesses are interviewed together they may be influenced by what the others say and if the cross-examiner brings out that the witnesses were interviewed together the jury could be left with the impression that counsel played a role in this tactic. Interviewing witnesses together does not promote independence of thought and no doubt opposing counsel will make that point if these witnesses corroborate each other in Court. It was held in *R. v. Chin*[24] that a special warning is required by the trial Judge regarding the credibility of a witness who has discussed evidence with other witnesses before trial.

The interviewing of witnesses by Crown counsel was the subject of Recommendation #107 by Commissioner Kaufmann at the Morin Inquiry. That recommendation stated as follows:

(a) Counsel should generally not discuss evidence with witnesses collectively.

(b) A witness's memory should be exhausted, through questioning and through, for example, the use of the witness's own statement or notes, before any reference is made (if at all) to conflicting evidence.

(c) The witness's recollection should be recorded by counsel in writing. It is sometimes advisable that the interview be conducted in the presence of an officer or other person, depending on the circumstances.

(d) Questioning of the witness should be non-suggestive.

(e) Counsel *may* then choose to alert the witness to conflicting evidence and invite comment.

(f) In doing so, counsel should be mindful of the dangers associated with this practice.

(g) It is wise to advise the witness that it is his or her own evidence that is desired, that the witness is not simply to adopt the conflicting evidence in preference to the witness's own honest and independent recollection and that he or she is, of course, free to reject the other evidence. This is no less true if several other witnesses have given conflicting evidence.

(h) Under no circumstances should counsel tell the witness that he or she is wrong.

(i) Where the witness changes his or her anticipated evidence, the new evidence should be recorded in writing.

(j) Where a witness is patently impressionable or highly suggestible,

---

24 B.C. C.A., Lambert, Anderson and Toy JJ.A., February 23, 1989, summarized at 17 W.C.B. (2d) 36.

counsel may be well advised not to put conflicting evidence to the witness, in the exercise of discretion.

(k) Facts which are obviously uncontested or uncontestable may be approached in another way. This accords with common sense.

It is important to ascertain at the outset whether the witness gave a statement to the police. The witness, for any number of reasons, may give counsel a statement that differs from the statement that he gave to the police. Counsel can be frustrated later to learn of this statement to the police after receiving disclosure pursuant to *Stinchcombe*.

When counsel has pre-trial disclosure material from the Crown he should go over the important will-say statements with any of the witnesses who will talk to him, to determine their accuracy and any modifications or implications or other explanations which are relevant. Although there is said to be no property in a witness, defence counsel should always be particularly careful in arranging for the interview of potential Crown witnesses to ensure that no allegations can be made that the witness has been harassed or tampered with in any way. Counsel must avoid becoming a witness in the case by becoming embroiled in answering such allegations. It is best for an interviewer other than counsel to conduct such interviews or to do so in the presence of a witness who can be called to testify if necessary. Also, it is probably wise not to approach a witness who is emotionally involved in the case, such as a victim.

Because Canadian police departments are making more use of both audiotaping and videotaping, it is no longer enough to ask witnesses if they made a written statement to the police. It is very important to know if witnesses have been audio or videotaped. It is, of course, possible that witnesses will not know whether they have been audiotaped. But at least in all cases where the taping was openly done, defence counsel will be aware that a form of statement other than a written one may well be in the investigating officer's possession which you will request if not yet provided by way of disclosure.

THE CHILD WITNESS

Mary Wells,[25] in her paper "The Child Witness: Issues and Strategies," makes the point that the threshold issue with respect to children is not whether they can truthfully recall what has happened but "How do we help children to articulate their memories?" This can only be done with the proper preparation of the child witness which is obviously more painstaking than preparing the adult witness.

---

25 M.S.W. North Toronto Counselling Services.

Children who are the victim of abuse often believe they are in some way responsible for the crime committed against them. Much work may be required long before Court to improve the child's self-image, so that he or she does not feel blameworthy with the result that the truth does not surface.

In order to relieve the child's anxieties, Ms. Wells suggests that the child be shown diagrams of the courtroom including the participants' situation in the courtroom. However, if the child is asked to identify the accused during his or her trial testimony and points to the prisoner's dock that evidence will be meaningless given that the child had been forewarned as to the accused's position in the courtroom. The child should be asked which participants are most worrisome and in what order. The child should then have those fears allayed.

The witness should be taken to an empty courtroom for a test run in the witness box and any fears should be identified and dealt with one at a time rather than "as an overwhelming mass." The child should be made aware that his or her fears are normal ones.

The Crown may have to consider whether or not to make an application pursuant to sections 486, 482.2 to 488.5 of the *Criminal Code* to have the public excluded, to have a support person of the witness's choice be present and close to the witness while testifying, or where the complainant is under the age of 18 years testify outside the courtroom or behind a screen or other device where there is a concern that to do otherwise would prevent a full and candid account of the acts complained of from the complainant. A practical consideration however in using this procedure is whether jurors would sympathize less with the complainant because the juror hears only a voice without human form and does not have as good an opportunity to assess demeanour as when the witness can be seen.[26] There is also provision pursuant to section 715.1 of the *Criminal Code* where the complainant is under 18 years of age to enter into evidence a videotape by the complainant describing the acts complained of if made within a reasonable time after the alleged offence if the witness adopts the contents while testifying.[27] The child's videotaped statement taken pursuant to section 715.1 cannot be a prior consistent statement by virtue of the wording of the section.[28]

---

26 In *R. v. Levogiannis* (1990), 2 C.R. (4th) 355 (Ont. C.A.), it was held that the jury should be instructed, where there is obstructed view testimony, that such procedure is permitted due to the age of the witness and has nothing to do with the accused's guilt or innocence. The Supreme Court of Canada in (1993), 16 O.R. (3d) 384 affirming the Court of Appeal, said that the use of the screen does not deprive the accused to a fair hearing.

27 See *R. v. Meddoui* (1991), 61 C.C.C. (3d) 345 (Alta. C.A.) describing the law in this area. This section was ruled unconstitutional in *R. v. L. (D.O.)* (1991), 65 C.C.C. (3d) 465 (Man. C.A.); *R. v. Thompson* (1989), 68 C.R. (3d) 328; *R. v. Christensen* (1989), 8 W.C.B. (2d) 13 (Ont. Dist. Ct.); *R. v. M. (J.L.)* (1991), 68 C.C.C. (3d) 344 (Sask. Q.B.). Contra *R. v. K. (J.)* (1990), 60 C.C.C. (3d) 413 (N.W.T. S.C.).

28 *R. v. Wing*, 2008 CarswellOnt 5241 (Ont. C.A.) at para. 1.

It is helpful to bring someone to Court as a support for the child. That person should not have an emotional investment in the trial nor be involved as a witness who will be subject to an order for exclusion of witnesses. It should be explained to the child that such a support person is not able to show their support from the body of the courtroom, otherwise the child may feel he or she is not doing a good job when looking at this support person and finding no favourable response. The result may have a detrimental effect on the witness's confidence and testimony.

The child should be prepared for those questions regarding the taking of the oath. Amendments to the *Canada Evidence Act* have simplified this aspect considerably for all involved. See the Chapter, "Competency and Compellability" for the changes.

The questions that the child will be asked at trial and the answers should be reviewed several times, but not to the point where it will appear that the answers have been memorized. The witness should be encouraged to be his or her natural self and to tell in as much detail exactly what he or she recalls.

Because very young children have difficulty in describing the time sequence of events, they should be prompted to try to relate the occurrence of the crime with some other notable event that stands out in their mind close to the time of the offence. Obviously the questions should be constructed so they are understandable to the child. Children are not good at describing height and length and so should be asked to compare the height of an individual with someone in the courtroom and describe length by comparing to the dimensions of the courtroom. To help put the child at ease simple background questions should start the examination-in-chief such as age, family and school type questions.

See later Chapter, "Cross-Examination of Child Witnesses."

The Well-Prepared Child Witness

Court Jesters Cartoons. Peter V. MacDonald, Q.C. and David Brown. Stoddart. © 1991 by Peter V. MacDonald and David Brown.

4

The Defence of Alibi

INTERVIEW OF ALIBI WITNESSES

The word alibi means "elsewhere." When the defence of alibi is raised the accused claims that as he was elsewhere he could not have committed the crime.[1] To constitute an alibi the evidence must be determinative of the final issue of the guilt or innocence of the accused, so that where the accused was charged with murder, the precise time of death not established and there was a wide range of times when the murder could have been committed, and the evidence of the alibi witnesses did not encompass the whole of the wide range of times, the trial Judge did not err by failing to provide the jury with the standard alibi evidence instruction[2] as enunciated in *R. v. Parrington* (1985), 20 C.C.C. (3d) 184 (Ont. C.A.) and *R. v. O'Connor* (2002), 170 C.C.C. (3d) 365 (Ont. C.A.). See last page of this chapter for trial Judge's charge on reasonable doubt as it relates to alibi.

Counsel should try to obtain statements from alibi witnesses as soon as the client advises of their existence. It may be many months before these witnesses are called to testify at which time they will no doubt be closely cross-examined as to details, particularly the date and times that are relevant. The witnesses will be able to refresh their memories from their signed statements and avoid being subject to the criticism that they are confused or are lying as to the date or time or other details relating to the alibi because the event took place a significant time earlier. If there are specific factors which help the witness recall the date and time and any other details then they should be included in the statement and given in testimony as, for

---

1 *R. v.Wright* (2009), 247 C.C.C. (3d) 1 (Ont. C.A.) at para. 19. This appeal turned on whether the trial Judge erred by characterizing the appellant's position as an alibi defence, which, absent timely disclosure, triggered an adverse inference instruction to the jury. It was held that the trial Judge was wrong in her characterization and therefore wrong to give the instruction to the jury.

2 *R. v. R. (M.)* (2005), 195 C.C.C. (3d) 26 (Ont. C.A.).

example, it was the witness's birthday which could be a trigger event for the witness's memory. If there are documents that are relevant to the alibi, they should be obtained. They may either support or debunk this defence. If the alibi witness is able to remember what he did both closely before and after the time in question that should be included in the statement as well, as the Crown will no doubt ask such questions. If the witness is unable to recall those areas surrounding the event the Crown will make the point that the credibility and/or reliability of the witness as to his recollection of the alibi time is suspect.

Where there is more than one alibi witness it is imperative that they be interviewed separately so that there can be no allegation that they influenced each other in stating facts they should not otherwise have remembered. They no doubt will also be questioned if they conferred before attending to give their statements.

The Issue of Fabrication

Fabrication of the false alibi may lead to an inference of guilt but this is not always so since the lie may have been due to panic, embarrassment, fear of authority, dread of conviction, etc.[3] It should be noted however that there is a difference between fabrication of an alibi and disbelieving the alibi. The former admits to the usual broad inference of fraud and the latter amounts to nothing more than an inability to prove the specific fact of alibi.[4] An important decision in this area of the law which applies equally to statements made by an accused which are not in the nature of an alibi is *R. v. Coutts*.[5] Doherty J. opines as follows:

> [13] This court has repeatedly drawn a distinction between statements made by an accused (or testimony of an accused), which are disbelieved and, therefore, rejected and those statements or testimony which can be found to be concocted in an effort to avoid culpability. The former have no evidentiary value; the latter can constitute circumstantial evidence of guilt: *R. v. Davison, DeRosie and MacArthur* (1974), 20 C.C.C. (2d) 424–428 (Ont. C.A.), leave to appeal to S.C.C. refused, [1974] S.C.R. viii; *R. v. Mahoney* (1979), 50 C.C.C. (2d) 380 (Ont. C.A.) at 389, affirmed without reference to this point (1982), 67 C.C.C. (2d) 197 (S.C.C.); *R. v. Sandhu* (1989), 50 C.C.C. (3d) 492 (Ont. C.A.) at 499–501; *R. v. Levy* (1991), 62 C.C.C. (3d) 97 (Ont. C.A.) at 100–103;

---

3   *R. v. Burdick* (1975), 27 C.C.C. (2d) 497 (Ont. C.A.); *R. v. Cole* (1980), 53 C.C.C. (2d) 269 (Ont. C.A.); *R. v. Nielsen* (1984), 16 C.C.C. (3d) 39 (Man. C.A.), reversed (1988), (sub nom. *R. v. Stolar*) 40 C.C.C. (3d) 1, (S.C.C.).

4   *R. v. Davison* (1974), 20 C.C.C. (2d) 424 at 428 (Ont. C.A.); *R. v. Tessier* (1997), 113 C.C.C. (3d) 538 (B.C. C.A.); *R. v. Witter* (1996), 105 C.C.C. (3d) 44 (Ont. C.A.). See also *R. v. Hibbert* (2002), 163 C.C.C. (3d) 129 (S.C.C.).

5   (1998), 126 C.C.C. (3d) 545 (Ont. C.A.), leave to appeal refused (1999), 131 C.C.C. (3d) vi (S.C.C.).

R. v. Witter (1996), 105 C.C.C. (3d) 44 (Ont. C.A.) at 52–53. In an oft-quoted passage from *Mahoney, supra,* Brooke J.A. said, at p. 389:

> *If the jury accepted the evidence of the Crown witnesses that the appellant was the killer, disbelief of the appellant's denial was inevitable, but that disbelief could not be treated as an additional item of circumstantial evidence to prove guilt.* In my view, the jury ought not, routinely, to be instructed with respect to the inferences that may be drawn from the fabrication of a false alibi in the absence of a proper basis for that instruction, as for example, where there is extrinsic evidence of fabrication, or where the appellant has given different versions as to his whereabouts, one of which must be concocted. [Emphasis added.]

[14] The words of Brooke J.A. apply with equal force to statements made by an accused which are not in nature of an alibi, e.g. see *R. v. Levy, supra; R. v. Sandhu, supra.*

[15] This distinction between statements which are disbelieved and, therefore, rejected and those which can be found to be concocted and capable of providing circumstantial evidence of guilt cannot be justified as a pure matter of logic. In many, if not most cases, the inference of concoction flows logically from the disbelief of an accused's statements or testimony. The distinction made in *Mahoney* is, however, fully justified and, indeed, essential to ensure that the trier of fact properly applies the burden of proof in cases where statements of an accused are tendered or an accused testifies. If tiers of fact were routinely told that they could infer concoction from disbelief and use that finding of concoction as evidence of guilt, it would be far too easy to equate disbelief of an accused's version of events with guilt and to proceed automatically from disbelief of an accused to a guilty verdict. That line of reasoning ignores the Crown's obligation to prove an accused's guilt beyond reasonable doubt. By limiting resort to concoction as a separate piece of circumstantial evidence to situations where there is evidence of concoction apart from evidence which contradicts or discredits the version of events advanced by the accused, the law seeks to avoid convictions founded ultimately on the disbelief of the accused's version of events: *R. v. Tessier* (1997) 113 C.C.C. (3d) 538 (B.C. C.A.), *per* Ryan J.A. at 556, *per* Southin J.A. at 561; *R. v. Pleich* (1980), 55 C.C.C. (2d) 13 (Ont. C.A.).

Alibi evidence often accompanies identification evidence. Normally, if the alibi evidence does not stand up, that should not be the end of the matter as the prosecution must still prove identification beyond a reasonable doubt.[6] But in reality this does not happen when there is a jury. Experience has shown that if a jury does not accept an alibi the defence becomes tainted and the identification becomes fortified. Given that jurors are often swayed by honest but mistaken identification, this is another reason why an eye witness identification case should be tried before a Judge alone who will

---

6   *R. v. Tzimopoulos* (1986), 54 C.R. (3d) 1 (Ont. C.A.), leave to appeal refused (1987), 54 C.R. (3d) xxvii (S.C.C.); see also *R. v. Penman* (1985), 82 Cr. App. R. 44 (C.A.).

abide a discreet body of law that has developed around the dangers of identification evidence.

However, it is not sufficient for consciousness of guilt inference to be made unless a reasonable jury could infer that the alibi was deliberately fabricated and the accused was a party to the fabrication.[7] It is not enough that the alibi is found to be unworthy of belief or that the evidence implicating the accused is so compelling as to demand rejection of the alibi evidence.[8] Mere rejection of the alibi evidence as untruthful or unreliable does not constitute affirmative evidence of guilt.[9]

In order for there to be an inference of consciousness of guilt there must be independent evidence of fabrication and the trial Judge is required to provide such an instruction.[10]

Notice of Alibi

In *R. v. Wright*[11] Justice Doherty noted "there are qualifications on the accused's right to silence. One such qualification arises where an accused advances an alibi defence. If the accused fails to make timely disclosure to the prosecution of the substance of the alibi (or fails to testify in support of the alibi) the trier-of-fact may, not must, draw an adverse inference against the defence for that failure: *R. v. Noble*, at para. 111; *R. v. Cleghorn*; *R. v. Crawford*, 1995 CanLII 138 (S.C.C.); (1995), 96 C.C.C. (3d) 481 (S.C.C.) at pp. 494-5; *R. v. Chambers*, at p. 343; *R. v. P. (M.B.)*, 1994 CanLII 125 (S.C.C.), (1994), 89 C.C.C. (3d) 289 at pp. 304-5; *R. v. Hill*, 1995 CanLII 271 (ONCA), (1995), 102 C.C.C. (3d) 479 (Ont. C.A.) at pp. 476-7." . . . . . "The qualification can be justified only when the rationale for that qualification actually operates. Thus if the alibi defence is disclosed in time to permit meaningful investigation of the defence then there can be no justification for the instruction. See *R. v. Hogan* (1982), 2 C.C.C. (3d) 557 (Ont. C.A.) at p. 566, *R. v. Cleghorn*, 1995 CanLII 63 (S.C.C.), (1995), 100 C.C.C. (3d) 393, para 305." In *Cleghorn*, it was held that the "criteria of timeliness and adequacy of cure thus evaluated on the basis of whether a meaningful investigation could have been undertaken as a result of the disclosure."[12]

---

7 *R. v. Witter* (1996), 105 C.C.C. (3d) 44 (Ont. C.A.).

8 *Ibid.*

9 *Ibid.*

10 *R. v. Baltovich* (2004), 73 O.R. (3d) 481 (C.A.); *R. v. Maracle* (2006), 206 C.C.C. (3d) 36 (Ont. C.A.); *R. v. O'Connor* (2002), 170 C.C.C. (3d) 365 (Ont. C.A.).

11 (2009), 98 O.R. (3d) 665 (C.A.) at paras. 18, 19. See also *R. v. Hill* (1995), 102 C.C.C. (3d) 469 (Ont. C.A.).

12 *R. v. Laverty* (1977), 35 C.C.C. (2d) 151 (Ont. C.A.); *R. v. Parrington* (1995), 20 C.C.C. (3d) 184 (Ont. C.A.).

The Failing Alibi

"Is it simply your unsupported word, or did anyone actually <u>see</u> you on the night in question writing a biography of Jane Austen?"

Miscellaneous.

Producing alibi for the first time at trial cannot be subject to criticism if the accused referred to it in his or her statement and the police failed to investigate[13] or where the alibi witness had been turned up by the police.[14]

It was held in the case of *R. v. Ford*,[15] that an alibi to be properly disclosed should provide the Crown with full particulars of the alibi defence

13 See also *R. v. Mearow*, 2006 CarswellOnt 6140 (Ont. C.A.).

14 *R. v. Mahoney* (1979), 50 C.C.C. (2d) 380 (Ont. C.A.), affirmed (1982), 67 C.C.C. (2d) 197 (S.C.C.).

15 (1993), 78 C.C.C. (3d) 481, 1993 CarswellBC 1134 (B.C. C.A.), leave to appeal refused (1993), 157 N.R. 399 (note) (S.C.C.).

including names of witnesses and the disclosure should be at a time when an investigation may uncover something. Disclosing the alibi by mailing the names and addresses of the witnesses and details of what is expected that they will say at trial leaves witnesses open to questioning by the police. This alternative raises concerns with some that the police may not record completely or accurately what the alibi witness says or, in some cases, opens the door to the exercise of pressure to have the witnesses retreat from their proposed testimony. To have alibi witnesses interviewed by the police in the presence of counsel or someone delegated by counsel may or may not be acceptable to the police and may at trial put the defence counsel's office in conflict with the police on what was actually said at the interview, unless of course it is recorded by audio or video tape. Also this method of investigating the alibi will not preserve evidence for trial under section 715 of the *Criminal Code* nor will the alibi evidence receive a "test run" as it would at a preliminary hearing.

It is my preference that it should normally be at the preliminary hearing when defence counsel presents its alibi witnesses so the client is within the rule of giving timely disclosure before trial of the alibi to the prosecution. While the preliminary hearing may not be held for a significant time after arrest the Crown will have the opportunity to closely cross-examine the alibi witnesses to determine their credibility and reliability. In addition this procedure will preserve the alibi evidence to be read in at trial if for some reason an alibi witness or witnesses are unable on that date to appear for trial. The evidence is preserved by section 715 of the *Criminal Code* or by the principled approach to hearsay evidence.[16]

By having the alibi witness's testimony scrutinized at the preliminary inquiry, defence counsel can determine how his or her client's alibi will stand up at trial. If the evidence is untrustworthy or the alibi cannot be satisfactorily established, counsel no doubt will choose not to call it at trial. There is, in my view, no obligation to notify the Crown before the trial that the alibi called at the preliminary hearing will not be called at trial.[17] How-

---

16 *R. v. Russell* (1936), 67 C.C.C. 28 (S.C.C.); *R. v. Paradis* (1976), 38 C.C.C. (2d) 455 at 459-460 (Que. C.A.), leave to appeal refused [1977] 1 S.C.R. xi (S.C.C.); *R. v. Parrington, supra*; *R. v. Speid* (1988), 42 C.C.C. (3d) 12 (Ont. C.A.); *R. v. Cleghorn* (1995), 100 C.C.C. (3d) 393 (S.C.C.); *R. v. Dunbar* (1982), 68 C.C.C. (2d) 13 (Ont. C.A.).

17 Counsel should be aware of the decision in *R. v. Gillespie* (May 13, 1986), Borins D.C.J. (Ont. Dist. Ct.) (Released May 18th, 1986), summarized at 16 W.C.B. 491, where the Crown was permitted to introduce into evidence a letter from the accused's counsel that the intended defence of alibi would no longer be relied upon at trial on the basis that a false alibi could be used as evidence of consciousness of guilt. In *R. v. Witter* (1996), 105 C.C.C. (3d) 44(Ont. C.A.), Doherty J.A. expressed doubts whether an alibi notice by counsel constituted a statement by the accused and felt the Court did not have the benefit of full argument on this issue in *R. v. Gillespie*. He further expressed doubt that an alibi notice was admissible as part of the Crown's case as was held in *R. v. Gillespie*. He felt

ever, if the evidence is not impressive at the preliminary hearing it may only be due to a nervous witness who will be more comfortable at trial with the preliminary hearing experience behind him.

If the trial is to be held in the provincial Court, it will of course be necessary to disclose the alibi by other means than at a preliminary hearing, such as by a notice in writing as referred to earlier in *R. v. Ford*. It is of interest to note that Recommendation 94 from The Commission Proceedings Involving Guy Paul Morin states:

> Where the defence discloses the existence of an alibi in a serious case, police should be encouraged to have the alibi investigated by officers other than those most directly involved in investigating the accused. Often, the investigation of an alibi need not draw extensively upon the knowledge of the investigating officers themselves. This recommendation permits a more objective, less predisposed approach to the potential alibi.

If counsel chooses to mail in the alibi then it would be fruitful to make reference to Recommendation 94 and insist that the alibi be investigated by officers other than those involved in the investigation.

Improper disclosure of the alibi can only weaken an alibi, it will not exclude it. It does not give rise to an inference of guilt.[18]

Disclosure of an alibi may be given by a third party who has a witness to the alibi.[19]

The Alibi at Trial

Do not lead the alibi witness in Court as to the date and time because these matters are essential to the alibi, and leading questions will detract from their weight. Ask such questions as: Did you learn that Mr. X was arrested on the charges before the Court and from whom did you hear? How long after the charges did you learn about them? As a result of learning about the charges did you speak to anyone from my office? Did you give a statement in writing? Did you sign it? When did you give that statement? (Witness may wish to refer to the statement for the date or generally refreshing her memory.) Then launch into questions detailing the alibi. You may then wish to finish off by asking whether the witness had been questioned about his or her alibi by the Crown Attorney or the police. Indeed, you may enhance the credibility of your witnesses by eliciting that they had been questioned by the police earlier, had given a statement and even testified at the preliminary hearing if such was the case. The trier-of-fact will then know

---

it should only be admitted after the accused has testified in direct examination "in a manner which gives the notice impeachment potential."

18   *R. v. Cleghorn, supra.*
19   *Ibid.*

that the witness did not come forward at the eleventh hour and the prosecution had foreknowledge of what the witness would say at trial, and could prepare an attack on the witness's credibility. If that witness is left unchallenged or unscathed in cross-examination, his or her testimony will be bolstered.

If the alibi witness was called upon to remember the facts supporting the alibi some time after the event, he or she may be cross-examined to show that they may be mistaken as to the exact day and time he or she is referring to, i.e., they could be off in their recollection by a single day. Hopefully the witness could point to some memorable event that would have triggered their memory as, for example, a birth date or other memorable circumstance.

The Crown can lead evidence as part of its case to show an accused attempted to concoct a false alibi to support an inference of consciousness of guilt.[20]

Most often alibi witnesses are close members of the accused's family or are very good friends of the accused. No doubt in cross-examination of those alibi witnesses the Crown will highlight the closeness of the relationship and obtain an easy admission they would not want to see anything bad happen to the accused and will do so again in his or her jury summation. Defence counsel should be mindful of the words of the Lord Chief Justice in *R. v. Turnbull* wherein he stated:[21]

> "[W]e think that the way the comment was left was unfortunate in that the learned Judge did not go on to point out to the jury that as the appellant's alibi was that he was at home with his wife, who else could he have called to support it? This is a situation which not infrequently arises. In such circumstances it will almost be present in the jury's mind that the witness is the defendant's wife and they will no doubt make what they think is the proper allowance for this fact. They should, however, be warned in most, if not all, similar cases that they should not necessarily regard the fact that the witness is the defendant's wife as derogating from the worth of her evidence when the nature and content of the defence is such that anyone would expect her to be called as a witness in any event."

---

20 *R. v. Babinski* (1991), 67 C.C.C. (3d) 187 at 189 (Ont. C.A.), affirmed (1992), 76 C.C.C. (3d) 286 (S.C.C.); *R. v. Witter, supra*; *R. v. Biddle* (1995), 96 C.C.C. (3d) 321 at 331 (S.C.C.)

21 (1976), 63 Cr. App. R. 132 at 143 (H.L.). See also *Cloutier v. R.* (1960), 34 C.R. 60 (Que. C.A.); *R. v. Andrade* (1985), 18 C.C.C. (3d) 41 (Ont. C.A.) per Martin J. at 64 and 66; and *R. v. Belanger* (1975), 24 C.C.C. (2d) 10 (Ont. C.A.), where it was held to be improper to cross-examine the accused's wife, an alibi witness, that she had provided an alibi for her husband in an earlier trial as this was not so unusual as to be inherently improbable. The Court added that the wife's previous alibi could have been relevant if the prior evidence had been fabricated, or if it was strikingly similar to her present evidence, and it was improbable that the same events coincidentally happened twice.

The Crown will also cross-examine alibi witnesses regarding any discussions between them and with the accused in an attempt to at least infer collusion.

Failure to Call Supporting Alibi Witnesses

It was held in *R. v. Carey*[22] that a jury instruction permitting an adverse inference due to the defence failure to call witnesses who might have been expected to provide relevant evidence for the defence with respect to alibi should be used with caution particularly when the names of the witnesses were disclosed as a result of the Crown's cross-examination and not put forth by the accused himself. The trial Judge should point out there may be valid reasons for not calling these witnesses and the jury should not speculate as to those reasons.

While the trier-of-fact is entitled to draw an adverse inference when the accused or spouse who is in a position to support the alibi fails to testify in support of the alibi, by virtue of section 4(6) of the *Canada Evidence Act*, the Crown and Judge are forbidden to comment on such failure.[23] It was held by the Quebec Court of Appeal that this subsection has no application where the trial Judge is sitting alone.[24]

Counsel for an accused is permitted to comment on the failure of a co-accused to testify[25] but the trial Judge may use her discretion in not permitting counsel to use his co-accused's failure to testify as a piece of evidence pointing to his guilt.[26]

For a more complete reference to the case law the reader is referred to the Chapter – Further Limitation and Obligations – and the subheading – Duty to Call Witnesses which surveys cases that permit adverse comment for failure of the defence to call witnesses.

The *Sophonow* Inquiry Recommendations

Justice Peter Cory's recommendations in The Inquiry Regarding Thomas Sophonow with respect to alibi witness and their investigation by police are as follows:

---

22 (1996), 113 C.C.C. (3d) 74 (Que. C.A.). See also *R. v. Simon* (2001), 154 C.C.C. (3d) 562 (Que. C .A.).

23 *R. v. Noble* (1997), 114 C.C.C. (3d) 385 (S.C.C.); *R. v. Milec* (1996), 110 C.C.C. (3d) 439 (Ont. C.A.); *R. v. Miller* (1998), 131 C.C.C. (3d) 141 (Ont. C.A.).

24 *Pratte v. Maher* (1963), 43 C.R. 214 (Que. C.A.).

25 *R. v. Creighton*, [1995] 1 S.C.R. 858.

26 *R. v. Leon-Uzarraga* (1998), 123 C.C.C. (3d) 291 (B.C. C.A.) at para. 47; *R v. Noble*, *supra*, at 429. See also *R. v. Oliver* (2005), 194 C.C.C. (3d) 92 (Ont. C.A.) per Doherty J. at para. 65.

1. The alibi defence should be disclosed within a reasonable time after the Crown disclosure has been completed and the Defence has reviewed it and is in a position to know the case that must be met. When that disclosure should be made by the Defence will vary from case to case. It will obviously depend upon the extent of the Crown disclosure, how long it will take the Defence to review that disclosure and how quickly Defence Counsel can prepare the alibi evidence disclosure. To the extent that it is possible, the disclosure of the alibi evidence should be in the form of statements signed by the witnesses. Alibi evidence may well establish innocence and the Defence should spend all the time and energy required to put forward a complete and detailed position on the alibi evidence.

2. How should the police investigate the alibi evidence? Obviously, it is incumbent upon them to ensure that the alibi defence is credible. However, because of the importance of the evidence, the same care should be taken in interviewing the alibi witnesses as is taken with the interviews of suspect. That is to say, wherever possible, the interview should be videotaped and, if that is not feasible it must, at the very least, be audiotaped. The entire interview must be on tape. Anything which is alleged to have been said that is not transcribed should be considered inadmissible.

    The interviewing of alibi witnesses should be undertaken by officers other than those who are the investigators of the offence itself.

    It has been suggested that it should be done by members of other police forces. However, this is cumbersome and may be unnecessarily expensive. If the interview is conducted by an officer other than one involved in the investigation of the crime itself and if the interview is videotaped or audiotaped, this will provide sufficient safeguards.

3. The alibi witnesses should not be subjected to cross-examination or suggestions by the police that they are mistaken. The alibi witnesses should be treated with respect and courtesy. They should not be threatened or intimidated or influenced to change their position. However, I agree that it is appropriate for the police to instruct the witnesses that it is essential that they tell the truth and that a statement can be used as proof of its contents. The witnesses should be advised that they should be careful to tell the truth and of the consequences of a failure to do so.

4. If, as a result of the disclosure of the alibi and the interviewing of the alibi witnesses, the Crown deems it appropriate to conduct further interviews of Crown witnesses expected to be called at the trial, a procedure similar to the interrogation of the alibi witnesses should be followed. That is to say, if there is to be a further interview of a Crown witness, it should be conducted by someone other than the investigating officers. The police conducting the interview should make every effort

to avoid leading questions or questions which suggest the position of the police on the case.

4(a) it is essential that any further interviews of Crown witnesses following the disclosure of the alibi evidence should as well be videotaped or, if that is impossible, audiotaped. Every portion of the interview should be transcribed. Any statement alleged to have been made by the witness and which does not appear on the tape recording should be deemed to be inadmissible.

The Trial Judge's Charge on Alibi and Reasonable Doubt

The trial Judge's charge with respect to alibi must relate the principle of reasonable doubt to the evidence of the defence as follows: that if the jury believed the alibi testimony given in support of the defence then they must acquit; if they did not believe the evidence in support of the alibi defence but were left with a reasonable doubt by it, they are required to acquit; finally, if they were not left with a reasonable doubt by the evidence in support of the alibi, they must determine whether they were convinced beyond a reasonable doubt of the accused's guilt.[27]

---

27 *R. v. Parrington* (1985), 20 C.C.C. (3d) 184 (Ont. C.A.) per Cory J.

5

Presenting Evidence-In-Chief

OBJECTIVES

In comparison to the study of the art of cross-examination, direct examination is the neglected child of the trial advocacy family. However, more cases have been won by evidence given in-chief than by evidence given in cross-examination and it is unfortunate that when examination-in-chief does not receive the respect it deserves from counsel, a case which could have been won may be lost.

The primary objective of examination-in-chief is to present through the witness all that can be said which is relevant, admissible and favourable to the proponent's case. When a witness testifies to an event or a conversation, the more legitimate detail that can be recalled about that event or conversation, the better the chances that the witness's credibility and/or reliability will be enhanced. This should be kept in mind when your witness is being interviewed, particularly the client. The unpractised lying witness often does not become very specific or is vague in their testimony because he or she is unable to recall events as there is nothing for them to recollect, and they may even have to resort to making up evidence as they go along, in which case they become more vulnerable in cross-examination.

Weaknesses, if disclosed first in cross-examination, can destroy otherwise good impressions made earlier in direct examination. Examination-in-chief must therefore be used not only to present a case but also to lessen the impact of damaging questions that counsel anticipates will be put to the witness by the opponent by way of cross-examination. This, of course, means that the questioner must anticipate the cross-examination of the witness when preparing for examination-in-chief. An obvious example is where the accused has a criminal record. A witness's criminal record should always be disclosed during examination-in-chief to reduce the likelihood that the opponent will mention it in cross-examination. Even if the record is mentioned in cross-examination its impact on jurors will have been minimized since they will have already heard the information directly from the witness. It is also possible that a jury will be left with a good impression of the witness's credibility since the information was voluntarily revealed.[1] See later chapter on Criminal Records.

When revealing a weakness in the testimony of one's own witness, counsel should try to phrase questions in such a way to minimize any potentially damaging effect. In one case,[2] for example, the previous conviction of a witness was disclosed in-chief by Sir John Simon, K.C. in the following sympathetic manner:

> Q: I am sorry to have to ask you, Mr. Newton, but I had better ask it here. Have you been convicted of forgery?
> A: Yes, I have, Sir John.
> Q: In the year 1907. I suppose that would be the year . . . and you served a sentence in respect of it?
> A: I did, yes.[3]

Because the principles of "primacy" and "recency" state that people generally remember best what they heard first and last, the appropriate place to have a witness volunteer any weakness in-chief would be somewhere in the middle of the testimony. The weakness will have less impact if the witness makes a good impression at the outset because it appears to be a law of human nature that first impressions are lasting ones which are difficult to change even when subsequently met with unfavourable facts.

Another example where counsel may wish to meet a weakness in-chief is when the witness has given different versions of what he or she saw or heard. Attempting to explain the inconsistency in examination-in-chief may lessen any impact of damaging questions on cross-examination, unless the chosen tactic is to deal with it in re-examination if not explained in cross. However, in *R. v. Pinkus*[4] this approach was held to be oath-helping and would weaken cross-examination.

In experienced hands, examination-in-chief may also be used to trap opposing counsel. By touching only lightly on certain aspects of the case and thus enticing the cross-examiner into more detailed questions which the witness has been prepared to answer effectively, greater impact may be achieved than if those questions had been asked during the examination-in-chief. If opposing counsel is caught off-guard by these responses he or she may not be able to think of appropriate follow-up questions quickly enough to neutralize any damage.

---

1 More has been said about this topic in Chapter, "Client and Witness Interviews."
2 Ed. C.E. Bechhofer Roberts (see also J.H. Munkman, *The Technique of Advocacy* (London: Stevens, 1951), p. 47).
3 *Ibid.*, p. 261.
4 This approach was disapproved of in *R. v. Pinkus* (1999), 140 C.C.C. (3d) 309 (Ont. S.C.J.) *per* McKinnong as it was held to be oath-helping and would weaken cross-examination.

SOME BASIC RULES

Testimony in direct examination should be presented in a logical and orderly sequence so that it will have the greatest possible impact on the triers-of-fact. A disconnected story is to be avoided as jurors will be more likely to remember a story told in a chronological and sensible sequence. The scene should be set before describing the action so that the juror will understand what happened in context and the questioner will not lose the effectiveness of the evidence by having to interrupt the testimony to provide additional background information. However, there can be no hard and fast rules in this regard as there may be times when counsel wishes to present the most significant testimony at the outset of the trial when the jurors are usually most alert. The lead-up to the most dramatic testimony could be lengthy and tedious and the jurors' minds may have started to wander by the time the crucial testimony is presented. A model examination-in-chief can be found in *The Tichborne Case*[5] where the defendants were attempting to show there were tattoo marks on the arm of the missing heir. There were no such tattoos on the arm of the false claimant. As John Munkman[6] states:

> Notice the orderliness, the thoroughness at each state, the precision with which the witness is guided to the exact point without leading (there are in fact a few leading questions), and the economy of words.

> *Introductory questions. First topic: knowledge of missing heir.*
>   'I believe you were educated at Stonyhurst?'—'I was.'
>   'Were you there with Roger Charles Tichborne?'—'Yes.'
>   'During what years were you with him?'—'1847 and 1848.'
>   'Were you both philosophers?'—'Yes.'
>   'Where did you live?'—'At a house called the seminary.'
>   'Did you both live in the seminary?'—'We did.'
>   'During the years you were at Stonyhurst, did you see much of Roger Charles Tichborne?'—'I did during the two years that we were together.'
>   'Were you in the same class?'—'We were not in the same class exactly.
>   'Where did you see most of him—At what parts of the day?'—'During recreation.'
>   'Now, have you a recollection of the appearance of Roger Charles Tichborne?'—'I have.'

> *Second topic: refusal to identify the claimant.*
>   'You were in Court, I think, during the time the claimant was under examination and cross-examination?'—'I was during the cross-examination.'
>   'For how long did you see him?'—'For about three hours.'
>   'Did you form your judgment whether he is the Roger Tichborne whom you knew in 1847 and 1848?'—'I did.'

---

5 Viscount Maugham (1936), pp. 301-303.
6 J.H. Munkman, *The Technique of Advocacy* (London: Stevens & Sons Limited, 1951), pp. 47-49.

'What was the judgment?'—'I could discover nothing that put me in mind of Roger Tichborne.'

'In your judgment and belief, is he or is he not the man?'—'In my judgment and belief he is not the man.'

Third topic. tattoo marks (notice the orderly and thorough procedure).

'Now, do you remember during the time you were at Stonyhurst with Roger Charles Tichborne, doing anything to either of his arms?'—'I remember tattooing one of his arms.'

'Which arm was it you tattooed?'—'The left arm.'

'At the time you tattooed it, was there, or was there not, upon the arm any other tattoo mark then existing?'—'Yes, there was.'

'What was that then existing mark?'—'It was a heart, a cross, and an anchor.'

'What was it that you tattooed upon the arm?'—'I tattooed R.C.T.'

'Will you . . . point out to the jury the position on the arm that you tattooed those initials?'—'The initials were tattooed about there—about that distance from the wrist . . .'

'Where were the other marks that you have mentioned?'—'They were above it . . .'

'Now will you tell us how you tattooed it; what materials you used?'—'Indian ink, and three needles inserted into a small handle of deal.'

'Besides the marks you have just told us, the letters you tattooed, was there any other mark either upon the arm or upon the wrist, so far as you recollect?'—'There was a small mark on the wrist.'

'What was that small mark on the wrist?'—'It was probably the result of tattooing, but badly done; it was like a splotch.'

Fourth topic: facts showing that the marks would still be here.

'After you had tattooed the letters you have mentioned, did you see Roger Tichborne's arm bare after you had done it?'—'Oh, frequently.'

'Up to the time of his leaving Stonyhurst?'—'Yes.'

'Were the marks you have described to us, including what you put on his arm yourself, still remaining there the last time you saw his arm?'—'They were.'

'Now, at or about the time you tattooed Roger Charles Tichborne, was there anything done with your arm, or to your arm?'—'At the same time he tattooed an anchor on my arm . . .'

'What materials was that done with?'—'With the same material and the same instruments.'

'The same material and the same instruments; the same ink?'—'The same ink.'

'Have you that mark remaining on your arm now?'—'I have . . .'

'. . . The mark which you have shown to the jury was done on the same day, with the same instruments, and with the same ink?'—'It was; probably during the same hour.'

The questions should be kept simple and brief. Rolling up two or three questions into one is not advisable as a multiple question can be difficult to answer. Use simple language. Remember, what is simple to counsel may not be simple for the jurors. For example, do not use the word "subsequent" when "after" will be more readily understood by all. Explain or reduce technical language to more commonly understood language. Ambiguous and double negative questions will not only be confusing to the jury but also to the witness who will in turn reply with ambiguous and indefinite answers. A clear question should evoke a clear answer. It is important to remember that it is not enough that counsel and the witness understand each other. The jurors must understand what is occurring between counsel and the witness. Counsel and the witness start off with an understanding of the background of the case; jurors do not. The questioner should not hesitate to spoonfeed the jurors, if necessary.

The following segment of the examination-in-chief by Norman Birkett of his client, Mancini, charged with the murder of woman he claimed to have loved is an example of brief, simply phrased, succinct questions evoking succinct responses by the accused, as is seen in the above example, *The Tichborne Case.*

'Were you in any way responsible for the death of Violette Kaye?'
'I was not, sir.'
'Did you ever use the hammer in any way at all?'
'I have never even seen it.'
'Did you live with Violette Kaye at Brighton?'
'I did, sir.'
'Where did she get money?'
'She was a loose woman and I knew it.'
'Did she appear to be in fear?'
'Yes. That's why we were always on the move.'
'Was she often intoxicated?'
'Often.'
'How did you get on together?'

For the first time Mancini hesitated. When at last he spoke his voice was very low.

'Strange as it is,' he said, 'I used to love her.'
'Had you any quarrels?'
'None.'
'Does that cover the whole time you were together?'
'Every second she was alive.'
'How did she behave when she came to the Skylark Café on Thursday, the 10th of May?'
'She was staggering a little. She wasn't herself. She was affected by something. All that week she had been rather strange.'
'What time did you get home that night?'
'About half-past seven.'
'What did you do when you saw her lying on the bed?'

'At first glance I thought she was asleep. I caught hold of her shoulder and I said, "Wake up." Then I saw blood on the pillow and on the floor.'

'When you found she was dead, why didn't you fetch the police?'

It was the key question of the whole examination. Mancini's answer, set of by Birkett's imaginative strategy, created an immense impression on the Court.

'I?' he said. 'I fetch the police? With my record?' He drew himself up and took a long breath. 'Where the police are concerned, a man who's got convictions never gets a square deal.'[7]

Refrain from eliciting irrelevant or unimportant testimony, otherwise the jurors may become bored or confused and thereby miss what is really important. The witness should be controlled in a way that directs attention away from irrelevant and unimportant evidence. The questions should have an object that is relevant to the case. The important testimony should be reached quickly, developed and stopped. The more issues that counsel brings out in-chief means there is more grist for the opponent's cross-examination.

Generally, counsel should not simply ask the witness to tell his own story. The witness in all likelihood will tell a rambling and disjointed tale and forget some of the important details. The witness should be guided by questions to the essential point and only then be asked to give his or her account. If the witness gives these essential details of the most important parts of his testimony without any guidance from counsel it will be much more impressive than doing so in answer to a number of questions.

If the witness begins to stray from a logical order the questioner should interrupt and guide him or her back on track. A witness telling the story well in his own way should not be interrupted with questions. Unlike cross-examination, during examination-in-chief counsel should stay more in the background and permit the witness's personality, if a pleasing one, to dominate.

On a rare occasion, counsel will have a client or other witness who is unpredictable or uncontrollable and any preparation with that witness only serves to prevent counsel from collapsing when the witness does not follow the game plan. Experienced counsel will have an easier time recovering than those newer to the bar. David C. Day, Q.C., of the Newfoundland bar was faced with a runaway client, the petitioner in a divorce proceeding. After some questions were put to his client, she testified: "No more questions. We'll get to it now." Mr. Day, a very experienced counsel, kept his composure and steered the client through some humorous testimony to the desired conclusion.[8]

---

7 From *Defender's Triumph*, by Edgar Lustgarten, published by Wingate.

8 Pages 5 to 9.

Boring the Jury

"...*but I digress.*"

Trial Diplomacy Journal's Cartoon Album. David M. Freedman, Ed. © 1980 Court Practice Journal, Inc.

Mr. Day:

Q. I refer next to paragraph 6 of the Petition Mrs. . . ., to ask you about your knowledge of your allegation—I summarize in my words—that your incontinent husband consorted with another woman. To begin, tell His Lordship how you—.

A. It wasn't that way at all Your Honour. It happened right in our marriage bed in Foxtrap. He's the whoremaster. She isn't much better.

Q. Mrs. . . ., I promise to come to that part of your story in a few questions.

A. No need for any more questions. We'll get to it now.

Q. When did you first suspect your husband was having sexual contact with another woman?

A. When I seen him in my bed with her.

Q. You came into the bedroom unexpected and found your husband and another woman in the sheets?

A. You can say that. Part under, part on the sheets. Anyway, I didn't walk in or nothing. I heard he was rampsing with this one and that one on Friday nights when I go to town [St. John's] to bingo. Then the rampsing became something more than just rampsing.

His Lordship:
You know what "rampsing" is, do you Mr. Day?

Mr. Day:
Ramming? No. No. I know the term as "rompsing". Never experienced, at least I don't think so.

His Lordship:
"Rampsing", also known as "rompsing" in the Dictionary of Newfoundland English.

Mr. Day:
Q. Mrs.—

A. Playing around innocent like. But what happened later was no innocent matter. She was a real sailor's man. I heard she's contacted everything there is to get.

Q. How did you learn the rampsing became romantic?

A. I hid in the closet one night. I loaned my car to my girlfriend that time so he'd think I was in town. Two o'clock there's noise downstairs, then on the stairs, then in the bedroom. I came out. Dead on the floor. My husband is alone, a skinful in, being on the beer.

Q. False alarm?

A. Yes, but there was nothing false the next Friday. I didn't go to bingo that time. I and my girlfriend got in my car and kept a watch. Sure enough, ten o'clock, he and the trooper come to our house, go in, lights on downstairs, then upstairs in the bathroom, back down in the kitchen, back up to the bathroom, then the bedroom, then lights out. And they closed the curtains.

Q. And when the curtains came down and the lights went out in your home in Foxtrap that night in June, what, praytell, what did you do?

A. Plenty.

Q. Let us in on it.

A. Well, we had the plan in place. My friend is a social worker so you can imagine it was all above board. She got advice from a lawyer. And we had two tension ladders. And secret like, we put the two of them up handy to the bedroom window about 2 a.m. when the business is done and all is quiet. But things didn't stay quiet. I got up on one ladder. It got stuck first and wouldn't expand up. Anyway, we got them up.

Q. The two ladders?

A. Yes. The social worker up one and me up the other. Almost fifteen feet off the ground. And I think she had the light. Yes, she had the flashlight. I had the axe. I smashed out the window. The storm window and the inside window and the transit. And ripped down the curtains.

Q. The transom? The wooden bar in the window?

A. Yes. The whole shagging thing. Glass and wood chips and sheers all over the place. The axe got loose from me and hit the bed. And then I shined the light in. No, I mean the social worker shined the light in. And what a sight. I did the looking. The two darlings fast to sleep. Anyway, she shined the light in. The trooper was under the sheets or at least part under and part on the sheets. He was asleep on his back. About the same time they both sat up and they stared right into the light. My husband and her.

Q. What next happened?

A. I didn't stick around to find out. But I know he went to the Mounties next day and tried to charge me with breaking and entering. But I certainly didn't enter. I only did the breaking. He was the one entering. So we both should be charged. But nothing came of it.

When counsel has received the desired answer, the question should not be asked again for emphasis as the witness may feel the questioner was not satisfied with the answer the first time and may answer differently on the next occaston, opening up an obvious line of cross-examination. Do not repeat the answers the witness gives as some advocates do. It is annoying. As Sir David Napley stated: "Echoes may be fascinating in the Tyrolean foothills, but they are tedious in a Court of law."[9] However, if returning after a break in the trial, as for example, overnight, counsel may wish to bring the judge or jury back to the point where he or she left off by reminding them, through the witness, of the answer or series of answers given just before the break.

Some counsel are most comfortable writing out in full their questions for examination-in-chief. The danger with this method is that it can cause too heavy a reliance on notes. The result can be a stilted, boring presentation destroying the naturalness of the testimony. Counsel should avoid as much as possible looking at his or her notes while asking questions. Otherwise, he/she will give the impression of being indifferent to the witness's answers and may signal to the jury that a scripted answer is forthcoming or that they too should be uninterested in the responses of the witness. In this regard Sir Frederick Wrottesley[10] stated:

Do not hold the brief before you like a book from which you are reading, (that is) you will inevitably examine the witness as if you were hearing him repeat a catechism he has learned instead of gathering from him information which he possesses but you do not.

Counsel's presentation should be as lively and as interesting as possible. The important words of each question should be jotted down. If

---

9 D. Napley. *The Technique of Persuasion*, 3rd ed. (London: Sweet and Maxwell, 1983), p. 125.

10 F.J. Wrottesley, *The Examination of Witnesses in Court,* 3rd ed. (London: Sweet & Maxwell, 1961), p. 49.

counsel feels more confident with the questions written out, the key words should be underlined so that, at a glance, the eye can quickly pick them up and thereby stimulate the memory. In this way the questioner's attention can be focused on the witness, following his/her demeanour, being alert to his/her answers so that the questioner can be prepared to react accordingly.

When preparing questions, regard must be had for the personality and character traits of the witness. If counsel feels the witness will not be pleasing to the jury or judge then that witness should be tightly controlled, and shorter answers should be sought. If the witness has a manner which will create a favourable impression, then the witness should be given more freedom to express himself or herself. An examination should not interfere with the spontaneity of the answers, since such responses are usually the most convincing ones that a witness can give.

EMPHASIS

Verbal

Some two thousand years ago Quintillian stated:

> Indifferent discourse well delivered is better received by a popular audience than a good discourse badly delivered. It is not so important what our thoughts are, as in what manner they are delivered, since those whom we address are moved only as they hear.

Quintillian's opinion is good advice for the examiner-in-chief.

As indicated, the questioner should ask questions as if genuinely interested in the answers and give the impression that he/she is hearing the answers for the first time. If counsel appears uninterested or bored a similar response may be triggered in the jurors. With proper emphasis, the questioner can maintain the jurors' attention, particularly with respect to the important answers.

Dramatic emphasis can be achieved by tone and inflection, by showing enthusiasm, humour and personality. Counsel's voice should be raised so that all can hear. As indicated earlier, the questioner's head should not be buried in his or her notes, reading his prepared questions verbatim in a monotone. This will only result in monotony and a loss of interest by the jurors.

Choice of phrasing can be effective, such as prefacing the appropriate question with: "Please tell the jury, Mr. Smith . . .", prompting the witness to turn his face toward the jury. Repeating key phrases or words throughout your examinations can help to bring home your point.

Emphasis

"A unique and stirring plea, counsellor."

Counsel should ensure that the witness's voice is raised and that the witness speaks in a definite manner so that each juror can hear every word. Counsel should not place himself or herself in a position to question the witness which allows the witness's head to turn away from the triers-of-fact. A good place for counsel to stand is at the end of the jury box so that the witness's voice will travel toward the jurors on its way to the counsel.

In a non-jury case, counsel may direct questions from the counsel table. It will be easier for the trial Judge to hear the witness. If the witness speaks quietly it would be advisable to stand back in order to encourage the witness to raise his or her voice to allow the trial Judge to hear the witness.

Counsel should watch the mood and attention of the jurors. If some jurors appear restless or bored counsel should change the pace or proceed immediately to another subject-matter which will be more interesting or at least inject more enthusiasm into his or her presentation.

It is generally felt by experienced counsel that professionalism and sometimes tactics dictate that the questioner should maintain the same impassive face during favourable and unfavourable testimony from one's own witness. However, if it becomes necessary for you to impeach your own witness, as for example, by employing section 9 of the *Canada Evidence Act*, there may be no reason to hide your annoyance particularly because you would not want the triers-of-fact to think that you were expecting such testimony.

Demeanour of counsel is of the utmost importance. You should generally be pleasant and mannerly and, without being overbearing, should convey that you are the master of the courtroom. Such a posture will give the jurors confidence in following your submissions to them at the end of the trial.

A witness's background can enhance his/her credibility and reliability. Evidence which goes to stability such as marriage, children, work history, executive positions, work in the community, etc., should be adduced.

When the opportunity presents itself counsel should have the witness testify as to any special means of knowledge, opportunities of observation, reasons for recollections or belief, or other circumstances increasing the witness's competency to speak of the particular case. Joseph Sedgwick[11] gave the following examples:

> You may have witnesses for your defense of alibi. It is not enough for such witnesses to say bluntly that the accused could not have been at the scene of the crime at the time alleged because he was then playing poker five miles away. The witness must come to that slowly; he must be asked if he remembers the 5th of March; and why he remembers that day so clearly out of all the days gone by; it may be that it was his birthday—or pay day—or some other day which for an assigned reason was especially memorable. If he remembers a time, you must get his special peculiar reason for remembering it—he may have had a new watch which he consulted, as one does with new watches, every few minutes. If he can remember the weather, a bad snowstorm, or Hurricane Hazel—you can confirm his recollection by the meteorological reports for that day—it will greatly add to his credibility. Only after you have

---

11   J. Sedgwick, "Presentation of the Evidence," Special Lectures, 1959, Law Society of Upper Canada (Toronto: Richard DeBoo Ltd., 1959), pp. 89-100.

explored all of the circumstances that probably would fix the date and time in the memory of the witness should you come to the question of the poker game and the presence there of the accused. Or let us suppose that it is a question of observation. It will not do merely to ask the witness what he saw without first fixing him in his position, showing how far away he was from the thing observed; the light or lack of it; what attracted his attention to the occurrence—and, in short, every item however trivial that will serve to impress on the jury not merely the truthfulness of the witness but also his competence.[12]

If the witness is giving a conclusionary answer it will obviously be much more effective if the detailed reasons for that conclusion are given. It is one thing to testify that the accused was drunk but there will be a greater impact on the triers-of-fact if the reasons for that conclusion were given, for example, his speech was slurred, he staggered when he walked, there was a strong smell of alcohol on his breath. In order to build the pyramid of questions counsel should ask himself—if the witness's conclusion is correct what else would be true?

PUTTING THE WITNESS AT EASE AND *CRIMINAL CODE* PROTECTIONS

A witness should not be brought directly to the heart of the issue after he or she has been sworn. Most non-professional witnesses are nervous at the start of their testimony probably due to the unfamiliarity of being in the witness-box, the seriousness of the matter and all eyes are on them. They should be given time to settle down and relax. The best way to help put the witness at ease is to ask some easy preliminary questions that are easy to answer—Where do you live? How old are you? Are you married? Do you have children? What is your occupation? How long have you been at that job? These types of questions also go to establishing the reliability of the client.

Prior to the trial you will have explained, when necessary, the Court procedures, some basic rules of evidence, what the issues are, what to expect by way of cross-examination, how the witness should present himself or herself in the courtroom, that you have the right to re-examine the client to deal with matters that were left unsaid or vague in cross-examination, that you will object to any improper questions as well as other advice discussed earlier, all of which should help to make the witness or your client less nervous.

Special procedures are provided by the *Criminal Code* in sections 486, 486.1 to 486.5 to help put persons at ease who are testifying and are under the age of 18 or a witness who has a mental or physical disability. Such

---

12 *Ibid.*, pp. 95-96.

procedures can be: excluding members of the public from the Court so that the interests of the witnesses under the age of 18 are safeguarded; that a support person of the witness's choice be permitted to be close to the witness while testifying; and where the witness is under 18 years of age and has difficulty in communicating due to a physical or mental disability may testify outside of the courtroom or behind a screen or other device; where the accused is under the age of 18 not to be personally cross-examined by the accused; and the Court may make an order that any information that could identify the complainant or a witness not be published in any document, broadcast or be transmitted in any way with respect to the offences enumerated.

Where the witness is under 18 years of age, section 715.1 allows a videotape made within a reasonable time after the alleged offence, which describes the acts complained of, to be admissible if the witness, while testifying, adopts the contents of the videotape. See later in this chapter further discussion of section 715.1 – Videotaping of Witness Testimony.

Section 486.2 also provides protections for witnesses who are testifying with respect to criminal organizations charged with enumerated offences, a terrorism offence or enumerated offences set out in the *Security of Information Act*. Those protections include testifying outside the courtroom if the Judge or Justice feels it is necessary to protect the safety of the witness and testifying outside the courtroom or behind a screen or other device that would allow the witness not to see the accused if the Judge or Justice is of the opinion that the order is necessary to obtain a full and candid account from the witness of the acts complained of.

See also Chapter, "Cross-Examination of Child Witnesses" and later in this Chapter under heading, "Videotaping of Witness Testimony."

HUMANIZING THE CLIENT

You want your client to be humanized as much as possible, particularly if he will not be testifying. You can do this of course with character evidence. (See Chapter, "Character Evidence"). Sometimes you can elicit good character evidence from Crown witnesses as well as your own. But you want as much flesh on the bones as possible during the Crown's case as the jury will in many instances only be hearing negatives through the Crown's questioning of his/her witnesses.

How should counsel refer to her client during the trial? The accused sits in the prisoner's dock even though he is presumed to be innocent. Police or sheriff's officers sit on either side of him. He is made to look like a prisoner which carries an aura of guilt. No doubt the Crown will refer to him as the accused and the judge may too. Recommendation 83(a) from the Commission on Proceedings Involving Guy Paul Morin states that "absent the existence of a proven security risk, persons charged with a criminal offence should be entitled, at their option, to be seated with their counsel, rather than in the prisoner's dock". While this is a welcome suggestion any experienced counsel knows that some clients sitting at counsel table can be very distracting. Recommendation 83(b) states that Crown counsel and the Court should be encouraged to refer to the persons charged by name, rather than "as the accused". There is absolutely no reason for the defence counsel to refer to his client as the accused. The client should be personalized. The client should be called by his Mr. or Mrs. last name and as the trial progresses the client's first name should be used in the appropriate places. James McElhaney[13] states:

> This natural progression helps the jury feel they are becoming acquainted with someone rather than having familiarity thrust upon them. . . . But when your client is older than you, using his/her first name may be a signal mistake. This is especially true if a juror might think you are condescending towards your client or towards some racial or ethnic group by using your client's first name—no matter how friendly you might be with your client outside the Court.

It is important, however, not to overdo calling the client by his/her first name as it will seem too contrived.

Sometimes ingenuity in referring to a client by name can be very effective. The late Ross McKay of Toronto defended a young man about 19 years of age in a drug conspiracy trial. His client's surname was Barron. The two co-accused were in their early forties. Mr. McKay sparingly (but often enough to make the point effectively) referred to his client as "the boy Barron." This nicely contrasted his client's youth and experience against that of his two older co-accused who were alleged to be the ringleaders.

If the client is a "character type" with a number of rough edges he should be seen as his natural self. There is something appealing about a "character," particularly as there seems to be so few of them around nowadays. They are usually humorous with a degree of warmth and their naturalness shines through. If the client has some habits which counsel knows will not be appealing to the triers-of-fact he should be told so in a constructive way.

The accused should have close members of her family in Court, as well as close friends, sitting in the same seats each day if possible, close to the client and in clear view of the jury. This shows they are supportive and care and the accused is worth caring for. If the family is presentable it reflects on the accused. The jury will know that by convicting the accused there are others who will be hurt by the verdict.

---

13   J.W. McElhaney, *Trial Notebook* (A.B.A., Litigation Section, 1981), p. 8.

Getting to Know You

"Ladies and gentlemen of the jury, say hi to my client."

The New Yorker Book of Lawyer Cartoons. New Yorker Magazine Eds. (Illus.). Alfred A. Knopf Inc., 1997. © 1993 by The New Yorker Magazine, Inc.

The jurors watch the prisoner in the prisoner's dock. They watch to observe how he or she reacts to the testimony or to any number of happenings in Court. The way in which the client sits in the prisoner's dock can be of some significance. There is nothing more unappealing than an accused who sits back with his hands spread across the back of the seats like he owns the world or who is inappropriately laughing or making faces.

The jurors will watch counsel and how counsel interacts with his/her client. Jurors probably feel that the defence counsel knows whether or not his client is really guilty or innocent. A juror may feel that if counsel ignores his client inside or outside the courtroom he does not like the client or may even feel that the client is guilty, and the juror may be influenced accordingly. Counsel should speak with his client and smile with her when it is appropriate.[14]

The jurors will watch the accused outside the courtroom in the hallways, and perhaps even on the elevator. They will note how he acts with

---

14 In Professor Monroe H. Freedman's article for the Symposium on Professional Ethics entitled: Professional Responsibility of The Criminal Defence Lawyer: The Three Hardest Questions, he noted at p. 1471 that ". . . Effective trial advocacy requires that the attorney's every word, action, and attitude be consistent with the conclusion that his client is innocent . . ."

family members or others. This is all part of the atmosphere of the trial and both client and counsel should be ever-aware of their conduct as it may well have a bearing on how some of the jurors will assess the accused.

Finally, although counsel can never give his opinion on the innocence of his client, counsel's demeanour throughout the trial should convey that his client is innocent for if less than that is conveyed it will be noticed by the jurors with obvious results.

VIDEOTAPING OF WITNESS TESTIMONY

There are different scenarios which allow for witness testimony to come from other than the witness stand. One such instance is the principled approach to hearsay which is discussed in detail in the Chapter, "The Hearsay Horror."

Sections 714.1 to 714.4 permits a witness inside or outside of Canada "by means of technology" in the circumstances described to have his or her evidence received by the Court.

714.1 A court may order that a witness in Canada give evidence by means of technology that permits the witness to testify elsewhere in Canada in the virtual presence of the parties and the court, if the court is of the opinion that it would be appropriate in all the circumstances, including

(a) the location and personal circumstances of the witness;
(b) the costs that would be incurred if the witness had to be physically present; and
(c) the nature of the witness's anticipated evidence.

1999, c. 18, s. 95.[15]

714.2 (1) A court shall receive evidence given by a witness outside Canada by means of technology that permits the witness to testify in the virtual presence of the parties and the court unless one of the parties satisfies the court that the reception of such testimony would be contrary to the principles of fundamental justice.

(2) A party who wishes to call a witness to give evidence under subsection (1) shall give notice to the court before which the evidence is to be given and the other parties of their intention to do so not less than ten days before the witness is scheduled to testify.

1999, c. 18, s. 95

---

15 In *R. v. Y. (C.)* (2000), 150 C.C.C. (3d) 317 (Sask. C.A.) the Court refused the Crown's application to have an important witness's evidence in a murder case heard by video conference pursuant to section 714.2 as there was no evidence that the witness would be inconvenienced or that he was not fully accessible for attendance at trial. Cost of requiring attendance at trial not significantly more than would be incurred for trial.

714.3 The court may order that a witness in Canada give evidence by means of technology that permits the parties and the court to hear and examine the witness elsewhere in Canada, if the court is of the opinion that it would be appropriate, considering all the circumstances including

(a) the location and personal circumstances of the witness;
(b) the costs that would be incurred if the witness had to be physically present;
(c) the nature of the witness's anticipated evidence; and
(d) any potential prejudice to either of the parties cause by the fact that the witness would not be seen by them.

1999, c. 18, s. 95

714.4 The court may receive evidence given by a witness outside Canada by means of technology that permits the parties and the court in Canada to hear and examine the witness, if the court is of the opinion that it would be appropriate, considering all the circumstances, including

(a) the nature of the witness's anticipated evidence; and
(b) any potential prejudice to either of the parties cause by the fact that the witness would not be seen by them.

1999, c. 18, s. 95

As indicated in the Chapter, "Cross-Examination of Child Witnesses," pursuant to section 715.1 there is provision for a witness under 18 years of age to testify via video for certain enumerated offences.

715.1 (1) In any proceeding against an accused in which a victim or other witness was under the age of eighteen years at the time the offence is alleged to have been committed, a video recording made within a reasonable time after the alleged offence, in which the victim or witness describes the acts complained of, is admissible in evidence if the victim or witness, while testifying, adopts the contents of the video recording, unless the presiding judge or justice is of the opinion that admission of the video recording in evidence would interfere with the proper administration of justice.

(2) The presiding judge or justice may prohibit any other use of a video recording referred to in subsection (1).

R.S.C. 1985, c. 19 (3rd Supp.), s. 16; 1997, c. 16, s. 7; 2005, c. 32, s. 23

In *R. v. S. (P.)*[16] the Court held that in considering whether a videotape has been made within a reasonable time, a number of factors are to be balanced, the most important being the reasons for the delay and the impact of the delay on the child's ability to recall the events. The Court found in

---

16 (2000), 144 C.C.C. (3d) 120 (Ont. C.A.), leave to appeal refused (2001), 266 N.R. 400 (note) (S.C.C.). See also *R. v. L. (D.O.)*, [1993] 4 S.C.R. 419, 85 C.C.C. (3d) 289 (S.C.C.) where the Court announces other factors that can be considered in determining what is a reasonable time. Also, *R. v. Scott* (1993), 87 C.C.C. (3d) 327 (Ont. C.A.); *R. v. M. (S.)* (1995), 98 C.C.C. (3d) 526 (Alta. C.A.) where the Court relied on the natural reluctance of the child and the mother to make a report to the authorities.

this case that the late disclosure was probably because of the child's timidity and an inability to communicate because of fear and embarrassment. There was also the consideration that the child did not want to put in jeopardy the accused, her older cousin. The Court also felt it may have been difficult to disclose due to the child's confusion given she had been victimized by her brother before and after the incident. The Court held that while two years was a long delay the complainant was not so young (12 years at the time of the incident) that the delay would raise serious concerns about her ability to accurately recall the incident. Also, there was no suggestion that anything happened during the two year delay which would cast doubt upon the reliability of the videotaped statement.

In *R. v. F. (C.)*[17] the Court held that a *voir dire* was necessary to determine admissibility and the judge has the discretion to exclude if prejudice outweighed probative value. If there is conflicting evidence as to how useful the video statement can be in providing an honest and complete account of the complainant's story the statement should be admitted unless the trial judge feels that to admit it would interfere with the truth-finding process. The statement is considered "adopted" within the section if the witness recalls giving the statement and when giving it was attempting to be honest and truthful. It is not relevant that the witness is unable to recall the events discussed in the statement or if the witness has an independent memory of the events. If the trial judge rules that the statement has been adopted the video and the *viva voce* evidence given at trial comprises the witness's evidence-in-chief. Credibility and the reliability of the overall evidence all go to the weight, not the admissibility of the evidence.[18]

If the conditions of the section are not met the video statement may still be admissible if the principles of necessity and reliability are met.[19]

The video does not become an exhibit and therefore does not go into the jury room.[20]

DEFENCE DUTY TO CALL WITNESSES

An issue arises as to what is the duty on the part of defence counsel to call a particular witness when a witness who can support an accused's

---

17 [1997] 3 S.C.R. 1183, 120 C.C.C. (3d) 225.

18 The contents of the complainant's videotaped statement which are adopted by the complainant on the witness stand is not corroborative of the witness's evidence-in-chief as it is not independent evidence. See *R. v. Aksidan* (2006), 209 C.C.C. (3d) 423 (B.C. C.A.); *R. v. S. (K.P.)* (2007), 224 C.C.C. (3d) 62 (B.C. C.A.) at 29, leave to appeal refused (2007), 384 N.R. 385 (note) (S.C.C.).

19 *R. v. F. (W. J.)* (1999), 138 C.C.C. (3d) 1 (S.C.C.); *R. v. Burk* (1999), 139 C.C.C. (3d) 266 (Ont. C.A.).

20 *R. v. K. (J.)* (1990), 60 C.C.C. (3d) 413 (N.W.T. S.C.).

testimony is not called to testify; and what can the Court or Crown say in such circumstance?

The answer is easily resolved when that witness is the spouse of an accused or the accused. The *Canada Evidence Act* states that the failure of a husband or wife of a person charged or the failure of the accused to testify is not to be made subject of comment by the Judge or prosecution, see later in this chapter.[21]

With respect to other such witnesses who are not called to testify it was recognized by Justice Binnie in *R. v. Jolivet* that:

> "It is clear from those authorities that it will be rarely appropriate for the trial Judge to comment on the failure of the Crown to call a particular witness, and even more rare to do so with respect to the defence."[22]

Binnie J. in *Jolivet, supra,* at para. 38 stated that there are many reasons for calling certain evidence that are unrelated to the truth of the witness's testimony and named, for example, that the point has been adequately made by another witness, or that an honest witness has a poor demeanour.

In *R. v. Zehr,*[23] a case which involved the failure by the defence to call supporting alibi witnesses, it was held that the trial Judge was wrong in charging the jury that it may infer that the reason one might fail to call a witness in support of a position is that such witness may not have supported the position taken. The Court of Appeal held:

> "While permissible in some cases, comment on the failure to call a witness should only be used with great caution. This kind of comment from a trial Judge can seriously affect what might otherwise be the jury's assessment of the credibility of those who do testify and perhaps, more importantly the integrity of the case. Such comment and instruction whether referable to the prosecution or the defence is really a comment on the conduct of the case and the instruction gives it some evidentiary significance. There are many reasons why counsel may choose not to call a witness, and our courts will rarely question the decision of the counsel, for the system proceeds on the basis that counsel conducts the case. Often the witness is not called and if the reason is known, it would not justify an instruction that an adverse inference might be drawn from the witness not being called."[24]

In *R. v. Lapensee*[25] the Ontario Court of Appeal noted that "in a criminal case the principle must be applied with due regard to the division of responsibilities between the Crown and defence," referring to *Jolivet* at para. 26, "Drawing an adverse inference against an accused in a criminal trial raises the danger of placing a burden of adducing evidence on the defence."

---

21 Section 4(6) of the *Canada Evidence Act.*
22 *R. v. Jolivet,* [2000] 1 S.C.R. 751 at para. 39.
23 (1980), 54 C.C.C. (2d) 65 (Ont. C.A.).
24 *Ibid* at 68. See also *R. v. Belowitz,* (1990), 56 C.C.C. (3d) 402 (Ont. C.A.).
25 (2009), 99 O.R. (3d) 501 (C.A.).

In *R. v. Marshall*[26] the accused failed to call certain witnesses who were his friends and whom he claimed could in part corroborate his defence. No reason was given for failure to call these witnesses. The Court of Appeal held it was proper for the Crown to cross-examine the accused on his failure and it was not improper for the trial Judge in drawing the jury's attention to the fact that the accused's version of events was unsupported by any other witness. The jury was properly urged to draw an adverse inference because of this failure.

Even where an adverse inference charge is given the trial Judge must instruct the jury that there is no obligation on defence to call a particular witness and that there may have been a perfectly valid reason for not doing so.[27]

In *R. v. Lane*[28] it was held that counsel is permitted to address the Court as to the reason for not calling a witness. The trial Judge, if she accepts the explanation may refuse to draw an adverse inference. See *R. v. L.P.* (2003), 172 C.C.C. (3d) 195 (C.A.) (Q.L.) at para. 14; see also *R. v. Jolivet* at para. 26.

In *R. v. Rooke*,[29] the British Columbia Court of Appeal held that comment on the failure to call a witness should only be made where the witness is of some importance to the case. If an adverse inference is to be drawn it is a matter which goes to credibility of only the particular issue on which it appears the missing witness could have given cogent evidence and that if the witness were called his evidence would have been unfavourable to the accused with respect to a certain specific instance or instances and those ought to have been spelled out with some particularity. The Court further noted that unless there was a clear logical basis for drawing an adverse inference there would be a shifting of the burden of proof to the accused and the jury should be so instructed. Adverse comment on the failure to call a witness is only to be made if the circumstances are such that a reasonably competent defence counsel would recognize there were logical grounds for

---

26 (2005), 200 C.C.C. (3d) 179 (Ont. C.A.), leave to appeal refused (2006), 2006 CarswellOnt 5556, 2006 CarswellOnt 5557 (S.C.C.); see also *R. v. Charrette* (1982), 67 C.C.C. (2d) 357 (Ont. C.A.) where in the circumstances the trial Judge was entitled to draw an inference adverse to the credibility of the accused.

27 *R. v. Zehr, supra*; *R. v. Koffman & Hirschler, supra.*

28 (2008), 240 C.C.C. (3d) 16 (Ont. C.A.) at para. 79, leave to appeal refused 2009 CarswellOnt 6206, 2009 CarswellOnt 6207 (S.C.C.).

29 (1988), 40 C.C.C. (3d) 484 (B.C. C .A.). See also *R. v. Scott* (2002), 157 O.A.C. 246 (Ont. C.A.) at para. 9; see also *R. v. Koffman & Hirschler, supra*; see also *R. v. S. (C.R.)* (1999), 133 C.C.C. (3d) 559 (N.S. C.A.) where the Nova Scotia Court of Appeal held that the ruling of an adverse inference against the party failing to call a witness should only be the subject of comment by the trial Judge where the witness is of some importance and not where they only had a collateral or peripheral involvement with the main issues. See also *R. v. Solomon* (2002), 2002 CarswellOnt 4526 (Ont. S.C.J.); *R. v. Rooke, supra*; *R. v. S. (C.R.), supra*, at 571.

drawing an adverse inference: circumstances such as where the accused would have greater access to the witness than the Crown; where the witness is in a position to corroborate the defence on a significant issue; and if no reason appears from the evidence why the accused cannot call the witness and would not be acting reasonably in calling him.

In *R. v. Koffman & Hirschler*[30] the witness not called was involved in drugs and Martin J.A. stated that he was one whom, understandably, neither the defence nor the Crown might wish to call and the jury should have been so advised rather than being left with the impression that they could draw an adverse inference against the defence in the absence of evidence as to why he was not called.

The adverse inference can be drawn is not one of guilt, but if that witness were called, his testimony would be unfavourable.[31]

With respect to defence not calling alibi witnesses, see Chapter, "The Defence of Alibi."

Defence counsel's decision as to whether or not to call a witness will be made easier when the witness that counsel considered is called by the Crown, thereby giving counsel the advantage of cross-examination while his opponent is limited to the rules of examination-in-chief. But if this Crown witness turns out to be obviously favourable to the accused because of his or her relationship, it would be a wise tactic to avoid leading questions even though in cross-examination they are permitted. If leading questions are used, the trial Judge and jurors will be quick to recognize that counsel is putting words in the witness's mouth and that the witness is quite ready to give the desired answer. The Crown will obviously ask the triers-of-fact not to credit those answers with much weight. Evans J.A., in *R. v. McLaughlin*,[32] said for the Ontario Court of Appeal:

> The impact of evidence on the trier-of-fact is determined by many factors, including the interest of the witness, his demeanour, as well as the form in which the questions are put to the witness by counsel.[33]

The fact that care was taken not to put leading questions to the friendly witness even though it was permissible could be pointed out to the jury in defence counsel's final address in order to buttress that witness's testimony.

CROWN DUTY TO CALL WITNESSES

It sometimes occurs that the police have taken a statement from a witness which contains evidence favourable to the defence, or the police

---

30 (1985), 20 C.C.C. (3d) 232 (Ont. C.A.).
31 *R. v. Koffman & Kirschler, supra* and *R. v. Rooke, supra.*
32 (1974), 2 O.R. (2d) 514 (Ont. C.A.).
33 *Ibid.*, 524.

have at least interviewed a witness who can assist the accused. The Crown, however, may elect to not call the witness. This can create a dilemma for defence counsel. There may be reasons why the defence does not wish to call that witness but does want the testimony to be heard because it helps his client; or at least insists on the unfolding of the narrative; perhaps counsel would much prefer to cross-examine the witness, or does not wish to call any evidence at trial and hopes to be successful on a directed verdict, or wants to address the jury last, or it may be there are some nagging concerns about how the witness will stand up to cross-examination by the Crown attorney. Can the defence in certain circumstances force the Crown to call a witness?

The Supreme Court in *R. v. Cook*,[34] discussed the various arguments which the defence would argue favours a Crown obligation to call witnesses. The Court, in dismissing the arguments held that the decision how to present the case must be left to the Crown absent evidence that this discretion was being abused. The Court held that failure to call a witness of an oblique motive is akin to failure to disclose or an abuse of process.[35] If the conduct of the Crown falls short of an abuse, this can be a factor in influencing the trial Judge to call the witness. Such a case was *R. v. Giroux*[36] where the Crown refused to call an analyst to testify as to the deceased's alcohol level. The defence had possession of the analyst's report. The trial Judge found that there was no oblique motive by the Crown in refusing to call the analyst but found that in the circumstances of this case, namely, because this evidence was relevant to the narrative, the evidence was potentially exculpatory and the Crown had provided no reason as to why the prosecution was not calling the witness, who was reliable, the Court would call the witness. Also, the accused's right to address the jury last was preserved.

In *R. v. Onigbinde* (2010), 251 C.C.C. (3d) 15 (Ont. C.A.) at paras. 45-46, it was held that when the Crown in an opening statement told the jury that a certain witness was anticipated to testify but failed to call that witness, the defence "was at least entitled" to make the submission that if the witness had been called, his evidence would have been unhelpful. The Court noted that "there is a long and well-established practice in civil and criminal cases in this province that in certain circumstances – such as these – counsel can invite the trier-of-fact to draw an adverse inference when opposing counsel declined to call a witness from whom it is anticipated relevant evidence will be tendered."

---

34 (1997), 114 C.C.C. (3d) 481 (S.C.C.). See also *R. v. V. (J.)* (1994), 91 C.C.C. (3d) 284 (C.A. Qué.).
35 See also *R. v. Lemay* (1951), 102 C.C.C. 1 (S.C.C.); and *R. v. Yebes* (1987), 59 C.R. (3d) 108 (S.C.C.).
36 (2002), 166 C.C.C. (3d) 427 (Alta. Q.B.).

Oblique motive has been interpreted in earlier cases to mean an improper motive[37] such as holding back evidence which is in favour of the accused[38] or which would prevent the narrative from unfolding accurately.[39] The argument that a particular witness should be called is a hollow one if based on speculation. It should be supported, as for example, by reference to a statement by the witness or a transcript of the witness's testimony at the preliminary hearing or perhaps from something that is contained in the disclosure.

SHOULD THE ACCUSED TESTIFY?

The Ethical Nightmare

There are times when the most difficult decision defence counsel must make in a trial is whether or not to call his client to testify. Like the patient who cannot tell the doctor how to operate, the client cannot advise counsel on how to conduct the trial. However, there are recognized exceptions to this cardinal rule and it appears to be generally accepted that the accused has the right to make the decision to testify. In the case of *R. v. Smith*,[40] the Ontario Court of Appeal indeed held that it is in fact the client's decision whether or not to testify. In my view the accused should have the final say on how his/her personal liberty should be decided. It is rare, however, that an accused person will make such a choice without input from counsel, requested or otherwise. Most often the accused will accept counsel's advice and counsel should, of course, be prepared to make a recommendation. As will be seen later, considerations can differ depending on whether the trial is before a judge alone or with a jury.

The "ethical nightmare" dreaded by any responsible defence counsel occurs when he/she knows that his client will tell a false story under oath. It appears to be a basic rule of professional ethics that counsel should not call to the stand a witness whom he/she knows will commit perjury.[41] To

---

37 *R. v. Yebes, supra; Adel Muhammed El Dabbah v. Attorney-General for Palestine*, [1944] 2 All E.R. 139 (U.K. P.C.); *R. v. Jewell* (1980), 54 C.C.C. (2d) 286 (Sask. Q.B.); *Cunliffe v. Law Society (British Columbia)* (1984), 40 C.R. (3d) 67 (B.C. C.A.); *R. v. Nugent*, [1977] 3 All E.R. 662 (U.K.); *R. v. Singh* (1975), 27 C.C.C. (2d) 197 (B.C. C.A.); *R. v. McFayen* (1967), 60 W.W.R. 11 (B.C. C.A.); *R. v. O'Donnell* (1982), 3 C.C.C. (3d) 333 (N.S. C.A.), reversed [1985] 2 S.C.R. 216.

38 *R. v. Lemay, supra*, at 6.

39 *Cunliffe v. Law Society (British Columbia), supra.* An example of an oblique motive can be seen in *R. v. Fletcher* (February 14, 1989), Haliburton Co. Ct. J. J. (N.S. Co. Ct.), summarized at 8 W.C.B. (2d) 581.

40 (1997), 120 C.C.C. (3d) 500 (Ont. C.A.). *R. v. Archer* (2005), 202 C.C.C. (3d) 60 (Ont. C.A.) at para. 139; *R. v. McKenzie* (2007), 51 C.R. (6th) 316 (Ont. C.A.) at paras. 67, 68.

41 *Nix v. Whiteside*, 475 U.S. 157 at 173 (U.S. Iowa, 1986).

do otherwise would be to risk being charged with the crime of subornation or perjury. But what happens when a client insists on testifying?

In a publicized American case, Miami lawyer Ellis Rubin asked to be excused from the case on the morning of the trial of his client, Russel Sanborn, who had been charged with murder, after the defendant directed counsel to present evidence and/or testimony and argue facts which counsel knew to be false. The trial judge refused Rubin's request because of the lapse of time since the commission of the crime, the inconvenience to witnesses and the possibility that "any new counsel will be confronted with the same conflict." The Florida Appellate Court confirmed the trial judge's decision. The Appellate Court's proposed solution was to hold that Rubin should allow the "defendant to take the stand and deliver his statement in a narrative form" and "decline to elicit the perjurious testimony by questioning" and refuse to "argue the false testimony during closing argument." Rubin refused to act on the basis that the lawyer would be a knowing instrument of totally unethical and dishonest conduct and that "silence here is participation; it is co-operation with evil." Rubin was held in criminal contempt and sentenced to 30 days.[42]

The American Bar Association's view was that defence counsel should be required to tell all if the client cannot be persuaded to tell the truth and rejected the solution put forth by the Florida Appellate Court in *Rubin*.[43]

Professor Monroe Freedman has opined that "the attorney who prevents his client from testifying only because the client has confided his guilt to him is violating that confidence by acting upon the information in a way that will seriously prejudice his client's interests."[44] Professor Freedman goes on to say that the most common method for avoiding the ethical problem is for the lawyer to withdraw from the case, at least if there is sufficient time before trial for the client to retain another attorney. But he points out that the client, now realizing that the obligation of confidentiality is not what it has been represented to be, will in all likelihood withhold incriminating information or the fact of his guilt from his new counsel. Professor Freedman feels that on ethical grounds the practice of withdrawing from a case under such circumstances is indefensible, since the identical perjured testimony will ultimately be presented. More important is that the new counsel will be ignorant of the perjury and therefore will not be in a position to attempt to discourage the client from presenting it. Only the

---

42 *Rubin v. State*, 490 So. 2d 1001 (Fla. 3d DCA 1986), rev. denied 501 So. 2d 1283 (Fla. 1986), cert. denied 483 U.S. 1005.

43 *Ibid.*

44 Reporter, Commission on Professional Responsibility, American Trial Lawyers Foundation.

original counsel who knows the truth has the opportunity but he loses it in the very act of avoiding the ethical problem.[45]

In 1978, when Chief Justice Charles Dubin was a practising lawyer, he made certain suggestions during a panel discussion given by the Law Society of Upper Canada about the problems that arise when counsel learns that his client is going to tell an untrue story. First, he said, counsel must tell the client that he cannot put him in the witness-box because he is going to commit perjury. Counsel should then advise the trial Judge that there has been a fundamental disagreement with the client which has just arisen and the client no longer has counsel's confidence, and as counsel no longer has the confidence of his client he can ask for a mistrial. Counsel must not tell the trial Judge or anyone else about the nature of the disagreement because of solicitor-client confidentiality.[46] However, would a trial Judge permit a counsel to withdraw from a trial when to do so would abort a lengthy trial? Would not such a solution allow some accused persons to cause mistrials at their convenience? When Warren Burger, former Chief Justice of the United States, was a Judge of the United States Court of Appeals, Washington, D.C., he said:[47]

> It is perfectly clear, not only in the legal profession in the United States, but in all common-law countries where witnesses are called and examined under the adversary system, that the lawyer must tell his client that he will not be proffered as a witness once the lawyer knows that he will testify falsely. But it has happened that, even after he has agreed on this before the trial, the defendant, in the midst of trial, insists upon taking the stand. Obviously the lawyer cannot physically or otherwise prevent him from walking to the witness chair and taking the oath. If in those circumstances the lawyer's immediate withdrawal from the case is either not feasible, or if the Judge refuses to permit withdrawal, the lawyer's course is clear: he may not engage in direct examination of his client to facilitate known perjury. He should confine himself to asking the witness to identify himself and to make a statement, but he cannot participate in the fraud by conventional direct examination. Since this informal procedure is not uncommon with witnesses, there is no basis for saying that this tells the jury the witness is lying. The Judge may infer that such is the case but lay jurors will not.

One could choose to disagree with Justice Berger's opinion about what lay jurors might think. They certainly could wonder why defence counsel would be acting in such a fashion and might well conclude the reason is that counsel does not think much of his or her client's testimony.

---

45 M.H. Freedman, "Professional Responsibility of the Criminal Defence Lawyer; The Three Hardest Questions" (1966), 64 Mich. L. Rev. 1469.

46 *Tuckiar v. R.* (1934), 52 C.L.R. 335.

47 W.E. Burger, "Standards of Conduct for Prosecution and Defence Personnel: A Judge's Viewpoint" (1966), 5 Am. L.Q. 11 at 13 (1966).

British Columbia rules[48] of conduct dictate that the lawyer must advise his client of his duty to withdraw from the case if the client chooses to lie. See also New Brunswick Professional Conduct Handbook[49] stating that not only must counsel seek to withdraw from the case when learning about the fraud perpetrated on the Court but should also advise the Court and adverse party of the fraud. The C.B.A. Code[50] states that the lawyer should withdraw or seek leave of the Court to do so if the client persists to perjure himself despite the lawyer's attempt to prevent the perjury.

Professor Freedman argues that the only alternative is "to put the client on the stand to be examined in the usual way, and to argue the case based on the evidence." He goes on to say that counsel have a duty to discourage the client from testifying falsely on the grounds of "law, morality and results" and advise that the client may be found out with the result that he or she may be charged with perjury. But Freedman holds the decision must be the client's. Freedman argues that counsel would not be suborning perjury because there is no wilful procuring of false evidence because the lawyer has attempted to convince the client not to testify falsely but accepts the client's decision. Professor Freedman's conclusion is hard to swallow as an ethical result but is difficult to criticize logically. *Quaere* however why counsel could not tell the client that he or she will be forced to advise the Court that the client intends to commit perjury given that it has been held disclosure of future crimes to one's counsel are not privileged communications?[51]

If the client unexpectedly perjures himself/herself, the C.B.A. Code and the Ontario rules call for counsel to make disclosure to the Court and do all he or she can to reasonably rectify the problem subject to the rules regarding withdrawal of services and confidential information.[52]

What does counsel do when he or she suspects, as opposed to knows, that his client's version of the events is a lie and that the client will lie on the witness stand? Joseph Sedgwick, Q.C. opined that even though he may not believe his client, somebody else may and if the client elects to take the witness stand and be sworn, his counsel has no right to assume he will commit perjury.[53] Indeed, if the client tells his lawyer two different versions, the second version being the one the witness will testify to, why should counsel take it upon himself to disbelieve the second version? In very practical terms, if an accused is unable to convince his own counsel that he is telling the truth, will he be able to persuade the Court? The oft-quoted

---

48 Chapter 8, rule 2.
49 Part B, Rule 8.
50 Chapter ix, Commentary 4; Ontario rule 10, Commentary 3(b).
51 Norman Lefstein "Client Perjury in Criminal Cases: Still in Search of an Answer" (1987-88) 1 Georgetown Journal of Legal Ethics, 521 at pp. 524-525.
52 C.B.A. Code, Chapter 9, Commentary B; Ontario rule 10, Commentary 3(a).
53 1968 Law Society of Upper Canada Lectures, p. 279.

dialogue between Dr. Samuel Johnson and his biographer Boswell may assist counsel who feels morally restricted in calling to the stand a client whom he feels is guilty and suspects will be lying:

Boswell:	But what do you think of supporting a cause that you know to be bad?
Johnson:	Sir, you do not know it to be good or bad until the Judge determines it. . . . An argument which does not convince yourself may convince the Judge to whom you urge it; and if it does convince him, why then, Sir, you are wrong and he is right. It is his business to judge; and you are not to be confident in your own opinion that a cause is bad, but to say all you can for your client, and then hear the Judge's opinion.
Boswell:	But Sir, does not affecting a warmth when you have no warmth, and appearing to be clearly of one opinion when you are in reality of another opinion, does not such dissimulation impair one's honesty? Is there not some danger that a lawyer may put on the same mask in common life in the intercourse with his friends?
Johnson:	Why, no, Sir. Everybody knows you are paid for affecting warmth for your client, and it is therefore properly no dissimulation: the moment you come from the Bar resume your usual behaviour. Sir, a man will no more carry the artifice of the Bar into the common intercourse of society than a man who is paid for tumbling upon his hands will continue to tumble upon his hands when he should walk upon his feet.[54]

Factors to Consider

There are a number of reasons why a client may not wish to testify or why counsel would be concerned about a client testifying: the client may be unable to withstand cross-examination, have a prejudicial criminal record, or an unpleasing personality and attitude, or become easily nervous and confused on the witness stand, or is clearly a liar; the accused in testifying on his own behalf may have to point his finger at his co-accused or some individual not charged which the accused does not wish to do. The most difficult consideration for counsel is when the client maintains his or her innocence (and you may believe the client) but some of the above-mentioned factors cannot be ignored.

As a general rule when there is a jury, I would always wish to call my client unless there is very good reason against it. If, after considering the

---

54 1963 Law Society of Upper Canada Lectures, p. 90. It is generally accepted that more than mere suspicion is required and that a lawyer does not have a duty to correct false testimony unless there is no doubt as to the falsity. See *Lawyers and Ethics, Professional Responsibility and Discipline* (Toronto: Carswell 1993) 7-15 by G. MacKenzie.

pros and cons I am still in doubt, then I opt for calling the accused to testify. The reason for this choice is that, as empirical studies have shown,[55] the likelihood of conviction is increased enormously when the accused does not testify. However many experienced Crown Attorneys would probably admit they are happy to see the accused testify so they can put their theories to the accused for the jury's consumption, ask questions which embarrass the accused such as inconsistencies in their testimony or expose an incriminating demeanour; in effect, giving a first jury address. An example of a witness the Crown might welcome to the witness stand is the fraudsman. Such clients might survive examination-in-chief but his or her penchant for being manipulative or less than genuine could be apparent in cross-examination when the accused is not in control of the dialogue.

In many cases the choice of whether or not the accused should testify is an easy one. If the defence calls an alibi the accused should in most cases testify but there is no rule of law or practice which precludes evidence in support of an alibi being tendered in the absence of testimony by the accusd.[56] See Chapter, "The Defence of Alibi." By virtue of section 4(6) of the *Canadian Evidence Act*,[57] the failure of the accused to testify in support of his alibi cannot be the subject of adverse comment by the Judge or Crown although it may be considered by the triers-of-fact on their own or the alibi may be rejected on appeal.[58]

If the accused's state of mind is in issue such as intent or knowledge, or the evidence requires an answer or explanation by the client on a material issue, then his or her testimony is normally very important. If counsel chooses to call any evidence, then in most instances the accused should testify. By calling other witnesses to the stand the client's failure to testify will be highlighted. However, it is recognized that there are instances when the accused simply cannot be called even though it is necessary to call other evidence.

The choice not to testify can be easy when the client has a significant criminal record, particularly for similar offences or where the accused will make a poor witness because there are questions which he cannot adequately answer or where there is a fear that he will convict himself from his own

55 H. Kalven and H. Zeisel, *The American Jury* (Boston: Little, Brown, 1966), p. 60. Edward Bennett Williams, famed U.S. counsel, interviewed in the American Bar Association magazine, Litigation, (Winter, 1986), stated that based on his own research 95% of persons who did not testify were convicted.

56 *R. v. Sophonow (No. 2)* (1986), 25 C.C.C. (3d) 415 (Man. C.A.), leave to appeal to S.C.C. refused at (1986), 54 C.R. (3d) xxviin (S.C.C.).

57 R.S.C. 1985, c. C-5.

58 *R. v. Vezeau* (1976), 34 C.R.N.S. 309 (S.C.C.); *R. v. Steinberg* (1931), 56 C.C.C. 9 (S.C.C.); *Catellier v. R.* (1948), 6 C.R. 466 (Que. C.A.); *R. v. Hutton* (1953), 16 C.R. 136 (B.C. C.A.); *R. v. Sgambelluri* (1978), 43 C.C.C. (2d) 496 (Ont. C.A.). See also *R. v. Noble* (1997), 114 C.C.C. (3d) 385 (S.C.C.).

mouth. However, even though simulated studies suggest that a jury will more readily convict if it is aware of an accused's criminal record[59] counsel should not reject calling his or her client too quickly. If the charge before the Court is fraud, for example, and the accused's record involves violence and driving offences, then counsel can point out to the jury the lack of relationship between the charge and the criminal record and the fact that the criminal record, not being one of dishonesty, does not reflect negatively on the accused's credibility. Counsel must also be mindful of the decision of the Supreme Court of Canada in *R. v. Corbett*,[60] which now gives the trial judge a discretion in limiting the Crown's cross-examination of the accused as to his or her criminal record. (Corbett applications are discussed in more detail in the Chapter, "Criminal Records.")[61]

Where trial is by judge without a jury concern about your client's criminal record will probably not be as great if there was a jury. If you chose not to call your client, the judge would no doubt conclude that the client has a criminal record in any event or at least may have something to hide. This conclusion however should not lead to a conviction unless the prosecution meets its burden of proof through its own witnesses and/or the cross-examination of defence witnesses.

Where the accused's criminal record is very old, counsel may choose not to disclose it in examination-in-chief. If the Crown does ask about this record, defence counsel may say to the jury in his or her final address that although it is the Crown's right to ask about prior convictions, is it not unfair to do so where the convictions are old and unrelated; and when the Crown resorts to such questions, does it not indicate the weakness of the Crown's case and by bringing out this old record the Crown is attempting to bias the jury against the accused?

Counsel should not be deterred from calling the accused when his last conviction was many years prior to the charge before the Court because jurors may give the accused credit for changing his ways since his last conviction. Defence counsel can emphasize this fact in his or her final address. In any event, a judge on a Corbett application may not permit any cross-examination on a dated criminal record.

The choice of whether or not to call the accused is made easier when the cross-examiner is able to paint a clear picture of the defence through the Crown witnesses or when the Crown introduces an exculpatory statement

---

59   V.P. Hans and A.N. Doob. "Section 12 of the *Canada Evidence Act* and the Deliberations of Simulated Juries" (1975-76), 18 Crim. L.Q. 235; A.N. Doob and H.M. Kirshenbaum, "Some Empirical Evidence on the Effect of Section 12 of the *Canada Evidence Act* Upon an Accused" (1972-73), 15 Crim. L.Q. 88.

60   [1988] 1 S.C.R. 670 (S.C.C.).

61   See the chapter on Criminal Records for a more detailed discussion of *R. v. Corbett* and the trial judge's discretion, and *R. v. Underwood* which allows a *Corbett* application to be made before the accused elects to testify.

which would be the same as or close to the evidence the accused would give under oath. In such instances counsel may choose not to risk other problems the client could be facing if he or she took the stand for the sake of merely repeating what was in the statement. This is especially so if no other defence evidence was to be called. Defence counsel would have the opportunity of addressing the jury last if no defence evidence was called.

Should the opportunity to address the jury last be a real consideration in not calling any evidence? It is thought by many counsel that by addressing the jurors last, the jurors would recollect better what defense counsel had to say over that of Crown counsel, and also that defense counsel would be in a better position to deal with the Crown's submissions rather than trying to anticipate everything the Crown would argue by having to address the jury first. In *R. v. Rose*,[62] the majority of the Supreme Court held there was no fundamental advantage to the Crown in addressing the jury last and that trial judges could redress any unfairness resulting from the order of addresses by virtue of additional instructions to the jury and even permitting the defence a limited reply when the Crown addressed the jury last. There are experienced counsel however who do not mind addressing the jury first. Some even prefer it. These counsel believe that they will be able to persuade the jury to the defence side and once they are there the Crown will have a difficult time changing the jurors' minds; and if both Crown and defense were addressing the jury on the same day, the jurors' attention would probably not be as focussed in the latter part of the day. My own view is that much really depends on the circumstances. But in the normal course, I do not feel the opportunity to address the jury last should be an overriding factor in deciding whether or not to call any evidence, including your client to the witness stand.

Should the accused be called to testify when the case against him or her is weak? When the case is being tried before a judge without a jury there is not the concern than if there is a jury. How often has the "weak case" in front of the jury turned into a devastating loss? This happens because the jurors will sometimes be swayed by a bias, speculation, suspicion or the emotionalism of the case. Even with the "weak case" it is my view that a jury in most instances will want to assess the accused and his or her side of the story. Most jurors are now sophisticated enough about the law to know that the accused is permitted to testify and will question why he/she did not. In my experience it was once thought that the best that counsel could do to counteract such thinking when the accused is not called to testify is to tell the jurors in their final address that the responsibility for the conduct of the case, including what witnesses to call, lies with counsel and that if the jurors have any criticism about the way the case has been conducted they should blame counsel and not the accused. When no evidence whatsoever is called

---

62 [1998] 3 S.C.R. 262.

counsel can explain that by not calling any testimony he or she is allowed the tactical advantage of addressing them last and that the prosecution's case is so weak there is no need to call evidence to refute it. In *R. v. Smith*,[63] the Ontario Court of Appeal held that counsel was able to say to the jury that they could blame counsel for any shortcomings they saw in the conduct of the defence but counsel was not permitted to state that the responsibility for the accused not testifying was counsel's alone. It is the client's decision whether or not to testify.

Smith also held it is wrong for defence counsel to give his personal opinion about the strength of the Crown's case and to suggest this decision not to call the client was tactical so he could address the jury last. Because of the media attention given to the rise in crime, particularly violent crime, and the outpouring against the perception of leniency and mollycoddling of criminals by the courts, juries are, in my view, convicting more often. Defence counsel must give them something beyond just his or her adversarial skills. Counsel must give them a credible denial of guilt from the accused's own mouth. I have no doubt that an accused's chances of being convicted increase significantly when he or she does not testify. However, there are always exceptions to every rule and I appreciate that there are experienced counsel who lean away from calling their client unless they feel under the circumstances it is absolutely necessary. If counsel is unable to call the client, even with a weak Crown case, then in my view serious consideration must be given to electing trial by judge alone.

Some cases, such as murder cases, in my view often dictate that the accused testify because of the serious consequences that would attach to a conviction.[64] If a convicted accused claims that he is innocent, he may never forgive his counsel for the advice that the client ought not to testify as to his innocence. Defence counsel may also have haunting doubts for years to come. With a very serious charge, the negative factors for not testifying will have to be very strong to outweigh the benefit of a denial of guilt under oath. In this situation, a bad criminal record alone may not be a sufficient reason to keep the accused from the witness stand. It may well be that the circumstances of the case will permit counsel to argue that the accused's criminal record, rather than the nature of the evidence against him or her, made the client an obvious target of suspicion: and if the client did not have this criminal record, he or she probably never would have been charged, the evidence being so weak.

In the last analysis, it is my view that by calling your client to testify, the entire focus of the trial changes. All eyes are on the accused. If he or

---

63 (1997), 120 C.C.C. (3d) 500 (Ont. C.A.).

64 I appreciate that there are experienced counsel who disagree with me and that there can be significant reasons why you would not wish to call your client, but I have found that such circumstances are rare in a murder case.

she makes a good impression, the heretofore incriminating evidence may be overwhelmed. If the client makes a bad impression, a weak Crown case can be bolstered. There are some accused who, for any number of reasons, give a bad impression just sitting there in the prisoner's dock. It may be, however, that when they speak they give the very opposite impression. The look and sound of your client may be a factor in whether he or she should take the stand. However, we have all had cases where to call the client would in all likelihood result in a conviction because the client could not withstand cross-examination for any number of reasons. The only hope for a favourable result is to create reasonable doubt through cross-examination and/or calling other defence witnesses.

Defence counsel is often faced with the feeling that the accused will probably be convicted if he does not testify and will probably be convicted if he does testify. Why should the client not then testify? By testifying, she will have had the opportunity to put her side of the story before the Court to be weighed with the rest of the evidence and there can be no recriminations later that her counsel did not give her this opportunity. (Though there can be recriminations that he did!) If the client wishes to testify against your advice, the client's wish is paramount. You hopefully have laid the groundwork as best you can. If the client comes across as a sympathetic one on the stand she may gain an acquittal or a conviction on a reduced charge although technically guilty of the charge in the indictment. Whether or not the client is expected to be a good, mediocre or bad witness will be an important consideration in any decision whether the client should testify. This involves your judgment in whether the client is able to be convincing in responding to the hard questions and assessment of the client's demeanour in the witness box.

Defence counsel may be able to explain away a poor performance by the client in the witness-box by the fact that he was uneducated or unsophisticated, that he was nervous because there was so much at stake, that she was not used to testifying, or that she could not be exact because he did not keep notes at the relevant time about the events in question.

At the very least, counsel can always console herself with the fact that the cross-examination of the accused enabled him to better anticipate what the prosecutor would say in her jury address.

Normally an accused accepts counsel's advice to testify or not, particularly when the reasons are properly explained. If there is a concern of later client recriminations it is better for counsel to protect himself by having the client acknowledge in writing that notwithstanding counsel's advice to the contrary, (and setting out the reasons for that advice) the witness chooses to testify or not to testify.

While by virtue of section 4(6) of the *Canada Evidence Act*, neither the Judge nor the Crown can comment on an accused's failure to testify, or the accused's spouse's failure to testify, this section does not preclude a co-accused's counsel from commenting on the accused's or his spouse's failure to testify.[65] This may be an important consideration for counsel in deciding whether or not to call his or her client. So often where there are co-accused, each blames the other in an attempt at exoneration. See section on Cutthroat defences. If one co-accused testifies and points the finger at his co-accused who did not testify the latter will have problem enough. But that problem will be magnified when the final submissions are made and counsel for the former accused makes within-bound comments about the co-accused's failure to testify.

Section 4(6) does not prevent defence counsel from commenting on the failure of her own client to testify. Defence counsel may explain that an accused is not obligated to testify, which does not open the door for the Judge or Crown to comment.[66] Defence counsel will stress an accused's right to remain silent and the jury can infer guilt from that silence.

Section 4(6) is applicable only where there is a jury[67] and does not apply on a *voir dire*[68] or where the trial judge is sitting alone. While some courts have held that a trial Judge sitting alone may draw any necessary conclusions from the accused's failure to testify,[69] the Supreme Court in *R. v. Noble*[70] held that a trial Judge may never infer guilt from the failure of an accused to testify. It is not always appropriate for a Judge to draw an adverse

---

65   *R. v. Naglik* (1991), 65 C.C.C. (3d) 272 (Ont. C.A.). This however does not permit counsel free rein to encourage the jury to speculate or draw unwarranted inferences. The fact that co-counsel can comment on the failure of a co-accused to testify is not grounds for a separate trial and does not infringe section 11(c) of the Canadian *Charter of Rights and Freedoms*, Part I of the *Constitution Act, 1982*, being Schedule B of the Canada Act 1982 (U.K.), 1982, c. 11. See *R. v. Cuff* (1989), 49 C.C.C. (3d) 65 (Nfld. C.A.). See also *R. v. Oliver* (2005), 194 C.C.C. (3d) 92 (Ont. C.A.), leave to appeal refused (2006), 216 O.A.C. 397 (note) (S.C.C.) wherein Doherty J. stated that "an accused who testifies is entitled to ask a jury to consider the co-accused's failure to testify when assessing the respective merits of the defences advanced by the co-accused. The submission is particularly appropriate when the defences conflict. . ." But Counsel for the co-accused is not permitted to use the accused's failure to testify as evidence of guilt. See *R. v. Leon-Uzarraga* (1998), 123 C.C.C. (3d) 291 (B.C. C.A.); *R. v. Noble* (1997), 114 C.C.C. (3d) 385 (S.C.C.) at 429. See also *R. v. Naglik, supra; R. v. Creighton*, [1995] 1 S.C.R. 858.

66   *R. v. McConnell* (1967), [1968] 1 C.C.C. 368 (Ont. C.A.), affirmed [1968] 4 C.C.C. 257 (S.C.C.)

67   *R. v. Bouchard*, [1970] 5 C.C.C. 95 (N.B. C.A.); *R. v. Binder*, [1948] O.R. 607 (N.B. C.A.); *R. v. Johnson* (1993), 79 C.C.C. (3d) 42 (Ont. C.A.), leave to appeal refused (1993), 84 C.C.C. (3d) vi (S.C.C.). If the jury asks the trial Judge whether the accused was entitled to testify, it is proper for the Judge to say that the accused was entitled to give evidence or call evidence on his behalf but there is no onus on him to prove his innocence, the onus remaining on the Crown. See *R. v. François* (1993), 14 O.R. (3d) 191 (C.A.), affirmed (1994), 19 O.R. (3d) 322 (note) (S.C.C.).

68   *R. v. McDonald* (1948), 91 C.C.C. 30 (Alta. C.A.).

69   *Pratte v. Maher*, [1965] 1 C.C.C. 77 (Que. C.A.); *R. v. Bouchard*, note 96 above, at p. 106.

70   (1997), [1997] 1 S.C.R. 874 (S.C.C.).

inference if the defendant fails to testify – this is so when the prosecution's case is weak. However, if the prosecution's case, standing alone, could support a finding of guilt beyond a reasonable doubt, in the absence of defence evidence, including the failure of the accused to testify, then an adverse inference could be drawn.[71] Where the facts cry out for an explanation and the accused is in a unique position to provide it and does not, or his or her explanation comes solely from an out-of-court statement and untested by cross-examination the Judge or jury may properly draw an unfavourable inference.[72] See also, Defence Duty To Call Witnesses, earlier in this chapter.

Although section 4(6) prohibits certain comment, the jury may still draw an adverse inference from the accused's failure to testify even though they cannot be told they may do so.[73] Also, an appellate Court may draw an adverse inference from the accused's failure to testify when deciding whether there was a substantial wrong or miscarriage of justice or an unreasonable verdict at trial.[74] But the trial Judge is not permitted to instruct the jury that they are entitled to draw an adverse inference from the failure of an accused to testify in support of his alibi defence.[75]

If the client has a concern that by testifying, what he says can be used to incriminate him in another proceeding then his attention should be drawn to his protection in section 13 of the *Charter* which is discussed in the Chapter, "Self-Incrimination."

Lastly, it may be that an accused's choice to testify will depend on whether or not a statement she gave is ruled admissible and the Crown chooses to introduce it into evidence. If her statement is exculpatory and is evidence before the jury the client may well not choose to testify thereby avoiding any significant challenges to her credibility.

---

71 *R. v. Noble, supra*, at para. 87. Section 4(6) does not prevent a trial Judge from telling the jury that an issue is uncontradicted. *R. v. Noble* at para. 97.

72 *R. v. Johnson, supra*; *R. v. Lepage* (1995), 95 C.C.C. (3d) 385 (S.C.C.); *R. v. Grosse* (1996), 107 C.C.C. (3d) 97 (Ont. C.A.); *R. v. Milec* (1996), 110 C.C.C. (3d) 439 (Ont. C.A.); *R. v. Noble* (1996), 106 C.C.C. (3d) 161 (B.C. C .A.), affirmed (1997, 114 C.C.C. (3d) 385 (S.C.C.). In *R. v. Biladeau* (2008), 241 C.C.C. (3d) 374 (Ont. C.A.) Justice Sharpe commented there was a difference between commenting on the failure to testify "and commenting on the fact that the accused has the right not to testify."

73 *R. v. Corbett* (1973), 25 C.R.N.S. 296 (S.C.C.). The Court stated: "There is no practical way of preventing a jury from drawing an improper inference from silence."

74 *Ibid., R. v. Noble, supra.*

75 *R. v. Miller* (1998), 131 C.C.C. (3d) 141 (Ont. C.A.). Charron J. commented that section 4 (6) assures that "no greater weight will be placed upon his failure to testify by reason of a comment by the prosecutor or the Judge."

Why Did I Ever Testify?

"We find the defendant charming, ingratiating, eloquent, witty, disarming and guilty."

National Law Journal. © New York Law Publishing Co.

ADVISING CROWN WHETHER CLIENT WILL TESTIFY

The Crown may ask defence counsel at some point before the defence is called if the accused will be testifying. This may be because the Crown will want to know whether or not to prepare for cross-examination. There is no obligation on defence counsel to so advise the Crown or the Court. Also there may be a tactical reason for this question by the Crown. If counsel advises the Crown that the client will not testify then the Crown may call witnesses it might not otherwise have called. If the Crown is made aware the client will testify, the Crown may hold back certain witnesses to call in reply, subject to any ruling that it would be impermissible to do so if the Crown was splitting its case. Defence counsel may also wish the Crown to call a particular witness that he wishes to cross-examine.

ACCUSED TESTIFYING ON THE *VOIR DIRE*

Defence counsel may wish to have a full-dress *voir dire* to determine a *Charter* issue or the voluntariness of his client's alleged statements to the police. Counsel may be even more concerned with testing the evidence of the police officers as preparation for cross-examination of those officers in the main trial.

It is, of course, not always necessary for an accused to testify on a *voir dire* to argue successfully for the exclusion of an alleged confession. The onus is on the Crown to prove beyond a reasonable doubt the voluntariness of any statements; namely that the statement was not obtained from the accused either as a result of fear of prejudice or hope of advantage exercised or held out by a person in authority[76] and that the statement reflects the operating mind of the accused at the time he or she gave the statement.[77] Other persons who can give evidence for the accused may have been present; the police may testify as to circumstances which cast doubt on the voluntariness of the statement; or counsel, through cross-examination of the police officers, may secure helpful answers. However, in most cases it will be necessary for the accused to testify on such relevant matters as force, threats of force, inducements, psychological factors and the accused's state of mind as it may have been affected by alcohol, drugs or other factors.

If the accused is seeking to exclude the confession based on a *Charter* argument, for example, that he or she was not given the right to counsel, then the onus shifts to the accused on the balance of probabilities. This can increase the necessity for the client to testify.

---

76 *Ibrahim v. R.*, [1914] A.C. 599 (P.C.).

77 *Ward v. R.* (1979), 44 C.C.C. (2d) 498 (S.C.C.); *R. v. Clarkson* (1986), 25 C.C.C. (3d) 207 (S.C.C.); *Nagotcha v. R.* (1980), 51 C.C.C. (2d) 353 (S.C.C.).

What then are the risks facing an accused who testifies on his or her *voir dire?* The Supreme Court of Canada in *DeClercq v. R.*[78] held that an accused may be asked on a *voir dire* whether the statement he made was true. Such an admission can only be used in determining the question of credibility on the *voir dire* issue. An accused cannot be asked on the *voie dire* questions as to his innocence or guilt.[79] The evidence on the *voie dire* may not be used on the trial proper.[80] The accused may testify on the *voie dire* without prejudice to his privilege not to testify on the trial proper.[81] Even if the witness were to admit that the statement was true the trial judge can find that it was involuntarily given and inadmissible.[82] *DeClercq* should be looked at again by the Supreme Court of Canada in view of the fact that it was based on the English decision in *R. v. Hammond*[83] which was later overruled by *Wong Kam-ming v. R.*[84] *DeClerq* was disapproved by the Privy Council in *Wong Kam-ming.*[85]

Section 13 of the *Charter* states: A witness who testifies in any proceedings has the right not to have any incriminating evidence given used to incriminate that witness in any other proceedings, except in a prosecution for perjury or for the giving of contradictory evidence. *Voir dires,*[86] retrials,[87] preliminary hearings,[88] bail hearings,[89] and public inquiries[90] fall within the meaning of "any other proceedings" for the purpose of section 13 of the *Charter.* However section 13 does not prevent the witness from being cross-examined on that evidence for the purpose of impeaching credibility[91] but such evidence cannot be introduced to establish proof of its contents. In *R.*

---

78 [1969] 1 C.C.C. 197 (S.C.C.).

79 *R. v. Erven* (1978), 44 C.C.C. (2d) 76 (S.C.C.).

80 *Ibid.* It was held to be impermissible for the trial Judge to use evidence from a *voir dire* to bolster the complainant's testimony. See *R. v. H. (J.)* (2011), 2011 ONCA 207 (Ont. C.A.) (endorsement).

81 *Ibid.*

82 *R. v. Van Dongen* (1975), 26 C.C.C. (2d) 22 (B.C. C.A.).

83 [1941] 3 All E.R. 318 (C.C.A.).

84 [1979] 1 All E.R. 939 (P.C.).

85 Notwithstanding the compelling reasons not to follow *DeClercq v. R.,* it has been held that it is not open to a provincial Court of Appeal to reconsider the issue. See *R. v. Guérin; R. v. Pimparé* (1987), 38 C.C.C. (3d) 380 (Que. C.A.); *R. v. Sawchyn* (1981), 22 C.R. (3d) 34 (Alta. C.A.).

86 *R. v. Tarafa* (1989), 53 C.C.C. (3d) 472 (Que. S.C.); *R. v. Skinner* (1998), 42 C.C.C. (3d) 575 (Ont. C.A.).

87 *R. v. Kuldip* (1990), 61 C.C.C. (3d) 385 (S.C.C.); *R. v. Darrach* (2001), 148 C.C.C. (3d) 97 (S.C.C.).

88 *Lucas v. Saskatchewan (Minister of Justice)* (1995), (sub nom. *R. v. Lucas*) 97 C.C.C. (3d) 89 (Sask. Q.B.).

89 *R. v. B. (T.B.)* (1988), 62 C.R. (3d) 306 (Ont. Prov. Ct.); *R. v. Sicurella* (1997), 120 C.C.C. (3d) 403 (Ont. Prov. Ct.).

90 *Phillips v. Nova Scotia (Commissioner, Public Inquiries Act),* [1995] 2 S.C.R. 97 (S.C.C.).

91 *R. v. Kuldip, supra.*

v. Calder,[92] in a case that involved a statement ruled inadmissible because the accused's right to counsel was violated, the Supreme Court held that only in very limited circumstances could such evidence be used to challenge the credibility of the accused. In *R. v. Noël*[93] the Supreme Court held that when the prior evidence was incriminating when given, its subsequent use is to be totally prohibited even if it was tendered for the limited purpose of testing credibility, unless there is no real danger of incrimination. If the prior evidence was not incriminating, it may be used to challenge credibility in another proceeding.

ORDER OF WITNESSES

As a general rule the accused's case should unfold in a logical order that is likely to make the most sense to the triers-of-fact. There are times when an orderly presentation cannot be accomplished as a witness may not be able to come to Court at a particular time because of circumstances, such as being out of town, illness or other reasons. Counsel should explain to the Court that he is calling the witness out of order and give the reason so that the jurors do not feel there is something missing from the unfolding of the narrative.

It would be ideal to start the day with a witness who makes a favourable impression and is not shaken in cross-examination. It puts the triers-of-fact in a receptive mood for the questioner's case. It is also important, when possible, that the jurors go home at the end of the day with a favourable impression of the case as that impression will stay with them for the rest of the day and overnight. The final witness for the defence should be a strong one as normally that witness's testimony will be most present in the minds of jurors when they deliberate. However, we do not live in an ideal world and we do not conduct trials where ideal situations always present themselves.

All witnesses on the same subject-matter should be called successively so that the evidence will be easier to follow and the repetition of the same evidence will present to the jury the greatest impact of the points to be made. If one witness does not make a favourable impression, his or her failures can be overcome by the cumulative weight of all the witnesses.

Counsel should not proceed from one boring subject-matter to the next. Where possible, interesting witnesses should be interspersed to keep the listeners' attention. Break up the monotony of a series of lengthy and uninteresting witnesses by calling witnesses who will be brief. The less

---

92 (1996), 105 C.C.C. (3d) 1 (S.C.C.).
93 (2002), 168 C.C.C. (3d) 193 (S.C.C.).

important witnesses should be heard during the middle of the day when the jury is bored or fatigued and its attention span has decreased.

It is best to place a weak witness between stronger witnesses on the same subject. The stronger witnesses can buttress the weaker witness.

When calling an expert to whom counsel intends to pose a hypothetical question it will usually be appropriate to call him or her as the last witness since the hypothetical question will be based upon the testimony heard before. Normally the expert will be providing extremely important testimony and by calling the expert last, the questioner will be giving his/her evidence its due emphasis. See Chapter, "The Expert Witness."

In some cases counsel will choose to call his client first because this is the only way the case would make any sense to the jurors. To call other witnesses first may leave them testifying in a vacuum because the client's testimony provides the best source for setting the scene properly. This concern may be obviated if defence counsel wishes to make an opening address to the jury painting an overview of the defence and explaining the order of witnesses to be called if necessary. Defence counsel may also wish to call her client first where the client has shortcomings or where counsel has doubts about how the accused will withstand cross-examination and she knows there are other witnesses such as a witness corroborative of the accused, a strong character witness or an expert witness, who can overcome any negative impression left by the accused. Another approach would be to call character witnesses first with the hope that the accused will gain credibility from their testimony. If counsel is confident the client will be an impressive witness, then in my view the client should testify last.

Defence counsel normally requests an order excluding witnesses so that the witnesses who follow each other to the witness stand will not consciously or subconsciously tailor their evidence to match the earlier testimony. (See Chapter, "Cross-Examination of Police Officers" for a further discussion of this topic). There is no rule of law or practice that states that where such an order is made the accused must be called first. The decision on the order of calling witnesses is entirely that of counsel for the accused, even where alibi witnesses are called. The trial judge can neither direct the calling of the accused nor the order in which the accused will testify.[94] But it appears from *R. v. Angelantoni* and *R. v. Smuk*[95] that there

94   *R. v. Smuk* (1971), 3 C.C.C. (2d) 457 (B.C. C.A.); *R. v. Sparre*, Ont. Co. Ct., Borins Co. Ct. J., October 4, 1977, summarized at 1 W.C.B. 611; *R. v. Angelantoni* (1975), 31 C.R.N.S. 342 (Ont. C.A.) not following the opposite view in *R. v. Archer* (1972), 26 C.R.N.S. 225 (Ont. C.A.); see annotation A.G. Campbell "The Order of Defence Witnesses" (1974), 26 C.R.N.S. 277. However, in *R. v. Chambers* (1987), 13 B.C.L.R. (2d) 153 (B.C. S.C.), Trainor J. of the British Columbia Supreme Court held that although it would normally be wrong for the trial judge to dictate the order of witnesses, it is not

is nothing preventing the Crown from pointing out to the jurors in summation that the accused's testimony must be considered in light of the fact that it was defence counsel who requested an order excluding witnesses to prevent the tailoring of evidence yet the accused testified after hearing all of his own witnesses. This may be an acceptable risk for defence counsel depending on the circumstances of the case. However Professor Robert Keeton[96] has provided an answer for any such comment by the Crown. He argues that:

> The justification for calling the client after other witnesses is that the most truthful witness will make mistakes, particularly when subject to skillful cross-examination. The ability of the witness who can observe and tell the facts is as much at stake as his honesty. The danger of damaging mistakes in your client's testimony is reduced when he has been afforded the opportunity of hearing the testimony of his supporting witnesses, and observing the techniques of the opposing lawyer on cross-examination, before he takes the stand.

Related to Professor Keeton's comment is another reason to call the client as the last witness, and a very practical tool. If the accused testifies before other defence witnesses, it may be that a witness called thereafter will testify to something that the client did not address or contradicts the client on some point. In either case, the client may have evidence to offer which could satisfactorily answer any negative impression that had been left by such earlier testimony, but would be unable to do so having already testified.

Counsel may also wish to call her client last because she feels that the accused's defence will have its greatest impact that way as it could be the last evidence the jury hears.

When there are a number of character witnesses it would be advisable to call at least some of them prior to the accused testifying because they will prepare the jurors to be in a very receptive mood before hearing the accused's testimony. If the accused has not made a good impression then calling character witnesses afterwards will not change anything. Where the accused is fortunate enough to have a number of very good character witnesses, defence counsel will not wish to bore the jury by calling one character witness after another to say basically the same thing. It is suggested that some character witnesses be called before the client testifies, perhaps interspersed between other witnesses where it does not break up the order of things, and that the strongest character witness be called after the accused testifies.

---

improper to do so where opinion evidence would be given and the Court would first have to determine if the proper foundation had been laid.

95 *Ibid.*

96 R.E. Keeton, *Trial Tactics and Methods* (Boston: Little, Brown, 1954), p. 22.

AFTER-THE-FACT CONDUCT (CONSCIOUSNESS OF GUILT) EVIDENCE

It is not an unusual feature of a trial for the Crown to lead after-the-fact or consciousness of guilt evidence. Some examples of post-offence conduct are, "flight from the scene of the crime; attempts to resist arrest; failure to appear at trial; and acts of concealment such as lying, assuming a false name, changing one's appearance and hiding or disposing of evidence,"[97] as well as the influencing of witnesses. In the *Morin* trial there were other examples including demeanour evidence which has been discussed in detail in the Chapter, "Observation and Recollection." The courts have expressed concerns about the risk of this kind of evidence in that it will be overemphasized by the trier of fact.[98] In this regard Commissioner Kaufmann made <u>Recommendation 76A(a)</u>:

> (a) Purported evidence of "consciousness of guilt" can be overused and mis-used. Crown counsel and the courts should adopt a cautious approach to the tendering and reception of this kind of evidence, which brings with it dangers which may be disproportionate to the probative value, if any, that it has. Crown counsel and police should also be educated as to the dangers associated with this kind of evidence. This recommendation should not be read to suggest that such evidence should be prohibited.

In *R. v. Diu*,[99] the Court recognized that after-the-fact conduct (consciousness of guilt evidence) can be problematic where more than one offence is charged or where the issue is level of guilt. Where such conduct might provide the basis to infer guilt for one of the offences charged it does not necessarily mean it is logical for inferring guilt for all of the offences charged.

USE OF INTERPRETERS

Where the client or a witness is unable to understand the English language an interpreter is obviously required. The accused bears the burden

---

97 *R. v. Turcotte* (2005), 200 C.C.C. (3d) 289 (S.C.C.).

98 See *R. v. B. (S.C.)* (1997), 119 C.C.C. (3d) 530 (Ont. C.A.) where the Court stated the risk is best avoided by a judicious use of the power to exclude prejudicial evidence even though it has some probative value and *R. v. Campbell* (1998), 122 C.C.C. (3d) 44 (B.C. C.A.), affirmed (1998), 130 C.C.C. (3d) 223 (S.C.C.), per Hall, J.A. *R. v. Peavoy* (1997), 117 C.C.C. (3d) 226 (Ont. C.A.), the Ontario Court of Appeal was critical of the term "consciousness of guilt" suggesting a more neutral term such as "after-the-fact conduct."

99 (2000), 49 O.R. (3d) 40 (Ont. C.A.).

of demonstrating that he requires an interpreter on the balance of probabilities.[100]

Section 14 of the *Charter* elevates the right to an interpreter to a constitutional guarantee for a witness in any proceeding who does not understand or speak the language of the Court or who is deaf.[101] The interpretation must be continuous, precise, impartial, competent and contemporaneous.[102] In *R v. Potvin*[103] the Court held that when an order is made that the trial be held in the official language of the accused, pursuant to section 530 of the *Code*, it is necessary that the trial Judge and the Crown not only understand the official language but speak it in Court. A trial will not necessarily be vitiated every time a few words are spoken in an official language other than that of the accused; but a unilingual trial pursuant to section 530 must be essentially consistent with the provisions of section 530.1.

Where an accused requests an interpreter, formal training as an interpreter is not required. The standard that must be met in interpretation is not one of perfection, but is one of continuity, precision, impartiality, competency and contemporaneousness. The general standard is word-for-word translation of everything an English-speaking accused would hear although minor variations from this standard would not necessarily contravene the accused's rights. While there is no constitutional right to an accredited interpreter, there is a right to a competent interpreter. The ultimate issue is whether deficits in the assistance of an interpreter made the trial fundamentally unfair.[104]

The rights of the accused by virtue of the combined effect of sections 530 and 530.1 of the *Criminal Code* are not violated when co-accuseds are charged jointly as participating in a common enterprise and seek to be tried in different languages of choice and severance is refused.[105]

A difficulty arises when the witness does speak and understand some English but is more proficient in his or her native language or he or she is fairly proficient in English but still has problems with some of the language. When should an interpreter be requested? An interpreter slows down the trial processes and the evidence can lose its impact when given through an intermediary. However, I would make the case that an interpreter should be used. The client may only fail to understand a few words but they may be vital in how he or she interprets or responds to a question or the proceedings.

---

100 *R. v. R. (A.L.)* (1999), 141 C.C.C. (3d) 151 (Man. C.A.), reversed [2001] 11 W.W.R. 413 (S.C.C.).
101 *R. v. Tran* (1994), 92 C.C.C. (3d) 218 (S.C.C.).
102 *Ibid.*
103 (2004), 69 O.R. (3d) 641 (Ont. C.A.).
104 *R. v. Sidhu* (2005), 203 C.C.C. (3d) 17 (Ont. S.C.J.).
105 *R. v. Sarrazin* (2005), 75 O.R. (3d) 485 (C.A.).

There is also a tactical advantage for the witness who does not understand some English. While the interpreter is interpreting the question, the accused, no doubt understanding at least part of the question in English, will have extra time to consider the question and his answer so that he or she can respond correctly. This could be a disadvantage for the accused when it is the Crown witness who requests an interpreter but not the accused.

Defence counsel should make it clear to the Judge and the jury at the outset that the accused does understand some English but counsel feels that his or her client will miss the meaning of some words which could be important. If this is not made clear when an interpreter is requested the Court and/or the jurors may come to feel that after hearing the accused at times lapse into English that he has requested an interpreter for an ulterior motive, such as stalling for time after a question to come up with the right answer for his defence.

In *R. v. Johal*[106] it was held that a Judge should be "generous and open-minded" and appoint an interpreter where it is apparent the accused is having trouble expressing himself or understanding the proceedings, or if the accused requests an interpreter and the Judge feels the request is justified.

It is of practical importance that the interpreter, if he or she is the same one who is assisting the accused in instructing counsel, be warned by the trial judge that the solicitor-client privilege applies to the interpreter.[107]

A violation of section 530 is substantially wrong and therefore section 585(1)(b) of the *Code* has no application.[108]

THE INEFFECTIVE INTERPRETER

There are times when it becomes obvious that the interpreter is ineffective. This may not be discovered unless and until the accused, family members or friends who speak both English as well as the foreign language of the witness bring this problem to the attention of counsel. Counsel must put on the record when made aware of the mistakes of the interpreter, advise as to what those mistakes were, to support a potential motion for a mistrial or to at least for a change of interpreters.

---

106   (2001), 155 C.C.C. (3d) 449 (B.C. C.A.).
107   *R. v. R. (A.L.), supra.*
108   *R. c. Ohelo* (*sub nom. R. v. Ohelo*) (2009), 98 O.R. (3d) 788 (Ont. S.C.J.).

6

The Objectives of Cross-Examination

". . . a lawyer can do anything with cross-examination if he is skillful enough not to impart his own cause upon it."[1]

CREATING REASONABLE DOUBT

It has been said that the overall objective of cross-examination for the defence is to create reasonable doubt, not to remove it. It is therefore fundamental that the cross-examiner have a defence theory so that when he or she rises to cross-examine each witness he or she has a clear objective or even more than one objective in mind which fits within that blueprint. That blueprint will have in mind the nature of your defence, the evidence which supports it, how to overcome any obstacles to that defence and any evidence which relates to issues of law that will be relevant throughout the trial.

Robert Keeton,[2] in my view, correctly sets out the aims of cross-examination:

(1) Discrediting the testimony of the witness being examined;
(2) Using testimony of this witness to discredit the unfavourable testimony of other witnesses;
(3) Using the testimony of this witness to corroborate the favourable testimony of other witnesses;
(4) Using the testimony of this witness to contribute independently to the favourable development of your own case.

I would add this caveat: the jury should be made aware of the defence's position as soon as possible, usually through cross-examination of the Crown witnesses and not for the first time when counsel is called upon to

---

1 The latter part of John Henry Wigmore's quotation that begins with: "Cross-examination is the greatest legal engine ever invented for the discovery of truth."
2 R.E. Keeton, *Trial Tactics and Methods* (Boston: Little, Brown, 1954), p. 87.

present the defence. Often counsel will receive what he/she believes to be favourable answers for the defence in cross-examination but the jurors will not necessarily understand the significance of those answers until counsel makes her jury address. There are times when counsel, either through inexperience or purposely (perhaps out of a fear that the Crown may later be able to undo the harm), refrains from exposing the full face of the defence until after the Crown's case has been completed. As a result the judge or the jury may be somewhat uncertain as to what parts of the evidence fit the defence theory or what line the defence is attempting to pursue.

Although there may be the rare occasion when the cross-examiner receives an answer that he may wish not to pursue until the right moment later, it is urged that the defence theory be clear to the jury as soon as possible in order that the jurors can scrutinize the evidence with that theory in mind. Counsel wants the jurors to know his client's side of the case as soon as possible. If the defence tries to illuminate its position for the first time during the final address it could be too late if the jurors have become impressed with the Crown's evidence. Indeed, a study in the U.S. some years ago showed that approximately 85 percent of prospective jurors chose a favourite side early in the trial and then distorted the evidence to fit that tentative preconception.[3] Indeed, studies in the U.S. show that approximately 75 percent of jurors decide the case after the opening statement. If this is so, defence counsel should try as quickly as possible to diminish the impact of the Crown's opening address. After decades at the Bar I have come to the conclusion that most cases are decided before the final argument. Where possible counsel should use cross-examination to argue his or her case in the form of questions in order to present the defence position to the Judge and jury. Of course, counsel will again present the defence position to the Court in his or her final address but it cannot be gainsaid that it is a good strategy to repeat the defence position as often as possible.

Notwithstanding any question of tactics, there is a duty to cross-examine, drawing the attention of the witness to any particular point on which it is intended to suggest that the witness is not speaking the truth.[4] The witness should be given the opportunity of making any explanation open to him, by drawing his attention to any defence to be called later which will contradict him, unless it is perfectly clear from the surrounding circum-

---

3 The study published in the June 2001 issue of Journal of Experimental Psychology; Applied (Reported in Globe and Mail, June 25, 2001.)

4 *Cross on Evidence*, 4th ed. (Toronto: Butterworths), p. 227; *Phipson on Evidence*, 13th ed. (1982), p. 806; *R. v. Verney* (1993), 67 O.A.C. 279 (Ont. C.A.); *Browne v. Dunn* (1893), 6 R. 67 (U.K. H.L.), per Lord Herschell, adopted by Duff J. in *Peters v. Perras* (1909), 42 S.C.R. 244 (S.C.C.); *R. v. Jackson* (1974), 20 C.C.C. (2d) 113 (Ont. H.C.); *R. v. Mandzuk* (1945), 85 C.C.C. 158 (B.C. C.A.); *R. v. Foxton* (1920), 34 C.C.C. 9 (Ont. H.C.); *R. v. Moke* (1917), 28 C.C.C. 296 at 305 (Alta. C.A.); *R. v. Miller* (1959), 125 C.C.C. 8 (B.C. C.A.).

stances that it is intended to impeach his story.[5] This has come to be known as the *Browne v. Dunn* principle. See Chapter, "Further Limitations and Obligations in Examining Witnesses," for a more detailed discussion on Duty To Cross-Examine: The Browne and Dunn Rule. In *R. v. Dyck*,[6] the British Columbia Court of Appeal went rather far when it held that it was wrong to allow the accused to call contradictory evidence when the accused failed to cross-examine on the point. Surely this impropriety could have been rectified (as appears to be the normal course) by permitting the Crown a rebuttal to that contradictory evidence and/or by a judicial comment that no such allegations were put to the witness by the defence so that the witness had an opportunity to deny them.[7] This rebuttal evidence by the Crown would be the last piece of evidence that the jury would hear on the issue near the end of the trial and therefore has the potential to be very detrimental to the offending party's case.

The other great danger of not putting the defence case to the prosecution witnesses in cross-examination is that the trier-of-fact, especially a Judge sitting without a jury, might make the inference that the defence case, as developed for the first time in examination-in-chief, must be of recent invention (that is, since the Crown case was put in) otherwise it would have been put to the prosecution witnesses in cross-examination. This is a negative inference that no defence counsel should blindly run the risk of incurring. However, there is probably no counsel that has not been guilty of oversight and it may well be that counsel inadvertently failed to put a question or questions that they should have posed.

Alerting the trier-of-fact to your client's defence during the Crown's case can be accomplished by arguing the case in the form of questions put in cross-examination, as exemplified in one fashion by Edward Greenspan, Q.C. in the following trial extract where the police officer had testified in-chief that he had found counterfeit money which had fallen from behind a picture hanging on the wall in the house of the accused. The defence was that the money was planted by the police.

Q. I am showing you what purports to be the original information in this case. The names are Antonio and Grace Stalteri, is that correct?
A. Yes, sir. That is what it says.
Q. How does the name "Grace" get on the information in this case?
A. I have no idea, sir.
Q. And you have never seen the indictment in this case?

5 *R. v. Foxton, ibid.*; *R. v. Moke, ibid.*; *R. v. Nepp* (1927), 48 C.C.C. 275 (Man. C.A.); *R. v. Vanmeer* (1950), 97 C.C.C. 241 (Ont. Co. Ct.); *R. v. Hart* (1932), 23 Cr. App. R. 202 (Eng. C.A.); *R. v. Mandzuk, ibid.*; *R. v. Miller* (1959), 125 C.C.C. 8 (B.C. C.A.).
6 (1969), [1970] 2 C.C.C. 283 (B.C. C.A.).
7 *R. v. Nicolaides* (April 8, 1987), Doc. 1975/85 (Ont. Dist. Ct.), summarized at 1 W.C.B. (2d) 417; *R. v. MacDonald* (1989), 48 C.C.C. (3d) 230 (N.S. C.A.); P.K. McWilliams, *Canadian Criminal Evidence*, 2nd ed. (1984), p. 1049 .

A. Not that I am aware of, sir.

Q. If I were to tell you that the original indictment in this case said the name "Grace Teresa Stalteri," what would your answer be as to how the name "Grace" became involved?

A. I am afraid I don't have an answer for it, sir. I don't know how it got there. I didn't type it up.

Q. Let me suggest an answer to you. You were told by Rose Stalteri that her mother's name was "Teresa." I suggest to you, sir, you know as a fact there was another Antonio Stalteri in Toronto and that he has a wife whose name is "Grace."

A. I would have to disagree, yes, sir.

Q. I would suggest to you further, Officer, that you do know that there is another Antonio Stalteri and his wife's name is "Grace" and that Antonio Stalteri has a criminal record.

A. I have since heard this to be true, sir, but I haven't any factual knowledge of it.

Q. I suggest to you as well that before you went to the home of this Antonio Stalteri that you knew that there was an Antonio Stalteri with a criminal record and a wife whose name was "Grace"?

A. No, sir.

Q. I suggest to you as well, Officer, that you also knew that there was another Antonio Stalteri that you and other officers felt were linked with other people in connection with a matter that had occurred the day before this raid on August 1st, 1971.

A. I'm sorry, sir. I missed the last part of what occurred.

Q. Occurred the day before August 1st, 1971.

A. We were told, sir, when we went there there was an Antonio Stalteri living there. This was one of a part of a number of raids made the same time on that day.

Q. There was a shooting in a plaza in North Toronto, isn't that correct?

A. Yes, sir, there was.

Q. And as a result of that shooting in a plaza in North Toronto there were a number of raids in homes in what is commonly known in Toronto as Little Italy, isn't that correct?

A. Yes, sir, I believe so.

Q. One of the homes you raided was the home of Mr. Antonio Stalteri and his wife Teresa?

A. Yes.

Q. Rose Stalteri told you her mother's name was "Teresa." Can you give any explanation why the name "Grace" appears on the original information and the original indictment in this case?

A. No, sir, I cannot.

Q. If I suggested to you you were of the belief that the name was "Grace" because you were at the wrong home and you were at the home of the other Antonio Stalteri, would that not be correct?

A. No, sir.

Q. If I were to suggest to you as well, Officer, upon charging into this home you expected to find many things, that is why you came with six officers, after an hour and five minutes of searching through the home of a man whom you know now does not have a criminal record and never involved with the police, after an hour and five minutes, because of a sense of frustration, a sense of over zealousness, you put that money behind the picture.

A. No, sir. I did not.

Q. I suggest to you as well, sir, that when you went out with this money to Antonio Stalteri, you went out there with the knowledge that you could not convict a man who had money in a house unless you could get something more from him and that in fact Antonio Stalteri, my client, never said anything to you out there.

A. That is absolutely untrue, sir.

Q. I suggest to you as well, sir, whatever statement you say was made by Antonio Stalteri was done in collaboration with other officers and never made to you in that form.

A. It was made in the form I read to you as I remember it, sir.

Q. If I suggest to you that Antonio Stalteri, when you showed him the money, looked at you and said, "I don't know," and that is all that he said to you and, if anything else, he said to you he had no knowledge of it and that is all he said to you.

A. No, sir. I disagree.

Q. You know that Antonio Stalteri now has no criminal record and has never been involved with the police?

A. So I have been informed, sir.

Q. You know that Mrs. Stalteri as well has never been in any trouble and never been involved with the police?

A. So I have been informed, sir.

Q. You have no answer for me why you charged her as "Grace"?

A. I did not charge her.

Q. You have no answer for me why she was charged as "Grace Teresa"?

A. No, sir, I have not.

Q. Rose Stalteri told you her mother's name was "Teresa"?

A. That's correct, sir.

Q. You now know about this other Antonio Stalteri?

A. I don't know about him, personally.

Q. Do you know about an Antonio Stalteri that has a criminal record and you know that that Antonio Stalteri's wife's name is "Grace"?

A. No, sir, I do not.

Q. My suggestion to you [is that] you were in the wrong house.[8]

In the above cross-examination which contributed to an acquittal, Mr. Greenspan obviously knew the officer would not be agreeing with his suggestions. Positive responses were not really the object of the exercise nor were they expected. The goal was to put forth the defence side of the story in the form of questions so that the jury would not become settled in

---

8 From the transcript of *R. v. Stalteri*, Ont. Dist. Ct., September 13, 1972.

with the one-sided prosecution story which they might find difficult to put from their minds by the time the defence was called, when for the first time they hear a denial of the officer's evidence. In reality, the cross-examiner is making an early mini-jury address. The jury, once alerted to the defence position, will pay even closer attention to the questions and answers which follow to see how they fit in with either side of the story. The accused's later denial will have received a psychological boost if his counsel has forcefully put the accusatory questions, provided that counsel has credibility with the jurors. As well, defence counsel has fulfilled his or her obligation by giving the witness the opportunity to refute what the accused or his witnesses will testify to and what counsel will be alleging in his jury address, namely that the counterfeit money found at the Stalteri residence was a result of a police "plant."

There are some writers of advocacy techniques who make the point that phrases such as the commonly used "I suggest that" as a prefix to a question should not be used. Why this suggestion has been made is not clear, unless these writers suggest that something similar could happen as that which occurred to Bob McGee, when as an assistant Crown attorney in Toronto he wound up a long cross-examination of an accused charged with murdering a rival mobster and his girlfriend:

> Q. I suggest to you that when you swear that you did not murder these people, you sir, are a liar.
> A. And I suggest to you sir, you are full of shit.
> The accused's wife, who was sitting in the body of the courtroom applauded and shouted: "Good for you, dear."[9]

There are, of course, other ways to argue a case in the form of questions without using the "I suggest to you" prefix. The questions themselves should paint the picture that the defence wants to place before the Court. Alan Gold cross-examined an undercover police officer (posing as a wealthy Texan) on behalf of his female-stripper client who was a go-between in a drug purchase and pleaded not guilty to trafficking.[10] At this moment no more will be said as to his purpose so as to allow the reader to make out the picture that is being painted:

> Q. I mean, these bars that you mentioned are so-called adult bars, where the dancers wear less than a full complement of clothing?
> A. That's correct.
> Q. They make their money by tips from customers?
> A. By table dancing.

---

9 P.V. MacDonald, *Court Jesters: Canada's Lawyers and Judges Take the Stand to Relate Their Funniest Stories* (Toronto: Methuen, 1985), p. 65.

10 From the transcript of *R. v. Miles*, Ont. Dist. Ct., Weiler Dist. Ct. J., November 13, 1986, a mistrial declared unconnected with the cross-examination illustrated.

. . .

Q. These girls aren't particularly sophisticated, are they? You can't answer that?
A. I don't know.

. . .

Q. And the girl, my client, you were dealing with, was one of these table dancers?
A. Right.

. . .

Q. And so was this Jessica who introduced you to my client?
A. That's correct.
Q. All right. Is this the first time you had been in any of these bars, Gilmores, Filmores, Cocomo's and the others? Is this the first time you had been in these bars?
A. Yes, I believe it was.

. . .

Q. It's not the sort of place you frequented, aside from your professional capacity, is it?
A. No.
Q. These are the sorts of places that advertise in the *Sun*, "13 Nude Girls," that sort of thing?
A. I have seen the advertisements in the *Sun*.
Q. Officer, the girls dancing in these places are all trying to find a way of dancing out of those places, aren't they?
A. I wouldn't know that.
Q. Officer, you and Officer Downs, I mean, you are a good looking guy, so is Officer Downs, would you agree with that, as far as these girls are concerned?
A. Thank you.
Q. You were certainly a cut above the other customers in this place, weren't you?
A. No, I would not say that.
Q. You wouldn't say that?
A. No, I would not.
Q. Do you think they get a lot of wealthy Texans in these bars, Officer?
A. Offhand, I wouldn't say so.
Q. Officer, do you think real wealthy Texans would, in the ordinary course of human experience, walk into these bars and be interested in your average table dancer?
A. No.
Q. I mean, if there really happened to be one in a million love stories come true, would "Bar girl marries rich boy," be one of them?
A. I believe so.

. . .

Q. You called my client throughout Rene, is that right?
A. That's correct.
Q. And even in the course of testifying in the court proceedings, you would occasionally slip into calling her Rene, is that true?
A. That's true.
Q. That's how you knew her?
A. Yes, it is.

. . .

Q. Officer, I mean, let's not be nonsensical about this. You make contact with Jessica, and you pretended you were a big Texas playboy who wanted to buy drugs, isn't that what happened?
A. That's correct.
Q. And I mean, if the girl wanted to impress you, or get in good with you, helping you out in your desires would be the way to do it, isn't that right?
A. That's correct.
Q. I mean, do you think it's unreasonable for a girl in her situation to get in good with a wealthy Texan playboy, it isn't, is it?
A. That's correct.
Q. I mean, that's a pretty good temptation, isn't it Officer?
A. That's a very good temptation.
Q. So you propositioned her for some cocaine, did you?
A. I would believe yes, I did.
Q. That's what you wrote.
A. I wrote that I did that.
Q. I mean, she wasn't coming up to you and trying to force cocaine down your throat against your will, was she?
A. Not at all.

. . .

Q. And similarly, with Miss Miles you made it clear to her in no uncertain terms that you were heavily involved in drugs, and you talked to her about cocaine prices here and in Texas, is that right?
A. That's true.
Q. I mean, you made it very clear you wanted to purchase cocaine, right?
A. True.
Q. And I mean, she wasn't walking through the bar saying, "Cocaine for sale. Anybody want to buy cocaine?" was she?
A. Not at all.
Q. Any discussion about purchasing cocaine came about because you made it clear that is what you wanted to do, isn't that fair?
A. I would say that would be fair.
Q. Officer, you wanted to meet the male, as it were, that you thought was giving instructions to Renalda Miles, isn't that fair?
A. I would say, I guess.

Q. Officer, on several occasions Miss Miles said to you, "I wish he would meet with you," didn't she?

A. That's correct.

Q. I mean, in that, you were on the same wave length. She kept telling you, to quote her, "I'm so fucked up. I wish he would meet you."

A. That's correct, she did say that.

Q. And you wanted that too, didn't you?

A. I would go along with that.

. . .

Q. Well, in any event Officer, your posture with both girls was that you were wealthy, and you were prepared to pay for the cocaine, right?

A. That's correct.

Q. And Officer, it wasn't just that you wanted, sort of, the cocaine in the abstract, your story was that you were on the verge of leaving Canada, having completed your business, is that correct?

A. Correct.

Q. And you were sort of going to throw a going away party for yourself, am I right so far?

A. Correct.

Q. And that you had rented a chalet up north in some ski area?

A. Correct.

Q. And that you wanted enough coke for everybody at the party, right?

A. Correct.

Q. For about 50 people, was your estimate, right?

A. I can't recall. I said for all the people I had done business with here, and prior to my leaving.

. . .

Q. So this wasn't, as it were, to obtain . . . I mean, the understanding, that all the people you were dealing with, was that you had a substantial party in mind, and this was the recreational drug that was to be consumed at the party, correct?

A. Correct.

. . .

Q. And in fact, as I recall your evidence-in-chief, you emphasized you wanted good stuff because it was for you and—?

A. And my friends.

. . .

Q. Officer, on two occasions you have already mentioned in your evidence-in-chief, you offered Miss Miles money for her part in this endeavour, didn't you?

A. I did, yes, in an abstract way.

Q. I didn't mean you pulled out a wallet, you said, "keep the change," as it were?

A. That's true.

Q. Her response was no thanks, what was it, "Blow me out"?

A. Correct.

Q. "Let me have my portion at the party," is that correct?

A. Yes.

Q. Was she very worried about being invited to the party?

A. Worried about being invited?

Q. Do you remember what she said to you that night at her house, "If I don't get if for you, am I still invited to the party?", do you remember that?

A. That's true.

Q. She wanted to be invited to this party, didn't she?

A. It would seem that way.

Q. And her understanding of who was going to be at this party was that you, a wealthy Texan, was going to have at least several dozen of your business associates, right?

A. That's correct.

Q. Presumably people of your same stature and wealth, or similar thereof? A desirable group of people for a girl in her position to get in with, is that reasonable?

A. Reasonable.

. . .

Q. Officer, posing as a wealthy Texan . . . By the way, did you pose as an eligible bachelor, or as a separated man, or a—

A. I cannot recall whether I was separated, or a bachelor; it was one of the two.

Q. You certainly didn't emphasize to her you had a little wife waiting at home, or anything like that, did you?

A. No, I did not.

Q. Officer, then can we agree really where we are at, you, posing as a wealthy Texan, made it clear you wished to purchase cocaine, right?

A. Correct.

Q. And that she agreed to help you, to try to help you make that purchase, isn't that correct?

A. That's true.

. . .

Q. Somebody else was going to set the price for sale to you?

A. That's correct.

Q. And the arrangements for the sale, she was being given information by somebody else, wasn't she, as far as you could tell?

A. As far as I could tell, yes.

Q. Do you remember on February 9th, Officer, one of the conversations . . . Do you remember on the morning of February 9th, as I think you recounted in your evidence-in-chief, she said that the friend's father was paranoid, and that, "He has changed his mind and would only sell me two ounces," is that right, and then you acted a little upset.

A. (Peruses notes) I have found it, yes. "Her friend's father was paranoid, had changed his mind, and would sell me two ounces."

Q. And you acted upset, and she apologized and said it wasn't her fault. She was worried you would be mad at her, is that right?

A. Well, she was worried what I would think about it.

Q. Then what does your notebook say, the next sentence?

A. She said that he would sell me the other six ounces tomorrow, that the price would still be the same.

Q. Is that what you wrote?

A. Yes.

Q. She said that he would sell you the other six ounces, right?

A. That's right.

Q. This was not, "we will sell you." She never said, "we will sell you"?

A. Well my recollection is she said that he would sell.

Q. Not that we'll sell you, or she'll sell you. What you've done in your book is, "he'll sell you," right?

A. Correct.

. . .

Q. And then, on February 7th, the next day, at 10:15, you arrived at the bar and then you went over and invited her to your table, didn't you?

A. That's correct.

Q. And I mean, Officer, you knew you were an undercover officer doing all this in the course of your duties, but she didn't know that at the time, did she?

A. No, she did not.

Q. To her you were a wealthy Texan inviting her to your table, and that would obviously be taken as a compliment, wouldn't it?

A. That's correct.

. . .

Q. Officer, I am going to suggest to you, the only reason she went to work that night was to see you, which might be a little bit different than to talk to you. Are you really sure, sir, at this stage, whether it was to talk to you, or to see you?

A. No, I could not. It could be to see me, or to talk to me.

Q. To see you. If she said it was to see you with a twinkle in her eye, that might indicate some kind of fondness, wouldn't it?

A. No, there was no twinkle in her eye.

Q. Officer, she asked you to sleep with her?

A. She asked me, stressing the fact it was sleeping.

Q. She asked you to sleep with her and stresses the sleeping. Can you tell me how she does that?

A. Well, to use the words, I couldn't. She looked at me in a friendly sort of way, and said, "Would you like to go up to sleep for a while?" We had been up all night.

Q. What did she . . . I am stressing the word, "sleep" Officer.

A. It's the way she said it. I used the word to stress I didn't trust myself.
Q. She would take that as a compliment?
A. She would indeed.

. . .

Q. Officer, I was about to ask you about the Aquarius. Is it the Aquarius Lounge, is that what it is called?
A. I'm not sure. I could tell you what I called it when I made my notes. What night was that?
Q. February 7.
A. The Aquarius Tavern I called it.

. . .

Q. It was your idea to go to that place?
A. That's correct.
Q. Was this on street level?
A. No, it was not.
Q. Where is it located?
A. It's—I believe I wrote the address down when I found out where it was. It's located on top of 55 Bloor Street West.
Q. That's the Manulife Building, is it?
A. The Manulife Building, yes.
Q. This is a lounge, isn't it, at the top of the building?
A. Yes, it is similar to a piano bar.
Q. With a beautiful view of the city?
A. Yes.
Q. With sparkling lights and all of that?
A. Yes.
Q. Floor to ceiling windows?
A. That's correct.
Q. Dark?
A. As a lounge would be, as a piano bar would be.
Q. Romantic?
A. It could be taken that way.
Q. And there was just you and my client?
A. That's correct.
Q. You had trouble finding this place, did you?
A. I did.
Q. My client didn't seem to know where it was, did she?
A. No, she didn't.
Q. She had never been there before, had she?
A. I don't believe she had been.
Q. Certainly a cut above Gilmores and Filmores, wasn't it?
A. Obviously.
Q. And in the course of that conversation at that location, you already testified in-chief—let me just focus on one part of your evidence—there were a

series of questions about what you did, what your father did, and that sort
of thing, is that right?

A. That's right.

. . .

Q. I mean Officer, you would agree with me if your story were true, and you
really were interested in her, you know, like, boy-girl stuff, I mean, that
would be a matter of some interest to her, wouldn't it?

A. It would. However, I believe she was asking the questions in regards to the
deal.

Q. That's my point, Officer. That is your interpretation, isn't it?

A. Yes, that's my interpretation.

Q. And your interpretation is influenced by the fact that you know you are a
police officer, and you know what you are interested in in that setting, is
that right?

A. That's correct.

Q. Again, you are not possessed of any special ability to read her mind, are
you?

A. None whatsoever.

Q. Again, we are faced with the fact we really can't reconstruct exactly what
was said for the jury to decide what was mean, can't we Officer?

A. No, we can't.

Q. And Officer, the fact is, whatever else was said or meant, there are two
things I would like to specifically ask you about in completing my cross-
examination. She specifically asked you, and you noted it, if she didn't get
the cocaine for you, whether she would still be invited to the party, or would
you just disappear. She asked you that, didn't she?

A. She did ask that, yes.

. . .

Q. Your summary is, as you read it—this is your notebook—she stated she
was still trying to decide whether or not to do it for you. This is what you
wrote?

A. Yes, that's the last part of it.

The defence of Ms. Miles was that she was the agent for the purchaser,
not for the seller. Note how Mr. Gold paints his client, a stripper and heavy
user of cocaine, as a sympathetic object being pursued by the handsome
undercover officer posing as a wealthy Texan businessman, whom she
viewed as a knight in shining armour. She didn't want any money for herself,
she was trying to obtain the cocaine at the behest of the officer and she
wished that the purchaser could deal with the supplier directly. Ms. Miles
did not testify but her story was told better through the questions of her
counsel than it could have been by herself and she did not have to face a
penetrating cross-examination which would have helped to convict her co-
accused.

It becomes particularly important to argue the defence position through cross-questioning if it is not intended to call a defence. Otherwise the jury could be left with a host of answers in a vacuum and a theory which would be difficult to argue in the closing address. This point was brought to my attention years ago by a young counsel who advised that he had conducted his cross-examination of the material Crown witness in a guarded manner on the understanding that his client would be testifying. By going only so far with his questions the young counsel was hoping to prevent the Crown from anticipating his client's testimony. However, as the Crown's case came to a close, the client panicked and refused to testify. The unfortunate defence counsel probably made the shortest jury address of his career.

However, it must be remembered that the questions alone are not the evidence. If the witness denies or does not adopt what the question alleges, then defence counsel has nothing to rely on in his final address except the hope that the jurors remember the questions and that they analyze the evidence in their glow. It should also be remembered that there is a limit as to how far counsel can go in asking questions which allege something he is not prepared to substantiate by evidence.[11]

SILENT CROSS-EXAMINATION: LESS CAN BE MORE

The first question counsel must consider is whether or not the witness should be cross-examined. Some counsel, particularly those who are inexperienced, are fearful that if they do not cross-examine the witness, the client or others will feel that they are not doing their job. However, it has been said before that we earn our fees as much as by what we do not say as by what we do say. It should be considered a cardinal rule of trial advocacy that if the witness does not harm the accused's defence and counsel knows that he will be unable to elicit favourable testimony from the witness in cross-examination, the only words to be spoken by counsel are "No questions." Hopefully, a message will be sent to the trier of fact that this witness in no way harmed your client. Do not feel that you have to cross-examine on all inconsistencies. There is no need to cross-examine on minor inconsistencies which mean nothing in the long run and may show up the weakness in your case if that is the best you can do, unless there are numerous ones which may impede on the witness's reliability and/or credibility.

There is nothing sadder than seeing the cross-examiner use an aimless and scattergun attack on the prosecution witnesses hoping that something fruitful will occur for the defence. The almost inevitable result will be that the prosecution's case is made stronger by this Russian roulette approach

---

11   That limit is discussed in the Chapter, "Further Limitations and Obligations in Examining Witnesses."

as the cross-examiner fills in gaps in the Crown's case or, because he/she foolishly repeats the same questions as those asked in-chief, the witness repeats the same damaging answers. Worse, it may distract attention from the genuinely strong parts of the defence case. The best that such a cross-examination will achieve is to try the patience of the judge and the jury who will no doubt entertain serious doubts about the credibility of the defence. It may be that a naive client will be happy with his/her counsel and will tell all in his jail corridor about what a great fighter he/she was; but there can be little pride for the lawyer who, like the fisherman, was dragged into the river by his catch.

THE FAVOURABLE ANSWER

Once counsel has obtained a favourable answer, the objective has been achieved. Unfortunately there are some counsel who wish to accentuate this favourable response or feel that it may be forgotten by the judge and jury and therefore attempt to make the same point again by later asking the witness to restate the answer. Counsel is then surprised and dismayed to hear the witness's answer to the question is not as favourable as before. As a result the cross-examiner has to go off-track in an attempt to resurrect the previously favourable answer which will not be forthcoming because the witness will say that he or she must not have expressed himself or herself clearly or had misunderstood the original question. When counsel has received a favourable response he/she should not ask for a curtain call. Usually the Judge will have the response in his notes and if the judge does not the Court reporter is sure to have it.

Any experienced cross-examiner knows that there will be many times when she will be unsuccessful in attaining all or even any of her objectives. There are limits to what cross-examination can achieve—it cannot win a hopeless case. Cross-examinations may disclose weaknesses but they may not be significant enough to win the day. It is hoped, however, that what follows in the ensuing chapters will give counsel their best chance of success so that when the trial is over the client will feel that her counsel protected her interests to the utmost and professionally; and the public, whether members of the jury or those following the trial, will feel that the administration of justice was well served.

7

Preparation for Cross-Examination

The greatest attributes of the best advocates are their common sense, judgment, ingenuity and understanding of human nature combined with their ability to perform well with little sleep. Without these qualities as a foundation, it will not matter how knowledgeable counsel is in the law, or how articulate or intelligent; success in the courtroom will be elusive. But even these attributes are not enough unless they are used in a studied preparation for the cross-questioning of the witness.

Because of the considerable media attention that has been focused on the consequences of crime, the public has become aroused to the extent that, in my view, we live in a law-and-order society as never before. No group recognizes this more than politicians, particularly when seeking election. It is substance that dominates the outcome of a trial and it will be the rare jury that could be swayed by histrionics, fancy phrases and impassioned pleas without the supporting evidence. It is therefore important for counsel to know everything that can affect both sides of the case for it is that knowledge and counsel's ability to use that knowledge that will have a significant impact on the outcome of the trial.

DISCLOSURE

Counsel will want to be certain that she has the important disclosure from the Crown before a trial date is set, for example: the witnesses' statements, reduced to writing or otherwise, such as by video or audio; the up-to-date criminal records, outstanding charges and police occurrences for each of the witnesses, other contacts the witnesses have had with the police; copies of any photographs, sketches or videos taken by the police; experts' reports; and any 911 calls to the police. Third party records, such as from a psychiatrist or a counsellor are not the subject of Crown disclosure and require an application to the Court.

The disclosure you receive or the information provided by your client or from other sources may lead you to request additional disclosure. See

Chapter, "Crown Disclosure" for a more detailed discussion on the topic of disclosure. It is of course important to carefully go through the Crown disclosure with the client.

THE CLIENT

Preparation obviously starts with the client. Detailed interviews will not only provide his version of the events but will also provide counsel with information with which to seek out other evidence. Where the client is capable of doing so, it is often helpful to have him or her write out what he or she recollects about the events and, where appropriate, make diagrams. It is part of the human experience for many people, I feel, that if left in a quiet room with time to think, the client will be able to recall more than if they are in a strange office answering questions. The most relevant questions can be asked by counsel after reviewing the client's written version and Crown disclosure. See also Chapter, "Client and Witness Interviews."

WITNESSES

Interviewing Crown witnesses is, of course, permissible as there is no property in a witness even when under subpoena by the Crown.[1] However, it would be potentially dangerous and probably futile to attempt to interview a witness who is emotionally involved, such as the victim of a sexual assault. Such a witness would be understandably hostile which might lead to accusations against the interviewer. It is best to have the witness interviewed by someone other than counsel on the case. A law student or a private investigator of integrity should take the witness's statement or at the very least be present taking notes of the dialogue between counsel and the witness. With such precautions, if the witness denies giving this statement or changes what he has said, or even accuses his interviewer of some impropriety in taking or recording the statement, then counsel will not be put in the embarrassing position of having to take the witness stand to confirm the statement or to refute the allegations of impropriety. Other examples of such allegations include putting words in the witness's mouth or attempting to get the witness to change her story or forget part of it. If such allegations are made and there are no corroborating witnesses for counsel, counsel is faced with having to retire from the case as it would be unseemly to argue his own credibility before the Court. When the witness to be interviewed by the defence is important enough and there is some uncertainty about how she will react to an interview, counsel might consider, if it is affordable,

---

1   *R. v. Cook* (1960), 127 C.C.C. 287 (Alta. C.A.); *R. v. Gibbons*, [1946] O.R. 464 (Ont. C.A.).

having the statement taken under oath by a Justice of the Peace or a commissioner in the form of an affidavit. The fact that a statement is sworn will carry considerable weight[2] and if the witness were to contradict her sworn statement she could be subject to an allegation of committing perjury or giving inconsistent evidence under oath, both of which are offences under the *Criminal Code*. Even if unsworn an application could be made to the Court to declare the witness hostile. See Chapter, "Prior Inconsistent Statements" under the heading "The Common Law Hostile Witness."

Defence counsel should ascertain from the witness whether he has given a statement to the police. Caution should be exercised here because often when this question is asked a witness will deny giving a statement only because he thinks "a statement" means a signed statement and does not associate a statement with an oral interview with or utterance to the police. If the witness has given a previous statement it could be at odds with the statement given to the defence counsel with the obvious result that if counsel were to call that witness at trial, he could be discredited in cross-examination. This problem is mostly negative with the Crown's duty to make timely disclosure.[3] There could be a valid reason, such as fear, for the contradictory statement, but counsel should be aware of such a statement and the surrounding circumstances so as not to be caught by surprise.

The witness should be interviewed as soon as possible after the event and a signed statement taken. This is when the witness's recollection will be best. A statement taken months later could result in the loss of valuable evidence due to a fading memory and is subject to attack on the basis of inaccuracy. This is particularly so if the witness is asked to recollect a rather ordinary event in his or her life and might have difficulty relating it to a specific day. It is especially vital that an alibi witness be interviewed and provide a statement as soon as possible. Such a witness may not be called upon to testify until many months after the event when not only a recollection of a particular day is required but a particular time is important. The witness who has given a statement shortly after the event will not be subject to an attack that their memory may well be at fault by the time the matter comes to trial when he/she is able to testify that their memory was refreshed by reading over the statement he/she gave so shortly after the incident.

The signed statement can, not only, be used by the witness to refresh his or her memory later but can also form the basis of an application to cross-examine one's own witness under section 9 of the *Canada Evidence Act*,[4] or can be used to cross-examine the witness if he or she is called by the opposite side.

---

2 The reader is referred to in the Chapter, "Client and Witness Interviews," heading "The Witness's Statement."

3 *R. v. Stinchcombe*, [1991] 3 S.C.R. 326.

4 R.S.C. 1985. c. C-5.

If the witness refuses to be interviewed then this fact may be used in cross-examination to show perhaps a bias for the side which calls the witness, particularly if the witness gave a statement to that side. Such a situation may also permit counsel to plant the seed in the mind of the trier-of-fact that the witness may have something to hide. This type of questioning is not recommended for the alleged victim in the case as a victim's failure to cooperate with the accused's counsel is understandable.

Even where counsel knows that the witness will not be helpful to her case, counsel should still take a detailed statement from that witness in order to prevent being surprised at trial. If the witness testimony contradicts his statement in any significant way, he can be impeached and even though his testimony at trial was damaging, the conflicting evidence will affect his credibility. It is also a good idea to include in the statement those essential or collateral matters which the witness did not see or hear, so that he cannot change his position later at trial without being impeached. See also Chapter, "Client and Witness Interviews."

PRIVATE INVESTIGATORS

Private investigators can be very useful in such matters as seeking out and interviewing witnesses, finding potential exhibits, viewing scenes and taking measurements and photographs. In retaining investigators it is important to consider how their credibility will be assessed as witnesses because they must often testify about their investigations and will often have to contradict what other witnesses have said.

VISITING THE SCENE

Visiting the scene of the incident in many cases is vitally important as it will give counsel a better understanding of the events which will be of assistance in framing questions for cross-examination. By taking measurements and noting obstructions, for example, counsel will have a better insight into what could or could not have happened. Counsel may even wish to have photographs taken or scale diagrams made of the scene to assist in her cross-examination. By asking questions which indicate to the witness that the cross-examiner has visited the scene, the witness will be convinced that the cross-examiner knows about what she is asking. The witness will not fudge his or her answers regarding any questions about the scene for fear of being contradicted by counsel's first-hand knowledge. At the very least, the Judge and jury will be impressed that counsel's questions stem from first-hand knowledge.

TAKING A VIEW

Counsel may wish to have the trier-of-fact visit the scene to take a view to facilitate a better understanding of the evidence.[5] It is of course important that before counsel requests a view that she has been to the scene previously and is confident that a view will be helpful to the client's defence. Counsel will want to make certain that conditions have remained the same as they were on the day of the alleged offence. If not, counsel for the other party would argue, where relevant, that the weather conditions and/or temperature are different, that the physicality of the scene has changed, the lighting is different, etc. In other words, the scene presently is misleading for the trier-of-fact. Section 652 of the *Criminal Code* provides:

View

652. (1) The judge may, where it appears to be in the interests of justice, at any time after the jury has been sworn and before it gives its verdict, direct the jury to have a view of any place, thing or person, and shall give directions respecting the manner in which, and the persons by whom, the place, thing or person shall be shown to the jury, and may for that purpose adjourn the trial.

Directions to prevent communication

(2) Where a view is ordered under subsection (1), the judge shall give any directions that he considers necessary for the purpose of preventing undue communication by any person with members of the jury, but failure to comply with any directions given under this subsection does not affect the validity of the proceedings.

Who shall attend

(3) Where a view is ordered under subsection (1), the accused and the judge shall attend.

In considering what is "in the interests of justice" the Court in *R. v. Pringle*[6] stated that the view ". . . have the capacity to add something to the evidence that *viva voce* evidence or demonstrative evidence cannot provide and which is essential to the determination of the issues before the Court. In that way, a view adds a value to the evidentiary phase already available to the trier-of-fact that cannot be added in any other way."

While a language of section 652 speaks of a "jury" taking the view, it now appears to be accepted that a Superior or Provincial Court Judge trying an indictable case under Part XIX without a jury can order that the view be taken.[7]

By virtue of the wording of section 652(1) it would appear that the order to take a view which would be made after the jury is sworn could still

---

5 *R. v. W. (F.D.)* (1997), 120 C.C.C. (3d) 68 (B.C. C.A.).
6 2002 CarswellAlta 1137 (Alta. Prov. Ct.).
7 *R. v. Prentice* (1965), 47 C.R. 231 (B.C. C .A.).

be made while the jury is deliberating.[8] The discretion of the trial Judge to make or not to make the order on the basis of whether the interests of justice is served or not, is a discretion which is not likely to be interfered with unless exercised judiciously.[9]

DOCUMENTARY EVIDENCE

In addition to the transcript of the preliminary inquiry, it is important to gather relevant memoranda, letters, notes, reports, documentation and previous statements or testimony of opposing witnesses, as there are fewer more effective moments in a trial for the cross-examiner than when the witness is impeached with what he or she had written or spoken on the subject on some previous occasion. Documentary evidence which is admissible pursuant to the provisions of the *Canada Evidence Act* may also provide ammunition for cross-examination. When there is a related civil domestic matter, such as a custody battle or other civil suit, such as a claim for damages, Court documents may provide helpful information. Other documents such as counselling or psychiatric records will require third party applications because of rights to privacy issues.

PHYSICAL EVIDENCE

Defence counsel should always take the time to study the physical materials seized by the police, whether or not the Crown intends to introduce those materials at trial.

Physical evidence takes many forms, of course, and much of this evidence appears to speak for itself, such as a crowbar used as an offensive weapon. But there are pieces of physical evidence which bear close inspection and this need for inspection particularly arises when various items are seized from an accused or at his residence.

The Crown may advise the defence about what has been seized and even introduce the seized items into evidence at the preliminary hearing without identifying the real significance of that evidence, thereby complying with disclosure rules but at the same time perhaps hoping to catch the accused unawares at trial. An example of such physical evidence might be the accused's diary which contains an appointment or a name which appears incriminating.

There are also items which are purposely not introduced at the preliminary inquiry either because they could be helpful to the defence or because

8 *R. v. W. (F.D.), supra.* See *R. v. Arroyo*, 1999 CarswellOnt 4596 (Ont. S.C.J.).
9 *R. v. Paradis* (1976), 38 C.C.C. (2d) 455 (Que. C.A.), leave to appeal refused [1977] 1 S.C.R. xi; *R. v. Grant* (1950), 98 C.C.C. 401 (Sask. C.A.).

their significance is not grasped by the police or Crown, or even by the client who, in the circumstances, fails to advise his counsel about them. Several years ago the police had arrested four accused on a train in northern Ontario for the murder in Toronto of Emanuel Jacques in the celebrated "Shoe-shine Boy" case. It was not the Crown's intention to introduce into the evidence the contents of the suitcase of one of the accused. Defence counsel at first knew nothing of the contents. Neither the police nor the Crown advised him of the contents, perhaps because they did not realize there was any value in them. The Crown, at the defence's request, arranged for an inspection of the accused Werner Gruener's suitcase at the police property department. Gruener's suitcase disclosed a wealth of material which confirmed his unusual thinking processes and supported the psychiatric testimony called on his behalf. This evidence was instrumental in leading to the accused's acquittal.

THE PRELIMINARY INQUIRY

A properly conducted preliminary inquiry is the best preparation tool for defence counsel. (See the later chapter devoted to the Preliminary Inquiry.) Therefore, in preparing the cross-examination at trial, counsel should read the evidence of the witnesses at the preliminary inquiry in detail. This will enable counsel to know what the witness will probably say and will also help in preparing additional questions that counsel did not think of at the preliminary inquiry. No doubt counsel will also learn that there are some questions which should not be asked. Additional leads to evidence may come to mind for the first time after careful reading of the transcript of the preliminary inquiry. Just as at trial, counsel will look for such things in the transcript as internal conflicts in the witness's testimony, statements which are illogical, answers which conflict with answers of other witnesses or with materials of which counsel is aware, and even statements which are helpful to the defence.

A good method of preparation is to break down the cross-examination into headings and to jot down in short-form the questions to be put to the witnesses under those headings. Draw about a one-and-a-half inch margin down the right hand side of the page and put there the page number and line of the preliminary inquiry transcript which refers to the same question and answer that will be asked at trial. If the witness contradicts himself or herself counsel can quickly refer to the contradictory answer in the preliminary inquiry transcript and impeach the witness or at least refresh the witness's memory if he or she has forgotten or watered down a favourable answer. Within that margin counsel can also write, beside the appropriate question, references to any other documents or other witnesses' testimony which bear on the question and which counsel may wish to put to the witness.

ANTICIPATING THE WITNESS

In preparing questions for cross-examination, counsel should consider all the possible answers the witness might give to a damaging question so that counsel can close all the escape routes the witness might take. The witness must be committed to a position from which he or she is unable to escape.[10] Also, by anticipating certain answers by the witness counsel may have at the ready follow-up questions that will negate any effective response by the witness.

FLOW CHARTS

There are cases, such as fraud, which can entail lengthy and complicated facts, many dates, times, figures, and documents. In this kind of case, it is highly recommended that counsel prepare a chronological analysis which sets out the relevant dates and times with a short reference to the facts beside each date. A flow chart with this overview of the history of events means the evidence can be considered in a clearer and more insightful way and, as a result, counsel may be able to spot something out of place or which does not make sense in the testimony either within the evidence of a particular witness or as it relates to other evidence in the case. This kind of analysis may provide counsel with other ideas which, without the chart, would not have come to mind. You may wish to use such a chart as a visual aid when addressing the jury to enable the jurors to better understand the salient points you wish to underscore.

THE LAW

At some point before the trial, not necessarily at the beginning when you do not have all the facts, you should be fully aware of all the legal issues with which you will be confronted. This may require significant research of the law in preparation for argument before the Court. As your experience grows, research will still be important but you will not require it as often.

Having a good grasp of the law that relates to the changes that the client is facing will not only help you to identify the issues in your case but will also assist you in formulating needed questions, whether they be to your own witness or in cross-examination. To cross-examine a witness at the preliminary inquiry on a charge of sexual assault in order to show that

---

10 This approach is discussed in further detail in the Chapter, "General Techniques of Cross-Examination." An example of this can he seen in the cross-examination of a police officer on his notebook in the Chapter, "Cross-Examination of Police Officers."

the accused was drunk and therefore did not have the necessary intent to commit the offence would be a waste of time as far as a "not guilty" plea is concerned since sexual assault is not a "specific intent" but a "general intent" offence.[11] Unfamiliarity with the case law surrounding identification evidence may result in the failure to ask important questions about proper line-up procedure. These are only two examples which point out that it is necessary for counsel to have a sound knowledge of the law as it relates to the client's case before any of the evidence is heard.

If the client is aware of the legal issues and what his counsel's objectives are she may think of helpful facts which will assist counsel in his cross-examination and overall preparation as well as being better prepared in responding to the cross-examination.

DURING THE TRIAL

Counsel will of course continue to prepare for cross-examination during the opponent's examination-in-chief of the witness. Most authors on this subject indicate that copious notes of the direct examination should not be made by the cross-examiner but instead the witness should be studied carefully for body language. Some of the following are usually noted: tell-tale facial expressions, body or hand movements and changes in voice tone, an over or under emphasis at a certain point, an obvious omission, long pauses or speaking too quickly or with less confidence in a particular area, breathing too deeply, lack of directness in answering or any other conduct which may be a signal of the witness's lack of veracity or candour.

I do not completely agree with the view that notetaking is not as important as watching the witness, particularly when counsel is involved in a lengthy trial. With careful notetaking of the important parts of the testimony, counsel in attempting to impeach the witness on cross-examination, can put to the witness her exact words in-chief; counsel's jury address will be constructed from his notes; and counsel may be called upon later in the trial to look back at his notes for the purpose of arguing questions of law or refreshing his memory, including disputes with the trial judge or his opponent over what a witness said in his earlier testimony. There are few counsel who have total recall or the luxury of an assistant (such as a junior lawyer or law student) present throughout the trial to take down complete notes of what was said by the witness in every case and so the cross-examiner must do it.

---

11   *R. v. Chase* (1984), 13 C.C.C. (3d) 187 (N.B. C.A.), reversed [1987] 2 S.C.R. 293.

Knowing The Law

"'Ignorance of the law is no excuse.' Golly! *I* never
heard *that* one! Did *you* ever hear *that* one?"

The New Yorker Book of Lawyer Cartoons. New Yorker Magazine Eds. (Illus.) Alfred
A. Knopf Inc., 1997. © 1993 by The New Yorker Magazine, Inc.

    The witness should be watched but counsel will always find time to
do that witness but certainly does not have to stare constantly at a witness
to detect changes in speech pattern or tone. Any experienced counsel knows
that a witness's mannerisms can be misleading. A good liar may present
himself or herself very well to the jury where an honest witness, because of

nervousness or his or her own peculiarities, may appear as a dishonest witness. In any event, if the witness has testified at the preliminary inquiry, counsel at trial should have a good reading of that witness and it would be extremely rare that this witness would surprise counsel by his or her mannerisms or testimony at trial.

It would be helpful for counsel to draw a margin about one-and-a-half inches wide down the right side of the pages being used to record the examination-in-chief. Within that margin he can jot down reminders of questions that arise from the testimony he has noted which are in addition to the questions he has already prepared. Within that margin counsel can also make a mark beside a piece of evidence which will bear on his or her jury address.

Most counsel have devised their own short-form system for keeping up with the witness but if counsel falls behind he should not hesitate to ask for the answer to be repeated by the witness or the Court reporter.

The judge is worth watching during the examination of witnesses, particularly when the accused has elected trial by judge alone. Counsel should observe when the trial judge is not making notes as this will be an obvious indication about the evidence the judge feels to be insignificant. Counsel will then have to decide whether to concentrate on other areas of the evidence or to try harder to convince the trial judge of the significance of the evidence he or she has not been noting. If the trial judge is making notes, so should counsel.

Counsel should also watch the jury. It is often too difficult to read what the jurors are thinking but some jurors' faces and body language do reflect interest or lack thereof and whether a juror is for the examiner or against the witness. After such signals counsel may wish to change her approach or make a note of when a juror shook his head in disbelief so that counsel will remember to refer to it in her jury address.

Counsel should listen carefully to the answers she receives instead of concentrating on getting to her next planned question. Not listening carefully to the answers is usually more of a problem for inexperienced counsel who may suffer from nervousness. As a result, the cross-examiner is concentrating on her questions and her own performance, thereby creating an inner turmoil which distracts her attention from the answers to her questions. Counsel must not miss the helpful answer she was not expecting, as that answer could be very significant to the case. If such an answer is given, the cross-examiner may then have to abandon part or all of her prepared cross-examination and embark on a new line of inquiry. She will have to ask questions she may not have anticipated. Careful preparation should never inhibit mental flexibility as the examiner's ability to be opportunistic could make the difference between acquittal and conviction.

When the witness testifies to something which counsel was not expecting, thereby disturbing part of her carefully planned cross-examination, or when the examination-in-chief may have been a lengthy one, giving rise to additional questions which counsel may not have thought of prior to the trial, she may wish to have some time to marshal her thoughts and notes before continuing on her cross-examination. In those circumstances, counsel should not hesitate to ask the judge for a short recess for that purpose. Such requests should, of course, be kept to a minimum.

ORDER OF CROSS-EXAMINATION WHEN MORE THAN ONE DEFENCE COUNSEL

When there are co-counsel, the order of cross-examination may be important. In Ontario the practice is that the cross-examination proceeds according to the order of the accuseds' names on the information or indictment, unless there is an agreement among the counsel otherwise and the trial Judge agrees. There are a number of considerations in deciding in what order counsel wishes to cross-examine if he or she was to have a choice, some of which are mentioned below.

The order of cross-examination normally dictates the order of the jury addresses. If you cross-examine last, you address the jury last which may be important because you would want to know what your co-counsel may say to the jury with respect to your client and be in a better position to respond, if necessary. And if there are many counsel whose addresses would spread over a number of days, then being the last one to address the jury could be advantageous to the extent that your submissions would be fresher in the jurors' minds when they retire to consider their verdict.

Counsel who cross-examine first usually carry the weight of the cross-examination for the defence or at least a significant portion thereof. This is usually because the Crown places the most seriously implicated accused at the beginning of the indictment and that accused is normally involved in most of the evidence. Counsel may well wish to be first in such circumstances to establish his client's position and set the tone. This lead could be helpful to less experienced counsel who cross-examine subsequently. It may be that counsel wants to cross-examine later in the order because it is tactically better for the client to take a low profile given the circumstances or because counsel will be in a better position to protect the client's interests from an attack by co-counsel who cross-examines before.

Where there are a number of defence counsel the witness may not know which accused you represent. If you have reason to believe that the witness would be more sympathetic to your client than your co-accused, introduce yourself to the witness by identifying your client. This may result in less damaging answers, depending on the circumstances of the offence.

8

Manner of Cross-Examination

Developing a courtroom style does not come easily and it will no doubt take many trials over perhaps many years before counsel accomplishes the manner with which he or she is most pleased and most comfortable. Like an athlete, the advocate should try to stay within himself or herself. Many young counsel who come to admire a particular senior counsel may try to emulate that style but because their personalities and attributes are different, the young lawyer does not appear to be natural and no counsel wishes to taint his client's case by appearing to be less than real. In the last analysis it is best to remember that style is one thing and substance is another. The judge charges the jury only on the latter and the Court of Appeal is persuaded by what is or is not on the printed page.

THE DON'TS

There are certain approaches to cross-examination which should be avoided. Do not frustrate the Court with lengthy and pointless cross-examinations. If you cross-examine on irrelevant matters, the judge will stop you, your momentum is weakened and, if done often enough, the judge and the jury may conclude you have no case. Less experienced counsel may feel they have to ask something that relates to every point that was made in-chief; at times they may even be uncertain as to which points are worth responding to. Choose the important ones to respond to and that is where your understanding of the objectives of cross-examination, discussed earlier in this book are helpful.

Do not prejudice the jury against the client by showing a quick temper, a grating personality or by using seemingly unfair tactics. Do not adopt mannerisms such as walking back and forth and sideways or with hands always waving, which will distract the jurors from the point that is being made. Do not ridicule or be sarcastic with a witness or treat almost every witness as if he or she is a scoundrel or perjurer, unless, of course, sufficient facts are established in a particular case to show that the witness is being dishonest. Do not gain the reputation as a lawyer who misrepresents the facts, uses false insinuation or sly innuendo with the witness. Avoid these types of cross-examinations because, although they may upset or frustrate certain witnesses and even confuse them, the only real result is that jurors will feel sympathetic toward the put-upon witness and antagonistic toward the examiner.

The Over-Zealous Defence Counsel

"We find the defendant innocent but his attorney despicable."

© National Law Journal

Do not fall into the trap of arguing with the witness. It is usually a sign that the cross-examiner is receiving damaging answers and it makes the lawyer look unprofessional. Counsel should not become angry except when, as a tactic, righteous indignation would be appropriate. When a witness tried to insult Lord Carson, the latter replied with a smile and said: "It's not a bit of use being impertinent to me. I am too old a hand to be put off by that—you'll have to answer my questions I'm afraid."

Do not harp on minor inconsistencies, for a judge or jury will understand that honest people can make such errors. The jurors may well feel that minor discrepancies mean very little and if that is the best that can be done with the witness by the cross-examiner then the witness's credibility stands undamaged and even fortified.

Do not distort the facts in your questions. You will be corrected by the trial judge or opposing counsel which will interrupt the flow of your questions and may affect your credibility if done too often. It is fair for counsel to attack the witness's character in order to impeach credibility but it is quite improper to make such an attack without any purpose other than to humiliate the witness. It may occur that a client who is angry or revengeful will give his counsel information for cross-examination which will do nothing to advance the client's case and will only serve to shame or disgrace the witness. Any counsel who surrenders to the importuning of a client who wishes to degrade the witness, without any hope of impeaching the witness's credibility, lacks the judgment to be a successful courtroom advocate. In such a case the cross-examiner will create sympathy for the witness and discredit himself or herself in the eyes of the jury. For example, if a witness has a criminal record do not confront him or her with it if it is very remote, is too minor or is not relevant. A conviction for dishonesty, if not too remote, obviously bears on credibility. A Crown witness conviction for assault would not assist the defence if the charge were fraud but would obviously affect the jury if the accused were charged with assault on the witness and his or her defence was self-defence (notwithstanding that a prior record goes only to the credibility of the witness.)

WHEN TO ATTACK

The perjured witness is far from the common witness. The witness who is honestly mistaken or inadvertently stretches the truth is more usual. At some point the cross-examiner's manner with the perjured witness may be different from the norm as the cross-examiner will want to indicate to the jury exactly what he or she thinks of this person who has falsely accused his or her client. These witnesses expect to be attacked. If it is not in your nature to vent at a deserving witness, be mindful of what the Hollywood mogul, Sam Goldwyn is credited with when he said decades ago: "The most important thing about acting is honesty, and once you've learned to fake that, you're in."

Another approach to the lying witness is not to be aggressive in manner but to lull that witness into a false sense of security employing one or more of the techniques discussed later with the ultimate goal to show the witness as a liar before he or she realizes what is happening. But the witness who is trying to be honest may well resent any attack and so if the cross-examiner's manner alerts the witness at the outset of his/her true purpose, that witness will set himself or herself to defy the questioner from the beginning. However, if such a witness is approached in a pleasant manner he/she may be disarmed and induced into a fair and friendly discussion which may disclose the weaknesses of his/her testimony. Sir Frederick Wrottesley[1] gives the following advice from a quote of Mr. Cox:

> There are two styles of cross-examination, which we may term the savage style and the smiling style. The aim of the savage style is to terrify the witness into telling the truth; the aim of the smiling style is to win him to a confession. The former is by far the most frequently in use, especially by young advocates, who probably imagine that a frown and a fierce voice are proofs of power. Great is their mistake. The passions arouse passions. Anger, real or assumed, kindles anger. An attack stimulates to defiance. By showing suspicion of a witness, you insult his self love—you make him your enemy at once—you arm his resolution to resist you—to defy you—to tell you no more than he is obliged to tell—to defeat you if he can.
>
> Undoubtedly there are cases where such a tone is called for, where it is polite as well as just; but they are rare, so rare that they should be deemed entirely exceptional. In every part of an advocate's career, good temper and self-love are essential qualifications; but none more so than in the practice of cross-examination.
>
> It is marvellous how much may be accomplished with the most difficult witness, simply by good humour and a smile, a tone of friendliness will often succeed in obtaining a reply which has been obstinately denied to a surly aspect, and a threatening reproachful voice. As a general rule, subject to such very rare exceptions scarcely to enter into your calculations, you should begin your cross-examination with an encouraging look, and manner, and phrase. Remember that the witness knows you to be on the other side; he is prepared to deal with you as an enemy; he anticipates a badgering, he thinks that you are going to trip him up, if you can; he has, more or less, girded himself for the strife. It is amusing to mark the instant change and demeanour in most witnesses when their own counsel has resumed his seat, and the advocate on the other side rises to cross-examine. The position, the countenance, plainly show what is passing in the mind. Either there is fear, or, more often, defiance. If you look fierce and look sternly, it is just what had been expected, and you are met by corresponding acts of defence. But if, instead of this, you use a pleasant smile, speak

---

1   F.J. Wrottesley, *The Examination of Witnesses in Court,* 3rd ed. (London: Sweet & Maxwell, 1961), pp. 94-95.

in a kindly tone, use the language of a friendly questioner, appear to give him credit for a desire to tell the whole truth, you surprise, you disarm him; it is not what he had anticipated, and he answers frankly to your questioning.

Wrottesley goes on to describe how different types of witnesses should be treated. He states: "Be mild with the mild—shrewd with the crafty—confiding with the honest—merciful to the young, the frail or the fearful—rough to the ruffian and a thunderbolt to the liar. But in all this, never be unmindful of your own dignity."[2] Any trier-of-fact would no doubt be impressed with counsel who conducted himself or herself in such a fashion.

COUNSEL'S PERSONALITY

It is basic to trial strategy that counsel should create an atmosphere in favour of his or her client. Such an atmosphere could, even subconsciously, influence a juror in favour of the accused. Counsel is both actor and director and should create a friendly atmosphere for his/her client by displaying a pleasant personality and an appropriate sense of humour, by showing courtesy to the participants and by being forthright with the Court, without being subservient.

The following has been said about counsel's demeanour:[3]

The lawyer must be poised in his attitude, confident in his approach to the problem, and ready both physically and mentally to go to trial. He must be confident without being overconfident.

. . .

The winning trial lawyer is not a facade. He is a sincere man . . . . and his battle is partly won when the jury realises that he is sincere and not posturing.

. . .

A lawyer should walk with shoulders back, chin up, radiating confidence but not cockiness, with a smile of genuine liking for his fellow human beings upon his lips. Courtesy should so permeate his mannerisms that it is distinctive, not a cloak donned for the occasion. This will reflect itself in the way in which he greets the jurors, the court, the court attendants, and his opponents.

A nervous counsel does not reflect confidence and nervousness may reflect poor preparation. Even when well prepared, David G. Humphrey[4] had this advice to disguise nervousness: "Speak slowly, and I mean very,

---

2 *Ibid.*, p. 92.

3 M.C. Roberts, *Trial Psychology* (Toronto: Butterworth Legal Publications, 1987), p. 104.

4 Later Mr. Justice Humphrey, Ont. Gen. Div. in the Advocates' Society Journal, Hilary Term, 1992.

very slowly. This has two advantages. Firstly people who speak slowly attract more attention than fast talkers. Secondly, slow speech will permit you to breathe properly."

MAINTAINING JURORS' INTEREST

"My little friend Bloopy, here, will translate into layman's terms some rather dry, legalistic material."

Trial Diplomacy Journal's Cartoon Album. David M. Freedman, Ed. @ 1980 Court Practice Journal Inc.

It is, of course, important that jurors do not become bored with the cross-examination, especially if it is a lengthy one. If the jurors are bored their minds will wander and they may lose the significance of the answers that help the client. In the normal course of a cross-examination counsel can only hope to make a few good points at the most from the witness and more often not even that. Less significant points will be forgotten by the time the jury comes to consider its verdict. Sometimes a tendency to cover too many points occurs in a vain attempt to satisfy clients. The cross-examiner should not let the jurors miss the good points because he/she has lost their attention due to a morass of less than meaningful questions or because they have been unable to retain so much information. A cross-examination which was a model of brevity was made by the colourful western Canadian lawyer Paddy Nolan decades ago. The complainant was a dairy maid who testified that when she was returning from the barn with a pail of milk the accused sexually assaulted her. The cross-examination went like this:

> How much milk were you carrying?
> A gallon.
> And what was the size of your pail?
> It was a gallon pail.
> Did it have a lid or cover of any sort?
> No, it had no cover.
> Your milk must have pretty well filled the pail?
> It was filled to the brim.
> And when you arrived home after meeting the accused, how full was your pail then?
> It was still filled to the brim.
> I have no further questions.

Nolan's address to the jury was equally short. "Gentlemen, this young woman says that she lost her virtue, but saved her milk. What do you think about it"?

"Not guilty" was what they thought.[5]

Another model example of brevity with effective punchy questions can be seen in the cross-examination of Dr. Crippen who was convicted of murdering his wife. He had panicked at the police investigation and fled with his mistress to Europe en route to Canada:

> By Mr. Muir—You thought you were in danger of arrest:—Yes.
> And so you fled the country:—Yes.
> Under a false name:—Yes.
> Shaved off your moustache:—Yes.
> Left off wearing your glasses in public:—Yes.
> Took Le Neve with you:—Yes.
> Under a false name:—Yes.
> Posing as your son:—Yes.
> Went to Antwerp:—Yes.
> Stayed in a hotel there:—Yes.
> Sayed indoors all day:—Oh, no.
> Practically all day:—We did not; we went to the Zoological Gardens and walked all over the place.
> Enjoying yourselves:—Certainly.[6]

The jurors should be kept interested in the cross-questions by appropriate voice inflections, facial expressions and hand movements which will

---

5 P.V. MacDonald, *Court Jesters: Canada's Lawyers and Judges Take the Stand to Relate Their Funniest Stories* (Toronto: Methuen, 1985), p. 130.

6 Excerpt from Notable British Trial Series.

command attention. As stated in the Chapter, "Presenting the Evidence-In-Chief," the questions should be brief and simply put to ensure that everyone understands them. Lengthy or complicated questions can leave the witness with more than one way to answer the question or give him or her the opportunity to ask the questioner to repeat or rephrase the question in order to gain time to search for an appropriate answer. If the witness makes a habit of asking that simple questions be repeated, the reason for doing so will become apparent to the Judge and jury. If, however, the questions are lengthy or counsel uses big words and fancy phrases the jury will sympathize with the witness's difficulty.

The cross-examiner's voice should project so that it is heard not only by the witness but also by the judge and jury. Although there are times when counsel must move close to the witness-box, such as when producing an exhibit, the usual position for counsel should be near the end of the jury-box so that the witness's voice will be forced to reach him or her through the hearing zone of the jury-box.

Always keep in mind a basic truism of courtroom advocacy – while you may have a facility with the English language, your voice is resonant and you have great presence, at the end of the day when the time comes to judge the case, it is not the questions, it is the answers that count.

THE DAMAGING ANSWER

On occasion even the best of cross-examiners will receive a damaging answer which he/she instinctively knows cannot be changed by ensuing questions. When this occurs counsel should display no outward sign that this has happened but should move quickly to the next question and hope that the jurors will be affected by counsel's demeanour more than by the answer.

9

Observation and Recollection

Observation and recollection of events are very often significant aspects of any criminal trial. There is probably nothing more important for a trial lawyer than to appreciate human fallibility when it comes to these realities and how to approach a witness in these circumstances.

The primary function of most witnesses is to give their recollection of events. The classroom experiment wherein a group of actors burst into the room unannounced before the unprepared students and play out a scene is a scenario many of us have heard about in different forms. The students are required to answer a number of questions about what occurred including questions regarding descriptions of the individuals, the number of people involved, their clothing, any weapons involved and what was said. We have come to learn that in these tests the different answers given are almost as numerous as those giving the answers.

Why do different people honestly perceive the same event differently? The simple answer is that human beings are not computers, movie cameras or tape-recorders. They are subject to conscious and subconscious influences which will have impact on their recording and recall. Experts tell us that our powers of observation and our recollections are affected by such things as past events in our lives, and by prejudices, habits and our imaginations. Recollection can also be affected by such matters as suggestion, state of mind or health or the effects of alcohol or drugs at the crucial moment. If the event happened quickly and unexpectedly or if the witness was frightened or surprised at the crucial moment then the witness's ability to record the event accurately in his or her mind will be even more negatively affected. Other factors affecting testimonial trustworthiness can be the age or the intelligence of the witness; whether or not the witness had impaired eyesight or hearing; whether the witness was thinking of something else, such as business or family worries, at the time of the event; whether the witness was interested in what was happening, whether there were any distracting sounds such as a loud radio; and how good was the opportunity to observe, taking into consideration such matters as distance, lighting, atmospheric conditions and obstructions. The aforementioned are all areas that can be ripe for cross-examination.

Sounds can play tricks on the mind. Regular sounds are often *assumed* to be heard rather than actually being heard. But familiar sounds which do occur may not be noticed, such as by those people who live near railway tracks and fail to hear the train whistle; yet a new sound will capture their attention.

In *The Technique of Advocacy*[1] John Munkman discusses how some of the aforementioned factors affect observation:

> Opportunity to observe is not in itself enough. There is a familiar experiment in which a picture is shown to several people, and after they have looked at it for a few moments they are asked to write down the details. Most people are unable to write down very much. Exceptionally, a trained observer, such as a police officer, may notice every detail of a scene. As a rule, the ordinary man does not notice much unless his attention is attracted and his interest aroused. *Interest and attention* are pre-conditions of accurate observation. Every day, numerous things are said and done in our presence which we hardly notice. It follows that evidence given by a witness about matters in which he took no interest at the time is likely to be vague: positive statements by such a witness are likely to be unreliable, as they may have been built up after the event by inference and imagination. Thus in the ordinary road accident case, a bystander is unlikely to see much until his attention is attracted by a loud crash. Likewise, where a third party reports a casual conversation which he heard some months before, and which has become important only because a dispute has afterwards arisen, it is improbable that he noticed or remembered the exact words which were used.
>
> There are other limitations to accuracy: if events happen quickly, or there is a great deal of talk going on within a short space of time, an impartial witness will see or hear only a fraction of what is happening. Surprise, excitement and rush make the picture confused and its details obscure. If the witness has a personal interest or bias, his attention will tend to be concentrated on facts or remarks which are favourable to him, to the exclusion of others. Prof. Swift says ([Prof. E.J. Swift, *Psychology and the Days Work*] p. 307):
>
>> 'Attention is rigorously selective, and this selection is based on the relative importance of the details; but it should be remembered that the choice of what is important is a personal matter.'
>
> He is referring, of course, not to a deliberate choice, but to one which takes place subconsciously. It is well to realize that bias can intervene, without any dishonest intent, even at the stage of observation, before memory and imagination have got to work.
>
> Pausing here, it is evident that there is great scope for the technique of *probing* in testing the accuracy of observation. One familiar device, where a

---

1   J.H. Munkman, *The Technique of Advocacy* (London: Stevens and Sons Ltd., 1951), pp. 19-21.

witness claims to have seen certain details, is to lead him to say something more, which can be disproved. In one case a police witness gave evidence identifying a man, and Sir Henry Curtis-Bennett, K.C., led him on to deny that the man had a limp: the limp, however, was proved to be real. A similar device can be used where a witness swears that certain words were never used: he is led on to say he never heard certain other words, and it is proved that those other words were in fact spoken.

A further factor which may interfere with accuracy is the presence of intense pain or shock, or strong emotion: all of these things may prevent the senses from operating in a natural way, and may produce pictures or sounds which are distorted, or totally imaginary. Hallucinations, which are an extreme example, may originate from drugs, or drink, or from illnesses affecting the brain. A person who is seriously ill may easily hear imaginary voices, and be quite convinced that they are real. The reason is that, in abnormal physical states, there is less interest in exterior happenings and the imagination takes the place of the exterior senses. Strong emotion may have the same effect as shock or pain, though the effect is not so obvious. Any condition which concentrates attention on one's own interior feelings—mental or physical—is open to suspicion, because it draws attention away from the outside world and gives scope to the imagination.

There are times when pride will affect the witness's testimony. Some witnesses will resent any attack on their recollection and as a result they will stand firm on what they said in examination-in-chief when it would appear they should be retreating from their original testimony. There is the witness, who out of a sense of pride, will use his or her imagination and try to fill in the gaps or rationalize because he or she is not prepared to admit an inability to remember all that is being asked about. With the effluxion of time a witness may confabulate by filling in those gaps testifying about what he thinks he should have said or done rather than what was actually said or done. The witness may use the most logical explanation that later comes to mind, or be influenced by the suggestions of others. The more this reconstruction is repeated, the firmer it takes root in the witness's recall. Again, these are areas to be explored in cross-examination. In these circumstances the cross-examiner should at first approach the witness in a pleasant way to appeal to his sense of fairness in an attempt to achieve a change or modification from his/her testimony in-chief.

A line of questioning will open up for the cross-examiner if the witness did not give a statement shortly after the event, a statement from which the witness could refresh his or her memory before testifying. If the witness is asked to give a statement or recollect the event for the first time, perhaps weeks or months after the event, the questioner might ask the witness in the name of fairness whether or not he could agree that he may not be reporting accurately or completely what he is trying to remember so long after the event. Counsel may wish to inquire in a subtle way whether there was any reason for the witness to recall the event in question so that the details would be impressed on his/her memory. Was the witness interested and attentive at the time of the event so that the incident would be more readily imprinted in his/her mind? An unusual event will be more readily remembered than commonplace, trivial or unimpressive events. And, of course, if the witness is prepared to admit that the matter was relatively insignificant or routine to him at the time and that there was no particular reason to remember it, doubt may be cast on the accuracy of his/her observations. Here is an example:

> Q. When this took place, almost three years ago, you did not think you would need to recall it so long afterwards?
> A. I guess that's right.
> Q. You did not know 36 months ago that you were going to be a witness in this case?
> A. No.
> Q. When did you first learn that you would be a witness in this case?
> A. About a month ago.
> Q. Is that when you were first asked to recall what happened?
> A. Yes.

The above questions obviously show there is no reason for the details of a conversation to be impressed on the memory of the witness. The questions below show that there would be no reason to remember accurately the details of a conversation because it took place during a similar routine that had gone on for a lengthy period of time and there was nothing to make it memorable. Assume a bank teller had testified in-chief as to what the accused had told her when depositing the money:

> Q. How long have you worked at the bank?
> A. For one year.
> Q. And how many customers would you say that you deal with on an average day?
> A. About 100.
> Q. So that in one week you would deal with approximately 500 customers.
> A. Yes.
> Q. And many of them would have short conversations with you?
> A. Yes.
> Q. And if you worked 50 weeks during the year you would have dealt with about 25,000 customers, according to my calculations?
> A. I guess that's right.
> Q. And you would have routine conversations with many of those customers?
> A. Yes.
> Q. And the conversation you told us about would be classified as a routine conversation?
> A. Yes.
> Q. You did not write it down?
> A. No, I did not.

In an English case which captured wide interest at the time and eventually became the basis of a London play and subsequently a movie, The Winslow Boy, a 13-year-old cadet at the Royal Naval College by the name of George Archer-Shee in 1908 was charged with the theft of a five shilling postal order which was subsequently cashed at the local post office. The postal order had in fact been purchased by another cadet, "B," who had put it in his locker at school. He returned to his locker later in the day to find it missing. Two cadets only had been given leave to go to the post office on the afternoon in question, Archer-Shee and "A." The postmistress saw that "A" bought a postal order and shortly after another cadet asked her to cash a postal order for five shillings which was endorsed by "B" and immediately afterwards the same cadet asked her for a postal order for fifteen-and-six. It was not disputed that Archer-Shee had gone to the post office that afternoon to obtain a postal order for that amount.

As a result the boy was requested to withdraw from the college. Rufus Isaacs represented the Crown and reduced the case to a simple issue — "was the boy who bought the fifteen-and-six order the same boy who cashed the five-shilling order?" If the jury believed he was then the boy was guilty. The postmistress, who was obviously an honest witness, testified that she was certain that it was the same cadet who cashed the five-shilling order as bought the one for fifteen-and-six. The following is the cross-examination by Edward Carson of the postmistress.[2] His purpose was to show that she may have been mistaken and probably was. Carson does not attempt to show her as a lying witness.

CARSON: Is there anything in your books to show the order in which the postal orders are dealt with, or the time?
WITNESS: No.
CARSON: So that, on the point whether the same person cashed the five-shilling postal order as bought the one for fifteen-and-six, we must rely on your memory?
WITNESS: Yes.
CARSON: Are not all these cadets very much alike?
WITNESS: Yes.
CARSON: All smart, good-looking boys about the same age?
WITNESS: Yes.
CARSON: When did you first know anything was wrong?
WITNESS: The petty officer came up that night and asked me if a cadet had cashed a postal order who had no right to it.
CARSON: It was he who first suggested to you it was a cadet?
WITNESS: Yes.
CARSON: Did he say he had given leave only to two cadets?
WITNESS: Yes.

2   *Carson* by H. Montgomery Hyde, Publisher William Heinemann Ltd., Melbourne, London, Toronto.

CARSON: Was he in a very excited condition?

WITNESS: I thought so, but I have never seen him before. I have said that he was almost raving.

CARSON: Did you say a word that evening about it being the same boy who bought the fifteen-and-six order who had cashed the five-shilling order?

WITNESS: I did not say it to the petty officer.

CARSON: Did you ever say it was a cadet who cashed the order before you saw Commander Colton the next day?

WITNESS: If I said 'I did not' to Mr. Elliot, K.C., it must be correct.

CARSON: Can you remember anyone else at all having a transaction or conversation with you that day?

WITNESS: No.

CARSON: Do you remember the appearance of anyone?

WITNESS: No.

CARSON: Do you remember if any of the cadets' servants came?

WITNESS: No.

CARSON: Were you ever asked about the cadets' servants by anyone?

WITNESS: No, I do not remember being asked as to anybody else.

CARSON: So you paid no attention to anyone else that day?

WITNESS: No.

CARSON: No one has attempted to test your memory on that point until now?

WITNESS: No.

On the 4th day of the trial Rufus Isaacs told the jury it need not be troubled further and that George Archee-Shee was innocent of the charge.

In the following example police officers Ca. and Co. were charged with obstructing justice for helping officers M. and L. plant drugs on J.B. This supposedly occurred at the police station. The whereabouts of the officers in the police station at particular times became important as a result of evidence given by the Crown witnesses M. and L. Detective Smith testified on behalf of the accused placing them at certain areas at certain times in the police station which was helpful to their defence. Crown Attorney James Stewart attempted to show the unlikelihood of Detective Smith's accurate recollection because his attention was first drawn to what would be a routine event long after its occurrence:

Cross-Examination by Mr. Stewart:

Q. Officer, that particular night was a routine night.

A. It was a routine and busy night, yes.

Q. And you were processing other people?

A. My partners were.

Q. All right, and were you involved in assisting any of them in processing anybody else?

A. I may have done an information here and there, but not a key role in assisting them, no.

Q. Well, do you remember if you were involved?

A. No, I don't.

Q. You don't. Why did you become aware that this night—when did you become aware that this was not just a routine night at the division?

A. When Constables Co. and L. and M. and Ca. were arrested.

Q. And how long afterwards, approximately?

A. After they were arrested?

Q. No, from the night that we're talking about to the night you became aware that it wasn't an average night at the station, how long would that time period be, approximately?

A. Well, from October 14th when it happened to whenever they were arrested. I don't recall when they were arrested.

Q. Can you give even an approximate?

A. Well, the trial date was set for J.B., so I imagine it was six months.

Q. And between the night we're talking about and the night you became aware that it wasn't an ordinary night, I suppose there were a lot of routine nights at the station.

A. Yes.

Q. And the processing of J.B. was a very routine matter.

A. Yes.

Q. He wasn't fighting, you didn't have to restrain him, nobody died at the station, it was a routine night.

A. Yes.

Q. And I would suggest to you that a lot of what we've been talking about in relation to things, it's vague for you.

A. Yes.

Q. Very vague.

A. Yes.

. . .

MR. STEWART: Q. And when questions were being asked about this, or whatever, I suppose you're trying to in some way reconstruct what happened because you have some of the paper work, or whatever, but you're trying, this is my normal practice, I do this, I do that.

A. Yes, and I can pull a visualization out of my head about certain things that happened, but some things I am vague on, yes.

Q. The time, you have no idea in regards to the times.

A. Not without refreshing my memory from a Record of Arrest, or . . .

Q. That type of thing.

A. Yes.

Q. But otherwise the time period, you just, you can't help us.

A. Not without looking at paper work, no.

Q. Well, you don't have times in your book. You don't know the time period at all.

A. No.

Q. Okay, and whether M. and L. ended up over at some time in the Youth Bureau office or not you weren't sitting there saying, "Oh, there goes

Officer L. out. He must be going somewhere." It wasn't that type of thing at all.

A. No, I wasn't doing that at all.

Q. No, and you weren't keeping track of where all your other fellow officers were at every point in time.

A. No, I don't do that.

Q. So, there could have been times when officers were talking together and you wouldn't be aware of it, or if you were aware at the time you wouldn't remember now. Is that fair.

A. It's quite possible, yes.

As seen in some of the examples above and from our own experience, witnesses are often called upon to testify many years after the event as to what they observed, heard, or what they themselves said. It is important to make clear to the trier-of-fact that the first time the witness's memory was tested about that event (orally by police questioning) was significantly after it occurred and try to evoke from that witness an admission that their memory about that occasion may be vague or faulty due to the passage of time. Below is an example of an approach by Douglas Hunt Q.C. in a fraud trial regarding details of an event that occurred many years prior:

Mr. Hunt:

Q. Mr. Smith, would you agree with me that as a general proposition one's memory for details is not going to be as good 10 or 15 years after an event as it would be at the time of the event?

A. I agree.

Q. And it's particularly true if one, for whatever reason, didn't have occasion to or the need to make an accurate record of the details of the event at the time it happened?

A. I agree.

Q. And would you agree it's particularly true of meetings when one has to attend numerous meetings in the ordinary course of business on a day to day, week to week, month to month basis?

A. I agree.

Q. And that in those circumstances, details such as who was present, who said what, what the response was, when there are no notes involved, makes it very difficult to have an accurate memory?

A. I agree.

Q. And on a number of occasions you have quite candidly said I'm not 100 percent sure when you were giving an answer, and I'm going to suggest that when you used that phrase what you really meant was that you didn't have particularly precise recollection of the details of the event that you were being asked to recall?

A. I agree.

Q. And on a number of occasions when Justice Fairgrieve intervened, you quite candidly corrected yourself and you indicated that you didn't really have a clear recollection of the event and you were trying to reconstruct certain events?

A. Yes, that's true.

Q. And you used words from time to time like I would have, or he would have, or they could have, and those were efforts to attempt to reconstruct from whatever memory you might have of an event? Agree?

A. Yes.

Q. And so too, when you used words like I probably would have, or he probably would have, these were attempts to reconstruct from the memory that you did have?

A. You're right.

Q. Okay. And so would it be fair and would you agree that the Court should exercise caution when assessing your evidence where you have qualified it in those ways?

A. Yes.

MR HUNT:

Q. And would you agree with me that there's a risk that after so many years that memory that you actually do have might be faulty with respect to details?

THE WITNESS:

A. To some degree yes, you're right.

An approach such as above could be thwarted if the witness gave a signed statement to the police shortly after the event and refreshed her memory from that statement before testifying. That is why it is important to ascertain from the witness how long after the event their attention was first drawn to it.

A witness may genuinely not remember or may be fearful of being pinned down to a specific time, measurement, weight, temperature, etc. You may be in a position to refresh the witness's memory from transcripts of their prior testimony or from other materials. Also, counsel should not readily accept the witness's answer that he or she is unable to remember but press the witness, as for example, by using the elimination process, as in the following example.

Q. Mr. Brown, you say you do not know what month it was last year that you last saw my client?

A. Yes.

Q. Was is during the winter or warmer days?

A. Warmer days.

Q. Did you have to wear a coat?

A. No.

Q. It was in the summer months?

A. Yes.

Q. Was it closer to spring or fall?

A. I'm not sure – I think the leaves were about to change colour.

If the witness has trouble remembering during cross-examination but had no such memory loss during examination-in-chief the cross-examiner should point this out to the witness and emphasize this selective memory in his final address.

Imagination has a habit of taking over where there is a vagueness in recollection. Munkman writes about this syndrome as follows:[3]

> Vagueness in recollection, whether there was vagueness at the start or not, is the greatest of all sources of error. To quote Prof. Swift again:
>
> > 'The undetected vagueness of memory-details of the witnesses furnishes a fertile soil for the growth of imaginary pictures. The attempt to see faces in the moon is comparable to their experience. With a dim outline, or a sketch with several possibilities, there is always a strong tendency to fill in the outlines, usually with what is in one's mind.'
>
> Attention may now be drawn to several factors which *accentuate* this natural tendency for the imagination to supplement the memory.
>
> The first of these factors is a sudden happening, *just after* the events in question, which rivets the attention of the observer, previously roving at large and in a superficial manner. Such a happening is the crash of a motorcar collision, or a sudden quarrel. On these occasions, the mind of the observer flashes back at once to the preceding events and commences to reconstruct them. Afterwards, the vague impression received at the time will be blended with the reconstruction, and both will be remembered together as a single vivid picture seen at the time.
>
> Apart from such dramatic incidents, as soon as any happenings become a matter of controversy the witnesses are liable to talk them over and think about them. Each time the picture may be filled out a little, or something may be omitted, and when it is again recalled the memory has again been modified.
>
> A third factor, especially in murder cases, may be Press publicity or local rumour, which the witnesses unconsciously absorb and which forms a prejudicial background to their evidence. A somewhat similar result may be produced if one witness reads the statement of another: anything which puts a vivid picture before the witness is liable to influence his imagination.
>
> Finally, there is the effect of suggestive questions—and it is for this reason that an impartial investigator is careful to avoid suggestive questions in the early stages of his inquiries: the technique of insinuation, which is inherently suggestive, is brought to bear only when the evidence has crystallised in a one-sided form, as is the case at the stage of cross-examination. Prof. Swift quotes an impressive illustration of the effect of suggestion, in a murder case which occurred in the American Middle West and was investigated thirty years afterwards. Among other things it was alleged that the body had been taken away in a covered wagon, hidden under a buffalo robe. He says:
>
> > 'The detectives, as they secured one fact after another, collected the information by suggestive questions and statements to those with whom they conversed. When, for example, a prospective witness said that there was a buffalo robe in the wagon the detectives would ask if it covered the

---

3   *The Technique of Advocacy, ibid.*, pp. 30-32.

outlines of a human form. The man would think it likely, and soon that it did... It is a well-known principle of psychology that if you tell a man something often enough he finally accepts it; and as he continually repeats it, even as a possible fact, it ends by becoming firmly fixed. Then he believes he saw or heard it.'

Throughout all this ferment of memory and imagination, the emotions, or bias, or wishful thinking, exercise a pervading influence, both in suppressing real facts and in causing the acceptance of fresh details which are imagined. Prof. Swift sums up the whole subject as follows:

'. . . memory is exceedingly plastic and prone to error; and it is always exposed to the deflecting influences of repeated narration, with it generous mixture of error, continuous thinking about the affair with numerous fictitious insertions, intended actions not carried out, biased opinions, and suggestions.'

A witness testifying about an event should be questioned not only as to the details of the event but also the details shortly before and after the event. If the witness is unable to remember these events with any accuracy then counsel could argue against the accuracy of his recollection about the key event.

Sir Frederick Wrottesley, in *The Examination of Witnesses in Court,* has this to say about memory and perception:[4]

One of the most effective ways to discredit a witness is to enquire closely into the sources of his knowledge. For instance, when a witness has given, in detail, a narrative of a past transaction and you wish to show to the court and the jury that he was mistaken, you should picture the scene in your own mind, place, persons, and accessories. You should then have the witness repeat his narrative, taking care to note his congruity or want of congruity with the accompanying circumstances, then you are apt to detect improbabilities and even impossibilities. You put yourself in the place of the witness, and see as he saw, you notice how he was prejudiced, how he formed too hasty conclusions, etc. We all know how erring the senses are and how unreliable and frail the human memory is.

It is said that Sir Walter Raleigh tore up the manuscript of the second volume of his "History of the World", because he was unable to ascertain the true cause of a fight which took place under his own observation beneath the window of his room in the tower where he was imprisoned, remarking that if he could not obtain an accurate account of such an occurrence, it must be impossible to give a correct narrative of events which occurred in ages long past and in remote corners of the globe.

Where honest witnesses make conflicting statements, and it is necessary to ascertain which has sworn truly, much depends upon the powers of perception and memory of the witnesses, upon their ability to narrate correctly events

---

4 F.J. Wrottesley, *The Examination of Witnesses in Court,* 3rd ed. (London: Sweet & Maxwell, 1961), p. 78.

which they witnessed, for in order to give a true account of what he has seen, a witness must have a correct perception of what he saw, and a memory which is retentive enough to enable him to recall with accuracy all that passed in his presence. The line of demarcation between imaginary and memory, however, is sometimes hard to draw, and it is unquestionably true that witnesses testify to things which they imagine have occurred, but which in fact have had no existence: the memory is deceitful and unreliable, and things which are stored away in it received colour from existing impressions and experiences; the new things are mingled with the old. A writer of ability says upon this matter:

> 'Men have seen a very simple fact; gradually when it is distant, in thinking of it, they interpret it, amplify it, provide it with details, and these imaginary details become incorporated with the details, and seem themselves to be recollections.'

An instance is related by Ram of witnesses in a trial in Scotland, who were unable to separate what they had read in a newspaper from what they had heard from the parties. The experienced cross-examiner, therefore, will not take the statements of honest witnesses for granted, but will investigate thoroughly and endeavour to show that they are mistaken as to what they think they heard or saw, and will, in the mildest and most patient manner, prove, by his examination of a witness who believes that he is telling the truth, that, from the surrounding circumstances and the testimony of the other witnesses as well as from the unreasonableness of his story, his evidence cannot be relied upon.

There will be times when counsel feels quite sure that an honest witness is incorrect in his or her testimony and it is difficult to understand why this witness testified about a certain matter in the way he or she does. This may be the time when, as Frances L. Wellman[5] submits, that unconscious partisanship takes over. Perception and recall can be affected by the witness's desires. Unconscious partisanship occurs when the witness wants to be favourable to the side who calls him or her because the witness feels complimented by the confidence placed in him. It is human nature to prove worthy of that confidence and so there is unconscious dilution or a colouring of the evidence in favour of the side who called the witness. It is also human nature to want to see "your side" win and so the witness may lose any feeling of objectivity when he or she is asked questions the answers to which he or she perceives could hurt the side calling him or her. Accordingly the witness will testify in a way to fit his or her prior conclusions. Although not deliberately telling an untruth, this witness may stretch the truth or withhold the whole truth.

Cross-examining a witness to show there were a number of interviews he or she gave to the police and Crowns and the length of those interviews

---

5 FL. Wellman, *The Art of Cross-Examination,* 4/e, revised and enlarged by Frances L. Wellman. Copyright 1903, 1904, 1923 and 1936 by Macmillan Publishing Company; renewed 1931, 1932, 1951 and 1964 by Ethel Weilman.

may allow you to show that a partisanship developed in favour of the prosecution which built up over a period of time as the parties came to know each other better. As a result the witness became more willing to provide answers the prosecution was seeking. In addition the point can be made that with a number of interviews the witness became trained or scripted.

There is also the witness who becomes a partisan because of negative things told to him or her about the accused by the police officers, the prosecution counsel or other witnesses. The witness may have been told by the police that there is other evidence which points to the accused. As a result the witness will presume the accused is guilty and his/her evidence could be influenced accordingly, recalling matters to fit his/her now coloured perception of the accused, or strengthening any uncertainties the witness may have had. In this regard see recommendations by Commissioner Kaufman from the Morin Inquiry in the Chapter, "Cross-Examination of Police Officers." The cross-examiner should therefore ask the witness about the content of discussions with the police and the Crown and other witnesses, how many such discussions took place, and for how long. However, if the witness responds by detailing uncomplimentary things that the police or others have told him or her about the accused, those answers could greatly prejudice the accused in the eyes of the jury. It would be best to ask such questions at the preliminary hearing stage and the answers given may dictate whether a re-election to trial by judge alone should be considered.

DEMEANOUR EVIDENCE OF THE ACCUSED

Demeanour evidence came under close scrutiny at The Commission Proceedings Involving Guy Paul Morin. The Commissioner's Recommendation 76A(b) stated:

> Purported evidence of the accused's 'demeanour' as circumstantial evidence of guilt can be overused and misused. Crown counsel and the courts should adopt a cautious approach to the tendering and reception of this kind of evidence, which brings with it dangers which may be disproportionate to the probative value, if any, that it has. Crown counsel should be educated as to the merits of this cautionary approach and the dangers in too readily accepting and tendering such evidence. In particular, where such evidence of strange demeanour is brought forward after the accused is publicly identified, Crown counsel, the police and the judiciary should be alive to the danger that this 'soft evidence' may be coloured by the existing allegations against the accused. The most innocent conduct and demeanour may appear suspicious to those predisposed by other events to view it that way.

Mark Sandler, one of the Commissioner's counsel cross-examined the witness Patterson regarding a statement she made to the police about the accused Morin's apparent lack of caring when she had discussed Christine

Jessop's death with him. Note Mr. Sandler's approach which is consistent with the above recommendation:[6]

> Q. Now, I'm going to refresh your memory about another item that you tes-
> tified to in the conversation, and you testified at both the first and second
> trial that in response to a suggestion on your part, he had said something
> like, "Things like that happen, what can you do? She was a sweet, innocent
> little girl." Do you remember that?
>
> A. Yes, I do remember that.
>
> Q. And interestingly, this actually appears to have become the most significant
> item in many ways in your evidence because you describe the way in which
> he said those words. Do you remember what you said about that?
>
> A. Somewhat. I think he was very carefree, like very uncaring I guess you
> would call it, when he did say it. I just—the whole thing that really upset
> me about the conversation was the fact that he just seemed like he didn't
> really care too much about the situation, and I guess that's where I just sort
> of think that compared to the person that I thought he was, it was just very
> unusual.
>
> Q. Okay. Now, you described that part of the conversation that he sounded
> uncaring, and it was opposite to anything that you'd ever discussed with
> him before. Do you remember saying words to that effect?
>
> A. Right.
>
> Q. I take it, just analysing the conversation a little bit, when he indicated to
> you that things like that happen in response to your suggestion that whoever
> had done it had to be a sick person; do you remember that?
>
> A. Yes.
>
> Q. "Things like that happen, what can you do. She was a sweet, innocent girl."
> It was the tone that struck you rather than the contents, as I understand your
> evidence; is that right?
>
> A. Right. Yeah, he just—no expression.
>
> Q. Okay. So that there was nothing in the words that were unusual or inappro-
> priate, it was the manner in which he expressed them that struck you at the
> time; do I have that right?
>
> A. Right.
>
> Q. And I guess I want to ask you this, had you ever seen him grieve the loss
> of a friend or relative?
>
> A. No.
>
> Q. Or seen him celebrate the birth of a family member or a family occasion of
> any sort?
>
> A. No.
>
> Q. Or had you ever seen him angry, that you can recall?
>
> A. Not that I can recall.
>
> Q. Had you ever seen him really, really upset?
>
> A. No.
>
> Q. No. And you hadn't been to his home, you"ve said, and he hadn't been to
> your home; am I right?

---

6 Vol. 67, p. 11, June 25th, 1997.

A. Right.

Q. And I guess what I want to ask you is, with the benefit of some reflection and hindsight, and so on, that really, you"d had very little, if any, exposure to the range or lack of range of emotions that Guy Paul Morin showed in those kinds of situations; am I right?

A. Right. The only emotions that I really had that he had showed to me was just the relationship that we had, basically.

Q. So that how he expresses his losses or how he expresses anger or how he expresses grief or bitterness, you didn't know anything about those aspects of his personality, I take it?

A. No.

Q. Is that fair?

A. Mm-hmm.

Q. And as I understood the answer that you gave to Mr. Scott at the first trial and to Mr. McGuigan at the second trial, what struck you here was that his tone was basically the tone that you would have in every day conversation, there was nothing other than an every day tone that he used when he spoke those words; am I right?

A. Right.

Q. Did you know when you spoke to him in April of 1985 how many times he had or hadn't discussed with neighbours, or friends, the Christine Jessop death between January and April of 1985, or her disappearance between October '84 and April of 1985? Did you have any idea about how many times he has had to or chosen to discuss this matter before he spoke to you about it?

A. No.

Q. Did you make any assumptions about whether he had discussed it a number of times before he discussed it with you?

A. No. I think I had a lawyer ask me in one of the trials that question.

. . .

Q. Okay. Now, I want to jump ahead to April the 22nd of 1985, and we've heard that Guy Paul Morin was arrested on that date and I take it that was knowledge that came to your attention on that date. It permeated the media.

A. Yeah, it wasn't actually that date, it wasn't until the next day that I found out.

Q. Okay. That became known to you on April the 23rd of 1985. And knowing that Guy Paul Morin was now arrested and charged with Chrstine Jessop's murder, what did you do, or what did you think?

A. At the time I was probably in shock, I was very scared, it was the first time in my life anything like this had ever happened to me. I was a new mom at the time and I was home by myself with my daughter, and I called my mom.

Q. Okay. And did you harken back to the conversation that you had had with Guy Paul Morin the previous week?

A. Did I think about it?

Q. Did you think about it?

A. Oh, yeah.

Q. Sure. And had you thought about it as being significant until Guy Paul Morin was arrested?

A. No. Actually, I think when we left band that night after we talked to him, my girlfriend and I, we sort of looked at each other and kind of went, jeez, you know, I wonder if Guy did this to Christine. And you know, I think we just sort of laughed it off and though, you know, like it was just kind of silly. I think we were kind of concerned at the way that the conversation had come about with him, and how he had seemed to us, like, that he was very uncaring, or he had seemed to me, and that was probably about it as far as thinking anything like that. But that was just like more or less hearsay and just a little comment and I never ever dreamed in a million years that he would be arrested for it after the conversation.

Q. Sure. And I guess what I was asking you is, did the conversation acquire some added significance to you when you heard that Guy Paul Morin was arrested?

A. Oh, when I heard he was?

Q. Yes.

A. Oh, okay, I thought you said before he was. Well, a little bit, just because of some of the feelings that I had when I was talking with him just over the fact that he was a little unconcerned compared to what I thought that he might be like. And that's why I was very upset, emotionally upset at this time, and my mom came and picked me up and took me to her home and that's when I actually told my mom about what he, you know, about the conversation that I had had with him. And that's when she said to me that, you know, maybe I should tell the police, maybe it would make me feel better.

Q. All right. Did you infer at that point that Guy Paul Morin was likely guilty because of what he had told you?

A. No.

Q. Did you have any opinions when you heard that he was arrested as to whether he was guilty or not guilty of the offence? And I want you to look back now, look back to that time and not with the benefit of hindsight and what we now know, okay?

A. Yeah.

Q. How did you feel when you heard he was arrested?

A. Shocked.

Q. Did you feel he was guilty?

A. I don't think—I don't think I really thought he was guilty or not guilty. I think I—because I was young at the time and like, if it would have been nowadays when I'm older and it's a lot clearer to me, I think back then, when somebody got arrested like that, I think it was just automatic, you know, police think they have the bad guy and they have the bad guy.

Q. Right. But I guess one of the things that the Commissioner is exploring here, is how to prevent an innocent person from being convicted in the future, so we kind of think about how evidence becomes formulated in people's minds. And do you think, with the benefit of hindsight, that the fact that Guy Paul Morin was arrested and charged with the murder by police officers, affected the significance that you gave to this conversation?

A. At the time—I know at the time that I did give my statement to the police, I wasn't giving my statement to the police because I thought it was evidence. I was giving my statement to the police because my mother thought I should, just for my overall benefit of feeling a bit better. I know I had the conversation with him and if, for some reason, there was something in that conversation that would help the police, then that's why I gave my statement.

Q. So, correct me if I'm wrong, what I'm hearing you say is that you gave the statement so that if there was something in the contents of what he had said, that might be significant, the police would know about it and not because you were of the view that the way in which he'd given his statement was evidence, or you regarded as evidence; do I have that right?

A. Yes.

. . .

Commissioner Kaufmann referred to the following writings and evidence in support of his recommendation regarding demeanour:

In an article entitled "Guilt and the Consciousness of Guilt: The Use of Lies, Flight and other 'Guilty Behaviour' in the Investigation and Prosecution of Crime,"[7] Andrew Palmer wrote:

Guilty demeanour [as opposed to tangible guilty conduct] is both more difficult to define, and identify. Perceptions of guilt based on demeanour are likely to depend on highly subjective impressions which may be difficult for the witnesses to articulate, let alone convey to a jury. The greatest obstacle to the use of guilty demeanour, therefore, will usually be the difficulty of establishing that the accused did indeed behave in a way which might be thought consistent with guilt. Even if this can be established, however, the significance of the behaviour will often be fairly equivocal. It may, therefore, be difficult for the jury to eliminate possible innocent explanations for the behaviour. Because of this, guilty demeanour will usually provide a far less secure basis for an inference of guilt than the evidence in the other four categories of guilty behaviour.

. . .

As a general rule, one would expect somone who has committed a crime—or at least a bloody one—to experience some sort of immediate psychological or emotional reaction to that fact. Birch, for example, has argued that '[f]ailing to show any emotion after committing murder is so unusual' that 'if the question is which of two mentally normal men committed a murder, evidence that one was upset afterwards ought to be relevant.'

---

7 (1997), 21 Melbourne University Law Review 95.

. . .

Another arguably relevant emotional response to an alleged crime occurs when the accused's behaviour and emotional responses depart from the behaviour and responses which would have been expected if the hypothesis consistent with innocence were true. For example, the idea that Lindy Chamberlain's failure to publicly cry over the death of her daughter Azaria meant she had probably murdered her, was based on beliefs about the ways in which bereaved others supposedly behaved.

. . .

I would argue, however, that while departure from the stereotype might legitimately arouse the suspicions of investigators, an inference of guilt cannot be safely drawn from it . . . The most that can be said is that the accused's emotional responses to the event appeared to be unusual. Guilt would, of course, be one explanation for the apparently unusual nature of the accused's responses; but another equally plausible one would be the accused's *general* emotional responses or levels of expressiveness differed from the norm. Without recourse to a battery of psychological testing, or the admission of a host of evidence about how the accused had responded in other, comparable, situations (if indeed any could be found), it is difficult to see how the jury could ever eliminate this possible explanation.

. . .

In a recent Canadian drugs case, for example, the accused's 'nervous reaction' was listed as one of the items of evidence against him:

> Officer Coderre, who knew the appellant, reached him first, took away his weapon and informed him that they wanted to question him in the context of their ongoing investigation with respect to marijuana plants in the area. In response to this, the appellant reacted nervously and told the officers that he was in the process of hunting, that he had done nothing wrong and he asked them to let him leave.
> [*R. c. Couture* (1994), 93 C.C.C. (3d) 540 (C.A. Qué.)]

It is difficult to see how the jury could possibly have eliminated the many conceivable innocent explanations for the accused's alleged nervousness; and if the jury could not eliminate those explanations, then knowing that the accused reacted nervously could not have assisted them to make a rational decision about the accused's guilt or innocence.

. . .

In the Canadian case referred to above, the supposedly unconvincing denial of guilt occurred in court, so that the jury would have been able to decide whether or not the denial was that of a guilty man on the basis of their own perceptions. In most cases, however, the unconvincing denial will have occurred out of court, and the jury would have to decide whether the denial was that of a guilty person purely on the basis of a witness's account of that denial. Yet the supposed difference between the denial of the guilty and the denial of the innocent clearly turns subtle nuances of tone and timing, matters which are particularly difficult to convey accurately to a court. I would therefore argue that an accused person's out of court denial of guilt, no matter how unconvincing it might have seemed to those who heard it, should never be offered as evidence from which the accused's guilt can be inferred. As Lowe J. said—with the addition by myself of the word parentheses—'by no torturing of the statement "I did not do that act" can you (safely) extract the evidence "I did do the act".'

In summary, as diverse as the behaviour contained in this category is, it does tend to share the two following characteristics: difficulty in satisfactorily establishing the fact of the behaviour, and difficulty in eliminating any innocent explanations for it. These two characteristics mean the evidence of guilty demeanour should seldom, if ever, be admitted.

Demeanour evidence was advanced against Susan Nelles when she was wrongly charged with the murder of four infants at the Hospital for Sick Children in Toronto. In discharging Ms. Nelles at the preliminary inquiry, His Honour Judge Vanek found that no inference of guilt could be drawn from a doctor's evidence as to Ms. Nelles' demeanour:[8]

> Several . . . items of evidence relate to utterances and conduct following closely after the death of baby Justin Cook on Sunday, March 22nd, at about 5:00 a.m. Dr. Fowler testified that he did not see Nelles that morning until he was about to leave the hospital; and that as he was leaving he saw Nelles sitting at one of the desks in the nurses' station apparently writing up the final report in Cook's medical chart. He said he knew she had been involved with Pacsai and had given the digoxin before and was anxious to see what she looked like at this time. He glanced in her direction and said that she had very strange expression on her face and no sign at all of grief. He said he thought this was very strange that this would be her appearance at a time such a terrible thing had happened. With respect, while it appears that Dr. Fowler went to school with Nelles' father many years ago and may have had some isolated transactions with him since then, he barely knew Susan Nelles, if at all; he knew nothing about her emotional range, her reaction to stress, or her manner of expressing her grief. I am unable to find any evidence of guilt from what a doctor thought from a passing glance was "a very strange expression" on the face of a young woman he barely knew, who had suffered a most harrowing experience, and was engaged in the very emotionally disturbing duty she was bound to perform of writing up the final death note as part of her other difficult duties on the occasion of the death of a baby in her care.

The cross-examination of Dr. Fowler by Austin Cooper Q.C. was in part as follows:

> Q. Now, as to Susan Nelles, was she a close friend of yours?
> A. No.

---

8 *R. v. Nelles* (1982), 16 C.C.C. (3d) 97 at 124-125 (Ont. Prov. Ct.).

Q. Did you ever visit her house?

A. Never.

Q. Or her apartment?

A. Never.

Q. Has she ever visited your house?

A. Never.

Q. I think you said you knew her one year?

A. Just because she was on the ward.

Q. On the ward?

A. Her brother is a resident on the ward and I knew her father.

Q. Have you ever had lunch with her?

A. Never.

Q. Or coffee?

A. Never.

Q. Or dinner?

A. Never.

Q. Ever had any sort of meaningful conversation with her about anything other than whether a baby has or hasn't had its medication or has turned blue?

A. Never.

Q. Okay, so you never worked a twelve hour shift in her company?

A. Never.

Q. Did you ever see her since her arrest on March 25th? Other than around the Court or whatever?

A. No, I've never seen her since then.

Q. Did you ever see her grieving after a relative had died?

A. I have never seen her grieving after any because I don't know her. I've never seen –

Q. Did you ever she her upset, ever?

A. Never.

Q. Ever see her cry?

A. No.

Q. Did you ever see her angry?

A. No.

Q. Did you ever see her depressed or elated?

A. No.

Q. Did you ever see her sad or shocked?

A. No.

Q. Well, I'm going to suggest that you really don't know much about the lady's emotional range; you'll agree with that?

A. I've seen many nurses who are looking after sick patients and her reaction, again, was very unusual.

Q. Well, I didn't ask you that. I asked you – I suggested that you don't know much about her emotional range?

A. No.

Q. You just don't know much about it?

A. No, except that it's unusual. Under the circumstances, for a person to have that reaction.

Q. And Doctor Jedeikin, was he upset and crying?

A. No.

Q. Was Doctor –

A. He was very upset but he wasn't crying.

Q. He wasn't crying, do you expect a Doctor to cry after a death?

A. No, not often.

Q. Doctor Kantak, was he there?

A. No, I didn't see him.

Q. Do you know what other Doctor was there?

A. It was just Doctor Jedeikin and me that I can remember.

Q. Okay. Well, a number of witnesses here have described Susan Nelles as being a cheerful person. Do you know her well enough to even know about that?

A. No.

Q. She's easy to get along with. Do you know her well enough to even know that?

A. No. I don't work with her.

Q. You don't work with her. She's conscientious and eager. You don't even know that, I guess?

A. No. I don't know that. I presume that she does her job well or she wouldn't have been working in the ward.

Q. Do you think those people, whether nurses or Doctors, who have worked on shift with her, would be in a better position than you to describe her emotional state. Someone who knew her well and worked with her on shift. Do you think?

A. I'm not talking about her emotional state, I'm talking about her appearance under a certain situation and I explained what she looked like. And I don't know anything about her reactions, her emotional reactions.

Q. Well my question was, do you think those who have worked on shift with her over a period of weeks or a year, twelve hours a day, would be in a better position than you to describe Susan Nelles's emotional state?

A. Well, I'm not sure about that.

Q. You're not sure about that?

A. Because they haven't seen her in exactly the same situation that I saw.

Q. Oh, I see. Well, we've had some witnesses here who spoke about that. There was a Mrs. Ober who gave evidence in this courtroom and I've got it exactly as I can that "After Justin Cook's death, Susan Nelles looked tired and strained and pretty upset." Is that the type of reaction you would have expected from a nurse after a death?

A. Yes.

Q. We have Mr. Cook himself, Justin Cook's father who gave evidence here just a couple of weeks ago. He said, "There were tears in Susan Nelles's eyes and she said she was sorry." Is that the type of reaction you would have expected from a nurse after the death of an infant that she was looking after.

A. Yes, that's what I would have expected.

Q. You would have expected that. Another nurse, Susan Reaper, said in this courtroom under oath, after the death of Justin Cook, "Susan Nelles was upset. She was smoking a cigarette." Is that the type of reaction you would have expected?

A. I'm not sure. I don't know.

Q. Mrs. Lyons, Evonne Lyons, one of the nurses on 4B gave evidence in this courtroom that "Susan Nelles was upset" Marie Mandel, one of the other nurses, I believe on 4B, said, " Susan Nelles, after the death of Justin Cook seemed to be in shock." Is that the type of reaction you might expect to see after the death of a child who you were looking after?

A. I don't know what that term means, I'm not sure.

Q. Well you said she looked strange. Do you know what that term means?

A. Yes.

Q. Phyllis Trayner, who is the same lady Mr. McGee asked you about and whom you said you knew by sight anyway, the head nurse?

A. I just know her by sight just the way I know Miss Nelles.

Q. She swore in this courtroom, just a couple of weeks ago, that "After Justin Cook's death, Susan Nelles was very upset. There were tears in her eyes."

That's the type of reaction you would have expected?

A. That's what I would have expected but there was no evidence of that at all when I witnessed her.

Q. When you witnessed her. Bertha Bell, a nurse on 4B, swore in this courtroom some short time ago that, "After the death of Justin Cook, Susan Nelles was upset. She was very quiet. I know Susan Nelles well, I know when she was upset."

That's the sort of thing you'd expect after the death of a child you were looking after?

A. Yes.

Q. Janet Brownless, a nursing assistant, a registered nursing assistant, on 4A, said that, "Susan Nelles helped Brownless bathe Justin Cook after the death of Cook and that Susan Nelles was upset."

Again, that's the type of reaction that would be normal?

A. Yes.

Q. And Mrs. Whittingham, who was also on duty, I believe, on 4B said, "everybody was upset and feeling badly after Justin Cook's death, including Susan Nelles."

Again, that's how you'd expect the nurses to react?

A. Yes.

The New Brunswick Court of Appeal also commented unfavourably on determining credibility on the basis of demeanour evidence:[9]

> In determining credibility, the trial judge ... made the following comments:

---

9   *R. v. B. (S.P.)* (1994), 90 C.C.C. (3d) 478 at 482-483 (N.B. C.A.).

... certainly if the accused had not been near [M.] when he was alleged to have kissed her, he would have made this known to the police when questioned about the matter.

Mr. [B.] also testified that he had never kissed a girl in his life, that he did not know what a passionate kiss was, and that if he had a girl-friend, he did not know if he would kiss her any differently from the manner in which he would kiss his mother. I find this evidence difficult to believe and rather preposterous.

I think that even the most naïve, sheltered and unworldly 17-year-old would know better than that.

Most importantly I want to mention that in my opinion [he] lacked the sense of outrage while testifying concerning the allegations, which one would expect if he were the subject of fabricated allegations or innocently distorted memories. If the evidence in the question against him had been totally made up, one would have expected to see a young man much more upset and much stronger in his denials of the accusations.

Again one would have expected a very strong denial from the accused had he not been kissing the young girl as alleged.

. . .

Similarly, I would refuse to determine the credibility of an accused person by relying on a stereotyped degree of reaction, outrage or denial that one subjectively might expect from someone who is falsely accused.

Two of the systemic witnesses before me warned of the dangers of demeanour evidence. Professor Ericson said:

[I]t's highly problematic to make that kind of inference [of guilt] from expressions of human emotion or paraticular human actions. There can be very many inferences that are made, and very many different actions that are taken as a result of those inferences.

I think what you're dealing with here is of course—I mean, this is a basis of human culture and human judgment generally that we're constantly making these inferences in order to read the character of people and to take action in relation to people. When it gets into a very serious matter, like a serious criminal trial, of course, there should be much more vigilance over whether or not that kind of information is allowed to be admissible, or those kinds of inferences are allowed to be admissible. And I'm basically agreeing with what I take to be the basis of your statement, that it's just highly problematic, and certainly should not be a grounds for concluding that somebody was actually motivated by what you're inferring from the accused.

Mr. Brodeur also pointed out that demeanour is culturally sensitive. He cited the example of aboriginals in Australia. Non-aboriginal Australians can make hasty and erroneous interpretations of aboriginal behaviour. Aboriginal body language and behaviour is markedly different than that of non-aboriginals. Looking someone in the face, for instance, is a mark of disrespect to the former and a mark of truth to the latter. Mr. Brodeur stated that aboriginals very often lose custody of their children because judges misinterpret their (apparently evasive) behaviour in court.

The more recent case of *R. v. Levert*[10] held that the probative value of demeanour evidence is suspect because perceptions of guilt based on demeanour are likely to depend on highly subjective impressions that may be difficult to convey to a jury.

It is not unusual to hear a police officer opine that the accused appeared calm during his arrest. Although this may appear to be neutral evidence in a trial before judge alone, a juror may feel that if the accused was innocent he would be in a more excited state if he was wrongfully charged. This scenario suggests the following questions in cross-examination:[11]

1. that the officer never met your client before
2. that the officer never spoke to your client before
3. that the officer has never seen your client in any manner of crisis to observe his/her reaction
4. that the officer has no special qualifications as an expert in the area of psychology or human behaviour
5. that the officer is in no position to dispute the fact that your client was in fact in a state of shock at the time of his arrest.

In *R. v. Perlett*[12] it was held that a Court should not infer consciousness of guilt from an accused's silence or unusually calm reaction after very disturbing circumstances.

Demeanour evidence was not held to be admissible in the circumstances as it was not evidence of equivocal conduct or conduct inconsistent with supposed societal norms given by a person without a special relationship with the accused.[13]

---

10 (2002), 159 C.C.C. (3d) 71 (Ont. C.A.) at 73. See also *R. v. F. (J.)* (2003), 177 C.C.C. (3d) 1 (Ont. C.A.); *R. v. Bennett* (2003), 179 C.C.C. (3d) 244 (Ont. C.A.), leave to appeal refused (2004), 2004 CarswellOnt 1325, 2004 CarswellOnt 1326 (S.C.C.).

11 Steven Skurka, Criminal Lawyers' Newsletter - For the Defence, September/October, 2000, p. 41.

12 (2006), 82 O.R. (3d) 89 (Ont. C.A.), leave to appeal refused 2007 CarswellOnt 5633 (S.C.C.).

13 *R. v. Clark* (2004), 69 O.R. (3d) 321 (Ont. C.A.).

DEMEANOUR EVIDENCE OF THE COMPLAINANT

In *R. v. A. (J.)* (2010), 78 C.R. (6th) 40 (Ont. C.A.) at paras. 12, 18, application/notice of appeal 2010 CarswellOnt 6224 (S.C.C.) the Court held that it was permissible for the trial Judge to rely on a complainant's post-event emotional state and the post-event demeanour is a matter for the trial Judge's discretion.[14]

DEMEANOUR WHEN TESTIFYING

Credibility

It is trite to say that so often the guilt or innocence of an accused rests on findings as to the credibility of witnesses. Much has been said by our courts over the years about this issue of credibility and those comments are helpful to counsel in assessing witnesses and in preparing questions for both examination-in-chief and cross-examination. In *R. v. White*[15] Mr. Justice Estey stated in part about credibility:

> It is a matter in which so many human characteristics, both the strong and the weak, must be taken into consideration. The general integrity and intelligence of the witness, his powers to observe, his capacity to remember and his accuracy in statement are important. It is also important to determine whether he is honestly endeavouring to tell the truth, whether he is sincere and frank or whether he is biased, reticent and evasive. All these questions and others may be answered from the observation of the witness's general conduct and demeanour in determining the question of credibility.

And in *Faryna v. Chorny*,[16] O'Halloran J.A. speaking for the British Columbia Court of Appeal, stated:

> The credibility of interested witnesses, particularly in cases of conflict of evidence, cannot be gauged solely by the test of whether the personal demeanour of the particular witness carried conviction of the truth. The test must reasonably subject his story to an examination of its consistency with the probabilities that surround the currently existing conditions. In short, the real test of the truth of the story of a witness in such as case must be its harmony with the preponderance of the probabilities which a practical and informed person would readily organize as reasonable in that place and in those conditions.

---

14 See also *R. v. Varcoe* (2007), 219 C.C.C. (3d) 397 (Ont. C.A.) at para. 33; *R. v. Boss* (1988), 46 C.C.C. (3d) 523 (Ont. C.A.).

15 [1947] S.C.R. 268 (S.C.C.) at 272.

16 (1951), 4 W.W.R. (N.S.) 171 (B.C. C.A.) at 174. See also [1952] 2 D.L.R. 354 at 356-358 (B.C. C.A.).

In *R. v. Norman*,[17] a case involving the sexual assault of a child, Finlayson J.A. held that an assessment of credibility based on demeanour alone of Crown witnesses is insufficient as grounds to base a conviction when there are significant inconsistencies in their testimony. The reliability of the evidence is paramount.

In *R. v. G. (M.)*,[18] the Ontario Court of Appeal held that the most valuable means in assessing the credibility of a crucial witness is to determine the consistency of what the witness said in the witness box and what the witness said on other occasions, whether or not under oath, on material matters about which an honest witness is unlikely to be mistaken. See Chapter, "Client and Witness Interviews."

Refreshing the memory of one's own witness normally arises when that witness is honestly forgetful due to the passage of time or is overly nervous (although it is also a preliminary step to be taken before your own witness can be declared hostile. See Chapter, "Prior Inconsistent Statements" under the heading "The Common Law Hostile Witness"). The witness may even have given a different answer than in a previous statement. Obtaining evidence from a co-operating witness whose memory with respect to that evidence has failed or partly failed can be accomplished by two different doctrines which have been referred to by Wigmore as "past recollection recorded" and "present recollection revived."[19]

---

17 (1993), 16 O.R. (3d) 295 (Ont. C.A.); *R. v. Gostick* (1999), 137 C.C.C. (3d) 53 (Ont. C.A.); *R. v. S. (W.)* (1994), 29 C.R. (4th) 143 (Ont. C.A.), leave to appeal refused (1994), 35 C.R. (4th) 402 (note) (S.C.C.).

18 (1994), 93 C.C.C. (3d) 347 (Ont. C.A.), leave to appeal refused (1995), 95 C.C.C. (3d) vi (note) (S.C.C.).

19 3 *Wigmore on Evidence* (Chadbourn rev. 1970), §758; *Salutin v. R.* (1979), 11 C.R. (3d) 284 (Ont. C.A.); *Mooney v. R.* (1977), 35 C.C.C. (2d) 392 (C.C.C.).

REFRESHING THE WITNESS'S MEMORY

"*Does this, by any chance, refresh your memory, Mr. Fillgate?*"

The New Yorker Book of Lawyer Cartoons. New Yorker Magazine Eds. (Illus.).
Alfred A. Knopf Inc., 1997. © 1993 by The New Yorker Magazine, Inc.

Past Recollection Recorded

This doctrine assists counsel who is faced with an honestly forgetful witness who is unable to remember an earlier statement with the result that the statement is admitted into evidence. In *R. v. Rouse and McInroy*,[20] Estey J. discussed the doctrine of past recollection recorded at pages 497 to 498 as follows:

> The rule is of long standing in the law of evidence that documentary evidence will be admitted through a witness in the witness box who, although the witness cannot recall the substance of the document or perhaps the precise event described or recorded therein, is able to swear to its truth at the time of the trial.
>
> Such documents may take the form of business records or deeds where the witness has either made the entry in the document or signed the instrument,

---

20 (1978), 42 C.C.C. (2d) 481 (S.C.C.). See also *R. v. McBride* (1999), 133 C.C.C. (3d) 527 (Ont. C.A.).

acknowledging execution or other event. Where time has elapsed or where the witness in his daily life participated in a large number of such events or transactions, it is entirely unrealistic to expect a witness to say, or indeed to believe him if he did say, that upon examining the instrument he was able to recall his entry or the event. The law in acknowledging these realities has long recognized the procedure whereby the witness may incorporate in his testimony the contents of such deeds or documents when he adopts those contents as part of his testimony.

The witness must be unable to recall the facts which have been recorded before the writing becomes admissible.[21] The witness may rely on the document if it was made or verified by the witness contemporaneously with the event.[22] The witness must be able to verify that the record relied upon actually represents the knowledge of the witness at the time the record was made, as for example, verifying that he made the record or adopted it or because it was within the witness's general routine of work and is a reliable source.[23] The document itself should be entered as an exhibit as it is the evidence on the issue. What is contemporaneous should depend on when the facts were still fresh in the witness's memory so as to catch any inaccuracies.[24] In one reported case the Court sanctioned a 22-day lapse between the event and the time of recording.[25]

The Supreme Court of Canada has held that hospital records were admissible in evidence *as prima facie* proof of the facts stated therein where the nurse's notes were made contemporaneously by someone having personal knowledge of the matters being recorded and under a duty to make the records.[26] In *Salutin v. R.*,[27] Dubin J.A. held that it is the record which is the evidence where the proper foundation, for example, contemporaneity and accuracy, is laid. A copy of the record will be admissible if certified as a true copy but there should be evidence that the copy was prepared with the original notes or that it was read over by the witness and verified as correct.[28]

---

21 *Mooney v. R., supra.*
22 *Fleming v. Toronto Railway Co.* (1911), 25 O.L.R. 317 (Ont. C.A.); *R. v. Davey*, [1970] 2 C.C.C. 351 (B.C. C.A.).
23 *Mooney v. R., supra.*
24 Archbold, *Pleading, Evidence and Practice in Criminal Cases*, 42nd ed., S.G. Mitchell and P.J. Richardson (eds.) (London: Sweet & Maxwell, 1985), p. 396, §4-297; *R. v. Davey, supra.*
25 *R. v. Fotheringham* (1975), 72 L.S.G. 551; see also *R. v. Graham*, [1973] Crim. L.R. 628 where the witness was an accomplice.
26 *Ares v. Venner*, [1970] S.C.R. 608 at 626 (S.C.C.).
27 *Supra.*
28 *R. v. Armstrong* (1977), 28 N.S.R. (2d) 431 (N.S. Co. Ct.); *R. v. Davey, supra*; *R. v. Simons* (1991), 68 C.C.C. (3d) 97 (Alta. Q.B.).

In *R. v. Fliss*[29] the Supreme Court of Canada held that evidence will be admissible as past recollection recorded if it meets Wigmore's four criteria which are:

(1) The past recollection must have been recorded in same reliable way.

(2) At the time of recording, it must have been sufficiently fresh and vivid to be probably accurate.

(3) The witness must now be able to assert that the record accurately represented his knowledge and recollection at the time. The witness is to affirm that "he knew it to be true at the time."

(4) The original recording itself must be used, if it is procurable.

Present Recollection Revived

In *R. v. Gwozdowski*,[30] the Ontario Court of Appeal adopted the following passages from *Phipson*:[31]

> A witness may refresh his memory by reference to any writing made or verified by himself concerning, and contemporaneously with, the facts to which he testifies; but such documents are not evidence *per se* of the matters [therein] contained.
>
> ....
>
> The writings may have been made either by the witness himself, or by others, providing in the latter case that it was read by him when the facts were fresh in [the] memory, and he knew the statement to be correct.
>
> ....
>
> The document must have been written either at the time of the transaction or so shortly afterwards that the facts were fresh in his memory. A delay of a fortnight may not be fatal; but an interval of several weeks, or six months, has been held to exclude.

But in *R. v. B. (K.G.)*[32] the Ontario Court of Appeal sanctioned witnesses refreshing their memories from statements they had given to the police two and one-half and three and one-half years after the occurrence they were testifying about. The Court noted that in *Gwozdowski* the refreshing memory problems occurred when the witnesses were in the witness box but in *B. (K.G.)* memories were refreshed from police statements well before

---

29 [2002] 1 S.C.R. 535 at paras. 63, 64. See also *R. v. Thom* (2010), 2010 ONCJ 492 (Ont. C.J.).

30 (1972), 10 C.C.C. (2d) 434 at 437 (Ont. C.A.); J. Buzzard, R. Amlot and S. Mitchell, *Phipson on Evidence*, 11th ed. (London: Sweet & Maxwell Limited, 1970), pp. 632-634.

31 *Ibid.*, pp. 632-633, art. 1528.

32 (1998), 125 C.C.C. (3d) 61 (Ont. C.A.). See also *R. v. Muise (No. 1)* (1974), 22 C.C.C. (2d) 487 (N.S. C.A.).

trial. The Court stated that *Gwozdowski* mistated the law if it meant to say that a witness cannot refresh his/her memory from a statement not recorded contemporaneously with the facts set out in it as it is inconsistent with authorities such as *R. v. Coffin* (1956), 114 C.C.C. 1 (S.C.C.). In *B. (K.G.)* the Court noted that defence counsel was free to cross-examine the witness to determine whether the witness had a present memory of events about which he/she testified. "What triggers recollection is not significant." Any external source or event may be used to refresh a witness's memory.[33] It is not necessary that the witness wrote the document from which memory is refreshed as it is not the document but the recollection of the witness that is the evidence.[34] The fact that the witness refreshed his/her memory from a statement not made contemporaneously can go to the weight of that evidence.[35]

In *R. v. Bengert et al (No. 5)*,[36] the British Columbia Court of Appeal held that the view held by many lawyers that a witness may only refer to notes that he/she made reasonably contemporaneously with the event, or if someone else made the notes, and the witness verified the accuracy of the notes when the events were contemporaneous in his/her mind, is a misconception. The Court adopted what was said in Wigmore, Vol. III (1970), p. 125, s. 758. The concern the witness may be reconstructing rather than actually having memory revived depends on the circumstance. It will depend on the nature of the narrative and the importance of the observation to the witness. Detailed or routine matters may require that the record be made within a short time of the event. However, if memory can be stimulated by some special circumstance, then the recollection should be a matter of weight and not admissibility.[37]

When a witness is refreshing her memory from notes previously made, he/she may not simply read from those notes or an earlier prepared statement, because this is seen as more than just refreshing one's memory. What often happens however, particularly with police officers, is that they virtually read *verbatim* from their notebooks. It is not unusual to see counsel, particularly Crown counsel, read aloud or have the witness read aloud that part of the statement being used to fresh the witness's memory. Sometimes the witness, without being asked, will commence to read the statement aloud. This procedure should be the subject of objections by opposing counsel. The witness should be given a copy of the statement to read silently rather than to read aloud because the statement is not the admissible evi-

---

33   See *R. v. Thom, supra; R. v. B. (K.G.)* (1998), 125 C.C.C. (3d) 61 (Ont. C.A.).

34   *Ibid., B. (K.G.)*, at 67. It does not matter who made the notes. See *R. v. Thom, supra*.

35   *Ibid., B. (K.G.)*

36   (1980), 53 C.C.C. (2d) 481 (B.C. C.A.).

37   *R. v. Richardson*, [1971] 2 All E.R. 773 at p. 777; *R. v. DaSilva*, [1990] All E.R. 29 (C.C.A.) at pp. 32, 33; Newark and Samuels, Refreshing Memory, [1978] Crim. L.R. 408 at p. 409.

dence.[38] The witness will then give her testimony without reading from the material which has refreshed her memory.[39] Although it is not objectionable for the witness to periodically look down at their notes to refresh memory.

While it is clear that opposing counsel may inspect the notes referred to in Court by the witness to refresh memory, there are differing opinions as to whether the trial Judge has a discretion or whether she must permit counsel to inspect the notes referred to by the witness where memory was refreshed outside of the courtroom shortly before testifying.[40] However, the common practice seems to lean strongly toward permitting counsel to inspect the notes in such circumstances. But with present rules of disclosure the defence normally receives a copy of the police officer's notes.

There appears to be an exception to the contemporaneity rule when refreshing one's memory from the transcript of a preliminary hearing, perhaps because evidence given under oath may be more trustworthy than evidence not under oath.[41] But it would be improper for the witness to read the testimony of other witnesses in the transcript.[42]

In *R. v. Fliss, supra,* at para. 45, Binnie J. for the majority stated that an officer was entitled to refresh his memory from the transcript of an intercepted private communication that was held to be admissible as "it was his recollection, not the stimulus that becomes evidence." Binnie J. goes on to say "The stimulus may be hearsay, it may itself be largely inaccurate, it may be nothing more than the sight of someone who had been present or hearing some music that had played in the background. If the recollection here had been stimulated by hearing a tape of his conversation with the accused, even if the tape was made without valid authorization, the officer's recollection—not the tape—would be admissible."

When counsel hears his witness straying from an earlier statement and wishes to have the witness refresh his memory by drawing his attention to that earlier statement he may ask leading questions.[43]

Counsel may cross-examine a witness on a writing which a witness relied on to refresh his memory without having to worry about making the writing evidence and in this respect present recollection revived differs from past recollection recorded.[44]

---

38   *R. v. Laurin (No. 5)* (1902), 6 C.C.C. 135 (Que. K.B.).
39   *R. v. Fliss, supra.*
40   *R. v. Catling* (1984), 29 C.C.C. (3d) 168 (Alta. Q.B.); *R. v. Lepine* (1962), 38 C.R. 145 (Sask. Dist. Ct.); *R. v. Musterer* (1967), 61 W.W.R. 63 (B.C. Mag. Ct.); *R. v. Lewis,* [1969] 3 C.C.C. 235 (B.C. S.C.); *R. v. Kerenko, supra. R. v. Muise (No. 1)* (1974), 22 C.C.C. (2d) 487 (N.S. C.A.). See also Chapter, "Inconsistent Statements."
41   *R. v. Husbands* (1973), 24 C.R.N.S. 188 (Ont. Co. Ct.).
42   *Ibid.*
43   *R. v. Williams* (1853), 6 Cox C.C. 343; *R. v. Coffin,* [1956] S.C.R. 191 (S.C.C.).
44   *R. v. Brown* (1927), 49 C.C.C. 37 (Sask. C.A.) at 41; *R. v. Laurin (No. 5), supra.*

When a witness, usually a police officer or other investigator takes the stand to testify the Crown normally asks if the witness made any notes and if so does she wish to refer to these notes to refresh her memory for the purpose of giving her testimony. If the witness says yes the Crown's questions normally go like this:

Q. Who made the notes?
A. I did.
Q. Officer, when did you make your notes?
A. At the time or shortly thereafter.
Q. Were the events fresh in your mind at the time?
A. Yes.
Q. Have there been any additions or deletions or any changes whatsoever to your notes since you first made them?
A. No.
Q. Do you have an independent recollection of the events in questions?
A. Yes.
Q. Would it assist you at times to refer to your notes to refresh your memory?
A. Perhaps for some parts.

The Judge would then inquire of opposing counsel if he or she has any questions of the witness. The answer is usually no. the Judge will then permit the witness to refresh his or her memory from their notes if needed and sometimes gives the warning to the witness not to read aloud.

While opposing counsel has the right to question the witness as to whether the above preconditions have been met, counsel invariably agrees to the officer being able to refresh his memory before the Crown has even finished her qualifying questions. Normally the preconditions for note-taking have been met, and in any event counsel wants the opportunity to see the witness's notes which he can only do if the witness has refreshed her memory from them. This consideration becomes academic if the notes have been part of disclosure.

If the original notes are no longer procurable the witness has been permitted to refresh his memory from a copy of the notes if the authenticity of the copy is proven.

When counsel wishes to refresh a witness's memory from a previous statement that the witness made she will produce that statement to the witness (counsel may wish to advise the trial Judge first of her purpose) and seek an admission that the statement is the witness's statement by identifying his signature or by recognizing his handwriting or the circumstances. When that has been done counsel must then seek an admission after the witness has read the statement if it helps to refresh his memory about the relevant part. If the witness answers yes then counsel will repeat the question that was originally asked. If the answer is no, counsel may have to resort to section 9 of the *Canada Evidence Act* or the common law regarding a hostile witness. See Chapter, "Prior Inconsistent Statements."

10

General Techniques of Cross-Examination

CONTROLLING THE WITNESS

Unlike examination-in-chief where the witness is the center of attention, the cross-examiner is at center stage during cross-examination. His or her Court style and demeanour are vital and will command attention. The cross-examiner should be confident, always in control of what is happening, like an orchestra leader. If there is one commandment for cross-examination, it should be: "Thou shalt control the witness." Control is essential as the witness must be prevented from moving the examination into areas where he or she wishes to go thereby giving answers which could be potentially detrimental to the questioner's position.

Open-ended Questions

The easiest way for the cross-examiner to lose control of the witness is to ask open-ended questions. The cross-examiner should always resist asking "why," unless it becomes necessary to take the risk or counsel does not care what the answer will be or counsel is confident the reply cannot hurt his or client. Asking "why" allows the witness to give a full explanation, which may be damaging to the cross-examiner's side, or at the very least, neutralize any favourable answers previously received. Guard against being so frustrated by a position the witness is taking that you ask a "why" question. When you ask such a question you can open up the opportunity for the witness to respond with otherwise inadmissible answers giving opinion evidence you don't want to hear, and you find yourself objecting to answers you provoked. Jurors won't be impressed and your side will appear to be losing. An example of the "why" question being used effectively can be seen in the cross-examination of Oscar Wilde, part of which is reproduced under "The Vain Witness" in the Chapter, "Cross-Examination of Certain Categories of Witnesses."

The questions put to the witness should be closed-ended. The best way to accomplish this is by asking leading questions. The cross-examiner makes the witness say what he wants him to say. The leading question should be framed to elicit a continuing series of "yes" or "no" answers as much as possible.[1] An example of such leading questions can be seen in the cross-examination of the doctor later in this chapter under the heading, "Closing Off Avenues of Escape."

Knowing the Answer to the Question: The Step-by-Step Approach

It has been often stated that the cross-examiner should never ask a question unless he or she knows the answer. This proposition should certainly be endorsed for examination-in-chief. It is not asking much from counsel that his preparation enable him to know beforehand what his own witness will say. However, in cross-examination the situation is different. One writer[2] put it this way:

> Unfortunately, cross-examination is too complicated and subtle a process to be patient of such dogmatic instructions. The most that can be said is that the questions should be so chosen, and so framed, that unjustifiable risks are avoided ... An example of a wholly unjustifiable risk is to be found in the situation where the answer to the question cannot materially strengthen the cross-examiner's case, and may seriously weaken it.

American trial advocate, Irving Younger,[3] points to two exceptions to the rule that counsel should know the answer to the question before it is asked. He stated them as follows:

> First exception: you may ask a question to which you don't know the answer if you don't care what the answer is. Be very sure you really don't care what the answer is because if there is an answer anywhere in this universe that could possibly hurt you, that is the one you are going to get. Make sure that there is nothing that could hurt you. The best illustration is the question that is asked for rhetorical effect. You've really done a job on somebody. It is not just that you laid gloves on him, you had him against the ropes, he's bloody and bowed and you want to finish it off with a kind of flourish, so you might say, "Sir, aren't you ashamed of yourself?" And sit down. You don't know the answer to that question but you can ask it because you don't care what the answer is.

> The second exception: You're impeaching a witness. There is a desperately important question you'd like to ask but you don't know the answer. It could

---

1 An example of this technique can be seen later in this chapter, in the cross-examination of the doctor under the heading "Closing Off Avenues of Escape".

2 G. Colman, Q.C., *Cross Examination. A Practical Handbook* (Capetown, South Africa: Juta and Company Limited, 1970).

3 Speech to Advocacy Symposium (150th Anniversary) in Toronto, 1982, sponsored by the Canadian Bar Association, p. 238.

be answered yes or no. A "no" answer is very good for you, a "yes" answer blows you out of the water. You don't know. You can't risk asking, but wait—there may be preliminary questions that you can ask. You don't know the answers to those preliminary questions until you hear them, but no answer to any of those preliminary questions can devastate your case, and the answers to the preliminary questions tell you what the answer to the payoff question will be. So that you escalate right there on your feet in the courtroom to the point where you know the answer to the payoff question and then you ask it . . .

G. Arthur Martin[4] described the step-by-step approach this way:

> Sometimes you ask questions in a probing type of examination in an effort to find the weak spot in the witness's evidence, not knowing what the answer will be but no matter what the answer is it can't seriously damage your case. If you find you are not making any progress toward your objective, you retreat gracefully, acting as though you are quite satisfied that you have elicited some information helpful to your case and embark on a new line of approach. Sometimes, however, you are forced by circumstances to embark on a line of cross-examination which can be dangerous to your case. When this is necessary, you proceed step by step so that the previous answer affords a certain amount of protection before you proceed to the next question.

When Lizzy Borden was tried for murder of her parents in Massachusetts in 1892, George D. Robinson, her counsel, wanted to show through his cross-examination of the maid that the family was not quarrelsome as was commonly thought, but that they lived in harmony. Robinson did not come right out and ask the witness to confirm that the family was not quarrelsome. He led the witness along, obtaining safe answers as stepping-stones to the final question and answer. Here is how it went:

Q. Did you have any trouble [at the Borden home]?
A. No sir.
Q. [Was the Borden home] a pleasant place to live?
A. Yes.
Q. [Was the Borden family] a pleasant family to be in?
A. I don't know how the family was. I got along all right.
Q. You never saw anything out of the way?
A. No sir.
Q. You never saw any conflict in the family?
A. No sir.
Q. You never saw any quarrelling or anything like that?
A. No, sir, I did not.[5]

If during this "feeling-out" process the witness stated she did not like working or residing in the Borden home then the cross-examiner would

---

4 Law Society of Upper Canada Lectures on Expert Evidence.
5 E. Lustgarten, *Verdict in Dispute* (Allen Wingate. 1949). p. 227. See also pp. 251-253.

have safely gone to another topic as he would be alerted that the witness's answers to the important question would have been unfavourable.

The risk of asking a question to which counsel does not know the answer to has been lessened with the necessity for complete Crown disclosure and pre-knowledge of witnesses' testimony at the preliminary hearing.

The Crown however is in a different position as it is not generally entitled to disclosure of the defence case and so it is more usual for the Crown to have to ask chance questions. It has been said by one Crown Attorney that the Crown does not have to feel they let the state side down if the answer hurts the prosecution as the Crown's role is to seek the truth.[6]

Asking One Question Too Many

Even the most experienced counsel have suffered the ignominy of asking one question too many and end up chastising themselves for not recognizing when they had achieved their objective or at least can go no further on the subject. This occurs when the cross-examiner is successful in achieving a series of favourable answers leading up to the last question which drives home the point. Does the cross-examiner ask that last question or does he or she hold back, waiting to argue in his or her jury address that since the witness answered favourably to the lead-up questions that the hoped for answer must be the obvious result? The latter course is the safest because the witness is not there to give the cross-examiner a bad answer. But perhaps counsel feels for whatever reason, that the final blow must be struck. Irving Younger[7] stated:

> The temptation may be induced by more than the desire of an orderly mind to round things off logically. There is great personal satisfaction in bringing of a dramatic coup: and it impresses one's client and one's audience, whereas silence, or an undramatic and possibly unfruitful cross-examination on other aspects of the case, will not.

The following is an example of how the final blow boomeranged and control was lost. The accused was charged with biting off the victim's nose. The defence lawyer cross-examined:

Q. Where were the defendant and the victim when the fight broke out?
A. In the middle of a field.
Q. Where were you?
A. On the edge of the field.
Q. What were you doing?

---

6 Brian McLure, assistant Crown Attorney, Peel Crown's Office. Paper to Ontario Bar Association, 2008 Institute of Continuing Legal Education, February 2nd 2008.
7 I. Younger, *The Art of Cross-Examination* (American Bar Association Monograph Series), "Litigation," p. 30.

A. Bird-watching.
Q. Where were the birds?
A. In the trees.
Q. Where were the trees?
A. On the edge of the field.
Q. Were you looking at the birds?
A. Yes.
Q. So your back was to the people fighting?
A. Yes.

This would have been a good place to stop, and then later in summation argue that the witness could not possibly have seen the nose being bitten off. But counsel opted for the *coup de grâce* by asking for an explanation by asking an open-ended question.

Q. Well, if your back was to them, how can you say that the defendant bit off the victim's nose?
A. Well, I saw him spit it out.

In the short cross-examination by Paddy Nolan[8] earlier, note that he did not ask the complainant: "Well witness, if you were sexually assaulted how come your pail still remained full to the brim with the milk?" No doubt Mr. Nolan was concerned that the witness might have had a reasonable answer.

Recognizing the one question too many in some instances will be easy, in other instances it will be more difficult. Asking the witness to explain is one way of asking one question too many. James W. McElhaney[9] says that:

> Any time you hear yourself saying, "Well, if that is true, then how can you say ...?", you are asking one question to many ... Asking one question too many is like asking "why?" It gives the witness a chance to explain. It surrenders control.

Chris Evans, of Calgary, sends along the following portion of his cross-examination with respect to a charge of fraud relating to switching price tags at a discount house. This example shows that it is not unusual for experienced counsel to fall prey to the one question too many.

Mr Evans: Now, you say you saw my client in the stationery department, and he removed a price tag from a small packet of confetti, and placed it on a packet of Smurf whistles.
Witness: Yes.
Mr. Evans: And you say you also saw him remove the Smurf whistle tag, and discard it in a bin.

---

8 P.V. MacDonald, *Court Jesters: Canada's Lawyers and Judges Take the Stand to Relate Their Funniest Stories* (Toronto: Metheun, 1985), p. 130. See Chapter, "Manner of Cross-Examination, 4. Maintaining Jurors' Interest" for quote.

9 J.W. McElhaney, *Trial Notebook* (American Bar Association, 1981), p. 132.

Witness:	Yes.
Mr. Evans:	And how far away from him were you at that time?
Witness:	About 15 feet. I was up high, in an observation booth.
Mr. Evans:	Are you telling this court that, at 15 feet, you were able to clearly see those little tags, and what my client was doing with them?
Witness:	[Calmly] I saw absolutely clearly.
Mr. Evans:	[Sarcastically] I suppose you were using x-ray vision?
Witness:	No, as a matter of fact, I was using binoculars.
Mr. Evans:	Moving on quickly.

If counsel has any doubt about asking the one question too many it is best to remember the words of James Jeans:[10]

> Remember, the consummation comes at closing argument. Cross-examination supplies the facts from which the arguments will be made at a later and more propitious time. When the urge arises to go all the way remember, "coitus interruptus isn't half bad."

When the Witness Answers the Question with a Question

Another aspect of controlling the witness in cross-examination occurs when the witness answers a question with a question. At times, this is done innocently, perhaps seeking clarification, and at other times it is done aggressively, or in an attempt to be evasive by stalling for the purpose of thinking of the right answer to give. The problem for the questioner is that if the witness's question makes sense and counsel does not answer it the jury may well feel that the witness scored. In fact, the witness may have made such a good point that counsel may be unable to give a satisfactory response. Other times counsel may be able to snap back with a very effective answer that enhances his or her case. However, counsel does not want to be thrust into a position of arguing with the witness as that will show weakness.

There are different ways you can respond to the questioning witness depending on how you view the witness's motives. A mild reply would be: "I'm sorry Mr. Smith, but the rules of evidence do not allow me to answer your question. If I was permitted to do so I would be more than happy to tell you what you should have done in the situation." Stronger retorts are: "Witness, I would be more than happy to reply to your question but my function is to ask questions, it is your job to answer. Please do so."; or "Just answer the question, please. You are testifying and I am not."; or "Witness, if you and I are both asking the questions, there will be nobody to answer." The last thing you want to do is to respond in such a way as to encourage the witness to ask more questions allowing him some credibility.

---

10   J.W. Jeans, *Trial Advocacy* (St. Paul: West Publishing Co., 1975), p. 325.

If counsel does have a good response or can think of one by the time of her jury address she can remind the jurors of the witness question and suggest the answer in her final address.

If the witness continues to disrupt the cross-examination by asking questions counsel should ask the Court to instruct the witness to be responsive. The witness who so conducts himself or herself will not be looked upon favourably by a judge or jury and in final summation counsel can harken back to the tactic of the witness attempting to avoid answering questions.

Closing Off Avenues of Escape

There are some witnesses who will try to avoid giving a helpful answer to the opponent. Included are the untruthful witness, the witness who shades the truth and the evasive witness. There will be times when the witness can be brought to his or her knees quickly with a prior inconsistent statement. When counsel does not have this luxury, he or she should not put a crucial question to the witness without first asking questions the answers to which will prevent the witness escaping from giving a favourable response to this crucial question. This method of controlling the witness is normally referred to as closing off the avenues of escape. It calls for a step by step approach to gain admissions from the witness which unknown to him or her will prevent evading the damaging question that is coming. In order to put the witness off-guard counsel might start this gradual approach of shutting the doors behind the witness at the outset of his or her cross-examination. To prevent the witness from being alerted, the blocking questions should appear innocuous and should not be asked one after the other but instead should be posed during different parts of the cross-examination.

In order to determine which doors should be shut, the cross-examiner should put himself in the witness's shoes and ask himself what answers could be given in order to escape the damaging question.

If the witness attempts to break out of the corner into which he has painted himself, counsel will push him back by drawing his attention to his earlier answers to the seemingly innocuous questions.[11] Note the following two examples:[12]

---

11 An example of this technique can be seen in the Chapter, "Cross-Examination of Police Officers" where the officer is cross-examined on an important omission in his notebook. In this example the avenues of escape are closed by securing from the officer admissions as to why it is important to make complete and accurate notes about what he heard or observed.

12 Current Criminal Law Evening Sessions, September-October, 1978. Sponsored by the Department of Continuing Education, L.S.U.C.

You are cross-examining a pathologist in a murder case. The victim has died as a result of a single gunshot wound with the bullet penetrating just above the eyelid. No gunpowder residue has been found on the victim's skin. You, as defence counsel, realize how important it is to show that there may well have been powder residue present but that the pathologist has done something which may have wiped away the powder residue which may have been present. The defence position in the case is that the victim accidentally shot himself and of course, in cases of this nature, your research has indicated that powder residue should be present. The theory of the Crown is that the victim was shot at a distance of some 6 to 7 feet and therefore that is the reason why no powder residue exists. We know from the preliminary hearing that the pathologist used a wet cloth when washing the dried blood off the wound. At the trial, the pathologist indicates that he used a dry cloth in wiping the blood away. You of course, as defence counsel, wish to demonstrate that the pathologist may have wiped the powder residue away by the use of a wet cloth.

Q. Doctor, you said you used a dry cloth to wipe the wound?
A. Yes.
Q. Do you recall giving evidence at the preliminary hearing in this matter?
A. Yes.

The doctor is then read the following question and answer from the preliminary hearing:

Q. What did you use to wipe the dried blood off the wound?
A. A wet cloth.

The doctor then agrees with you that he was under oath at the time of the preliminary hearing and that he must have used a wet cloth and that he has been mistaken in the evidence that he gave today at trial as to his use of a dry cloth. You then ask your next question which is:

Q. Do you think, doctor, that you might have wiped away some of the powder residue by using a wet cloth?
A. Possibly, or possibly but not likely.

The example given illustrates several things. First, when the lawyer has reached the crucial question, namely whether or not the doctor may have wiped away the powder residue by using a wet cloth, the lawyer has not trapped the doctor. The reason for this is due to the fact that the lawyer has been too hasty to arrive at the crucial area and has not set it up right. You have allowed the doctor to get out of his prior inconsistency by simply saying he was mistaken, something which every juror can certainly understand and sympathize with. Furthermore, you have asked the crucial question without having set the matter up in such a way that (a) the doctor cannot get out of it and (b) the jury really has no understanding of what it is you are trying to do. You may know everything about gunpowder residue and close-up shots as opposed to distance shots, but the jury likely knows nothing about it.

The following illustration accomplishes much more:

Q. Now doctor, you have indicated that you removed the blood from the piece of tissue over the eyelid with a dry cloth.
A. Yes

Q. Is that correct?

A. Yes.

Q. And while there may be other reasons for using a dry cloth, I suggest to you that one of the main reasons, and perhaps the most important is that there might be powder residue on the surface of the tissue which you would not want to disturb when removing the blood.

A. Yes.

Q. And you have been a pathologist for 15 years?

A. Yes.

Q. And of course, over these years, as a result of your vast experience, you are aware of the fact that the existence or non-existence of powder residue on the wound can be of very great importance?

A. Yes.

Q. It of course has special significance in terms of deciding how far the barrel of the gun was from the victim when it was fired. Is that so?

A. Yes.

Q. And it is generally recognized that if the barrel of the gun is held within 18" of the wound, one is likely to find powder residue? Is that so?

A. Yes.

Q. And, as you have already indicated, the existence or non-existence of powder residue may be a crucial factor in a case of this nature?

A. Yes.

Q. That is why you were so careful to use a dry cloth as opposed to a wet cloth when you removed the blood from the piece of tissue? Isn't that so?

A. Yes.

Q. Because if you had used a wet cloth you might well have wiped away any powder residue that might still have been on that piece of tissue.

A. Yes.

Then you go to the preliminary hearing as above and destroy one doctor.

In example 2, it can be seen that skillful cross-examination has put the doctor in a position which he cannot get out of when confronted with his inconsistency at the preliminary hearing. And further, the significance of the point has been brought home to the jury since you have shared your knowledge of powder residue and distance of gunshot wounds with them.

THE "SKIP-ROUND" TECHNIQUE

If counsel does not cross-examine in an orderly sequence or in the same order as direct examination but instead randomly skips from one part of the evidence to another it may prevent the untruthful witness from seeing what is coming and he or she will therefore become confused and unprepared for the crucial questions. However this technique can also be confusing for jurors to follow what is attempted to be accomplished.

OTHER POSSIBLE INTERPRETATIONS

The more witnesses that defence counsel must challenge the more difficult it becomes to defend the case successfully. It is simply a matter of common sense that a jury may disbelieve one or two witnesses who contradict what the client testifies to but it becomes virtually impossible to create reasonable doubt by urging that many are lying against the accused as if in some mass conspiracy—as the Crown would put it in her final submissions.

Often evidence can have more than one face—a guilty one, an innocent one and even a neutral one. Therefore, before counsel challenges the witness evidence he/she should consider whether or not there is another alternative'such as accepting the witness's testimony but placing another interpretation on it—an interpretation which fits in with the client's defence or at the very least is a neutral interpretation. This tactic is especially important even when there is only one witness testifying against the accused, such as a police officer.

One approach is accomplished by first asking the witness a series of questions designed to show that he or she could well have been mistaken or did not consider or have the opportunity to consider other relevant factors with respect to some of his or her answers. The cross-examination would culminate with a question such as: "Mr. Smith, given these new facts, which in fairness, you did not have the opportunity to consider when you testified in examination-in-chief, are you now prepared to change your evidence (or "is there some doubt in your mind?") when you say that . . .?" If these new factors are strong enough to make any fair and reasonable person entertain doubts about their original testimony but the witness stubbornly sticks to his or her original evidence you will ask the trier-of-fact to discredit such a witness as being biased. During this type of approach it would be best to ask the questions in a friendly and conversational tone since counsel will be asking the witness to change his or her mind.

Another approach is to show that the evidence is also consistent with another explanation without adding any additional facts. In the following example the accused was charged with possession of heroin for the purpose of trafficking. The officer had testified that certain items—syringes, baggies, dextrose to dilute the heroin, and scales—were found in the accused's apartment and were consistent with items that a drug trafficker would have. The cross-examination by Austin Cooper, Q.C. was designed to show that the Crown's evidence was consistent with simple possession.

Cross-Examination of First Officer
Q. You did find equipment in the apartment that led you to believe—or on his person—that led you to believe that Mr. Simmons was a user of heroin?
A. Yes, we did.
Q. Syringes, spoon, that type of thing?

A. Yes, spoon, syringes, scales, Baggies—as I said, syringes. The Dextrose was not on his person.

Q. Not on his person. All of those items are consistent with a person being a user as well as a trafficker, isn't that right?

A. Yes. There was a good quantity of certain things.

Q. A person who uses likes to check how much he has bought and make sure he has not been fooled, is that right?

A. Yes, with the money they're paying, they like to see they're getting their money's worth.

Q. And the scales would be necessary in order to be able to weigh whatever he has bought, is that right?

A. Could be used for that.

Q. Syringes, of course, are used to administer the heroin into the user, isn't that right?

A. Yes sir.

Q. And the spoon is a common item found among users, that right?

A. Yes sir.

Q. This stuff is called "the works" isn't it?

A. Yes.

Q. Syringes, spoon, something to tie the arm to expose the vein?

A. Yes, there was a bandage there also.

Q. There was a bandage there also. And Dextrose is commonly found amongst those who use heroin to perhaps make their supply go further by cutting it down to the point where they can use it over a longer period of time, that right?

A. Yes sir.

Q. And Baggies are found amongst users of heroin because [that] is what they use to transport the things—the heroin that they use, is that right, or the heroin that they buy?

A. Yes, they carry it in these bags.

Q. There were some contraceptives found. I understand?

A. Yes, there was.

Q. Which again are used by users to transport that which they use, heroin?

A. It's another method used.

Q. Another method used. Did you look at Mr. Simmon's arms?

A. I did not, no.

Q. Did he tell you that he was a user?

A. I heard him say that to someone there.

Q. All right, did you overhear him saying he had been a user for about a year and a half?

A. I don't recall the time, just said he was a user and had been doing it for a while.

Q. Doing it for a while. And you overheard him say that to one of the other officers, in the apartment, that right?

A. Yes, this was in the apartment.

Q. How long after he had been arrested and cautioned?

A. Well it was during the hour we were there, somebody made this comment to him about being a user, and I heard his answer.

Q. Did you overhear him saying then yes, that he had a heavy habit?
A. Yes, I believe that is one of the expressions he used.
Q. A gram a day, or a gram and a half a day?
A. I have the amount of a gram on my mind, I think that's—
Q. Something sticks in your mind that he told the officers his habit was as much as a gram a day, is that right?
A. I believe he said around a gram a day.
Q. A gram a day. That, from your experience as a morality officer, is a pretty heavy habit, isn't it?
A. Yes sir.

Second Officer Cross-Examination
(In direct testimony the officer testified that carrying of heroin in the mouth was commonly associated with *trafficking* in heroin).
Q. Can you assist me as to who first had contact with the accused when he entered the apartment?
A. I did.
Q. How did that contact take place, what form?
A. The accused unlocked the door, as he did I threw the door open, I seized him by the throat.
Q. Any particular reason why you did that, officer?
A. Yes, it's standard procedure, especially when the suspect is suspected to be a dealer in narcotics, especially heroin.
Q. Well, what is the purpose of the throat seizure?
A. Well, its not uncommon for people who carry heroin to carry it in their mouths, usually wrapped in sort of plastic, commonly a condom.
Q. What was your intent with respect to that seizure, what did you hope to accomplish by seizing him by the throat?
A. To prevent him from swallowing any material he did have.
Q. Did he have anything in his throat?
A. I thought not.
Q. Now you seized the accused by the throat because you were concerned that if he were carrying something in his mouth he might swallow it, is that right?
A. Yes sir.
Q. And I suggest to you that those who use or deal in heroin often carry in their mouth whatever supplies they have, is that right?
A. Yes sir.
Q. So when you said that because he was suspected of being a dealer in heroin you seized him by the throat, you would do the same if he were suspected of being a heroin addict carrying his own supply in his mouth?
A. Yes sir.
Q. Which he might swallow, is that right?
A. Yes sir.[13]

---

13 For a further example see the cross-examination of the psychiatrist in Chapter, "Cross-Examination of the Expert Witness," under heading "Challenging the Expert by Means of Recognized Authority."

MATCHING WITNESSES' TESTIMONY

This approach involves asking different witnesses basically the same questions with respect to a specific area and presupposes that there has been an order by the trial judge excluding witnesses so that they will not consciously or sub-consciously tailor their evidence to each other. If different witnesses give significantly different answers to the same question then at least one of the witness's credibility is open to attack—or even more than one if the defence theory is that there is a conspiracy of lies.[14]

ENLARGING ON DETAILS

This technique is concerned with enlarging the cross-examination to cover points not directly connected with the main story which the untruthful or unreliable witness may be unable to answer and thereby appear to be unworthy of acceptance.[15]

THE BEGINNING AND THE END OF CROSS-EXAMINATION

The Beginning

The beginning of the cross-examination is important as it can set the tone and grasp the interest of the jurors. This accords with the principle of primacy, the concept that what is first heard is best retained.[16] To quote the words of Douglas Laidlaw (a Toronto civil counsel, now deceased):

> You should never let the witness get ahead of you at the start. The first engagement between you and the witness is one of the most important. You should choose a point upon which you are not going to lose, or a point that if you lose you can move away from very quickly.[17]

An effective approach is to unnerve the witness or throw him or her off balance with a surprise question that makes a telling point and influences the jury's thinking against the witness throughout his or her testimony. During a demonstration at an Osgoode Hall Law School summer advocacy programme, David Humphrey, Q.C.[18] cross-examined one Laura Hobson

---

14 More is said about the exclusion of witnesses in Chapter, "Cross-Examination of Certain Categories of Witnesses" under heading "The Lying Witness."
15 *Ibid.*
16 J.W. James, *Trial Advocacy* (West Publishing Co. 1975).
17 Speech to Advocacy Symposium (150th Anniversary) in Toronto, 1982, sponsored by the Canadian Bar Association, p. 250.
18 Now His Honour Judge Humphrey of the Ontario Court of Justice (General Division).

who had admitted in examination-in-chief her involvement in a drug trafficking scheme with the accused. But Miss Hobson was not charged in
return for her testimony against the accused. Attacking the witness at his or
her weakest point at the opening of cross-examination is tactically best at
times because the witness is most nervous. The witness has just been examined-in-chief by a friendly counsel and may be tense waiting for the
cross-examiner whose style is unknown. The witness is therefore less prepared at the outset of cross-examination facing the unknown. Later, having
become more accustomed to the cross-examination, the witness will have
gained confidence and if the same questions are posed at the beginning they
may be answered in a different, less helpful way. Mr. Humphrey's first
question was: "Miss Hobson, you admit you are guilty of this offence, my
client denies his guilt. Can you tell us why you are sitting in the witness
stand and my client is in the prisoner's dock?" This question not only caused
laughter but immediately alerted the triers-of-fact to the gut issue of accomplice testimony and that a deal was made between the witness and the
prosecution in return for her testimony against the accused. Obviously any
juror would be interested in the following questions by virtue of this opening
salvo and its sarcastic tone. It should be noted, however, that this opening
salvo suffers from the fact that the witness is asked the "why" question
which could lead to a devastating answer if the witness had had her wits
about her. She could have said something such as: "I was always a bit player
and the police told me if I was truthful on the witness stand they would not
charge me because your client was a major drug dealer who was the one
that really deserved to be charged." Instead of asking the last question it
would have been safer, although perhaps not as catchy, to ask "Q. You say
you are guilty, yet you are in the witness-box, are you not? A. Yes. Q. And
he says he is not guilty and he is in the prisoner dock is he not? A. Yes. Q.
And the reason for this rather strange occurrence is because you made a
deal with the prosecution . . ."

Another example of an opening question which has gained the reputation of a classic occurred in the trial of Alfred Rouse who was charged
with murder.[19] The Crown's theory was that the accused picked up a hitch-
hiker, killed him and set fire to his car so as to make any identification
impossible. Rouse wanted to leave the impression that he himself was killed.
The defence called an expert to establish that the fire could have been started
accidentally. Sir Norman Birkett opened his cross-examination for the
Crown this way:

Q. What is the co-efficient of the expansion of brass?
A. I'm afraid I cannot answer that question offhand.
Q. If you do not know, so say.

---

19 S. Tremayne (ed.), *Trial of Alfred Arthur Rouse*. Noteable British Trial Series, (Toronto:
    Canada Law Book, 1931), p. 244.

A. What do I mean by the term? You want to know what is the expansion of the metal under heat?

Q. I asked you what is the co-efficient of the expansion of brass, do you know what it means?

A. Put that way, probably I do not.

Q. You are an engineer?

A. I dare say I am. I am not a Doctor, nor a crime investigator nor an amateur detective, I am an engineer.

Q. What is the co-efficient of the expansion of brass? You do not know?

A. No, not put that way.

The expert was immediately thrown off balance by this question and his expertise was thrown into doubt.

Another example of Norman Birkett's love for the opening salvo came when he cross-examined the prosecution expert, Sir Bernard Spilsbury in the Mancini trial.[20] It was the Crown's theory that the deceased's body (a prostitute) was found in a trunk beaten over the head with a hammer, although morphine was found in her body. Spilsbury gave his "decided an unqualified opinion" that the fracture to the head of the deceased had been produced by a blunt object, possibly a hammer which was discovered in the cellar; the fracture being received when she was alive and was the cause of death. Birkett, in attempting to show Spilsbury's opinion was not based on fact, and obviously feeling that a "theory" leaves a weaker impression, began:

Q: "Your views are rightly described as theories, are they not?"

Spilsbury was an honest and shrewd witness.

A: "I am not quite sure that is right, when my opinion is based on experience."

Q: "They are the results of your experience, but are mere theories without question?"

A: "They are, in the sense that they are not facts."

and later

Q: "You will concede at once that there are many other possible theories available to account for the death of this woman?"

Another approach to throw a witness off balance and gain an early advantage with the jury at the outset of the cross-examination is to catch that witness in a contradiction—not necessarily on a major point—with a previous answer given under oath or by a document or letter. In this way counsel can immediately change any favourable impression the witness made with the jury on direct examination. The witness, now wary of the

---

20 *Defenders' Triumph* by Edgar Lustgarten, Publisher Wingate — Norman Birkett defending Tony Mancini.

cross-examiner, may be more willing to co-operate in answering leading questions.

Oscar Wilde prosecuted the Marquess of Queensberry for criminal libel because the latter alleged he had committed indecent acts with young boys. Wilde had testified in-chief that he was 39 years of age. Edward Carson, who cross-examined Wilde, knew that Wilde was not 39. On this point, he cross-examined thusly:[21]

> Q. You stated your age was 39. I think you are over 40. You were born on the 16th October, 1854? (holding up his birth certificate)
> A. I have no wish to pose as being young. I am 39 or 40. You have my certificate and that settles the matter.
> Q. But being born in 1854 makes you more than 40?
> A. Ah! Very well.
> Q. What age is Lord Alfred Douglas? (His alleged lover and son of the Marquess of Queensberry.)
> A. Lord Alfred Douglas is about 24, and was between twenty and twenty-one years of age when I first met him.

Although it would appear at first blush that Wilde was impeached on a small point, it was a stupid lie which would have impacted on the jury. It was highlighted by the follow-up question, comparing his age to Lord Alfred Douglas whom Wilde had admitted to staying with in different cities.

Some years ago in the Ontario Supreme Court Assizes the accused John Brown was charged with defrauding the government. He had operated the Browndale Schools for emotionally disturbed children and received government funding based on the budget he had given the government, with his costs to be supported by audited statements. These statements were alleged to be false. Mr. Brown was also a Member of Parliament. The trial had lasted some 40 to 50 trial days before the cross-examination began. The following is a reconstruction of the opening of Irwin Koziebrocki's cross-examination on behalf of the Crown.[22]

> Q. Mr. Brown, you testified in examination-in-chief that you had nothing to do with the running of a Corporation known as Browndale International Ltd. and that you did not hold an executive position with that company?
> A. That is correct.
> Q. Do you recall a recent civil action commenced in the Supreme Court of Ontario against Browndale International Ltd.?
> A. Yes.
> Q. I'm showing you an affidavit filed in the Supreme Court of Ontario in that civil matter. Will you look at this affidavit and tell me whether it is yours?
> A. Yes it is.

---

21 *The Trials of Oscar Wilde,* William Hodge and Company Ltd. (London, Edinburgh, Glasgow) edited by H. Montgomery Hyde, Barrister-at-Law of the Middle Temple.

22 From the transcript of *R. v. Brown.*

Q. Did you sign it before a commissioner of oaths?

A. Yes I did.

Q. Please read paragraph one of your affidavit aloud.
[witness reads]

Q. Is it not true to say the paragraph you just read, and sworn to be true, states that you are the president of Browndale International Ltd. and have knowledge of the workings of the corporation?

A. Yes.

Q. How do you reconcile your evidence today with what you swore to in your affidavit?

A. [long pause—no answer given]

MR. K. My Lord may Mr. Brown's affidavit be the next exhibit?

HIS LORDSHIP. Yes, Exhibit 1501.

Q. Since you are unable to answer my last question Mr. Brown, let's see if you can answer this one. You testified that you were personally unfamiliar with the provisions and workings of the Children's Mental Health Centres Act which came into effect in Ontario on April 1, 1971?

A. That's right.

Q. Do you recall whether you were a member of the Provincial Legislature in 1970 and 1971?

A. Yes I was.

Q. Is it not true that during that time you were the health critic for the New Democratic Party?

A. Yes I was.

Q. How can you say that you had no knowledge of the workings of the Children's Mental Health Centres Act under the control of the Ministry of Health when you were the health critic for the opposition at the time this legislation was debated and passed.?

A. I personally had nothing to do with the passing of the Act.

Q. Well let me read to you a speech made by yourself in the Ontario Legislature as recorded in Hansard dated March 15, 1971.
[At which time a lengthy passage from Hansard was read in which Mr. Brown congratulated the government at length for its farsightedness in passing an important piece of legislation as the Children's Mental Health Centres Act and praising the virtues of various provisions contained in that Act.]

Q. Mr. Brown, in light of your own words as recorded in Hansard, how can you maintain that you did not have any knowledge of the provisions of the Children's Mental Health Centres Act?

A. [no answer]

Shortly thereafter Court adjourned for the day. The next day John Brown changed his plea to guilty of defrauding the government of Ontario of several millions of dollars.

Mr. Brown had testified some five days in-chief. Irwin Koziebrocki's cross-examination lasted approximately 45 minutes. Mr. Brown had been destroyed at the very outset of the cross-examination by contradictory material to the point where he could not recover. It should be noted that while Mr. Koziebrocki asked some open-ended questions giving the witness the opportunity to explain his inconsistencies, the witness was unable to do so, a result which Mr. Koziebrocki was no doubt confident.

In the book, *Sir Patrick Hastings: His Life and Cases*[23] the author recounts Hastings' first question to the plaintiff who was suing for damages as a result of an alleged serious injury caused by a box of falling oranges. The plaintiff and his family had apparently made many claims against insurance companies over the past years. Hastings had carefully rehearsed his first question, which was: "I am going to suggest to you that this case is a deliberate fraud, and that for years past you and your family have lived by making fraudulent claims upon insurance companies." According to the author, the "judge sat up, obviously puzzled, the jury came rapidly to attention, and plaintiff's counsel seemed frankly amazed. As for the plaintiff, he looked most uncomfortable and glanced miserably around the Court."

In 1910, Dr. Crippen was convicted of murdering his wife. At a time when the police investigation was at a dead end Crippen panicked and with his mistress fled to Europe en route to Canada. The following is an extract from the opening cross-examination by Mr. Muir of Dr. Crippen as reported in the Notable British Trial series.

Q: On the early morning of first February you were left alone in your house with your wife?

A: Yes.

Q: She was alive?

A: She was.

Q: Do you know of any person in the world who has seen her alive since?

A: I do not.

Q: Do you know of any person in the world who has ever had a letter from her since?

A: I do not.

Q: Do you know of any person in the world who can prove any fact showing that she ever left that house alive?

A: Absolutely not. I have told Mr. Dew (Scotland Yard Inspector) exactly all the facts.

In a few short questions counsel secured from the accused that he was probably the last person to have seen or heard from his wife. Damming stuff.

A German named Gruban who became naturalized in England retained Patrick Hastings to sue Handel Booth for damages for fraud. It was just at the time of WWI and Gruban had been advised to speak to Booth so as to be able to gain favours for the former's company with the Minister of

---

23 H. Montgomery Hyde.

Munitions. Booth wanted a secret commission of 10% of a 65,000 pound contract. At the time Gruban refused. Booth had already written out 600 pounds on a piece of paper which he crumpled up and threw in a wastebasket in anger. Booth told Gruban he would become interned and the only way to remain free was to hand over his shares in his company and let Booth act as his trustee, with Booth taking no more part in his company. Booth was scared and agreed but was subsequently interned. The following opening salvo by Hastings to Booth who had vehemently denied demanding a secret commission resulted, according to the author,[24] in shaking Booth's confidence profoundly and shows how counsel effectively used a document to help destroy a witness:

> 'Mr. Handel Booth, would it be dishonest for a director of a company to seek for himself a secret commission on his company's earnings?'
> To which Booth with great emphasis said, 'Of course it would.'
> 'If you did such a thing, would you consider yourself a rogue?'
> To which Booth answered even more empathetically: 'Of course.'
> 'Did you do that very thing when you were a Director of Gruban's company?'
> To which Booth, almost speechless with indignation, shouted: 'Never, never, never!'
> 'Very well,' said Hastings quietly, 'take a look at this piece of paper.'
> It was the piece of paper on which Booth had made his note, and which he had thrown angrily into the waste paper basket when Gruban had refused to agree to the commission, and which Gruban had later picked out and kept. Booth turned the paper over and over again, and as he did so Hastings read out the words written on it: 'Full ten percent to F.H.B. Say £600 or £650.'
> 'Who is F.H.B.?' said Hastings.
> The answer was, 'I know only one, myself.'
> 'What was the ten percent on?'
> 'I do not know.'
> 'What was the amount of the Birmingham contract?'
> 'Six thousand pounds.'

When Seddon was tried for the murder of Miss Barrow by arsenic he was prosecuted by Rufus Isaacs, considered the great cross-examiner of his day. Rufus Isaac's first question: "Mr. Seddon, did Miss Barrow live with you from July, 1910 till September, 1911?" "Yes." said Seddon. "Did you like her?" Seddon was taken aback by the subtlety of the question and repeated the question. "Did I like her?" He could not say yes because the jury had already heard of her repellent nature, but if he said no, that answer could strengthen his motive to kill her. Seddon displayed dexterity of mind in his response. "She wasn't a woman you could have been in love with,

---

24 *Six Great Advocates. A Series of Talks* by Lord Birkett, Penguin Books.

but I sympathized with her deeply." Apparently the jury did not feel he sympathized with her enough and convicted Seddon of murder.[25]

Sir Patrick Hastings, a renowned English barrister, rose to cross-examine the plaintiff in a civil case.[26] He had learned from Edward Carson, another renowned English barrister that if counsel was to accuse a witness of fraud he should make this abundantly clear at the very outset of his cross-examination. Hastings' first question was carefully planned and rehearsed:

> "I am going to suggest to you that this is a case of deliberate fraud, and that for years past you and your family have lived by making fraudulent claims upon insurance companies."

In this carefully thought out question Hastings made the jury aware of his client's side of the story from the outset of the trial. He captured the jurors' complete attention with this startling opening salvo while no doubt unsettling the witness. He then followed up with a series of questions that were connected to his first question. Hastings began with his first claim of which his clients had detailed knowledge:

> 'Five years ago, did you father buy a derelict house at this address?' Hastings then gave him the address.
>
> 'I don't know.'
>
> 'Did your brother repair that house?'
>
> 'I don't know.'
>
> 'Did you yourself redecorate that house?'

As the witness hesitated, Hastings proceeded to prod his memory.

> 'Please don't say you don't know, because I hold in my hand your actual bill that was sent in to the insurance company.' He handed him the bill.
>
> 'Is that your bill?'
>
> 'It seems to be.'
>
> 'Is that bill grossly excessive?'
>
> 'Certainly not.'
>
> 'Did any living person ever see what work you did upon those premises, except your father, your brother and yourself?'
>
> 'I don't know.'
>
> 'Within two days of your work being completed, was that house burned to the ground?'

---

25 *Six Great Advocates. A Series of Talks* by Lord Birkett, Penguin Books.
26 Although this was a civil case there is much to learn for criminal counsel.

'There was a fire.'

'And were your family responsible for those premises being set alight?'

Before the witness could answer this question, his counsel sprang indignantly to his feet in protest. What possible relevance, asked Mathews, could there be in such a question? How dare Hastings attack his client like this? It was an outrage, and he asked the judge to disallow this and any more questions on the same lines.

The judge appeared to hesitate for a few moments. Then he sternly addressed the defendants' counsel.

'Mr. Hastings, I understand you are alleging that the claim in the present action is a fraud?'

Hastings bowed in agreement.

'And you are proposing to attack the plaintiff's character by alleging that he has been a party to earlier frauds?'

'I am, my lord.'

'Very well. I shall not disallow the questions. But I must point out to you that you are incurring a grave responsibility and may well be running considerable risk. You understand that to charge a man with being a party to a fraud of this nature is a matter of the utmost gravity?'

There was now no turning back for Patrick Hastings.

'I do, my lord,' he said, 'and I am going to suggest that this witness and his family have been parties to the same fraud on no less than thirteen previous occasions, and for precisely the same purpose – namely to swindle insurance companies.'

It is not always possible or even desirable to commence a cross-examination with the aforementioned approaches. The questioner may wish to put the witness off-guard and lull him or her into a false sense of security. He or she may use the building blocks approach in order to obtain the desired result, as for example, attempting to trap the witness by closing off all of his possible escape routes. Counsel will, therefore, want to commence by putting the witness at ease, making the point he or she wishes to make in an easy manner. There may be some doubtful areas that the cross-examiner wishes to ask about. If such questions are put at the beginning of the cross-examination the significance of any unfavourable testimony elicited may not be as appreciated or remembered as it might if dealt with later on.[27]

The End

It is always ideal to finish with a question which elicits a strong answer favourable to the questioner's case. This is the last answer the triers-of-fact

---

27 Counsel should employ the step by step or probing approach discussed in the previous heading "The Beginning."

will hear and accords with the principle of recency—the concept that the last heard is the last retained. But this is easier said than done even when counsel has carefully prepared a strong finish because the earlier course of cross-examination may not have followed the path he or she originally planned.

A real judgment call for the cross-examiner occurs when counsel does make a telling point but has not yet completed his or her planned cross-examination. Should counsel sit down with this strong finish or should he or she continue with the rest of the prepared cross-examination? Much of course will depend on how much of the cross-examination is left and the number of significant points yet to be made. However in a proper case counsel should not be hesitant about foregoing the remainder of the cross-examination if he or she can sit down having scored heavily against the witness with his or her last question. The jury will remember this telling point which may not have had the same impact if the cross-examination continued dealing with lesser points.

Some counsel, when ending their cross-examinations, will summarize several points that have been made throughout cross-examination in order to emphasize that which is favourable to their client. For example, in an identification case:

Q. If we can summarize some of your testimony then Mr. Smith—you first saw the accused when he crossed the street.
A. Yes.
Q. You had just looked up from working on a car.
A. Yes.
Q. You saw the accused for no more than three seconds as he passed by you.
A. Yes.
Q. You really saw him from a side view only.
A. That's right.
Q. He was wearing a hat with the brim pulled down over his forehead.
A. Yes.
Q. He was wearing sunglasses.
A. Yes.
Q. The collar of his coat was pulled up.
A. Yes.
Q. You did not see him in a line-up.
A. No.
Q. The first time you saw him since then was today, as he sits here in the prisoner's dock 11 months after.
A. Yes.
Q. You were told by Sgt. Black when you came to court the man who committed the robbery would probably be in the courtroom.
A. Yes.
Q. And you know that the man who would be charged with the robbery would be sitting in the prisoner's dock.

A. Yes.

Such a technique can be useful, particularly before a jury, as it presents a cohesive and succinct picture of the salient points made during cross-examination, which may have been lengthy. Some of the points may not have been easily made during the cross-examination and may have taken some time to achieve so that the jury may then have lost something when compared to the forceful impact that summarization can accomplish.

An example of the lying witness who was destroyed by Norman Birkett (later Lord Birkett of Ulverston), occurred in a civil case when Birkett's client was suing a cab company for damages as a result of the plaintiff being injured in one of the defendant's cabs. The plaintiff claimed that the cab driver was driving too fast given the greasy state of the roads. The driver testified he was going at a slow pace the whole time.[28] Here Birkett succinctly summed up parts of the witness's testimony incorporating some of what others had said and after he delivered his punch line one can imagine the jurors, with smiles on their faces, nodding in agreement.

BIRKETT: You say you were travelling quite slowly?
WITNESS: Yes.
BIRKETT: Not fast at all, but quite slowly?
WITNESS: That's right.
BIRKETT: And you drew out to pass another vehicle?
WITNESS: Correct.
BIRKETT: Still not going fast?
WITNESS: Yes.
BIRKETT   (after a pause): Let us just see, Mr. —. You skidded slightly?
WITNESS: Yes.
BIRKETT: Mounted the pavement?
WITNESS: Yes.
BIRKETT: Hit a plate glass window and smashed that?
WITNESS: Right.
BIRKETT: Knocked over two or three stalls, loaded with fruit and vegetables outside a shop?
WITNESS: Correct.
BIRKETT: Knocked down one policeman and two pedestrians?
WITNESS: I'm afraid I did.
BIRKETT: And finally knocked down a lamp-post?
WITNESS: Yes.
BIRKETT: (after a further pause): Well, now, I wonder if you would like to estimate how much more damage you might have done if you had been going fast?

---

28 *The Life of Lord Birkett of Ulverston* by H. Montgomery Hyde, Published by Hamish Hamilton, London.

In the manslaughter trial of four Toronto police officers[29] charged with the killing of Otto Vass an eyewitness had described during examination-in-chief how two of the officers had beaten Mr. Vass, whom according to the witness, Ms. P, was powerless to resist. The witness had not seen how the altercation started when Mr. Vass had suddenly and unprovoked struck one of the two officers. The following questions in cross-examination sum up a portion of the witness's evidence-in-chief in a way which makes the thrust of the witness's evidence-in-chief appear illogical or help to confirm the defence position that Mr. Vass was in a manic state when pain would not affect him as it would a normal person. Either conclusion was helpful to the defence and at the very least neutralizing the damaging effect achieved during examination-in-chief.

Q. Ms. P, it is true, is it not, that the officers were struggling with this man when he was kicking at them?

A. Yes.

Q. And it is true that they were trying to restrain him, or at least one of them, the officer who had him in the headlock. Is that correct?

A. I believe so.

Q. And Mr.—Mr. Vass, the man who was on the ground, he was—when he was no longer resisting, the officers stopped trying to restrain him?

A. Could you repeat that, sir, please?

Q. When Mr. Vass was no longer resisting, the officers stopped trying to subdue him, stopped hitting him.

A. Yes.

Q. So let me understand if I have all this right. Mr. Vass is lying on his back. Correct?

A. Correct.

Q. One officer is at the head of him in a squat position with a headlock on him. Correct?

A. Yes.

Q. And as you say punching him a number of times. That's your position?

A. Yes.

Q. Is that correct?

A. Yes.

Q. And whilst this is going on, he's being beaten with a billy on his legs.

A. Yes.

Q. And he is screaming.

A. Yes.

Q. And at the same time, he is kicking out a number of times and is able to kick a baton out of the officer's hands.

---

29 *R. v. Lemaitre, Duncan, Bevalaqua and Le*, Ontario Court of Justice, September, October, 2003, before Justice Lesage. Mr. Vass had a long history of mental illness and at times, without reason, would become violent. Although he died suddenly when the fray was over, his injuries were all superficial, non life-threatening. The cause of death was debated at trial.

A. Yes, sir.

Q. And it would appear that the blows you describe to the face did not make him dizzy enough or at least cause him to stop kicking.

A. Can you please repeat that?

Q. Apparently, the blows you described did not make him dizzy enough to stop him from resisting.

A. I guess not.

Q. Right. And the blows from the billy and whatever pain resulted from that did not stop him from kicking out with enough accuracy to kick the baton out of the hands of the officer. Is that right?

A. Yes.

Counsel, however, should be cautious with reiteration of this kind. If the witness has not been cemented to the answers given earlier he or she may take the opportunity during the summarization to change or waffle on some of the answers previously given, which will detract from what the cross-examiner is trying to achieve. If this happens, the cross-examiner will have lost considerably because he will not only be unsuccessful in his goal but he will also have to go back and try to resurrect the earlier evidence. His rhythm will have been destroyed and it will be difficult to hide his obvious frustration.

THE EMBARRASSING QUESTION

There are times when it is necessary to ask a witness an embarrassing question. Counsel should not retreat from asking such questions if they are relevant to his or her case even though they may evoke tears or an emotional outburst from the witness. However, the questioner does not wish to incur the hostility of the jury or create sympathy for the witness by asking intimate personal questions which cause the witness to feel shame or hurt. In order to deal with this situation a statement should be made to the witness before asking the question, indicating that a question or questions that may be embarrassing or painful will be asked, that counsel dislikes doing so but that it is necessary in order to develop the case. If the witness is having difficulty answering because of an emotional upset, the cross-examiner should, before the opponent has the opportunity to do so, suggest that he is not opposed to a short recess so that the witness can regain her composure.

THE WITNESS WHO IS BOTH FAVOURABLE AND UNFAVOURABLE

The objectives of cross-examination break down into two categories: eliciting favourable testimony or discrediting or neutralizing the witness or his testimony. There will be times when both of these categories apply to the same witness. When this situation presents itself counsel should begin with eliciting the favourable testimony. If counsel commences his or her cross-examination in the destructive mode the witness may not be in any mood to be forthcoming later with favourable evidence.

If counsel can elicit significant favourable testimony and also feels he or she can severely damage the credibility of the witness then an important choice will probably have to be made. Although not always true, damaging the credibility of the witness can impact on a witness's entire testimony with the result that the favourable testimony will be undermined. A jury could be understandably skeptical of the counsel who argues that you can have your cake and eat it too, although the jury would normally be charged that it can believe some, none, or all or a witness's testimony. In some cases therefore, counsel may have to decide whether it is more worthwhile to forego the destructive part of her cross-examination and that decision will depend on how damaging the witness was as opposed to how helpful he or she may be.

WATCHING THE CLOCK

Adjournments, whether for coffee breaks, lunch, overnight or for the weekend may negatively affect what appears to be a fruitful cross-examination. Counsel's momentum will be broken and the witness, given a breather, can collect his or her thoughts or speak to others, including witnesses on the same side. The cross-examiner should therefore keep his or her eye on the clock so that there is time to ask those questions which should be asked before there is a break in the cross-examination.

It would be helpful to inquire of the trial judge (or the Court clerk) at the outset what are his/her normal break times during the day. If during cross-examination you feel that you require the lunch hour or overnight or even a short break to rethink some of your planned cross-examination it has been my experience that the trial judge would be amenable, particularly if you are close to a break time. Do not be fearful or embarrassed to tell the trial judge that you are nearing the end of your cross-examination and you would like some time to review your notes. You may even wish to request a break after examination-in-chief so that you can review your notes before starting your cross-examination.

11

Cross-Examination of Certain Categories of Witnesses

"Lies are like cockroaches, if you see one there are bound to be others."[1]

THE LYING WITNESS

During the first few years of young counsel's courtroom practice he or she may feel that 50 per cent of the witnesses testifying against his or her client are lying. By the time counsel has travelled the road to senior status that figure has no doubt dropped drastically. This change of attitude comes with life experienced both inside and outside the courtroom. During the early years when youth is so idealistic, defence counsel often feel that they must automatically accept everything their clients tell them as the truth. They find it difficult to distinguish between a stranger to the truth and an honestly mistaken witness. As times goes on they still hopefully take a strong position on behalf of the client but their visions become less blurred as they learn more about life. It becomes easier to distinguish between the honestly mistaken witness and the lying witness or the witnesses who shade the truth by placing undue emphasis on some parts of their testimony or too little emphasis on other parts. In the later years defence counsel come to realize that some witnesses fool themselves as to what the truth really is. They even come to doubt some of their own clients.

Unearthing a motive to lie is obviously very helpful in exposing a liar. There are of course many different reasons for a witness to lie or exaggerate the truth: vengeance, monetary gain such as a reward or because of an ongoing civil suit or domestic claim against the accused or even an application for compensation before a criminal injuries compensation board; a preconceived bias or dislike of the accused, or to deflect blame from a friend

---

1 Nelson DeMille: Night Fall

or close one, or themselves, or to gain favour from the authorities with respect to criminal or immigration issues.[2] Such motives can be easily identifiable but often there are motives to lie which exist but cannot be identified. For this reason it should not be held against the defence that a motive to lie does not appear in the evidence. In any event, to require the defence to show a motive to lie would be to place upon the accused the burden to prove his or her innocence which of course is unacceptable.[3] The absence of a demonstrative motive to make a false allegation does not necessarily mean there is no such motive and an absence of a motive does not establish that the witness is telling the truth.[4]

It is an error for a trial judge to conclude that an accused has a motive for not telling the truth because he or she does not want to be convicted. Such reason is contrary to the presumption of innocence and creates an almost insurmountable disadvantage for the accused.[5]

How does one tell an untruthful witness? Often it is not possible to do so because some liars are very adept at their deceit, while witnesses who are nervous due to their inexperience in the witness stand may give off false impressions as to their credibility. However, there are physical warning signals which telegraph that point in the witness's testimony where he or she may be in distress. Shifting about in the witness-box, averting the eyes, fleeting facial expressions that betray what a person is actually thinking, placing a hand to the mouth, evasiveness, sudden changes in voice level, pregnant pauses before answering, quarrelsomeness, a tightening of the lips to suppress anger, smiling without using the muscles around the eyes, answering questions with questions, or a sudden loss of memory or hazy recollection when there was no such impairment in direct examination are some of the signs indicating a witness who may be less than truthful.[6]

However, I would make the point, as in *R. v. Norman*, and other cases referred to in the Chapter, "Observation and Recollection," that the content of the witness's testimony is a more significant test of credibility and reliability than a number of the accepted physical signs of a false witness. In this regard you will seek self contradictions from the witness, conflicts with the testimony of other credible witnesses and documents, and testimony

---

2   The reader is referred to the Chapter, "Cross-Examination of the Jailhouse Informant and Analogous Witnesses" for additional possible motives to lie.

3   *R. v. F. (A.)* (1996), 30 O.R. (3d) 470 (Ont. C.A.).

4   *R. v. Batte* (2000), 49 O.R. (3d) 321 (Ont. C.A.).

5   *R. v. B. (L.)* (1993), 82 C.C.C. (3d) 189 (Ont. C.A.) at 190; *R. v. Murray* (1997), 115 C.C.C. (3d) 225 (Ont. C.A.); *R. v. Trombley* (1998), 126 C.C.C. (3d) 495 (Ont. C.A.), affirmed (1999), 134 C.C.C. (3d) 576 (S.C.C.).

6   The May 17th 1999 edition of the Toronto Star reported some findings of a study to be presented that week to the American Psychiatric Association which found that during a deception, nasal tissues became engorged with blood causing them to swell with the scratching of their nose. The study refers to 23 other non-verbal and language indicators, including: leaning forward when talking, averting their gaze and speech errors.

that is improbable or offends common sense. The demeanour of fraudsmen belies their purpose, yet fools their victims, and the child who can lie with a straight face is not that unusual. It has been said that nervous indications from the witness or quarrelsomeness reflect on a witness's credibility but that witness may exhibit those characteristics in their everyday life.

It is important for counsel to decide how she will approach the witness in cross-examination. If the decision is to approach the witness as a liar rather than as an honestly mistaken witness counsel should make sure that she has a good chance of success because if she fails, the witness's evidence-in-chief will be fortified. The cross-examiner's opponent will underscore to the jury that the witness withstood a searching cross-examination and therefore should be believed. A witness who stands up well under cross-examination will obviously be more impressive than a witness who looks good during examination-in-chief.

Recognizing the Lying Witness

"The witness is perjuring himself, your honor."

© Criminal Lawyer's Newsletter.

The questioner's manner with the witness who is being attacked as a liar will not always be the same and will depend on the nature of the evidence that the witness gives. If the witness has given obviously damaging testimony against a client, such as an accomplice who testifies that he or she saw the client commit the offence, then there is no need to use a friendly approach. Neither the witness nor the jury will expect that. It may be desirable to use a certain tone to convey disbelief or disapproval of the witness's answer. This approach may cause some weaker or slow-thinking witnesses to become less certain about their responses and to reconsider or backtrack about some of their evidence. With such witnesses questions should be put quickly and forcefully so that the witness does not have time to invent answers and will be overcome by the strong personality of the cross-examiner.

There may be situations where the cross-examiner does not want the witness to know that he or she will be attacking his credibility. Counsel may wish to

1.   close off later avenues of escape before springing the trapdoor shut,[7]
2.   elicit favourable testimony first, or
3.   lull the witness into a false sense of security.

In such instances counsel will employ a friendly attitude so that the witness hopefully will feel relaxed and will not set himself or herself against the cross-examiner from the outset. The questioner should conceal his purpose by not letting his voice or manner show that he wants a "yes" response or he may receive a "no" answer. It may do no harm to flatter a witness to obtain favourable testimony, but a clever witness will probably become extra-cautious. With such a witness, the tact that both he and the examiner are mutual seekers of the truth could be fruitful.

A technique that has been used with success is to let the witness think that the cross-examination is over and just as the witness is about to leave the stand counsel says: "Oh, I have one further question." That one further question should be an important one which counsel has purposely kept back for this moment. Because the witness has relaxed his or her tension and mental concentration he or she may be caught off-guard, producing good results for the cross-examiner.

In preparing for cross-examination a recommended exercise for counsel is to picture the scene or situation in his or her mind and follow it through, asking himself or herself—did this witness say or do what a reasonable person would have done or said in the same circumstances? The following questions have been suggested as ones counsel should ask himself or herself about the witnesses: How did the witness come to be there? What was he doing? How much would he have seen or heard? Why does he remember? How does he know that? What would he have done if that really happened? Whom would he have told? How did they find him! Why should he lie? In the last analysis, the triers-of-fact will not believe that which goes against their human experience. Counsel will therefore look to find improb-

---

7   This technique is discussed in detail in Chapter, "General Techniques of Cross-Examination."

abilities or a story that is internally inconsistent or inconsistent with other evidence.

Many of the techniques described in the Chapter, "General Techniques of Cross-Examination" are applicable to the lying witness.

One method that has been suggested to confuse the lying witness is the "skip-around" technique. With this technique counsel might start his or her cross-examination in the middle of the story, skip to the end, and then back to the middle. It is said that the truthful witness will not be confused because he or she is speaking from impressions on the mind, but where the witness is lying he or she is speaking from an invented story memorized in chronological order and which will break down when tested with this technique. By changing this subject-matter back and forth and creating a lack of continuity an untruthful witness will become confused with prepared answers.

However, to use this technique could become confusing and boring for the jurors at trial as they will have trouble following the evidence, particularly since they will have less knowledge of the background of the case than the witness. Also, if the witness is caught in an inconsistency he has the excuse of saying that he was confused because of the lack of an organized pattern of questioning. With this hip-hop technique it would be difficult to use the transcript of the preliminary hearing for impeachment purposes at trial because there was no logical line of inquiry pursued by the cross-examiner at the preliminary hearing and the jurors might become lost as to what you are attempting to achieve.

One of the best approaches to use when dealing with the lying witness is the same approach as for the honestly mistaken witness—ask questions regarding collateral matters or minor details surrounding the event not directly connected to the main story which the witness has not prepared. It will be difficult for the witness to answer such questions because he has no impressions on his mind to draw upon. The witness will have to invent his evidence. The questioner's approach, therefore, is to have the witness enlarge on the details of his story in order to increase the chances of contradicting his evidence, showing that his story is improbable or showing that the witness does not remember things which he should remember if his story is true.

This technique of enlarging on details is used by Crown attorneys in testing the truthfulness of an alibi. Where a particular time of the day is an issue, the Crown will ask questions not only bearing on the date and time in question but also on what the witness did in the earlier and later parts of the day, evening, or even week. This is to ascertain if the witness can remember those events or is confused or is inconsistent within himself or with others, so as to cast doubt on the witness's recollection or veracity about the material time. That is why it is important to obtain a signed statement by the alibi witness as soon after the event as possible. If the witness is cross-examined at trial months after the event as to how she could recall with any accuracy the date and time of the accused's whereabouts she will be able to testify that she refreshed her memory just before testifying from the statement she gave so close to the time of the event in question. See Chapter, "The Defence of Alibi."

Counsel can increase the difficulty for the witness by asking questions in a rapid-fire manner so that the witness does not have time to fabricate proper answers. As the witness continues to invent, without time to think, the risk increases that his or her answers will come in conflict with indisputable facts. If the witness is answering truthfully he will not hesitate in his answers but if answering falsely he will be detected. If these questions are asked at a preliminary inquiry and are then repeated at trial, particularly in a different order, the witness may well answer differently and become entangled in self-contradictions and could be contradicted by others. An example of such rapid-fire cross-questioning is described by Wrottesley as follows:[8]

Q. Where was the conversation held?
Q. What time of day?
Q. Who was present?
Q. Were they sitting or standing?
Q. How did he come to the place?
Q. Who did he meet on the way?
Q. How was he dressed—and the other party?
Q. Did they speak loud or low?
Q. Did they eat or drink together—and what?
Q. Did anyone come in while they were talking?
Q. Were they together?
Q. When they parted which way did they take?
Q. Who did he meet afterwards?
Q. What time did he reach his home?

The technique of seeking contradictions between witnesses by using the matching technique referred to in the earlier chapter, whether on the main points or on trivial or collateral matters, requires that the witnesses be excluded at the outset of the trial so that they will not be influenced by each other's testimony.

Normally it is the defence who requests such an order. When defence counsel fails to make such a request then Crown counsel should be wary. If the Crown witnesses are unrelated to each other insofar as their evidence on key issues is concerned, defence counsel may prefer not to request the order because he or she has a number of witnesses, some of whom do support each other and therefore there is more to gain by having his or her

---

8 F.J. Wrottesley, *The Examination of Witnesses in Court,* 3rd ed. (London: Sweet & Maxwell, 1961), p. 128.

witnesses remain in the courtroom. In such a case it would be the Crown who should seek the order for exclusion of witnesses. However, I would suggest counsel for both sides should keep their witnesses out of the courtroom during the testimony of the other witnesses as it reflects best on the Court proceedings and does not give your opponent the opportunity to criticize the credibility of your witnesses because they heard what other witnesses had to say before they testified.

The trial judge has the discretion of whether or not to grant or to refuse a party's application for an order excluding witnesses.[9] Almost invariably a judge will grant the order without counsel having to give reasons.[10] Wigmore makes the following strong argument that a motion to exclude witnesses should be granted in all cases:[11]

> It seems properly to be demandable as a right, precisely as is cross-examinatton . . . Finally, it cannot be left with the judge to say whether the resort to this expedient is needed; not even the claimant himself can know that it will do him service; he can merely hope for its success. He must be allowed to have the benefit of the chance, if *he* thinks that there is such a chance. To require him to show some probable need to the Judge, and to leave to the latter the estimation of the need, is to misunderstand the whole virtue of the expedient, and to deny it in perhaps that very situation of forlorn hope and desperate extreme when it is most valuable and most demandable.

Wigmore also stated:[12]

> But when all allowances are made, it remains true that the expedient of sequestration is (next to cross-examination) one of the greatest engines that the skill of man has ever invented for the detection of liars in a court of justice.

Experienced counsel normally ask for "the usual order" excluding witnesses so that no juror feels that the accused is requesting something special because he or she has something to fear.

Breach of an order to exclude witnesses from the courtroom does not preclude the witness from testifying but is a factor in assessing the weight of the witness's evidence.[13]

The opportunity that probably arises most often allowing counsel to attack the credibility of a witness is when the witness is caught in a contradiction between his or her testimony and a prior statement under oath or a document, letter or oral statement to another individual. Counsel may wish

---

9 P.K. McWilliams, *Canadian Criminal Evidence,* 2nd ed. (Aurora: Canada Law Book, 1984). pp. 996-997; *R. v. Dobberthien* (1974), 13 C.C.C. (2d) 513 (Alta. C.A.) *per* Allen J.A., affirmed [1975] 2 S.C.R. 560 (S.C.C.).

10 W.H. Carleton, Q.C., "Exclusion of Witnesses" (1977), Crown's Newsletter (December 1977/January 1978) p. 1.

11 Wigmore, *supra,* p. 467.

12 *Ibid.,* p. 463.

13 *R. v. Dobberthien, supra.*

to ask the witness to explain the contradiction. Asking for an explanation is usually the one question too many. If the witness is given the opportunity to explain he or she may be able to do so through modification, by claiming misunderstanding, that he or she misspoke or by any other invention. However, where one of the contradictory answers is favourable to the accused then counsel will wish to press the witness to accept that answer as being the true answer. On the other hand, counsel may wish to leave the contradiction without pinning the witness down to either answer so that counsel can later argue during submissions the witness's lack of trustworthiness.[14] See the chapter on "Prior Inconsistent Statements."

Impressing the witness with your foreknowledge may make her have second thoughts about fudging any of her answers. Professor Hegland[15] gives the example where the cross-examiner wishes to show that the witness had been drinking heavily in a bar before the accident occurred. The witness will want to play down the amount he drank. Before the witness is asked how much he had to drink the following questions are put:

> Q. Mr. W., now when you were in the bar, you were sitting next to Bud Jones, isn't that correct?
> Q. And the bartender's name is Paul, isn't it?

As Professor Hegland points out it really doesn't matter if Bud or Paul know how much the witness had to drink and it really doesn't matter whether they will testify. What matters is the witness thinks they know and they might testify. This should keep the witness honest.

Professor Hegland also points out that the way the question is asked is important:[16]

> Ask the witness with such authority and confidence that the witness will think the sky will fall if he is answers "no." If the question is asked in an unsure way the witness will sense that uncertainty and the witness will answer accordingly. So with confidence and authority the question will be asked thusly: "Now before you left the bar you had at least 5 beers, isn't that right?"

Let us suppose you have caught the witness in one or more contradictions. You may have done so by using the transcript of the preliminary hearing or a document. You now wish to ask an unrelated question of some importance. But now you do not know whether the witness will answer truthfully and in your favour. You have nothing with which to contradict him or her. Just before asking this question or even during it, open your file or the transcript of the preliminary inquiry or noticeably look at some document. The question you ask is a leading one. The witness, knowing

---

14 See also Chapter, "Prior Inconsistent Statements."

15 K.F. Hegland, *Trial and Practice Skills in a Nutshell* (St. Paul: West Publishing Co., 1978).

16 *Ibid*, p. 66.

that he or she has been contradicted earlier by something reduced to writing, should in all likelihood give you the desired answer for fear of being contradicted again by whatever you were looking at or holding in your hand.

THE HONEST WITNESS

The honest witnesses will become readily apparent to counsel by virtue of his or her demeanour, lack of bias or motive, the inherent consistency and rationality of his or her evidence and the legitimate detail that permeates their testimony. Their demeanour and evidence has the ring of truth. From this witness you will attempt to seek all that you can that confirms or supports the client's defence. Attacking the honest witness that has damaging testimony against your client only serves to give her the opportunity to re-emphasize what she stated on examination-in-chief. When you feel that you are cross-examining an honest witness to obtain helpful testimony, try to appeal to their sense of fairness and reason at the appropriate moment in your cross after you feel you are making in-roads in your cross-examination.

An example of counsel appealing to a witness's sense of reason and fairness is in the following case, *R. v. Ahmadoun*, where the accused was charged with personation of a peace officer in that he falsely passed himself off as a Court officer to a receptionist in order to serve one of the employees of the company with a summons. As a result the receptionist paged the employee to come to the reception area where she was served with the summons by the accused. The defence was that the accused told the receptionist witness that he was there to serve Court papers on the employee, not that he was a Court officer. The cross-examination went thusly:

Q. Ms. D, you told the Court that you were first interviewed by the police about this matter some two months after it occurred.

A. Yes.

Q. You had to cast your mind back some two months to recall what you were told by the accused.

A. Yes.

Q. You did not write down what Mr. Ahmadoun told you.

A. I did not.

Q. You would admit, just like any other human being that your memory is not as complete and accurate as a tape recorder?

A. I guess that's right.

Q. But you do recall hearing words as 'Court' and 'papers'?

A. Yes.

Q. I'm asking you to be fair here, Ms. D. Given the two month time period that passed since you were first asked to recall by the police what was said to you by the accused, is it not possible that what you heard him say was that he had Court papers to serve, not that he was a Court officer with papers?

A. Well, yes, I guess so.

In circumstances where the questioner will not be able to directly shake the witness as to the material parts of his or her testimony, a collateral attack could prove beneficial; for example, asking questions as to memory and opportunity to observe in order to qualify, modify, minimize or neutralize the testimony of this kind of witness. You challenge the witness's reliability rather than her credibility.[17] For example, if the witness is quite able to describe what the accused was wearing in a case relying on identification evidence, was the witness able to describe what other persons close by were wearing, or indeed what the witness himself or herself was wearing? If the witness is open to challenge through this route then it may be argued later that the witness could also be mistaken on the major part of his or her evidence.

It is also worthwhile to inquire of this kind of witness as well as the lying witness whether the Crown or police hinted at what other witnesses said or whether they were interviewed in the presence of other witnesses so as to be influenced against your client. Did they learn anything about the case through the media? Did the Crown or police denigrate the accused in the witness's presence? Did the police tell the witness they had other witnesses to the accused's guilt or otherwise reinforce the accused's guilt to influence the witness?

The Commission on Proceedings Involving Guy Paul Morin made Recommendation 82:

> Trial judges should be alert to the concern that honest witnesses' perceptions of events may be coloured by the existence of criminal charges against the accused, the notoreity of the crime which he or she faces, or the fact that the authorities, whom they respect, admire, and deal with, are supportive of the prosecution. Where this concern arises on the evidence, trial judges should instruct the jury to be mindful of potential colouration in assessing the evidence of these witnesses and that miscarriages of justice have been occasioned in the past due to honest, but faulty, accounts of witnesses whose perceptions were coloured by criminal charges or other external influences.

See Chapter, "Observation and Recollection."

THE MISTAKEN WITNESS

It is rare that a witness will ever admit that he or she is mistaken. A good example is in identification cases where the witness honestly believes in the correctness of his or her identification even though in cross-examtnation he or she has been shown the probabilities of mistake. The record of proven cases of mistaken identification is well documented. In most cases

---

17   See Chapter, "Observation and Recollection."

it is useless then to ask the witness outright if he is positive about his or her testimony or whether he could be mistaken.

Sir Frederick Wrottesley[18] suggests the following approach in cross-examining the mistaken witness:

> The witness has detailed an occurrence at a certain time or place, and it is your purpose to show that he was mistaken in some of the particulars, and that the inferences he drew from them were incorrect, or not justified by the facts. Your first proceeding to this end is to realise the scene in your own mind. Your fancy must paint for you a picture of the place, the persons, the accessories. You then ask the witness to repeat the story, you note its congruity or otherwise with the circumstances that accompanied it; you detect improbabilities or impossibilities. You see as he saw, and you learn in what particulars he saw imperfectly, and how he formed too hasty conclusions; how prejudice may have influenced him; how things dimly seen were by the imagination transformed into other things in his memory.

Counsel must endeavour to show, just as he or she would with the lying witness, that the mistaken witness's testimony is impossible, improbable or inconsistent within itself or with that of other witnesses or with common sense experience. This is the kind of witness that often can be approached in a friendly manner indicating that you are not challenging their honesty but after pointing out where their evidence is contradicted on other evidence or they are mistaken in some areas of their testimony, gently pushing the witness to agreeing to some doubt about his/her original evidence that hurt your client. Where the witness is intransigent, ask if he/she has ever been mistaken about what they have heard or observed. We all have been and if the witness claims perfection then his/her credibility will be questioned by the trier of fact.

An example of challenging the witness with the improbability of his damaging testimony occurred when Arthur Martin Q.C. defended the accused Lytton some decades ago after obtaining a new trial for Lytton who had been convicted of murder. Mr. Martin described the background to the *Lytton* case[19] and his approach to cross-examining a key Crown witness on a very important aspect of his testimony:

Mrs. S. left the accused Lytton's employment because of some allegedly improper conduct by him toward Mrs. S.'s 14-year-old daughter. She told her husband and brothers about this conduct with the result that K. went to Lytton's home and gave him an unmerciful beating. The next day Mr. & Mrs. S. and K. came to Lytton's home to fetch some of their daughter's belongings. Lytton, fearful of the beating warned them not to come into the house, that he had a gun. They broke down the door and Lytton shot Mr. S.

---

18 F.J. Wrottesley, *supra*, pp. 108-109.
19 Speech by Arthur Martin, as he then was, at Advocacy Seminar, April 1989, Edmonton.

in the stomach. K. ran and Lytton ran after him shooting K. three times in the back, killing him.

A neighbor saw all of this from his verandah, having been awakened by the noise. He testified that Lytton had gone back into the house, stayed there for some five minutes, came outside, saw Mr. S. getting to his feet and killed him by repeatedly hitting him over the head with a heavy rifle.

The accused's position was that he was guilty of manslaughter, not murder on the basis that there was no five minute interval before he killed Mrs. S., that this all happened in one continued sequence of events when Lytton, crazed with fear and anger went completely out of control, killing K. and Mr. S. The defence had to wipe out the five minute interval testified to by the neighbour or else Lytton would be convicted of murder.

Mr. Martin's plan was not to be aggressive and accuse the neighbour of purposely lying but to show the improbability of his testimony. His cross-examination was a model of succinctness. Here is how it went:

> Q. Mr. Jones, the deceased Stewart was well-known to you as well as a friend?
> A. Yes.
> Q. When you saw him stagger out of the house, holding his stomach and collapse on the front lawn, you realized he must be seriously hurt?
> A. Yes.
> Q. Did you phone the police?
> A. No.
> Q. Did you call your wife to phone the police?
> A. No.
> Q. Did you phone for an ambulance or a doctor?
> A. No.
> Q. When the accused Seth Lytton came out of the house and raised the rifle above his head, did you call Seth, 'don't do it, don't hit him'?
> A. No.
> Q. Did you raise your hand or your voice during all this time to get assistance or do anything to prevent happening what occurred?
> A. No.

At this point the neighbour may well have felt he did not look very good standing there with a ringside seat to a fight and doing nothing to help the deceased. Counsel took him off the hook with an opportunity to redeem himself.

> Q. Mr. Jones, the fact is, that you were not standing there for five minutes. The interval between the first shot and the striking of Stewart all happened so quickly that you didn't have time to do anything, did you?
> A. (By a grateful witness) No.

The witness was a decent man and just like in the example of the Honest Witness, when he saw how improbable his story was, he was ready to back down.

In attempting contradictions with other witnesses, whether they be an honest or lying witness, the witness's testimony should be anchored to the same event on all of the important details such as time, place, people present and statements. Counsel should place the witnesses' evidence against each other by asking each witness the same questions to determine if there will be significantly contradictory answers. This technique should be employed at the preliminary hearing, as, for example, with witnesses who claim to have seen the same event. This way the questioner will know what not to ask these witnesses at trial and can focus on the contradictions elicited at the preliminary hearing.

The cross-examiner should inquire into the witness's observation and recollection.[20]

When challenging an answer as mistaken (or as a lie), a technique that has been employed with the witness whom has previously given a proven or about to be proven mistaken answer is to ask what was a reported favourite question of the renowned English barrister, Marshall Hall: "Are you as sure of that as of everything else you have said?"

THE BIASED WITNESS

A witness may be biased for any number of reasons, such as, greed, love, hate or revenge. The witness may not even realise that he is biased as when he feels some loyalty to the party that has called him and who he has come to like through a series of interviews; or has been unconsciously influenced by what the Crown or police or the media have told him about the accused; or feels obliged because the Crown has stayed or withdrawn his charges. A question to such a witness as: "Do you feel by testifying for the prosecution that you are on the Crown's side?," could be revealing.

Directly accusing the witness of bias will achieve nothing for counsel, as the witness will obviously deny any such allegations. Counsel's approach is to ask in a gradual way about those factors which will paint a picture of bias, such as building up the close relationship or enmity between the witness and the accused, or the numerous discussions between the witness and the police prosecutor and the negative things which the prosecutor told the witness about the accused. If counsel is confident of the witness's answer he can finish this part of the cross-examination with questions such as: "You are very close to the accused? You do not want to see him go to jail, do you? You love your son. You can't believe he'd do something like this. This has to be a mistake. You really don't like the accused? The police made it quite clear the accused is not a nice person? That's the way you feel about the accused too?" However, if counsel feels that any such questions may be

---

20 See Chapter, "Observation and Recollection."

the one question too many with that witness he should not ask it but make his point as to bias in his or her jury address.

There will be witnesses who have negative feelings against certain groups of people with the result that their testimony can be affected by their bias. As Colman[21] states:

> Pointers to such prejudice are such things as these: a note of contempt or bitterness in the voice of the witness when speaking of the relevant group or type of persons; a tendency to avoid using a person's name when it would be natural to do so; a tendency to mispronounce the name, or be uncertain about it when that is not to be expected, the use of generalizations (the word "they" is often significant).

Counsel of course should try to expose the prejudice using questions such as: "What do you mean 'they'? What do you think about those type of people?"

When the witness seems eager to say negative things about your client, it has been suggested that such phrases as: "don't try so hard to convict my client" and "I thought you'd try and get that in" would bring the point home nicely.

THE VAIN WITNESS

A vain or self-assured witness may be mistaken but it will be very difficult for such a witness to change or modify his or her testimony as the witness would perceive the slightest admission or error as a loss of self-esteem. The cross-examiner would therefore have to indicate by his or her questions that any modifications or corrections by the witness would not reflect adversely on himself. It may be that the best approach for the cross-examiner is to reveal the witness's vanity in all its glory so that his or her testimony will be judged accordingly, as for example: "Have you never made a mistake when adding up figures? Not even going back to high school? You are unusually gifted?" Or just say nothing and when making your final submissions point to the vanity of the witness who was too proud to admit that he or she could be wrong.

Then there is the vain witness who is not mistaken but is so full of himself or herself that he or she might say something out of vanity that will come back to haunt the witness. Perhaps one of the most vain witnesses ever to testify was Oscar Wilde, who unsuccessfully prosecuted the Marquess of Queensberry for criminal libel. The Marquess had alleged that Wilde had committed indecent acts with a number of young boys including

---

21   G. Colman, Q.C., *Cross-Examination: A Practical Handbook* (Capetown, South Africa: Juta and Company Limited, 1970).

his son, Lord Alfred Douglas. The following occurred during part of Wilde's cross-examination by Mr. Edward Carson which was described in the book, *The Trials of Oscar Wilde*.[22] Throughout the cross-examination it is said that Wilde scored repeatedly against Carson, but then came near the end of the cross-examination. Here, the vanity of Wilde leads him into trouble by his answer to one question. This is an excellent example of a cross-examiner seizing the moment when an unexpected answer occurs and not letting go until the damage has been done. This cross-examination is also an example of how counsel deals with an evasive witness. Note also how Carson uses the usually forbidden open-ended question "Why?" dramatically in back-to-back instances to not allow Wilde off the hook when he knows that there will be no answer that can hurt him.

Q. Do you know Walter Grainger?

A. Yes.

Q. How old is he?

A. He was about sixteen when I knew him. He was a servant at a certain house in High Street, Oxford, where Lord Alfred Douglas had rooms. I have stayed there several times. Grainger waited at table. I never dined with him. If it is one's duty to serve, it is one's duty to serve; and if it is one's pleasure to dine, it is one's pleasure to dine.

Q. Did you ever kiss him?

A. Oh, dear no. He was a peculiarly plain boy. He was, unfortunately, extremely ugly. I pitied him for it.

Q. Was that the reason why you did not kiss him?

A. Oh, Mr. Carson, you are pertinently insolent.

Q. Did you say that in support of your statement that you never kissed him?

A. No. It is a childish question.

Q. Did you ever put that forward as a reason why you never kissed the boy?

A. Not at all.

Q. Why, sir, did you mention that this boy was extremely ugly?

A. For this reason. If I were asked, why I did not kiss a door-mat, I should say because I do not like to kiss door-mats. I do not know why I mentioned that he was ugly, except that I was stung by the insolent question you put to me and the way you have insulted me throughout this hearing. Am I to be cross-examined because I do not like it?

Q. Why did you mention his ugliness?

A. It is ridiculous to imagine that any such thing could have occurred under any circumstances.

Q. Then why did you mention his ugliness, I ask you?

A. Perhaps you insulted me by an insulting question.

Q. Was that a reason why you should say the boy was ugly?

---

22 William Hodge and Company Ltd. (London, Edinburgh, Glasgow) edited by H. Montgomery Hyde, Barrister-at-Law of the Middle Temple at p. 150.

Following this last question, Wilde had trouble articulating several answers which was most unusual for such a renowned articular and glib speaker. His efforts were not made easier by Mr. Carson's "sharp staccato repetition: Why? Why? Why did you add that?" Finally Wilde answered: "You sting me and insult me and try to unnerve me; and at times one says things flippantly when one ought to speak more seriously. I admit it."

You may be in a position to bring to the witness's attention other honest evidence which contradicts what the witness has said. "Having regard to that evidence witness, do you still claim that . . .?" If the witness keeps to his/her position despite more abundant evidence to the contrary, the trier of fact will not be impressed.

THE TALKATIVE WITNESS

There are some witnesses who want to keep talking though they have answered the question. The most effective way to control such witnesses is to promptly ask the next question so that they have to direct their attention to a new answer.

However, if the witness's answers are irrelevant, irrational, nonsensical or inconsistent, encourage the continuation of such answers as they will no doubt provide you with further ammunition to impair the credibility of the witness.

THE EVASIVE WITNESS

The evasive witness also calls upon counsel's abilities to control the cross-examination. This evasion becomes apparent by the witness's tone, lack of responsiveness, slowness in answering, repeating counsel's questions before answering or asking counsel to repeat his or her questions, and relying on such answers as "I can't remember," "I don't know," and "I'm not sure."

Counsel generally should not become perturbed by this tactic. Such evasiveness will become apparent to the jury and the witness will fall into disfavour. Counsel can even continue to ask questions which would have the effect of encouraging the evasiveness. The evasiveness can be highlighted by rapid-fire questioning.

There are other ways of dealing with the evasive witness. If the witness does not respond directly to counsel's question but continues talking, counsel can highlight the witness's failure to respond by saying something such as: "Now witness, my question was—did you not tell the police that the accused was not present when the assault took place? Please answer that question." If the witness fails to respond, put the same question to him again in a firmer tone. If the witness continues in the same fashion ask the trial judge to direct the witness to answer the question.

Another approach is after the witness completes his evasive answer, ask the reporter to read back your last question and then say to the witness, "Will you answer that question please?"

Do not let the witness dance around your question. Evasiveness by the witness will be noticed by the jury and no doubt the cross-examiner will emphasize it in his or her jury address, pointing out that the trial judge had to ask the witness to answer the question. Sometimes it pays to be persistent when the witness does not respond frankly. The following is a small portion of a cross-examination of a witness called at the Kaufman Inquiry who had testified at trial how Mr. Morin had held his shears supposedly indicating a guilty mind.

> Q: Did you say (at trial) "I recall that he did seem to be holding his shears very tightly when he talked to us."
> A: I said it, but I don't remember it.
> Q: Alright. And that's not true, that's a lie under oath, is that correct?
> A: It's not accurate.
> Q: It's a lie under oath.
> A: It's not accurate.
> Q: Well, there's a difference between something not being accurate and some-thing being a lie. I'm suggesting to you that when you say, I recall that he did seem to be holding his shears very tightly when he talked to us, is a lie.
> A: Okay.[23]

The cross-examination of Oscar Wilde under the heading, "The Vain Witness" is another example of confronting the evasive witness where Edward Carson kept pushing Wilde as to why he mentioned Grainger's ugliness, causing Wilde to become argumentative and evasive.

If the witness keeps repeating the questions before answering or asks the questioner to repeat his questions this habit should be drawn to the witness's attention by pointing out that the questions are simply put and that the witness should not be having difficulty with them and that he or she should not be stalling for time in order to formulate an answer. Counsel might say to the witness something like the following: "Come now, witness, you had no trouble answering questions from my friend. Don't you want to be as fair with me as you were with him?" Accuse the witness of having a

---

23 The Commission on Proceedings Involving Guy Paul Morin, Report Vol 2, pp. 960-961. The inquiry was held to ascertain why Mr. Morin was wrongfully convicted of murder after DNA proved his innocence.

The Evasive Witness

"The witness is being evasive, your honor!"

© Cartoon Bank.

selective memory if he/she continues to respond with "I can't remember" or "I don't know" when they had no memory loss for your opponent's questions. You may of course have to resort to transcripts to refresh the witness's memory about their answers on a prior occasion.

When the witness fails to answer counsel's question within a normal time for response it should be underscored, not only for the jury, but for the record in case the matter goes to an appeal. When there is a lengthy pause after a question counsel might say: "Witness, my watch tells me 40 seconds have now passed without an answer to my question, speak please."; or "Did you hear the question witness? Did you understand the question? Then why don't you answer it?" or, "How much longer must the jury wait for your answer, witness?" Statements such as these highlight for the record these lengthy pauses which would not otherwise be detectable in a reading of the transcript.

THE EXAGGERATING WITNESS

The cross-examiner is not interested in controlling the exaggerating witness. If it appears that the witness will exaggerate his testimony he should be given every opportunity to do so including leading him into exaggerations. The exaggerations will become readily apparent to the triers-of-fact as they build up or as they are shown to come into conflict with the objective facts. This technique is often employed by Crown attorneys or those defence counsel representing police officers where allegations of brutality by the accused or complainant are made against a police officer. The cross-examiner has the medical information as to the lack of injuries suffered by the accused or evidence of lack of complaint by the accused to medical officers or other police. The cross-examiner is therefore happy to lead the accused into answers describing serious injuries or at least noticeable injuries which are not borne out by the evidence.

The exaggerating witness can be contradicted by other witnesses, documents, photographs or even videotapes, such as in an impaired driving case showing where the accused is brought into the police station to blow into the breathalyzer machine. If the arresting officers exaggerate the accused's signs of impairment in their notebooks and/or their testimony they may easily agree with your conclusion that your client was close to being a falling-down drunk. If the video which was taken very shortly after arrest shows that the client was not swaying when walking or slurring his words, you will have destroyed the officer's credibility.

An example of the cross-examination of an exaggerating witness using the transcript of the preliminary hearing is at the beginning of the Chapter, "The Preliminary Inquiry."

SYMPATHETIC WITNESSES

Counsel is somewhat at a disadvantage with a sympathetic witness such as an elderly person, a child or a victim. Their demeanour is often attractive and there can be the ring of truth about their testimony. They should be treated gently. See Chapter, "Client and Witness Interviews" under heading "The Child Witness."

Elderly witnesses should be treated with respect at all times. To do otherwise would arouse the sympathy of the jury for the witness. This is so even when bias or falsehoods by the witness are exposed. The cross-examiner should question closely the powers of perception of elderly people.[24] Are there gaps in the witness's memory that are significant with respect to an important part of the evidence which permits you to cast doubt on the

---

24   See, particularly, those areas referred to in the Chapter, "Observation and Recollection."

reliability of the witness's testimony? What was the witness's mind-set at the relevant time? How accurate were his observations? Are there any prior inconsistent statements?

Do not try to prove your intellectual superiority over the witness by being sarcastic or patronizing. The trier-of-fact will not be happy that you are taking advantage of an uneven playing field by seemingly going out of your way to embarrass these witnesses.

You may be able to turn the opposite party's sympathetic witness to a helpful witness for the defence by having him contradict a Crown witness and support some aspect of the defence case.

THE FRIENDLY HELPFUL WITNESS

There will be times when the prosecution calls a witness who can be quite helpful to the defence. This witness would appear to have a bias in favour of the accused by virtue of friendship or being a family member or other reason. The Crown has to call this witness for a proper unfolding of the narrative or to prove some point. In this instance, it would add more weight to the answers on cross-examination if the questioner stayed away from leading questions to this obviously friendly witness and proceeded as if on examination-in-chief.

As indicated earlier when there are multiple accused the witness may not know which of them you are representing when the witness takes the stand to destroy. If you have reason to believe or feel the witness may have some sympathy for your client, or at least is not hostile against your client as opposed to the other accused, you may want to start your cross-examination by introducing yourself and whom you represent. Depending on the circumstances you may get better answers.

12

Prior Inconsistent Statements

A. THE OPPONENT'S WITNESS

There are fewer more effective moments than when counsel is able to impeach a witness with what he or she had written or spoken on a prior occasion. A study was completed a number of years ago in Oregon which showed that what Oregon jurors enjoyed most about a trial "was watching a witness squirm when being impeached with a prior inconsistent statement."[1]

The purpose of the prior inconsistent statement is that it is admitted "for the limited purpose of negating the witness's credibility, so that in substance, the jury is left with nothing if they believe the prior statement was in fact made by the witness and that it countermands the testimony given in open Court."[2]

A prior inconsistent statement may come from evidence given previously which is evidenced by a transcript, a letter or other writings or an oral statement or a statement on video or audiotape. It may even be from an intercepted communication.[3] It would also include a written document expressly adopted by the witness.[4] Defence counsel have received some assistance in obtaining prior statements as a result of the Supreme Court of Canada decision in *R. v. Stinchcombe*,[5] which holds that the defence must be provided with disclosure of all statements taken from persons who have given relevant information to the authorities notwithstanding the Crown

---

1 J.W. McElhaney, Trial Notebook (Chicago: A.B.A., Litigation Section 1).

2 *R. v. Rouse (sub nom. McInroy v. R.)* (1978), 42 C.C.C. (2d) 481 per Estey J. concurring in the result, at p. 500. See *R. v. B. (K.G.)*, [1993] 1 S.C.R. 740 later in this chapter for the substantive admissibility of prior inconsistent statements based on the principled approach to the admissibility of hearsay testimony.

3 *R. v. Nygaard* (1987) 36 C.C.C. (3d) 199 at 203 (Alta. C.A.).

4 *Falovitch v. Lessard* (1979), 9 C.R. (3d) 197 (Que. S.C.).

5 [1991] 3 S.C.R. 326.

does not wish to call those persons to testify. A more detailed examination of *Stinchcombe* and disclosure is dealt with in the Chapter, "Crown Disclosure."

A word about statements given on video or audiotape that are not accompanied by transcripts of the interviews. If you feel that it may become necessary to cross-examine on these prior statements you could have difficulties without an acceptable transcript. It seems that the Crown is not always having transcripts made of interviews, perhaps because of the cost, and it will be necessary to have your own transcript made from the disc of the interview that is provided in disclosure. Reading over a transcript is a great source for preparing cross-examination, even better than the video, unless you are interested in the demeanour of the witness when being interviewed. If cost is a factor preventing you from ordering a transcript in your preparation, watch the video and mark down those times that are shown at those places where you feel you may have to contradict the witness by playing that portion of the video during cross-examination. This part of preparation is of course time-consuming and can give an aspirin a headache.

THE *CANADA EVIDENCE ACT*

Previous inconsistent oral statements are covered by section 11 of the *Canada Evidence Act*[6] which allows counsel to call evidence to refute the witness's denial of a prior statement. Section 11 provides:

> 11. Where a witness, on cross-examination as to a former statement made by him relative to the subject-matter of the case and inconsistent with his present testimony, does not distinctly admit that he did make the statement, proof may be given that he did in fact make it, but before the proof can be given the circumstances of the supposed statement, sufficient to designate the particular occasion, shall be mentioned to the witness, and he shall be asked whether or not he did make the statement.[7]

Section 11 would appear to apply to any inconsistent former statement and not just oral statements.[8] An "inconsistency" for the purposes of this section was liberally interpreted in *R. v. Dollan*,[9] to include when the witness claimed not to remember some of the details contained in the statement.

With respect to previous statements by witnesses in writing or reduced to writing the law in this regard is partly covered by section 10(1) of the *Canada Evidence Act* which provides:

---

6 R.S.C. 1985, c. C-5 [as am. S.C. 1994, c. 44, s. 86].

7 This section is discussed in more detail in Chapter, "Self-Incrimination."

8 A. Bryant, "The Adversary Witness: Cross Examination and Proof of Prior Inconsistent Statements" (1984), 62 The Canadian Bar Review 67.

9 (1982), 65 C.C.C. (2d) 240 (Ont. C.A.).

10.(1) On any trial a witness may be cross-examined as to previous statements made in writing, or that have been reduced to writing, or recorded on audio tape or video tape or otherwise, relative to the subject-matter of the case, without the writing being shown to the witness or the witness being given the opportunity to listen to the audio tape or view the video tape or otherwise take cognizance of the statements, but, if it is intended to contradict the witness, the witness's attention must, before the contradictory proof can be given, be called to those parts of the statement that are to be used for the purpose of so contradicting the witness, and the judge, at any time during the trial, may require the production of the writing or tape or other medium for inspection, and thereupon make such use of it for the purposes of the trial as the judge thinks fit.

With regard to what is a statement in writing or reduced to writing, it has been held that a police officer's notes of an interview with a witness that were not confirmed by the witness cannot be considered as a statement in writing or reduced to writing.[10] A videotape itself is not a statement reduced to writing, but a transcript of the videotape is.[11]

Sections 10 and 11 of the *Canada Evidence Act* permit cross-examination of the witness on previous statements by the witness and not on statements made by counsel or agents on behalf of the witness. An accused could therefore not be cross-examined at trial on statements made by his counsel at the bail hearing, especially so if the accused did not adopt such statements.[12]

THE PRIOR INCONSISTENT STATEMENT OF AN ACCUSED

The Crown is entitled to cross-examine an accused on his inconsistent statement and tender it into evidence provided there has been compliance with section 10 or 11 of the *Canada Evidence Act* and provided it has not breached the rule against the Crown splitting its case. If the statement is made to a person in authority the Crown must prove it was made voluntarily whether it is for substantive use or to impeach credibility.[13] If there has been a *Charter* breach in obtaining the statement it is impermissible for the Crown to use it.[14]

---

10 *R. v. Handy* (1978), 45 C.C.C. (2d) 232 (B.C. C.A.); followed in *R. v. Cassibo* (1982), 70 C.C.C. (2d) 498 at 512 (Ont. CA.). However, see *R. v. Carpenter (No. 2)* (1982), 1 C.C.C. (3d) 149 (Ont. C.A.).

11 *R. v. Parks* (1993), 15 O.R. (3d) 324 (C.A.); *R. v. Wood* (1989), 51 C.C.C. (3d) 201 (Ont. C.A.).

12 *R. v. Peebles* (1989), 49 C.C.C. (3d) 168 (B.C. C.A.) per Craig J. If the accused had adopted his counsel's statements at trial, then he is bound.

13 *Hébert v. R.* (1954), (*sub nom. R. v. Hebert*) [1955] S.C.R. 120; *R. v. Calder*, [1996] 1 S.C.R. 660. The Crown can use the evidence given by the accused on a *voir dire* if the statement is held to be admissible. See *R. v. Tarrant* (1981), 63 C.C.C. (2d) 385 (Ont. C.A.). See also *R. v. Henry* (2005), 202 C.C.C. (3d) 449 (S.C.C.) re compelled evidence.

14 *R. v. Cook*, [1998] 2 S.C.R. 597; *R. v. Calder, ibid.*, at paras. 34-35.

IMPEACHING WITH PRIOR STATEMENTS

At times, counsel will have to deal with the witness whom he or she does not want to bring gently back to a prior inconsistent statement. It may well be that the examiner wants to show that this witness has given two different answers to the same question on different occasions and will probably tell the jury in his final address that if the witness were to be asked the question a third time there would no doubt be a third different answer. The cross-examiner's position will be that the witness is a liar and that only one of the contradictory answers is true—the answer that supports the cross-examiner's position; or that neither answer is true.

The examiner must first anchor the witness to the contradiction. This can be achieved by having the witness repeat the part of his or her evidence-in-chief which it is intended to contradict. The examiner can then ask the witness if he or she recalls giving evidence on a certain date at the preliminary inquiry, emphasizing that the answers given were under oath; then from an appropriate point the examiner can read those questions and answers given by the witness from the transcript of the preliminary inquiry leading up to the crucial contradictory answers to the ones given in-chief. The cross-examiner can then ask the witness whether those questions were asked and those answers given. If the witness says "yes" then the questioner asks if the answers given were true. If the reply is "yes," the cross-examiner has his or her contradiction. The next questions might go something like this: "You knew you were testifying under oath at the preliminary hearing, just like today? Both answers cannot be true, can they? The true answer is the one you gave at the preliminary inquiry." Or—"Neither answer is true, you just can't get your story straight." Or—"So when you testified at the preliminary hearing you lied (or were mistaken)." Your questions will depend on what you want to achieve—whether you want the witness to adopt what he or she said on a prior occasion or whether you want to show the witness to be a liar or honestly mistaken. But when counsel has the witness in this position of giving a prior inconsistent statement, he or she should not ask "why" questions such as—"Why did you tell two different stories?—unless counsel does not care what answer the witness gives—because if given the opportunity, the witness just may be able to explain away the inconsistency. It is often best for counsel to wait for the final address and then make what he or she will of the contradiction without the witness there to respond.

In the following example,[15] Chris Evans, Q.C., of Calgary, is cross-examining the complainant who claims that the accused, a police officer, assaulted him after arrest. In this particular example, the prior inconsistent statement was not given under oath but is from the transcript of the witness

---

15 From the transcript of *R. v. W.* (February 19, 1981), Doc. No. 0141044391 (Alta. Prov. Ct.).

videotaped statement to the police. Note how Mr. Evans, who is facing a witness who has given numerous inconsistent statements (not all of which are reproduced here) is not just satisfied with pointing out inconsistencies but is forcing the witness to admit on a number of occasions that he has lied which had a devastating effect on his credibility and led to an acquittal.

Q. Oh, yes. You went to see them [the police] twice, didn't you? You gave them a statement, which you know they took a note of and took down and taped—

A. Yes, sir.

Q. —you knew that? When I say, "taped" they were recording what you told them—

A. Yes, sir.

Q. —On one occasion, sir? And then you went back on August the 12th, didn't you, to give them a further statement?

A. Yes.

Q. And you knew that was tape recorded?

A. Yes.

. . .

Q. MR. EVANS:—of 1981 at about 10 minutes to 3 in the afternoon, and you were with Sergeant Meikle in his office. Does that put the date to mind? The second time you went to talk to the police, they had some more questions for you, didn't they?

A. Yes, they did.

Q. Resulting from your complaint against my client, the police officer?

A. Yes.

Q. Okay. Now, I'm going to put to you some questions that were asked of you early on in that interview, and I'll ask whether you remember the answer I'm going to read to you, and whether you recall being asked the question, giving the answer. It's page two, sir.

And it's about one-third of the way down the page, Sergeant Meikle asked, "Had—" He was talking about your friends, "Had they been drinking that night?" Answer, "No." Meikle, "Neither of them?" And yourself, "Maybe one or two beers, like we weren't impaired or anything."

Do you remember being asked those questions, giving that answer?

A. Yes.

Q. And then the next question, "Had you been using drugs?" That is you, then, "Your friends?" Answer, "No."

Do you recall being asked that question, giving that answer?

A. Yes.

Q. And that was a lie, wasn't it? Because later on you told the sergeant that you d had a joint, just as you told the Court, here? Right?

A. Yes.

Q. So, you lied to Sergeant Meikle?

A. (NO AUDIBLE ANSWER)

Q. Well, simple, it was opposite of the truth.

THE COURT: I didn't hear your answer.

A. Yes.

Q. MR. EVANS: Okay. And then you were asked, "At what point were you advised that you were under arrest?" Answer, "I wasn't." Question, "Never?" Answer, "No." Question, "Not even in the police car when you were sitting in the police car?" Answer, "No."

Do you recall asking those questions and giving those answers?

A. Yes.

Q. And those were lies too, weren't they?

A. No.

Q. Well, you told the Court today, that when you were pulled over, the policeman came up to you, you knew he was a police officer, and he said, "You're under arrest for dangerous driving and impaired driving." Right?

A. Yeah.

Q. Well, then you must have been lying to Sergeant Meikle, weren't you?

A. Yeah.

Q. Yes. Well, so when you said you weren't lying, that was a lie too, wasn't it?

A. Yeah.

Q. So, you lied to this Court. Is your answer, "Yes"?

A. Yeah.

Q. I guess it doesn't really bother you whether you lie or tell the truth, does it?

A. Sure it does.

Q. Mmm hmm. Well, why do you use the truth so recklessly if it doesn't bother you?

A. (NO AUDIBLE ANSWER)

Q. Can you answer my question?

A. I don't know.

. . .

Q. Let's go to your—the transcript that's before the Court, your interview with Sergeant Meikle on August the 12th; and lets start—

MR. EVANS: Your Honour, it's one-third of the way down the page, starting, "While en route".

Q. Let me ask you whether you were asked some questions and you gave certain answers.

MR. BOURQUE: Sorry, Mr. Evans, what page was that?

MR. EVANS: Oh, 4, sir, in transcript number 2.

Q. Question, "While en route to Headquarters was there a verbal exchange between yourself and Whitty and his partner?" Answer, "Well, we said a few things to each other, yeah." Do you recall being asked that question, giving that answer?

A. Yes, I do.

Q. Then, was that the truth?

A. Yes.

Q. Well, why did you tell the Court today, under oath, in this courtroom, that there was no conversation on the way to the Police Station?

A. I don't know.

Q. You lied to the Court today, didn't you?

A. Yeah.

Q. Yes. And then we get down to—

MR. EVANS: Sir, two-thirds of the way down the page.

Q. "Did you ever use the name of Dickie Dumont?" Answer, "Yeah." "Can you relate for me how you used the name?" "Oh. I just said to Constable Whitty that Dickie Dumont would probably be talking to you." Question, "What did you mean by that answer?" "Well, I just said Dickie Dumont will probably be talking to you." Question, "What did you mean, were you threatening the officers?" Answer, "No, I wasn't threatening." Do you recall being asked those questions by Sergeant Meikle and giving those answers, Mr. Hauer?

A. Yeah.

Q. And in each case—now, first of all, that was more conversation you had in the police vehicle, right?

A. Yeah.

Q. Okay. And also those were lies, weren't they, because you've told the Court today that you threatened the police officers, didn't you?

A. Yeah.

Q. And you told the Court today that you threatened my client that Dickie Dumont, an unlikely appellation, was going to blow him away with a shotgun, didn't you?

A. Yeah.

Q. And so you lied to Meikle, didn't you?

A. Yeah.

Q. And you lied to the Court today, didn't you?

A. Yeah.

. . .

Q. How much beer did you have that evening, by the way, Mr.—

A. Five beers.

. . .

MR. EVANS.: Two-thirds of the way down the page, Your Honour.

Q. Question, "You say you just had one beer the entire evening?" Answer, "Two beers, maybe. Actually two beers, that's all I had." Do you recall being asked that question and giving that answer?

A. Yeah.

Q. And now you've come to court and said, well you had five, right?

A. Yeah.

Q. So, you lied to Meikle again?

A. Yeah.

Q. Now, let's get this straight. About two weeks after this event you come in and see a senior police officer, and you complained about the conduct of this man towards you when you were drunk, right?

A. Yeah.

Q. When you had threatened to blow him away, right?

A. Yeah.

Q. An in complaining about the conduct of this man, in order to get him charged with this offence that's before the Court, and drag his name through the mud, you told a bunch of lies to Sergeant Meikle, didn't you?

A. Mmmm hmmm.

Q. You said you had a 3-inch lump on your head?

A. Somewhere's around there, yeah.

Q. 3 inches? So, you have a lump sticking out from you head about this far? Just look at my pen, will you? Is that your evidence under oath, you got a lump sticking out of your head about as far as I'm showing you, this part of the pen sticking out of my head?

A. It wasn't quite that big.

Q. Oh. I see.

A. It was quite noticeable, though.

MR. EVANS: Like Pinocchio. Thank you.

Frances Wellman[16] described the proper way to deal with a letter written by the witness which contradicts his testimony:

> If you have in your possession a letter written by the witness, in which he takes an opposite position on some part of the case to the one he has just sworn to, avoid the common error of showing the witness the letter for identification, and then reading it to him with the inquiry, "What have you to say to that?" During the reading of this letter the witness will be collecting his thoughts and getting ready his explanations in anticipation of the question that is to follow, and the effect of the damaging letter will be lost.

> The correct method of using such a letter is to lead the witness quietly into repeating the statements he has made in his direct testimony, and which his letter contradicts. "I have you down as saying so and so; will you please repeat it? I am apt to read my notes to the jury, and I want to be accurate." The witness will repeat his statement. Then write it down and read it off to him. "Is that correct? Is there any doubt about it? For if you have any explanation or qualification to make, I think you owe it to us, in justice, to make it before I leave the subject." The witness has none. He has stated the fact; there is nothing to qualify; the jury rather likes his straightforwardness. Then let your whole manner toward him suddenly change, and spring the letter upon him. "Do you recognize your own handwriting, sir? let me read you from your own letter, in which you say."—and afterward—"Now, what have you to say to that?" You

---

16 F.L. Weilman, *The Art of Cross-Examination,* Reprinted with permission from *The Art of Cross-Examination,* 4/e, revised and enlarged by Frances L. Wellman. Copyright 1903, 1904, 1923 and 1936 by Macmillan Publishing Company, renewed 1931, 1932, 1951 and 1964 by Ethel Wellman.

will make your point in such fashion that the jury will not readily forget it. It is usually expedient, when you have once made your point, to drop it and go to something else, lest the witness wriggle out of it. But when you have a witness under oath, who is orally contradicting a statement he has previously made, when not under oath, but in his own handwriting, you then have him fast on the hook, and there is no danger of his getting away; now is the time to press your advantage. Put his self-contradictions to him in as many forms as you can invent:—

"Which statement is true?" "Had you forgotten this letter when you gave your testimony to-day?" "Did you tell your counsel about it?" "Were you intending to deceive him?" "What was your objective in trying to mislead the jury?"[17]

When counsel is impeaching a witness with a prior inconsistent statement contained in a letter or document, the witness should be made to read aloud the contradictory portion to dramatize that contradiction and increase the pressure on the witness.

It is vital that the cross-examiner not use his or her conflicting material until sure that there is a clear conflict. The witness should be tied down to his or her answers so as to be unable to explain his or her way out of the difficulty by claiming confusion or by some other invention. If the witness can successfully explain the seeming conflict, then counsel will face the embarrassment of having taken up the time to read to the witness the prior alleged inconsistent statement without obtaining the expected result.

Sometimes the witness has qualified his or her answer in another portion of the transcript of the preliminary inquiry. If opposing counsel, after the cross-examiner has appeared to impeach the witness with a prior inconsistent statement, requests that the cross-examiner in fairness, read to the witness a qualifying answer in another part of the transcript, that once seeming impeachment will fall flat with the result that the witness's credibility will be bolstered and counsel may lose credibility.

It is therefore important for the cross-examiner to have carefully read through the witness's evidence in the transcript. The impeachment technique should be saved for the important contradictions. Overuse of minor contradictions will dilute the impact counsel is trying to achieve as the jury will not be impressed with nit-picking. If, however, there are numerous minor inconsistencies, the numbers may wear the witness down and the cumulative effect of the many inconsistencies could damage the witness's credibility.

When it is intended to contradict the witness on a previous oral statement, the approach is the same as it would be if the statement was reduced to writing. The conditions precedent are set out in section 11 of the *Canada Evidence Act* as noted at the beginning of this chapter.

If there is concern that the witness will attempt to wiggle out of the answer given at the preliminary inquiry, as for example, by claiming he or

---

17 *Ibid.*, p. 131.

she did not understand what was being asked, then counsel should commence reading the transcript from a point somewhere prior to the crucial questions and answers, stopping every so often to ask the witness if those questions were asked, and those answers given, and if so, were the answers true? If the cross-examiner receives "yes" answers all along the way and then a sudden denial or claim of confusion from the witness with respect to one question only, followed by another build-up of "yes" answers to subsequent questions, the witness should lose credibility.

This technique should also be used by Crown attorneys when questioning the accused on his or her signed statement and should also be used by defence counsel when cross-examining the witness on a signed statement.

When the maker of the statement attempts to depart from any part of his or her statement, the cross-examiner will of course point out any initialling of corrections made by the accused or other witness and the signing at the bottom of each page by the witness which would indicate that the statement was carefully read over before signing on the bottom of the last page. Not only will the cross-examiner elicit that the witness read over the statement before signing it, he will ask the witness if she asked the officer taking the statement to change it to reflect the witness's new version.

There is a difference of opinion amongst the provinces as to whether a prior inconsistent statement of the witness upon which the witness has been cross-examined at trial can be made an exhibit. In the province of Ontario, the statement could not be made an exhibit as the accused would be prejudiced because the jury would have, in the jury room, a written account of the Crown's evidence.[18] British Columbia and Alberta leave the trial judge a discretion as to whether the statement should be marked as an exhibit.[19]

---

18   *R. v. Rowbotham* (1988), 41 C.C.C. (3d) 1 at 54 (Ont. C.A.); *R. v. McShannock* (1980), 55 C.C.C. (2d) 53 (Ont. C.A.). However, in *R. v. Campbell* (1990), 57 C.C.C. (3d) 200 (Alta. C.A.), *R. v. Smith* (1983), 35 C.R. (3d) 86 (B.C. C.A.), *R. v. Newall* (1983), 9 C.C.C. (3d) 519 (B.C. C.A.) and in *R. v. Rodney* (1988), 46 C.C.C. (3d) 323 (B.C. C.A.), the western courts have taken the position that the trial judge has a discretion whether or not to have the prior statement marked as an exhibit. If there is an extensive cross-examination on the prior statement, as in *R. v. Smith* and *R. v. Newall*, then it may be necessary to have the statement marked as an exhibit so that the trier-of-fact may properly understand the extent to which the witness has been contradicted or impeached. If the cross-examination has not been extensive, then the proper exercise of the discretion under s. 10(1) may lead the judge to permit only edited parts of the writing or none of them to be marked as exhibits. In *R. v. Adolph B.* (1997), 33 O.R. (3d) 321 (Ont. C.A.), the Ontario Court of Appeal held that there can be exceptions to the rule that out-of-court statements used to impeach a witness will not be marked as exhibits, such as where defence counsel suggested in cross-examination of a police officer that there was a difference between the handwritten notes and the typed will-say statement. In this case the notes and typed statement were made exhibits to enable the jury to determine the differences and any impact.

19   *Ibid.*

IMPEACHMENT BY OMISSION

At times we have all been surprised, after reading witnesses' statements and their evidence at the preliminary inquiry, to hear the witnesses at trial for the first time add something to his or her testimony which hurts the defence. In attempting to make the point to the trier-of-fact that this is eleventh hour testimony that has no credibility, counsel has to impeach the witness by his or her prior inconsistent statements. The witness may respond by saying that he or she was never asked about that particular point by the police or at the preliminary inquiry; the witness may say he or she simply forgot or wasn't feeling well when testifying, or that they were too nervous at the time. The following is the kind of cross-examination that illustrates how counsel can approach such evasion by the witness:

Q: Mr. Smith, you were interviewed by the police approximately two hours after the shooting.

A: Yes.

Q: The police asked you specifically to describe the shooter.

A: Yes.

Q: At that time you knew it was important to give the police as accurate a description of the shooter as you could because the police wanted to find this man.

A: That's right.

Q: You tried to be as complete and accurate and truthful as possible in giving that description.

A: I did.

Q: Then six months ago at the preliminary hearing you were asked by the prosecutor when you were under oath to describe the shooter.

A: Yes, yes.

Q: Again you knew how important your evidence was.

A: Yes.

Q: Again you tried to be as complete and accurate and truthful as possible and you gave the same answer you gave to the police officer.

A: I did.

Q: Today, you were again asked to describe the shooter by the prosecutor.

A: Yes.

Q: You told the members of this jury that the shooter had a beard—a rather full beard.

A: Correct.

Q: Something that would be hard to miss I guess?

A: Right.

Q: Mr. Smith, you at no time when you spoke to the police two hours after the shooting tell them that the shooter had a beard.

A: I don't know, I can't recall.

Q: Well, let me show you your statement to the police. Those are your initials on each page and your signature on the last page. Dated December 10th, 1997?

A: Yes.

Q: You see here on page two you are specifically asked to describe the shooter. (Quote out loud the question and answer.)

Q: Were you asked that question and did you give that answer?

A: Yes.

Q: Was your answer true?

A: Yes.

Q: You at no time here or anywhere else in your statement say the shooter had a beard. Is that not right?

A: You're right. I must have been nervous and forgot. I had witnessed a shooting you know.

Q: You gave a description to the police about other features of the shooter, did you not? You even were able to describe his eyebrows?

A: I guess.

Q: The beard you described would be more obvious than the shooter's eyebrows.

A: I don't know, maybe.

Q: Your statement took up three pages of questions and answers. At no time did you ever mention that you were nervous or your memory was faulty.

A: Okay.

Q: Again at the preliminary inquiry when you swore under oath to tell the truth you were asked to describe the shooter and at no time when you gave that description under oath did you mention he had a beard.

A: If you say so.

Q: Are you prepared to accept that you did not mention the beard during your evidence? The Crown Attorney I'm sure will correct me if I'm wrong about what you didn't say at the preliminary inquiry.

A: Okay, I'll accept what you say.

Q: By the time the preliminary hearing rolled around you weren't still nervous about what you saw?

A: I don't know about that.

Q: Mr. Smith, on two previous occasions, once on the very same day of the event within a couple of hours after, and later under oath you were given full opportunity to describe the shooter and you did not mention he had a beard. Today, you see my client sitting in the prisoner's dock with a beard and for the first time you have added that beard to your description. In all honesty do you not see your description being influenced by the beard you see in the prisoner's dock?

A: (pause) I'm not sure. Maybe.

In the above example the questions at the outset are designed to show that there were two previous statements by the witness and that he was aware of the importance of the answers he gave under oath regarding his descriptions and that it would have been very unlikely he would have forgotten such an obvious feature as a beard even though forgetful or nervous. Questions were designed to show that he had two earlier opportunities to describe the beard and only did so on the third occasion because the accused had a beard sitting before him in the prisoner's dock. You don't mind posing the open-ended last question at the end of this cross because even if the witness answers in the negative the trier-of-fact will doubt him. This last question can be effective as a mini-jury address which should be employed in your cross-examinations whenever the opportunity presents itself so that the trier-of-fact is alerted to your defence at the earliest opportunity. In the above example you have not made an aggressive attack on the witness's credibility as a truth teller, but have created a significant crack in his reliability in that he was unduly influenced by a man in the witness-box wearing a beard.

In the chapter on the Preliminary Inquiry, it is suggested that you ask the witness with your last question if there is anything the witness would like to add to his or her testimony. You will have asked the witness to take his or her time to think about it. Usually the witness has nothing to add. Assuming the witness testified at the preliminary inquiry that the Court was told everything that the witness could remember, this response can be read back to the witness at trial if he/she adds anything new to his/her testimony which hurts your client.

This technique is especially effective in the cross-examination of a witness who may be expected to remember in great detail, either because the event described is significant or because he has a duty or responsibility to remember or record all the details, as in the case of an investigating police officer. When a witness is told at trial he or she is testifying about something that the witness never said before, the response often heard is that "I was never asked about it." Counsel will then be able to read from the preliminary hearing transcript to show that the witness was given an opportunity to tell everything he or she knew and did not mention this new evidence.

You may wish to take a risk and inquire of the witness whether he/she has told the Crown or police about this additional evidence. If you have not received up-to-date disclosure about it the chances are likely that the witness has not told the prosecution and your risk in asking the question is considerably lessened. The eleventh hour testimony would then be even more glaring if the prosecution was not told. If the witness in fact did tell the prosecution it was no doubt very late in the day which would still leave the witness's credibility vulnerable to attack and you would have a complaint against the prosecution for failing to disclose, with a possible remedy.

For a further example of impeachment by omission, see Chapter, "Cross-Examination of Police Officers."

COAXING WITH PRIOR STATEMENTS

The transcript of the preliminary inquiry provides those statements reduced to writing that most often present counsel with the opportunity to contradict the prosecution witness. When the witness testifies differently at trial than he or she did at the preliminary inquiry counsel may, without trying to attack the witness's credibility, wish to coax the witness back to adopting his or her testimony at the preliminary inquiry. The following is an example of how this may be achieved:

Q. Mr. Smith, you told my friend that the man who robbed you was about 6 feet tall.
A. That's right.
Q. You testified at the preliminary inquiry in this matter at Provincial Court on January 5th, some eight months ago?
A. Yes
Q. The evidence you gave was under oath?
A. Yes.
Q. You told the truth when you testified there?
A. Yes, I did.
Q. Mr. Smith, I'm going to read back to you a question put and an answer made and then I'm going to ask you whether or not it was your answer?
A. Yes, sir.
Q. Your Honour, I'm referring to page 8, line 16 of volume 1 of the transcript of the preliminary inquiry which I believe you have:
  Q. How tall was the man who robbed you?
  A. I'd say 5 foot 2 inches—no taller than 5 foot 3 inches.
Q. Do you recall being asked that question and giving that answer at the preliminary inquiry?
A. Yes, I do now.
Q. Was the answer that you gave the preliminary inquiry true?
A. Yes.
Q. I take it your memory of the robbery was much clearer in your mind at the time you testified at the preliminary inquiry some eight months ago than it is now?
A. Yes, that's fair.
Q. And therefore more accurate?
A. Yes.
Q. That is only human nature I suggest. Our memories tend to become faultier with the passage of time. You would then agree that the man who robbed you was no taller than 5 foot 3 inches tall.
A. Yes.

When attempting to have a witness change or backtrack on their evidence, your effort becomes easier if you can give that witness a face-saving escape hatch rather than an obvious attack on the witness's credibility which could cause the witness to become intransigent.

When the prior statement is not contained in a transcript of the preliminary inquiry but in some other document such as the police officer's notebook, the cross-examiner will first seek the witness's admission that his or her answers which were reduced to writing were complete and accurate at a time shortly after the incident in question.

> Q. Mr. Smith, you recall speaking to Sergeant Jones and Sergeant Black after the robbery at the police station?
> A. Yes.
> Q. And they asked you questions about the robbery?
> A. Yes.
> Q. And they asked you to try and remember what the robber looked like?
> A. Yes sir.
> Q. And you tried your best to be as complete and accurate as possible in giving your description?
> A. Yes.
> Q. And the police were making notes of what you said?
> A. Yes.
> Q. And you knew it was important to be as accurate as you possibly could?
> A. Yes.
> Q. And your memory of what the robber looked like two hours after the robbery was a great deal fresher than it would be now, a year later?
> A. Yes.
> Q. And did you not tell those two police officers that the robber had red hair, not black hair?
> A. I don't remember.
> Q. Well, if you did would you not agree your memory would be more accurate when you spoke to the police than now?
> A. I guess so, but I don't remember.
> Q. If we hear from the police officers that they have it in their notebook that you told them that the robber had red hair, would you accept that that was what you told them and it was the truth to the best of your knowledge?
> A. I guess I'd have to.

Because the witness did not admit to making his or her prior contradictory statement in the second example, the cross-examiner, pursuant to section 11 of the *Canada Evidence Act*, may call one of the police officers to testify about that prior contradictory statement.

ADOPTION OF PRIOR STATEMENT BY WITNESS

When using the transcript of the preliminary inquiry or other written materials in order to contradict the witness, remember to ask the witness if the answers or statements made on the prior occasion were true so as to come within the basic rule of evidence which states that when a witness adopts the answers given in his or her previous testimony that testimony can be considered as evidence at the trial.[20] If the witness does not adopt

---

20 In *R. v. McCarroll* (2008), 238 C.C.C. (3d) 404 (Ont. C.A.) at para. 40, the Court stated

what was said on a prior occasion as true, that prior inconsistent statement can only be used by the triers-of-fact to assess the witness's credibility.[21] The trial judge "must caution the jury in the strongest terms with respect to the danger of accepting that evidence and failure to do so will result in a new trial."[22]

However the Supreme Court of Canada case of *R. v. B. (K.G.)*[23] has brought about a significant change in the law regarding prior inconsistent statements. There are now circumstances in which such statements may be admissible for their truth even though not adopted by the witness at trial if there are sufficient guarantees of necessity and reliability attached to the taking of the statement. The necessity requirement would be met if the witness in Court recanted his/her prior out-of-court statement or because evidence of the same quality cannot be obtained at trial.[24] The indicia of reliability must be a substitute for the lack of an oath, lack of contemporaneous cross-examination and the inability of the trier-of-fact to observe the demeanour of the witness at the time the prior statement was made. The substitutes could be a statement under oath, solemn affirmation or declaration, a videotaped statement and the ability of the defence to cross-examine the witness at trial. These substitutes can also have their own substitutes as suggested in *R. v. B. (K.G.)*.[25] A *voir dire* is to be held to determine if the statement is to be admissible for its truth. The procedure on the *voir dire* is described in *R. v. B.((K.G.)*.

The most recent case on the issue of admitting hearsay evidence under the principled exception when there is a prior inconsistent statement is *R. v. M. (J.)*,[26] which holds that the focus of the reliability inquiry is on the comparative reliability of the prior statement and the trial testimony. To meet the requirement of reliability the party seeking to admit the hearsay should:

   1.   Show there is no real concern about the truth of the hearsay state-

---

that to adopt a prior statement the witness must admit making the statement and verify the accuracy of its contents based on his or her present memory of the events referred to in the statement.

21 *R. v. Deacon* (1947), 89 C.C.C. 1 (S.C.C.); *R. v. Duckworth* (1916), 26 C.C.C. 314 (Ont. C.A.); *R. v. Mannion* (1986), 28 C.C.C. (3d) 544 (S.C.C.) at para. 8; *R. v. Rouse, supra*.

22 *Binet v. R.* (1953), [1954] S.C.R. 52 (S.C.C.).

23 (1993), 79 C.C.C. (3d) 257 (S.C.C.). For oath substitutes see *R. v. Mohamed* (March 18, 1997), MacDonnell Prov. J., [1997] O.J. No. 1287 (Ont. Prov. Div.); *R. v. Sharpe* (1997), [1997] M.J. No. 127 (Man. Prov. Ct.) Corrin Prov. J. where the courts looked at the surrounding circumstances to conclude the declarants appreciated the seriousness of their statements. A transcript can suffice. See *R. v. Hawkins* (1996), 111 C.C.C. (3d) 129 (S.C.C.) 162-163.

24 *R. v. U. (F.J.)* (1995), 101 C.C.C. (3d) 97 (S.C.C.); *R. v. B. (K.G.), supra*.

25 (1993), 79 C.C.C. (3d) 257 (S.C.C.).

26 (2010), 251 C.C.C. (3d) 325 (Ont. C.A.), following *B. (K.G.)*.

ment because of the circumstances in which the statement came
about; or
2. Show that no real concern arises from the fact that the statement is
    offered in hearsay form because, in the circumstances, its truth and
    accuracy can nonetheless be sufficiently tested in the proceedings.
    Relevant circumstances include, but not limited to, the timing of
    the statement in relation to the event reported; the absence of a
    motive to lie on the part of the declarant; the presence or absence
    of leading questions or other forms of prompting; the nature of the
    event reported; the likelihood of the declarant's knowledge of the
    event, apart from its occurrence, and confirmation of the event
    reported by physical evidence.

    R. v. U. (F.J.)[27] appeared to have signaled a relaxing of the indicia
requirements of trustworthiness with respect to prior inconsistent statements
being admissible for their truth. The complainant in a sexual assault case
was asked by the police when she last had sex with her father. She replied,
"last night." After the father was arrested he was asked the same question
and he responded "last night." The complainant recanted her statement at
trial and the father denied at trial sexually abusing his daughter. The Supreme Court held there was a "striking similarity" between what the daughter and her father said and this feature was therefore an adequate substitute
for an oath and videotape.

    It was further held in *R. v. B. (K.G.)* that the issue of whether or not
the prior inconsistent statement is admissible for its truth is to be determined
on a *voir dire*. When the party who calls the witness successfully invokes
section 9 of the *Canada Evidence Act* it must then state its intention in
tendering the statement. If the party states it only wishes to use the statement
to impeach credibility, then the matter proceeds under the orthodox rule.
But if the party gives notice that it wishes to make substantive use of the
statement, the trial judge must determine on the balance of probabilities
whether the indicia of reliability are present. If only some or none of the
deemed list of indicia of reliability are present the Court must satisfy itself
that, on the balance of probabilities, there are sufficient substitutes circum-
stantially guaranteeing the reliability of the statement.

    The Court also noted that before the prior inconsistent statement could
be admissible, it would have had to be admissible as the witness's sole
testimony, *i.e.,* if the witness could not have made the statement during
examination-in-chief or cross-examination, as for example, because it was

---

27 (1995), 101 C.C.C. (3d) 97 (S.C.C). The Court set out certain preconditions before this
    kind of "striking similarity" evidence was admissible.

hearsay testimony or in breach of a *Charter* right, it could not be admitted through the reformed prior inconsistent statement rule.[28]

On the *voir dire,* the trial judge does not have to be satisfied that the prior statement was the true statement over the witness's trial statement. This determination is for the trier of fact.

If the prior inconsistent statement reports a confession by the accused, even where there has been a warning and oath given and the statement videotaped, or sufficient substitutes established, the trial judge will still have a discretion to refuse the jury permission to make substantive use of it particularly when the circumstances surrounding the taking of the statement by the police are suspect and would offend the rules for taking a voluntary statement from an accused by a person in authority or other forms of investigatory misconducts, or where the conduct of a person in authority would bring the administration of justice into disrepute.

See Chapter, "The Hearsay Horror" and sections therein on "Necessity and Reliability" as preconditions to the principled approach admissibility of hearsay testimony.

ESTABLISHING THE ACCURACY OF THE TRANSCRIPT

Sometimes after the cross-examiner has read back a portion of the transcript to the witness, the witness will say he or she does not recall being asked those questions nor giving the answers being read back. In such instances, there are several alternatives open to the cross-examiner. He or she can tell the witness that the transcript is certified as being correct by the Court reporter and ask if the witness is prepared to admit the accuracy of the questions and answers put to him or her at the preliminary inquiry. In the alternative, counsel can ask the Crown attorney if he or she is prepared to admit that the transcript has been certified as being correct and if the answer is "yes" the witness in all likelihood will accept the Crown's admission. Finally, counsel can always resort to the trouble of calling the Court reporter to testify to the accuracy of the transcript by reference to the certification signed by the Court reporter in the transcript. Often the witness will volunteer that if it is in transcripts then he must have said it.

When attempting to impeach the witness on his or her prior statement in a transcript, it is wise if the cross-examiner stands beside the witness and

---

28   See *R. v. Devine* (2008), 232 C.C.C. (3d) 1 (S.C.C.) at para. 13. The Supreme Court confirmed *B. (K.G.)* at p. 784 that a prior inconsistent statement can only be admitted for the truth of its contents under the principled approach if the evidence in the statement would be admissible through the witness's testimony at trial. In *Devine* the complainant's identification evidence could only be admitted under the principled approach if the identification was not itself based on hearsay. See also *R. v. Couture* (2007), 220 C.C.C. (3d) 289 (S.C.C.).

reads aloud from the transcript, pointing with his or her finger to the part he or she is reading. This will not only keep up the pressure, but will also impress upon the witness that his or her answers were recorded.

ADDRESSING THE PRIOR INCONSISTENT STATEMENT DURING EXAMINATION-IN-CHIEF

Counsel (probably more often, the Crown) knowing that her witness has made a prior inconsistent statement, as a tactic to blunting cross-examination may wish to bring out from that witness an explanation as to why the witness is contradicting his prior statement. In *R. v. Pinkus*[29] the Court held this procedure to be impermissible as it was oath-helping and would weaken cross-examination. However counsel would have reply if it was relevant.

CROSS-EXAMINATION BY ACCUSED ON CO-ACCUSED'S PRIOR STATEMENT

Generally, the Crown cannot cross-examine an accused on his or her prior inconsistent statement to the authorities unless it has been proven to be voluntary or when excluded during the Crown's case for violating the *Charter*.[30] However, when the accused voluntarily enters the witness box the co-accused is entitled to treat him or her as any other witness and is able to cross-examine the accused on his or her prior inconsistent statement notwithstanding the statement has not been proven voluntary or introduced by the Crown and even where the accused alleges his or her 10(b) rights under the *Charter* have been violated.[31]

B. CROSS-EXAMINATION OF YOUR OWN WITNESS (THE HOSTILE WITNESS)

When counsel calls a witness he or she normally does so expecting that witness to advance his or her case in some fashion. A problem occurs when the witness gives unfavourable testimony or does not come up to proof with respect to anticipated favourable testimony for the side which calls the witness. There are a number of options open to the examiner-in-

---

29 (1999), 140 C.C.C. (3d) 309 (Ont. S.C.J.).

30 *R. v. Calder* (1996), 105 C.C.C. (3d) 1 (S.C.C.).

31 *R. v. Logan* (1988), 46 C.C.C. (3d) 354 (Ont. C.A.), affirmed (1990), 58 C.C.C. (3d) 391 (S.C.C.); *R. v. Pelletier* (1986), 29 C.C.C. (3d) 533 (B.C. C.A.). See also *R. v. Creighton* (1995), (sub nom. *R. v. Crawford*) 96 C.C.C. (3d) 481 (S.C.C.) as to whether one accused could cross-examine a co-accused on the latter's failure to give a statement to the police.

chief to deal with such a witness. What follows is a look at those options involving: The Common Law Hostile Witness and Section 9(1) and 9(2) of the *Canada Evidence Act.*

THE COMMON LAW HOSTILE WITNESS

By virtue of the common law, if the examiner-in-chief can convince the trial Judge to declare the witness hostile, the questioner may conduct a cross-examination at large with all of the rules of cross-examination applying.[32] This procedure has nothing to do with section 9 of the *Canada Evidence Act.*[33]

It is significant to note that counsel does not have to be concerned with a prior inconsistent statement when there is an application to declare the witness hostile at common law although in most cases a hostile animus would be shown by demonstrating that the witness's evidence was inconsistent with a prior statement. In addition a witness at common law is hostile when he shows from the manner in which he gives his evidence-in-chief that he is not giving the evidence fairly and is not desirous of telling the truth because of a hostile animus toward the prosecution.[34] The trial judge will observe the witness's demeanour, attitude and the substance of his or her evidence.[35] However, it is unusual to find a witness who overtly displays animosity toward the party calling him. Indeed, a clever witness who attempts to veer from the truth may hide any such overt animosity.

---

32 *Hanes v. Wawanesa Mutual Insurance Co.*, [1961] O.R. 495 at 528 (Ont. C.A.), reversed [1963] 8 S.C.R. 154 (S.C.C.); *R. v. Marshall* (1972), 8 C.C.C. (2d) 329 at 340 (N.S. C.A.); *R. v. Deacon*, [1947] S.C.R. 531 (S.C.C.); *R. v. Cooper* (1969), [1970] 3 C.C.C. 136 (Ont. C.A.); *R. v. Cassibo* (1982), 70 C.C.C. (2d) 498 at 514 (Ont. C.A.).

33 R.S.C. 1985, c. C-5.

34 *R. v. Coffin* (1956), 23 C.R. 1 (S.C.C.) *per* Kellock J.; in *R. v. Malik* (2003), 194 C.C.C. (3d) 572 (B.C. S.C.), the Crown submitted that the witness could be declared hostile at common law relying on *R. v. Cassibo*, *supra*; *R. v. Coffin* and *R. v. Haughton (No. 3)* (1982), 38 O.R. (2d) 536 (Ont. Co. Ct.). The Crown submitted that the witness demonstrated a consistent failure to tell the truth during his examination-in-chief, (without pointing to any prior inconsistent statements) and that his lack of veracity was manifest. The trial Judge held that "hostile animus was more than an interest at variance with the Crown." There was no inconsistent prior statement and the manner and demeanour of the witness did not reflect an animus nor was there any suggestion that the Crown had been misled regarding the nature of the witness's testimony. The Application was dismissed.

35 *Hanes v. Wawanesa Mutual Insurance Co.*, *supra*; *R. v. Marshall*, *supra*; *Coles v. Coles* (1866), L.R. 1 P. & D. 70 (U.K. Ct. Div. & Matr.); *R. v. May* (1915), 23 C.C.C. 469 (B.C. C.A.); *R. v. Marceniuk* (1923), 20 Alta. L.R. 53 (Alta. C.A.); *R. v. Haughton (No. 3)* (1982), 38 O.R. (3d) 536 (Ont. Co. Ct.).

SECTION 9 OF THE *CANADA EVIDENCE ACT*

If the circumstances are not present to apply to have the witness de-clared hostile pursuant to the common law, another option for the examiner-in-chief is to utilize section 9 of the *Canada Evidence Act* which states:

(1) A party producing a witness shall not be allowed to impeach his credit by general evidence of bad character, but if the witness, in the opinion of the court, proves adverse, the party may contradict him by other evidence, or, by leave of the court, may prove that the witness made at other times a statement inconsistent with his present testimony, but before the last mentioned proof can be given the circumstances of the supposed statement, sufficient to desig-nate the particular occasion, shall be mentioned to the witness, and he shall be asked whether or not he did make the statement.

(2) Where the party producing a witness alleges that the witness made at other times a statement in writing, reduced to writing, or recorded on audio tape or video tape or otherwise, inconsistent with the witness's present testi-mony, the court may, without proof that the witness is adverse, grant leave to that party to cross-examine the witness as to the statement and the court may consider the cross-examination in determining whether in the opinion of the court the witness is adverse.

It has been held that the purpose of section 9 is to give redress to a party who calls a witness in the legitimate expectation that the witness will give material evidence essential to its case in accordance with previous statements and finds that the witness has changed his or her testimony.[36]

When section 9(1) or 9(2) [as amended S.C. 1994, c. 44, s. 85] is employed, counsel will normally be attempting to deter the witness from his or her trial testimony and adopt what he or she said in an earlier statement. It is, of course, trite law that what the witness does not adopt as true in his or her prior statement is not evidence and the triers-of-fact can only view the inconsistent statements as going to the credibility of the witness.[37] If counsel wishes to go beyond just attacking the credibility of the witness by proving the truth of the contents of that statement (and why not) that can be accomplished if the witness were to adopt his prior statement as being true. In that unlikely event counsel will have to make a *B. (K.G.)* application which would involve a *voir dire* wherein the trial Judge will assess the reliability of the statement. The necessity requirement has been met because the witness has recanted.[38] See chapter on the Hearsay Horror.

Subsections 9(1) and (2) are separate and distinct and one does not rely on the other. If the circumstances permit, there is nothing to prevent an

---

36 *R. v. Chisholm*, [1995] O.J. No. 3300 (Ont. Gen. Div.).
37 *R. v. Deacon* (1947), 3 C.R. 265 (S.C.C.); *R. v. Rouse* (1978), 5 C.R. (3d) 125 (S.C.C.).
38 *R. v. U. (F.J.)*, [1995] 3 S.C.R. 764 at para. 48.

application being brought under section 9(1) without first applying under section 9(2) as was done in *R. v. Haughton (No. 3).*[39]

Section 9(1), *Canada Evidence Act*

The common law rule codified by section 9(1) of the *Canada Evidence Act* is that counsel cannot impeach his or her witness's credit by general evidence of bad character. Section 3 of *England's Criminal Procedure Act, 1865,*[40] declaratory of the common law, prohibits any attempt to impeach the credit of one's own witness by general evidence of bad character, which includes not asking any questions about the witness's bad conduct on former occasions.[41] The Crown is entitled in direct examination to adduce the criminal record of its own witnesses pursuant to section 12 of the *Canada Evidence Act* but not where the Crown's motive is to show that the accused associated with disreputable persons thereby discrediting the accused's character.[42]

But section 9(1) does permit counsel to contradict his or her own witness by other evidence where the witness proves adverse or with leave of the Court, prove that the witness made at other times a statement inconsistent with his or her present testimony.[43] Note that such a statement is not required to be in writing or reduced to writing in section 9(1). Section 9(2) requires the statement to be in writing, reduced to writing or, by virtue of a recent amendment, audio tape or video tape or otherwise.

While section 9(1) refers to a witness being "adverse," it does not define this term. Some cases have treated the term as synonymous to "hostile."[44] In addition to allowing the proof of the existence of a prior inconsistent statement under section 9(1), such a finding of adversity/hostility allows the examiner to cross-examine the witness at large. Other cases have considered adversity to be something less than hostility.[45] In *Hanes v. Wawa-*

---

39 (1982), 38 O.R. (2d) 536 (Ont. Co. Ct.).

40 28 & 29 Vic., c. 18.

41 R. Cross and C. Tapper, *Cross on Evidence*, 6th ed. (London: Butterworths, 1985), p. 273.

42 *R. v. Boyko* (1975), 28 C.C.C. (2d) 193 (B.C. C.A.).

43 Although the wording of the section suggests that a finding of adversity is required before a party may contradict his or her own witness with other evidence, the section has not been interpreted in this manner. See Alan Mewett, Q.C., *Witnesses*, pp. 14-15 to 14-16.

44 See, e.g., *R. v. McIntyre*, 43 C.R. 262, [1963] 2 C.C.C. 380 (N.S. C.A.); *R. v. Collerman*, 46 W.W.R. 300, 43 C.R. 118, [1964] 3 C.C.C. 195 (B.C. C.A.); *R. v. Marceniuk*, [1923] 3 W.W.R. 758 (Alta. C.A.); *R. v. Brennan* (1962), [1963] 3 C.C.C. 30, 40 C.R. 329 (P.E.I. S.C.). As well, the recent case of *R. v. Soobrian* (1994), 76 O.A.C. 7 (Ont. C.A.), appears to equate the concepts of adversity and hostility.

45 *Hanes v. Wawanesa Insurance Co.*, [1961] O.R. 495 (Ont. C.A.); *R. v. Gushue* (1976), 30 C.R.N.S. 178, 32 C.C.C. (2d) 189 (Ont. C.A.), affirmed (1979), 50 C.C.C. (2d) 417 (S.C.C.); *R. v. Cassibo* (1982), 70 C.C.C. (2d) 498 (Ont. C.A.).

nesa Insurance Co., the Ontario Court of Appeal considered section 20 (now section 23) of the Ontario it *Evidence Act* to be the same as section 9(1) of the *Canada Evidence Act* and it was held that the meaning of "adverse" was not limited to hostility but included a witness who, although was not hostile, was unfavourable in the sense of assuming by his or her testimony a position opposite that of the party calling him or her.[46]

If the concept of adversity is something less than hostility, one must consider what consequences flow from a finding that a witness is adverse. The prevailing view is that, like a hostile witness, an adverse witness may be cross-examined at large by the party calling him or her. However, it may be argued that on this approach, notwithstanding a difference in terminology, there is little practical difference between an adverse witness and a hostile witness; why then draw a distinction at all? An alternative view would confine the cross-examination of an adverse witness under section 9(1) to the issue of the prior inconsistent statement.[47] It is the author's view that the former approach is preferable and conforms with established practice. Concerns regarding possible abusive cross-examination of adverse though not hostile witnesses can be dealt with by the trial Judge in the exercise of his or her discretion to control the trial process and protect witnesses. Thus the degree of cross-examination allowed may vary with the degree of adversity or hostility displayed by the witness.

The procedure under section 9(1) is detailed by Martin J.A. in *R. v. Cassibo*.[48] In that case, the Court found that a trial Judge may receive evidence of the making of a previous inconsistent statement by the party's own witness on the preliminary issue of whether the witness is adverse. Moreover, both oral and written statements may be taken into account on the *voir dire* that has to be held to determine whether the witness is adverse.[49] There may not be a prior inconsistent statement but section 9(1) would permit other circumstances to be proven to show that the witness is adverse, such as bias, fear, self-interest, etc.[50] After hearing evidence with respect to the making of a previous oral statement, the Judge may refuse to declare the witness adverse or may refuse to grant leave to prove the statement in

---

46 *R. v. Milgaard* (1971), 14 C.R.N.S. 34 (Sask. C.A.); *R. v. Rouse* (1978), 5 C.R. (3d) 125 (S.C.C.); *R. v. Cassibo, supra*; *R. v. Soobrian* (1994), 76 O.A.C. 7 (Ont. C.A.). See also Sopinka, Lederman and Bryant, *The Law of Evidence in Canada* (Toronto: Butterworths, 1992) at p. 86; also Sheppard, "Evidence", *Canadian Encyclopaedic Digest*, 3rd Edition (Toronto: Carswell, 1988) at s. 441.

47 See, for example, Michael E. Webster, "Cross-examination on a finding of adversity?" (unpublished, 1997), where it is argued that cross-examination at large of an adverse witness may coerce the giving of false testimony and should thus not be allowed. In support of this position, Webster relies on *Haynes v. Wawanesa Mutual Insurance Co., supra* and *R. v. Cronshaw* (1976), 33 C.C.C. (2d) 183 (Ont. Prov. Ct.).

48 *Ibid.*, at 514.

49 *Ibid.*

50 *Ibid.*

the trial proper because the evidence with respect to its making is too conflicting, unsatisfactory because it was made as a result of confusion, duress, emotional upset or the words allegedly spoken are ambiguous.[51] In some circumstances, a judge may find a witness to be adverse solely on the basis of a previous inconsistent statement.[52] On the *voir dire*, the witness should only be examined, not cross-examined, on the prior inconsistent oral statement.[53]

In *R. v. Williams*,[54] it was argued that a declaration of adversity could be made on the basis that there is "some" evidence that there was a prior inconsistent statement. Martin J.A. held the trial judge "must be satisfied to some degree that the statement which constitutes the basis for finding that the witness is adverse was made."

If it appears the witness honestly does not recall something, then the trial judge should not declare the witness adverse.[55] Not so, however, where the witness has a selective memory.[56]

What happens when the Crown who calls the witness already knows or has reason to suspect that the witness will now be unco-operative although he or she was co-operative earlier and gave a statement supporting the Crown's case? It has been held that such foreknowledge should not prevent cross-examination.[57] However, in a section 9(2) application, the Ontario Court of Appeal held that it was not permissible for the Crown to call a witness it knew or anticipated would be inconsistent with a prior statement for the real purpose of throwing a shadow over the defence absent evidence to support a contention that the witness was acting in collusion with the accused. Without a link between the witness's alleged lies and the evidence which the Crown expected would be tendered by the defence, the witness's evidence was irrelevant, or at least of minimal probative value. Its prejudicial effect was severe in that it suggested the defence was a fabrication, without any evidence of the accused's involvement in fabricating it.[58]

---

51 *Ibid.* See also *R. v. O'Hara* (December 18, 1990), Doc. CA 1105/87 (Ont. C.A.) following *R. v. Cassibo* approving the principle that there is a two-step process where the trial judge has a discretion: first, to find the witness hostile or adverse; second, to permit cross-examination. In this case, the Ontario Court of Appeal found no reviewable error in the trial judge exercising his discretion to refuse cross-examination.

52 *Ibid.*

53 *Ibid.*, at 521.

54 (1985), 50 O.R. (2d) 321 (Ont. C.A.).

55 *R. v. Rouse, supra*; *R. v. Gushue* (1976), 30 C.R.N.S. 178 at 182, 14 O.R. (2d) 620 (Ont. C.A.), affirmed (1979) (sub nom. *Gushue v. R.*), [1980] 1 S.C.R. 798 (S.C.C.); *R. v. Waddilove*, Ont. Co. Ct., 1976; *California v. Green*, 479 P. 2d 997 (Calif. S.C., 1971).

56 *R. v. Rouse, supra*; *R. v. Gushue, ibid.*

57 *R. v. Casssibo* (1982), 70 C.C.C. (2d) 498 (Ont. C.A.); *R. v. Mann* (1972), 56 Cr. App. R. 750 (U.K. C.A.).

58 *R. v. Soobrian* (1994), 96 C.C.C. (3d) 208 (Ont. C.A.). See also *R. v. Lake* (November 24, 1997), McCombs J., [1997] O.J. No. 5447 (Ont. Gen. Div.). *R. v. Chisholm* (1995),

Section 9(2), *Canada Evidence Act*

A remaining option open to the examiner-in-chief and the one most often employed, particularly by Crown Attorneys, occurs when the witness has made a prior inconsistent statement in writing or reduced to writing and section 9(2) of the *Canada Evidence Act* is utilized. A signed statement by a witness can be a devastating weapon for the Crown Attorney if the witness is hostile. By cross-examining on a prior inconsistent statement, in writing or reduced to writing, or recorded on audio tape or video tape or otherwise, the witness can be shown to be lying to protect the accused. Even if the witness does not adopt his or her prior statement, the impact on the jury will be enormous unless the inconsistency is satisfactorily explained.

However, when the examiner sees that the witness is testifying inconsistently with the witness's prior statement or where it appears that the witness is conveniently forgetting what he or she saw or heard, then the examiner should not immediately launch into an application under section 9(2). Rather, the examiner should inquire of the witness whether he or she had made an earlier statement as defined in section 9(2) and whether his or her memory would have been better at the time of making that statement. Finally, the witness can be asked whether he or she might not wish to refresh his or her memory from that statement. This procedure was given sanction in *R. v. Coffin*[59] and it seems clear that such a procedure may be demanded by the trial judge.[60] If the witness's memory is accurately refreshed after reading the relevant part of the statement and the witness responds accordingly then the necessity of using the procedure under section 9(2) is obviated. If the witness's memory is not refreshed then the examiner is free to try to invoke section 9(2). When the witness refreshes his or her memory from a prior statement he or she is not to read the statement aloud.[61]

The accepted procedure for section 9(2) was set down by Culliton C.J.S. in *R. v. Milgaard*[62] as follows:

(1) Counsel should advise the court that he desires to make an application under section 9(2) of the *Canada Evidence Act*.

[1995] O.J. No. 3300, 1995 CarswellOnt 3712 (Ont. Gen. Div.) where the Court found that the Crown knew before the witness testified what answers she would give; that the witness fell within the definition of adverse but the plan was to impeach her evidence through prior inconsistent statements to enable the Crown to suggest she had collaborated with the accused, her husband, in fabricating the defence. Section 9 was not intended for that purpose. The fact that the witness was the wife of the accused creates no presumption of collusion.

59 *Supra*.

60 *R. v. Stewart* (1976), 31 C.C.C. (2d) 497 (S.C.C.).

61 *R. v. Laurin (No. 5)* (1902), 6 C.C.C. 135 (Que. K.B.), followed in *R. v. Marshall, supra*, and affirmed in *Lizotte v. R.* (1950), 11 C.R. 357 (S.C.C.).

62 *Supra*, 15 at 49-50 and approved in *R. v. Rouse, supra*.

(2) When the Court is so advised, the Court should direct the jury to retire.

(3) Upon retirement of the jury, counsel should advise the learned trial Judge of the particulars of the application and produce for him the alleged statement in writing, or the writing to which the statement has been reduced.

(4) The learned trial Judge should read the statement, or writing, and determine whether, in fact, there is an inconsistency between such statement or writing and the evidence the witness has given in Court. If the learned trial Judge decides there is no inconsistency, then that ends the matter. If he finds there is an inconsistency, he should call upon counsel to prove the statement or writing.

(5) Counsel should then prove the statement or writing. This may be done by producing the statement or writing to the witness. If the witness admits the statement, or the statement reduced to writing, such proof would be sufficient. If the witness does not so admit, counsel then could provide the necessary proof by other evidence.

(6) If the witness admits making the statements, counsel for the opposing party should have the right to cross-examine as to the circumstances under which the statement was made. A similar right to cross-examine should be granted if the statement is proved by other witnesses. It may be that he will be able to establish that there were circumstances which would render it improper for the learned trial Judge to permit the cross-examination, notwithstanding the apparent inconsistencies. The opposing counsel, too, should have the right to call evidence as to factors relevant to obtaining the statement, for the purpose of attempting to show that cross-examination should not be permitted.

(7) The learned trial Judge should then decide whether or not he will permit the cross-examination. If so, the jury should be recalled.

It is noteworthy that the procedure under section 9(2) provides for cross-examination with respect to a prior inconsistent statement in writing or reduced to writing, for example, the transcript of a preliminary hearing, or from another proceeding,[63] a statement in the witness's handwriting or one signed by the witness,[64] a statement to the police by the witness that was tape-recorded and transcribed.[65] (Section 9(2) now specifically includes a statement recorded on audio tape or otherwise.) Also included is another person's record of what was said on an earlier occasion by the witness. The balance of authority, at least in Ontario, appears to require that the witness read over the statement or signed it provided that the record was made contemporaneously and it is reliable, for example, a police officer's notes of what the witness told the officer.[66] If the trial Judge decides that the

---

63 *R. v. Haughton (No. 3), supra.*

64 *R. v. Milgaard, supra; R. v. Rouse, supra.*

65 *R. v. Gerow* (1981), 22 C.R. (3d) 167 (B.C. C.A.).

66 *R. v. Carpenter* (1982), 31 C.R. (3d) 261 (Ont. C.A.). This case seems to run contra to *R. v. Handy* (1978), 5 C.R. (3d) 97 (B.C. C.A.) and *R. v. Cassibo* (1982), 70 C.C.C. (2d) 498 (Ont. C.A.), which held that a police officer's notes of an interview, that were not

previous statement is sufficiently inconsistent then he or she has a discretion to allow cross-examination on the inconsistent statement.[67] There is no need to prove the witness is adverse in this situation.[68] Counsel seeking to cross-examine would appear to have the burden to show to "some degree" that there was a prior inconsistent statement.[69] If the burden is satisfied, the cross-examination is limited to the inconsistency between the witness's testimony and the prior statement.[70]

However, if the cross-examination on the inconsistent statement shows that the witness is not only inconsistent but that he or she is also adverse, the trial judge can permit counsel to cross-examine his or her own witness at large.

If counsel is permitted to cross-examine his or her own witness, is counsel entitled to continue the cross-examination in re-examination? Mr. Justice Watt's unreported ruling in *R. v. Turchiaro and Prette*[71] held that cross-examination continued during re-examination, although the scope of re-examination remained as always. It seems to make sense that once the witness is cloaked with the mantle of hostility or adversity that the witness continues to wear that cloak throughout his or her testimony.

With increased use by police audio and videotaping of witnesses' statements, the transcripts of the tapings or the tapings themselves may well be offered more frequently for section 9(2) purposes.

If the trial judge finds that the witness chooses not to remember and was therefore lying about his or her recollection, then a finding of inconsistency can be made.[72]

An example of the proper procedure and of the manner in which section 9(2) may effectively be used, is found in the examination by Douglas Hunt, Q.C., appearing for the Crown in a prosecution for conspiracy to commit personation arising out of an attempt to gain illegal entry into the United States from Canada. One of the main Crown witnesses, whose entry into the United States was the object of the conspiracy, had given a signed statement to an investigating officer implicating all of the accused. When

---

confirmed by the witness, cannot be considered as a statement in writing or reduced to writing within section 9(2).

67 *R. v. Carpenter, ibid.*

68 *R. v. Rouse, supra; R. v. Cassibo, ibid.; R. v. Gushue, supra.*

69 *R. v. Williams,* note 23 above. This case deals with section 9(1) but it is suggested that the discretion exercised in section 9(1) should be no different than in section 9(2). *R. v. Meade* (1974), (Ont. Co. Ct.), held that the burden of proof is on the balance of probabilities.

70 *R. v. Polley* (1971), 5 C.C.C. (2d) 94 (N.S. C.A.); *R. v. Milgaard* (1971), 14 C.R.N.S. 34 (Sask. C.A.); *R. v. Marshall* (1972), 8 C.C.C. (2d) 329 (N.S. C.A.); *R. v. Rouse* (1978), 5 C.R. (3d) 125 (S.C.C.); *R. v. Cassibo, supra.*

71 (January 15, 1988) Toronto Assizes. See also *R. v. Moore* (1984), 15 C.C.C. (3d) 541 (Ont. C.A.), leave to appeal refused (1985), 15 C.C.C. (3d) 541n (S.C.C.).

72 *R. v. Rouse, supra; R. v. Gushue, supra.*

called to testify at trial, the witness's evidence during examination-in-chief differed in several significant respects from his statement to the officer. Notice how Mr. Hunt first has the witness admit he made the prior statement and seeks the witness's admission that his memory would have been better at the time he gave his prior statement than it was presently. When the witness isn't certain he is then asked if he would like to refresh his memory with respect to the events that occurred earlier and the witness says yes and then after refreshing his memory denied remembering any of his answers to the questions put by Mr. Hunt. Mr. Hunt then advises the trial Judge he wishes to raise a section 9(2) application on a *voir dire* in the absence of the jury and seeks a ruling of inconsistency by the witness with respect to his evidence and prior statement. He files the statement as an exhibit. When the witness would not accept that he made the prior statements, Mr. Hunt had to call the Customs and Immigration Officer to prove the statement. The trial Judge found there were inconsistencies and as a result permitted Mr. Hunt to cross-examine on the inconsistencies only, but not cross-examine at large.

Q. Mr. Saitta, you told the court this morning that it was your idea to use Mr. Collucci's name and his Certificate of Citizenship when you got to the border, is that correct?

A. Yes, it was my idea.

Q. And you told us that you had no discussion about that with the accused men before you produced Mr. Collucci's Certificate of Citizenship to the Customs official?

A. That's right.

Q. You also testified that it was you who decided where you would sit in the car, and what you would say if questioned about the purpose of your trip?

A. Yes.

Q. All right. Now, were you asked by a Customs official to go into a building?

A. Yes.

Q. When you went inside the building, do you recall being interviewed by a Customs and Immigration Officer?

A. Yes, an officer spoke to me.

Q. Did that officer take a statement from you that you signed?

A. I signed some papers that he gave me, yes.

Q. Mr. Saitta, would your memory with respect to the events that occurred on January 8th have been better at the time that you spoke to that officer than it is now?

A. I don't know, maybe.

Q. Well, would you like to refresh your memory of those events by reading the statement that you gave to that officer?

A. Sure, it doesn't matter to me.

Q. Mr. Saitta, I am placing before you a two page document headed "United States Customs and Immigration Service," and below that "Statement of Detainee." Do you recognize your signature at the bottom of page 2?

A. Yes it is my signature, but I don't remember these things in it.

Q. Well, Mr. Saitta, just read this statement to yourself.

(Witness reads Statement)

Q. Have you finished reading your statement?

A. Yes, I read it but I don't remember these things.

Q. Does that statement refresh your memory as to whose idea it was for you to use Mr. Collucci's name and his Certificate of Citizenship when you were attempting to cross the border?

A. No.

Q. Does it refresh your memory as to whether or not you had any discussion with the accused men before you produced Mr. Collucci's Certificate of Citizenship?

A. No.

Q. Does it refresh your memory as to who decided where you would sit in the car and who decided what you should say about the purpose of your trip if you were questioned?

A. No.

Mr. Hunt: Your Honour, at this point I would like to raise a matter concerning section 9(2) of the *Canada Evidence Act*. I believe it would be more appropriate if this was done in the absence of the jury.

His Honour: Yes. Members of the jury, I am going to ask you to retire at this time while I deal with this matter. Thank you.

(Jury retires.)

Mr. Hunt: Your Honour, it is my position that this witness has testified in a manner that is inconsistent with a signed statement that he provided to the police. I am passing up to Your Honour a copy of that signed statement. I have highlighted the areas in respect of which I am alleging inconsistency on the part of Mr. Saitta during his examination-in-chief. Counsel for the accused have copies, Your Honour. I would ask Your Honour to rule that the evidence given by this witness is in fact inconsistent with this statement and that I be allowed to proceed to prove that this statement is, in fact, his.

His Honour: Yes, this statement will be Exhibit "A" on this voir dire. On reading the witness's statement to the officer I find that it is inconsistent in a number of areas with the evidence that he has given in this Court. The Crown may prove the statement. May I ask you, Mr. Hunt, how do you intend to proceed?

Mr. Hunt: Well, in view of the answers that the witness has just given, I believe that I should put the statement to Mr. Saitta and see if he is prepared to admit that it is his. Given his previous answers, I don't know what his position will be. In the event that he does not admit it, I will call the officer who took the statement from him.

His Honour: Very well, proceed.

Mr. Hunt: Thank you, Your Honour. Mr. Saitta, you have testified that on January 8th of this year you arrived at the American border in Niagara Falls, New York?

A. Yes.

Q. And you were asked by a Customs and Immigration Inspector to go inside a building where you were met by other Customs and Immigration Officers?

A. Yes.

Q. How many other officers did you meet?

A. Three or four.

Q. Were you required to remain inside the building for some period of time?

A. Yes.

Q. While you were inside the building do you recall being asked questions by one of the officers?

A. Yes.

Q. Can you recall whether the officer who asked you the questions wrote down the questions and your answers?

A. He was writing something.

Q. Mr. Saitta, I am going to ask you to listen while I read Exhibit "A" to you, and then I am going to ask you questions about what I have read.

    (Exhibit "A" read to the witness.)

Mr. Hunt: Now, Mr. Saitta do you recall being asked those questions?

A. I remember being asked questions but I don't know if it was those questions.

Q. Do you recall giving those answers that I read to you?

A. No, I don't recall that.

Q. Do you have any recollection of the answers that you gave to the questions that were asked of you by the officer?

A. No, I don't.

Q. Mr. Saitta, I am showing you Exhibit "A" and I am pointing to the bottom of page 2. You have already indicated that you recognize your signature there?

A. Yes, I signed that but I didn't look at the papers that he gave to me.

Q. Do you recognize your initials at the bottom of page 1?

A. Yes, but I didn't read it. I didn't read anything.

Mr. Hunt: Your Honour, it is apparent that Mr. Saitta has not admitted that Exhibit "A" is, in fact, his statement. I believe that I am now in the position of having to call the officer who took the statement in order to prove it. I would ask your permission to do so at this time.

His Honour: Yes, Mr. Saitta I would ask you to wait outside please. You will be recalled. Just remain in the Witness Room across the hall.

    (Witness retires.)

His Honour: Yes, please proceed.

Mr. Hunt: Thank you, Your Honour, I now call Officer Eugene Retkowski.

    (Witness sworn.)

Examination-in-chief by Mr. Hunt:

Mr. Hunt: Mr. Retkowski, you are a Customs and Immigration Officer assigned to the United States Immigration Service, am I correct?

A. Yes, sir.

Q. In your capacity with that Service you are a criminal investigator?

A. That is correct.

Q. How long have you been so employed?

A. Nine and a half years.

Q. What are the nature of your duties?

A. I investigate any violations of the United States immigration laws and pursue either administrative or criminal proceedings when I detect one.

Q. Were you so employed on January 8th of this year?

A. Yes, I was.

Q. Were you asked to attend at the Rainbow Bridge in Niagara Falls, New York on that date, shortly after 10 o'clock in the morning?

A. Yes, I was.

Q. At that time did you have occasion to speak to the previous witness, Mr. Saitta?

A. Yes, I spoke to him at some length in connection with a suspected attempt by a number of people to smuggle him into the United States.

Q. Did you take a statement from Mr. Saitta?

A. Yes, I did.

Q. What form did that statement take?

A. I asked Mr. Saitta a series of questions and I recorded his answers.

Q. Did you do this in writing?

A. Yes, I did.

Q. I am showing you a document marked Exhibit "A," do you recognize that?

A. Yes, I do. This is Mr. Saitta's statement. It is in my handwriting. I recorded the questions that I asked Mr. Saitta and his answers.

Q. Do you recognize any initials and/or signatures on that statement?

A. Yes, my initials, along with Mr. Saitta's, are on page 1 and my signature is at the bottom of page 2 beside Mr. Saitta's.

Q. Did Mr. Saitta affix his initials and his signature to this statement in your presence?

A. Yes, he did.

Q. Did Mr. Saitta read the statement before initialing and signing it?

A. Yes, he appeared to. When I had completed recording his last answer I read it over myself and then I asked him to read it. He took the statement and appeared to read it. I asked him if he was satisfied that it was correct and he nodded his head in the affirmative. I then asked him if he was prepared to initial page 1 and to sign page 2. He did so.

Q. Did you record your questions precisely as asked and his answers precisely as they were given?

A. Yes, I wrote out the questions before I asked him. I did my best to record his exact answers and I believe that I did so.

Q. Thank you, sir. Those are all my questions, Your Honour.

(Cross-examination by counsel for the accused)

Mr. Hunt: Your Honour, it is my submission that officer Retkowski has proved that this statement, Exhibit "A," is the statement of Mr. Saitta. I would ask that I be permitted to cross-examine Mr. Saitta with respect to the evidence that he has given which is inconsistent with this statement.

His Honour: Yes, I will permit cross-examination on the inconsistencies found in this statement. I am not permitting you at this point to cross-examine Mr. Saitta on any other issues. Mr. Clerk, please bring in the jury. Recall Mr. Saitta, please.

(Jury returns)

Cross-examination by Mr. Hunt

Q. Mr. Saitta, you are still under oath.

A. Yes.

Q. Mr. Saitta, this morning you told us about the incident at the Rainbow Bridge on January 8 of this year.

A. Yes.

Q. After you were asked to go inside the building at the Rainbow Bridge you were interviewed by Officer Eugene Retkowski, an officer with the United States Immigration Service, isn't that correct?

A. I was interviewed by someone, I don't remember his name.

Q. Mr. Saitta, I am suggesting to you that it was Officer Retkowski who interviewed you, and that you gave him an account of how you came to be at the Rainbow Bridge that is very different from the story that you have told to this Court.

A. I don't remember what I told anyone at the Rainbow Bridge.

The Hostile Witness

"Your witness."

Trial Diplomacy Journal Cartoon Album. David M. Freedman, Ed. © 1980 Court Practice Journal, Inc.

Q. Mr. Saitta, I am going to read to you a number of questions and answers and I would like you to listen to them please.

(Certain questions and answers read to the witness.)

Q. Now, Mr. Saitta do you recall being asked those questions by Officer Retkowski?

A. No. I was asked some questions but I don't remember them now.

Q. Do you recall giving those answers to Officer Retkowski?

A. No, I don't.

Q. Well, Mr. Saitta I am going to suggest to you that you did give those answers to Officer Retkowski on January 8th of this year, and that you gave them to him because they were true, do you agree with me?

A. Well, I can't remember if I said those things or not. It was sort of confusing to me to be there. I didn't know what was happening when I was asked to go inside the building.

Q. I am placing before you the same document that I asked you to read a little while ago. It is the document that I have just read that series of questions and answers from. It is headed "United States Customs and Immigration Service" and below that "Statement of Detainee." Mr. Saitta, you have already indicated that you recognize your signature at the bottom of page 2, am I correct?

A. Yes.

Q. And are those your initials at the bottom of page 1?

A. Yes.

Q. All right, Mr. Saitta, let's deal with these questions and answers, one at a time . . .

It isn't enough to simply refer to the fact that there are inconsistencies between the witness's evidence and what that witness said earlier. Counsel should be prepared to assist the trial Judge by pointing to the areas in the evidence which differed from the witness's earlier statement. In the example above Mr. Hunt accomplished this by handing to the trial Judge the witness's prior statement highlighting the areas where he was alleging an inconsistency, thereby making the Judge's role easier. He also made it clear to the trial Judge that he was embarking on a section 9(2) application.

In contradistinction to Mr. Hunt's control of a hostile witness is what occurred in *R. v. Situ*[73] where the Crown had a difficult Crown witness and gradually the questioning became more persistent with the Crown commencing to challenge the witness by asking leading questions and by reminding him, improperly, that he could be subject to a perjury prosecution. The Court held that the following excerpt of cross-examination went from a controlled examination into a cross-examination and impeachment without the Crown asking for a declaration that the witness was hostile or an adverse witness or making an application under section 9(2) of the *Canada Evidence Act* for leave to cross-examine the witness on prior inconsistent statements. Note the Court's comments in paragraph 16 of the judgment which follows:

Q. Okay, and so –

A. Like I – like I told you before, he had nothing to do with this stuff.

. . .

---

73 (2005), 200 C.C.C. (3d) 9 (Alta. C.A.).

Q. Okay, can you – as to what information he gave you about the house, would it help you to refresh your memory as to what he actually told you to do to the house if you read your preliminary hearing transcript over?

A. Yeah, I guess. Yes.

. . .

Q. And you start at question that's on line 16.

A. Okay.

Q. And there's another question at line 18, and then your answer at line 19.

A. Like I said, he just gave me the address.

Q. Okay, does that refresh your memory as to the words that actually came out of his mouth?

A. No, it doesn't.

Q. Okay, so –

A. Because there was nothing coming out of his mouth.

Q. Okay. Do you recall testifying at the preliminary inquiry at 220 and giving this answer about the words that came out of his mouth? Just read it over to refresh your memory, sir. Line 19.

A. I don't think he said that anyways.

Q. All right. Okay what words did he say then if he didn't say these words you testified to at the preliminary inquiry?

A. He said, Here, have that, here's the address. And that's all.

[14] After a further exchange between Crown counsel and the witness regarding what may or may not have been said by the appellant about the address, the examination continued at A.B. 294/45:

Q. Okay, did anyone ever say these words, Do this one, to you?

[15] At that point, the defence counsel ("DC") objected that Crown counsel ("CC") was cross-examining his own witness:

DC: This in my view, is – is both leading and if my friend is –

The Court: It's cross-examination.

DC: Yes, sir and –
The Court: But we can get there if we have to.
DC: Yes, sir through the hostile – the inconsistent, previous statement or the other – or a hostile witness procedure, but. . .
CC: My Lord, I take the position that leading questions are not allowed in the Court. It is that the weight given to the answer then is entitled to the weight that the trial Judge puts on it, because of the leading nature of the question. It certainly is leading.
DC: Well, at any time that my friend seeks to get a different answer from the one that was given by the witness, this is going beyond simply being a leading question. It's a form of cross-examination.
The Court: Well if you look at section 9 of the *Canada Evidence Act*.
DC: Yes, sir.

The Court: It says if a witness in the opinion of the Court proves adverse, the party may contradict him by other evidence or, by leave of the Court, may prove that the witness made at other times a statement that is inconsistent with his present testimony. But before the last mentioned proof can be given, the circumstances of the supposed statement sufficient to designate the particular occasion shall be mentioned to the witness and he shall be asked whether or not he did make the statement. Now that's a pretty clear exposition of what the law is.

After further discussion, the transcript continues at A.B. 296/32:

CC: He's read it. I've asked him does it refresh his memory. He says yes. And then I asked him a question. I was now just about, which my friend objects to – just about to ask a leading question to which I take the view is that they are –

The Court: But word –

CC: – leading questions are – the answer gets less weight. It's not that you're not allowed to ask him, but the answer sure gets less weight.

The Court: But word for word from the transcript –

CC: Well, I'm not – I'm not putting word for word from the transcript to him yet. My question simply was. . . In dealing with this Hamptons robbery, did anyone say – and I was about to give these words to him.

The Court: All right. Did anyone say what?

CC: Yes, my question is, In dealing with the robbery in the Hamptons. . . did anyone say, in giving you the address, quote, "do this one."

Q. Did you hear that question, Mr. Cree?

A. Yes.

Q. Okay.

A. Well, it says that right down here, but. . .

Q. Okay. No, but we want to know from you, sir. So I'll repeat the question. The Hamptons robbery. . . in getting the address to the Hampton's, did anyone say "do this one"?

A. I guess so, because it's down here. I don't remember.

Q. Okay, so you –

A. Like I say, it's been a long way.

Q. I see, you don't remember now?

A. Yeah.

Q. So reading the preliminary transcript, were you under oath at that time?

A. Yes.

Q. And were you trying to be truthful?

A. Yes.

Q. And you knew you were in a courtroom.

A. Yes.

Q. There was a judge there, right?

A. Yes.

Q. Lawyers were asking you questions?

A. Yes.

Q. Okay, both for the prosecution and the defence?

A. Yes.

Q. Okay. So you're doing your best to make truthful statements?

A. Yes.

Q. Okay. Knowing that if you lie, it's a crime, right?

A. Yes.

Q. Get added – it might get added to your long jail term?

A. Yes.

Q. Okay. So my question to you, sir, is when you got the address from Mr. Situ, this Hamptons address –

A. Yeah.

Q. – that he said was his friend's house –

A. Yes.

Q. – did anyone, when you got the address, say, "do this one"?

A. Yes.

Q. Who's that?

A. Mr. Situ, but I don't – I didn't – I didn't recognize this or as – hear him that good. So I thought he – that's what he said.

Q. Okay, so you –

A. That's why I said –

Q. – you thought he might have said "do this one," but you're not 100 percent sure.

A. Yes, I'm not 100 percent sure.

Q. Okay.

A. That's why I said that in the last Court hearing.

Q. Okay. Now can you just tell us about the things that you would have –

The Court: Just so the record is clear, you've read that –

A. Yes.

The Court: Mr. Cree, and –

A. But I just – everything –

The Court: Just a minute, and the words are there.

A. Yeah.

The Court: And what you are telling me then is that, if you said it, you don't remember saying it, or are you –

A. No, I do remember saying it, but I don't know if it's true fact.

The Court: Okay.

A. – that he said that.

The Court made the following comments:

[16] Crown counsel then continued with further cross-examination as to what the appellant had or had not said, specifically whether Situ said "do this one" or "don't do this one," and the following exchange occurred at A.B. 300/5-11:

A. No, I said he probably said, maybe don't do – or don't do this one. . . and I thought that he said do this one. That's what it says right there.

Q. Okay, but your memory is – is what, sir, of what he said when he gave you the address?

A. "Do this one."

[18] The procedure adopted by the Crown counsel at trial leaves us without any record by which to assess the extent of the inconsistency, if any, between Cree's trial and preliminary inquiry testimony. Excerpts from the preliminary inquiry were neither read in nor made an exhibit at trial. We assume that there was an inconsistency and recognize that Crown counsel could have applied, pursuant to section 9 of the *Canada Evidence Act*, for leave to cross-examine the witness on prior inconsistent statements, or as an adverse or hostile witness. Indeed, the trial Judge suggested this to him. Alternatively, Crown counsel could have made a K.G.B. application (pursuant to the principles outlined in *R. v. B. (K.G.)*, [1993] 1 S.C.R. 740, 79 C.C.C. (3d) 257) to have the preliminary inquiry transcript admitted in evidence. See also Ron Delisle, Don Stuart & David Tanovich, *Evidence, Principles and Problems* 7th ed. (Toronto: Carswell, 2004) at 462; *R. v. Glowatski* (2001), 47 C.R. (5th) 230, 2001 BCCA 678, 160 C.C.C. (3d) 525. The prior inconsistent statement could then be weighed by the trial Judge, along with the trial testimony, to permit the Court to determine what evidence should be found reliable: *Glowatski* at para. 22. Unfortunately, the Crown counsel chose not to pursue any of these avenues. We cannot now speculate on what the results would have been had the proper applications been made.

[19] We allow the appeal and order a new trial on Counts 1, 2 and 3, the three home-invasion robberies.

13

Re-Examination

THE LAW

When cross-examination is finished, opposing counsel may re-examine his or her witness to explain ambiguities, qualify admissions or to put answers given in cross-examination into proper perspective.[1] If the witness's evidence can be strengthened by re-examination, it will carry a tactical advantage as it is the last evidence the jurors will hear from the witness. It is not hard to appreciate therefore that if re-examination is done well it can be most effective.

The law relating to re-examination is simple. No leading questions may be put in re-examination,[2] and because an accused is entitled to know about all of the evidence against him or her before he or she is obliged to answer, re-examination can be used only to explain or to qualify answers given in cross-examination and no new material may be introduced unless with leave of the Court.[3] In other words, re-examination is limited to what was raised in cross-examination, otherwise it is against the rule of splitting one's case.[4] However, trial judges often give leave to the examiner-in-chief to introduce new matters in re-examination which were omitted in-chief through inadvertence.[5] When such leave is given, opposing counsel will be given an opportunity to cross-examine on the new material.

---

1 *R. v. Evans* (1993), 82 C.C.C. (3d) 338 (S.C.C.), per Cory J. at 339.
2   *R. v. J. (J.)* (2002), 168 C.C.C. (3d) 44 (Ont. C.A.).
3 *R. v. Moore* (1984), 15 C.C.C. (3d) 541 (Ont. C.A.), leave so appeal to S.C.C. refused (1985), 15 C.C.C. (3d) 541n (S.C.C.).
4 *Evans, supra*, at 349.
5 *R. v. Smith* (1986), 71 N.S.R. 229 (C.A.). However, in *R. v. Burk* (1999), 139 C.C.C. (3d) 266 (Ont. C.A.) it was held that where the Crown made a tactical decision not to cross-examine a witness on what turned out to be an important point, the Crown should not have been permitted to re-examine on that point.

If inadmissible matters are introduced in cross-examination, the right to re-examine on the inadmissible evidence remains and this rule holds true even where the witness volunteers the inadmissible evidence.[6]

A question often employed, particularly by Crown counsel after a prosecution witness has been bruised in cross-examination, is: "Are you still certain about your testimony in-chief when you testified that . . .?" This is not proper re-examination as it does not explain or qualify testimony in-chief. It is also oath-helping. On one occasion I walked into a courtroom in Toronto to watch the marvellous trial lawyer, Arthur Maloney, Q.C. defend. At the time I entered the courtroom, Mr. Maloney had just risen to re-examine his expert. Mr. Maloney asked this one question: "Dr., there are probably a number of questions I could ask you but I'll ask only this one—have any of the questions my friend asked caused you to change your mind about the answers you gave to me in examination-in-chief?" The answer was obviously "No." I had not heard any of the cross-examination but I remember thinking, "What a well-put and economical question to preserve the evidence-in-chief." But as much as I might admire the artistry of that question I do not believe it to be a proper re-examination for it is really the same question that the Crown puts in re-examination when he or she asks whether the witness has any doubts about his evidence given in-chief.

WHEN TO RE-EXAMINE

Re-examination should be confined to the really essential matters in cross-examination which emerged to the client's disadvantage. According to Mortimer Hays, the trial judge and jurors:[7]

> [H]ave a sense of proportion and counsel must not be too concerned about minor inaccuracies. The attempt to review each and every incident and offer an explanation may create a bad impression, as the witness's testimony is left with a long series of explanations of inaccuracies on his part. It is much better to have them relegated, where possible, to the broad field of unimportant and immaterial matters. By concentrating upon the major issues (particularly if . . . the direct examination of the witnesses, the re-direct examination, and the summation hammer upon these pivotal points and indicate the total immateriality of other details) counsel will help the jury to arrive at the conclusion that the other matters are unimportant.

However, if counsel, affecting indifference, can dismiss the cross-examination by saying: "I have no need to re-examine the witness," it is all for the better.

---

6 *R. v. Nöel* (1903), 7 C.C.C. 309 (Ont. C.A.).
7 M. Hays, "Tactics in Direct Examination," August 1, 1951, Practicing Law Institute.

It is really quite impossible to teach re-examination by examples because so much depends on what is brought out in the cross-examination in each particular case. However, there are some areas that can be identified as usually requiring re-examination:

1. Where the witness is cut off in his or her answer in cross-examination so that he or she is not able to give a desired explanation.

2. A good cross-examiner will try to lead the witness through a series of "yes" or no answers in order to control the witness. The re-examiner can give the witness the opportunity to explain and amplify his or her one-word or multi-word answers in re-examination.

3. If there is an important inconsistency between what the witness testified to in-chief and in cross-examination it will be necessary to ask the witness to explain the inconsistency. A glaring inconsistency left alone will be maximized by the opponent in summing-up and counsel has therefore nothing to lose in asking for an explanation even though he or she may not know the answer. There may be a mitigating answer, such as misunderstanding by the witness of one of the questions. Here the re-examiner may lead to identify the inconsistent answers.

4. If there has been a suggestion of recent fabrication, the re-examiner is entitled to rehabilitate the witness by bringing forth an earlier consistent statement.[8]

5. If the cross-examiner questions only on part of a conversation or part of a document the re-examiner may re-examine to bring out the rest of the conversation or contents of the document if it serves his or her purpose.

6. The cross-examiner may, by his or her questions and the answers received, be satisfied to reach a certain point without asking the final question to nail the coffin shut, probably because he or she is not sure of or is afraid of the answer. But in final argument, the cross-examiner will urge that there is an obvious inference that can be drawn from the answers given and of course that inference will be unfavourable to the opponent. In re-examination counsel can prevent this tactic by asking that question which the cross-examiner was fearful of posing. A simple example would be where the alibi witness called to testify for an accused is his wife. The Crown's cross-examination would go something like this:

Q. Mrs. Smith, do you love your husband?
A. Yes, sir.
Q. You do not want to see him go to jail?
A. No, I don't.

8　*R. v. Lalonde* (1971), 5 C.C.C. (2d) 168 (Ont. H.C.); *R. v. St. Lawrence* (1949), 93 C.C.C. 376 (Ont. H.C.).

Q. You would do everything you could to prevent that?

A. Well . . . yes, yes I would.

The cross-examiner may not wish to ask the next question—"and that includes lying for him"—because the wife's answer would be obvious. The obvious inference left and to be underscored in the jury summation by the cross-examiner is that the wife might even lie about the alibi to prevent her husband from being convicted. The re-examination should be:

Q. Mrs. Smith, by doing everything you could to prevent your husband from going to jail are you including unlawful acts such as committing perjury before this court?

A. Oh no, sir, I could never do that.

Another example in this area is when questions are put in cross-examination about witnesses speaking to each other about the case, inferring or alleging a joint recollection or even collusion about what was seen or heard. The re-examination might go something like this after it was established what the witnesses discussed:

Q. Did you try to influence X (about what she saw or heard)?

Q. Did X try to influence you (about what you saw or heard)?

Q. Was your recollection influenced (by what you saw or heard) or has your evidence been a result of yur own independent recollection?

There is an important piece of advice that counsel can give his or her witness before testifying: although the witness may be concerned while on the stand that he is not answering as he would ideally like to do in cross-examination, he should not panic or fumble to explain because his own counsel will have the opportunity in re-examination to go over the evidence that the witness gave in cross-examination and to give him the opportunity to explain or qualify any of the answers requiring explanation or amplification.

COUNSEL SPEAKING TO WITNESS BETWEEN CROSS-EXAMINATION AND RE-EXAMINATION

Different law societies may take different views as to whether counsel may speak to her witness after cross-examination and before commencing re-examination. Those rulings are related to ethical considerations. The case law seems to favour two different positions: either it is improper or that consent should be obtained from the opposite side, or from the Court.[9]

---

9   *R. v. Montgomery* (1998), 126 C.C.C. (3d) 251 (B.C. S.C.); *R. c. Brouillette* (1992), (*sub nom. R. v. Peruta*) 78 C.C.C. (3d) 350 (Que. C.A.), leave to appeal refused (1993), 81 C.C.C. (3d) vi (note) (S.C.C.); *Emil Anderson Construction Co. v. British Columbia Railway*, 1987 CarswellBC 1242 (B.C. S.C.) per MacDonald J.

14

Reply, Surreply and Collateral Questions

REPLY (REBUTTAL) EVIDENCE

The Crown is only entitled to call rebuttal or reply evidence in order to meet new facts or issues raised by the defence which the Crown could not reasonably be expected to anticipate and call as part of its case. The accused is entitled to know the entire case for the prosecution before electing to call evidence and therefore the Crown is not entitled to split its case by calling evidence in reply.[1] This rule prevents the accused from being taken by surprise and being deprived of an adequate opportunity to make a proper investigation with respect to the evidence. It also prevents a piece of evidence from being unduly emphasized in relation to other evidence.[2] The reply evidence is not to be merely confirmatory of the Crown's case, but must be directed solely to rebutting the new evidence led by the defence.[3]

Even if the new evidence relates to a particular defence being put forth by the accused which the Crown knows will be raised, the Crown will not necessarily be precluded from calling reply evidence where the issue had not become a live issue during the Crown's case and its precise nature was not clear until the defence witnesses testified.[4] This should not however give the Crown the right to ambush the defence. In *R. v. Demeter*[5] the Court underscored the trial Judge's discretion with respect to the admissibility of

---

1 *R. v. Campbell* (1977), 38 C.C.C. (2d) 6 (Ont. C.A.). See also *R. v. John* (1985), 23 C.C.C. (3d) 326 (S.C.C.); *Krause v. R.* (1986), 29 C.C.C. (3d) 385 (S.C.C.).

2 *Ibid.*

3 *Ibid. R. v. Therien* (1943), 80 C.C.C. 87 (B.C. C.A.).

4 *R. v. Stevenson* (1990), 58 C.C.C. (3d) 464 (Ont. C.A.) at 490-1; *R. v. Pangelen* (1996), 31 O.R. (3d) 504 (Ont. C.A.) held that if the evidence was not introduced during the Crown's case because it was of marginal importance, but takes on added significance during the defence case, the trial Judge has a discretion to admit the evidence as not offending the rule against the Crown splitting its case provided the evidence would not be unfair to the accused.

5 (1975), 25 C.C.C. (2d) 417 (Ont. C.A.).

the reply evidence by stating that although strictly admissible, the evidence was of such slight probative value that the trial judge would have been justified in excluding it.

McIntyre J., on behalf of the Supreme Court of Canada, wrote the following in *Krause v. R.*[6] regarding reply evidence:

> The plaintiff or the Crown may be allowed to call evidence in rebuttal after completion of the defence case, where the defence has raised some new matter or defence which the Crown has had no opportunity to deal with and which the Crown or the plaintiff could not reasonably have anticipated. But rebuttal will not be permitted regarding matters which merely confirm or reinforce earlier evidence adduced in the Crown's case which could have been brought before the defence was made. It will be permitted only when it is necessary to insure that at the end of the day each party will have had an equal opportunity to hear and respond to the full submissions of the other.
>
> In the cross-examination of witnesses essentially the same principles apply. Crown counsel in cross- examining an accused are not limited to subjects which are strictly relevant to the essential issues in a case. Counsel are accorded a wide freedom in cross-examination which enable them to test and question the testimony of the witnesses and their credibility. Where something new emerges in cross-examination, which is new in the sense that the Crown had no chance to deal with it in its case-in-chief (*i.e.*, there was no reason for the Crown to anticipate that the matter would arise), and where the matter is concerned with the merits of the case (*i.e.*, it concerns an issue essential for the determination of the case) then the Crown may be allowed to call evidence in rebuttal. Where, however, the new matter is collateral, that is, not determinative of an issue arising in the pleadings or indictment or not relevant to matters which must be proved for the determination of the case, no rebuttal will be allowed. An early expression of this proposition is to be found in *Attorney-General v. Hitchcock* (1847), 1 Ex. 91, 154 E.R. 38, and examples of the application of the principle may be found in *R. v. Cargill*, [1913] 2 K.B. 271 (C.C.A.); *R. v. Hrechuk* (1950), 98 C.C.C. 44, 10 C.R. 132, 58 Man. R. 489 (Man. C.A.); *R. v. Rafael* (1972), 7 C.C.C. (2d) 325, [1972] 3 O.R. 238 (Ont. C.A.), and *Latour v. The Queen* (1976), 33 C.C.C. (2d) 377, 74 D.L.R. (3d) 12, [1978] 1 S.C.R. 361. This is known as the rule against rebuttal on collateral issues. Where it applies, Crown counsel may cross-examine the accused on the matters raised, but the Crown is bound by the answers given. This is not to say that the Crown or the trier of fact is bound to accept the answers as true. The answer is binding or final only in the sense that rebuttal evidence may not be called in contradiction.

---

6   (1986), 29 C.C.C. (3d) 385 at 391-392 (S.C.C.). See also *R. v. John* (1985), 23 C.C.C. (3d) 326 at 329 (S.C.C.) and *R. v. Daigle* (1988), 39 C.C.C. (3d) 542 at 558-559 (Que. C.A.); *R. v. Lavoie* (1992), 72 C.C.C. (3d) 83 (Que. C.A.); *R. v. Lawrence* (1989), 52 C.C.C. (3d) 452 (Ont. C.A.); *R. v. Vickerson* (2005), 199 C.C.C. (3d) 165 (Ont. C.A.).

CHARACTER EVIDENCE IN REPLY

Character evidence may be called in reply to rebut evidence of good character adduced by the defence, but it cannot be evidence of specific acts of bad conduct. It has to be evidence of general reputation, criminal record of the accused "or possible expert evidence of disposition."[7] The one exception to this rule are acts that would be evidence of similar acts.[8]

SURREPLY (SURREBUTTAL)

If the Crown adduces new evidence in rebuttal, the Court may permit the accused to call evidence in surrebuttal to contradict or qualify this new evidence.[9] Once surrebuttal is permitted, the defence cannot be limited in calling its evidence for full answer and defence.[10]

COLLATERAL QUESTIONS

The collateral fact rule states that if a party elicits an answer from an opposing witness relating to a collateral matter, that party is bound by the answers and is not permitted to contradict the witness by other evidence. The Oxford Dictionary[11] defines a collateral fact as additional, but subordinate; contributory; aside from the main subject, course etc.

While normally reply evidence that goes only to credibility is collateral and held to be inadmissible as reply evidence[12] the case of *Aalders v. R.*[13]

---

7   *R. v. Brown* (1999), 137 C.C.C. (3d) 400 (Ont. C.A.).

8   *Ibid.*

9   *R. v. Demeter, supra; R. v. Therien, supra; R. v. Wong On (No. 3)* (1904), 10 B.C.R. 555 (B.C. C.A.); *R. v. Higgins* (1902), 36 N.B.R. 18 (N.B. C.A.); *R. v. Morgentaler (No. 3)* (1973), 14 C.C.C. (2d) 453 (Que. Q.B.); *R. v. Ewert* (1989), 52 C.C.C. (3d) 280 (B.C. C.A.).

10 *R. v. Rhodes* (1981), 59 C.C.C. (2d) 426 (B.C. C.A.); *R. v. Ewert* (1989), 52 C.C.C. (3d) 280 at 283 (B.C. C.A.); *R. v. Morgentaler (No. 3)* (1973), 14 C.C.C. (2d) 453 (Que. Q.B.).

11 Oxford English Reference Dictionary 2nd ed. Rev. 2002, Oxford University Press. For decisions relating to whether certain facts are collateral, see *R. v. Fife* (2004), 186 C.C.C. (3d) 361 (B.C. C.A.); *R. v. Moghaddam* (2006), 206 C.C.C. (3d) 497 (B.C. C.A.); *R. v. McNeil* (2009), 238 C.C.C. (3d) 353 (S.C.C.); *R. v. Hoeving*, 2008 ABQB 479 (Alta. Q.B.); *R. v. Towpich*, 2008 ABQB 382 (Alta. Q.B.); *R. v. Jones*, 2008 ABQB 559 (Alta. Q.B.). My thanks to Laura K. Stevens, Q.C. for this list of cases: The Collateral Facts Rule: In Whose Eyes Beholding? 2009 National Criminal Law Program, Vol. 1.

12 *R. v. Dussiaume* (1995), 98 C.C.C. (3d) 217 (Ont. C.A.). See also *Phipson on Evidence*, 14th ed. (1990) para 12-33; *R. v. Gassyt* (1998), 127 C.C.C. (3d) 546 (Ont. C.A.), leave to appeal refused (1999), 136 C.C.C. (3d) vi (S.C.C.).

13 (1993), (sub nom. *R. v. Aalders*) 82 C.C.C. (3d) 215 (C.S.C.). In *R. v. R. (D.)* (1996), 107 C.C.C. (3d) 289 (S.C.C.), it was held that where the credibility of the children was central to the disposition of the case, credibility was not collateral.

held that the collateral rule was not breached if the rebuttal evidence was related to an essential issue that may be determinative of the case (as opposed to whether the Crown seeks to introduce evidence which is determinative of an essential issue). In *Aalders* it was held that in certain circumstances the credibility of the accused on a secondary issue could be essential in ascertaining his intention on the main issue. In *R. v. P. (G.)*,[14] Justice Rosenberg stated that the determination of whether evidence is collateral involves a consideration whether the evidence is "relevant to some issue in the case other than to merely contradict the witness."

The reasoning behind the rule that there must be a finality of answers to collateral questions is that if contradictory evidence is permitted with respect to collateral matters the trial could become submerged in side issues and the jurors deflected from the main issues.[15]

There are therefore two distinct considerations with respect to reply evidence: does the evidence breach the collateral fact rule or does it amount to a splitting of the Crown's case? In either instance, the evidence is inadmissible.

Some exceptions to the collateral fact rule are:

(1) Bias. Should the witness deny on cross-examination being biased evidence can be called to refute the denial,[16] or where the witness can be discredited due to corruption or the like.[17]

(2) Prior Convictions. Section 12 of the *Canada Evidence Act* permits proof of prior convictions when the witness denies such fact or refuses to answer.

(3) Reputation for Truthfulness. A witness may testify as to his or her personal opinion that the opponent's witness is untruthful and would not believe that witness under oath.[18] However in *R. v. Clarke*,[19] it was held impermissible for the witness to be asked if he/she would believe the Crown witness under oath.

(4) Medical evidence to show that the witness suffers from some disease or defect or abnormality of the mind that affects the reliability of his or her evidence.[20]

---

14 (1996), 112 C.C.C. (3d) 263 at 275 (Ont. C.A.).

15 *Krause v. R., supra*, at 392.

16 *R. v. McDonald* (1959), 126 C.C.C. 1 (S.C.C.); *Wigmore on Evidence*, Vol. 3A (Chadbourne Revision, 1976) at 784-800; *R. v. Bencardino* (1973), 15 C.C.C. (2d) 342 (Ont. C.A.). In *R v. S. (A.)* (2002), 165 C.C.C. (3d) 426 (Ont. C.A.) testimony of a witness was allowed in reply from which bias of a defence witness could be inferred.

17 Wigmore, *Evidence in Trials at Common Law*, reversed by Chadbourne 1970, Vol. 3A at 1009-1011.

18 *R. v. Gonzague* (1983), 4 C.C.C. (3d) 505 (Ont. C.A.); *R. v. T. (S.)* (1986), 31 C.C.C. (3d) 1 (Ont. C.A.).

19 *Supra*. See Chapter, "Character Witness."

20 *Toohey v. Metropolitan Police Commissioner*, [1965] 1 All E.R. 506 (U.K. H.L.); *R. v.*

(5) Sweeping Claims. Where a witness has made a wide and exaggerated statement of fact which, if left unanswered, would leave the jury with a distorted picture and could reasonably affect the verdict.[21]

(6) To refute evidence of good character introduced by the accused.[22] See also section 666 of the Criminal Code permitting introduction of the accused's criminal record in reply if accused puts forth evidence of good character.

(7) Alibi. However in *R. v. Biddle*[23] it was held that because the accused had given his alibi to the police before trial, the identity of the accused was an issue at trial and that the accused's presence at the scene of the crime was an essential element of the Crown's case to be proven in-chief, and that this was not a case where the Crown did not know exactly what the defence would allege, the Crown should not have been allowed reply evidence to contradict the accused's alibi.

(8) To show a prior inconsistent statement by the witness that relates to an issue in the case.

As a general proposition it would appear that even when the Crown suspects that a particular defence will be raised, it does not have to respond in its case in-chief to a defence which the accused might possibly raise as it does not know exactly what allegations to refute.[24]

The trial Judge has a discretion to exclude relevant reply evidence if its prejudicial effect outweighs its probative value.[25]

Hawke (1975), 22 C.C.C. (2d) 19 (Ont. C.A.); *R. v. Chaulk* (1990), 62 C.C.C. (3d) 193 (S.C.C.).

21 This is an American concept discussed in Moss, "The Sweeping Claims Exception and Federal Rules of Evidence," [1982] Duke L.J. 61; *McCormick on Evidence*, 4th ed., Vol. 1 (1992) at 229-232.

22 *R. v. Morris* (1978), 43 C.C.C. (2d) 129 (S.C.C.).

23 (1995), 96 C.C.C. (3d) 321 at 331 (S.C.C.).

24 *R. v. Chaulk, supra,* at 238.

25 *R. v. Clair* (1995), 411 A.P.R. 101 at 107 (N.S. C.A.). This weighing process also obtains for the rule against the admissibility of collateral facts. See *R. v. B. (A.R.)* (1998), 41 O.R. (3d) 361 (Ont. C.A.), leave to appeal refused (1999), 243 N.R. 198 (note) (S.C.C.), affirmed (2000), 48 O.R. (3d) 640 (S.C.C.).

15

Reopening The Case

CROWN REOPENING

Lamer J., in *R. v. P. (M.B.)*,[1] stated the law:

The keystone principle in determining whether the Crown should be allowed to reopen its case has always been whether the accused will suffer prejudice in the legal sense—that is, will be prejudiced in his or her defence. A trial judge's exercise of discretion to permit the Crown's case to be reopened must be exercised judicially and should be based on ensuring that the interests of justice are served.

Traditionally, courts in Canada and in England have treated the stage reached in a proceeding as correlative to prejudice and injustice to the accused. That is, a court's discretion with respect to reopening will be exercised less readily as the trial proceeds. The point is illustrated by taking the following three stages in a trial:

(1) before the Crown closes its case,

(2) immediately after the Crown closes its case but before the defence elects whether or not to call evidence (most commonly, this is where the defence has moved for a directed verdict of acquittal for failure by the Crown to prove some essential ingredient of its case), and

(3) after the defence has started to answer the case against it by disclosing whether or not it will be calling evidence.

In the first phase, before the Crown has closed its case, a trial judge has considerable latitude in exercising his or her discretion to allow the Crown to

---

1   (1994), 89 C.C.C. (3d) 289 (S.C.C.). See also *R. v. G. (S.G.)* (1997), 116 C.C.C. (3d) 193 (S.C.C.), where the Court held it was impermissible in the circumstances to permit the Crown to re-open its case to call a new witness after the defence closed its case. An example of where the Crown was not permitted to re-open after the defence was closed is *R. v. Guimond* (2000), 139 C.C.C. (3d) 97 (Man. C.A.). In *R. v. P. (M.B.)* (1994), 89 C.C.C. (3d) 289 (S.C.C.) it was held that the trial Judge was in error to permit the Crown to re-open and call evidence after the Crown closed its case and defence started to answer its case. At this juncture the trial Judge's discretion to permit re-opening is very restricted.

recall a witness so that his or her earlier testimony can be corrected. Any prejudice to the accused can generally be cured at this early stage by an adjournment, cross-examination of the recalled witness and other Crown witnesses and/or a review by the trial judge of the record in order to determine whether certain portions should be struck.

Once the Crown actually closes its case and the second phase in the proceeding is reached, the trial judge's discretion to allow a reopening will narrow and the corresponding burden on the Crown to satisfy the court that there are no unfair consequences will heighten. The test to be applied by the trial judge is generally understood to be that reopening is to be permitted to correct some oversight or inadvertent omission by the Crown in the presentation of its case, provided of course that justice requires it and there will be no prejudice to the defence.

Lastly, in the third phase after the Crown has closed its case and the defence has started to answer the case against it (or, as in much of the case-law, the defence has actually closed its case), a court's discretion is very restricted and is far less likely to be exercised in favour of the Crown. It will only be in the narrowest of circumstances that the Crown will be permitted to reopen its case. Traditionally, an *ex improviso* limitation was said to apply to this stage of the proceeding; that is, the Crown was only allowed to reopen if some matter arose which no human ingenuity could have foreseen. At this late stage, the question of what "justice" requires will be directed much more to protecting the interests of the accused than to serving the often wider societal interests represented by the Crown, the latter being a more pressing consideration at the first and, to a lesser extent, the second phase

. . .

What is so objectionable about allowing the Crown's case to be reopened *after* the defence has started to meet that case is that it jeopardizes, indirectly, the principle that an accused not be conscripted against himself or herself. In *Dubois*, this court interpreted the privilege against self-incrimination contained in s. 13 of the Charter as preventing the Crown from indirectly conscripting the accused to defeat himself by using his previous testimony against him—something which the Crown is directly prohibited from doing under s. 11(c) of the Charter. In my opinion, a similar danger is involved when the Crown seeks to reopen its case *after* the defence has begun to answer the case against it—that is, there is a real risk that the Crown will, based on what it has heard from the defence once it is compelled to "meet the case" against it, seek to fill in gaps or correct mistakes in the case which it had on closing and to which the defence has started to respond. To ensure that this does not in fact happen, the Crown should not, as a general rule, be permitted to reopen once the defence has started to answer the Crown's case.

. . .

I have suggested that it will only be in special circumstances that a trial judge should entertain an application by the Crown to reopen after the defence has begun answertng the case against it. Two examples of such circumstances have been provided: where conduct of the defence has contributed to an omission by the Crown, or where matters of form rather than substance are involved. There may be other exceptional circumstances in which reopening will be justified.

. . .

Clearly, where the interests of the accused warrant reopening the Crown's case, a trial judge should exercise his or her discretion accordingly, no matter how late in the proceeding it may be.[2]

DEFENCE REOPENING

Where the trial is before judge sitting without a jury and there is a finding of guilt, the trial judge is not functus officio until he or she has imposed sentence. The trial judge therefore has the discretion to vacate the finding of guilt and reopen permitting the accused to call further evidence. This discretion should be exercised only in exceptional circumstances and where clearly called for.[3] It has been held that there must be a reasonable explanation advanced for earlier failure to adduce the evidence sought to be introduced and that such evidence must be admissible, credible and which might reasonably affect the verdict.[4] An application to re-open evidence based on nothing more than a desire to reverse an earlier tactical decision

---

2 See *R. v. G.* (1994), 90 C.C.C. (3d) 97 (B.C. C.A.), where the Crown was permitted to reopen its case just prior to the jury addresses in order to call a witness because it did not know till after defence closed its case that the witness had material evidence to give and the accused was not prejudiced in the circumstances. Where the jury verdict is an unambiguous verdict of acquittal, the accused is entitled to an immediate discharge and the Court is not entitled to re-open the case. *Head v. R.* (1986), 30 C.C.C. (3d) 481 (S.C.C.).

3 *R. v. Lessard* (1976), 30 C.C.C. (2d) 70 (Ont. C.A.). In *R. v. Clarke*, 2009 CarswellOnt 6281 (Ont. S.C.J.) it was held that reopening is permitted when it is in the interests of justice to do so, i.e., when the evidence is material, what is prejudice to the other party and the effect of reopening on the orderly and expeditious conduct of the trial.

4 *R. v. Sarson* (1992), 77 C.C.C. (3d) 233 (N.S. C.A.). An example of the defence not being allowed to re-open because of a failure to demonstrate that the witness it wished to recall had any relevant evidence to give on substantive issues or could establish a possible defence can be seen in *R. v. Scott* (1990), 61 C.C.C. (3d) 300 (S.C.C.). In *R. v. Arabia* (2008), 235 C.C.C. (3d) 354 (Ont. C.A.) at para. 46, following *R. v. Kowall* (1996), 108 C.C.C. (3d) 481 (Ont. C.A.), leave to appeal refused (1997), [1997] 1 S.C.R. viii (note (S.C.C.); see also *R. v. Hayward* (1993), 86 C.C.C. (3d) 193 (Ont. C.A.), the Court held that once a trial Judge convicted an accused, as compared to a defence application to reopen its case prior to conviction, the test is more stringent. The test to admit fresh evidence is the Palmer test for the admission of fresh evidence on appeal. The party seeking to introduce the evidence must show: the evidence could not have been found by the exercise of due diligence; it is relevant evidence that bears upon a decisive or potentially decisive issue; it is credible evidence; and it could have reasonably been expected to have affected the result.

could properly be refused as being detrimental to the orderly conduct of the trial.[5]

The Judge, however, has no power to re-open the case after a jury verdict.[6]

5 *R. v. Hayward* (1993), 86 C.C.C. (3d) 193 (Ont. C.A.).
6 *R. v. Lessard*, above; *R. v. Gostick* (1991), 62 C.C.C. (3d) 276 (Ont. C.A.).

16

Further Limitations and Obligations in Examining Witnesses

SUGGESTING FACTS COUNSEL CANNOT PROVE

Is counsel permitted to make an allegation which he or she does not intend to prove if the answer is a denial? This question has finally been decided in *R. v. Lyttle*[1] by the Supreme Court of Canada holding that a question may be put to a witness by the defence in cross-examination about matters that need not be proved independently, provided counsel has a good faith basis for the question. Good faith comes from information available to the cross-examiner and his or her belief in its likely accuracy and purpose for which it is put. A reading of this decision implies that it applies only to the defence, not to the Crown. However counsel cannot suggest facts counsel knows to be false.[2]

Lyttle is an important decision as it broadens the scope of cross-examination for the defence.

ASKING A WITNESS TO COMMENT ON ANOTHER WITNESS'S CREDIBILITY

Neither Crown nor defence can ask a witness if another witness is lying, or pass comment on the credibility of another witness.[3]

---

1 (2004), 180 C.C.C. (3d) 476 (S.C.C.). See paras. 48 and 49. This holding applies to an expert as well.

2 See Law Society Upper Canada Rule 4.01(2)(e).

3 *R. v. Markadonis* (1935), 63 C.C.C. 122 (N.S. C.A.), new trial ordered (1935), 64 C.C.C. 41 (S.C.C.); *R. v. R. (A.)* (1994) 88 C.C.C. (3d) 184 (Man. C.A.). See also *R. v. Read* (Alta. C.A.), May 7, 1984; *R. v. Bell (No. 2)* (Ont. Dist. Ct.), Vannini Dist. Ct. J., April 14, 1984, summarized at 11 W.C.B. 488; *R. v. Logiacca* (1984), 11 C.C.C. (3d) 374 (Ont. C.A.). See D.H. DeRusha and P.G. Reddam, "Abusive Cross-Examination: Asking the Accused Whether Other Witnesses are Lying" (1980), 28 Chitty's L.J. 1 at 3 for a discussion of this

This type of question is often heard from Crown attorneys when an accused or a defence witness contradicts the testimony of a police officer. The Crown will seek, as a stratagem, to juxtapose the witness credibility beside that of the police officer trusting that the Judge or jury will normally choose the evidence of an officer of the law. The question by the Crown would perhaps be: "Mr. Smith, you say it was dark outside. Officer Jones says it was not. Does that mean Officer Jones is lying?" This is a tactic to which vigorous objection should be taken.

KNOWINGLY POSING INADMISSIBLE QUESTIONS

Asking inadmissible questions is obviously improper and if intentionally done such impropriety calls for the Court's reprimand. If it bears on a vital issue or is repeated and the gain to the offending counsel is substantial and cannot be rectified, a mistrial should be considered. The mere fact that the question is asked causes the mischief,[4] because if counsel is forced to object the jury may well feel his or her side has something to hide and if counsel does not object a Court of Appeal may not give much credence to any ground of appeal based on that question. So, for example, counsel may not suggest to a jury, through cross-examination or otherwise, the contents of documents which are inadmissible.[5]

DEFENCE SUBPOENA TO CROWN COUNSEL

When defence counsel wishes to call Crown counsel to testify it must be shown that it is likely the Crown can give material evidence. A fishing expedition with the hope that something helpful may turn up does not meet the onus.[6] In *R. v. Elliott*[7] the Court stated that only in exceptional circum-

---

issue; *R. v. Yakeleya* (1985), 20 C.C.C. (3d) 193 (Ont. C.A.) at 195, 196; *R. v. Brown* (1982), 1 C.C.C. (3d) 107 (Alta. C.A.) at 109, 110, affirmed (1985), 21 C.C.C. (3d) 477 (S.C.C.); *R. v. S. (P.)* (Ont. C.A.) summarized at 7 W.C.B. (2d) 58; *R. v. Diamantopoulos* (Ont. C.A.), summarized at 7 W.C.B. (2d) 99; *R. v. Bevan* (1991), 63 C.C.C. (3d) 333 (Ont. C.A.); *R. v. White* (1999), 132 C.C.C. (3d) 373 (Ont. C.A.), where the Court found the question by the Crown not improper because the Crown did not ask the accused to explain why some other witness had lied but did ask the accused to confirm what the witness did say was a lie.

4 *Hyndman v. Stephens* (1909), 19 Man. R. 187 (Man. C.A.); *Loughead v. Collingwood Shipping Co.* (1908), 6 O.L.R. 64 (Ont. Div. Ct.).

5 *R. v. Yousry* (1914) 11 Cr. App. R. 13. See also *R v. W. (R.S.)* (1990), 55 C.C.C. (3d) 149 (Man. C.A.).

6 *R. v. Stupp* (1982), 70 C.C.C. (2d) 107 (Ont. H.C.); *R. v. Harris* (1994), 93 C.C.C. (3d) 478 (Ont. C.A.); *McCormick on Evidence* (4th ed.), p. 68; *Sopinka The Law of Evidence in Canada*, p. 598; *Phipson on Evidence*, 14th ed. (Sweet & Maxwell (U.K.), p. 140;

stances should opposing counsel be called as a witness. Relevance and necessity of counsel's evidence must first be shown.

ADMISSIBILITY OF PLEA DISCUSSIONS

It periodically arises that the Crown wishes to call defence counsel to testify as to the contents of a failed plea bargain discussion. Such was the case in *R. v. Lake*.[8] A crown witness, Currie, was charged separately from Lake, with murder. Currie's counsel unsuccessfully requested that the Crown withdraw the charge of murder and accept a plea of conspiracy to commit robbery on the basis that Currie was present at the murder scene but had abandoned the agreement to rob before the actual robbery took place and the victim was killed. At Lake's trial Currie denied he was present at the murder scene thereby contradicting his counsel's representations to the Crown.

The Crown argued that such statements by counsel in the course of resolution discussions are not protected by solicitor-client privilege but are admissible for their truth under the exception to the hearsay rule enunciated in *R. v. B. (K.G.)*. The Crown also argued that although the law recognizes a further public interest privilege in protecting the confidentiality of resolution discussions the privilege is not absolute and should give way to the more important public interest, namely the search for the truth in criminal proceedings.

Justice McCombs, after referring to certain authorities held:

> In my view, a ruling favourable to the Crown in the circumstances of a case such as this would have a profound chilling effect upon resolution discussions, an essential component of the administration of justice, and would do irreparable damage to the public interest in the proper administration of justice. This public interest is of such importance that it must outweigh all other considerations.

The resolution discussions were held to be privileged.[9]

Stanley and Douglas (1951), [1952] 1 S.C.R. 260 at 270 (S.C.C.); *R. v. Brown*, 1997 CarswellOnt 5991 (Ont. Gen. Div.).

7 (2003), 181 C.C.C. (3d) 118 (Ont. C.A.). The fact that Crown Counsel was present at meetings where the conduct of the police officer involved in the investigation was discussed was held not to be a sufficient foundation.

8 [1997] O.J. No. 5447 (Ont. Gen. Div.) per McCombs J. (Ont. Gen. Div.); *R. v. Legato* (2002), 172 C.C.C. (3d) 415 (Que. C.A.).

9 In Ontario at least, judicial pretrial discussions are accepted as being privileged. Often, defence counsel will encase their plea resolution discussions in the form of a hypothetical, but why should counsel have to resort to this silly camouflage.

Michael Proulx and David Layton, co-authors of Ethics and Canadian Criminal Law[10] state:

> "Communications between defence counsel and prosecutor during plea discussions are confidential and privileged. Public policy encourages full and candid discussion between the parties, and whatever has been revealed during those discussions is not admissible at trial. However, there may be circumstances where the privilege is set aside, most particularly when the client later waives privilege by alleging a denial of the right to effective assistance of counsel."

POSING QUESTIONS CONTAINING COUNSEL'S PERSONAL KNOWLEDGE

Consider the question: "Witness, I suggest you were wrong when you say you definitely picked my client out of the line-up because I was present and heard you say that you were not sure it was my client." In this blatant example counsel would be giving evidence without being sworn under oath and subject to cross-examination. This is obviously improper.

A further difficulty arises because counsel may have to shed the role of the advocate and take on the role of a witness to contradict the testimony of the opponent's witness. No counsel should place himself or herself in such a position by taking on a brief where there is a chance he or she may have to testify. It would be unseemly to be both counsel and a witness at the trial since counsel may then have to argue his or her own credibility before the Judge or jury.

EXPRESSING PERSONAL OPINION

It is impermissible for counsel to express in the courtroom his or her personal belief in the evidence and the accused's innocence or guilt.[11] The case law which universally accepts this rule is most often breached during counsel's final jury address but can arise during examination of witnesses. Mr. Justice Rose in a lecture to the students at Osgoode Hall Law School decades ago stated the reason why the existence of this rule:

> Your duty to your client does not call for any expression of your belief in the justice of his cause. . . . The counsel's opinion may be right or wrong, but it is not evidence. If one counsel may asset his belief, the opposing counsel is put at a disadvantage if he does not state that it is his belief his client's cause or defence is just. If one counsel is well-known and of high standing, his client

---

10   Irwin Law, 2001 at p. 417. John Sopinka, Sydney N. Lederman and Alan W. Bryant echo these views. See also R. v. Legato (2002), 172 C.C.C. (3d) 415 (Que. C.A.).

11   R. v. R. (A.J.) (1994), 94 C.C.C. (3d) 168 (Ont. C.A.).

would have a decided advantage over his opponent if represented by a younger, weaker, or less well-known man.

THE DUTY TO CROSS-EXAMINE: THE BROWNE AND DUNN RULE

The English civil case of *Browne v. Dunn*[12] is no doubt the most often quoted case when it comes to defence counsel's duty to cross-examine. Lord Herschell of the House of Lords in that case defined the rule thusly:

> "Now, my Lords, I cannot help saying that it seems to me to be absolutely essential to the proper conduct of a cause, where it is intended to suggest that a witness is not speaking the truth on a particular point, to direct his attention to the fact by some questions put in cross-examination showing that that imputation is intended to be made, and not to take his evidence and pass it by as a matter altogether unchallenged, and then, when it is impossible for him to explain, as perhaps he might have been able to do if such questions had been put to him, the circumstances which it is suggested indicate that the story he tells ought not to be believed, to argue that he is a witness and worthy of credit. My Lords, I have always understood that if you intend to impeach a witness you are bound, whilst he is in the box, to give him an opportunity of making any explanation which is open to him; and, as it seems to me, that is not only a rule of professional practice in the conduct of a case, but is essential to fair play and fair dealing with witnesses.

Lord Herschell continues as follows:

> Of course I do not deny for a moment that there are cases in which that notice has been so distinctly unmistakably given, and the point upon which he is impeached, and is to be impeached, is so manifest, that it is not necessary to waste time in putting questions to him upon it. All I am saying is that it will not due to impeach the credibility of a witness upon a matter on which he has not had any opportunity of giving an explanation by reason of there having been no suggestion whatever in the course of the case that his story is not accepted."

The Supreme Court of Canada in *R. v. Palmer*[13] recognized *Browne v. Dunn* also stating that the effect to be given to the absence or brevity of cross-examination depends on the circumstances of each case. In *R. v.*

---

12 (1893), 6 R. 67 (U.K. H.C.).

13 (1979), 50 C.C.C. (2d) 193 (S.C.C.). See also *R. v. MacKinnon* (1992), 72 C.C.C. (3d) 113 (B.C. C.A.); *R. v. Letourneau* (1994), 87 C.C.C. (3d) 481 (B.C. C.A.), additional reasons at (1995), 55 B.C.A.C. 130 (B.C. C.A.), leave to appeal refused (1995), 102 C.C.C. (3d) vi (S.C.C.), at pp. 521-523 [C.C.C.]; *R. v. Dyck* (1969), [1970] 2 C.C.C. 283 (B.C. C.A.).

Paris[14] the Court stated that the relevance of the failure to cross-examine on the credibility of the witness should depend on: the nature of the matters on which the witness was not cross-examined, and the overall tenor of the cross-examination and conduct of the defence. Where the position of the defence on matters not put to the complainant is clear even without cross-examination or where the areas not touched upon in cross-examinations are not significant in the case, the failure to cross-examine will have no significance in the assessment of the accused's credibility. However, where the focus of the complainant's evidence is left untouched or is even implicitly accepted in cross-examination, then the failure to cross-examine may have a negative impact on the accused's credibility.

In *R. v. Henderson*[15] the Court stated that where a thorough cross-examination of a witness challenges the account of events by the witness, the defence is not required "to put the Crown on notice of every detail that the defence did not accept." Also, in *R. v. Khuc*[16] it was held that counsel is not required to ask contradictory questions about straight forward matters of fact on which the witness has already testified and unlikely to change. Counsel does not have to embark on a futile cross-examination but can rely on the judgment of the jury as to what evidence it will accept. In *R. v. H. (S.)*[17] the Court held it is not necessary to put every contradictory detail to a witness but fairness required that where the accused gave a very detailed description of events when the sexual assault took place but failed to put those details to the complainant in cross-examination, the rule in *Browne v. Dunn* was breached as several parts of the description were significant enough and different from the complainant's version that the complainant

---

14 (2000), 150 C.C.C. (3d) 162 (Ont. C.A.), leave to appeal refused (2001), 276 N.R. 395 (note) (S.C.C.); *R. v. Marshall* (2005), 200 C.C.C. (3d) 179 (Ont. C.A.), leave to appeal refused 2006 CarswellOnt 5556, 2006 CarswellOnt 5557 (S.C.C.); *R. v. Giroux* (2006), 207 C.C.C. (3d) 512 (Ont. C.A.), leave to appeal refused 2006 CarswellOnt 7126, 2006 CarswellOnt 7127 (S.C.C.).

15 (1999), 134 C.C.C. (3d) 131 (Ont. C.A.); See also *R. v. Verney* (1993), 87 C.C.C. (3d) 363 (Ont. C.A.). Noting that *Browne v. Dunn* is a rule of fairness preventing the ambush of a witness by not giving him an opportunity to state his position with respect to later evidence which contradicts him on an essential matter. It is not however an absolute rule and counsel is not obliged to slog through a witness's evidence-in-chief, putting him on notice of every detail the defence does not accept.

16 (2000), 142 C.C.C. (3d) 276 (B.C. C.A.).

17 2010 CarswellOnt 5215 (Ont. C.A.) (endorsement). The Court of Appeal concluded that the trial Judge in the circumstances of this case, and citing *R. v. Giroux, supra*, was correct in exercising his discretion by taking into account the *Browne v. Dunn* breach in assessing the credibility of the witness giving the contradictory evidence. In this case the Court did not accept counsel's argument that the trial Judge should have permitted the complainant to be recalled to answer questions because during submissions the trial Judge indicated how he was going to treat the credibility of the accused due to the breach of the principle; defence counsel, having been put on notice, did not request that the witness be called.

should have been given the opportunity to respond given that the complainant would be impeached on those differences.

The first option for the Court when the witness is unable to tell his side of the story is to explore whether the witness is available for recall and the complaining party can decide whether to decline the opportunity and if so, no special instruction to the jury is required. If the witness can not be recalled or if the Judge feels it is inappropriate then it is within the Judge's discretion as to whether the jury should be given a special instruction that in assessing the weight to be given to the uncontradicted evidence, they may take into account that the opposing witness was not questioned about it and take this into account in assessing the credibility for the opposing witness.[18]

THE CUT-THROAT DEFENCE

In *R. v. Creighton*, the Supreme Court observed that while the Crown is unable to cross-examine an accused with respect to various aspects of the evidence on the basis of exclusionary rules born from policies of fairness to the accused, the accused is not so limited in attacking his co-accused in what has been described as the "cut-throat defence." One accused therefore may cross-examine his co-accused on a statement which has not been established as voluntarily given,[19] or may comment on the fact that his co-accused did not testify at trial,[20] or comment on the failure of his co-accused to make a statement to the police when first arrested.[21] One accused may cross-examine or lead evidence on the disposition or propensity of his co-accused to commit the offence for which both have been indicted.[22] However one accused is not permitted to cross-examine a co-accused on the facts that underlie charges of which the co-accused was acquitted.[23]

While a successful application to sever the trial may seem to be the just way for the beleaguered accused to escape the finger-pointing from his co-accused, the Supreme Court in *Crawford* held that although the trial Judge has a discretion to order separate trials where the "cut-throat defence" is employed by the co-accused, the discretion must be based on principles of law which include that severance is not to be granted unless it is established that a joint trial will work an injustice to the accused. In this regard

---

18 *R. v. McNeill* (2000), 144 C.C.C. (3d) 551 (Ont. C.A.).

19 *R. v. Young* (1981), 64 C.C.C. (2d) 13 (B.C. C.A.); *R. v. Logan* (1988), 46 C.C.C. (3d) 354 (Ont. C.A.), affirmed [1990] 2 S.C.R. 731 (S.C.C.).

20 *R. v. Cuff* (1989), 49 C.C.C. (3d) 65 (Nfld. C.A.).

21 *R. v. Creighton* (1995), (*sub nom. R. v. Crawford*) 96 C.C.C. (3d) 481 (S.C.C.).

22 *R. v. Creighton, supra*, at 495; *R. v. Kendall* (1987), 35 C.C.C. (3d) 105 (Ont. C.A.); *R. v. McMillan* (1975), 23 C.C.C. (2d) 160 (Ont. C.A.), affirmed (1977), 33 C.C.C. (2d) 360 (S.C.C.); *R. v. Jackson* (1991), 68 C.C.C. (3d) 385 (Ont. C.A.) at 434, affirmed (1993), 86 C.C.C. (3d) 385 (S.C.C.).

23 *R. v. Akins* (2002), 5 C.R. (6th) 400 (Ont. C.A.) at 405.

the Supreme Court held that a "cut-throat defence" is not in itself sufficient for a severance. The cases do go on to say that a careful jury instruction must be given in such circumstances.

An accused may find himself testifying against his co-accused without wanting to, when charged separately with the same offence, and the Crown has subpoenaed him for that purpose. This is permissible provided that the predominate purpose is not to obtain evidence against the accused compelled to testify but is for some legitimate public purpose such as gaining evidence against the accused being tried.[24]

The compelled witness is guaranteed "use immunity" by virtue of section 13 of the *Charter* in any subsequent proceedings and the trial Judge has discretion to exclude derivative evidence. See Chapter, "Self-Incrimination."[25]

PRIOR CONSISTENT STATEMENTS

Where the witness has made a statement to the police shortly after a relevant event that is consistent with the evidence which the witness gives in-chief, it would be advantageous to counsel to reveal the details of the earlier statement to demonstrate this consistency as a sign of a truthful witness. However, this self-corroboration or oath-helping to enhance credibility is not permitted by the rules of evidence and the witness normally may not be asked in-chief whether he or she formerly made this prior consistent statement. A statement is not made more trustworthy because it has been repeated.[26]

Even the rule permitting the Crown to elicit a recent complaint in sexual assault cases in order to show consistency, but not for the truth of the complainant, has been abrogated by virtue of section 275 of the *Criminal Code*.[27]

---

24 *British Columbia (Securities Commission) v. Branch* (1995), 97 C.C.C. (3d) 505 (S.C.C.). Normally, those who are charged separately or are unindicted co-conspirators are compellable witnesses for the prosecution at the trial or preliminary hearing of another separately charged accused. See *R. v. Primeau*, [1995] 2 S.C.R. 60; *R. v. Jobin*, [1995] 2 S.C.R. 78. A co-accused who pleads guilty during a joint trial is a compellable witness against the defendant. See *R. v. McKee* (1960), 126 C.C.C. 251 (Ont. C.A.).

25 *R. v. S. (R.J.)* (1993), 80 C.C.C. (3d) 397 (Ont. C.A.), affirmed (1995), 96 C.C.C. (3d) 1 (S.C.C.).

26 Although the rule is normally applied in examination-in-chief, it can also apply in cross-examination particularly when the cross-examiner is not adverse in interest but attempting to seek self-serving statements from the witness on behalf of the accused. See *R. v. Wood* (1989), 51 C.C.C. (3d) 201 (Ont. C.A.), leave to appeal refused (1990), 56 C.C.C. (3d) vi (note) (S.C.C.); *R. v. Campbell* (1977), 38 C.C.C. (2d) 6 (Ont. C.A.).

27 R.S.C. 1985, c. C-46, as amended R.S.C. 1985, c. 19 (3rd supp.), s. 11. Although the rules of respecting recent complaint were abrogated, the defence is still entitled to cross-examine the complainant as to his or her failure to make a recent complaint. See *R. v.*

Some exceptions to this oath-helping rule are statements qualifying as *res gestae*[28] or within the Supreme Court of Canada ruling in *R. v. Khan*,[29] or as narrative.[30] In *R. v. Ay*[31] it was held that because the evidence of prior complaint was admissible as narrative it did not go to the consistency of the complaint and therefore the credibility of the complainant's evidence at trial. A prior complaint becomes part of the narrative if it advances the story from offence to prosecution or if it explains why so little was done to terminate the abuse or bring the offender to justice. *R. v. Ay* also holds that the complaint must be described in general terms only, without detail as to what actually was said, i.e., only the fact the complaint was made; so the jury would not draw the inference of the truthfulness of the complaint. The Crown is not entitled to lead evidence as to the manner in which the statements were taken from the complainant, including the length of time to take the statement and the emotional state of the complainant at the time.[32]

Further exceptions to the rule forbidding prior consistent statements referred to elsewhere in this book are statements made upon incriminating evidence being located and statements of prior identification of the accused by the witness, and statements indicative of the person's physical condition, emotions and state of mind which are relevant. In addition section 715.1 of the *Criminal Code* permits the admission of a prior videotaped statement

---

Widdifield (1991), 13 W.C.B. (2d) 184 (Alta. C.A.), and the trier-of-fact can still draw an adverse inference depending on the circumstances. See *R. v. O'Connor* (1995), 25 O.R. (3d) 19 (Ont. C.A.), leave to appeal refused (1996), 104 C.C.C. (3d) vi (note) (S.C.C.); *R. v. H. (J.)* (1996), 108 C.C.C. (3d) 97 (Ont. C.A.), additional reasons at (1996), 110 C.C.C. (3d) 533 (Ont. C.A.).

28   *R. v. Jones* (1988), 66 C.R. (3d) 54, 1988 CarswellOnt 84 (Ont. C.A.).

29   (1990), 79 C.R. (3d) 1 (S.C.C.).

30   *R. v. F. (J.E.)* (1993), 85 C.C.C. (3d) 457 (Ont. C.A.), when prior complaints are allowed into evidence as part of the narrative, the jury has to be told that these prior complaints were not admissible for the truth of their contents but to help it understand what occurred and why, as for example, the complainant finally divulged her secret and how the matter came to the attention of the police. See also *R. v. B. (O.)* (1995), 103 C.C.C. (3d) 531 (N.S. C.A.); *R. v. Foster* (1995), 128 Sask. R. 292 (Sask. C.A.), leave to appeal refused (1996), 152 Sask. R. 316 (note) (S.C.C.); *R. v. Ay*, 93 C.C.C. (3d) 456, 1994 CarswellBC 1112 (B.C. C.A.); *R. v. Codina* (1995), 95 C.C.C. (3d) 311(Ont. C.A.), leave to appeal refused (1995), 100 C.C.C. (3d) vi (note) (S.C.C.); *R. c. Dinardo* (2008), (*sub nom. R. v. Dinardo*) 231 C.C.C. (3d) 177 (S.C.C.); *R. v. Stirling* (2008), 229 C.C.C. (3d) 257 (S.C.C.).

31   *Ibid.*

32   Not every gap in a story has to be filled with narrative evidence but only if it was necessary to provide chronological cohesion and eliminate gaps in order that the story makes sense. See *R. v. Curto* (2008), 230 C.C.C. (3d) 145 (Ont. C.A.) at paras. 34, 35 and *R. v. (F. (J.E.), supra.* In this latter case Finlayson J. at page 474 stressed that it will not always be necessary to fill in every gap to understand the story and properly assess the witness's credibility.

of a witness under 18 years of age who adopts the contents of the video while testifying.

Perhaps the most significant exception is when opposing counsel alleges or implies that the witness's testimony is of recent fabrication; for example, that a certain fact testified to was not mentioned previously.[33] A previous consistent statement then becomes admissible as the witness is permitted to be rehabilitated.[34] The prior consistent statements must have been made before the point at which fabrication is alleged.[35] However an allegation of mere fabrication does not create an exception to the rule prohibiting prior consistent statements when the defence position is that the witness is fabricating from the beginning.[36]

The courts have applied this exception to the general rule against the admission of self-serving statements by the accused where no direct allegation of recent fabrication has been made. In *R. v. Giraldi* (1975), 28 C.C.C. (2d) 248 (B.C. C.A.). McFarlane J.A., speaking for the Court (McFarlane, Branca, Carrothers JJ.A.), said at p. 253.

> I find the reasoning of the judges in this case impelling. That reasoning does not support the proposition that the only basis for applying the exception and admitting the evidence is the fact that cross-examination of the witness has been of such a nature as to lay a foundation for inferring a recently fabricated or contrived story. On the contrary it supports the view, which in my opinion is the correct one, that that foundation may be laid in other ways including the whole circumstances of the case and the conduct of the trial. Moreover, it is very much a matter for the trial Judge who is required to consider the question of admissibility with great care before allowing the earlier self-serving statement to be admitted.
>
> I think also this view that a suggestion of recent fabrication need not necessarily be made expressly but may arise implicitly is supported on a careful consideration of the judgments of the Ontario Court of Appeal in *R. v. Pappin* (1970), 12 C.R.N.S. 287, and *R. v. Rosik* (1970), 2 C.C.C. (2d) 351, [1971] 2 O.R. 47, 13 C.R.N.S. 129 (appeal in the latter to the Supreme Court of Canada dismissed, 2 C.C.C. (2d) 393*n*, [1971] 2 O.R. 89n, [1971] 5.C.R. vi).

And in *R. v. Campbell* (1977), 38 C.C.C. (2d) 6 at pp. 18-9, 17 O.R. (2d) 673, 1 C.R. (3d) 309 (Ont. C.A.), Martin JA., speaking for the Court (Arnup, Martin and Lacourcie're JJ.A.), said:

---

33 *R. v. Campbell, supra.*

34 *R. v. Simpson*, [1988] 1 S.C.R. 3 (S.C.C.), per McIntyre J., *R. c. Dinardo, supra*, at para. 37; *Welstead v. Brown* (1951), [1952] 1 S.C.R. 3 (S.C.C.); *R. v. Wannebo* (1972), 7 C.C.C. (2d) 266 (B.C. C.A.); *R. v. Lalonde* (1971), 5 C.C.C. (2d) 168 (Ont. H.C.); *R. v. Giraldi* (1975), 28 C.C.C. (2d) 248 (B.C. C.A.), leave to appeal refused (1975), 28 C.C.C. (2d) 248n (S.C.C.); *R. v. Racine* (1977), 32 C.C.C. (2d) 468 (Ont. C.A.); *R. v. Campbell, supra.*

35 *R. v. Ellard* (2009), 245 C.C.C. (3d) 183 (S.C.C.) at paras. 32-34.

36 *R. v. McDonald* (2000), 148 C.C.C. (3d) 273 (Ont. C.A.).

I accept the proposition that an express allegation of recent fabrication in cross-examination is not necessary before the exception with respect to rebutting an allegation of recent fabrication becomes operative, and that a suggestion that the accused's story has been recently contrived may also arise implicitly from the whole circumstances of the case, the evidence of the witnesses who have been called, and the conduct of the trial. Where the circumstances are such as to raise the suggestion that the accused's evidence is a recent fabrication, counsel may properly anticipate the allegation of recent fabrication in cross-examination, and examine the accused in chief with respect to previous statements to other persons, prior to his being cross-examined: see *R. v. Giraldi* (1975), 28 C.C.C. (2d) 248, [1975] W.W.D. 166; *R. v. Racine* (1977), 32 C.C.C. (2d) 468 at p. 473; *Previous Consistent Statements*, at pp. 86-7, by R.N. Gooderson.

In *R. v. Conway*, Mr. Justice Moldaver made the following observations as they related to the facts in that case:

While it is true that at page 20 of the decision of *R. v. Campbell* (1977), 38 C.C.C. (2d) 6 (Ont. C.A.), the Court of Appeal indicated that where the failure of a witness to mention some circumstance on an earlier occasion when he might have done so is made the basis for a suggestion of recent fabrication, then evidence is admissible that, on a still earlier occasion, he did mention that circumstance, the Court of Appeal cited as authority for this proposition the Australian case of *Nominal Defendant v. Clements* (1960), 104 C.L.R. 476. Upon reviewing the case of *Nominal Defendant*, the following passage is found at page 479 of Chief Justice Dixon's judgment, and I quote:

If the credit of a witness is impugned as to some material fact to which he deposes upon the ground that his account is a late invention or has been lately devised or reconstructed, even though not with conscious dishonesty, that makes admissible a statement to the same effect as the account he gave as a witness if it was made by the witness contemporaneously with the event or at a time sufficiently early to be inconsistent with the suggestion that his account is a late invention or reconstruction.

I read that quote from Chief Justice Dixon as indicating that the prior statement need not have occurred prior to the statement in which a certain piece of evidence was left out, so long as it is made contemporaneously with or so shortly thereafter as to rebut a suggestion that it has been recently fabricated.

In this regard, I rely as well on the authority of *R. v. Simpson and Ochs* (1988), 38 C.C.C. (3d) 481 (S.C.C.).

Further, in coming to this conclusion, I am mindful of the fact that it is not every attack on a witness's credibility that opens the door to the admissibility of otherwise self-serving evidence. Indeed, a general attack upon a witness to show the improbability of his or her evidence may, and often does not bring into play the doctrine the recent fabrication. The nature of the attack must, at the very least, create the suggestion that the present account of the witness has been fabricated since the event in question. The authority for this proposition comes from the following case: *R. v. Campbell, supra.*

PRIOR CONSISTENT STATEMENT OF ACCUSED

If counsel seeks the admission of his client's prior consistent statement a starting point would be the accepted proposition that evidentiary rules may be relaxed where it is necessary for the fair trial of an accused and to ensure that all relevant probative and reliable evidence is before the trier-of-fact. See *R. v. Finta* (1994), 88 C.C.C. (3d) 417 (S.C.C.) at 526-28, reconsideration refused (June 23, 1994), Doc. 23023, 23097 (S.C.C.).

Notwithstanding the above, the door has been opened, at least in the province of Ontario, to lead a prior consistent post arrest exculpatory statement of an accused person where it amounts to "more than mere consistency or repetition of the subject-matter but touches on a live issue at trial, such as the state of mind of the accused at the moment of first accusation. . ."[37]

Prior to *Liu*, the Ontario Court of Appeal per Doherty J. in *R. v. Suzack*[38] noted the general rule that prevents an accused from introducing self-serving exculpatory statements through the cross-examination of other witnesses. In that case, the post arrest comments were not part of the same narrative as the pre-arrest utterances and each statement was an isolated comment made under very different circumstances and therefore inadmissible. But he also noted that when post arrest exculpatory statements are made by the accused's own testimony the dangers inherent in admitting such self-serving statements are considerably reduced as the accused can be cross-examined.[39]

---

37 *R. v. Liu* (2003), 172 C.C.C. (3d) 79 (Ont. S.C.J.) per McKinnon J.

38 (2000), 141 C.C.C. (3d) 449 (Ont. C.A.), leave to appeal refused (2001), 80 C.R.R. (2d) 376 (note) (S.C.C.).

39 Doherty J. found he did not have to decide this issue because the attempt to admit the statement was through cross-examination of a witness. See also *Lucas v. R.* (1962), [1963] 1 C.C.C. 1 (S.C.C.), per Kerwin C.J.C. for the majority. . . "It was open to the defence to obtain evidence from the appellant to the effect that he had made a statement to the police, following his arrest, which was similar to the evidence which he had given at trial." In *R. v. T. (W.P.)* (1993), 83 C.C.C. (3d) 5 (Ont. C.A.), Doherty J.A., on behalf of the Court made approving reference to *Lucas*. Other favourable decisions are: *R. v. Small*, [1991] O.J. No. 3693 (Ont. Gen. Div.), per Forestell J.; *R. c. Rozich* (1979),10 C.R. (3d) 364 (Que. S.C.); *R. v. Fischer* (2005), 197 C.C.C. (3d) 136 (B.C. C.A.), leave to appeal refused 2005 CarswellBC 3056 (S.C.C.). Contrary authority: *R. v. Terceira* (1998), 123 C.C.C. (3d) 1 (Ont. C.A.); *R. v. Campbell*, *supra*; *R. v. Horton* (1995), 1995 CarswellOnt 2427 (Ont. Gen. Div.). See *R. v. Mathisen* (2008), 239 C.C.C. (3d) 63 (Ont. C.A.) at paras. 104-5. In *R. v. Edgar* (2010), 101 O.R. (3d) 161 (Ont. C.A.), application/notice of appeal 2010 CarswellOnt 10099 (S.C.C.) the Court held that spontaneous exculpatory statements by an accused made upon arrest or shortly thereafter are admissible as an exception to the rule excluding prior consistent statements as they may be relevant to credibility and as circumstantial evidence bearing on guilt or innocence. However the accused must first testify to be open to cross-examination.

THREATENING CHARGE OF PERJURY

For the Crown attorney to threaten a witness with a charge of perjury is improper as it would prejudice the fair trial of the accused.[40] Nor should the trial Judge repeatedly remind the witness that he or she is under oath.[41]

ABUSIVE AND UNFAIR CROSS-EXAMINATIONS BY THE PROSECUTION

There has been a disturbing increase in the number of reported judgments (seemingly more in Ontario) regarding impermissible cross-examinations by Crown counsel. In *R. v. White* (1999), 132 C.C.C. (3d) 373 (Ont. C.A.) Justice Doherty noted the "well-established and unfortunately ever-growing line of authority relating to improper cross-examinations by Crown counsel."[42] Why that is so, one can only speculate. Are they being too influenced by American TV shows, such as *Law and Order*? Have their forensic skills become only a sideshow to their concern for being prepared to argue *Charter* motions? Have they lost focus as mini-ministers of justice whose role is to "exclude any notion of winning or losing" as proclaimed in *R. v. Boucher* (1954), 110 C.C.C. 263 (S.C.C.). The fact that this crossing-of-the-line keeps repeating itself in a number of areas leads me at least to ask the questions: Why don't some Crowns get it? They do have educational

---

40   *R. v. Provencher* (1955), 114 C.C.C. 100 (S.C.C.).
41   *R. c. Gagnon* (1992), 74 C.C.C. (3d) 385 (C.A. Qué.).
42   See also Labrosse J. in *R. v. Henderson* (1999), 134 C.C.C. (3d) 131 (Ont. C.A.).

Counsel Should Not Give Personal Opinions

"Let me tell you, folks—I've been around long enough to develop an instinct for these things, and my client is innocent or I'm very much mistaken."

The New Yorker Book of Lawyer Cartoons. New Yorker Magazine Eds. (Illus.). Alfred A. Knopf, Inc., 1997. © 1993 by The New Yorker Magazine, Inc.

programmes. Why does the defence not object more often? And why do some judges, as gatekeepers not step in and put an immediate stop to these breaches? It could at least mean less work for courts of appeal. The cases from the courts of appeal make it clear that if the trial judges do step in when these breaches occur and/or they give proper jury instructions negating improper cross-examination the trial can be saved.[43] What follows is a list of a number of the areas of impermissible cross-examinations, some of which have already been referred to in relevant chapters in this book:

---

43   *R. v. Henderson, ibid*; *R. v. Romeo* (1991), 62 C.C.C. (3d) 1 (S.C.C.).

The Bill Clinton-Solution

"Is it still perjury if I cross my fingers?"

NICK IN THE WALL STREET JOURNAL

© The Wall Street Journal.

- humiliating and demeaning the accused for lifestyle, etc.
  R. v. Robinson (2001), 153 C.C.C. (3d) 398 (Ont. C.A.);
  R. v. Rose (2001), 153 C.C.C. (3d) 225 (Ont. C.A.);
  R. v. Logiacco (1984), 11 C.C.C. (3d) 374 (Ont. C.A.);
  R. v. Ryder (October 17, 1994), (Ont. C.A.);
  R. v. R. (A.J.) (1995), 94 C.C.C. (3d) 168 (Ont. C.A.);
  R. v. Walker (1994), 90 C.C.C. (3d) 144 (Ont. C.A.);
  R. v. Kahn (1998), 126 C.C.C. (3d) 523 (B.C. C.A.).
  R. v. Carrière (2004), 190 C.C.C. (3d) 164 at 179 (Ont. C.A.).

- editorializing, sarcasm
  R. v. R. (A.J.) ibid. (You want the jury to believe that one too?...your
  testimony is "incredible.");
  R. v. Schell (2000), 148 C.C.C. (3d) 219 (Ont. C.A.) (Your usual
  larcenous instinct?);
  R. v. Robinson, supra;
  R. v. Kahn, supra.

- Crown stating own opinion in cross-examination
  R. v. R. (A.J.), supra.

- attacking accused's character (unless the accused puts his or her
  character in issue)
  R. v. Logiacco, supra.
  R. v. W. (R.S.) (1990), 55 C.C.C. (3d) 149 (Man. C.A.).

R. v. Rose, supra;

R. v. Robinson, supra.

See also Chapter, "Character Witnesses."

- Crown counsel bullying the accused and attempting to ingratiate himself with the jury and align himself with them against the accused, as for example, by prefacing numerous questions beginning with: "Is that your evidence under oath?" and "You are asking the jury to believe your evidence?"
  R. v. Kahn (1998), 126 C.C.C. (3d) 523 (B.C. C.A.), additional reasons at (2001), 145 B.C.A.C. 317 (B.C. C.A.), leave to appeal refused (2001), 275 N.R. 198 (note) (S.C.C.).

- whether evidence in another proceeding was rejected or disbelieved.
  R. v. Ghorvei (1999), 138 C.C.C. (3d) 340 (Ont. C.A.);
  R. v. Barnes (1999), 138 C.C.C. (3d) 500 (Ont. C.A.);
  R. v. Schmidt (2001), 151 C.C.C. (3d) 74 (B.C. C.A.).

- casting doubt on the credibility of accused's testimony because he has seen disclosure and tailored evidence accordingly
  R. v. White (1999), 132 C.C.C. (3d) 373 (Ont. C.A.);
  R. v. Schell (2001), 148 C.C.C. (3d) 219 (Ont. C.A.).

  See also Chapter, "Crown Disclosure."

  However, the accused may open the door allowing the introduction of such a question, such as where the accused referred to review of disclosure to bolster his explanation for having such a detailed memory of events.
  R. v. Cavan (1999), 139 C.C.C. (3d) 449 (Ont. C.A.), leave to appeal refused (2000), 142 C.C.C. (3d) vi (S.C.C.), leave to appeal refused (2000), 142 C.C.C. (3d) vi (S.C.C.), leave to appeal refused (2000), 142 C.C.C. (3d) vi (S.C.C.).

- asking the accused to comment on the credibility of his accusers or other witnesses, why they would lie or falsely implicate the accused.
  R. v. Markadonis (1935), 64 C.C.C. 41 (S.C.C.);
  R. v. Yakeleya (1985), 20 C.C.C. (3d) 193 (Ont. C.A.);
  R. v. R. (A.J.) (1995), 94 C.C.C. (3d) 168 (Ont. C.A.);
  R. v. Brown (1982), 1 C.C.C. (3d) 107 (Alta. C.A.), affirmed (1985), [1986] 1 W.W.R. 97 (S.C.C.), at 110 [C.C.C.];
  R. v. White (1999), 132 C.C.C. (3d) 373 (Ont. C.A.);
  R. v. Kusk (1999), 132 C.C.C. (3d) 559 (Alta. C.A.);
  R. v. N. (P.L.F.) (1999), 138 C.C.C. (3d) 49 (Man. C.A.);

R. v. Sevillano (1995), (sub nom. *R. v. DeFrancesca*) 104 C.C.C.
(3d) 189 (Ont. C.A.), leave to appeal refused (1996), 104 C.C.C.
(3d) vi (note) (S.C.C.), leave to appeal refused (1996), 104 C.C.C.
(3d) vi (note) (S.C.C.), leave to appeal refused (1997), 103 O.A.C.
240 (note) (S.C.C.);
R. v. Rose (2001), 53 O.R. (3d) 417 (Ont. C.A.);
R. v. Cole (1999), [1999] O.J. No. 1647, 1999 CarswellOnt 1380
(Ont. C.A.);
R. v. Masse (2000), [2000] O.J. No. 2687, 2000 CarswellOnt 2523
(Ont. C.A.);
R. v. Vandenberghe (1995), 96 C.C.C. (3d) 371 (Ont. C.A.).

However, the Crown may ask questions intended to negate any motives.

R. v. P. (H.P.) (1996), 112 C.C.C. (3d) 140 (Man. C.A.).

- going beyond the permissible limits of cross-examining the accused on his/her criminal record, which are: the name of the offence, date and place of conviction.

  See also Chapter, "Criminal Records."

- cross-examining accused for failure to make a statement upon arrest or to provide alibi, immediately after being informed or her right to remain silent
  R. v. Schell (2000), 148 C.C.C. (3d) 219 (Ont. C.A.);
  R. v. Parrington (1985), 20 C.C.C. (3d) 184 (Ont. C.A.).

  See Chapter, "Self-Incrimination."

- posing a hypothetical which assumes the guilt of the accused.
  R. v. W. (R.S.) (1990), 55 C.C.C. (3d) 149 (Man. C.A.).

- as to knowledge of section 13 *Charter* protection

  The Crown is not normally permitted to cross-examine a defence witness who has implicated himself and thereby exonerating the accused of the charged offence as to his knowledge that he could not be prosecuted as a result of his incriminating testimony. Without independent evidence of a motive to falsely testify, knowledge of s. 13 should not negatively impact on a witness's credibility. *R. v. Jabarianha* (2001), 159 C.C.C. (3d) 1 (S.C.C.). See also *R. v. Noël* (2002), 168 C.C.C. (3d) 193 (S.C.C.) at 226-227.

- Cross-examining accused to explain or be responsible for counsel's

tactical decisions is unfair and prejudicial
R. v. Henderson[44]

•   Crown personalizing role
R. v. S. (F.) (2000), 144 C.C.C. (3d) 466 (Ont. C.A.). In this case the Crown stated to the jury that his mission was to obtain a conviction; that he was an honest and just person and that if the jury was convinced of the accused's guilt it was because he failed to do his job; and that if there was no conviction that he and the jury would have to live with this sad result.

In *R. v. R. (A.J.)*,[45] the Ontario Court of Appeal stated that isolated incidents of transgressing the proper limits of cross-examination by the Crown may not be sufficient to overturn a verdict of guilty, but if the cross-examination prejudices the accused in his defence or is so improper as to bring the administration of justice into disrepute, the appellate Court will intervene.

In *R. v. Henderson*[46] the Ontario Court of Appeal has stated that "regardless of defence counsel's behaviour, Crown counsel should remain scrupulously fair."

The Canadian Bar Association Code of Professional Conduct (Chapter ix, commentary 2(k)) states that it is improper for a lawyer to needlessly abuse, heckle or harass a witness.

The reporting of cases wherein Crowns have displayed improprieties in their cross-examinations are important lessons for not only the Crown but the defence. The Crowns should be aware when the line of proper cross-examination has been crossed not only for the sake of their pride as an advocate but to prevent a guilty verdict from being overturned. The defence should be aware when that line has been crossed to properly object when it occurs, not only to protect the client's position on appeal but to let the offending Crown and the trial Judge know that the objections will keep coming if the Crown persists with his or her objectionable questions, with the result that the flow of cross-examination will be interrupted. If defence counsel sits silent the jurors may feel that the Crown's offending questions are permissible and they could settle in with an unfavourable view of the accused which may be difficult to overcome.

Defence counsel wants to be on firm ground with their objections. If those objections are continually overruled by the trial Judge the jurors may feel that counsel is improperly trying to prevent the prosecution's case from unfolding.

---

44   *Supra.*
45   *Supra.* See also *R. v. Ryder* (October 17, 1994), (Ont. C.A.).
46   *Ibid.*

While I have set out somewhat of a laundry list of what amounts to different aspects of improper cross-examination by the Crown, I feel that to better bring home these points to the reader it would be helpful to follow some portions of actual cross-examinations which have been the subject of negative comment by the courts.[47]

In *R. v. Carrière*,[48] the Ontario Court of Appeal set out what it described as "some of the most egregious examples of the Crown's serious level of misconduct during the trial and stated "it is important to note that these are but examples of the misconduct that occurred." This case also shows the misconduct carrying over into the Crown's jury address.

i) Excerpts from the trial Crown's opening address to the jury

I've personally been involved in this case for at least close to three years, since the actual murder of Marc Dubois. And the same pretty well applies to my colleague ... So you wouldn't be surprised to hear that *we have certain views about the case*, that I formulated various opinions in regards to the evidence...

Our purpose as Crowns is strictly to help you understand what this case is all about and hopefully again guide you to what we feel is the just and proper verdict.

. . .

I'm confident that once you know what we know about the case, you will be convinced that [the appellant] participated in planning the death of Marc Dubois and in the actual murder of Marc Dubois. [Emphasis added.]

ii) Excerpts from the trial Crown's cross-examination of the appellant

a) accusations that the appellant was lying and manipulating the jury

Q. Are you sure that this isn't what you're trying to do? Trying to dupe these people to my right ... with your stories?

Q. ...Do you begin to understand now why I'm suggesting to you that you're pretty good when it comes to playing little games and telling lies like that?

. . .

Q. Are you telling us a lie here ... or is this the truth?

b) the appellant's criminal antecedents and bad character

Q. ...Out of respect for Mr. Dubois, can I ask you to relate to us today where you would have placed his head...

---

47 The writer is grateful to Suhail Akhtar, Crown counsel, for the collection of a number of these cases reflecting improprieties in cross-examinations by Crown Attorneys, in his paper at the 2008 OBA Institute of Continuing Legal Education, 5 Shades of Cross-Examination.

48 (2004), 190 C.C.C. (3d) 164 (Ont. C.A.) at 179, leave to appeal refused 2006 CarswellOnt 308, 2006 CarswellOnt 309 (S.C.C.). The Court, in the circumstances of this case, dismissed the defence appeal.

. . .

Q. . . .Because — do you remember having photographs in your possession, all of the photographs showing Mr. Dubois' decapitated body, in your cell at a certain point in time in Ottawa?

Q. Do you remember making jokes about that...?

Q. . . .but did you not spend a good part of your life in jail?

Q. And I believe that you took some courses while you are in jail. There are courses offered in prison?

Q. And I understand it one of the courses offered was the butcher's course. Do you recall that?

. . .

Q. And that entailed decapitating animals, right?

. . .

Q. You didn't have a problem with doing an armed robbery. That wasn't something new for you.

Q. And you drank all afternoon because you commit robberies when you drink, right?

iii) Excerpts from the trial Crown's closing address to the jury

a) accusations that the appellant was lying and manipulating the jury

He can pretend all he wants; he can lie all he wants the truth betrays him.

. . .

Now I didn't mean to be offensive to the reality of the matter that Mr. Dubois' head, as you've heard, was never found. If [the appellant] was so respectful of Marc Dubois, he would have told the police something... His little show of emotion... that part about a good friend Marc Dubois out of respect I want the truth to come out. That was planned. That was faked. It was obviously a ploy to manipulate you, to manipulate your emotions. [The appellant] is fundamentally a dishonest person.

. . .

How can [the appellant] dare tell us that he's so sorry for what happened to poor old Mr. Dai.

Now some of the things [the appellant] says may be true but it's twisted by him. That's his game to twist the truth to his advantage. Hopefully again you've seen through that.

b) the appellant's criminal antecedents and bad character

Good morning. Now within a span of two weeks back in January 1994, the accused who stands before you, [the appellant] took away two lives . . . His guilt is crystal clear and his guilt should be crystal clear in your mind at this point. . . [The appellant] is a violent person. I think we've shown that. He's not only capable of doing such gruesome acts but he had a motive to do it and he had also the means to do it.

c) the trial Crown's personal opinion on the appellant's guilt and credibility

You now know everything that we know about what [the appellant] did to Marc Dubois. I guess that if you're not convinced by now with everything that you've heard and seen then I doubt that I have the skills or the ability to convince you otherwise. You have been presented with what I consider to be overwhelming evidence of guilt.

. . .

Now is the accused a credible person? Is he someone that can [be] believe[d]? I've already told you my view of [the appellant] and I think that this view, the Crown's view of [the appellant] is clearly supported by what we've heard and what we've seen in this courtroom.

d) comments suggesting that an acquittal would be an unfortunate result

If you conclude in your minds that [co-counsel] and I have failed in our task to convince you that this person is guilty then you will be bound by this unfortunate result.

e) personalizing the appellant's conduct

[Obstructing police] means that one is dishonest with a police officer. Have you been dishonest with a police officer lately?

f) examples of other improper suggestions to the jury

... I don't know what you're thinking. For all I know you may be thinking the Crown is stupid to think [the appellant] is guilty. But if I... was able to convince. . . one person that [the appellant] is guilty beyond a reasonable doubt and you are so convinced then I would ask ... this person or these persons to maintain their position. I would ask you not to cave into the pressure of your colleagues who . . . bought into this theory that Deslauriers did this. But the ones who have been convinced may have to show a great deal of courage in their conviction that [the appellant] is guilty. The bottom line is that I'm asking you not to collapse under the pressure of the majority if that's the case.

In *R. v. McIver*,[49] the accused was convicted of the offences of gross indecency and indecent assault. The complainant was 4 years old at the time of the offence but reported the incidents to the police 8 years later. At trial, the Crown asked the accused if he could explain why the complainant might lie. The following exchange occurred:

Q. In fairness you know of no reason or motive in your own mind at this moment in time why she would make this accusation that – against you?

---

49   1995 CarswellOnt 1261, [1995] O.J. No 1948 (Ont. C.A.).

A. No, sir. I do not.

In allowing the appeal, the Ontario Court of Appeal made it clear that the question was impermissible on the ground that it placed an onus on the accused to explain why the complainant was lying. The effect was "to turn him into an advocate in his own defence."

In *R. v. Henderson*,[50] the accused was charged with sexual assault. Three months after the alleged incident, the complainant and a friend spray-painted the words "You Rapist" on the accused's trailer prompting him to contact the police. Investigating the graffiti, the police questioned the complainant who told them she had been sexually assaulted by the accused. At trial, the accused admitted having sex with the complainant but insisted that it was consensual. The defence argued that the complainant had fabricated the complaint to conceal any infidelity from her boyfriend. At trial, the Crown decided to investigate the reason for the graffiti in the following way:

> Q. Sir, will you agree with me that if what [the complainant] told us about what happened at the time in the trailer is true, all the things that you have had to suffer since the phone calls and the spray-painting and the graffiti in the bar, even if they're not right, they are understandable if what [the complainant] says is true?
>
> A. I don't understand your question.
>
> ... Q. If what [the complainant] described in her evidence before this jury under cross-examination is true, then all these subsequent events that have been following you; the phone calls, the spray-painting and the graffiti, are at least understandable, are they not?
>
> A. I still don't understand your question.
>
> Q. They're consistent with someone's actions who have been raped?
>
> [Defence counsel]: That's not...
>
> Q. You'll agree with me, will you not...
>
> [Defence counsel]: That's not a matter that anyone could answer, Your Honour.
>
> A. [the appellant]: I don't think I'm in that position to say. If she felt she'd been raped, why didn't she come forward that night?
>
> Q. Well...
>
> [Defence counsel]: I say these are all improper questions.
>
> A. [the appellant]: I don't — I don't understand.
>
> [Crown counsel]: There's nothing improper, sir.
>
> [Defence counsel]: Oh, if...
>
> [Crown counsel]: If you're having some difficulty saying to this Court that if a girl was raped, it would be understandable that she might be angry and her friends might be angry and you might have some – the rapist, alleged, might have some actions taken against him? Are you having some difficulty saying that?
>
> A. No, I'm just not following where - what your question is.

---

50 (1999), 134 C.C.C. (3d) 131 (Ont. C.A.).

Labrosse J.A. (speaking for a five-member panel) expressed the following view:

> Crown counsel's questioning required the appellant to provide an alternate explanation for the complainant's behaviour that was not premised on his guilt. Such an explanation would have required the appellant to either comment upon the complainant's credibility or to give an opinion that he was clearly not qualified to give, explaining why her conduct was inconsistent with someone who had been sexually assaulted. Clearly questions of this nature are improper and unfair. [para. 15]

In *R. v. Schell*[51] the accused was charged with second degree murder. He testified that he owed the deceased $100 from a drug transaction. The accused testified that he killed the deceased in self-defence in the course of a struggle after the deceased entered his home without knocking and attacked him. At trial, the Crown put it to the accused that he had been in possession of the disclosure materials well in advance of the trial and that he had been present for the preliminary inquiry.

> Q. Mr. Schell, we are hearing this story, the jury, for the first time, the full version. Is that correct?
> A. Yes, Sir.
> Q. And you have had disclosure of the Crown's material, in terms of what witnesses would be testifying and what they are going to say?
> A. No, Sir, I did not. *[page 239]*
> Q. You did not read any of the statements?
> A. Some of them, Sir.
> Q. And you attended the preliminary hearing and listened to the witnesses?
> A. I did, sir.
> Q. So you have had an opportunity to think about it for the last 14 months?
> A. Think about what?
> Q. The evidence.
> A. No, sir.

Amongst other things, the Crown asked the accused whether he had testified at the preliminary inquiry, whether he had told anyone else his version of events and the fact that he had given a statement to the police.

Not surprisingly, the Court was most unimpressed by these events and ordered a re-trial on this and a host of other grounds. However, Rosenberg J.A. described the Crown's conduct as "the most serious ground of appeal."

> Crown counsel should not have led evidence from the arresting officer that the appellant had not made a statement upon arrest. The appellant had the right to remain silent and there was no permissible use of his silence: *R. v. Noble*, [1997] 1 S.C.R. 874 at p. 918. Standing alone, this error was of little consequence in this case. The evidence was extremely brief and the silence

---

51   (2000), 148 C.C.C. (3d) 219 (Ont. C.A.).

was not in response to any specific allegation the appellant might have been expected to deny. It was only when Crown counsel attempted to exploit the appellant's silence upon arrest and at the preliminary inquiry that the possibility of real prejudice arose. The trial Judge erred in law when he initially dismissed defence counsel's objection and allowed Crown counsel to continue this line of questioning. [para. 55]

It was also an error to permit Crown counsel to cross-examine the appellant on his use of disclosure. The appellant had a constitutional right to disclosure of the Crown's case through pre-trial disclosure and he had a statutory right to be present for the prosecution's case at the preliminary inquiry. [para. 56]

In *R. v. White*,[52] Doherty J.A. took exception to the following set of questions:

Q. Thank you. I want to ask you a bit about what information was given to you, and I concede any accused person gets this information, but you see this big red book in my hand?
A. Yes.
Q. That is the Crown brief of this case. You got that didn't you, or your lawyer got it?
A. Yes.
Q. You got to see before you testified every witness's statement, isn't that right?
A. That's right.
Q. You got to hear every witness that was called before this jury. Let's be correct. Ms. Kaforowski from CFS wasn't called at the preliminary inquiry and Dr. Thompson wasn't called at the preliminary inquiry and Michael Eleftherio wasn't called at the preliminary inquiry.

In addition, the Crown put to the accused that he had the opportunity to review all the exhibits and preliminary inquiry transcripts before testifying.

Doherty J.A. made it clear these questions should not have been permitted:

The line of questioning set out above seems calculated to suggest to the jury that the appellant's evidence was somehow suspect because he had received full disclosure and had not been subject to cross-examination prior to choosing to testify at trial. Not only are the suggestions improper, they are potentially prejudicial. As a matter of common sense, there may be considerable force to the suggestion that a person who gets full advance notice of the other side's evidence and testifies last is in a position to tailor his or her evidence to fit the disclosure. That inference, no matter how logical, cannot be drawn without turning fundamental constitutional rights into a trap for accused persons. Where any such suggestion seeps into the cross-examination of an accused, it must be eradicated by the trial Judge. [para. 20]

52　(1999), 132 C.C.C. (3d) 373 (Ont. C.A.).

Fortunately, in this case, the Judge did take the requisite steps with two immediate directions to the jury. This action was deemed sufficient by the Court to have cured any prejudice to the accused and prevented a re-trial.

In *R. v. S. (F.)*[53] the accused was charged with sexual offences against his stepdaughter which he denied. The Court of Appeal allowed his appeal. In its view the Crown had personalized his role in the trial stating to the jury that:

(1) His mission was to obtain a conviction and

(2) He, Crown counsel, was an honest and just person and that if the jury was not convinced of the accused's guilt it was because he had failed to do his job

(3) If there was no conviction that he and the jury would have to live with "this sad result."

In analyzing the Crown's cross-examination, Labrosse J.A. described the Crown as "inappropriately sarcastic, flippant and disrespectful towards the appellant" adding the following:

> When the appellant answered during his cross-examination that he was living with his stepson and his dog, Crown counsel retorted:
> Q. I assume your dog is not going to testify?
> When the appellant agreed that his stepson knew why the appellant was in Court, the next question from Crown counsel was:
> Q. He knows that you're not charged with shoplifting, right?
> And when Crown counsel sought to find out when the appellant ceased living with his wife, the following exchange took place:
> Q. Okay. When did you stop living with [your wife], sir?
> A. 28th of April '95, when I was charged. I was – they put me in jail for three days . . .
> Q. Okay.
> A. . . .until four o'clock and I came out on Monday...
> Q. I'm touched, sir, but that's not my question. My question is: when did you stop living with [your wife]?
> A. 28th of April, '95.

Labrosse J.A. concluded that the Crown had failed in its obligation to act in a scrupulous, fair manner and had crossed the line into behaviour that was both improper and unfair.

In *R. v. R. (A.J.)*[54] the accused was convicted of incest, sexual assault (on his daughter) and threatening. The complainant had been given up for adoption at birth and only located her father, the accused, when she was 20. She began living with him and, in her evidence, claimed that the sexual

---

53   (2000), 144 C.C.C. (3d) 466 (Ont. C.A.).
54   (1994), 94 C.C.C. (3d) 168 (Ont. C.A.).

assaults commenced immediately. The accused denied the offences claiming that he had not known that the complainant was his daughter and that she had consented to having sexual relations. Upon appeal, it was argued that the Crown's cross-examination was so prejudicial it had occasioned a miscarriage of justice. Doherty J.A. reviewed the conduct complained of:

> From the outset of the cross-examination, Crown counsel adopted a sarcastic tone with the accused and repeatedly inserted editorial commentary into her questions. I count at least eight such comments in the first eight pages of the cross-examination. During that part of the cross-examination, Crown counsel referred to one answer given by the appellant as "incredible." She repeatedly asked the appellant if he "wanted the jury to believe that one too." When questioned as to how he met T., the appellant said he was told by a friend that a relative would be coming to see him, whereupon Crown counsel remarked "so I guess you were expecting some long lost cousin in the old country." After the appellant had described his reaction to being told by T. that she was his daughter, Crown counsel sarcastically said "gee, I guess everybody would react the way you did."
>
> Crown counsel's approach from the very beginning of the cross-examination was calculated to demean and humiliate the appellant. She persisted in that approach throughout. For example, after the appellant said that he had allowed T. to move in with him shortly after they had met, Crown counsel said "you are just a really nice guy." At another point, she said, "tell me sir, do fathers usually have sexual intercourse with their daughters." Still later, after the appellant had testified that his girlfriend had left him but had told him that she wished to come back, Crown counsel said "you just have all these women running after you wanting to come back."

He made the following observation with respect to the Crown's tone and demeanour:

> The tone adopted by Crown counsel is not the only problem with her cross-examination. Crown counsel repeatedly gave evidence and stated her opinion during cross-examination. She also engaged in extensive argument with the appellant. For example, when the appellant gave contradictory explanations in the course of cross-examination, Crown counsel announced "you were lying," and when the appellant questioned Crown counsel's description of T. as "your victim" Crown counsel replied "certainly she is." Still later, after Crown counsel had very effectively cross-examined the appellant as to when he had learned that T. was his daughter, she proclaimed "you are playing games with me, with this jury." She followed that comment with the admonition "let's try and be honest." In several instances, the cross-examination degenerated into pure argument between the appellant and Crown counsel. After one lengthy exchange, Crown counsel announced: "It is hard to keep up with you sir because you keep changing your story."

He concluded:

Statements of counsel's personal opinion have no place in a cross-examination. Nor is cross-examination of the appellant the time or place for argument.

In *R. v. Walker*[55] the accused was charged with first degree murder of his common law wife. The Crown's position was that the deceased was a prostitute and he was her pimp. The motive to kill the deceased stemmed from the fact that she had returned home after doing a "trick" and had brought back insufficient monies to satisfy the accused and his need for drugs. The Crown was therefore allowed to lead evidence of the relationship between the two including the accused's mental and physical abuse of the victim in the years prior to her death. The Ontario Court of Appeal also agreed that this type of evidence was admissible. At trial, however, the Crown further explored the relationship in the following way:

Q. Isn't it true that the only enemy Monique Cloutier had in her life was you?
A. No, sir.
Q. You were the one that abused her physically?
A. I have, yes.
Q. You were the one that sent her out on the street to be subjected to all kinds of risks.
A. I have, yes.
Q. You were her one enemy, weren't you?
A. No, I don't think I was.
Q. No one else was her enemy, right?
A. She had no enemies. Everybody liked Monique. Everybody.
Q. You were doing her a great deal of harm, weren't you, Mr. Walker?
A. Yes, I was. I sure didn't help.
Q. You cared nothing for her welfare, did you, sir.
A. I cared nothing for myself at the time either.
Q. You agree with me then you cared nothing for Monique Cloutier's welfare?
A. Not intentionally.
Q. It was drugs that you craved and drugs that you loved.
A. Yes, it was.
Q. And when Monique couldn't come back with enough money you got angry and you killed her.
A. No, sir, I did not.

The Court stated the Crown attempted to portray the accused as "just the kind of person who was likely to have committed this crime and the above was just one excerpt that demonstrated the tenor of the cross-examination. There were others. Finlayson J.A. felt that the cross-examination went too far, putting the accused's lifestyle on trial and putting unnecessary emphasis on the point. Other examples included the following suggestions from the Crown:

---

55 (1994), 90 C.C.C. (3d) 144 (Ont. C.A.).

Counsel accused the appellant of taking her away from rehabilitation and putting her "back into that sleazy drug life that she'd been in for years."

He said, "You wanted her for your benefit to go out on the street and risk beatings, disease, arrest and further drug addiction, right?"

And he stated, "Mr. Walker, Monique Cloutier's life with you was a miserable, sole destroying grind, wasn't it?"

Finlayson J.A. concluded that otherwise admissible evidence had become inadmissible because of the Crown's cross-examination:

> What occurred during the case on appeal is somewhat unusual in that character evidence which was originally admissible because its probative value out-weighed its prejudicial effect became inadmissible because the improper cross-examination of the appellant elevated the prejudice to a point where it out-weighed the initial probative value. It is my view that the trial Judge should have stopped this abusive cross-examination when it became apparent that evidence which was let in for a proper purpose was now being used by the Crown for an improper purpose. I am aware that a criminal trial can be a demanding experience and that this Court should not be too quick to criticize excessive zeal on the part of counsel. However, this cross-examination, while not of itself sufficient to justify a new trial, is a significant factor in my proposed disposition of this appeal.

In *R. v. Bouhsass*,[56] the accused was charged with the second degree murder of his ex-girlfriend. According to the Crown, the accused, a visitor from Israel and of the Druze religion, had entered into a relationship with the deceased in an attempt to use her financially and gain Canadian citizenship. When she realized his intentions she broke off the relationship. Desperate for money, he entered her home at night and stabbed her to death as she lay in bed. After murdering her, he stole valuable jewellery that she had concealed in her bedroom and left the scene using her car. After describing the Crown's case as "formidable," the Court of Appeal turned its attention to the cross-examination conducted by the Crown. Its view could not be more scathing:

> In this case, the tone of the cross-examination was often sarcastic, personally abusive and derisive. The language used was emotive and it measured the appellant against a severe moralistic standard. The appellant was attacked for his lifestyle, including his relationship with women in general, his sexual activities, his supposed heroin addiction and his "thievery." While some of these maters (the thefts and the heroin addiction) were held by the trial judge to have probative value, as indicated, the Crown's questions focused largely on the prejudicial content of the evidence, rather than its probative content.
>
> In addition, the cross-examination broke, in a repetitive and persistent fashion, the following rules that have been spelled out time and time again by this Court:

---

56 (2002), 169 C.C.C. (3d) 444 (Ont. C.A.).

(1) It required the appellant to comment on the veracity of other witnesses.
(2) It improperly required the appellant to explain why certain witnesses were not being called to testify and in the same vein, it called upon him to answer for the fact that his evidence was not corroborated by anyone.
(3) It used the appellant's constitutional right to disclosure as a trap and portrayed him as a stage actor who, in light of disclosure, had carefully scripted his evidence to avoid the minefields in the case against him.
(4) Crown counsel repeatedly referred to the appellant as a bare-faced liar and he regularly injected his personal views and editorial comments into the questions he was asking.
(5) Crown counsel made a number of suggestions in cross-examination that were baseless but highly prejudicial to the appellant.
(6) Crown counsel mocked and unfairly challenged the appellant's adherence to his religious beliefs. [paras. 11 and 12]

Despite the strength of the Crown's case, the Court refused to apply the curative proviso and sent the matter back for a new trial. The re-trial is discussed later.

In *R. v. Robinson*,[57] the accused was charged with the sexual assault of his girlfriend. The trial Judge permitted the defence to lead evidence of prior sexual conduct between the appellant and the complainant which included sexual activity that was "out of the ordinary" including bondage, three-way sex, mutual urination and use of sexual aids. Rosenberg J.A. described how the Crown treated the evidence:

> Crown counsel repeatedly made use of this evidence in an attempt to portray the appellant as perverted and a sexual deviant. He used terms such as "bizarre" and "demented." He suggested that the appellant's evidence had all of the elements of a "demented version of a cheap crime novel." He made clear his own personal distaste and disgust for the appellant's sexual preferences and lifestyle. [para. 38]

> Crown counsel carried this theme on in his jury address, suggesting to the jury that the unemployment insurance misconduct and the sexual activities were "so insightful of the character of the accused." At the conclusion of the address, Crown counsel summed up the case as having all the features of a "bizarre, sadistic, albeit unsophisticated crime novel." The appellant had not put his character in issue. Crown counsel's jury address was an explicit invitation to the jury to use the evidence of other misconduct for the prohibited purpose of showing that the appellant was the type of person likely to commit these offences. [para. 39]

> As I have indicated, the cross-examination was also laced with sarcasm and was intended to demean the appellant. Crown counsel made clear his personal opinion of the appellant and his distaste for him and his lifestyle. He also on several occasions made suggestions to the appellant about various sexual acts

---

57   (2001), 153 C.C.C. (3d) 398 (Ont. C.A.).

that had no evidentiary foundation and had never been disclosed in the Crown's case in-chief. [para. 40]

According to Rosenberg J.A. the cross-examination had made the trial of the accused unfair:

> Credibility was critical in this case. The many acquittals show only that the case was finely balanced. The unfair attack on the appellant's character by the Crown and the improper attempt by Crown counsel to throw the weight of his office and his personal opinion into the balance may have tipped the case against the appellant. [para. 45]

Accordingly, I would allow the appeal from conviction and order a new trial. [para. 46]

Effect of Co-accused's Plea of Guilty

In *R. v. Caron*[58] the Ontario Court of Appeal stated that it is incumbent on the trial Judge to warn the jury that the plea of guilty by an accused who was also co-charged with the same offence is no evidence whatsoever of the guilt of the accused.

Voir Dire Evidence Forming Part of Trial

Voir dire evidence does not form part of the trial evidence unless there is an agreement to that effect and ambiguity in the use that could be made of that evidence is to be resolved in favour of the accused.[59]

TIMING OF INTRODUCING THE ACCUSED'S STATEMENT BY THE CROWN

A confession is normally offered into evidence by the Crown as part of its case. The Crown may choose not to introduce the statement because it is exculpatory. An issue arises however when the Crown does not introduce the statement during the prosecution's case but wishes to do so during the defence case. Normally the law regards it as unfair for the Crown to lie in wait for the accused and trap him with his previously untendered statement in order to contradict some part of his testimony.

---

58 (1971), 9 C.C.C. (2d) 447(Ont. C.A.). See also *R. v. MacDonald* (1974), 21 C.C.C. (2d) 87 (Ont. C.A.) at 92, affirmed (1977), 34 C.C.C. (2d) 1 (S.C.C.); *R. v. McGregor* (1981), 64 C.C.C. (2d) 353 (Ont. C.A.) at 357-58.

59 *R. v. Dela Cruz* (2007), 220 C.C.C. (3d) 272 (Man. C.A.) at paras. 28, 30.

The law in this regard is canvassed in *R. v. King*[60] where the Crown sought to cross-examine the accused on a prior statement to the police. No evidence about any statement by the accused was led by the Crown. The Court found that since the statement was exculpatory, it was only marginally, minimally or doubtfully relevant during the Crown's case such that the rule against splitting its case did not apply and the Crown could cross-examine. The statement was not "clearly relevant" to the Crown's case and only became so after the accused testified. The statement must first be found to be voluntary. The Crown may ask for a *voir dire* during the Crown's case and not use the statement unless the accused gives inconsistent testimony, or may wait to see if the accused gives contradictory testimony, ask for a *voir dire* during the cross-examination of the accused. If the accused does not admit making the statement, the Crown may prove it in rebuttal unless it is collateral.

In *R. v. Ament*[61] Grant J. of the Ontario High Court, in an oral judgment, ruled that if the statement is tendered by the Crown for the first time in cross-examination it can only be used for the purpose of impugning the credibility of the accused. If a statement has not been proven to be voluntary, the Crown cannot use it for any purpose including challenging the credibility of the witness.[62]

Defence counsel may require that additional portions or all of the statement be introduced if the Crown only intends to cross-examine on a portion thereof.[63]

CAUSING A DISTORTED VIEW OF THE EVIDENCE

If counsel attempts to leave a distorted view of the evidence by his or her cross-examination then the Court will rectify such false impressions by allowing the opposite side to introduce evidence it might not otherwise have been allowed to introduce. So where defence counsel criticized the police for not holding a line-up for this client on the issue of identification, the

---

60 [1998] O J. No. 662 (Ont. Gen. Div.). The leading case is *R. v. Drake* (1970), 1 C.C.C. (2d) 396 (Sask. Q.B.). See also *R. v. Chaulk*, [1990] 3 S.C.R. 1303; *R. v. Ament* (1972), 7 C.C.C. (2d) 83 (Ont. H.C.); *Lizotte v. R.* (1980), 18 C.R. (3d) 364 (Que. C.A.); *R. v. Ryckman* (1971), 19 C.R.N.S. 14 (Ont. H.C.); *R. v. Bruno* (1975), 27 C.C.C. (2d) 318 (Ont. C.A.); *R. v. Brooks* (1986), 28 C.C.C. (3d) 441 (B.C. C.A.), leave to appeal refused (1987), 86 N.R. 239 (note) (S.C.C.); but see *R. v. Pappajohn* (1978), 45 C.C.C (2d) 67 (B.C. C.A.) at 73, affirmed (1980), 14 C.R. (3d) 243 (Eng.) (S.C.C.).
61 (1972), 7 C.C.C. (2d) 83 (Ont. H.C.).
62 *Hebert. v. R.*, (sub nom. *R. v. Hebert*), [1955] S.C.R. 120 (S.C.C.).
63 *R. v. Drake, supra.*

Crown was permitted to lead evidence that the accused refused to go into a line-up when requested by the police.[64]

COMMUNICATION WITH WITNESSES GIVING EVIDENCE

The Law Society of Upper Canada has adopted certain rules for Ontario Counsel regarding communicating with a witness giving evidence. A commentary to Rule 4 states that if any question arises whether the lawyer's behaviour may be in violation of this rule, it will often be appropriate to obtain the consent of the opposing lawyer or leave of the tribunal before engaging in conversations that may be considered improper.

4.04 Subject to the direction of the tribunal, the lawyer shall observe the following rules respecting communication with witnesses giving evidence:
  (a) during examination-in-chief, the examining lawyer may discuss with the witness any matter that has not been covered in the examination up to that point,
  (b) during examination-in-chief by another lawyer of a witness who is unsympathetic to the lawyer's cause, the lawyer not conducting the examination-in-chief may discuss the evidence with the witness,
  (c) between completion of examination-in-chief and commencement of cross-examination of the lawyer's own witness, the lawyer ought not to discuss the evidence given in chief or relating to any matter introduced or touched on during the examination-in-chief,
  (d) during cross-examination but an opposing lawyer, the witness's own lawyer ought not to have any conversation with the witness about the witness's evidence or any issue in the proceeding,[65]
  (e) between completion of cross-examination and commencement of re-examination, the lawyer who is going to re-examine the witness ought not to have any discussion about evidence that will be dealt with on re-examination,[66]

---

64 *R. v. Marcoux* (1972), 18 C.R.N.S. 39 (Ont. Co. Ct.); *R. v. Brager*, [1965] 4 C.C.C. 251 (B.C. C.A.).
65 In *R. v. Savoy* (1977), 18 N.B.R. (2d) 489 (N.B. C.A.), the Court of Appeal was critical of the trial Judge agreeing to the Crown's request to speak to a witness whom the Crown called while the witness was under cross-examination.
66 In *R. v. Lawlor* (1999), 135 C.C.C. (3d) 249 (Nfld. T.D.). It was held that an accused should not be deprived of the right to speak to counsel during trial except during cross-examination and therefore was entitled to speak to his counsel after cross-examination and before re-examination. In *R. v. Montgomery* (1998), 126 C.C.C. (3d) 251 (B.C. S.C.). The Court held that the rule in British Columbia is that counsel is not permitted to speak to her own witness after cross-examination and before or during re-examination about evidence or issues in the case except with leave of the Court which in most cases should be readily given. The rule ought not to apply to accused, such that defence counsel may discuss the evidence with the accused before re-examination without requiring leave of the Court. This case canvasses the positions in other provinces on the issue.

(f) during cross-examination by the lawyer of the witness unsympathetic to the cross-examiner's cause, the lawyer may discuss the witness's evidence with the witness

(g) during cross-examination by the lawyer of a witness who is sympathetic to that lawyer's cause, any conversations ought to be restricted in the same way as communications during examination-in-chief of one's own witness

(h) during re-examination of a witness called by an opposing lawyer, if the witness is sympathetic to the lawyer's cause the lawyer ought not to discuss the evidence to be given by the witness during re-examination. The lawyer may, however, properly discuss the evidence with a witness who is adverse in interest.[67]

The Canadian Bar Association's position is that the lawyer should observe the local rules and practices concerning communication with a witness about the witness's evidence or any issue in the proceeding. The C.B.A. further says that generally, it is considered improper for counsel who called a witness to communicate with that witness without leave of the Court while such witness is under cross-examination.

ADMISSIONS AT TRIAL

Section 655 of the *Criminal Code*[68] provides that:

Where an accused is on trial for an indictable offence, he or his counsel may admit any fact alleged against him for the purpose of dispensing with proof thereof.

Section 655 also applies to the preliminary hearing.[69] For example, an accused may admit to the voluntariness of his or her statement thereby obviating the necessity of a *voir dire*. However, the waiver of a *voir dire* must be express, as a mere lack of objection will not constitute a valid waiver.[70]

This section can make life easier, particularly for the prosecution, since it could save the time, trouble and expense of calling witnesses. The Crown is not required to accept an admission and is entitled to call any evidence felt necessary, notwithstanding the admission.[71]

---

67 The Law Society's commentary to Rule 4 states that if any question arises whether the lawyer's behaviour may be in violation of this Rule, it will often be appropriate to obtain consent of the opposing lawyer or leave of the tribunal before engaging in conversations that may be considered improper.

68 R.S.C. 1985, c. C-46. There is a similar provision in the *Young Offenders Act*, ss. 58 and 59.

69 *Re Ulrich and R.* (1977), 38 C.C.C. (2d) 1 (Alta.T.D.).

70 *Park v. R.* (1981), 59 C.C.C. (2d) 385 (S.C.C.).

71 *R. v. Castellani*, [1969] 1 C.C.C. 327 (B.C. C.A.) at 340, *per* Bull J.A. In *R. v. Proctor*

Tactically, defence counsel should be prepared to make such admissions as they would save Court time and counsel is satisfied that the admissions would not help the prosecution because they relate to evidence of such a minor nature, or the Crown is in a position to prove that which counsel is prepared to formally admit. Defence counsel by such admissions could gain the favour of the jury and the trial Judge by offering in their presence to expedite the trial in such fashion. By formally admitting certain facts counsel may diminish a prejudicial atmosphere which surrounds the evidence in question.

If it becomes apparent that the accused's evidence is in conflict with any agreed statement of facts, the trial Judge should require the Crown to call the evidence on those matters in issue.[72]

Section 655 applies to summary conviction trials by virtue of section 795 of the *Criminal Code* and to indictable and summary conviction trials commenced by other federal statutes by virtue of section 27(2) of the *Interpretation Act*.[73]

Section 665 does not provide for admissions by the Crown. The Crown may, at common law, waive technicalities of proof by the accused.[74]

DEALING WITH MATTERS BEFORE JURY SELECTION

Section 645(5) of the *Criminal Code* states:

In any case to be tried with a jury, the Judge before whom an accused is or is to be tried has jurisdiction, before any juror on a panel of jurors is called pursuant to subsection 631(3) or (3.1) and in the absence of any such juror, to deal with any matter that would ordinarily or necessarily be dealt with in the absence of the jury after it has been sworn.

This section permits the trial Judge to rule on any issues pertaining to the trial, particularly the admissibility of evidence. The obvious benefit of this subsection is that a jury will not be continuously inconvenienced by having to leave the courtroom, sometimes for lengthy periods when matters of admissibility are argued. If the trial judge has to take time to consider his or her decision, the jurors will be inconvenienced further.

I have been concerned about whether jurors suspect that they are being asked to leave the courtroom because incriminating evidence against an accused person is being kept from them because of some legal technicality, especially when the defence is raising the objection. I have also had the

---

(1992), 69 C.C.C. (3d) 436 (Man. C.A.), Twaddle J.A. stated that the Crown is not entitled to refuse acceptance where the purpose is to keep an issue alive artificially for prejudicial purposes.

72 *R. v. Coburn* (1982), 66 C.C.C. (2d) 463 (Ont. C.A.).

73 R.S.C. 1985, c. I-21.

74 *Picariello v. R.* (1923), 39 C.C.C. 229 (S.C.C.).

concern that friends or relatives of jurors who drop in throughout the trial will hear the evidence that is being argued about and, even if ruled inadmissible, may tell a member of the jury about that evidence. Arguing the admissibility of the evidence before the jury is empanelled will obviate such concerns.

The early determination of evidentiary issues will also have the effect of assisting counsel with his or her trial tactics and preparation and counsel on both sides will be better able to determine what witnesses will be necessary and which potential witnesses can be dropped. In some cases the trial judge's rulings on admissibility of important evidence may influence either side to negotiate a plea. However, there may be the rare occasion you do not wish to argue the admissibility of a piece of evidence on a pre-trial motion because you are unsure whether you want that evidence in or out and you will not be able to make up your mind until you know how effectively the Crown's evidence on the issue will play out, or if the Crown decides to lead the evidence at all. Indeed, the Crown may be waiting to see how you deal with the issue on a pre-trial motion before deciding to lead the evidence.

17

The Expert Witness

YOUR EXPERT WITNESS

Admissibility

In *R. v. Fisher*,[1] Aylesworth J.A. of the Ontario Court of Appeal stated:

> It is trite to say that a witness may not give his opinion upon matters calling for special skill or knowledge unless he is an expert in such matters nor will an expert witness be allowed to give his opinion upon matters not within his particular field. Finally, opinion evidence may not be given upon a subject-matter within what may be described as the common stock of knowledge. Subject to these rules, the basic reasoning which runs through the authorities here and in England, seems to be that expert opinion evidence will be admitted where it will be helpful to the jury in their deliberations and it will be excluded only where the jury can easily draw the necessary inferences without it.

In *R. v. Mohan*,[2] the Supreme Court of Canada held that before expert evidence is admissible it must meet four criteria:

1. The expert evidence must be relevant.[3] Relevant evidence may still be excluded if:
    a) its probative value is outweighed by its prejudicial effect;

---

1 [1961] O.W.N. 94 (Ont. C.A.), affirmed (1960), 130 C.C.C. 1 (*sub nom. Fisher v. R.*) (S.C.C.).

2 (1994), 89 C.C.C. (3d) 402 (S.C.C.), reversing (1992), 71 C.C.C. (3d) 321 (Ont. C.A.). See also *R. v. Marquard* (1993), 85 C.C.C. (3d) 193 at 224 (S.C.C.).

3 In *Mohan*, Sopinka J. stated that "What is required is that the opinion be necessary in the sense that it provide information which is likely to be outside the experience and knowledge of a Judge and jury." To say that the evidence is necessary because it is "helpful" to the trier-of-fact "sets too low a standard" but necessity should not be judged by "too strict a standard."

    b) the time required to prove its admissibility is not commensurate with its value; or

    c) the trier of fact can be influenced out of proportion to the evidence's reliability and therefore should be excluded where it could be misused, distort the fact-finding process or confuse the jury who may be overwhelmed by the "mystic infallibility" of the evidence.

2. Necessity in assisting the trier of fact. Necessity should not be judged by too strict a standard. To be necessary, the evidence must provide information which likely is not within the experience and knowledge of the trier of fact. Experts must not usurp the function of the trier of fact so that as a result, the trial degenerates into a trial of experts, a danger that can occur with too liberal an approach to admissibility.

3. The evidence must not run afoul of an exclusionary rule.[4]

4. The expert must be one who is shown to have acquired a special skill or knowledge through study or experience in the area for which he or she has been called upon to testify.

Mohan went on to state that where the expert evidence advances a novel scientific theory or technique, it must be scrutinized to ascertain whether it meets a basic threshold or reliability, and, a satisfactory conclusion could not be reached without expert assistance. The closer the evidence approaches an opinion on an ultimate issue, the stricter the Court will be in applying the criteria of admissibility. The trial Judge should consider:

1. whether the theory or technique in question can be (and has been) tested;

2. whether it has been subject to peer review and publication;

3. its known or potential error rate;

4. the existence and maintenance of standards controlling its operation; and,

5. whether it has attracted wide spread acceptance within a relevant scientific community. (It is of interest to note that the syndrome of recovered repressed memories of traumatic incidents such as child sexual abuse, responsible for sending a number of accused to jail, has been severely criticized by the Canadian Psychiatric Association[5] and the Royal College of Psychiatrists in London, England.[6])

---

4 For example, bad character evidence and oath-helping, see *R. v. F. (J.E.)* (1993), 85 C.C.C. (3d) 457 (Ont. C.A.).

5 The Toronto Star, May 29th, 1996.

6 The Globe and Mail, January 13th, 1998, reporting an article from The Guardian. An example where an opinion was held to be inadmissible because the process by which it was formulated was not established to be scientifically valid can be seen in *R. v. Jmieff* (1994), 94 C.C.C. (3d) 157 (B.C. C.A.). For an example where it was held that expert evidence should not be mechanically excluded as defence evidence on the sole ground that the scientific community has not developed a psychological profile that is common to every offender who commits the crime charged, see *R. v. J. (J.-L.)* (1998), 130 C.C.C.

While it is trite law that neither an expert nor anyone else is permitted to testify as to whether a witness is telling the truth,[7] a body of law has developed in sexual and domestic assault cases which permit experts to testify as to matters which indirectly support the veracity of the complainant. In *R. v. Marquard*,[8] McLachlin J. speaking for the majority stated:

> A judge or jury who simply accepts an expert's opinion on the credibility of a witness would be abandoning its duty to itself determine the credibility of the witness. Credibility must always be the product of the judge or jury's view of the diverse ingredients it has perceived at trial, combined with experience, logic and an intuitive sense of the matter ... The expert who testifies on credibility is not sworn to the heavy duty of a judge or juror. Moreover, the expert's opinion may be founded on factors which are not in the evidence upon which the judge and juror are duty-bound to render a true verdict. Finally, credibility is a notoriously difficult problem, and the expert's opinion may be all too readily accepted by a frustrated jury as a convenient basis upon which to resolve its difficulties. All these considerations have contributed to the wise policy of the law in rejecting expert evidence on the truthfulness of witnesses. On the other hand, *there may be features of a witness's evidence which go beyond the ability of a lay person to understand, and hence which may justify expert evidence.* This is particularly the case in the evidence of children ... For this reason, there is a growing consensus that *while expert evidence on the ultimate credibility of a witness is not admissible, expert evidence on human conduct and the psychological and physical factors which may lead to certain*

(3d) 541 (Que. C.A.), reversed (2000), 37 C.R. (5th) 203 (S.C.C.). Evidence that was held to be properly excluded described profile or general behaviour patterns of persons who had been abused and that the complainant came within that profile because this evidence was based almost solely on the expert's own experience with no objective means of evaluating the reliability of that opinion. See *R. v. F. (D.S.)* (1999), 132 C.C.C. (3d) 97 (Ont. C.A.). *R. v. Clark* (2004), 182 C.C.C. (3d) 1 (Ont. C.A.) spoke to the issue of criminal profiling holding that expert evidence was inadmissible to explain why the crime was committed in a particular manner and who was likely to have committed it, because it was a novel field of scientific evidence and its reliability was not proven at trial. Clark also held that crime scene analysis, namely expert opinion as to what occurred at the crime scene and how the crime was committed was admissible as it was anchored in the evidence, as opposed to speculation or guesswork, and was not overly complex or technical as to overwhelm the jury.

7 *R. v. Taylor* (1986), 31 C.C.C. (3d) 1 (Ont. C.A.); *R. v. B. (F.F.)* (1993), 79 C.C.C. (3d) 112 (S.C.C.); *R. v. Kostuck* (1986), 29 C.C.C. (3d) 190 at 192 (Man. C.A.); *R. v. Marquard* (1993), 85 C.C.C. (3d) 193 (S.C.C.); *R. v. Jmieff* (1994), 94 C.C.C. (3d) 157 (B.C. C.A.). In *R. v. M. (B.)* (1998), 42 O.R. (3d) 1 (C.A.), the Court held that expert evidence about the nature of childhood memory and the effect of lengthy delay on the reliability of those memories was admissible. For an example, where it was held that expert evidence should not be mechanically excluded as defence evidence on the sole ground that the scientific community has not developed a psychological profile that is common to every offender who commits the crime charged, see *R. v. J.-L.* (1998), 130 C.C.C. (3d) 541 (Que. C.A.), reversed (2000), 37 C.R. (5th) 203 (S.C.C.).

8 *Ibid.*, at 228-229.

behaviour relevant to credibility, is admissible, provided the testimony goes beyond the ordinary experience of the trier of fact.

[Emphasis added].

Experts have been permitted to testify about general behavioural and psychological conditions supposedly consistent with child abuse, as for example: bed wetting, nightmares, anxiety, low self- esteem, depression, poor school performance, truancy, sexually acting out and promiscuity. The fact that such psychological and physical traits may be due to other causes such as death of a loved one, lack of love or caring from parents, poor school performance or emotional problems unrelated to abuse, etc., appear to be a matter of weight,[9] although in the United States, it has been held that such a "laundry list of possible behaviours does no more than invite speculation and should not be condoned."[10]

Testimony has been admissible from expert witnesses to explain evidence negativing credibility of a child victim of sexual abuse, such as a failure to complain or the recantation of an allegation of sexual abuse. Such behaviour is said to be consistent with a general pattern of child behaviour in other such cases and with child abuse.[11] However, the Supreme Court of Canada appears to have heeded prior remarks by the courts about the dangers of expert evidence by its upholding of an Ontario Court of Appeal decision in *R. v. D. (D.)*[12] which limits the admissibility of certain expert testimony and may lead the way for further such decisions. In *R. v. D. (D.)* the Crown called an expert on delayed disclosure of child sexual abuse who testified that standing alone, such delay signifies nothing and the significance of such delay depends on the circumstances of the particular victim. The Supreme Court held that the primary danger of such evidence is that the province of the jury may be usurped and jurors are more likely to abdicate their role as fact-finders and simply attorn to the opinion of the expert. Where there is no competing expert evidence, the jury will have no framework within which to evaluate the merit of the evidence and additional dangers arise because expert opinions are often derived from academic literature and out-of-court interviews. The expert evidence in *R. v. D. (D.)* was not unique or scientifically puzzling and was the proper subject for a simple jury instruction which would charge the jury that failure to make a timely complaint must not be the subject of any presumptive adverse assumptions of how persons, particularly children react to acts of sexual abuse;

---

9 See note 7 *infra*. The jury should be told to exercise caution with respect to this evidence.

10 *Com. v. Dunkle*, 602 A.2d 830 (Pa. 1992) at 834-835; See also *State v. Michaels*, 625 A.2d 489 (N.J. Super. A.D. 1993); *State v. Cressey*, 628 A.2d 696 (N.H. 1993).

11 *R. v. C. (R.A.)* (1990), 78 C.R. (3d) 390 (B.C. C.A.); *R. v. Marquard, supra; R. v. J. (F.E.)* (1990), 74 C.R. (3d) 269 (Ont. C.A.); *R. v. B. (G.)* (1990), 77 C.R. (3d) 347 (S.C.C.); *R. v. T. (S.)* (1986), 55 C.R. (3d) 321 (Ont. C.A.); *R. v. Beliveau* (1986), 30 C.C.C. (3d) 193 (B.C. C.A.).

12 (2000), 148 C.C.C. (3d) 41 (S.C.C.).

that some will make an immediate complaint, some will delay disclosure and some will never disclose the abuse. Delay may occur as a result of embarrassment, fear, guilt, or lack of understanding and knowledge. Timing is simply one circumstance and delay standing alone can never give rise to an adverse inference against the credibility of the complainant.

Where an expert gives an opinion that certain symptoms displayed by a child are consistent with sexual abuse and this opinion is based on her own clinical experience and the experience of her colleagues but there is no valid profile of the sexually abused child the probative value of such evidence is extremely limited and its prejudicial effect potentially overwhelming and such evidence should not be admitted.[13]

A child abuse expert was allowed to testify that young children do not have the motivation or sophistication nor the mental capacity to elaborately deceive or to manufacture a complex fabrication to achieve an ulterior purpose.[14]

In *R. v. Ryan*,[15] a psychiatrist was permitted to testify as to the dynamics of the psychiatrist-patient relationship in order to provide an explanation why the patient would remain in treatment and not actively resist unwelcome sexual advances from the psychiatrist.

An expert is entitled to testify regarding the myths and stereotypes about the battered wife and her responses to the batterer.[16]

In *R. v. Millar*,[17] the Ontario Court of Appeal recognized that the language of the experts, as for example, the phrase "child abuse," could have an emotional impact on a jury and held that the trial judge has a discretion to allow the evidence to be given in a less emotional but just as accurate a form.

The rule against oath-helping disallows a party calling evidence to bolster a witness's credibility,[18] otherwise a trial could become bogged down in a limitless number of witnesses testifying as to the credibility of other witnesses who are testifying as to the facts, causing confusion in the minds of the jury and deflecting it from the real issues.[19] As a result, a psychiatrist was prohibited from testifying that a complainant with the mental age of

13 *R. v. Olscamp* (1994), 95 C.C.C. (3d) 466 (Ont. Gen. Div.). See also *R. v. Diffenbaugh* (1993), 80 C.C.C. (3d) 97 (B.C. C.A.).
14 *R. v. W. (A.)* (1994), 94 C.C.C. (3d) 441 (Ont. C.A.). But see *R. v. Kyselka* in Chapter, "Character Witnesses" under heading "Oath Helping."
15 (1993), 80 C.C.C. (3d) 514 (B.C. C.A.).
16 *R. v. Lavallee* (1990), 55 C.C.C. (3d) 97 (S.C.C.).
17 (1989), 49 C.C.C. (3d) 193 (Ont. C.A.).
18 *R. v. Beland and Phillips* (1988), 36 C.C.C. (3d) 481 (S.C.C.) at 493; *R. v. Marquard, supra.*
19 *R. v. Kyselka* (1962), 37 C.R. 391 (Ont. C.A.).

between 10 and 11 was not imaginative enough to fabricate her evidence as this amounted to evidence that the complainant was telling the truth.[20]

It is not difficult to appreciate that there can be a fine line between what amounts to oath-helping and legally admissible evidence of experts in abuse cases. This distinction is demonstrated in *R. v. Marquard*,[21] where the Supreme Court of Canada permitted the expert to testify as to why children may initially lie to the hospital staff about the cause of their injuries, but found objectionable the expert's opinion that she disbelieved the child's version given at the hospital and accepted the version given at trial.

While evidence which is adduced only for the purpose of providing that a witness is truthful is impermissible, it will be admissible if there is a legitimate purpose. As a result, the Supreme Court of Canada found unobjectionable the following question and answer (psychiatrist witness): "Did at any time as far as you were aware she (the complainant) tell you something that was untrue?" "Not that I'm aware of" was the reply. McLachlin J. held that this evidence provided a foundation for the opinions which the psychiatrist had given about the complainant's behaviour, and these opinions would be weakened if he did not believe what she told him.[22] The Court also found permissible and inoffensive to the hearsay rule the expert's relating by the complainant of the history of sexual abuse she endured. This evidence was not admitted for the truth but to support the expert's diagnosis of the complainant's mental state and his explanation of her behaviour.

The above rationale appears to be supportive of earlier cases which hold that the consistency of the complainant's out-of-court accounts are admissible through the expert to support their views the complainant was not fabricating[23] or to show the foundation for the opinion that the complainant had been sexually abused.[24]

If an expert gives statistical evidence to support her opinion she may run afoul of the rule that she is commenting on the credibility of a witness. It was held to be objectionable that an expert from a child abuse unit testified that in her experience only one or two percent of children who complained of sexual abuse were lying.[25] Similarly, it was held to be objectionable that the expert's evidence that the literature suggested at least 90 percent of disclosures of sexual assault by children are true.[26]

---

20   *Ibid.*
21   *Supra.*
22   *R. v. B. (R.H.)* (1994), 89 C.C.C. (3d) 193 (S.C.C.).
23   *R. v. Manahan* (1990), 61 C.C.C. (3d) 139 (Alta. C.A.). This appears to be an exception to section 275 which abrogates the rules regarding recent complaint.
24   *R. v. Beliveau* (1986), 30 C.C.C. (3d) 193 (B.C. C.A.).
25   *R. v. Taylor* (1986), 31 C.C.C. (3d) 1 (Ont. C.A.).
26   *R. v. K. (P.V.)* (1993), 22 C.R. (4th) 332 (N.S. C.A.).

Where Do I Find My Expert

Many experts are now advertising in legal publications but in my view the best source for the expert you want are the opinions of experienced counsel who are normally easy to approach.[27] You will explain the issues on which the expert is required to give his/her opinions. You can bounce different names that you may have learned about with the experienced counsel you are consulting to determine which one they would choose. You want an expert who will be able to communicate well with the trier-of-fact, who does not come across as biased, who has a good reputation with the courts for honesty and integrity, and who has an impressive *curriculum vitae* indicating that he or she is well-qualified in the relevant area of expertise. Another source for experts is the various university departments that are concerned with your subject-matter.

Seeking the names of qualified experts during cross-examination of the prosecution expert who testifies at the preliminary hearing can be helpful. If you were to use that expert at trial the prosecution's expert could hardly deny your suggestion to him in cross-examination that your expert is very qualified in the relevant field.

Outside auditors are often hired to monitor forensic labs such as Ontario's Centre of Forensic Sciences, in order to receive accreditation in the lab's various disciplines. The auditor, every few years would investigate the lab to determine if it is complying with international standards, and if not, accreditation would not be granted. You can inquire from the lab or the Crown expert who testifies at the preliminary hearing as to who is their auditor and seek to retain that individual on behalf of your client. The Crown or its expert would have great difficulty in disagreeing with your expert's testimony.

Preparation of Your Expert

The expert witness has become an integral part of the trial process. Before the expert can be of any value to counsel, however, counsel must be of value to the expert. The expert should be made aware of exactly what the issues are in the trial. The expert should be given copies of materials such as transcripts of the preliminary inquiry, statements of the witnesses, photographs, medical and other reports, exhibits (where copies are available), and when necessary obtain releases for testing of exhibits pursuant

---

27   The listserv of the Criminal Lawyers Association of Ontario provides a list of experts. One can also put out a request on the listserv to CLA members for recommendations. Counsel needs to be a member of the association and this can be accomplished by e-mailing Anthony@criminallawyers.ca. The CLA's website is: www.criminallawyers.ca

to section 605 of the *Criminal Code*.[28] When appropriate, the expert should be granted access to the client.

It is important to review with the expert those questions counsel will be asking and prepare the expert for questions that might be posed in cross-examination. It is highly unlikely that counsel will ever hear the opposing expert witness admit in cross-examination that he or she is wrong. The cross-examiner is better advised to lead the expert to admitting that there is another possibility or probability that he or she cannot exclude or say is wrong. This is particularly so if the questioner can pose to the expert a changed set of facts on the evidence. It is therefore important for the expert to know all of the available information on the case so that the cross-examiner cannot surprise him with new facts that could cause the expert to change his opinion and damage the case he was called to support.

It goes without saying that the triers-of-fact should be able to understand everything that the expert has to say and therefore the expert witness should be warned beforehand to stay away from technical language and to speak to the jurors in layman's terms where possible. When this is not possible, the expert, either voluntarily or through questions put by counsel, should explain the language of his or her profession as simply and as clearly as is possible in the circumstances.

Qualifications of Your Expert

As indicated above only those persons who are shown to be qualified by some special skill, training or experience can be asked to give their opinion on a matter. Before a witness can give an opinion as an expert the Court must first rule whether the witness is qualified as such. Counsel is to advise the Court as to exactly what are the issues for which he is seeking to have his expert qualified.[29] The Court will hear the qualifications of the expert and permit cross-examination on the expertise issue before making a ruling. Deficiencies in the expertise of the witness go to weight and not admissibility.[30]

Because it is difficult to prevent an expert from being qualified, it is in most cases best not to forewarn the expert with your challenging questions at the qualification stage, but to wait until your cross-examination at large at the end of examination-in-chief. An exception to this tactic would of course be where you feel there is a good chance of damaging the expert's

---

28   R.S.C. 1985, c. C-46.

29   This view was strongly expressed by the Honourable Stephen T. Goudge, Commissioner of The Inquiry into Pediatric Forensic Pathology in Ontario, recommendation 129 (pgs 471-4). The trial Judge should stop an expert witness who strays beyond their recognized expertise.

30   *R. v. Marquard* (1993), 85 C.C.C. (3d) 193 (S.C.C.).

qualifications to the extent his or her opinion would be ruled inadmissible or you can show that the trier-of-fact can easily draw the necessary inferences without the expert testimony.

Counsel should obtain from the expert an up-to-date *curriculum vitae* containing the witness's qualifications, such as educational history in the field in question including degrees, diplomas, certificates and special courses related to the area of expertise; special awards or citations for work in the field of expertise; memberships in associations and societies in the relevant field; published works and speeches made or delivered in the area of expertise; practical experience in the field; previous Court experience stating the approximate number of courts which have accepted the witness qualifications and received his testimony as an expert in the area of concern, and the various levels of courts and the different provinces or jurisdictions in which the witness has testified. If, in the past, the expert who testifies as a defence witness has given evidence mostly for the prosecution, that fact should be brought to the jurors' attention, as it could be inferred that this exception means the expert feels especially strong about the position he or she is taking on behalf of the defence.

Counsel should not simply ask the expert to relate his qualifications in Court as he may sound less than humble or leave out some significant qualifications either out of a sense of humility or because he may feel they are not important. Counsel, not the expert, should place emphasis on the expert's qualifications. The questioner should therefore lead the witness through a statement of his qualifications permitting the witness to expand on these qualifications where appropriate. These introductory types of leading questions are considered permissible by the Court.

Opposing counsel may announce that he admits the expert's qualifications as a tactic in the hope that counsel will not detail the expert's curriculum vitae so as to prevent the jurors from becoming too impressed with the witness's background. It is important for the triers-of-fact to know the expert's qualifications in detail so that they can judge his opinion against that of the opposing expert's. It is also important for the judge to have a basis for ruling on the issue of the witness's qualifications as an expert and if there is an appeal to the Court of Appeal, to enable that Court to judge those qualifications, if necessary. When opposing counsel makes this offer, the questioner should thank him and point out that he feels that it is important for the jurors to hear the witness's qualifications so that they can properly judge his or her opinions, unless of course opposing counsel is also agreeing to accept those opinions.

Conceding The Expert's Qualifications

" YOUR HONOR, THE DEFENSE CONCEDES THAT THE PROSECUTION WITNESS IS AN EXPERT IN HIS FIELD! "

Trial Diplomacy Journal Cartoon Album. David Freedman, Ed. © 1980 Court Practice Journal, Inc.

There are times when counsel asks to be permitted to file his or her expert's *curriculum vitae* as an exhibit, usually on the basis that it is very lengthy and counsel has only dealt with part of its contents in examination-in-chief. Such a procedure should be objected to when there is a jury on the basis that, if filed, the *curriculum vitae* obviously becomes an exhibit which the jurors will have in the jury room during their deliberations, and the jurors may give undue and unfair emphasis to that document and testimony over other verbal testimony. This would be particularly unfair if the defence was not calling its own expert.

For some reason, counsel, particularly Crown attorneys, often feel that it is proper to file reports, such as a pathologist's report, as exhibits at trial. A trial is normally based on oral testimony. Written reports are at most used by the witness to refresh memory just as a police officer would refresh his memory from his notebook and should not be filed as exhibits in the ordinary course of events, just as a police officer would not be permitted to file his notebook.[31] However, if the trial is before a judge sitting without a jury, counsel should not have the same concern and no doubt the trial judge will appreciate not having to write out a lengthy *curriculum vitae* if it can be filed as an exhibit. Counsel may then only refer to highlights of the expert's C.V. after filing it as an exhibit. If you know that your expert's *curriculum vitae* is more impressive than your opponent's then you may wish to agree to filing them, particularly where there is a jury.

Counsel should be aware of section 657.3 of the *Criminal Code* relating to an expert's report which is set out later in this chapter.

Basis of Opinion By Your Expert

The expert should always be prepared to state the reasons for his or her conclusions and for greater impact should refer to any literature, tests or investigations that were carried out to support his or her conclusions. A better understanding of the evidence with a significant impact upon the jury can be achieved when the expert provides demonstrative evidence such as enlarged maps, graphs, plans, photographs, models, movies, etc., which should be entered as exhibits. Such evidence will help the jurors better remember the oral testimony that such exhibits relate to, particularly given that they will be in the jury room at the time of deliberations.

Although an expert can base his or her opinion on hearsay sources the claimed facts upon which the expert relies must be established before a Court can decide the weight that should be given to the opinion.[32]

In *R. v. Lavallee*,[33] the Supreme Court of Canada, following its decision in *R. v. Abbey*, held that an expert opinion is admissible if relevant, even if based on second hand evidence, i.e. hearsay. This hearsay is admissible to show the information on which the expert opinion is based, not as evidence going to the existence (or truth) of the facts on which the opinion is based. Where the psychiatric evidence is comprised of hearsay evidence, the problem is the weight to be attributed to the opinion. Before any weight can be given to that opinion, the facts upon which the opinion is based must be

---

31 See the distinction between present recollection revived and past recollection recorded in Chapter, "Presenting the Evidence-in-Chief," under heading "Refreshing the Witness's Memory." A ruling in support of this position was made by Watt J. in *R. v. Prette and Turchiaro,* January 25, 1988, Toronto assizes.

32 *Phillion v. R.* (1978), 37 C.R.N.S. 361 at 366 (S.C.C.); *R. v. Abbey* (1982), 29 C.R. (3d) 193 (S.C.C.); *R. v. Campeau* (1983), 42 A.R. 81 (Alta. C.A.); *R. v. Abadom* (1982), 76 Cr. App. R. 48 (C.A.); *Deschambault v. R.* (1985), 49 C.R. (3d) 151 (Que. C.A.).

33 (1990), 55 C.C.C. (3d) 97 (S.C.C.).

found to exist. Therefore, if an expert testifies as to what the accused told him and the accused does not testify, there are no facts to support the opinion of the expert witness unless there is other evidence such as the introduction of the accused's statement, medical records, other corroborating witnesses, etc.[34] Where the basis of the expert's evidence is based on admissible and inadmissible evidence, the trial judge must caution the jury that the weight of the expert's opinion is directly related to the quality of the admissible evidence on which it relies.

The expert may be asked to render his or her conclusion first, followed by directed questions as to the reasons why that conclusion was reached or begin with the reasons and end with the expert's conclusion.

> Although the building-blocks approach is probably best suited to inducing belief in a listener, if a witness's methodology for arriving at a conclusion is quite complex, the attorney may have the witness first state his conclusion and then proceed to support it.[35]

The Ultimate Issue Question

It is not uncommon for an expert to be asked to give an opinion on the very issue which the jury is to determine on the facts before it. The earlier case law held that the expert should not be permitted to do so. However, in *R. v. Marquard*[36] McLachlin J. for the majority stated:

> [T]here is a growing consensus that while expert evidence on the ultimate credibility of a witness is not admissible, expert evidence on human conduct and the psychological and physical factors which may lead to certain behaviour relevant to credibility, is admissible, provided the testimony goes beyond the ordinary experience of the trier-of-fact.

Expert testimony is admissible even if it relates directly to the ultimate issue which the trier-of-fact must answer. In *R. v. Burns* (1994), 89 C.C.C. (3d) 193 at p. 201 (S.C.C.) McLachlin J. writing for the Court said:

> While care must be taken to ensure that the Judge or jury, and not the expert, makes the final decisions on all issues in the case, it has long been accepted that expert evidence on matters of fact should not be excluded because it

---

34 In *R. v. Palma* (2001), 149 C.C.C. (3d) 338 (Ont. S.C.J.) it was held that whether introduced by defence or the Crown, secondhand information such as what the accused told the expert, but the accused does not testify, was admissible but the failure to testify was a factor to consider in assessing the weight of the opinion rendered on hearsay.

35 M.C. Roberts, *Trial Psychology* (Toronto: Butterworth Legal Publishers, 1987).

36 (1993), 85 C.C.C. (3d) 193 (S.C.C.). See also *R. v. R. (D.)* (1996), 107 C.C.C. (3d) 289 (S.C.C.) at paras. 38-40; *R. v. Graat* (1980), 17 C.R. (3d) 55 at 70-72 (Ont. C.A.), affirmed (1982), 2 C.C.C. (3d) 365 (S.C.C).

suggests answers to issues which are at the core of the dispute before the Court.[37]

Justice Sopinka in *R. v. Mohan*[38] observed at p. 414:

There is also a concern inherent in the application of this criterion that experts not be permitted to usurp the functions of the trier-of-fact. Too liberal an approach could result in a trial becoming nothing more than a contest of experts with the trier-of-fact acting as a referee in deciding which expert to accept.

These concerns were the basis of the rule that excluded expert evidence in respect of the ultimate issue. Although the rule is no longer of general application, the concerns underlying it remain. In light of these concerns, the criteria of relevance and necessity are applied strictly, on occasion, to exclude expert evidence as to do an ultimate issue.

THE EXPERT IS NOT AN ADVOCATE

"An expert witness should provide independent assistance to the Court by way of objective unbiased opinion in relation to matters within his expertise. An expert witness in the High Court should never assume the role of an advocate."[39] The expert who offends this rule will find his evidence rejected or receive little weight.

The Hypothetical Question

Where the expert witness has first-hand knowledge, such as the treating physician, he can give his opinion based on that knowledge. However, where the expert does not have first-hand knowledge the hypothetical question can be employed as the basis for the expert's opinion. The hypothetical question will contain a description of what occurred, the client's behaviour and what tests, investigations and examinations were carried out.

Arthur Martin, Q.C. (as he then was) opined that what is contained in the hypothetical question can be a second summation and should be used to outline and emphasize all those factors on which the defence is based—taking as many of the facts as possible from the testimony of opposing witnesses. The facts must have been testified to in Court and cannot come from statements by persons out of Court as that would be hearsay evidence.

---

37 See also *R. v. (D.)*.

38 *Supra.*

39 *Ikarian Reefer*, [1993] 2 Lloyd's Report 68 at 81. See also *Fellowes, McNeil v. Kansa General International Insurance Co.* (1998), 40 O.R. (3d) 456 (Ont. Gen. Div.); *Mathias v. Canada*, 1998 CanLII 7607 (F.C.); *Dulong v. Merrill Lynch Canada Inc.* (2006), 80 O.R. (3d) 378 (Ont. S.C.J.).

The hypothetical question put to the expert usually begins with such words as "Assume the following facts and I will then ask you your opinion based on those facts" and ends with "Are you able to express an opinion with reasonable (medical) certainty as to . . .? What is that opinion? Please tell the Court the reasons for your opinion." An example of a hypothetical question can be found in *R. v. Fisher*[40] where Dr. Easton, a psychiatrist, was asked the following:

> Now, I want to put certain facts to you in the form of a hypothetical question and ask you to assume the facts are as I state them. And I want to ask you what your opinion is on those facts, and on the facts, assuming it to be a fact, that the accused made that statement, Exhibit 60, I want to ask you your opinion as to his capacity to form the intent to cause the death of a person, and his capacity to form the intent to cause bodily harm that he knew was likely to cause death. Well, then, assuming the facts as follows: That at 8:30 p.m. on Thursday 9th of June, last, the accused went to the Wembley Hotel, and between then and 12:15 a.m., 10th June, drank four bottles of beer or more; that he then walked out of the hotel, spoke to a woman; then walked two blocks, got his car, and drove it back to the hotel; picked the woman up, the Wembley Hotel on the Danforth; and then drove to Eglinton Ave. and Midland, a distance of six miles or more; and that he then stabbed the woman fifteen times, and cut her left breast down one side and across the bottom and up the other side; that the stab wounds, six of them, were in the back, in the region of the left shoulder blade, one of which punctured the aorta, causing death, two of them were in the right elbow, one was on the—a superficial wound was the right forearm, one was on the right inner leg, above the knee and that there were three abdominal wounds, left of the medial line. . . . Assuming that those were the wounds, and that her death was caused as I stated; he pushed her out of the car and left her lying on the ground; and then drove the car directly or indirectly back home; and that the stabbing occurred roughly at . . . 1:00 a.m.; . . . then eleven days later . . . he made this statement to the police which is contained in Exhibit No. 60; now, assuming the facts to be as I have stated them, what is your opinion as to whether or not the accused in stabbing the woman and inflicting those wounds . . . had the capacity to form the intent to cause death?

Dr. Easton's reply was: "It is my opinion that he did have the capacity to form the intent."[41] The Crown then asked the follow-up questions: "Could you explain your reasons?" and "To what things do you refer?"[42]

In *Bleta v. R.*[43] Ritchie J. dealt with the situation where the expert was not asked a hypothetical question. The Supreme Court of Canada held that questions need not be put to the expert in the form of a hypothetical where

---

40 (1961), 34 C.R. 320 at 337 (Ont. C.A.), affirmed [1961] S.C.R. 535 (*sub nom. Fisher v. R.*) (S.C.C.).

41 *Ibid.*

42 *Ibid.*, at 338.

43 [1964] S.C.R. 561 (S.C.C.). See also *R. v. Swietlinski* (1978), 5 C.R. (3d) 324 (Ont. C.A.).

an expert testifies without empirical knowledge of the subject-matter but his opinion is based on the undisputed evidence. In the *Fisher* case the evidence was disputed with respect to such essential matters as the number of beers the accused consumed, his behaviour before and after the incident, and the issue of drunkenness. As a result it was necessary that Dr. Easton's opinion be given on the basis of hypothetical questions. An example of some questions put to Dr. Stokes in *Bleta,* which did not take the form of a hypothetical, were:[44]

> I think you have been present throughout practically all of this trial have you not?
>
> "And you were particularly interested in hearing the evidence of the witnesses who witnessed the episode that occurred on January 4 in the vicinity of Keele and Dundas St.?"
>
> "In addition you have studied a statement that was made to the police by the accused man?"
>
> ". . . did his [Bleta's] presentation of the facts as a witness in the witness box, was there anything about that that impressed you as a medical man?"
>
> "Doctor you have heard the evidence of Mrs. Degeer and Mrs. Trimbel?"
>
> "And he had an appearance about him that prompted one of them to say 'he didn't seem to be in this world'?"
>
> "Then you heard also the evidence of one of the ladies who said that after the stabbing he walked in a zig-zag fashion without any reason, sometimes on the sidewalks. Do you remember that part of the evidence?"
>
> "You heard the evidence of officer Kiekebelt he seemed dazed and confused, and to quote him exactly, he said, 'he didn't seem to be conscious of what I was doing'?"

Ritchie J. stated:

> This appears to me to be clear confirmation of the fact that all those concerned with the conduct of the trial who saw and heard the witnesses were satisfied that the proper basis had been laid for the admissions of the doctor's opinion. Under these circumstances it seems to me that, before excluding an expert's opinion, a court of appeal should be able to make a clear finding that there is no material before the jury to enable it to determine whether his conclusions were properly founded or not. I do not, with respect, consider that such a finding is justified in the present case.[45]

Richie J. stated the law to be as follows:

---

44 From transcript of *Bleta v. R., ibid.*
45 *Bleta, supra,* at 568.

Provided that the questions are so phrased as to make clear what the evidence is on which an expert is being asked to found his conclusions, the failure of counsel to put such questions in hypothetical form does not of itself make the answers inadmissible. It is within the competence of the trial judge in any case to insist upon the foundation for the expert opinion being laid by way of hypothetical question if he feels this to be the best way in which he can be assured of the matter being fully understood by the jury, but this does not, in my opinion, mean that the judge is necessarily precluded in the exercise of his discretion in the conduct of the trial from permitting the expert's answers to go before the jury if the nature and foundation of his opinion has been clearly indicated by other means.[46]

In *R. v. Swietlinski*,[47] the defence psychiatrist who had interviewed the accused on a number of occasions was asked:

You have, of course, been in here, in this courtroom, to hear the evidence tendered by Roman Swietlinski. In light of your interviews and in light of what you did hear in this courtroom, were you able to form any opinion as to whether or not on September 18th, Roman Swietlinski was not able to form a specific intent?[48]

The trial judge refused to permit this question on the basis that the witness would be giving an opinion based on the truthfulness of the accused which was the sole province of the jury. Hypothetical questions were then put to the witness. Martin J.A. stated:[49]

It is, in my view, not open to doubt that a psychiatrist who has examined an accused, may express his opinion as to the accused's mental state formed as a result of normal psychiatric procedures which, of course, include interviews out of Court with the accused, as well as statements made out of Court by others, which form part of the accused's psychiatric history. What is being adduced in such circumstances is the psychiatrist's expert opinion, and not the statements made by the accused and others as part of the patient's psychiatric history.

The degree to which the psychiatrist's opinion is dependent on statements made by the accused and others is a factor in assessing the weight, but does not affect the admissibility of the opinion: see *R. v. Lupien*, [1970] 2 C.C.C. 193 at pp. 199-201, [1970] S.C.R. 263 at pp. 272-5, 9 D.L.R. (3d) I at pp. 7-10, *per* Ritchie, J. (with whom Spence, J., concurred, and Hall, J., concurred on this point).

On the other hand, it is equally clear that where the facts are disputed, a medical witness may not express an opinion as to the accused's mental state based on the evidence that he has heard in Court because the opinion depends on the witness's assessment of the evidence. Where, however, the facts are

---

46 *Bleta, supra*, at 566-567.
47 (1978), 5 C.R. (3d) 324 (Ont. C.A.).
48 *Ibid.*, at 363.
49 *Swietlinski, supra*, at 364-365.

admitted, or are not in dispute, the trial Judge may, in the exercise of his discretion, permit the question to be put in that form: see *Bleta v. The Queen*, [1965] 1 C.C.C. 1, [1964] S.C.R. 561, 48 D.L.R. (2d) 139.

The question put by defence counsel to Dr. Orchard sought to elicit his opinion based not only on his interviews with the appellant but, also, on the evidence the appellant had given in the witness-box.

Accordingly, the trial Judge correctly ruled out the question in that form, since, as he stated, the assessment of the appellant's evidence was within the exclusive province of the jury.

Counsel for the appellant might, had he chosen to do so, have elicited Dr. Orchard's opinion as to the appellant's mental state, formed on the basis of his psychiatric examination of the appellant. Defence counsel could then have asked the witness a hypothetical question, whether, assuming the truth of the facts in evidence referred to in the question, they were consistent with or supported the opinion he had formed from his examination of the appellant. Defence counsel did not, however, adopt this course.

While the principal defence was that the appellant, because of intoxication, lacked the capacity to form the requisite intent, the identity of the killer of Miss McKenna was also in dispute. I am satisfied, on a fair reading of the discussion which ensued in the absence of the jury, with respect to the proper way in which the expert opinion as to appellant's mental state should be elicited, that the experienced defence counsel was content to confide the examination of the expert witness to hypothetical questions and did not wish to proceed on any other basis. He may, of course, have had what appeared to him to be valid reasons for so doing. It will be observed the trial Judge left the matter open in the event the circumstances dictated a different ruling. No application was made to the trial judge at a later stage to reconsider the matter. I am unable to conclude in all the circumstances that the trial Judge erred in the provisional ruling that he made at that time.

The following is an examination-in-chief of Dr. Danby in *Ref. re Truscott*[50] by G. Arthur Martin, Q.C. on behalf of Truscott to counter the Crown evidence that the lesions on Truscott's penis were traumatic in origin and therefore consistent with the accused raping the deceased. This examination-in-chief illustrates the qualifying of an expert using permissible leading questions, adducing the expert's opinion as a result of his own observations and the use of the hypothetical question based on observations of other persons:[51]

examination-in-chief—charles william elliott danby by mr. martin:

Q. Dr. Danby, you are a physician practising your profession in Kingston, Ontario. Is that correct?

A. That is correct, sir.

Q. You specialize in the fields of dermatology and syphilology?

50   [1967] S.C.R. 309 (S.C.C.).
51   From transcript of *Ref. re Truscott, ibid.*

A. That is right.

Q. I understand you graduated in medicine from Queen's University in 1940?

A. That is so.

Q. And after a period of internship at St. Joseph's Hospital in London you served as a medical officer in the Royal Canadian Navy from 1941 to 1945, except for a short period when you were on loan to the British Navy?

A. That is correct.

Q. During this period you were medical officer for the combined naval divisions of Montreal and Cartier from 1941 to 1945?

A. Not for that long. From 1942 to early 1943 in this particular appointment, and thereafter I was transferred to Toronto, to Esquimalt, to Vancouver and then back to be demobilized.

Q. After your discharge from the Navy you trained at the Montreal General Hospital for your specialist's certificate in dermatology and syphilology?

A. That is correct.

Q. You were certified by the Royal College of Physicians and Surgeons of Canada for dermatology and syphilology?

A. Yes, in 1948.

Q. You were admitted as a Fellow of the Royal College of Physicians and Surgeons of Canada in 1950 in the division of medicine in the specialty of dermatology and syphilology?

A. That is so.

Q. Since that time have you practised your specialty in Kingston?

A. Yes.

Q. You are an assistant professor of medicine at Queen's University?

A. Yes.

Q. You are the consultant dermatologist to the Department of Veteran Affairs?

A. That is so.

Q. You are the consultant in [dermatology] in the Canadian Forces Hospital in Kingston?

A. Yes.

Q. You are also a consultant to the Department of Justice in dermatology for the three Federal penitentiaries at Kingston, Collins Bay and Joyceville?

A. Yes.

Q. Have you ever treated Steven Truscott?

A. Yes.

Q. Under what circumstances did you treat him?

A. May I have permission to refer to my notes?

Q. Were they made at the time?

A. Yes, sir.

CHIEF JUSTICE TASCHEREAU: Yes.

MR. MARTIN: Yes, Dr. Danby, you may refer to your notes.

A. I had occasion to treat Steven Truscott first on January 30, 1964. Would you like a description or summary?

Q. Yes, would you summarize—How did you come to treat him?

A. He was referred to me by the prison doctor from Collin's Bay penitentiary, Dr. J. Gibson.

Q. He came to your office under escort?

A. Yes.

Q. Would you summarize what condition you found?

A. On his first examination he showed what I considered to be an infected dermatitis of the left side of his face extending from the level of his eyelid down to below his mouth and from the centre point of his eye out toward the ear, about three centimetres from the ear, this was the area. We saw it was oozing and scaling and crusted. I thought, as I said, that this was a secondarily infected dermatitis due to contact with some agent that had irritated his skin. He told me that it had been present for one year. He was seen on five subsequent occasions in my office, the last time being April 24. During this interval he showed good improvement up until about March the 1st. When he was seen in my office on April 15, which was his fifth visit, he showed a large, patchy nummular type of eczema—nummular means coin-shaped—involving the back part of his shoulders, the posterior aspect of his upper arms and his face and his ears. Now, on his last visit he had improved and his treatment was subsequently carried out and I did not see him again.

Q. What is the appearance of nummular eczema? You described it as a coin-shaped eczema. Can you further describe its appearance?

A. The appearance of nummular eczema is that of small or large round areas in the skin that are reddened and marked by innumerable small blisters which open and ooze and produce crusty—

Q. Is anything known as to the cause of nummular eczema?

A. It's a very difficult question to answer here because there are various theories advanced and we all have our own pet theories about the etiology of some of these more obscure disorders.

Q. There is no unanimity as to the cause?

A. I think we can say there is some unanimity in that the morphology is the same in each case, the appearance of the lesions are the same in each case, but as far as cause or causes is concerned it is sometimes difficult to pin down one or more causes as being the exactly correct one.

Q. Dr. Danby, I am going to refer you to certain evidence that was given at the trial of Steven Truscott. Evidence was given by Dr. Addison and Dr. David Hall Brooks who examined Steven Truscott in the guard house at the Royal Canadian Air Force base at Clinton about 10:45 p.m. on the evening of June the 12th.

CHIEF JUSTICE TASCHEREAU: What year was that?

MR. MARTIN: 1959; that was the night that he was arrested, my lord.

Q. Dr. Addison observed the condition of the parts which he described as follows, and commencing at page 640, line 20, Volume 3 (sic) of the evidence, he said—

MR. JUSTICE FAUTEUX: 640?

MR. MARTIN: 640, line 20, he commences to give his description.

MR. JUSTICE FAUTEUX: You said Volume 3; it must be 4?

MR. MARTIN: 4.

Q. He said as follows:

A. The penis on first examination appeared swollen and slightly reddened on the distal end.

Q. What is that?

A. The end farthest from the body. For a distance of about an inch and a half, and on closer examination, by stretching the skin, pulling it upwards towards the body, there were two large raw sores . . .

. . .

A. As I recall, that at the present time, they were like a brush burn. They were raw and there was serum oozing from the sores.

. . .

The two areas were on the shaft of the penis, "one on either side on the same location just behind the groove, just behind the glands". He further described it as "a raw sore, like a brush burn, with serum oozing from each of those large sores on the side". And further said, "They looked like a brush burn of two or three days' duration."

Then he further described them at page 652, line 28:

The whole area was pretty well involved, about the size of the ball of my thumb, about the size of a quarter. Little tiny red spots where the capillaries had been destroyed . . . it was one singular area on either side.

. . .

the ends had been scraped and they started to bleed through.

There was no scab on either lesion. There was a serum discharge on the lesion. This was said at page 654, line 28.

He further described them at page 661, line 12: B-2

The skin, on first appearance looked reddened and swollen and the full extent of the lesions showed up when I pulled it back and stretched it.

. . .

The lesion was on the skin and it wrinkled up and the full extent is not viewed until you pulled it back and saw the full extent of the lesions.

. . .

Q. Assume for the moment this description is correct. From that description would you be able to reach any conclusion as to the cause of the lesion?

A. Am I correct in understanding that this examination was of a lesion that is supposed to have been produced within the preceding three days?

Q. This was the view expressed by Dr. Addison, a brush burn of two or three days' duration, was his description. But that is part of the description. Assuming the size, the description of the raw sore, oozing, having the appearance of a brush burn of two or three days' duration; from that description would you be able to reach any conclusion as to the nature and cause of these injuries?

A. I would think that in the area where these lesions have been described, if it were an injury that had occurred three days before, or two days before, there would have been haemorrhage or bleeding visible in and around these lesions. Now, one must remember that in this area the skin is very thin. I would think a good comparison would be the thickness of the skin of your eyelid. If we remember that the skin is made up of two parts, the epidermis and dermis. For convenience, the epidermis is the outer layer of the skin, below which there are blood vessels ready to bleed and is not thicker than six one hundredths of a millimetre. It is tissue paper thin, I would think that if this had been due to injury there would have been haemorrhage.

Q. Would you be able to give any information as to the extent or the degree of the bleeding or haemorrhaging that would occur from injury of that kind?

A. I have in the past, and I still do occasionally, perform an operation called dermo-abrasion of the skin in which we abrade the skin in order to improve the appearance of scars. Now, we do not have to abrade it very deeply to get copious bleeding.

Q. Dr. Addison expressed his opinion as to the cause of these lesions as follows, at page 643, lines 9 to 13:

> There would have to be friction in an oval-shaped orifice. An oval-shaped knothole or something like that. Something of an oval shape and sufficiently rough to cause a friction or wear of the outer surface of the skin.

. . .

Then, he further stated on page 644, lines 9 to 13 that there was nothing inconsistent with this having been caused by the entry of the male organ into the private parts of a young small virgin. He further stated at page 645, line 30, that in his opinion these abrasions could have been caused by a boy of the size and age of Steven Truscott attempting to have intercourse or having intercourse with a girl aged twelve. He further stated at page 646, lines 17 to 20, that these injuries could be caused by an attempt to enter a girl whose hymen had not been ruptured and who had not started to menstruate if it was a tight orifice. *What is your opinion as to whether the lesions which Dr. Addison described could be caused in that way?*

A. *I don't think they could have been caused in that way.*

Q. Evidence was given by Dr. Penistan, the pathologist, that in his opinion that this child was raped by whoever did rape her after she was dead or while she was in the process of dying. Now, assume those facts, would that have any effect on your opinion?

A. It would not alter it.

Q. Dr. David Hall Brooks gave evidence as follows, page 835,—this would be Volume 5—page 835, line 13 to line 23:

> this was a circumcised male organ and the skin was wrinkled for a larger distance than usual. In other words, it was much more conspicuous. So I picked up this organ and put this skin, which is normally, for a certain distance wrinkled in any circumcised male, put in on the stretch just sufficiently to expose an area underneath, and found a region . . . a lesion on each side only. Not top and bottom. On each side of the shaft of this male organ from the groove extending towards the body, a lesion about

the size of one and a quarter inches by one inch would cover the whole thing on each side.

. . .

He further stated at page 835, line 27 to line 33:
It was the area where the skin, the most superficial layers had been rubbed away and was an area bigger than, just bigger than a twenty-five cent piece on each side, so there were two areas like that. At the top there was nothing and at the bottom there was nothing. The groove, itself, was perfectly all right. There was no frank bleeding. There was oozing. By this time the oozing was stagnant.

. . .

He then said:
That the area involved was of a size slightly bigger than a quarter.

. . .

This is at page 850, line 8 to line 19:
That the area involved was of a size slightly bigger than a quarter. The most superficial layer of skin had been rubbed away. There were no scratch marks in this area. That area was eighty percent of an area larger than a quarter piece on each side, or the area where there was no skin visible. The topmost layer of skin. There were capillaries, the smallest type of blood cells there are. There was no oozing from them. There was some sticky fluid coming away from these, not dropping away. It had got to the state of being tacky, sticky.

. . .

And further:
This injury was still oozing serum. It would seem fairly new and there was early signs of healing. There was no frank bleeding and just the pinpoint areas where you could see blood vessels showing through.

. . .

Page 851, line 9 to 15.
Q. Now, again assuming the correctness of Dr. Brooks' description, does this affect the opinion you have just expressed?
A. I don't think so.
Q. Dr. Brooks expressed an opinion as to the cause of the lesions. And he says at page 838, line 12 to line 30:
That the lesions could have been caused by the penetration or the attempted penetration of the organ into the private parts of a young girl such as Lynne Harper.
Q. What is your opinion with respect to that?
A. I don't think it could have happened—
MR. JUSTICE FAUTEUX: I am sorry, I don't hear you.
A. I don't think it could have happened in that way.

MR. MARTIN:

Q. Now, in your practice as a dermatologist do you see lesions of various kinds on the penis?

A. I do, sir.

Q. And in your experience as a naval officer, have you ever—did you see lesions on the penis?

A. Yes, sir.

Q. Have you seen injury to the penis attributed to force in intercourse?

A. I have seen lesions on the penis which sailors, particularly, had told me were incurred during the act of intercourse.

Q. What kind of injuries were they?

A. Well, I have only seen about six or seven of these, and those were a laceration or tearing of that small fold of skin which extends from the tip of the bottom—or, rather the bottom of the tip of the penis down to the underside of the foreskin. This is called the praetutium. And this has been torn in intercourse, allegedly.

Q. Have you ever in your experience as a dermatologist or your experience as a naval officer ever seen lesions on the side of the penis of the size described by Dr. Brooks and Dr. Addison attributed to force in having intercourse?

A. No, Sir.

Q. Have you seen lesions of any size on the sides of a penis attributed to force in intercourse?

A. No, sir.

Q. Are you aware of any medical literature describing lesions such as described by Dr. Addison and Dr. Brooks that attributed such lesions to force in intercourse?

A. I am not aware of it.

Q. Dr. Penistan, who was the pathologist who performed the post mortem upon the body of the deceased described an abrasion to the right labium majus of the deceased, at page 146. This would be Volume 1.

CHIEF JUSTICE TASCHEREAU: What page, Mr. Martin?

MR. MARTIN: 146.

CHIEF JUSTICE TASCHEREAU: Volume 1?

MR. MARTIN: Yes. Line 10 to 15. This is the description of the injury to the deceased.

> On the external private parts, on the right hand side of what is to the anatomist known as the labium majus, there was a superficial abrasion of the skin, just beside the entry into the vagina, measuring about one-third of an inch in diameter. There was no bleeding from this. It was too superficial for that. Nor was there any oozing or any scab upon it.

This is the description of the abrasion on the deceased.

> And then, Dr. Brooks in giving evidence stated—again we revert to Volume 5, page 826, line 19 to line 23:
> And on the external genitals, on the right hand side and the lowest part of the right lip there was an area where the skin, the superficial topmost layer of skin had been ripped right away over an area about the size of one of my ordinary fingernails.

With relation to the cause of this injury and the relationship of this injury and lesion, the lesions to the penis of Steven Truscott, the doctor testified as follows, at page 839, line 38 to page 840, line 1:

Q. Would that injury which you observed on the outer lip, the labium of the deceased, could that have any relationship in your opinion, to the injury which you observed on the private parts of the accused?

A. Yes, it is consistent in that the whole aspect of the case, as I saw the body first, was this of a very inexpert attempt at penetration. And this area damaged with pressure was up in the direction of the girl's entrance and at the time it was quite possible this . . . during the pressure of being carried forward, this got carried in too, and ripped the skin off.

Q. Again assuming the correctness of the description of that abrasion on the right labium, have you any opinion as to whether that kind of abrasion could be caused by a male organ in an attempt to make entry?

A. I think it is very unlikely, if not impossible this could occur in the area described.

Q. Now, Dr. Danby, Steven Truscott in giving evidence yesterday, said at page 155, line 5—I am going to read this evidence:

Q. I want you to describe as best you can the condition you think obtained that night—that is the night of the examination.
so far as you can remember what the sores looked like?

A. They were well on the way to healing. Dr. Addison described them as oozing, and there was no oozing whatsoever.

Q. How long had they been like that, in the condition they were that night?

A. About two weeks.

Q. I want you to listen to this next question quite carefully and apply your mind to it. What did the condition of your penis look like when you first noticed that there was something unusual existing there?

A. It was about six weeks before I was picked up. And it started off, what appeared to be little blisters, and continued to worsen from there until it was in the state it was when I was picked up.

Q. What caused it to worsen? How did its appearance change?

A. Well, one blister would break and it just seemed that more would appear.

Q. Do you know what caused them to break?

A. No, I don't.

Q. Now, when you first noticed this condition that you described did you tell your father about it?

A. No, I didn't.

Q. Now, Doctor, assuming for the purpose of your opinion that Steven Truscott has correctly described what the condition of his penis was when he first noticed it, does that description indicate any dermatological condition?

A. Of course, I think probably—

MR. JUSTICE FAUTEUX: Would you speak up a little louder please?

A. I think probably the most common lesion of the penis that is manifested by the appearance of small blisters is herpes simplex, which is the same type of thing as we know of as a cold sore. And certainly herpes simplex can occur on any area of the skin and membranes.

MR. MARTIN:

Q. Now, assuming that this condition originated in a number of blisters, could that condition have resulted in lesions the size described by Dr. Brooks and Dr. Addison, apart altogether from intercourse?

A. Oh, yes.

Q. What condition could bring about an appearance such as was observed?

A. In this particular area, if these were started out as a case of herpes simplex it is in an area where there is a lot of sweating, skin surfaces together a place very liable to secondary bacterial C2 infection, and irritation from day to day in the ordinary course of urination, and in, perhaps irritation from trousers or underwear. And these things could combine to produce lesions of this size or larger, and may make them persist for a longer period of time.

Q. Have you ever treated herpes lesions the size of a quarter?

A. I have seen herpes simplex involve an area of skin four square inches, not four inches square, but four square inches. That is the largest.

Q. Now, in your practice as a dermatologist have you made any observation as to whether it is usual or unusual for adolescents, boys, to tell their parents about skin problems in their genital area?

A. I think this must vary from boy to boy. Certainly my boys are not very quick to report anything like this.

MR. MARTIN:

Q. Now, just one final question, Dr. Danby. You were present in Court yesterday and heard the evidence of Dr. E.L. Marcinkowsky who, as I understand it, found two dermatological conditions present on Steven Truscott while he was in the Ontario Reformatory at Guelph. One was a dermatitis which Dr. Marcinkowsky considered was due to the fact that a burn had been treated with chloromycetin—is that the correct term?—and the boy reacted to the treatment and the treatment irritated the burn, which caused the dermatitis.

And he had a second type of dermatitis under the armpits, as I understand it, the axilla, which he said was a contact dermatitis and which he thought was caused possibly by detergents used in washing his clothes.

And then you have described the dermatological condition on his face which you saw in 1964 and the nummular axilla which then appeared on his shoulders and back.

Does the existence of those conditions indicate any proneness or susceptibility of this boy to skin conditions?

A. Well, certainly it does in the past show that he has had a tendency to develop skin reactions of this type.

MR. MARTIN: Thank you, doctor.

It is important to keep in mind the prejudicial effect of a hypothetical question and whether that prejudice outweighs its probative value. In *R. v. P. (C.)*,[52] a psychiatrist was permitted to testify as to why children recant allegations of sexual abuse by family members but Crown counsel was not permitted to ask a lengthy hypothetical question of a psychologist relating

---

52 (1992), 74 C.C.C. (3d) 481 (B.C. C.A.).

to recanting by a child because it so closely described the evidence of the complainant that the jury could view it as an invitation to believe the complainant notwithstanding her earlier recantation.

But the general rule is that when an expert lacks personal knowledge of the facts at issue and is required to give an opinion based on disputed facts or upon facts not yet proven, the opinion is to be elicited through a hypothetical question.[53] Counsel on the opposite side can of course put forth a hypothetical containing the disputed evidence that favours her side, followed by questions that seek favourable conclusions for her side.[54]

DISCLOSURE OF EXPERT EVIDENCE BY CROWN AND DEFENCE

The *Criminal Code* now mandates one of the very rare occasions when the defence is required to disclose part of its case to the prosecution. Section 657.3 which pertains to both defence and Crown states:

EXPERT TESTIMONY/Attendance for examination/Notice for expert testimony/If notices not given/Additional court orders/Use of material by prosecution/No further disclosure.

657.3 (1) In any proceedings, the evidence of a person as an expert may be given by means of a report accompanied by the affidavit or solemn declaration of the person, setting out, in particular, the qualifications of the person as an expert if

(*a*) the court recognizes that person as an expert; and

(*b*) the party intending to produce the report in evidence has, before the proceeding, given to the other party a copy of the affidavit or solemn declaration and the report and reasonable notice of the intention to produce it in evidence.

(2) Notwithstanding subsection (1), the court may require the person who appears to have signed an affidavit or solemn declaration referred to in that subsection to appear before it for examination for cross-examination in respect of the issue of proof of any of the statements contained in the affidavit or solemn declaration or report.

(3) For the purpose of promoting the fair, orderly and efficient presentation of the testimony of witnesses,

(*a*) a party who intends to call a person as an expert witness shall, at least thirty days before the commencement of the trial or within any other

---

53 Sopinka, Lederman and Bryant, *Law of Evidence In Canada*, (Toronto: Butterworths, 1990) at 537-540. See also *R. v. G. (P.)* (2009), 242 C.C.C. (3d) 558 (Ont. C.A.). In *G. (P.)* the Court noted that the use of hypotheticals ensures that the expert does not express an opinion as to the credibility of a witness thereby usurping the function of the jury.

54 See also *R. v. G. (P.)* (2009), 242 C.C.C. (3d) 558 (Ont. C.A.). In *G. (P.)* the Court noted that the use of hypotheticals ensures that the expert does not express an opinion as to the credibility of a witness thereby usurping the responsibility of the jury.

period fixed by the justice or judge, give notice to the other party or parties of his or her intention to do so, accompanied by

    (i) the name of the proposed witness,

    (ii) a description of the area of expertise of the proposed witness that is sufficient to permit the other parties to inform themselves about that area of expertise, and

    (iii) a statement of the qualifications of the proposed witness as an expert;

(*b*) in addition to complying with paragraph (a), a prosecutor who intends to call a person as an expert witness shall, within a reasonable period before trial, provide to the other party or parties

    (i) a copy of the report, if any, prepared by the proposed witness for the case, and

    (ii) if no report is prepared, a summary of opinion anticipated to be given by the proposed witness and the grounds on which it is based; and

(*c*) in addition to complying with paragraph (a), an accused, or his or her counsel, who intends to call a person as an expert witness shall, not later than the close of the case for the prosecution, provide to the other party or parties the material referred to in paragraph (b).

(4) If a party calls a person as an expert witness without complying with subsection (3), the court shall, at the request of any other party,

(*a*) grant an adjournment of the proceedings to the party who requests it to allow him or her to prepare for cross-examination of the expert witness;

(*b*) order the party who called the expert witness to provide that other party and any other party with the material referred to in paragraph (3)(b); and

(*c*) order the calling or recalling of any witness for the purpose of giving testimony on matters related to those raised in the expert witness's testimony, unless the court considers it inappropriate to do so.

(5) If, in the opinion of the court, a party who has received the notice and material referred to in subsection (3) has not been able to prepare for the evidence of the proposed witness, the court may do one or more of the following:

(*a*) adjourn the proceedings

(*b*) order that further particulars be given of the evidence of the proposed witness;

(*c*) order the calling or recalling of any witness for the purpose of giving testimony on matters related to those raised in the expert witness's testimony.

(6) If the proposed witness does not testify, the prosecutor may not produce material provided to him or her under paragraph (3)(c) in evidence without the consent of the accused.

(7) Unless otherwise ordered by a court, information disclosed under this section in relation to a proceeding may only be used for the purpose of that proceeding.

1997, c. 18, s. 80; 2002, c. 13, s. 62.

Criminal Code section 672.21

Section 672.21 provides that a statement made by the accused during the course and for the purposes of an assessment or treatment directed by a disposition, to the person specified in the assessment order or the disposition or to anyone acting under that person's direction is "protected" and is inadmissible in evidence without the consent of the accused. Subsection (3) lists certain exceptions.

CROSS-EXAMINATION OF THE EXPERT WITNESS

Preparation

No trial lawyer can escape the expert during his or her career and there can be no more difficult task for counsel than to tackle the expert on his or her own ground. A little bit of knowledge is truly a dangerous thing when cross-examining experts, therefore it becomes necessary for the cross- examiner to educate himself or herself on the subject-matter in question. One should also be mindful of the rules of evidence which relate to the admissibility of expert testimony, particularly given the conditions precedent for admissibility set out by the Supreme Court of Canada in *R. v. Mohan* (discussed earlier in this chapter).

Experts are usually intelligent and articulate people and many are experienced witnesses who are able to predict a number of the questions that they will be asked. In the majority of cases, the cross-examiner should seek out his or her own expert for consultation in helping to prepare the cross-examination of the opponent's experts. Counsel's own expert can refer him or her to the important and authoritative literature on the subject, as well as papers or books which may have been written on the subject by the opponent's expert which may be helpful for impeachment purposes. The expert can go over the materials and evidence with counsel and even assist counsel in preparing questions, which he or she may not have considered. Importantly, the expert will help counsel to avoid asking damaging questions.

Do not be hesitant in approaching the prosecution's expert for an interview. Most experts want to be fair or at least appear to be fair and will entertain the opposing counsel's questions. This is particularly so with the many forensic science experts, employed by the government-funded laboratories who testify regularly for the prosecution. These experts in the province of Ontario have always proven to be very receptive to taking the time to speak with defence counsel even though they know the same counsel will be cross-examining them at trial. There may even be times when such interviews will prove to be so enlightening and helpful for cross-examination purposes that defence counsel may decide not to retain his or her own expert.[55] Such an interview teaches which questions the expert should not be asked when the expert testifies. If an opposing expert refuses to talk to you notwithstanding there is no property in a witness, bring this fact out in cross-examination to show the witness's possible partisanship. It has been my experience that most government-funded witnesses pride themselves in not being partisan but they will advise the Crown of their interview with defence counsel. If you do speak to an opposing expert it would be best to have someone with you to guard against possible allegations of witness tampering, or if the expert says something different at trial than in your interview the witness can then testify on your behalf if you wish the Court to hear this discrepancy because it impacts on the expert's credibility and/ or you want the Court to be aware of what the expert told you as it is helpful to your client's defence.

If there is an order excluding witnesses and counsel knows that she may be calling her own expert witness, she should request the Court make an exception to that order so that her expert can hear the testimony, as it will be helpful to the expert in formulating his opinions, commenting on the evidence of the opposing expert, as well as advising counsel on additional lines of inquiry. With the expert sitting at the counsel table, the testifying expert will be careful not to make any exaggerated, rash or untrue statements.

However, if counsel does not call her expert to testify she may hear opposing counsel in his jury address rhetorically asking: "Why not?" Did this failure to call the expert sitting in Court to hear the evidence mean that he supported the other side? This can, of course, be answered if the expert evidence for the Crown has been largely neutralized in cross-examination but it is a factor to be borne in mind in deciding not to call a defence expert witness about whose presence the jury has been alerted.

Ascertain what you can about the expert on the opposite side from your colleagues or your own expert. Try Google. That expert may have a website. Knowing the extent of the opponent's expertise, his bias, if any, his writings

---

55 The present procedure in Ontario with the Centre of Forensic Sciences' expert is that your conversations with their experts will be relayed to the Crown. The Centre in Toronto in effect requests that you waive the umbrella of solicitor-client privilege if it does any lab work for the defence. Recommendation 27 from the Kaufmann Inquiry suggests that a protocol be established to facilitate the ability of the defence to obtain forensic work in confidence.

and his prior testimony, whether the expert has taken contradictory positions on other occasions will be of assistance in preparing cross-examination of that expert. If you do not receive the *curriculum vitae* of the expert by way of disclosure, request it. This will be of assistance in checking the background of the expert and anything he/she may have written on the topic in question. Make sure you have received disclosure of the experts' notes in addition to any reports made by them. At the very least ask to see the expert's file when he/she is on the witness stand, if you have not received it by way of disclosure.

In preparing for cross-examination of the expert it would be helpful to keep in mind the following hints in attempting to cast doubt on the expert's experience, methods and opinion:[56]

(a) Limiting the witness's apparent expertise. Narrow the extent of his/her expertise/experience by showing that it is not directly applicable to the case in question or, perhaps, by contrasting it to the experience of your expert.

(b) Showing the expert your knowledge of his/her subject. Know the meaning of the technical terms involved or the way in which any tests were carried out. He/she will be less inclined to dodge your questions!

(c) Inviting the witness to define technical terms and use common language. Some find this difficult.

(d) Showing that the witness has had less involvement/contact with the case than your expert, e.g., has only examined a party once; or viewed the machinery long after the accident.

(e) Challenging his/her methods, e.g., showing that there were other tests which the expert could/should have carried out which may have produced a different result.

(f) Inviting the witness to agree with the propositions which form the basis of your expert's opinion—he/she is unlikely to disagree with everything your expert says and you should know from your own expert those areas which are in dispute. Remember to 'put your case' to the expert by inviting him/her to deal with your expert's methods/opinions/conclusions.

(g) Inviting the witness to agree that, in his/her field, legitimate differences of opinion frequently occur between qualified experts; this shows that the witness is not infallible and that his/her evidence is 'opinion' only.

(h) Using hypothetical facts to test the strength of the expert's opinion: testing whether a different interpretation of the same facts or a slight change in those facts would affect the expert's opinion.

The preliminary hearing is a very useful procedure in preparing to cross-examine the expert at trial. Because they are not normally required in

---

56 Advocacy, Negotiation and Conference Skills, Inns of Court School of Law, 3rd ed. (Blackstone Press Ltd., 1991) at p. 244.

order to obtain a committal, and are too busy with other matters and expensive, it is not common for the Crown to call its expert witnesses at the preliminary hearing. In most cases, you should request the Crown to have its expert(s) at the preliminary hearing for you to call to testify. If you are aware it is not the Crown's intention to call the expert(s), subpoena them yourself. The importance of hearing the expert is that their evidence can turn out at trial to be more crucial than you originally thought in the early stages of the case. At the very least you want to pin the expert down to a position and seek answers that may be helpful to your defence. Their reports often do not tell the whole story which will emerge at the trial. Indeed, their evidence may even turn out to be helpful to your client. When possible you will have conferred with your own expert who can provide you with helpful lines of inquiry. The transcript of the expert's testimony at the preliminary hearing will be helpful to your own expert in preparing for trial.

By testing the Crown's expert's credentials at the preliminary hearing you can decide whether it is fruitful to do so at trial. You will ask the Crown's expert what writings he/she considers authoritative on the subject or what he/she has written on the topic. (This subject is discussed later in this chapter.) Inquire of the Crown's expert what other experts in the field commands his/her respect or if there are other experts the witness feels are more qualified than himself/herself. You may wish to retain one of these other experts for trial. You will explore with the expert any potential for bias to determine if you wish to pursue that avenue at trial. (This topic is discussed later in this chapter.)

At the preliminary hearing stage you can ascertain the thoroughness and completeness of the experts, interviews, examinations, and testing procedures, etc., potentially laying the groundwork for fruitful cross-examinations at trial. At the very least you will learn what questions not to ask at trial and what future investigations and preparation you should do for trial. At the preliminary hearing you can afford to take some risks with your questions that you don't want to take at trial, with the hope that some answers of benefit will result.

In the last analysis, the preliminary hearing should be used as a testing ground to determine the reliability of the expert's evidence, to define more clearly the issues that arise through the expert's testimony, to obtain discovery of evidence not already known, to seek confirmation of your own defence through the Crown's expert, and to tie the experts to their answers so that if they change their position at trial to your client's detriment you can impeach them with the transcript of their earlier testimony.

As indicated above, it may be that your opponent's expert can be helpful to your case. The following is an example of how defence counsel used the expertise of the Crown's expert to secure an acquittal. It is the opening of a cross-examination of the Crown's scientific expert by Edward

Clarke in the famous English trial of Adelaide Bartlett.[57] She was alleged to have murdered her husband by administering chloroform.

> "Dr. Stevenson, you have for many years given your attention to the subjects of this class?"
>
> "I have."
>
> "And you have had a long experience of the administration of chloroform?"
>
> "I have."
>
> "And you have also given study to the experience of other doctors?"
>
> "Yes."
>
> "And you have edited *The Principles and Practice of Medical Jurisprudence*, by Dr. Alfred Swaine Taylor, who is well-known as one of the greatest authorities in that branch of medical science?"
>
> "Yes."
>
> "And so far as your skill and experience have enabled you, have you taken care that it is complete in the subject with which it deals?"
>
> "Yes; it is fairly complete, I think."

Clarke, even though he was a defence counsel, had deliberately built up the expertise of the Crown expert as the man who knew all there was to know about dealing in chloroform. And then:

> "Can you refer me to *any* recorded case, *anywhere*, of murder by the administration of liquid chloroform?"

Stevenson answered as Clarke knew he must.

> "No," he said, "I know of none."

So if Mrs. Barlett had killed her husband by giving him liquid chloroform, she had performed a feat that was apparently unique.

> "There are no recorded cases of murder in this fashion" Clarke went on, "but have there not been deaths from the swallowing of chloroform by accident?"
>
> "Yes," said Stevenson.
>
> "How many?"
>
> "About twenty have been recorded."

So, by the test of statistics, accident was a more feasible hypothesis than murder.

With the above cross-examination as a start, Edward Lustgarten wrote that each question by Clarke that followed was designed to show that what Mrs. Bartlett was alleged to have done "would test the powers of a qualified physician and be utterly beyond her capacity and knowledge." Ms. Bartlett was acquitted.

This is one of those trials; like those surveyed in the chapter on cross-examination (The Beginning) where defence counsel begins his cross-examination with attention-getting questions which immediately alerted the

---

57 Edward Lustgarten, Publisher Allan Wingate, London & New York.

jurors to the realization that the ensuing questions would be important for the defence.

The Expert's Qualifications

If counsel is previously aware that the opponent's expert is well qualified, perhaps through questioning at the preliminary hearing, by reputation or as a result of other occasions in which he or she has heard the witness testify, counsel may wish to admit the expert's qualifications in an attempt to prevent the triers-of-fact from hearing them and being overly impressed. An experienced opponent will, as discussed earlier, refuse such a concession.

Often the expert's *curriculum vitae* will include qualifications which are impressive but do not relate to the issues involved in the case. Counsel should, in cross-examination, isolate those parts of the expert's qualifications that are irrelevant. If the expert testifies as to an impressive list of writings which are irrelevant to the issues at trial, he or she might be asked how those authorships helped him in coming to his or her conclusions. If the witness's expertise is based more on his or her academic credentials than practical experience, this fact should be underlined for the trier of fact. This should be accomplished in the general cross-examination of the expert as opposed to that point when counsel is given the right to cross-examine the expert on his or her qualifications before the witness is declared an expert and permitted to give opinion testimony. An obvious exception to this recommendation is where counsel is seriously hoping to prevent the witness from being qualified as an expert. However, with the liberal standards for qualifying experts currently prevailing, the witness will usually be permitted to give an opinion.

It would be a rare case where the cross-examiner could show that the expert is incompetent or dishonest. The advantage counsel seeks is to show her opponent's qualifications are less impressive than her own expert's qualifications. Counsel's own expert can help him or her in assessing any comparisons. One example is to show that the opponent's expert belongs to various (medical) societies whose admission is determined only by an application to join, while the cross-examiner's expert is a member of certain (medical) groups in which membership must be earned by special training or other qualifications.

In cross-examining the opposing expert the questioner is given the opportunity to trumpet the expertise of his own expert witness. In most cases the witness is aware of his opponent's expert's reputation and it would be the rare witness who would not agree that his opponent is well-qualified in the field or even admit, if the facts warrant, that the opponent's reputation or qualifications exceed those of the witness. It would be an ideal situation to be able to finish the cross-questioning of the expert witness with respect to the issue of qualification by asking—"Is it fair to say that there are a number of experts in the field who have more knowledge about the topic than you?"—and then name the cross-examiner's expert as one of those more knowledgeable.

Your opponent, in qualifying the expert will no doubt elicit the fact that the expert has testified in Court before and has been qualified as an expert on those occasions. If you are desirous of bringing out that the expert's opinion in a prior trial was rejected or disbelieved, be mindful of *R. v. Karaibrahimovic*[58] which held that such cross-examination is improper as a decision inconsistent with an expert's opinion does not mean that the opinion lacked merit as it might have been made for other reasons.

Bias

If the expert comes from the provincial government laboratory, counsel can point out that she is employed by the Solicitor General who is, in turn, the Minister responsible for policing in the province, that she and the police are responsible to the same Minister, that she works closely with the police and the Crown prosecutor in homicide or other types of cases, that whenever she has testified it has been for the prosecution or mainly for the prosecution, and, if borne out by the evidence, that when she met with the police they gave their theories as to what occurred prior to the witness forming an opinion. In order to counter some of the cross-examination aforementioned, the Crown should, when qualifying a government expert, point out that defence counsel has the right to use the government facilities as well (if such is the case) and that the expert has testified on behalf of the defence on occasion (if such is the case).

A question often arises about whether or not to elicit from the witness if he is being paid for his services as an expert. Those witnesses from the Solicitor General's laboratories are not paid specifically to testify for the Crown but are salaried employees. As far as other experts are concerned jurors will expect that a trained expert should be paid for coming to Court and offering his expertise. This is especially so since the expert would have to devote time to instruct counsel and some experts might have to cancel office appointments but still pay overhead in order to come to Court to testify. But if payment to the expert is substantial, some jurors may feel that his testimony may have been influenced by the payment, more particularly if it is significantly more than the fee being paid to the questioner's expert. On the other hand, it might be argued that the amount of the fee paid reflects the stature of the expert.

---

58   (2002), 164 C.C.C. (3d) 431 (Alta. C.A.).

If counsel can show that the witness has testified many times for the same side and/or the witness has earned a substantial part of his income from being a witness counsel may be able to persuade the jurors that this expert is a professional witness or a "hired gun." Your own expert may be of help here with this information.

Of course an obvious reason not to question the witness about fees is that the cross-examiner may be calling an expert who would then be subject to similar questions about his fees. *Quaere*: Can it be successfully argued that since the expert hired by defence comes under the umbrella of solicitor-client privilege that the fees agreement is also privileged? See Chapter, "Privileges."

If the expert comes from out-of-the-country at great expense to testify, you will want some answers—why could an expert not be found here? Was it because your opponent could not find anyone in this jurisdiction to support his or her position or was it because this expert was the very best expert on the subject, or it involved a rare specialty with no experts in the field in this jurisdiction? It would be best to obtain this information at the preliminary inquiry, perhaps from the officer-in-charge, so you will know whether to ask the question at trial.

The following is an example of attempting to create an aura of bias:[59]

Q: You receive referrals from the Children's Aid Society?

A: As do many in my profession.

Q: In fact, this very case came to you by referral from the Children's Aid Society?

A: Yes it did.

Q: The Children's Aid Society then pays the cost of your evaluation?

A: Certainly.

Q: Then, if you prepare a report that concludes there are signs of sexual abuse, your report is routinely sent to the Police Service.

A: It is, yes.

Q: Very often your report is forwarded from the Police Service to the Prosecutor's Office?

A: If the police feel it's warranted, yes.

Q: If there's a prosecution in relation to the same matter, you are often hired as a witness for the prosecution?

A: Oftentimes, yes.

Q: That's exactly what has happened here, isn't it?

A: Yes.

Q: In addition, sometimes there are civil cases that arise from such an evaluation, such as a divorce, custody, access, or an accounting of profits if there is a family business?

---

59 Prepared by Patrick J. Ducharme of Gignac, Sutts, Barristers and Solicitors, Windsor, Ontario for the Law Society of Upper Canada Continuing Education Seminar, Toronto, 1998.

A: Yes.

Q: You are sometimes retained on the civil case as well?

A: Again, almost everyone that I know in my profession is given business the same way.

Q: In this particular case you have been hired by the attorneys for Mrs. Jones in a civil case of that type, have you not?

A: Yes, I have.

Q: So you have been hired and paid by the Children's Aid Society, hired and getting paid today by the prosecutor, hired and about to be paid by the lawyers for Mrs. Jones?

A: Yes, but, I guess I just don't agree with what you're insinuating, Mr. Ducharme.

Q: Is it not true that you *never*, in the many cases where you have testified, even once testified for a defendant?

A: I've never been asked to.

Q: You have *only* ever been asked to testify by the prosecution, isn't that true?

A: Yes.

Q: Thank you.

An aspect of the Goudge Inquiry[60] was concerned with the bias of experts. In referring to the pathologist Goudge J.A. wrote that "the pathologist's role is to remain impartial and not to act as an advocate for either Crown or the defence." He warned against evidence from advocating experts that was "dressed up in scientific language which the jury does not easily understand and submitted through a witness of impressive antecedents."[61] He referred to authorities that were opposed to psychiatrists improperly testifying as to the credibility of witnesses.[62] Goudge J.A. noted that communications between the expert and retaining counsel are open to cross-examination by opposing counsel to determine whether such communications influenced the expert's opinion.[63] Counsel would therefore want to see any written communications that have passed between the two.

Opinion Evidence

An expert witness is permitted to give opinion evidence as indicated earlier. Counsel should attempt to obtain from the opposing expert the admission that honest differences of opinion often occur between qualified experts and that the witness in the past has had such differences of opinion

---

60 Stephen T. Goudge Commissioner of the Inquiry into Pediatric Forensic Pathology in Ontario (p. 179, Vol. 2).

61 *R. v. Mohan* (1994), 89 C.C.C. (3d) 402 (S.C.C.).

62 *R. v. Llorenz* (2000), 145 C.C.C. (3d) 535 (Ont. C.A.); *R. c. J. (J.-L.) (sub nom. R. v. J. (J-L.))* (2000), 148 C.C.C. (3d) 487 (S.C.C.).

63 *R. v. Stone*, [1999] 2 S.C.R. 290; *Browne (Litigation Guardian of) v. Lavery* (2002), 58 O.R. (3d) 49 (Ont. S.C.J.).

with other very qualified experts in his or her field. This line of questioning would have little meaning if the questioner was not calling his or her own expert.

Unreliability of Interviews

There are some experts such as psychiatrists and psychologists who, by the very nature of their work, interview patients or clients who may not have been fully truthful or reliable in what they reported to the expert either because of their mental instability or because of their vested interest in the outcome of the matter that brings them into contact with the expert. The cross-examiner should point out the unreliability of such interviews or at least make the point that the expert's opinion is based on the truthfulness and reliability of what she was told and that if the patient or client was untruthful her opinion would change. If there are versions in the evidence which are different than or in addition to what the expert received from her side, they should be brought to the attention of the expert who would then be asked if the particular opinion she gave would change in light of the new version, and if so, how would it change.

Be certain to ask in cross-examination to see the expert's notes and reports, if you have not already seen them, for they may reveal valuable information.

Thoroughness

It is not unusual for an expert to give his opinion even when it is not based on first-hand knowledge. This is particularly so when the witness answer is in response to a hypothetical question. In this situation counsel should obtain a witness's admission that it is always more advantageous to interview the witness himself or herself in order to have first-hand knowledge.

An attack on the expert's opinion can be made because when the expert gave her opinion she did not have all of the relevant facts. Examples include situations where the expert did not perform all of the tests he could have; his examinations were, for any number of reasons, not as complete as he would have liked; he did not speak to all of the people to whom he should have spoken to obtain background information about the accused or the offence, or where he did not speak to the accused. (Counsel should be cautious here if the accused refused permission to be so interviewed as this fact would be brought out by the Crown).

Where possible counsel should contrast the thoroughness of the opposing expert in arriving at a reliable opinion with that of his own expert, as for example, where there is an issue of insanity and counsel's expert has spent considerably more time interviewing the client than the Crown's psychiatrist who has spent a relatively short period of time with the client.

In the last analysis the cross-examiner should make the point that his expert had every opportunity to know the accused better than his opponent's expert and therefore his expert's opinion or conclusion is based on a more solid foundation and as a result more accurate.

Confirming Your Expert's Testimony

Techniques used with ordinary witnesses and detailed in other chapters are also applicable to experts. If it is counsel's plan to attack the opponent's expert, then before doing so he should use him to confirm as much as possible the testimony that his own expert will give or has already given. If the opponent's expert is familiar with the reputation of the cross-examiner's expert he will probably be prepared to agree to the fine reputation of his adversary.

Challenging the Expert by Means of Recognized Authority

A recognized technique in challenging the expert's opinion is to confront him with authoritative works or even his own writings which cast doubt on the correctness of his opinions. The rule, of course, is that counsel cannot cross-examine the expert on a text unless he admits he or she is familiar with the text and considers it authoritative.[64] If the witness acknowledges the authority of the work then counsel can read from it and to the extent the parts read are confirmed by the witness, they become evidence.[65] If the expert does not admit to knowing about the text, it may affect the weight of his opinion in the eyes of the jurors especially if he keeps refusing to admit knowledge of other writings brought to his attention. The cross-examiner, of course, could have his own expert testify that any knowledgeable person in the field would be familiar with the writings on which the opponent's expert has been cross-examined.

The witness should be asked at the preliminary hearing what writings he feels are authoritative on the subject in question. The expert may have testified in chief about articles or books he or she has written on the subject. After the witness has admitted knowledge of certain works, counsel should obtain them hopefully to uncover some relevant contradictory or helpful material.

---

64   *R. v. Marquard* (1993), 85 C.C.C. (3d) 193 (S.C.C.). It is not permissible for a trial Judge on his own motion to make reference to scientific works or reports setting out opinions of experts. See *R. c. Désaulniers* (1994), 93 C.C.C. (3d) 371 (C.A. Qué.).

65   *Ibid.*

Where the witness admits to a particular writing as a recognized authority, then that part which is inconsistent with his testimony should be read to him by counsel. The witness should then be asked whether or not he agrees with the part that has just been read. Whether the witness answers "Yes" or "No" he should be asked if he agrees that the statement just read was contrary to his opinion. The expert should normally not be asked to explain because he may be able to do so satisfactorily. Pray that the inconsistency is not rectified in re-examination.

An example of an expert witness being cross-examined on his own writings is seen in *Ref. re Truscott*[66] where G. Arthur Martin, Q.C.[67] cross-examined Dr. Simpson. In that case it was crucial for the Crown to prove the deceased died before 7:45 p.m., for if death occurred later Truscott could not be guilty of murder. Dr. Simpson testified for the Crown that having regard to the amount of food in the deceased's stomach, its character and the fact that very little passed into the small bowel, death occurred within two hours of the meal. The cross-examination of Dr. Simpson was conducted for the purpose of showing

1. that the stomach contents in relation to the time of consuming the last meal did not afford a reliable guide to the time of death within narrow limits and
2. that the post-mortem changes in the existence of rigor mortis however slight, at the time of the autopsy tended to indicate that death had occurred less than 48 hours before rather than confirm that death had occurred approximately 48 hours before.

Cross-examination proceeded as follows:

> Q. Now, you have written extensively, Dr. Simpson, in the field of forensic medicine.
> A. Yes.
> Q. Now, I have read a good many of your books and one of the books you have written is entitled *Forensic Medicine* and, as my learned friend Mr. Scott says, it has gone through five editions now?
> A. Yes.
> Q. And in the last edition, indeed, you say this edition has been combed to ensure it is abreast of the times. I notice at page 7 of the book—of course, I quite realize here you are dealing with a post-mortem event—you say under the heading of "Cooling":
>> "This is the only real guide to the lapse of time during the first eighteen hours after death, and its early measurement is often vital to the establishment of an approximate time of death."
> A. Yes, sir.

---

66 [1967] S.C.R. 309 (S.C.C.).
67 Later, Mr. Justice Martin of the Ontario Court of Appeal.

Q. Do you, anywhere in this book, suggest that the stomach contents and the state to which digestion has proceeded following the last meal is a reliable guide to the time of death?

A. No sir; I think that that is, as may be evident to you, a short book for the student.

Q. It would not have made it much bigger to put in a sentence indicating that stomach contents were also a reliable guide?

A. No sir; I appreciate that, but it is not intended to be a comprehensive work, of course.

Q. It should contain the things upon which there is greater consensus—

A. I think you may expect the next edition, sir, to contain some reference.

Q. You are going to change the next edition?

A. Each time I am writing I am learning and each case I have helps me to improve the next edition.

Q. I will throw this away and buy the next edition. You also deal with this in your 12th edition of Taylor, which you have edited?

A. Yes, sir.

Q. I should say, you do deal with the stomach contents.

A. There is a reference to the stomach contents there; it is a more comprehensive book.

Q. I think, to be fair, I should read everything that is here so I will not be taking it out of its context. The heading is "Inferences as to Time of Death"—it is page 210.

A. I think I know the paragraph you are referring to.

Q. "Inferences as to Time of Death from the State of Food. The site and state of digestion of the contents of the stomach and bowel may be used as an additional means of fixing the hour of death in relation to the last meal. Most elaborate tables have been prepared of the time taken by the stomach to digest certain articles of diet but these are wholly unreliable."

A. Could I stop there for a moment, if it will not interfere?

Q. No, it will not interfere.

A. I would draw a sharp difference between the state of digestion, which is a chemical process, and the emptying of the stomach. The state of digestion means the chemical process of digestion. I make a sharp distinction between these words.

Q. "The rate of digestion varies in different persons and according to the functional efficiency of the gastric mucosa."

A. Yes.

Q. The stomach cannot empty until the stomach digests the food?

A. No, the stomach can empty even in cases where the gastric juices are absent, or almost, into the bowels. The rate of emptying does not depend on the state of digestion.

Q. What I am quoting is irrelevant at this stage?

A. No; it appears to depend more on the state of stiffening of the food.

Q. I will come to something that is relevant.

"Gastric and intestinal activity is much retarded in cases of trauma and insensibility. Even without the paralysis of movement that is common to grave injury or deep insensibility, the process of emptying of the stomach may be much delayed."

A. Yes, sir.

Q. I am talking of something that is germane?

A. Yes, that is very apt.

Q. That is very apt?

A. Yes.

Q. You quote:

"Examination of the body of a woman strangled at about II pm. one February night showed meat fibre, intact peas, fragments of mint leaf and potato, together with some apple pips, still present in the stomach; very little had passed into the duodenum and none into the jejunum. She had had her last major meal—of roast lamb, peas, boiled potatoes, mint sauce, apple tart and custard at 2-2.30 p.m., no less than nine hours previously."

A. Yes, I remember that case.

Q. The description is remarkably—first of all, the cause of death was strangling?

A. Yes.

Q. The cause of death in this case was strangling. And the description of the stomach contents, is it not remarkably like the description given by Dr. Penistan, because it is said the examination showed meat fibre, intact peas, and intact peas I think were found here, fragments of mint leaf and potato, and in this case Dr. Penistan felt that he could not identify the material as potato, because it had passed into a discreet phase, although Dr. Brooks, I think in fairness, said he could see some pieces of potato. Do you agree—with apple pips still in the stomach the description is very muck like Dr. Penistan's?

A. Yes.

Q. Very little had passed into the duodenum. Again, that is remarkably like Dr. Penistan's?

A. Yes.

Q. The process seems to have gone farther in the case of the deceased, Lynne Harper, because he used the words "very little had passed through the duodenum." Is that correct?

A. Yes.

Q. You have these analogies in the two cases. And: "She had had her last major meal—of roast lamb, peas, boiled potatoes, mint sauce, apple tart and custard at 2-2.30 p.m., no less than nine hours previously."

A. Yes.

. . .

Q. Passing on to post-mortem changes.

A. Yes, sir.

Q. I think in fairness you say that rigor mortis is the most unreliable of post-mortem events?

A. Yes, sir.

Q. One could not, on the basis of the existence or the extent of rigor present, either on the afternoon of June the 11th or on the evening of June the 11th, pinpoint the time of death as between seven and seven-forty-five?

A. To start with "pinpoint" is not a word one could use to establish the time of death from one observation. It is not a matter of pinpointing; it is always an approximation.

Q. The words Dr. Penistan used were that he would put the time of death between seven and seven-forty-five. Those are relatively narrow limits. Putting the time of death, does that not indicate it was determining the time of death?

A. I do not think it was pinpointing, this giving a period of time and putting it in that period.

Q. Seven to seven-forty-five?

A. Yes.

Q. Does the existence of rigor and its extent on June the 11th enable you to place the time of death within that period?

A. No, sir. These are too variable.

Q. It is much too—

A. It is much too variable, the onset and duration of rigor mortis.

Q. Is the onset of rigor hastened by warm weather?

A. It tends to be, sir.

Q. Is the disappearance of rigor also hastened by warm weather?

A. It tends to be.

Q. And recognizing, as you have indicated, that rigor is an unreliable event, nevertheless, you do in your works give what you would expect, is that so, with respect to the passing off of rigor?

A. Yes, sir, I do give the sort of periods which are usual.

Q. I think you have a table in your small book?

A. Yes, sir; this is the student's guide that I first wrote. Oh yes.

Q. You give a table, I think at page 17, on rigor mortis. You say, "5-7 hours Rigor appearing in face, jaw, and neck muscles."

A. This is a start, the likely start, yes.

Q. "7-9 Spread to arms and trunk, and reaching legs. 12-18 Rigor fully established. 24-36 Rigor passing away in same order."

A. Yes, sir, those are the likely.

Q. These are the likely periods?

A. Yes, sir.

Q. But insofar as there is any value in rigor, the existence of the rigor that was observed by Dr. Penistan would point to less than a two-day interval?

A. It tends to, sir.

. . .

Q. You have heard the evidence given as to the atmospheric temperature?

A. Yes, sir.

Q. Quoting from memory I think 88 degrees on the 9th as a high, with a low of 65, or thereabouts; on the 10th, high of 92, low about 66; 11th a high of 90; a low of about 65. Those are very high temperatures?

A. Yes.

Q. And getting very close to the tropical temperatures you mentioned?

A. Yes.

Q. Of between 80 degrees and 100 degrees?

A. Yes, sir; that is certainly fair comment, sir.

Q. Also, again recognizing there may well be some variation in these post-mortem events, but, again, you give a table of what you would expect in respect to green staining in the flanks?

A. Yes, sir.

Q. You have put this as appearing in two days?

A. I think that is what I was saying there, that one would expect it in about two days.

Q. And you say in warm, hot months these processes are accelerated?

A. Yes.

Q. Because putrefaction may occur in 24 hours?

A. Yes, sir; I have seen it in Egypt and Cyprus.

Q. And the weather here would be comparable?

A. Yes, it is not very far away from it.

Q. As a matter of fact, if you were to assume that death occurred within two hours after the meal, as Dr. Penistan did, bringing the time of death to prior to 7:45 on the 9th, and Dr. Penistan started to perform his autopsy at 7:15 on the 11th, there would be a lapse of 48 hours?

A. Yes.

Q. And he does not mention any green staining?

A. No, I don't think there was any described.

Q. Again, if there had been a two-day interval, and I point out it was only half an hour less than two days, you would have expected—

A. Yes, sir.

Q. —green staining?

A. Yes, sir, I would. You may remember what I said earlier in evidence, I would expect it but it does not always appear.

Q. These are variable factors?

A. Yes.

Q. But, nevertheless, it is something you would expect?

A. Yes, sir, I think I would.

Q. The fact you do not find it, if it means anything, it tends to put the time of death later rather than earlier?

A. Yes, I think you put that very fairly, sir.

In addition to showing how an expert witness is cross-examined on his own writings, Arthur Maloney, Q.C., stated that:[68]

[T]he merit of this cross-examination is the wording of the first major question, viz., "Do you anywhere in this book say that the stomach contents are a reliable guide to the time of death?" I think a second merit of the cross-examination is the way in which the questions were put with respect to what Dr. Simpson

---

68   1971 Law Society of Upper Canada Lectures. Lecture on Expert Evidence.

would have expected in a way of rigor mortis or green staining if the deceased had been dead for 48 hours prior to the autopsy as the Crown contended.

The following is an example of the expert being confronted with an authoritative article by another expert in the field and the use made of it by the cross-examiner to show that the expert did not do all he could have in evaluating factors consistent with sexual abuse:[69]

Q. You are familiar, Dr. Armstrong, with this book that I hold in my hand, titled *American Psychiatric Press Review of Psychiatry Volume 10*?
A. I am familiar with it.
Q. If I'm not mistaken, you have this very book on your bookshelf at your office?
A. I believe I do, yes.
Q. You keep it right behind your office desk?
A. Yes I do.
Q. You are very familiar with the writings in the area of sexual abuse by its author, Dr. Yates?
A. Yes, he's one of many authors I have read.
Q. Dr. Yates is a well known and respected authority concerning allegations of sexual abuse?
A. Yes he is.
Q. You would be particularly familiar, I would assume, with Chapter 15 which deals with *false* and *mistaken* allegations of sexual abuse?
A. I have read it.
Q. I have a copy of Chapter 15 for you (presenting it to her). (I have given a copy to His Honour and a copy to the prosecutor.) Will you turn to page 326 in that chapter? At page 326, about half-way down the page, Dr. Yates outlines 9 different steps in making an effective evaluation of sexual abuse?
A. Yes he does.
Q. You are familiar with that 9-step evaluation?
A. Generally speaking I am.
Q. It is a good, thorough approach isn't it?
A. Yes, it is very good.
Q. Am I correct in saying that in your field Dr. Yates' 9-step evaluation method is used regularly?
A. Many evaluators do use it, yes.
Q. I have taken the liberty of reducing to writing those 9 steps in short form on the large board immediately to your right. As I'm asking you questions, Doctor, I would like you to refer to the writing on that board. I intend to ask you whether or not you used any or all of these steps in this case.
A. I can tell you right now I did not use all of them.
Q. First, Dr. Yates suggests that evaluators gather and review all background information and documents?

---

69   Prepared by Patrick J. Ducharme of Gignac, Sutts, Barristers and Solicitors, Windsor, Ontario for the Law Society of Upper Canada Continuing Education Seminar, Toronto, 1998.

A. Yes he does.

Q. You looked at a number of documents and did gather *some* background information, but you did not gather *all* background information?

A. I gathered all *relevant* background information.

Q. For this step, your assumption was that Annie's father, her brother, grandparents and aunts and uncles could *not* provide any *relevant* information?

A. Perhaps they could have, maybe. I should say I gathered what I considered to be the *most* relevant information.

Q. So, you believe that you gathered enough relevant background information to allow you to answer "yes" to Dr. Yates' Number 1 step?

A. Yes I do.

Q. Alright then. Please write 'YES' next to Number 1, Doctor.

Q. Second, Dr. Yates suggests interviewing all persons involved with the child. You did not do that?

A. No I didn't.

Q. Please write 'NO', then, next to Number 2.

A. Certainly.

Q. At step 3, Dr. Yates suggests that you should video-tape your assessment sessions with the child. You did not do that?

A. No I did not. First, I don't have the equipment and, secondly, I'm not sure I agree with Dr. Yates here.

Q. The reason that Dr. Yates suggests the assessment sessions should be video-taped is that anyone who wants to look at them later can determine for himself or herself the reaction of the child to your questions, correct?

A. I suppose you are correct. I suppose videotape would enable lay people to observe the sessions later.

Q. Lay people, like the 12 jurors who are required to weigh and consider your evidence presently?

A. Yes.

Q. Please wrote 'NO' next to Number 3.

Q. Step 4 suggests that you should have at least 10 sessions with the child to make an objective evaluation. You had only 7 sessions?

A. They were very extensive, involved sessions.

Q. So even though you conducted only 7 sessions, they were extensive and involved?

A. Yes.

Q. To be fair to you, why don't you write 'YES' next to Number 4?

Q. Step 5 suggests that you should provide the child who you're assessing with information about your role and the possible consequences of your evaluation. You definitely did not do that?

A. No, again that's not part of my experience. Children might be frightened by the prospect of knowing the consequences of their answers.

Q. But Dr. Yates suggests that you should tell the child, because knowing the consequences impresses upon the child the seriousness of telling the truth?

A. I don't agree with Dr. Yates, but certainly that is his reasoning.

Q. So you disagree with Dr. Yates on that point.

A. Yes I do.

Q. Will you please wrote 'NO' next to the Number 5?

A. Certainly.

Q. Step 6 suggests that you are to request all prior videotaped interviews. In this case, we have heard that there three prior videos taken by the Windsor Police. You did not view any of those?

A. I was not informed of any videotaped interviews.

Q. You did not make any inquiries to determine if there were any video-taped interviews?

A. I don't recall, I probably didn't. I'm sure I didn't.

Q. Please write 'NO' next to Step 6.

Q. Step 7 suggests that all "involved" adults should be assessed individually. You didn't do that?

A. I did not conduct interviews of all the "involved" adults, but they may have been done by others.

Q. If they were done by others, you never did receive any such report from anyone else, did you?

A. No, I didn't.

Q. Will you write 'NO' next to Number 7, please?

Q. Step 8 suggests that you observe the child with each parent. You definitely didn't do that, did you?

A. No, for the reasons I've already stated.

Q. Dr. Yates would suggest that it is important you see the child interact with her father so that you can assess them while they're together, but you had no such opportunity?

A. No, I didn't.

Q. Nor did you make any effort to have such an opportunity?

A. I was advised not to speak with Mr. Jones.

Q. Who advised you not to that, Doctor?

A. The Crown.

Q. Please write 'NO' next to Number 8.

Q. Step 9 asks that you note the degree of distress when the child is describing the sexual event. You did do that, somewhat extensively, didn't you?

A. Yes.

Q. Then write 'YES' next to Number 9.

Q. My review of the YES's and NO's, Doctor, is that you used only 3 of Dr. Yates' suggested 9 steps?

A. Yes.

Q. While you hold Dr. Yates' opinion in the field of assessing factors consistent with sexual abuse in high regard, your evaluation was considerably less detailed than what he recommends?

A. Less detailed, but valid.

Posing a Different Interpretation of the Facts

Another technique is to elicit a different interpretation of the facts to which the Crown's expert has testified, that is reasonable and favourable to the accused. An example of such an approach was used by G. Arthur Martin,

Q.C. (as he then was) in the cross-examination of Dr. Tennant in the *Gibbons*[70] case.

The defence of Gibbons was that he was insane and suffered from delusions that the Fitzmaurice brothers planned to kill him and while under the influence of his delusion he shot and killed the brothers in self-defence. The Crown's psychiatrist expressed the opinion that the accused was not suffering from mental disease or hallucinations or delusions: "He knew that when he fired a rifle it would hurt someone. He knew when he did it that it was wrong."

The facts were that when Gibbon's car became stuck in the snow near his farm and when the Fitzmaurice brothers approached in their sleigh, Gibbons shot them both dead. He then phoned the police and said, "I got one of them today." When the police arrived Gibbons said "Do you think I did the right thing?" Gibbons asked the police later if both brothers were dead and when he was told they were, Gibbons said, "Well, it is no more for two than one."

Gibbons had been objecting to the Fitzmaurice brothers crossing his land under a claim that they had a right of way and had once told them, "There will be blood spilt on the hill," if they came on his land again. The Crown's position was that Gibbons held a grudge against the Fitzmaurice brothers. Mr. Martin's cross-examination was in part as follows:

Q. Doctor, would you define a delusion?
A. A delusion is a false belief which has no foundation in fact, and which will not yield to reason or argument.
Q. Gibbons has consistently stated that the two Fitzmaurice brothers intended to harm him?
A. Yes.
Q. You are aware, of course, that on January 30th he drove thirteen miles on a cold winter night to Renfrew and requested assistance from the Police at one o'clock in the morning?
A. Yes.
Q. He told Sergeant Henderson that he feared the Fitzmaurice brothers intended to do him harm; you heard the evidence of Sergeant Henderson to that effect?
A. Yes.
Q. He asked Sergeant Henderson to provide him with police protection?
A. Yes.
Q. You are also aware that Sergeant Henderson thought that Gibbon's behaviour was so strange that immediately after Gibbons left he phoned his sister?
A. Yes.
Q. Have you been able to discover any evidence that the Fitzmaurice brothers intended to injure Gibbons?
A. No.

---

70 *R. v. Gibbons*, [1946] O.R. 464 (Ont. C.A.).

Q. Efforts were made by Sergeant Henderson to convince Gibbons that the Fitzmaurice brothers intended him no harm?

A. Yes.

Q. Do you know of any person who was able to convince Gibbons by an appeal to reason or argument that there was no basis for his belief that the Fitzmaurice brothers intended to injure him?

A. No.

Q. So if Gibbons believed that the Fitzmaurice brothers intended to injure him, and there was no basis for that belief that was a false belief.

A. Yes.

Q. And if he persisted in that belief in spite of reason or argument that belief was a delusion according to your definition?

A. Yes.

Q. The existence of a delusion is the hall-mark of insanity?

A. Yes.

Q. What is an hallucination?

A. An hallucination is a sensory perception without any external object to cause it.

Q. So, in other words, if a person sees objects that are not there or hears voices when non one is speaking those are hallucinations?

A. Yes.

Q. Did Gibbons tell you about an occasion when he was driving on the road and as he approached a hill he saw a tent on the hill and a hand came out of the tent and beckoned to him? He interpreted that as a sign from God that he was to join in a war against evil?

A. He told me that.

Q. Tell me Doctor, are your aware of anyone else who saw that tent and that beckoning hand?

A. There may have been a tent there.

Q. I don't think you answered my question, are you aware of anyone else who saw that tent and that beckoning hand?

A. No.

Q. If there was no tent there and no beckoning hand, that was an hallucination.

A. That may have been an hallucination.

Q. You have expressed an opinion that Gibbons knew that it was wrong to shoot the two men?

A. Yes.

Q. You have stated that you based your opinion on the fact that after the shooting Gibbons called the police and informed then what he had done and also on the fact that on being informed that both brothers were dead he said "Well, it is no worse for two than one?"

A. Yes.

Q. Now Doctor, I want you to assume these facts. You are sleeping peacefully in your bed, a burglar enters and menaces the life of your wife, and yourself and you are forced to kill the burglar in self-defence. Assuming the above facts occurred what is the next thing you would do?

A. I would phone the police.

Q. Why, you have not done anything wrong?

A. Well I would still feel obliged to report what occurred.

Q. Isn't that exactly what Gibbons did when he phoned the police?

A. I suppose that could be so.

Q. The second basis for your opinion that Gibbons knew what he did was wrong was the remark he made: "It is no worse for two than one."

A. Yes.

Q. You interpret that remark as meaning "they can only hang me once whether I have killed one or two"?

A. Yes.

Q. You have heard the opinions expressed by Dr. Doyle and Dr. Armour that Gibbons meant "that it was no worse for the two of them to be killed by Gibbons in self-defence than for Gibbons to be killed by them if he had not done what he did?"

A. I disagree with Dr. Armour and Dr. Doyle.

Q. When Gibbons met Constable McDermid at the door he said "Do you think I did the right thing?" Does not that indicate he expected the police to approve of what he did?

A. If that refers to the killing of the two men it would make me doubt if he knew what he was doing was wrong.

Arthur Maloney,[71] in analyzing the above cross-examination, had this to say:

> The merit of the cross-examination is that through a series of carefully worded questions the cross-examiner was able to select his own "battleground" to keep the witness from selecting another where he might stand a better chance of defending his opinion. The questions did not permit an argument to develop between the cross-examiner and the witness. The witness had to answer the question in a way which was bound to help the cross-examiner's case.

Counsel was therefore able to bring out a different interpretation of the facts.

Another example of placing a different interpretation on the facts than that put forward by the opposing side can be seen in the following cross-examination by Crown attorney Ken Rae, Q.C. in the case of *R. v. Everingham*.[72] The accused's defence was insanity. He had abducted an eight-year-old girl off a road near her cottage while he was driving his automobile and then drove to a secluded area, raped her and then unsuccessfully attempted to kill her by strangulation. Mr. Rae, using excellent tactical judgment, readily admitted in front of the jury that the accused did indeed have a disease of the mind, as he knew the evidence in this regard was overwhelming, but questioned whether the accused was so deep in the throes of a psychotic state at the time of the incident that he failed to appreciate the nature and quality of the act or to know that it was wrong. Mr. Rae was able, therefore, to concentrate on one front instead of two by staying away

---

71 *Supra.*
72 Owen Sound Supreme Court Assizes, February 1975.

from an area which he was bound to lose and possibly have a greater impact on the issue upon which he was basing his main attack.

In examination-in-chief Dr. J. Cooper testified that the factual circumstances surrounding the criminal acts were bizarre and helped convince him that the accused did not appreciate the nature and quality of his acts. The following extracts from the cross-examinations of Dr. Cooper and Dr. P. Rowsell relate only to the issue of whether or not the accused appreciated the nature and quality of his acts.

QUESTIONS TO DR. COOPER

Q. Is it harder to say what a man's mental condition was at a time in the past than to say what he is like right now?

A. Yes, definitely.

. . .

A. In trying to cast your mind back to a time when you were not present and Everingham was alleged to have attacked Sophia Vautour, am I right in assuming that it is of great importance that you have some evidence as to his conduct at the time?

A. That is correct.

Q. And if his conduct shows an absence of pattern or the result of reason, that is consistent with your diagnosis that at the time he was in a severely psychotic state?

A. Yes.

Q. Would the converse be true, that if there was a rational sort of explanation for why he did things, that that would tend to indicate that he was not in a severely advanced psychotic state at the time?

A. If you were to produce a reasonably rational description of what he did, then I would have to change my opinion.

Q. The mere fact of the raping of an 8-year-old child would not indicate you were psychotic?

A. No, definitely not. We might be mentally ill in another way but not necessarily psychotic.

. . .

Q. As I understand it, the blowing of the horn is significant to you as being, at the time of the abduction, as being a rash thing to draw attention to oneself as opposed to the classic rapist who would quietly seduce the person away from the scene?

A. Yes.

Q. And is it to your knowledge that the car had an inoperable passenger door?

A. No, I was not aware of that.

Q. Can you imagine if one held the little child across the steering wheel of the car, the chances of bumping into the horn ring would be present?

A. Well, you would have more knowledge in that area. I could not determine either way.

Q. With regard to the question of taking one's clothes off when driving, you find that that is a factor which leads you to the conclusion that he had this psychosis at the time because it would tend to put himself in a risk situation of being detected?

A. Yes, it is, I would say, with rapists I have seen, it is a very bizarre mode of behaviour.

. . .

Q. The other thing concerns the evidence of a certain towel. Did you hear Sophia Vautour give evidence about this towel?

A. Yes, I did.

Q. A person who was attempting to avoid detection would attempt to minimize the number of bloodstains that would be left about him and his clothes and his car?

A. Yes.

Q. So by taking his clothes off he would reduce the possibility of having such blood on his clothing, isn't that right?

A. That is possible; I never thought of that; yes.

Q. And by laying the towel on the seat of the car underneath the child he would reduce the chances of her blood being found on his car seat; isn't that correct?

A. That is possible, yes.

Q. And by disposing of the towel as well and being an unlikely thing to ever get connected back to him, there would be nothing in his car or the minimum amount of stuff in his car to be connected with that child?

A. Yes, if he did that in terms of taking off his clothes for those reasons then I would have to change my mind, if it would be proved that was the reason that he did it. You have introduced something now I had not thought about before.

CROSS-EXAMINATION OF DR. P. ROWSELL

Q. Dr. Cooper seemed to be impressed by the fact that he [the accused] took his clothes off while going down a public highway . . . the child was found at a place shown in exhibit #7 . . . it is pretty rugged territory out there and not many people about . . . no sign of life or habitation . . . a wild and remote area in which there are many places to which one can go and not have someone stumble upon them . . . would that relative privacy possibly indicate that there was a conscious rational thought that the deed to be done should be done privately?

A. Yes, it could.

. . .

Q. Would he, in your opinion, have appreciated that what he was doing when he grabbed the child was grabbing a child?

A. Yes.

Q. And when he hauled her away from the area, would he appreciate that he was hauling a little child away from her own place?

Q. Yes, I believe so.

Q. And when he said "fuck or die" did he know what the words meant?
A. Yes.
Q. When he raped her, would he know that he was putting a penis into a vagina without any question of consent, and that is rape?
A. I am sure that he did.
Q. When he tied up the ligature, would he know that is a stocking around the neck and the consequences of strangulation would very likely be death?
A. Yes.
Q. So he understands the nature and quality of these acts, does he?
A. Yes.

The cross-examiner was therefore able to induce one defence psychiatrist to contradict the other defence psychiatrist with respect to whether or not the accused appreciated the nature and quality of his criminal acts.

Imposing Different Facts—Putting Your Case to the Opponent's Expert

Where there is a debate as to the facts elicited from the opponent's expert that their opinion could change if the facts he or she relied on were not to be found in the evidence.

I am a believer in the trier of fact, whether it is a judge alone or jury, being made aware of the defence position as soon as possible during the Crown's case. I do not want my opponent's case standing alone, entrenched in the minds of the trier of fact without my client's side of the story being thought about until I call a defence, by which time it may be too late. The way to do this is to put your case to the Crown witnesses in cross-examination when the opportunity presents itself. Unless it is a weak position, repeating your client's position as often as possible can only help. This approach is discussed earlier in the book.

A technique which often presents itself with respect to expert witnesses is to establish that the expert has formed his or her opinion by relying on facts which can be disputed or without taking into consideration facts which have either been established, or which the cross-examiner hopes to establish, and which should modify the expert's opinion. At the very least the cross-examiner should try to show that the expert has relied on facts that can be disputed. A common place for this technique to occur is within the hypothetical question which has been posed in examination-in-chief. The hypothetical question is based on the fact situation which the examiner-in-chief relies upon. The cross-examiner's technique is to then ask the expert to assume other facts within the hypothetical question and if given those facts were true would his opinion change or be different, that is, in his client's favour. If the witness admits that his or her opinion would so change then since the cross-examiner would be relying on those facts as being true he or she could argue before the jury that the opposing witness really confirmed the defendant's position. If the witness states that his or her opinion would not change, then the cross-examiner should ask the triers-of-fact to find that the witness is not credible because he or she has a fixed opinion which would never change and relate that attitude to any bias the witness may have.[73] See earlier segment on the hypothetical question in this chapter under heading "The Hypothetical Question."

The hypothetical aside, there is nothing to prevent you from putting your case to the expert, as for example, inviting the expert to agree with the propositions and methods which form the basis of your expert's opinion. If there are versions in the evidence which are different from what the expert was aware, bring them to the expert's attention and ask the expert if his/her opinion would change in light of this other version and would that change of opinion support your client's defence. It would be productive to lead the expert to admitting there is possibly or even probably another conclusion that he/she can not exclude or say is wrong. At the very least obtain from the witness the admission that in his/her field of expertise legitimate differences of opinion occur between qualified experts in order to leave the impression that the witness's opinion is just that—an opinion, not carved in stone.

The following is an example[74] of the expert being cross-examined on facts about which the expert was unaware and counsel attempting to persuade the expert that his conclusion may have changed if he was aware of these new facts that counsel has now brought to his attention:

Q. All of your information came from Annie, her mother and the police?
A. That's right.
Q. You did not at any time speak to Mr. Jones, the father?
A. No I did not.
Q. You did not speak to Annie's older brother, John, who is 13?
A. No.
Q. You did not speak to any of the 4 grandparents?
A. No, I didn't.
Q. You knew that just a year and a half ago the grandparents had custody of this little girl for almost nine months?
A. No, I don't believe I was given that information.
Q. You also did not speak to the aunts or uncles of this child?
A. It was not necessary in this type of investigation to ask everybody questions.
Q. It was *you* who determined that the only people you neded to speak to where the mother, the child and the police?
A. Those are the people I interviewed.

---

73 See earlier segment on Bias.
74 By Patrick J. Ducharme of Gignac, Sutts, Barristers and Solicitors, Windsor, Ontario for the Law Society of Upper Canada Continuing Education Seminar, Toronto, 1998.

Q. The picture you developed in speaking to those persons was that this child was afraid of her father?

A. Very much so.

Q. She refused to even see her father?

A. That's right.

Q. She would cling to her mother looking for both physical and emotional support?

A. Yes.

Q. I am presenting to you a note. Look at it, please, and tell us if you have seen it before?

A. I don't believe I have ever seen this.

Q. Will you agree with me that the handwriting is Annie's?

A. It may be, it looks like hers, yes, I think it is.

Q. You have seen Annie's handwriting on a number of occasions?

A. Yes.

Q. You recognize this as hers?

A. It's similar, I believe it is.

Q. Will you read the contents to the jury, please?

A. "Daddy I love you and miss you, please come home".

Q. The note conveys a message inconsistent with the information that you've received from Annie's mother, doesn't it?

A. I was not given this information by Annie'ss mom, no, but it is not inconsistent with my conclusions.

Q. I didn't ask you, Doctor, if it was inconsistent with your *conclusions*, I asked if it was inconsistent with the *information* that you got from Annie's mother?

A. I was not told that Annie had written this note, nor was I told she missed her dad.

Q. Annie's mother had told you that Annie wanted nothing to do with her father?

A. Yes.

Q. The note suggests that Annie not only loves her dad, but that she wants to be with her dad?

A. There are possibly many reasons why she would write this note.

Q. One likely reason is that she loved her dad and wanted to be with him?

A. Yes, that's possible.

Q. Did you know that Annie had packed a suitcase with a favourate doll, a favourite book and some clothing, and had attempted to run away to find her dad?

A. I was not given that information.

Q. Did you know that Annie had made approximately 25 long-distance phone calls to her father somewhere between October 1st and January 1st?

A. I wasn't told that either.

Q. So, if contrary to the *information* you had, Annie in fact tried actively to contact her dad, wrote a note telling her dad she loved, and later tried to run away to find him, would you have come to a different conclusion?

A. Hypothetically, perhaps, but there are many factors that go into an assessment of factors consistent with sexual abuse and there are many factors which point to abuse. Perhaps this information can be explained.

Q. Surely if you had this information you would have had reservations about your conclusions?

A. Like I said, there are a number of factors that go into a decision, an opinion of sexual abuse, and my conclusion would stay the same.

Q. You certainly would have taken that information into account?

A. Of course, I take a lot of information into account.

Q. And with this information you may have come to a different conclusion?

A. Hypothetically it's possible, yes.

The above is an example where counsel may also have made something out of the fact that the expert was not as thorough as he might have been in gathering information for his conclusion. However it is tactically sound to give the witness a more graceful way out from his original opinion than a frontal attack on the quality of his or her expertise when attempting to have the witness admit that his or her conclusion was or may have been wrong. When it comes to your jury address you may wish to comment on the expert's thoroughness at that time and how pride may be preventing him or her from admitting the obvious.

Controlling the Expert

Experts are usually experienced witnesses who have been cross-examined many times by experienced counsel. Like experienced police officers they probably know many of the questions you will ask before you ask them. They are very comfortable in the witness box and most often have an air of credibility, particularly if from a government lab.

It is important that you do not depart from one of the golden rules of cross-examination—controlling the witness. If you lose control of the expert, allowing the witness to go where he/she wants to go and not where you want to go, you may find yourself in rough waters from which you may never escape. When preparing to cross-examine the expert, prepare leading questions. Don't ask open-ended questions unless you don't care what the answer is, or you are certain that you will receive a desirable answer, or you have nothing to lose by taking a chance. If it becomes necessary to coax or impeach the witness you will have at the ready the expert's report, notes, his/her evidence at the Preliminary Hearing, relevant photographs, sketches and writings on the subject by other experts or the witness which are helpful to your position.

Section 7, *Canada Evidence Act*

Section 7 of the *Canada Evidence Act* states that leave of the Court must first be obtained before calling more than five experts. If, due to oversight, leave is not sought, it may be granted retroactively when it has been discovered.[75]

---

75   *R. v. N. (R.O.)* (1991), 1 B.C.A.C. 81 (B.C. C.A.).

18

Cross-Examination of the Jailhouse Informant and Analogous Witnesses

Informer recants, convict freed

HAMILTON (CP)—A man who has spent nine years in prison for murder was ordered released on bail yesterday while he waits for his appeal to resume after a jailhouse informant recanted his testimony.

Chris McCullough, 29, had been convicted of the second-degree murder of Stoney Creek school teacher Beverly Perrin. McCullough had been found guilty and sentenced to life imprisonment with no chance of parole for 18 years.

"I can't believe it," said his mother Rossi McCullough, her eyes brimming with tears upon hearing her son was free. "I just can't wait to see him."

A jailhouse informant at the 1991 trial provided explosive testimony in the court of appeal last December about his role in the case.

The 40-year-old informant claims he received more than $8,000 in reward money from police for evidence he now claims was entirely fabricated.

The inmate informant also explained how his perjured testimony got him into the witness protection program, where he received between $10,000 and $15,000 more in rent and living expenses for himself and his family.

Key witness Tammy Waltham also recanted her testimony, which pointed to McCullough's involvement, shortly after the trial, saying she had lied under police pressure to protect her husband, Larry Pearce.

Police had told her Pearce's fingerprints had been found in Perrin's car. They weren't.

McCullough's appeal is expected to resume in late March.[1]

THE VETROVEC WARNING

In preparing to cross-examine the jailhouse informant, accomplice or unsavory witness it is important to keep in mind the law relating to the Judge's charge with respect to warning the jury about this type of witness.

---

1 Toronto Daily Star, February 12th, 1999.

You want to be able to bring out the kind of evidence which qualifies for what has been described as the *Vetrovec*[2] warning and to convince the trial Judge that he or she should warn himself or herself when there is no jury, or with a jury, about how to treat the evidence of these types of witnesses.

In *Vetrovec*,[3] the Supreme Court held that the trial Judge should instruct the jury to view the evidence of an accomplice or the unsavory witness with great caution, to look for other confirming evidence before convicting the accused and to indicate to the jury any such supporting evidence.[4] Dickson J. in *Vetrovec* stated that if the trial Judge believed the witness to be trustworthy, then, regardless of whether the witness is technically an "accomplice" no warning is necessary.[5] In *R. v. Bevan*,[6] the Supreme Court not only confirmed that when a *Vetrovec* warning is given the trial Judge has a duty to bring to the jury's attention evidence that is capable of supporting the testimony of the unsavory witness but held that it was not essential to refer to a piece of supporting evidence where the evidence was extremely prejudicial and its probative value did not outweigh its prejudicial effect. In *Bevan* the Court found it appropriate to give the warning where the witness was an accessory after the fact, had a lengthy criminal record, a strong motive to lie and a benefit to be gained.

A special warning that applies to an unsavory witness applies to any category of witness, including a victim.[7]

The most recent decisions about the *Vetrovec* warning from the Supreme Court are *R. c. Khela*[8] and *R. v. Smith*.[9] In *Khela* Fish J. stated: "a truly functional approach [to Appellate review of the adequacy of a *Vetrovec* warning] must take into account the dual purpose of the *Vetrovec* warning: first, to alert the jury to the danger of relying on the unsupported evidence of unsavory witnesses and to explain the reasons for special scrutiny of their testimony; and secondly, in appropriate cases, to give the jury the tools necessary to identify evidence capable of enhancing the trustworthiness of those witnesses." In *R. v. Smith* Fish J. stated: "In order to assess the risk of accepting testimony from an unsavory witness a jury must understand the reasons for special scrutiny. . . This requires identifying for the jury the

---

2   *R. v. Vetrovec* (1982), 67 C.C.C. (2d) 1 (S.C.C.).

3   *Ibid.*

4   In looking for confirmatory evidence of an unsavory witness's testimony, the trial Judge is to tell the jury this evidence needs to be independent and not tainted by its connection to the witness and it is to be material evidence related to an important and relevant aspect of the impugned testimony. See *R. v. Khela, infra* at paras. 39-43.

5   *Vetrovec, supra*, at p. 11.

6   (1993), 82 C.C.C. (3d) 310 (S.C.C.).

7   *R. v. Patrick* (2005), 202 C.C.C. (3d) 209 (Ont. C.A.).

8   (2009), 2009 SCC 4 at para. 47. In *Khela* the Court observed that where the guilt of the accused rested substantially on the testimony of a single witness of doubtful credibility, the danger of a wrongful conviction is strong, para. 2.

9   (2009) (*sub nom. R. v. James*), 2009 SCC 5.

characteristics of the witness that bring his or her credibility into serious question."

The courts have noted that ordinarily the trial Judge has a broad discretion whether to give a *Vetrovec* warning and the appellate courts will not be quick to interfere with that discretion, but that there are cases where a *Vetrovec* warning is required.[10] Two considerations are important when deciding whether to give the warning: the credibility of the witness and the importance of the witness's evidence to the case.[11] Considerations such as failure of the defence counsel to request a warning, the strength of the Crown's case apart from the evidence of the witness, the existence of confirmatory evidence, and the ability of the jury to properly assess the evidence of the witness absent a warning are all relevant to the application of the curative provisions in section 686(1)(*b*)(iii) of the *Code*.[12]

Marc Rosenberg[13] has written that "it is not whether the trial Judge personally finds the witness trustworthy but whether there are factors which experience teaches that the witness's story be approached with caution," for example: "involvement in criminal activities, a motive to lie by reason of connection to the crime or to the authorities, unexplained delay in coming forward with the story, providing different accounts on other occasions, lies under oath, and similar considerations." He further states that "the trial Judge must assess the importance of the witness to the Crown's case. If the witness plays a relatively minor role in the proof of guilt it is probably unnecessary to burden the jury with a special caution and then review the confirmatory evidence. However, the more important the witness the greater the duty on the judge to give the caution. At some point, as where the witness plays a central role in proof of guilt, the warning is mandatory."[14]

---

10 *Bevan, supra,* at pp. 326-327; *R. v. Brooks* (1998), 129 C.C.C. (3d) 227 (Ont. C.A.), reversed (2000), 30 C.R. (5th) 201 (S.C.C.), per Lakin, J.A. In *Brooks,* the *Vetrovec* warning was held to be appropriate as the witness was a jailhouse informant with a lengthy criminal record who was an informant on a prior occasion claiming the accused had confessed to him. For other appellate cases where the warning was held to be appropriate, see *R. v. Sauvé* (2004), (sub nom. *R. v. Trudel*) 182 C.C.C. (3d) 321 (Ont. C.A.), leave to appeal refused 2005 CarswellOnt 19, 2005 CarswellOnt 20 (S.C.C.); *R. v. Lamirande* (2002), 164 C.C.C. (3d) 299 (Man. C.A.); *R. v. Baltrusaitis* (2002), 162 C.C.C. (3d) 539 (Ont. C.A.); *R. v. Patrick* (2005), 202 C.C.C. (3d) 209 (Ont. C.A.); *R. v. Campbell,* 163 C.C.C. (3d) 485, 2002 CarswellNS 109 (N.S. C.A.).
11 *Brooks, supra,* per Laskin J.A.
12 *Brooks, supra,* per Laskin J.A.
13 *R. v. Bevan, supra,* per Major J.A.; "Developments in the Law of Evidence: 1992-1993 Term" (1994), 5 Sup. Ct. L. Rev. (2d) 421 at 463 by Marc Rosenberg [now Rosenberg J.A.].
14 Marc Rosenberg's paper, "Developments in the Law of Evidence: 1992-1993 Term" (1994), 5 Sup.Ct.L.Rev. (2d) 421 at 463, was quoted with approval when *R. v. Brooks* was decided in the Supreme Court of Canada (2000), 141 C.C.C. (3d) 321 (S.C.C.). See also *R. v. Marks* (2000), 48 O.R. (3d) 161 (Ont. C.A.).

A *Vetrovec* warning is not to be given with respect to defence witnesses.[15]

The inquiry into the wrongful conviction of Guy Paul Morin[16] put the role of the jailhouse informant under a microscope. Commissioner Kaufman not only heard evidence surrounding the weaknesses of the evidence by the two jailhouse informants who testified as to an overheard confession by Mr. Morin in his cell, he also heard evidence from various experts relating to the credibility of this type of witness and what safeguards could be employed against potentially false evidence. These experts included defence counsel and prosecutors from different common law countries. As a result the Commissioner made a number of recommendations regarding jailhouse informants, some of which will be alluded to here. Commissioner Kaufman defines in-custody informers in his Recommendation 37 as those who "are detained by authorities, either awaiting trial or serving a sentence of imprisonment." He noted in that recommendation that "the danger of an unscrupulous witness manufacturing evidence for personal benefit is a significant one."

It should be noted that Recommendation 52 from the Morin Inquiry also refers to analogous persons to jailhouse informants, such as a person facing charges. In *Vetrovec*, Dickson J. suggested witnesses should not be pigeon-holed into categories but that the trial judge should look at all the factors that might impair the credibility of a witness and then, if in his judgment the credit of the witness is such that the jury should be cautioned, then he may instruct accordingly.

Any experienced defence counsel knows that those who have lived criminal lives, who have learned to survive by their wits, have become experienced and believable liars. They can fool the police, the Crowns, judges and juries and this fact should be underscored in your final submissions, if not during the trial. As one witness at the inquiry stated about jailhouse informants: "The concept of truth really had no meaning to some of these people. They were to a large part, sociopaths." Evidence at the inquiry from the experts disclosed that jailhouse informants were creative, driven, manipulative, employing their street sense to fabricate believable lies.

There are many reasons why a jailhouse informant would lie: protection against outstanding charges or potential charges he or she could be facing, by seeking withdrawal of the charges; assistance with immigration problems; immunity or receipt of a light sentence; beneficial treatment in custody, including better food or other conveniencess; financial benefits such as a reward, future indemnity, as for example, payment of a past debt or to family; love of publicity; to divert suspicion from themselves or someone close; to minimize his/her role in a crime by enlarging the role of

---

15   *R. v. Hoilett* (1991), 3 O.R. (3d) 449 (Ont. C.A.) at 451-52.
16   The Commission on Proceedings Involving Guy Paul Morin.

others; being moved from a maximum security to medium security where life is easier (knowing that as a Crown witness he/she has to be moved for safety reasons); early parole; or it may be that the informant dislikes or is angry at the accused for any number of reasons including a slight which the accussed is unaware or becauses of the nature of the charge.[17] See "The Lying Witness" in Chapter, "Cross-Examination of Certain Categories of Witnesses."

R. v. Brooks[18] signals acceptance by the Ontario Court of Appeal of a number of observations by Commissioner Kaufman inquiring into the wrongful conviction of Guy Paul Morin where the evidence of two jailhouse informants played a central role. Laskin J.A. did not feel it was necessary for the purpose of deciding the appeal to adopt the recommendations of Justice Kaufman but he did recognize the validity of certain conclusions that were reached by the Commissioner.

Justice Laskin pointed to a number of reasons which underlie the need for a *Vetrovec* warning: the concern that without it a jury may not appreciate how unreliable a jailhouse informant can be and the jurors may be far too accepting of the testimony of these witnesses at face value; the jurors may associate the informants with the prosecution and assume the Crown would only call witneses who were truthful; the informants may make good witnesses because of experience in testifying and may have few scruples in perjuring themselves; they are highly motivated to testify because of potential rewards for doing so and may be able to gather information about the accused which makes their evidence more plausible; and the jurors may not be able to properly assess the credibility of the jailhouse informant's testimony as they are unlikely to be familiar with the workings of the jail ssystem and find it hard to accept that informants can gather so much information about the accused or the alleged crime from sources other than from converations with the accused; it would also be difficult to refute the evidence of a jailhouse informant because often no one else is present during his alleged conversation with the accused.

Laskin J.A., taking a lead from the Kaufman Inquiry, expressed that the Court should be concerned about an informant's motivation to lie whether he or she be in jail or not; that the informant's proclaimed "good citizen intentions in coming forward because of repugnance towards the crime charged or because a family member was a victim of a similar occurrence or because of lack of remorse by the accused should be viewed

---

17 For factors bearing on credibility, see *R. v. Bevan, supra*, per Major, J.A.; "Developments in the Law of Evidence: 1992-1993 Term" (1994), 5 Sup. Ct. L. Rev. (2d) 421 at 463, by Marc Rosenberg [now Rosenberg J.A.].

18 *Supra.*

skeptically. In the vast majority of the cases it is a benefit, real or perceived, for the informant or some third party that motivates the co-operation."[19]

The Successful Informant

"As I understand it, he made a hell of a stiff bargain before he turned state's evidence."

Drawing by Garret Price. ©1942, 1970 The New Yorker Magazine, Inc.

© The New Yorker Magazine.

When you are unable to point to a motive to lie or exaggerate, make it clear to the Judge or jury that there may well be a hidden motive that you are unable to identify, and perhaps only a psychiatrist may do so. It would be unfair to ask an accused to know so much about the informant's life so as to be able to ferret out a motive to lie. The Court should be reminded that the burden of proof is on the Crown, the defence need prove nothing, that burden never shifts to the defence, and for the accused to have to prove a motive would be to reverse the burden of proof. It is of interest to note that

---

19 "Report of the 1989-90 Los Angeles County Grand Jury Investigation of the Involvement of Jailhouse Informants in the Criminal Justice System in Los Angeles County" (1990), at p. 563.

Commissioner Kaufman in his report at p. 563 in rejecting the jailhouse informants' evidence that they were motivated to testify by their repugnance towards the crime stated: "Their attitude demonstrates that an informant's motive to lie may not be obvious—indeed, it may often be less conspicuous than that of the defendant."

Recommendation 47 by Commissioner Kaufman regarding disclosure by the Crown with respect to in-custody informers underscores that there should be a heavy onus on the Crown to make complete disclosure. The details of that recommendation are helpful to counsel in preparation for their potential cross-examination of witnesses in this area. That recommendation states:

> The current Crown policy reflects that the dangers of using in-custody inform-
> ers in a prosecution give rise to a heavy onus on Crown counsel to make
> complete disclosure. Without limiting the extent of that onus, the policy lists
> disclosure items that should be reviewed to ensure full and fair disclosure. The
> disclosure policy is generally commendable. Some fine-tuning of the items
> listed is required to give effect to the onus to make complete disclosure. The
> items should read, in the least:
>
> 1. The criminal record of the in-custody informer including, where accessible
>   to the police or Crown, the synopses relating to any convictions.[20]
> 2. Any information in the prosecutors' possession or control respecfting the
>   circumstances in which the informer may have previously testified for the
>   Crown ass an informer, including, at a minimum, the date, location and
>   Court where the previous testimony was given. (The police, in taking the
>   informer's statement, should inquire into any prior experiences testifying
>   for either the provincial or federal Crown as an informer or as a witness
>   generally.)
> 3. Any offers or promises made by police, corrections authorities, Crown
>   counsel, or a witness protection program to the informer or person associated
>   with the informer in consideration for the information in the present case.
> 4. Any benefit given to the informer, members of the informer's family or any
>   other person associated with the informer, or any benefits sought by such
>   persons, as consideration for their co-operation with authorities, including
>   but not limited to those kinds of benefits already listed in the Crown Policy
>   Manual.
> 5. As noted earlier, any arrangements providing for a benefit (as set out above)
>   should, absent exceptional circumstances, be reduced to writing and signed
>   and/or be recorded on videotape. Such arrangements should be approved
>   by a Director or Crown Operations or the In-Custody Informer Committee

---

20 In *R. v. Styles* (December 4, 2003), Clark J., [2003] O.J. No. 5824 (Ont. S.C.J.), the Court
    refused to order disclosure of any and all occurrence reports with respect to certain Crown
    witnesses whose credibility was in issue as they were not created in the course of or
    otherwise related to the investigation leading to the prosecution and were third party
    records which therefore had to be sought by way of an *O'Connor* application.

and disclosed to the defence prior to receiving the testimony of the witness (or earlier, in accordance with *Stinchcombe*).

6. Copies of the notes of all police officers, corrections authorities or Crown counsel who made, or were present during, any promises of benefits to, any negotiations respecting benefits with, or any benefits sought by, an in-custody informer. There may be additional notes of officers or corrections authorities which may also be relevant to the in-custody informer's testimony at trial.

7. The circumstances under which the in-custody informer and his or her information came to the attention of the authorities.

8. If the informer will not be called as a Crown witness, a disclosure obligation still exists, subject to the informer's privilege.

Recommendation 41 deals with matters to be considered by the Crown in assessing informer reliability before deciding to call that individual as a witness. Some of the matters referred to are also helpful to counsel in preparing to cross-examine this type of witness. This recommendation states:

The current Crown policy lists matters which Crown counsel may take into account in assessing the reliability of an in-custody informer. Those matters do not adequately address the assessment of reliability and place undue reliance upon matters which do little to enhance the reliability of an informer's claim. The Crown policy should be amended to reflect that the prosecutor, the supervisor or any Committee constituted should consider the following elements:

1. The extent to which the statement is confirmed in the sense earlier defined;

2. The specificity of the alleged statement. For example, a claim that the accused said "I killed A.B." is easy to make but extremely difficult for any accused to disprove;

3. The extent to which the statement contains details or leads to the discovery of evidence known only to the perpetrator;[21]

4. The extent to which the statement contains details which could reasonably be accessed by the in-custody informer, other than through inculpatory statements by the accused. This consideration need involve an assessment of the information reasonably accessible to the in-custody informer, through media reports, availability of the accused's Crown brief in jail, etc. Crown counsel should be mindful that, historically, some informers have shown great ingenuity in securing information thought to be unaccessible to them. Furthermore, some informers have converted details communicated by the accused in the context of an exculpatory statement into details which purport to prove the making of an inculpatory statement;

5. The informer's general character, which may be evidenced by his or her criminal record or other disreputable or dishonest conduct known to the authorities;

---

21 *R. v. Sauvé* (2004), 182 C.C.C. (3d) 321 (Ont. C.A.) is an example of where the Court noted that there was "little detail" in the statements attributed to the accused by the unsavoury witness.

6. Any request the informer has made for benefits or special treatment (whether or not agreed to) and any promises which may have been made (or discussed with the informer) by a person in authority in connection with the provision of the statement or an agreement to testify;
7. Whether the informer has, in the past, given reliable information to the authorities;
8. Whether the informer has previously claimed to have received statements while in custody. This may be relevant not only to the informer's reliability or unreliability but, more generally, to the issue whether the public interest would be served by utilizing a recidivist informer who previous traded information for benefits.
9. Whether the informer has previously testified in any Court proceeding, whether as a witness for the prosecution or the defence or on his or her behalf, and any findings in relation to the accuracy and reliability of that evidence, if known;
10. Whether the informer made some written or other record of the words alleged sopken by the accused and, if so, whether the record was made contemporaneous to the alleged statement of the accused;
11. The circumstances under which the informer's report of the alleged statement was taken (*e.g.* report made immediately after the statement was made, report made to more than one officer, etc.);
12. The manner in which the report of the statement was taken by the police (*e.g.* through use of non-leading questions, thorough report of words spoken by the accused, thorough investigation of circumstances which might suggest opportunity or lack of opportunity to fabricate a statement). Police should be encouraged to address all of the matters relating to the Crown's assessment of reliability with the informer at the earliest opportunity. Police should also be encouraged to take an informer's report of an alleged in-custody statement under oath, recorded on audio or videotape, in accordance with the guidelines set down in *R. v. K.G.B.*[22] However, in considering items 10 to 12, Crown counsel should be mindful that an accurate, appropriate and timely interview by police of the informer may not adequately address the dangers associated with this kind of evidence;
13. Any other known evidence that may attest to or diminish the credibility of the informer, including the presence or absence of any relationship between the accused and the informer;
14. Any relevant information contains in any available registry of informers.

Other informants such as accomplices can be motivated by some of the above-mentioned reasons, including such benefit as an annual stipend, moving expenses, bail consideration, or gaining entrance into the witness protection program (some can start their criminal lifestyle again without a past record). Even where police and witnesses deny that immunity from prosecution was offered, the Ontario Court of Appeal has held that the jury could find the witness was giving his testimony with the expectation of

---

22   (1993), 79 C.C.C. (3d) 257 (S.C.C.).

obtaining immunity from prosecution even though there was no expressed promise of immunity.[23] The issue is not just whether the informant received a benefit but whether he/she hoped to receive a benefit.[24]

The Unhappy Informant

"Informant 4972 is unhappy with his new identity."

Trial Diplomacy Journal, Cartoon Album, David M. Freedman, ed. © Court Practice Journal, 1980.

The Crown mantra at trial that the informant should be believed because he/she is relating details that only the real culprit could have conveyed or because the informant has first-hand knowledge because he or she was a co-participant in the crime, does not always accord with reality. Jurors have difficulty understanding the loneliness, the isolation and the need for human contact that impacts on an innocent defendant making him/her susceptible to the influences of those experienced prisoners who know how to use the system. Such informants can easily gain information from the inexperienced and lonely accused and twist exculpatory information into inculpatory evidence.

---

23 *R. v. Symonds* (1983), 9 C.C.C. (3d) 225 (Ont. C.A.).
24 *R. v. Brooks, supra.*

Informants are also known to have obtained information to use against an accused from media reports, from family and friends, jail visitors, trials and transcripts, co-accused, through impersonation; and through materials left by defence counsel with the client such as Crown disclosure. Commissioner Kaufman noted in his Recommendation 41 that "some informers have shown great ingenuity in securing information thought to be inaccessible to them. Furthermore, some informers have converted details communicated by the accused in the context of an exculpatory statement into details which purport to prove the making of an inculpatory statement." Some informants have been informants on prior occasions for benefit and are wiser for the experience.

When the witness is awaiting a sentence on his own charges at the time of testifying against the accused, his motive to carry on with his lies is strengthened as the accomplice-witness does not wish to upset the police or prosecution and spoil the bargain he has made. Such a circumstance is a factor for the Court in assessing the witness's credibility.[25] The calling of an accomplice against whom there are unresolved legal proceedings, for example, a key Crown witness who had pleaded guilty but had yet to be sentenced, was condemned in the *United States of America v. Schulman*, 2001 SCC 21 and quoted with approval in *R. v. Dowe* (2008), 235 C.C.C. (3d) 289 (S.C.C.); *R. v. Williams* (1974), 21 C.C.C. (2d) 1 (Can. Ct. Martial App. Ct.), leave to appeal refused (1974), 21 C.C.C. (2d) 1n (S.C.C.); *United States v. Shephard* (1976), [1977] 2 S.C.R. 1067 (S.C.C.). However, if the witness testifies against the accused after he has been sentenced, the prosecutor often tells the jury that even if the witness was lying to the police prior to trial, as defence counsel contends, the reason to do so no longer exists. This submission really does not accord with common sense. When possible, defence counsel must bring to the jury's attention through cross-examination that the witness has testified under oath at the preliminary inquiry against the accused and to change his or her testimony under oath later at trial could lead to a charge of perjury or a charge of giving inconsistent evidence. Often the prosecution has taken a sworn statement from the accomplice to impress this future witness with the seriousness of his or her accusations. There is usually an accompanying warning by the police when the statement is taken that if the witness goes back on his sworn statements he would be subject to a perjury charge. Obviously the witness does have reason to carry on with his lies after he has been sentenced. As well, the police or the Crown may have told the witness that to remove his/ her pointing finger from the accused later would result in a charge of public mischief or obstructing justice. The informer who changes his/her story at trial also knows that any bargain he or she made with the police, such as a

---

25   *R. v. Cruikshanks* (1990), 58 C.C.C. (3d) 26 (B.C. C.A.).

monetary reward or being placed in a witness protection program, would be lost. All of these motives to lie should be canvassed with the witness.

In approaching the informant, accomplice, or stool pigeon it is obviously important to explore with the witness and others, particularly at the preliminary hearing stage, any motive to lie and any possible means of the informant gaining knowledge other than from the accused or from participation in the crime. Obtain newspaper and other media reports of the offence from which the informant may have gained knowledge. Has the informant been an informant on prior occasions and if so was he/she reliable and was that evidence given in return for a benefit? Obtain, if possible, transcripts of the witness's earlier testimony as an informant. Does the informant have a psychiatric history which gives him/her a distorted sense of reality?[26] The answer to this question may only come after an application to the Court for disclosure of third party records. Obtain disclosure of the witness's criminal record, outstanding charges as well as occurrence reports with respect to prior police dealings, and supplementary reports, and other character evidence which points to disreputable and dishonest conduct. Inquire about the witness's discreditable associations and way of life. Is there available evidence that on past occasions the witness has lied under oath? These are questions, the answers to which could contribute to establishing a foundation for the judge to give a *Vetrovec*[27] warning.

Was there any request to a person in authority by the witness for benefits or special treatment for himself or a member of his/her family or anyone? Inquire of the Crown whether there in fact was any agreement between the witness and Crown or police and if it was in writing or audio or videotaped, or recorded in police officers' notebooks. Request a copy of these records. Similarly, obtain the Correction authorities' notes or records that relate to any such agreement. Ascertain how the informant came to the attention of the authorities. Was there any unexplained delay in coming forward with the story? Obtain copies of all statements and utterances by the informant, including debriefings, and any recordings of same. They may reflect internal inconsistencies or inconsistencies with the witness's testimony or be inconsistent with other credible evidence on material points. The witness may be adding to his/her statements each time he/she is interviewed and they may show that the witness has been influenced by promises or threats. Obtain if possible transcripts of the snitch's Court appearances as statements may have been made by the Crown, defence counsel or the witness on those dates which may provide ammunition for cross-examination, such as comments regarding a plea bargain. Did the witness change his or her story to only later implicate the accused? There may be individuals

---

26 This was one of the factors that led to Laskin, J.A. in *R. v. Brooks, supra*, to conclude that a *Vetrovec* warning should have been given by the trial Judge.

27 *Supra*, at p. 326-327.

you can locate, such as a disenchanted spouse, ex-lover, family member or former business associate, that are so upset at the witness that they will be willing to help the defence with ammunition against that witness. Such persons may at least be able to give bad character evidence against the informer.[28]

It will be important to note whether there is any confirming evidence of the informant's testimony. Commissioner Kaufman in his <u>Recommendation 39</u> stated that confirmation should be credible evidence or information, independent of the in-custody informer, which significantly supports the position that the inculpatory aspects of the proposed evidence were not fabricated. He also stated that one in-custody informer does not provide confirmation for another. It will be important to note how much detail is in the alleged inculpatory statement. It is easy to fabricate a statement with little detail. However, if the statement leads to the discovery of evidence known only to the culprit, the alleged statement obviously becomes significant evidence against the accused.[29]

In <u>Recommendation 67</u> Commissioner Kaufman stated that the trial judge should consider cautioning the jury in terms stronger than those often contained in a *Vetrovec* warning and do so immediately before or after the evidence is tendered by the prosecution, as well as during the charge to the jury.

In the following cross-examination, the witness Howard Smith testified for the Crown in the prosecution of a first degree murder charge involving the shooting death of a police officer during a break and enter.[30] The accused's defence was that he was not the man. In examination-in-chief, Smith testified in part that the accused had beaten him on his legs with a "little club" because Smith had held back some of the money from a different break and enter they were both involved in, and the accused said to Smith during the beating: "I should do the same thing to you as I did to that pig." The Crown, in order to lessen the impact on cross-examination and save the credibility of Smith by volunteering potentially damaging evidence in chief, led this witness through his criminal convictions and the fact that it was the witness who approached the police with the information in return for leniency with respect to an outstanding charge.

---

28 See Chapter, "Character Witnesses."

29 In *R. v. Sauvé* (2004), 182 C.C.C. (3d) 321 (Ont. C.A.) the Court held that it was inadmissible as oath-helping for a police officer to testify that the informant was the best informant he had used in 31 years and his recollection of events was uncanny. It was also inadmissible for the informant to testify that in addition to hearing the accused make inculpatory statements, other inmates had confessed to him in the past and subsequently pleaded guilty. The fact others confessed to him did not prove the accused confessed to him or that he was truthful because others pleaded guilty.

30 *R. v. York,* before Mr. Justice R. Clarke, Newmarket Assizes, February 26, 1992.

Smith is clearly a despicable person. There is no need for the cross-examiner to "float like a butterfly and sting like a bee." Defence counsel's objective is to make the jury quickly despise the witness, show up the inconsistencies in his story and that he is prepared to lie for gain and to detail his immoral lifestyle. Notwithstanding that the Crown Attorney went through the pro forma questions regarding Smith's criminal record, the cross-examiner explored in greater detail some of the convictions to paint an even more unflattering picture of the witness, as for example: by noting that Smith's conviction for obstruct justice meant that he lied in a matter relating to the justice system and that his conviction for communicating for the purposes of prostitution meant that he was a male prostitute and describing what that entailed. It was also brought out that he was charged with breaking into his own mother's home. Note that when there was a significant pause after a question was put the cross-examiner would highlight that by stating: "it's not a tough question."

The depth of preparation for the cross-examination is reflected when defence counsel questions the witness from a transcript of a plea of guilty by the witness. It was important that counsel elicited the fact that Smith had sworn an affidavit under oath for the prosecution to the truth of his story and was advised that if he changed his testimony from what was in the affidavit he could be charged with obstruct justice or perjury. The witness answers would be defence counsel's response to the Crown saying to the jury in his or her summation that there is no longer any motive for the witness to lie in Court because he or she had successfully made their deal before testifying. Defence counsel's position would be that the witness was boxed in by his affidavit and could not change his story at trial even if he wanted to.

Q. Mr. Burrow read out to you your criminal record, and one of those convictions was for attempt to obstruct justice. Is that correct?

A. That's correct.

Q. In other words, you attempted to defeat the course of justice.

A. That is correct.

Q. By something you did, by some lie.

A. That is correct.

Q. That relates to the justice system. That relates to courts. Is that right?

A. That is correct.

Q. And in 1987, you were convicted for communicating for the purposes of prostitution. Correct?

A. That is correct.

Q. You were a male prostitute.

A. That is right.

Q. Yes. And what did you do as a male prostitute?

A. I had sex for money.

Q. With men.

A. With women too.

Q. And with men.

A. That is correct.

Q. All right. And did you do that by standing out in the streets down in the tenderloin area of Toronto?

A. That is correct.

Q. And cars would come by and stop and you would hop in their cars. Is that right?

A. That is correct.

Q. And you didn't just kiss these men, did you? As a male prostitute.

A. I don't understand what you're saying, sir.

Q. What did you do to these men in the cars?

A. I was company, sir.

Q. Pardon?

A. Companying [sic].

Q. You were companing [sic].

A. Hired company.

Q. You were more than just hired company, you were hired sexual company. Isn't that correct?

A. Not always sir, no.

Q. Not always. Was there times that you were hired sexual company as a prostitute?

A. That is correct.

Q. And what did you do? What acts of sex did you commit? As a male prostitute. It's not a tough question. What acts of sex did you commit as a male prostitute?

A. All kinds of things.

Q. Do you find this funny?

A. Yes I do.

Q. Well just answer the question. There's a man charged here with first degree murder. It's not a funny situation. What acts of sex did you commit with men?

A. All kinds of acts of sex.

Q. Like what?

A. Like stuff that's just not public information, sir.

Q. We're all grown-ups here, we've heard it before.

A. I don't . . .

Q. At least a number of us have heard it before.

A. I had sex.

Q. Sex.

A. Sex.

Q. Okay. Did you take men's private parts into your mouth?

A. No I didn't.

Q. Did you commit oral sex on men?

A. No I didn't.

Q. Did they commit oral sex on you?

A. Yes they did.

Q. Yes. Did you commit anal intercourse with men?

A. No I didn't.

Q. Did they commit anal intercourse with you?

A. No I didn't. And I wear a condom too.

Q. There are also some outstanding charges in Nova Scotia, isn't that correct, against you?

A. That is incorrect.

Q. Did you not tell—in the video statement to the police—that there were outstanding charges against you in Nova Scotia?

A. That is correct.

Q. And what were they for?

A. Break and enter.

Q. How many?

A One count.

Q Break and enter to—against whom?

A. House.

Q. Whose house?

A. I forget.

Q. It was your mother's.

A. Was my . . .

Q. Two counts of break and enter against your mother's house. Isn't that correct?

A. That is correct. Excuse me, can I sit on this stool here.

THE COURT: No stand there, you'll be fine. The reporter has to hear what you say, that's why the microphone is there.

COUNSEL: Q. You've indicated it was you who approached the police with this information about Ronald York. Right?

A. That is correct.

Q. And you were in jail in Brampton at the time.

A. That is—that is incorrect.

Q. Where were you?

A. I was detained at the West Detention Centre, sir.

Q. You were charged with break, enter and theft.

A. That is correct.

Q. You could not get bail.

A. That is correct.

Q. And you told the police that you had read that Ronald York was arrested in March of '88. Is that right?

A. That is correct.

Q. And you came forward in September of '88.

A. That is correct.

Q. Some six months later.

A. That is correct.

Q. And you told the court here today that you did that because you were trying to make some deal—deal for yourself. Is that right?

A. That is correct.

Q. But when you testified at the preliminary hearing, you weren't so honest about that, were you? You weren't prepared when asked whether there was—you weren't prepared to admit that there was an advantage in it for

you. Remember that at the preliminary hearing? Well, maybe I'll read it to
you if you're having some problems.

A. Thank you.

Q. Page 17, Your Honour, line 25. Preliminary hearing was April 12, 1989.
Remember testifying in this courtroom preliminary hearing? Not this particular—sorry, this courthouse.

A. Yes, that's correct.

Q. Line 25.
"Question: Well, do I understand from what you said that, you did not get
any advantage as a result of coming forward and speaking to Staff Sergeant
Sorel?
Answer: That's correct."
Recall being asked those questions and giving those answers?

A. That is correct.

Q. So did you lie then?

A. No, I just interpreted the wrong way.

Q. You interpreted it the wrong way.

A. Yes. It was a court . . .

Q. Well I'm sorry, what—what was so difficult about it?

A. It was a court . . . .

Q. So how—how could you—let me read it again.

A. Okay.

Q. Help you out.

A. Okay.

Q. "Well, do I understand from what you said that, you did not get any
advantage as a result of coming forward and speaking to Staff Sergeant
Sorel?
Answer: That's correct."
Now, are you saying you misunderstood that?

A. No I didn't.

Q. No.

A. I didn't misunderstand that.

Q. So today you told the court quite openly . . .

A. Mmhm.

Q. . . . that you were looking for an advantage. And to get . . .

A. That's correct.

Q. And you got one. Correct?

A. That's correct.

Q. Okay. And I suggest to you what's happened is that since you've testified,
somebody along the way has told you, "Hey, just a second. You've got to
shape up. We want the truth. We know different." Someone on—either
from the police or the Crown's office has told you that they want the truth
out of you. Isn't that right? And not to lie like you did here.

A. My girlfriend tells me that too.

Q. Okay. So you're—you're a pretty well-known liar elsewhere, are you? Is
that right? Your girlfriend says you're a liar.

A. No, my girlfriend tells me to be honest.

Q. Well, she must be concerned about your honesty to tell you that.

A. No.

Q. Right?

A. No, we have an honest relationship.

Q. Well, we'll get to your relationship. Now, just before—just before you got this one day in jail, you received a 14-month sentence in Owen Sound for break, enter and theft. Is that right?

A. That is correct.

Q. What happened in this—the break, enter and theft in Brampton?

A. I got 14 months for break and enter.

Q. No no, not in—we're talking about the one in Brampton.

A. Oh Brampton. I got one day time served.

Q. Yeah, but what were the facts?

A. Facts were some people went away to Montreal, I was staying at that place for a while, some of my property was there when they went away. I needed some of my property, I went into the house illegally and when I was in there, I think I took a bottle of cologne, and I pleaded guilty to theft. Break and enter and theft.

Q. To what, cologne?

A. I—I—I pleaded guilty to the charge that they charged me with.

Q. All right. Well, what did you steal?

A. I stole cologne.

Q. That's it?

A. Yeah.

Q. Whose house was it that you broke into?

A. I can't recall.

Q. Well, were they friends of yours?

A. No. I just met.

Q. Where did you meet him?

A. Downtown Toronto.

Q. Downtown Toronto?

A. That's correct.

Q. Where?

A. At Yonge—Yonge and Bloor.

Q. Where on Yonge and Bloor? On the street?

A. No.

Q. Where?

A. At a bar.

Q. At a bar.

A. Yeah.

Q. And what, man, woman, two men?

A. Men.

Q. Two women?

A. Men.

Q. Two men?

A. Yeah.

Q. And well, what happened?

A. I was on the street and they offered me a place to stay for a few days till I got my act together.

Q. And is that why you went back? Just for a place to stay?

A. I don't follow you, sir.

Q. Did you go back for sex?

A. No I didn't.

Q. You remember pleading guilty to these charges in Brampton?

A. That's correct.

Q. And you remember that the Crown had gone into chambers, out of court to see the judge on your behalf to—for the purposes of telling the judge about your cooperation in this case.

A. To my knowledge, that is correct.

Q. All right. And you pleaded guilty that you broke, entered a dwelling house in Brampton on the 13th of August, 1988. Is that right? Recall that?

A. That is—that is correct.

Q. And you know what happens on a plea of quilty, a—the Crown attorney stands up and reads in a set of facts, and your lawyer after consulting with you on those facts that have been read in, then tells the court that those facts are accepted on the plea of guilty. That right?

A. That is correct.

Q. And then submissions are made by the Crown as to the sentence, and submissions are made by the defence lawyer, and then the judge makes up his mind. Right?

A. That is correct.

Q. And just going to read to you part of that transcript. Page 27, the Crown says that you met the two victims, Mr. Moran and Mr. Pollard. Your original meeting occurred in a bar in downtown Toronto, that as a result of their meeting, you were invited to return to their home in Brampton. Right?

A. That's correct.

Q. You agree with that? Okay. As a result of the invitation, you spent the night. Correct? Is that right?

A. Yeah, that's correct.

Q. And on or about August the 11th, these men left their residence for Montreal, locked their residence behind them when they left. On August the 14th one of them returns, and he finds that someone's been in the house, and he noted there's equipment or a V.C.R. specifically that was missing. Remember that being read in?

A. I don't remember, but it was probably read in. And since it's written in . . .

Q. Yes.

A. . . . probably true.

Q. Well, . . .

A. It's probably true. I don't recall words, but . . .

Q. August 31st, the other gentleman came back, found there were some clothing, some stereo equipment, jewellery and some cheques that were missing. Recall that?

A. I don't recall the wording or it, no.

Q. Do you want me to show it to you . . .

A. I recall pleading . . .

Q. Are you prepared to accept what I say as being—that I'm reading it accurately from the transcript?

A. I'm prepared to accept that whole book in your hand.

Q. All right. Well—and then several days after the incident, says three cheques were returned to one of the gentleman's bank—the ones that had been taken from the residence—and the cheques were all made out payable to you. Right?

A. That is correct.

Q. Okay. So there's no doubt about it, witness, you weren't being quite frank with this court when you said it was only cologne that was taken. Right?

A. No sir.

Q. You agree with me.

A. No I don't.

Q. No you don't.

A. I took them cheques when . . .

Q. And then—I'm sorry?

A. I took them cheques when I was staying at the residence, not when they went away.

Q. And did those gentlemen make the cheques payable to you?

A. No, I made them payable to me, sir.

Q. And on this—when you were arrested, it says you admitted to taking some of the articles, not all, but that you were in the presence of another individual who's named in this transcript, and in effect, were saying that both of you were involved in this—this break and enter. Is that correct? You want me to name you the name to refresh your memory?

A. Billy Keating?

Q. Yeah. You remember the total of the cheques?

A. You mean all three of them together, sum total or separate cheques?

Q. Mmhm. No, let's—let's just go for the total.

A. I say around in the area of $1500.

Q. Well, you're a little high. $1200.

A. Okay.

Q. And then there's some more discussions, and your lawyer stands up and says to the court at that time you were working as a male prostitute. Is that right?

A. That is correct.

Q. And after the submissions were made, the court found that you went there for the purposes of performing an act of prostitution. Isn't that correct?

A. Can you repeat that, sir?

Q. Says after submissions were made, the court found that you went there to perform an act of prostitution.

A. I do not recall that.

Q. Well, just let me show it to you. I don't want you to think that I'm misleading you.

A. Thank you.

Q. Have I read that correctly? From page 39?

A. That's the court saying that to me.

Q. That's—that's part of the court's finding. Isn't that right?

A. That's what the court is saying to me, yes. That's not what I'm saying to the court.

Q. All right. Now, you—you swore an affidavit for the Crown with respect to your evidence, right? With respect to your statement.

A. That is correct.

Q. And you know that once you—if you were to change your affidavit or go back on your affidavit, you would be in big trouble, because it's a sworn statement.

A. That is correct.

Q. You can be charged with perjury, obstruct justice, any number of such charges.

A. Yes sir.

Q. And for someone who sells his body to men and steals from his mother and has obstructed justice before, swearing this false affidavit means nothing to you, does it?

A. I don't understand what you're saying, sir.

Q. You don't mind swearing a false affidavit. That wouldn't bother you, would it?

A. I swore it to be the truth.

Q. I know you swore it to be the truth, I'm suggesting to you it's false, and—and—and it wouldn't bother you to swear a false affidavit.

A. That is your opinion, sir.

Q. Now, this beating that you say that Mr. York inflicted on you, vicious?

A. Pardon?

Q. Pretty vicious beating?

A. It was rage.

Q. Stand out in your mind?

A. Yeah, it does.

Q. Details of it?

A. Yeah it does.

Q. And you say that he took out a club from his coat pocket?

A. That is correct.

Q. And you've given two different answers on prior occasions with respect to what he beat you with, haven't you?

A. A bat, a club. It's the same thing to me.

Q. Pardon?

A. A bar and a club is the same thing.

Q. No no, you said baseball bat in your original statement to the police? You want me to read it to you?

A. No sir, I did say that.

Q. Baseball bat.

A. Yeah.

Q. Right. And then at the preliminary hearing, you said it was a little leather club with something in it.

A. That's correct.

Q. That is not a baseball bat, sir.

A. It is a bat.

Q. Yeah. A little leather club with something in it, is not a baseball bat.

A. It's a bat. I agree with that.

Q. Well, you may—but you called it . . .

A. I agree . . .

Q. . . . a baseball bat.

A. I agree with you, sir.

Q. This $800.00 rip-off that you talk about when you talked about it on the video, was like around $1,000.00, wasn't it? Is that the . . .

A. I don't recall, sir.

Q. . . . figure you—isn't that the figure you mentioned?

A. I do not recall. I think I said . . .

Q. Said about $1,000.00?

A. If that's what's on it, yes sir.

Q. Now you said that there was a—some job that you and him had done together, and that's why you—that's where this rip-off comes?

A. That is correct.

Q. And that was a break and enter?

A. That is correct.

Q. And—and where was that?

A. In Toronto.

Q. What? What kind of place?

A. Residential.

Q. Well again, you've given different answers, because you say in your statement to the police page seven, there was a furrier heist that York had done in the west end of the city, and you located some cash and didn't split the proceeds with York. Remember saying that to the police?

A. I don't recall.

Q. Oh. Read here, this is the typed version. You recall being beaten "because of a furrier heist he and York had done on the west end of the city. Smith located some cash and didn't split the proceeds with York who found out about it, and beat Smith for it." Did I read that correctly? Did I read it correctly?

A. Yeah, you did. Yes you did.

Q. Okay. By the way, up here you talk about beating him with a baseball bat.

A. That's correct.

Q. Two different answers as to where the break and enter took place—the business establishment or furrier, and a residential establishment. Is that correct?

A. It's in the book.

Q. Is that right?

A. It's—sorry sir, yes. It's in the book.

Q. You're having trouble getting your story straight, aren't you?

A. No sir, I'm not.

Q. Did you tell them at the hospital how you were injured?

A. No I didn't.

Q. I'm going to suggest to you that yes, Mr. York had hit you in the past—not with a baseball bat, not with a club—but he hit you because you called Val Groves names.

A. You can suggest anything you like, sir.

Q. And the one—the person that you were involved with physically more than anyone, was when you were living with Ramona Pilgrim when you used to beat her up. You used to beat up Ramona Pilgrim?

A. I used to beat her up?

Q. Yes.

A. I think we used to beat each other up.

Q. No, you used to beat her up.

A. No sir.

Q. Oh Mr.—. . .

A. No.

Q. . . . Mr—Mr. Smith.

A. Can you prove that?

Q. Excuse me.

A. Can you prove that?

Q. Pardon?

A. Can you prove that?

Q. I don't have to prove anything, and you . . .

THE COURT: Just answer the question.

COUNSEL: Q. . . . answer the questions, I'll ask them. All right?

A. That's correct.

Q. You would beat Ramona Pilgrim up, you would even draw blood by biting on her breasts. Isn't that correct?

A. That is incorrect.

Q. And it was Val Groves and Ronald York who used to come to your—to her rescue. On a number of occasions.

A. That is correct. Mona Pilgrim is a whore.

Q. And you were living with her?

A. Yes I was. That is . . .

Q. Does that give you the right to beat her up?

A. Doesn't give me the right to do anything, sir.

Q. You were living with her.

A. That is correct.

Q. Yes. Living off her earnings.

A. That is correct.

Q. You were that rare combination. You were both a prostitute and a pimp, weren't you?

A. I don't agree with that, sir.

Q. Now let me see here about what you say is in your—you were beaten I think you said, and it was your right leg in the thigh area. Is that what you said, swelling on the thigh?

A. I said that sir, yes.

Q. Transcript of your preliminary hearing, page 29. You're being asked the following about line eight:
"Question: What did you suffer by way of injury to your leg?
Answer: Swelling on the knee.
The Court: Swelling on the?
The Witness: On the knee. On my left leg."
Remember being asked those questions and giving those answers?

A. Sir, I recall when my leg's being swollen, whether it's my right, my left, it was swollen.

Q. You don't—I thought you had—could visualize this vicious beating in your mind's eye, Mr. Smith.

A. I recall, yes.

Q. Yeah.

A. I recall this, yes.

Q. Well, you've given different answers about it.

A. Well, I was beaten on my leg, sir. Which—whatever leg it was, I went to the hospital.

Q. Well, different answers as to where you were beaten, and different answers as to what leg you were beaten on.

A. I was beaten by Ronny York.

Q. Oh, I'm not going to quarrel with you there, sir. But it was a different beating for a different reason.

A. Sir, you're incorrect.

Q. Yes. Well, we only have your word for this statement, don't we?

A. That is correct.

Q. And your word really isn't worth very much, is it, Mr. Smith?

A. Not—not to you sir, it isn't.

COUNSEL: No further questions.

Normally when a witness is cross-examined on his criminal record and background the purpose is to show that he is a person of bad character and should not be believed. This often entails the cross-examination mantra of a simple mouthing aloud of the witness's criminal convictions and sentences. The following part of the cross-examination of the material Crown witness by Brian Greenspan in a murder trial goes beyond that mantra and is instructive in showing that when an individual's lifestyle is one of crime that the culture of the underworld presents the opportunity for broadening the cross-examination to significantly support the defence position.

D, the accused, was charged with first degree murder on the basis that he hired G to kill M. G plea-bargained his first degree murder charge to a plea of guilty to second degree murder with parole eligibility set at twelve years by agreeing to testify that D had hired him to commit the murder.

It was the defence position that it was in fact R that had hired G, not D. Mr. Greenspan, by detailing the offences committed by G, highlighting his associations in the criminal underworld and his misplaced sense of loyalty, particularly to R, depicted G as a vicious, unlikeable individual without moral scruples who enjoyed his life of crime and was the type who would be protecting R by falsely incriminating D.

Q. Let's talk about your criminal record. You – told us – you told Mr. Sherriff – on Friday that your record started when you were 18 years of age, is that correct?

A. That's correct.

Q. In fact you didn't wait long after you were an adult – you've got a conviction in Hull, Quebec on September 5th, 1991, which is about four months after your 18th birthday?

A. Yes.

Q. And it's got driving offences, property offences, and at that time you weren't – you weren't sent to jail the first time round, were you?

A. Bail I believe.

Q. And then shortly thereafter there is a failure to comply with your recognizance and then by February 7th of 1992 – and you're still 18 years old at that time, right?

A. Probably, yes.

Q. You got your first weapons offence, is that correct?

A. Yes.

Q. And your first jail sentence?

A. Yes.

Q. And then starting thereafter you're involved with break and enters?

A. Yes.

Q. You're involved in property offences, obstructing the police, possession of break-in instruments. I take it that as you got older – you became a – a little bit more seasoned in terms of how to commit crime?

A. Well, yes.

Q. Became an experienced criminal –

A. Yes.

Q. – right, and that's what you do for a living?

A. Yes.

Q. And as an experienced criminal who commits crime for a living, I take it that just as all of us like to do our work well, you liked to do your work well?

A. Yes.

Q. And you liked to prepare for your work, correct?

A. Yes.

Q. And as you got older and more experienced you prepared more carefully for your work?

A. Yes.

Q. And you started to, as we all do, when you get experience, you make mistakes, you try not to commit those mistakes again, is that right?

A. Yes.

Q. You learn from your mistakes, correct?

A. Yes.

Q. And as in all jobs, just like your job as a criminal – you took pride in the fact that you're getting better at it, you're getting more respected at it, people were recognizing you as a – as a good criminal, is that right?

A. That's right.

Q. That you were good at your job, correct?

A. That's correct.

Q. Because that's how you would acquire respect in the criminal world, by doing your job well, correct?

A. Correct.

Q. And so – as you graduated and you start committing more crimes and more sophisticated crimes it took better planning, correct?

A. Correct.

Q. And you started, I take it, to work with other people, not just alone?

A. Yes, several others.

Q. And that required a group of you getting together and mapping out a plan, correct?

A. Correct.

Q. Part of the plan is not only executing the offence but it's getting away with it, correct?

A. Correct.

. . .

Q. Because you told us that despite the fact that you've got a pretty impressive record

– you've got 11 separate entries between 1991 and 2003 – 11 separate times you came before the courts and 11 separate times you've been convicted of crimes, isn't that correct?

A. That's correct.

Q. And you didn't have much time during that period of 12 years to be out because most of the time you were in, isn't that correct?

A. That's correct.

Q. Particularly that long stretch on those robberies from Ottawa in 1996, which was where you met P and S?

A. Correct.

Q. Well you also said that you committed other crimes for which you weren't caught, correct?

A. Correct.

Q. Bank robberies –

A. Yes.

. . .

Q. Bank robberies. While armed?

A. Yes.

Q. Had guns?

A. Yes.

. . .

Q. Well you had loaded weapons with you –

A. Yes.

. . .

Q. And I take it – you were armed because you wanted to intimidate people, you wanted to scare them, you wanted to make sure that you got away with your robbery, is that right?

A. That's right.

Q. And – how many robberies did you commit for which you weren't caught?

A. Numerous; I don't recall how many.
Q. Five, 10, 20?
A. Over 20.

. . .

Q. And so clearly those were pretty well-executed crimes. You got in, you got out, you knew exactly what you were doing, you had a good plan and it worked, is that correct?
A. That's correct.
Q. I understand you had such a good plan that you robbed one bank repeatedly?
A. Yes, four or five times.
Q. The same bank four or five times. You got in and out of the same bank four or five times because you had such a good plan, isn't that right?
A. That's correct.
Q. Did you have a get-away car?
A. Yes.

. . .

Q. Right. You'd steal a car, come to the robbery and then you'd ditch the car, right?
A. Yes.
Q. And one thing you'd try to make sure of is you would steal a car that had nothing to do with you, right?
A. That's correct.
Q. Just a total stranger's car where you took it off the street somewhere in someone else's neighbourhood, not in your own neighbourhood, right?
A. That's correct.
Q. Because you didn't want the car to come back to you?
A. That's correct.

. . .

Q. In addition – you told us about the Gatineau, Quebec shooting that occurred after April the 6th of 2001, after the execution of Mr. M and Mr. P. You said that shooting was an accident, is that correct?
A. That's correct.
Q. You sort of tripped and shot him in the stomach?
A. No, no, he was lying on the bed and he kicked my – my handgun that I was carrying, and his legs were going up and down like this –
Q. Well you – you seem to –
A. – then he got up and he said "Fuck you, you shot me."
Q. And then you had a second accident?
A. No; I was beating him on the head.
Q. And it went off again?
A. Yes; he had powder burns.

. . .

Q. But you had a plan –

A. No –

Q. – right?

A. – it was a favour I owed somebody – beat the guy up and –

Q. It was more than a favour, it was a job?

A. Well it was more of a favour, because that favour I did for the guy, he used to take care of me in prison.

Q. All right. You got paid for it?

A. Yes.

Q. Right. So it was a favour for which you got paid, – you were at work, and your work was intimidating this man, threatening this man and accidentally your gun went off twice – once into his stomach and once across his head, isn't that correct?

A. That's correct.

. . .

Q. Safety issues. All right. All right. I don't want to put you in jeopardy. That's not the only crime though that you committed after the M/P homicides, is it?

A. No.

Q. There was a TTC robbery, wasn't there?

A. Yes.

Q. A good seventy thousand, $80,0000.00 robbery?

A. Yes.

Q. At gunpoint?

A. Yes.

Q. Gun's loaded?

A. Yes.

Q. Committed alone?

A. With S.

. . .

Q. And J is a – a life-long criminal – you knew him, you knew of him?

A. Yes.

Q. Associated with organized crime?

A. Yes.

Q. Just the type of people you wanted to get an in with?

A. Well, yes, to a certain degree. J was just like a – a big pet; you know he's not very smart.

Q. Not very smart. This organized crime figure – introduced to you by R, wasn't he?

. . .

Q. So R – he's your mentor now, I take it; you're now in Toronto, he's helped you find a job, he's helped; you with your apartment, he's helping you along, doing favours for you, correct?

A. Yes.

. . .

Q. All right. And you know the last time we talked, at the preliminary hearing, Mr. G, we – we talked about your time at – at Collins Bay on that long sentence – for the robberies, and it seems as if you wanted to get to Collins Bay, isn't that right?

A. That's correct. . . I had a few friends there.

. . .

Q. Well one of the things that you told us about on Friday was this fellow who was a Brinks robber?

A. Yes.

Q. And as I understand it, you knew him before you went into jail, isn't that correct?

A. That's correct.

Q. You had met him on the outside, is that correct?

A. That's correct.

Q. And – and you admired him as a – as a Brinks robber – that's a pretty important type of robbery?

A. That's correct.

. . .

Q. And so while you're there you – you meet S and P?

A. Yes.

Q. And they're people with lengthy – in the criminal world, lengthy and impressive criminal records, right?

A. That's correct.

Q. And – and while you're there - while you're – at Collins Bay – what do you do on a day in and day out basis at Collins Bay?

A. What do I do?

Q. Yes. – do you have a job there?

A. I run the – the canteen.

Q. Right. So you're running the canteen, and I take it you're – you're involved in programmes?

A. Yes.

. . .

Q. What sort of programmes were you involved in?

A. Anger management; cognitive skill programmes; different –

Q. So you're involved in anger management – and did you pass that course?

A. Yes.

. . .

Q. So after passing your anger management course, you come out and go to a halfway house and you put five bullets into the heads of two men, is that correct?

A. Yes, but Mr. Greenspan, I use violence as a tool not as a – you know jumping up and down but –

. . .

Q. You weren't angry when you killed them –
A. No.
Q. – is that correct? You were cold-blooded and direct and you didn't give a damn when you killed them isn't that right?
A. That's correct.

. . .

Q. But one thing – you've clearly said is that you can – you can apparently break every commandment that the community lives by – thou shalt not kill, thou shalt not steal; those things, you can break those – but the one thing you're not supposed to break is the commandment about loyalty, isn't that right?
A. To me, yes.
Q. Right. Because that's your commandment. Your commandment is you're a loyal guy and you're loyal to the people who are loyal to you, right?
A. That's correct.

. . .

Q. Well you had to be loyal to P, isn't that right –
A. Yes.

. . .

Q. Because part of this plea bargain with the police and the Crown, this plea bargain that you signed, your plea bargain made it clear that you wouldn't testify against P?
A. That's correct.
Q. And in fact your plea bargain made it clear you wouldn't testify against S?
A. I don't remember that part but if it's in there, I believe you.

. . .

Q. I suggest to you that you made a deal that said that you would only testify against the person who you identified as the person who had hired you; that's the only person you have to testify against – that's your deal, isn't that right?
A. That's correct.
Q. And your deal is that you point to and you say – and we're supposed to trust your word – the person that you say hired you, that's the only person you have to say anything about, isn't that correct?
A. That's correct.
Q. And we'll get to it a bit later, but what's perfectly clear is for several months R persistently told you to lay it on this man; blame him – that's what R told you repeatedly, isn't that correct?
A. No, he said tell the truth.
Q. No, he told you to nail D, isn't that correct?
A. Well he helped in my decision, yes.

Q. He also told you – when he was saying nail D, you knew that R hated D more than anybody on earth, isn't that right?

A. Um, that's putting it pretty roughly, but you know D had forged his name after – R helped him several times and D kept you know like forging his names and you know like not paying him for – for packages he put together on – on properties and – and even though you know like over the years R kept you know helping him, even though D kept fucking him, right.

. . .

Q. P and R kept telling you that D is a bad guy and both of them hated his guts, isn't that right?

A. No, but D is good to put you know big money projects together so –

. . .

THE COURT: – the question asked was very simple, there isn't anybody in this courtroom who didn't understand it, including you, the question was R and P told you that the accused D was a rotten man and that they hated him, is that right?

THE WITNESS: Yes.

MR. GREENSPAN: Q. When it comes to your loyalty, you told Mr. Sherriff that one of the things that you always look to as being very important was your canteen, correct?

A. Well it helps, yes.

. . .

Q. And so it was pretty important to get money into your canteen to buy your smokes –

A. Yes.

Q. – You said the other day that the food's rotten, so you need something to supplement your food, correct?

A. That's correct.

Q. And so having money in your canteen is pretty important –

A. Yes.

Q. – A lawyer's pretty important, when you need a lawyer?

A. That's correct.

. . .

Q. Who got you your lawyer on the murder charges to which you pleaded guilty?

A. R, but it was a Legal Aid lawyer, it wasn't like he paid for it.

Q. Who arranged for the lawyer?

A. R.

Q. Who in fact got you a lawyer who he said was the best you could get because he was experienced and knew Mr. Sherriff – that's what he told you, isn't it?

A. That correct.

Q. Who paid your canteen?

A. R.

. . .

Q. These guys who you were friendly with in Collins Bay – S, let's start with him for a moment. You knew him to have a pretty impressive criminal record?
A. Yes.

. . .

Q. An experienced life-time career criminal –
A. Yes.
Q. You – you had a falling out with him eventually I take it?
A. A falling out?
Q. Yes.
A. Yes.
Q. You're pretty upset with him because he's the one that pointed the finger at you?
A. That's correct.
Q. He's the one that gave a statement to the police that implicated you in these homicides.
A. That's correct.
Q. And he's the one who you refer to in one of the tapes, when you're talking to R, you called him a pathological liar, do you remember that?
A. Yes.
Q. Pathological liar means somebody who doesn't know how to tell the truth, right?
A. That's correct.

. . .

D was acquitted.

Brian Greenspan is a Toronto defence counsel.

19

Cross-Examination of Police Officers

Because most police officers are experienced at testifying under oath many have developed a very comfortable, pleasing and convincing style on the witness stand. Many officers are able to predict what questions will be asked before they are asked and as a result they are usually better prepared for the cross-examination than a civilian witness. I believe that the majority of police officers are honest witnesses, but if a police witness is going to lie then his or her motive for doing so can most often be attributed to a desire to see their arrest result in a conviction and perhaps potential job promotion, or to firming up a case against someone the officer believes to be guilty, or they do it out of a sense of loyalty to back-up a fellow officer. It may even be that the officer has a dislike for a particular accused for any number of reasons. Police are generally held in high esteem by the majority of the public and there is no doubt some jurors will accept their testimony merely because they are police officers. Successfully challenging the credibility of a police officer can be difficult for even an experienced counsel.

Because the guilt or innocence of an accused often depends on the testimony of a police witness, the officer's credibility and actions are usually under attack by defence counsel. However, what has been said about civilian witnesses also applies to police witnesses. They too resent aspersions cast upon their character or credibility and generally will be more responsive to a non-aggressive approach. Joseph Sedgwick made the following comments when discussing such an approach:

> Seldom we succeed by even the most vigorous cross-examination in getting an officer to swallow wholly what he has said in-chief. But if you have properly prepared yourself, you may get him to qualify what he has said, or, to bring out facts favourable to your client which he forgot, or conveniently did not see fit to mention. You will know the story of the accused, and of his witnesses, if any, and you will know in what respects those stories differ from the version given by the officer. By quietly putting to him the points of differences, you will not infrequently get him to agree that it might not be quite as he has said, thus you convert what was wholly black into a shade of grey. And so, when you go to the jury you can put to them those qualifications, which they may

seize, particularly if they are supported by your own witness. Juries are not prone to wholly disbelieve police witnesses, but they will accede to a reasonable doubt if you can raise one.

However, counsel should always keep in mind that police officers generally are biased in favour of the prosecution and some may suffer from the human tendency to shade the truth in favour of the prosecution. Even the most honest officer, with the rare exception, will not consciously volunteer any helpful information to the cross-examiner.

Often, the most defence counsel can expect to accomplish with a police witness is to underscore those matters the witness did not testify about in direct examination. So if the police witness testifies that the accused was drunk because he smelled of alcohol and his or her speech was slurred counsel should bring forth that there was nothing noticeably unusual about his or her walking or driving or else it would have been mentioned by the officer. Counsel should highlight how much the witness did not see to attack collaterally what he or she did see.

Other approaches to cross-examination are

1. to bring out the details of how the accused was co-operative so that it can be argued later that his or her actions were consistent with those of an innocent person and
2. to stress those matters with the witness that corroborate the accused's position.
3. elicit statements they received from witnesses which contradict incriminating testimony those witnesses gave at trial.

THE UNDERCOVER OFFICER

An undercover police officer's job is to play a role, such as a prospective purchaser of drugs. Some officers have considerable practice in role-playing. If, as a result of the officer's efforts, an arrest has been made, he or she has obviously been credible and believable in his or her deception. If counsel is challenging the credibility of the undercover officer it is useful to emphasize that the witness's job calls for him or her to be believable in his or her undercover role saying things that are not true to make the point that this ability can be transferred to the officer's testimony in the trial. This approach is probably more effective with a jury than when the trier of fact is a judge alone.

POLICE OFFICER'S NOTEBOOK

The police force in question will no doubt have a policy (perhaps obtainable on the Internet or upon request) setting out the best practices of the force with regard to note-taking and the use of the memorandum book. It is said that "The memorandum book is the first method of recording investigations, arrests and other significant events" and that these events must be recorded.[1] In *R. v. Karunakaran* it was held that while an officer's notes cannot be expected to record every minute detail, they must contain a complete and accurate record of significant events in the investigation so as to enable the Crown to fulfill its constitutional obligation to make full disclosure.[2] The police officer's notebook is defence counsel's most important tool in preparing for cross-examination.

Refreshing Memory

Police witnesses will most often request permission from the Court to refer to their notebook when testifying. If the officer has refreshed her memory from her notebook then counsel for the accused is entitled to see those notes. Counsel will probably have those notes provided in disclosure in any event. Before the officer is permitted to refresh her memory from her notebook there is a Crown mantra to be followed: Are these your notes? When were they made? (Close enough to the event), were any additions or deletions made to the notes since they were originally made? Did you consult with your partner in making your notes? Do you have any independent recollection of the events in question? Do you feel at times you may have to consult your notes to refresh your memory? This topic is discussed earlier in the book. See Chapter, "Presenting the Evidence-in-Chief."

Although the witness is permitted to refresh her memory by referring to her notes, she must not, strictly speaking, read verbatim from her notebook as if it were a prepared script because this would be more than refreshing her memory.

Impeachment

A police officer's notebook is a common area for attack by defence counsel. The notebook should be as complete and accurate as possible with respect to what the officer saw and heard regarding their investigation. If it is not and the officer's testimony differs from his notebook in any significant way, the officer's credibility could suffer and the case lost as a result. A properly recorded notebook can come to the officer's aid in unforseen ways

---

1 Toronto Police Service Policy and Procedural Manual #13-7 Memorandum Books.
2 *R. v. Karunakaran*, 2008 ONCJ 397(Ont. C.J.) at para. 25. The Court dismissed a charge of fail to provide breath sample where the arresting officer's notes "were little more than cryptic jottings" and the officer's evidence eight months after arrest was significantly more detailed.

when testifying many months after the event or when the Crown Attorney is asking questions of the officer during preparation of the case.

I recall hearing a trial Judge say that she was astounded at the number of police officers appearing before her who had not read their notebooks or transcript of their preliminary hearing evidence before testifying at trial. Officers who are cavalier with their notetaking and come to trial unprepared become easy targets on cross-examination. At the very least they look less than professional as they fumble to find the spots they are looking for, have trouble reading their own writing or realize that their notes are incomplete or inaccurate.

Counsel should ask to see the officer's notebook, preferably just before embarking on cross-examination, unless of course photocopies of the officer's notes have already been provided through disclosure. The questioner should ask the witness whether original notes were first jotted down on the back of the officer's notebook or on scraps of paper, which were used to refresh her memory later in order to flesh out her more complete notes in her notebook. These original notes should also be checked because they may differ from the more complete notes or give helpful information not contained in the fuller version. These scrap notes may also come to the aid of the police officer who has been challenged because of what is not in his/her notebook but is in fact in the officer's preliminary notes. If such preliminary notes were made but were not retained by the officer for production along with the notebook this may be a useful fact for cross-examination and comment at closing. A police officer may have made a supplementary report after she made up her notebook. Such a report may contain the additional information testified to that was not in the notebook but recalled shortly after making up the notebook.

The notebook may contain something favourable to the accused that the police officer intentionally or unintentionally left out of his or her testimony. The more common occurrence is where the notebook is silent about something damaging to the defence to which the officer has testified. In that instance the following is an example of the type of cross-examination that the cross-examiner could employ to attack the officer's credibility:

Q. Officer, you made up your notebook within an hour after the events when they would be fresh in your mind?
A. That's correct.
Q. In making up your notebook I take it you try to be as complete and accurate as possible as to what you saw and heard.
A. Yes.
Q. You learned to do that as part of your police training?
A. Yes.
Q. One reason you make up your notebook this way is because it may be a considerable time after the event that you are called upon to testify in court and you would want to be able to refresh your memory to testify accurately?

A. Yes.

Q. Another reason you would want your notes to be complete and accurate is that your expected evidence is typed for the prosecutor from your notes in order to help the prosecutor know the case that he has to present to court?

A. Yes.

Q. You want to be as helpful to the prosecutor as you can?

A. Yes.

Q. And a third reason you would want your notes to be complete and accurate is that if you testify to anything of any importance that is not in your notebook the defence lawyer in the case will challenge your credibility?

A. Yes, that happens.

Q. The defence lawyer will say if it is not in your notebook, you must have made it up later or your memory is not accurate.

A. That happens.

Q. You told the Court that after you advised my client he was under arrest you put your hand on his shoulder and he ran away?

A. Yes.

Q. Your touching of the accused was important in effecting the arrest?

A. Yes.

Q. There is absolutely not one word in your notebook that you touched my client on his shoulder before he ran away, am I correct?

A. Yes.

Suppose that the police officer tried to make excuses for the important omission in his notes. Has the above cross-examination closed off the possible escape routes? The cross-examination continues below, starting with the last question asked in the above scenario:

Q. There is absolutely not one word in your notebook that you touched my client on his shoulder before he ran away, am I correct?

A. Well no, but it was something I would never forget. I didn't have to put it in my notebook.

Q. But officer, you told us that you try to be as complete and accurate as possible when you make up your notebook.

A. That's right.

Q. And you left out the most important piece of your testimony on purpose, knowing your credibility would be challenged at trial? Is that what you're telling this jury?

A. Well, I probably forgot to put it in my notes and I remembered what happened later.

Q. Officer, is it not correct that you already told us that you made up your notebook shortly after the event because that is when the events were fresh in your mind?

A. Yes.

It might also be suitable to point out all the details, significant and insignificant, which the officer has quoted in his notes, particularly the details leading up to the missing notations in order to highlight by comparison those missing notations.

Another scenario which occurs relating to notetaking by police officers as well as others who make notes as part of their duty to record observations, such as doctors, is when the notetaker is asked by the Crown about some matter and he or she responds that they cannot recall or it is not in their notebook. Consider the following example:

> Q. Officer (doctor) can you describe the demeanour of the complainant when you spoke with her?
> A. (The witness looks through his/her notes.) I don't seem to have a note of it and I can't really recall, its been some time.

You of course want to emphasize in your final submissions that there was nothing out-of-the ordinary about the complainant's demeanour shortly after the alleged trauma he/she suffered.

> Q. Officer (doctor) would it not be fair to say that if the complainant had displayed upset or was badly shaken or appeared to be in shock, you would have in your normal practice made a note of that fact.
> A: I guess you're right.
> Q. And you made no such note
> A. I did not.

This same kind of approach can be taken when the officer's notebook contains no mention of a victim's injuries where there are charges of alleged violence.

No doubt most police departments have regulations as to how and when its officers should make up their notes. The Metropolitan Toronto Police have certain regulations that may not be unusual insofar as the rest of the country's police departments are concerned. Some of the regulations are designed to prevent police witnesses from later changing their notes. Mr. Justice Morand, in the 1976 *Report of the Royal Commission of Inquiry into Metropolitan Toronto Police Practices* stated:

> This evidence [about two police officers and their notebooks] disturbed me as an example of the willingness of police officers to alter their notebooks and evidence in order to buttress their case against an accused they believe to be guilty.[3]

Police Officers Conferring on Making Notes

It has, at least in some jurisdictions, become common practice for police officers to confer before making up their notebooks, when more than

---

3   (1976), p. 32.

one police officer has witnessed an event. The result, of course, is that their notes of the event are exactly the same or very close to being the same. Sometimes one officer will read over another officer's notebook and then initial the notes, thereby agreeing to their accuracy. There has, however, been some judicial condemnation of police collaboration on their notebooks. In *R. v. Vangent*,[4] Langdon then Prov. Ct. J. of the Ontario Provincial Court stated:

> It was obvious in assessing their evidence that *both relied heavily on the one set of notes that Officer Mortimer had prepared and which Officer Richard had adopted.* The Court cannot refrain from criticism of this system, (which it has observed in other cases in the past) of two officers purporting one to corroborate the other, and yet relying on one set of notes made up as an aid memoire, as a single aide memoire, by the two officers in collaboration, after the event. Why, the Court asks would the officers not have sat down and made their own notes based on their own independent recollection? Is it because they feared that their independent recollection recorded on the very day of the events might differ? How could it differ, if only the truth were recorded?

In *R. v. Charest*,[5] Salhany then Co. Ct. J. of the Ontario County Court, commented on police officers' collaboration in the preparation of note-books as follows:

> Though one can understand and expect two police officers who have witnessed an event or series of events to wish to sit down and discuss it, I fail to understand why it is necessary for them to also collaborate word for word in the preparation of their notes. What the Court expects and is entitled to hear is their own independent recollection of the event, not a recorded recollection which has been agreed to between them.

In *R. v. Barrett*,[6] Madam Justice Arbour of the Ontario Court of Appeal was critical of a police officer who witnessed an interview of the accused by another officer who made the notes on which the former initialled and later put in his own notebook. She held that "whenever possible, every officer in attendance at the interview who will want to refer to his or her notes as a memory and for the purpose of giving evidence should take contemporaneous, independent notes."

In *R. (Saunders) v. Independent Police Complaints Commission*[7] it was held that there is a real risk that when officers confer in making their notes they may in good faith include in their accounts recollections derived from other officers, or subconsciously suppress aspects that are inconsistent with accounts provided by others. There is also the risk that officers will delib-

---

4   (1978), 42 C.C.C. (2d) 313 at 326-327 (Ont. Prov. Ct.).

5   Ont. Co. Ct., Salhany Co. Ct. J., December 23, 1981, summarized at 7 W.C.B. 86, from the trial transcript. pp. 326-327.

6   (1993), 82 C.C.C. (3d) 266 (Ont. C.A.).

7   [2008] E.W.H.C. 2372 (Admin.) at para. 13.

erately fashion recollections to conform with others and may even involve substantial distortion.

Different people often see and hear things differently. Why it is felt that police officers, who may not have remembered the particular event in the same way, should be able to confer and arrive at a consensus, escapes logic. If they are the trained observers that the courts have often said they are, then there would be no reason for police officers to confer because it would be expected that their notes would compare favourably in any event. It would be extremely important to know whether some police officers remember an event differently because one officer's recollections may have accorded, at least in part, with the accused's or a defence witness recollection. However, it may be asking too much to expect a police officer, who writes up his notes in the same way as his fellow officer, to admit on the witness stand that originally he did not agree with his fellow officer's recollection. Where one police officer does not remember, he may well be influenced to fill in the gaps with a fellow officer's recollection. The unfairness of this practice can be shown to the Court by these questions:

Q. Officer, when you interview two accused persons for purposes of taking their statement, you interview them separately?

A. Yes.

Q. You do that because you don't want one accused's story to be influenced by the other accused's story?

A. Yes.

Q. When you interview more than one witness to an event, you interview them separately?

A. Yes.

Q. The reason for that is because you don't want one witness recollection to be influenced by another witness's recollection?

A. That's correct.

Q. That is standard practice.

A. Yes.

Q. But as you told my friend you and Officer Smith conferred with each other when making up your notebooks?

A. Yes.

If the officers deny jointly making up their notebooks you may be able to impeach their credibility by pointing out through cross-examination how many occasions they have included exactly the same or very closely the same wording in their notebooks. This was the situation in *R. v. Mattis*[8] where both officers testified they made up their notes separately and, in cross-examination, were unable to explain why their notes were virtually identical. The Court found it would be unsafe to base a conviction on that

---

8   (1998), 20 C.R. (5th) 93 (Ont. Prov. Div.).

evidence absent confirmation in material particulars. The Court quoted with approval the judgment of Malloy J. in *R. v. Green*[9] as follows:

> There are important reasons for requiring that officers prepare their notes independently. The purpose of notes made by a police officer is to record the observations made by that officer. The notes themselves are not admissible as evidence for the truth of their contents. An officer with relevant evidence to offer may testify at trial as to the act or observations made by him or her. However, that officer is not permitted to testify as to the information received from other officers for the purpose of proving their truth. Such evidence [is] hearsay and inadmissible.

> An officer's notes perform a valuable function at trial. It is usually many months, sometimes years, from the time of an occurrence to the time that the officer is called upon to testify at trial. Without the assistance of notes to refresh his or her memory, the evidence of the officer at trial would inevitably be sketchy at best. If the officer's notes are prepared without any indication of which is the officer's independent recollection and which is somebody else's recollection, there is every likelihood that that officer at trial will be "refreshing" his or her own memory with observations made by someone else. In effect, the officer will be giving hearsay evidence if it was his or her own recollection rather than the observations of somebody else written into the notes without attribution.

> . . .

The fact that officers have collaborated on their notes will always cause a trier of fact to give careful consideration to the reliability of that officer's evidence. There will, however, be situations in which such collaboration, although not good police practice, will not undermine the testimony of the officers. The extent to which the collaboration renders the evidence of the officers' unreliable will depend on the circumstances of each case and the explanation given by the officers. It is not unusual to hear that the only conferring the officers did was with respect to times, which would be hard to criticize.

In re-examination the Crown might ask the officer if there was any difference in recollection between the officers when the notebooks were made up. The answer will no doubt be "No." The cross-examiner can rhetorically ask the jury in his final address what reason would there have been to confer unless they were making up a story or there were some differences in recollection. Alternatively, it can be urged that the officers individually may not have had complete recall but by conferring they only succeeded in incorrectly stitching their fragments of recollection together.

---

9   (1998), [1998] O.J. No. 3598, 1998 CarswellOnt 3820 (Ont. Gen. Div.).

Statements by Accused Persons

At times counsel must listen to police officers relate lengthy verbal statements given by counsel's clients, and have no doubt been amazed to hear the officers say that they had accurately recorded the statements not at the time that they were given but an hour or two later when they arrived back at the police station. The accuracy of the officer's recollection can be important if there is a dispute by the accused as to what exactly he or she did say. In this situation counsel should try to draw out from the officer not only that he or she, moments ago, read out the client's statement in examination-in-chief from his notebook but that he also read the statement over before testifying, perhaps more than once. The officer should then be asked to close his notebook and repeat the statement. It is best to employ this technique at the preliminary inquiry stage. If the officer is unable to satisfactorily repeat the statement, counsel can bring this failure to his attention at trial and later argue before the jury that, if the officer were unable to repeat the statement accurately after having read the statement from his notebook and even after refreshing his memory earlier outside of Court, how can the jury find that he could record the so-called statement by the accused completely and accurately when it was made two hours earlier?

There is another way to make the same point in cases where the officer in charge of the investigation has been sitting in Court and listening to the witnesses and perhaps even making notes of their testimony. When this officer takes the stand to testify as to a lengthy oral statement allegedly made by the accused to the officer, that officer should be asked whether he can repeat word for word the testimony of a previous witness which was of comparable length to the accused's statement. It would be most surprising if he could.

There are instances when police officers have had the accused in the police interrogation room for an hour and yet only have fifteen minutes worth of notes. Even after excluding time to go to the washroom, to smoke a cigarette or have a coffee and make some small talk there is a significant amount of time not accounted for in the notebooks. Obviously there must have been a conversation with the accused which was not recorded unless the parties just sat and stared at each other. This gap could be important because the accused may have told his counsel of matters important to the defence which were not reflected in the officers' notes. If the officers have not recorded everything, they may have left out an exculpatory part of the statement or it may be argued on the *voir dire* on the voluntariness of the statement that such a significant time unaccounted for in the officers' notes reflects on the voluntariness of the statement because there could have been inducements, threats or physical abuse just as the accused testified.[10] If the

---

10   *R. v. Belanger* (1978), 40 C.C.C. (2d) 335 (Ont. H.C.).

officer testifies that he or she cannot remember what was said during the unrecorded period of time, the accused may be able to fill in the gap with answers which are consistent with his defence.

If the accused was given the standard police caution that anything he or she did say would be taken down in writing and used as evidence and if it is admitted that everything that the accused said was not recorded, then the officer's credibility may be in doubt. It could be suggested to the officer or argued later in closing that the police only entered into their notebooks that which would be helpful to the prosecution, at the very least the caution was a sham.

The accused may have given the police an exculpatory statement. In normal circumstances the law is clear that only the Crown can introduce this statement, not the accused. One exception to this rule is where the prosecutor in cross-examination alleges directly or by inference a recent fabrication by the accused. The accused would then be entitled to introduce his own exculpatory statement if it negates the allegation of recent fabrication and shows that the witness earlier told the police or others the same story.[11] See also "Statement by Accused Persons" in Chapter, "The Hearsay Horror."

Although the witness will not ordinarily be able to introduce the substance of his or her own exculpatory statement, can counsel be permitted to ask the police witness if the accused made a statement, the length of the statement, whether or not it was typed and whether or not it was signed, without asking about the contents of that statement. In this way counsel could say to the jury in his or her summation that it would no doubt be helpful to them to know what the accused said to the police immediately after the event, but only the prosecution, by the rules of evidence, can introduce the statement into evidence. Wouldn't the jurors like to know what was in that statement? Why didn't the prosecutor introduce it? Whether or not such a tactic would be permissible, if objected to by the Crown, is an open question as I am unaware of any reported cases that have dealt with the issue head on. However, in *R. v. Hamilton*[12] it was held that until a statement has been ruled admissible by a trial judge no mention should be made of it. In *Hamilton* it was the Crown who, without holding a *voir dire*, introduced the evidence that the police had interviewed the accused. It was held that the accused would be prejudiced as the jury could infer that the accused gave inculpatory statements. This reasoning would of course not apply where it is the accused who wishes to make reference to the statement.

---

11   *R. v. Lalonde* (1971), 5 C.C.C. (2d) 168 (Ont. H.C.); *R. v. St. Lawrence* (1949), 93 C.C.C. 376 (Ont. H.C.). See Chapter, "Prior Inconsistent Statements."

12   (1978), 42 C.C.C. (2d) 110 (Que. S.C.). In *R. v. Monk* (2005), 197 C.C.C. (3d) 126 (B.C. C.A.), the British Columbia Court of Appeal held that an accused is permitted to testify that he gave a statement to the police but was not permitted to testify as to its content.

However, *R. v. Suzack*,[13] *R. v. Liu*[14] and *R. v. Edgar*[15] are cases from the Ontario Court of Appeal which leave it open for the defence to lead a prior consistent post-arrest exculpatory statement of the accused provided the accused testifies.[16]

The Video or Audiotaping of Statements

The case law has been growing that casts a judicial shadow over statements taken by the police at the police station that have not been recorded.

In *R. v. Moore-McFarlane*[17] the Court observed there is no absolute rule requiring recording of statements, but the Crown bears the burden of establishing a sufficient record of the interaction between the suspect and the police, which can be readily satisfied by the use of audios, or better still, video-recording. When the suspect is in custody, recording facilities are readily available and where the police deliberately set out to interrogate the suspect without giving thought to making a reliable record, the non-recorded interrogation is suspect. A *voir dire* should be held to determine whether or not a sufficient substitute for an audio or videotape record has been provided to satisfy the heavy onus on the Crown to prove voluntariness beyond a reasonable doubt.

On the more recent decision of *R. v. Marshall* it was held that an accused's statement is not inherently suspect because the police have failed to record it. It becomes suspect only when the accused is in custody, recording facilities are readily available and police deliberately question the accused without giving any thought to making a record.[18]

In *R. v. Backhouse*[19] Justice Rosenberg stated: "That said I should not be taken as holding that it will always be an answer to the failure to videotape the statement that the suspect refused to participate. It could become all too

---

13   (2000), 141 C.C.C. (3d) 449 (Ont. C.A.), per Doherty J.A., leave to appeal refused (2001), 270 N.R. 193 (note) (S.C.C.).

14   (2003), 172 C.C.C. (3d) 79 (Ont. S.C.J.), per McKinnon J.

15   (2010), 101 O.R. (3d) 161 (Ont. C.A.), application/notice of appeal 2010 CarswellOnt 10099 (S.C.C.).

16   In *R. v. Monk* (2005), 197 C.C.C. (3d) 126 (B.C. C.A.), the British Columbia Court of Appeal held that an accused is permitted to testify that he gave a statement to the police but was not permitted to testify as to its content.

17   (2001), 160 C.C.C. (3d) 493 (Ont. C.A.). See also *R. v. Oickle* (2000), 147 C.C.C. (3d) 321 (S.C.C).

18   *R. v. Marshall* (2005), 200 C.C.C. (3d) 179 (Ont. C.A.), leave to appeal refused 2006 CarswellOnt 5556, 2006 CarswellOnt 5557 (S.C.C.).

19   (2005), 194 C.C.C. (3d) 1 (Ont. C.A.) at para. 118. See also *R. v. Lim* (1990), (sub nom. *R. v. Lim (No. 3)*) 1 C.R.R. (2d) 148 (Ont. H.C.); *R. v. Sabri* (2002), 166 C.C.C. (3d) 179 (Ont. C.A.); *R. v. Ahmed* (2002), 170 C.C.C. (3d) 27 (Ont. C.A.); *R. v. Ducharme* (2004), 182 C.C.C. (3d) 243 (Man. C.A.), leave to appeal refused 2004 CarswellMan 220 (S.C.C.).

easy for the authorities to attempt to avoid the impact of this Court's decision in *Moore-McFarlane* by attributing to the suspect a refusal to have his statement videotaped. It would still be open to the police to tape-record the statement, or at the very least electronically record the suspect's wishes, to avoid any later dispute. Depending on the context, the trial Judge might well view with concern a bare assertion by police officers that the suspect refused to be videotaped or even tape-recorded."

Just as the defence should interview witnesses separately in order to maintain and promote independence of thought so should the police when they are interviewing laypersons as well as other police witnesses. If not, much can be made of this in cross-examination.

OTHER SOURCES OF INFORMATION FOR CROSS-EXAMINATION

There are other sources of information that can be used to verify or challenge police testimony or provide additional leads in the case. The officer may have filed a supplementary report which contains information which is not in the officer's notebook, particularly if the notebook was made up during the incident or immediately thereafter. The supplementary report may confirm the officer's testimony or work against the officer's credibility or reliability if it does not contain the information to which the officer has testified. It may also contain information which contradicts or affects the evidence of other witnesses. Record of Arrest forms show the time the accused was brought into the police station, whether he or she had any complaints, if he or she had made a phone call, and if so, the telephone number called, as well as other information. In many police stations telephone calls made by the police and civilians to the station are recorded. Occurrence Reports, made up by the police, provide a detailed summary of witnesses interviewed and their statements together with other aspects of the investigation. Use of Force and Injury Reports may be required to be filed by many police departments when the use of force by a police officer has resulted in an injury, when a complaint about the use of force has been made or when a person is taken into custody with injuries which have not been caused by the police.[20] Police photographs (mug shots) taken after arrest could verify injuries at the time of arrest together with accompanying forms which describe the injuries and complaints. Police stations normally have video cameras showing the accused when he or she is brought into the station and presented for booking. The accused's physical appearance and demeanour can be noted and audio facilities permit counsel to hear what is

---

20 The Use of Force Report completed by a police officer pursuant to the Ontario *Police Services Act* falls within the parameters of the Crown disclosure obligations. See *R. v. Van Duzen* (2006), 214 C.C.C. (3d) 247 (Ont. C.J.).

said and whether or not the accused is given his or her rights at this time. If the client is kept in the local jail there could be records of recent injuries. There are affidavits in support of applications for search warrants on file which counsel is entitled to see and which may contain useful information for an attack on a search and seizure.[21] As a result of the *Charter of Rights*,[22] the law now permits the opening of the sealed packet containing the material in support of an application for an electronic interception.[23] This means that defence counsel, in testing the lawfulness of an authorization, is no longer required to show some evidence of fraud or material non-disclosure before looking at the affidavit in the sealed packet which supports the application for the electronic interception but can gain access to the affidavit on the basis of full answer and defence. Police accident reports normally depict the scene of the accident, provide details of measurements, road and weather conditions, times, names of participants and witnesses.

Request disclosure of criminal records, discharges or outstanding charges relating to the officer(s). Subpoena the officers personnel files to determine if there have been or there are any outstanding internal police hearings where the officer(s)' conduct has been found wanting and may be relevant to your defence. You may be met with right to privacy arguments when you subpoena an officer's personnel file.

However in *R. v. McNeil*[24] the Supreme Court broadened the obligation of the Crown to disclose with respect to police records involving the discipline and misconduct of officers that might be relevant. See Chapter, "Crown Disclosure" for detailed references to *McNeil*.

Can a police officer, or any witness be cross-examined on a prior judicial finding that he has lied under oath? Police officers, particularly ones on specialty squads, such as drugs, are often testifying and transcripts of their testimony at times become known, often as a result of speaking with other counsel. In *R. v. Ghorvei*[25] the witness, whose credibility was in question was a police officer. The Ontario Court of Appeal held that he could not be cross-examined on a prior judicial finding that he lied under oath. The evidence for which he was disbelieved in a prior case does not amount to discreditable conduct as such a finding was an opinion without the foundation of that opinion in order to assess it. If the lies had formed the basis of a conviction for perjury or giving contradictory evidence then

---

21 *A.G.N.S. v. MacIntyre* (1982), 65 C.C.C. (2d) 129 (S.C.C.).

22 Part I of the Constitution Act, 1982, being Sched. B of the Canada Act 1982 (U.K.), c. 11.

23 *R. v. Garofoli* (1990), 60 C.C.C. (3d) 161 (S.C.C.); *R. v. Dersch* (1990), (sub nom. *Dersch v. Canada (Attorney General)*) 60 C.C.C. (3d) 132 (S.C.C.).

24 (2009), 238 C.C.C. (3d) 353 (S.C.C.) at para. 15. See also paras. 35, 39, 42, 49, 53, 56, 59.

25 (1999), 138 C.C.C. (3d) 340 (Ont. C.A.).

the witness could be subjected to cross-examination on the underlying facts. See *R. v. Miller* (1998), 131 C.C.C. (3d) 141 (Ont. C.A.).

EXCLUSION OF POLICE WITNESSES

Because police officers often work in pairs, usually more than one officer testifies about the same conversation or occurrence. In such instances counsel has the opportunity to test one officer's evidence against the other by asking the same questions of each officer. It is therefore imperative that when police officers are testifying, an order excluding witnesses should be requested. This also applies when there is more than one civilian witness who can testify about the same circumstances.[26] If the officers contradict each other on significant matters with respect to the same questions then counsel should have at least been able to bruise their credibility.

A difficulty arises after the request for exclusion of witnesses when the Crown asks that the officer in charge of the investigation be allowed to remain in Court. Often the officer in charge is the last witness for the prosecution and has heard all of the evidence led by the Crown. At first blush this is a fair request as the Crown should be allowed to have someone knowledgeable about the entire case to assist him or her with the evidence just as defence counsel has his client to assist. The problem occurs when the officer in charge will be testifying on some important contested issue about which one or more other officers or even civilian witnesses will also testify. Sometimes the easiest solution is to have the officer in charge of the investigation testify first or else leave the courtroom when evidence is given by others which bears on his or her testimony and return when it is completed; or where the officer's partner will not be testifying, the partner should be the one designated to remain in the courtroom to assist the Crown, although this solution has its own obvious problem.

What happens when there is no such partner and the problem cannot be resolved easily? In the final analysis Canadian law seems to recognize that the decision to exclude witnesses is within the trial Judge's discretion.[27] However, defence counsel should press in all cases, when desired, for the exclusion of witnesses reciting Wigmore.[28] Wigmore states that the officer in charge of the investigation should be required to take the stand first and be exempt from the order of exclusion.

---

26 The topic of exclusion of witnesses has been discussed in Chapter, "Cross-Examination of Certain Categories of Witnesses."

27 McWilliams, *Canadian Criminal Evidence*, 2nd ed. (Aurora: Canada Law Book, 1984), pp. 996-997; *R. v. Dobberthien* (1974), 13 C.C.C. (2d) 513 (S.C.C.) *per* Allen J.A., affirmed (1975), 18 C.C.C. (2d) 449 (S.C.C.).

28 3 Wigmore on Evidence (Chadbourne rev.), vol. 6, p. 476.

THE OPINIONS OF POLICE OFFICERS WITH RESPECT TO IMPAIRMENT

Dickson J., in the Supreme Court decision of *R. v. Graat*,[29] warned that the courts must caution against the tendency to let the opinions of police officers overwhelm the opinions of other non-expert witnesses given that their evidence of opinion of impairment was being admitted under "the compendious statement of facts" exception rather than the "expert witness" exception. Accordingly there was no special reason to prefer the evidence of police officers over other witnesses. The evidence of police is entitled to no special regard even though the police may have seen more impaired drivers than non-police officer witnesses. He stated that "ordinary people with ordinary experiences were able to know as a matter of fact that someone is too drunk to perform certain tasks, such as driving a car." See Chapter "Opinion Evidence by Non-Experts."

---

29   (1982), 2 C.C.C. (3d) 365 (S.C.C.).

20

The Identification Witness

Mistaken identification is probably the most significant cause of proven miscarriages of justice leading to innocent persons being convicted. The identification witness is normally certain of the correctness of his or her identification even when confronted with factors which could lead to a mistake.[1] Because such witnesses are honest and without bias or motive they can be extremely convincing to a jury.[2] Over the years a body of legal precedent has developed recognizing the inherent dangers of identification testimony which can lead to honest error. For these reasons I would not hesitate to urge that, absent exceptional circumstances, where the prosecution's case depends on vulnerable identification evidence, the accused should elect to be tried by judge alone, particularly when you are doubtful about calling the client to testify.

In light of the inherent unreliability of eyewitness identification Crown counsel must ensure all relevant circumstances surrounding pre-trial identification procedures be fully disclosed to the defence and be made available to the trier of fact.[3] A preliminary hearing is particularly helpful in testing the identification evidence.

EXPERT TESTIMONY

The writings and teachings of various experts on the subject, such as social psychologists, explain many causes for mistaken identification. However, it would appear that such expert testimony is inadmissible when identification is in issue as such testimony would add little to what lay persons already know and the experts would be cautioning the jurors on the dangers of identification evidence, a function which is traditionally reserved

---

1 In *R. v. Burke*, [1996] 1 S.C.R. 474 at 498 (S.C.C.), Sopinka J. recognized that "progressive assurance that builds upon an original identification may be erroneous."

2 For an insightful statement distinguishing the credibility as opposed to the reliability of an eyewitness identification, see *R. v. Atfield* (1983), 25 Alta. L.R. (2d) 97 at 98-99 (C.A.).

3 *R. v. Miaponoose* (1996), 30 O.R. (3d) 419 (Ont. C.A.).

to the trial Judge.[4] In general the credit of a witness may not be impeached by evidence except through cross-examination and in special cases such as proof of prior inconsistent statements or bias unless the evidence tendered is also relevant to issues other than credibility. So that an expert's evidence would not be receivable to give his or her view that memory tends to get hazier as time elapses.[5] Likewise it has been held that a psychologist's evidence was inadmissible when called to instruct a jury that all witnesses have problems with perception and recall with respect to an occurrence that is brief and stressful; or that members of one race tending to think that members of another race all look alike. The expert would be reminding the jury of matters within their normal experience.[6]

However, in *R. v. Sophonow (No. 2)*,[7] O'Sullivan J.A. held that in certain circumstances an expert may be able to assist a jury, not to impeach the credibility of witnesses who saw the assailant but to impeach the trustworthiness of sketches and a composite sketch drawn by a police officer. An expert was permitted to explain the phenomenon which he described as "unconscious transference." Without scientific caution or explicit jury instruction the jury might not have realized that it was likely that the eyewitness might have been pointing out resemblances between the composite sketch and the accused rather than between the accused and the eyewitness's untainted memory of what he or she saw at the scene of the crime.

In the United States expert testimony has been ruled admissible as to factors that affect eyewitness reliability, particularly where there is not any significant corroboration.[8]

---

4 *R. v. Audy (No. 2)* (1977), 34 C.C.C. (2d) 231 (Ont. C.A.). The Court held that it was not holding in every case such evidence should be excluded, but this was not such a case. See also *R. v. Fengstad* (1994), 27 C.R. (4th) 383 (B.C. C.A.) where the Court held that the "problems of identification are clearly within the general knowledge and comprehension of judges and properly instructed juries. . ." Also see *R. v. McIntosh* (1997), 117 C.C.C. (3d) 385 (Ont. C.A.), leave to appeal refused [1998] 1 S.C.R. xii (S.C.C.). The Honourable Justice Cory recommended in the Sophonow Inquiry "that judges consider favourably and readily admit properly qualified, expert evidence pertaining to eyewitness testimony" but his recommendation does not seem to have gained favour.

5 *R. v. Sophonow (No. 2)* (1986), (sub nom. *R. v. Sophonow (No. 2)*) 25 C.C.C. (3d) 415 (Man. C.A.), leave to appeal refused (1986), 25 C.C.C. (3d) 415n (S.C.C.).

6 *R. v. McIntosh* (1997), 117 C.C.C. (3d) 385 (Ont. C.A.).

7 *Supra.* See also *R. v. Marinelli* (June 20, 1988), Doc. 1859/88 (Ont. Dist. Ct.), which held that an expert's evidence on the frailties of human perception and recall is admissible where the identification was made four months after the offence and the witness had, in effect, testified that his memory had improved the accuracy of his identification. The Court held that notwithstanding *R. v. Audy (No. 2)* advances in scientific knowledge were such that the Court should be exposed to that research as an aid in assessing the evidence.

8 *People v. McDonald*, 690 P.2d 709 (Cal. 1984); *U.S. v. Downing*, 753 F.2d 1224 (3rd Cir. (Pa.) 1985); *U.S. v. Smith*, 736 F.2d 1103 (6th Cir., 1984).

The evidence of a trained police officer, but without special training or experience in eyewitness identification, may be mistaken in his identification just as any civilian witness.[9]

PHYSICAL CHARACTERISTICS

The statement, "That is the man" is only the expression of an opinion which is valueless unless the witness can associate distinguishing features such as height, weight, clothing, scars, etc., which impart a degree of particularity to the description of the accused. "A description which fits fifty men equally can identify no one of them."[10] In *R. v. Miaponoose*,[11] the Court quoted with approval the Law Reform Commission of Canada Study Paper on Pretrial Eyewitness Identification Procedures (1983). The Commission pointed out that an opinion "that is the man" is partly based on a number of psychological and physiological factors, many of which are not totally understood by jurists. However, in *R. v. Mongovius (No. 1)*[12] the British Columbia Court of Appeal backed off somewhat from its earlier decisions when the Court found that a witness does not have to be as detailed in his identification of the alleged perpetrator as might be concluded from the judgments in *R. v. Browne*[13] and *R. v. Harrison*.[14]

The Supreme Court of Canada in *Chartier* has stated that regardless of the number of similar characteristics a witness's statement may reveal, if there is one notable dissimilar feature there can be no identification.[15] In *R. v. Blackman* the Ontario Court of Appeal held that the *Chartier* instruction to a jury on eyewitness identification applies to cases where there is a clear dissimilarity in the witness's identification coupled with a lack of supporting evidence.[16]

---

9 *R. v. Dunn* (2006), 211 C.C.C. (3d) 307 (P.E.I. C.A.), additional reasons at 2007 CarswellPEI 35 (P.E.I. C.A.).

10 *R. v. Smith* (1952), 103 C.C.C. 58 at 61 (Ont. C.A.); *R. v. Browne* (1951), 99 C.C.C. 141 (B.C. C.A.); *R. v. Yates* (1946), 85 C.C.C. 334 (B.C. C.A.); *R. v. Spatola*, [1970] 4 C.C.C. 241 at 249 (Ont. C.A.); *R. v. McDonald* (1951), 101 C.C.C. 78 (B.C. C.A.); *R. v. Harrison (No. 3)* (1951), 100 C.C.C. 143 (B.C. C.A.); *R. v. Simpson* (1954), 109 C.C.C. 366 (N.S. C.A.).

11 *Supra.*

12 (October 5, 1982), McFarlane, Taggart and Hinkson JJ. A. (B.C. C.A.), summarized at 8 W.C.B. 458.

13 *Supra.*

14 *Supra.*

15 *Chartier v. Quebec (Attorney General)* (1979), 9 C.R. (3d) 97 (S.C.C.). *R. v. Boucher* (2000), 146 C.C.C. (3d) 52 (Ont. C.A.); *R. v. Bennett* (2003), 179 C.C.C. (3d) 244 (Ont. C.A.), leave to appeal refused (2004), 2004 CarswellOnt 1325, 2004 CarswellOnt 1326 (S.C.C.).

16 (2006), 215 C.C.C. (3d) 524 (Ont. C.A.), affirmed (2008), 232 C.C.C. (3d) 233 (S.C.C.).

SOME FACTORS AFFECTING IDENTIFICATION

The leading English case of *R. v. Turnbull*[17] makes it clear that the circumstances in which the identification was made by each witness should be examined closely. Such circumstances are: How long did the witness have the accused under observation? At what distances? In what light? Was the observation impeded in any way? Had the witness ever seen the accused before? What length of time elapsed between the original observation and the subsequent identification to the police? Was there any material discrepancy between the description of the accused given to the police or others by the witness when first seen and the accused's actual appearance? Other factors include consistency of the witness's description, his degree of attention and awareness at the time of the crime and the witness's reaction at subsequent encounters with the accused.[18] Notwithstanding that the witness has a good opportunity to observe and accurately record in her mind the appearance of her attacker, a witness during a terrifying and prolonged attack on her person is not expected to observe and mentally record all of the salient features of her attacker or be completely accurate in her recollection of those observations.[19] Even though a witness in such circumstances recollects features consistent with the appearance of the accused, where there are other parts of her description which do not fit the accused, it is cause for considerable concern in assessing the reliability of the identification.[20]

The age of the identifying witness may be significant. If the witness is a child, a detailed and careful examination by the trial judge will be required in his or her charge to the jury.[21] An older witness may have visual problems.

A witness may also admit to difficulties in differentiating between members of a specific racial group.[22]

---

17 (1976), 63 Cr. App. R. 132 (Eng. C.A.); see also *R. v. Browne, supra*; *R. v. Harrison, supra*; *R. v. Yates, supra*; *R. v. Louie* (1960), 129 C.C.C. 336 (B.C. C.A.); *Mezzo v. R.* (1986), (sub nom. *Mezzo v. R.*) 27 C.C.C. (3d) 97 (S.C.C.); *R. v. Smierciak* (1946), 87 C.C.C. 175 (Ont. C.A.), at 177, sets out a number of factors to be considered in assessing identification evidence.

18 *Mezzo v. R., ibid.*, per Wilson J.

19 *R. v. Quercia* (1990), 75 O.R. (2d) 463 (Ont. C.A.). In *R. v. Reitsma* (1998), 125 C.C.C. (3d) 1 (S.C.C.), it was held that frailties of identification may be most pronounced where the accused was not known to the complainant before the offence and the opportunity to observe was limited to a brief, stressful encounter.

20 *Ibid.* See also *Chartier v. Quebec (Attorney General), supra*.

21 *R. v. Yates, supra*, at 345. See also A.D. Yarmey, *The Psychology of Eye Witness Testimony* (New York: Collier Macmillan, 1979), Chapter 9; L. Taylor, *Eyewitness Identification* (Charlottesville, VA. The Michie Co., 1982). p. 16.

22 Loftus, *Eyewitness Testimony* (Cambridge: Harvard University Press, 1979), p. 135; C.C. Thomas, *Eyewitness Identification in Criminal Cases,* 3rd ed., p. 122.

Whilst most identification witnesses are attempting to be honest there may exist with a particular witness a motive to fabricate, such as animosity, hope of reward, attention-seeking. (See Chapter, "Cross-Examination of Certain Types of Witnesses" heading "The Honest Witness.")

PHOTOGRAPHIC DISPLAYS

Although it may be necessary for police to show photographs to a witness as an investigative procedure to discover the identity of the culprit prior to arrest, a single photograph of the accused should not be shown[23]—instead a series of photographs should be displayed. See the recommendations of Justice Cory in The Inquiry Regarding Thomas Sophonow that follows in this chapter. There should be a similarity of faces in the photographs displayed.[24] Many police departments have computers capable of grouping a series of similar photographs. Mug shots should not be shown to the witness.[25]

Where photographs are shown in order to assist in the search of an accused, it is most objectionable to provide such photographs for inspection by more than one person at a time. Each witness should be required to make his or her own inspection and reach his own conclusion without the opportunity for consultation with others and the risk of being influenced by others.[26] However, once a witness has been shown a photograph, even as an investigative aid, his or her later evidence of identification of the accused in a line-up or in a prisoner's dock is weakened by this fact and a jury must be so warned.[27]

After arrest, showing a photograph of the accused to a witness is prejudicial and can destroy the value of the evidence.[28]

Obviously the exact words the witness says when pointing to the accused's photograph or what the witness says with respect to any other photographs in the line-up are important. How certain was the identification by the witness? Counsel should also inquire whether or not the witness has asked the officer if the identification he made was correct. It would be wrong if the witness were told the guilty party was in the photographs or the witness

---

23 *R. v. Smierciak* (1946), 2 C.R. 434 (Ont. C.A.).

24 *R. v. Faryna* (1982), 3 C.C.C. (3d) 58 (Man. C.A.).

25 *R. v. MacLean* (1975), 27 C.C.C. (2d) 57 (B.C. Co. Ct.); *R. v. Dean* (1942). 77 C.C.C. 13 (Ont. C.A.).

26 *R. v. Armstrong* (1959), 125 C.C.C. 56 at 60 (B.C. C.A.).

27 *R. v. Goldhar*; *R. v. Smokler* (1941), 76 C.C.C. 270 (Ont. C.A.); *R. v. Dwyer*; *R. v. Ferguson* (1924), 18 Cr. App. R. 145 (C.C.A.); *R. v. Sutton* (1970), 3 C.C.C. 152 (Ont. C.A.).

28 *R. v. Baldwin* (1944), 82 C.C.C. 15 (Ont. C.A.); *R. v. Watson* (1944), 81 C.C.C. 212 (Ont. C.A.); *R. v. Dwyer, ibid.*

was told subsequently that the guilty party was identified.[29] Even if the officer tells the witness that he cannot answer that question the witness should be asked whether he feels that being subpoenaed to testify is confirmation of the correctness of his identification therefore causing him to be more certain than ever in his prisoner dock identification.

The cross-examiner should also be alert as to what is said between the witness and the Crown attorney and the police. Was the witness told by the Crown or the police that the accused is a bad person or has a criminal record or that the rest of the case is strong? This type of influence may cause the witness to believe that the correctness of his or her identification has been bolstered.

The method used to recall or refresh the recollections of a witness who is to be relied upon to identify a person suspected of wrong-doing or who is under arrest is a matter of the utmost importance. The greatest care should be used to ensure the absolute independence and freedom of judgment of the witness. His or her recognition should proceed without suggestion, assistance or bias created directly or indirectly. If the means employed to obtain evidence of identification involve any acts which might reasonably prejudice the accused the value of the evidence may be partially or wholly destroyed.[30]

Eyewitness identification recommendations were made by Justice Peter Cory, the Commissioner to the Inquiry regarding Thomas Sophonow who was wrongfully convicted of murder. Justice Cory's recommendations with respect to photographic line-ups are as follows.[31]

Photo pack line-up

- The photo pack should contain at least 10 subjects
- The photos should resemble as closely as possible the eyewitnesses' description. If that is not possible, the photos should be as close as possible to the suspect.
- Everything should be recorded on video or audiotape from the time that the officer meets the witness, before the photographs are shown through until the completion of the interview. Once again, it is essential that an officer who does not know who the suspect is and

---

29 *R. v. D'Amico* (1993), 16 O.R. (3d) 125 (Ont. C.A.); *R. v. Tarrant* (1985), 14 W.C.B. 220 (Ont. Dist. Ct.); *R. v. Beal* (1985), 15 W.C.B. 311 (Ont. C.A.).

30 *R. v. Smierciak, supra.*

31 In *R. v. Slater* (2010), 2010 ONCA 376 (Ont. C.A.) (endorsement) the Court held that although the police did not follow the procedure for photo line-ups suggested in the Sophonow Inquiry, the photo line-up evidence was sufficiently representative, photos were shown sequentially to the eyewitness, the witness was told that the suspect's picture might or might not be included and the witness was not influenced by the investigating officer.

who is not involved in the investigation conducts the photo pack line-up.

- Before the showing of the photo pack, the officer conducting the line-up should confirm that he does not know who the suspect is or whether his photo is contained in the line-up. In addition, before showing the photo pack to a witness, the officer should advise the witness that it is just as important to clear the innocent as it is to identify the suspect. The photo pack should be presented by the officer to each witness separately.
- The photo pack must be presented sequentially and not as a package.
- In addition to the videotape, if possible, or, as a minimum alternative, the audiotape, there should be a form provided for setting out in writing and for signature the comments of both the officer conducting the line-up and the witness. All comments of each witness must be noted and recorded verbatim and signed by the witness.
- Police officers should not speak to eyewitnesses after the line-ups regarding their identification or their inability to identify anyone. This can only cause suspicion on any identification made and raise concerns that it was reinforced.
- It was suggested that, because of the importance of eyewitness evidence and the high risk of contaminating it, a police force other than the one conducting the investigation of the crime should conduct the interviews and the line-ups with the eyewitnesses. Ideal as that procedure might be, I think that it would unduly complicate the investigation, add to its cost and increase the time required. At some point, there must be reasonable degree of trust placed in the police.

The following is part of a transcript of an interview between the investigating police officer and a witness regarding the identification by the witness of an accused through photographs. Note how the witness starts off by saying that person in the photograph looks "a bit" like the suspect and doesn't seem sure, and how the officer leads him into saying he is in fact the suspect and how the officer lets the witness know the person in the photograph has a criminal background by referring to the Montreal police and a mugshot.[32]

> R [Police Officer]: But I'd just like you to look at this and see if you recognize any of these pictures as being a person that was in that restaurant that day. Take your time. (Pause). Look at them all. (Pause). You're staring at one picture, what picture are you staring at? What picture are you staring at?

---

32 *R. v. Son Long and Tran Tat* (March 23, 1992), VanCamp J. (Ont. Gen. Div.).

Tran [Witness]: This one.

R: Yeah, does he look like the third guy?

T: He look a bit like the third guy but, he, something about this picture. . .

R: Well, don't. . .

T: . . . doesn't look right.

R: . . . don't re-, don't forget that the picture, you're pointing right now at No. 7, picture No. 7, is that right?

T: Yeah.

R: Don't forget that these pictures might have been taken a couple of years ago, so, you know, when a, when you see a person in a picture the hair might be a little bit different or the weight might be a little different.

T: That's right.

R: What do you mean by that?

T: Well what I mean is, when I was talking to him, he didn't respect, like, I could tell by the way he said that, he didn't respect people when he talk to him. Like he had no respect for people.

R: Right.

T: And he was really mean and sarcastic.

R: And you never seen either one of these two people before. . .

T: Never.

R: Before this trip or before the restaurant?

T: Never.

R: Okay now you're certain you your own mind, right now, that they, those two were definitely the two of three people that were in the restaurant.

T: Yeah.

R: OK, now, I've prepared a photographic line up that has twelve pictures in it and (pause), BUC SING's picture won't be in here.

T: Yeah, that's right.

R: You think that No. 7, how about the rest pictures, any of the other pictures?

T: No.

R: No. So number 7 looks like the guy that was the third guy, is that what you're saying?

T: That's right.

R: Okay, and if I clip that up, can you just read to me what the number is on the back of that picture?

T: 5-9-4-6-1-9-0.

R: Okay, that's not a one, that's a slash, right. It's just a slash so it's . . .

T: Five. . .

R: . . .5-9-4-6, ninety. You see what it is, it's a number that's given for a picture that was taken in 1990.

T: Oh.

R: Okay? Okay. Now, this number 7, you feel that was the third guy (clears throat), that you didn't see with a gun, is that correct?

T: He looks the most like the third guy.

R: Okay. (Pause). Now, I'm going to show you some pictures. (Background noise). Okay, now that you picked out that, I've got another picture of that same number 7 I'm going to show you and maybe it might help you with it. Does that look any. . .

T: Oh, my God, it looks like that. Yeah. . .

R: That picture?

T: But he's skinnier now, yes.

R: Okay, that's the picture that we got given.

T: Do you have. . .

R: . . .pardon?

T: . . .a picture with the rest of his head?

R: No, that was ah, given to us by the Montreal Police Force and in this picture here, he's not wearing ah, a shirt, is that right?

T: Yeah, that's correct.

R: Okay, now that's the best picture we have, it. . . it was not ah, official police ah, mug shot. But there, as I say, in his face looks a little bit skinner.

T: Yeah, that's right.

R: Now, when you look at that picture, does that help you at all? Is that look more. . .

T: Yeah, ahm, it look more than the one in. . .

R: Okay. So would you say that's the third guy?

T: I would say so, yeah.

R: Okay.

POLICE LINE-UPS

There is no obligation for a suspect to take part in a line-up; however, if the accused raises the absence of a line-up when he has refused to partic-ipate, his refusal would become admissible.[33] Failure to conduct a line-up so that the accused is identified for the first time in Court may draw an adverse inference against the adequacy of the Crown's case.[34]

The witness should be taken to a line-up after the accused's arrest and should not be shown photographs.[35] The value of a line-up is weakened substantially when a witness is shown photographs of the identified partic-ipant prior to the line-up as there is a danger that the witness will be influenced by memory of the photograph.

The other persons in a line-up should not be conspicuously different from the suspect in age and build, colour and complexion, costume or any other particular.[36] An improperly conducted police line-up can lead to little

---

33 *R. v. Leclair* (1989), 67 C.R. (3d) 209, (sub nom. *R. v. Ross*) 46 C.C.C. (3d) 129 (S.C.C.); *R. v. Marcoux (No. 2)* (1975), 24 C.C.C. (2d) 1 (S.C.C.).

34 *R. v. Ross, supra; R v. Williams* (1982), 66 C.C.C. (2d) 234 (Ont. C.A.); *R. v. Todish* (1985), 18 C.C.C. (3d) 159 (Ont. C.A.); *R. v. Holberg and Russell* (1979), 42 C.C.C. (2d) 104 (Ont. Co. Ct.); *R. v. Browne and Angus* (1951), 99 C.C.C. 141 (B.C. C.A.).

35 *R. v. Smierciak, supra; Marcoux v. R.* (1975). 24 C.C.C. (2d) 1 at 19 (S.C.C.), *per* Dickson J.

36 *R. v. Goldhar; R. v. Smokler, supra; R. v. Opalchuk* (1958), 122 C.C.C. 85 (Ont. Co. Ct.); *R. v. Todish, supra.* See also *R. v. Malcolm* (1993), 81 C.C.C. (3d) 196 (Ont. C.A.); *R. v. McDonald* (1951), 101 C.C.C. 78 (B.C. C.A.); *R. v. Cosgrove (No. 2)* (1977), 34 C.C.C.

or no weight being attached to a resultant identification.[37] It is recommended that the police take a photograph of the identification parade to confirm the fairness of the line-up at trial. There should be at least ten persons in the line-up.

A line-up first held two and one-half years after the incident severely undermined the value of the identification.[38]

Witnesses should not be permitted to view the line-up together as any identification could be influenced. The investigation officers, after giving brief instructions should not communicate with the witness to avoid influencing the witness. The accused should not be made to repeat a significant statement alleged to have been made at the scene. The officers should not give any information about a suspect to a witness who has made a tentative identification. The witnesses should not communicate what their position was at the line-up so as to reinforce each other.[39]

The witnesses and police should be questioned as to whether the witness was influenced in any way prior to the line-up, as for example, if the witness was driven by an officer to the line-up and was told that the suspect would be in the line-up or told what kind of individuals would be in the line-up.

(2d) 100 (Ont. C.A.); *R. v. Armstrong* (1959), 125 C.C.C. 56 (B.C. C.A.); *R. v. Klusoczky* (1979), 4 W.C.B. 52 (Que. C.A.).

37 *R. v. Faryna, supra.*

38 *R. v. Harvey* (2001), 57 O.R. (3d) 296 (Ont. C.A.), affirmed (2002), 7 C.R. (6th) 1 (S.C.C.).

39 Mark Sandier, Bensen Cowan and Marlys Edwardh, Criminal Lawyers' Association Annual Conviction and Education Programme, 1996.

The Line-Up

The New Yorker Cartoon Album 1975-1985. The New Yorker Magazine, Inc. Penguin Books, 1985. © The New Yorker Magazine, Inc. 1975, 1976, 1977, 1978, 1979, 1980, 1982, 1983, 1984, 1985.

Justice Peter Cory's Recommendations in the Inquiry Regarding Thomas Sophonow as to live line-ups are as follows:

Live line-up

- The third officer who is present with the prospective eyewitness should have no knowledge of the case or whether the suspect is contained in the line-up.
- The officer in the room should advise the witness that he does not know if the suspect is in the line-up or, if he is, who he is. The officer should emphasize to the witness that the suspect may not be in the line-up.
- All proceedings in the witness room while the line-up is being watched should be recorded, preferably by videotape but, if not, by audiotape.

- All statements of the witness on reviewing the line-up must be both noted and recorded verbatim and signed by the witness.

- When the line-up is completed, the witness should be escorted from the police premises. This will eliminate any possibility of contamination of that witness by other officers, particularly those involved in the investigation of the crime itself.

- The fillers in the line-up should match as closely as possible the descriptions given by the eyewitnesses at the time of the event. It is only if that is possible, that the fillers should resemble the suspect as closely as possible.

- At the conclusion of the line-up, if there has been any identification, there should be a question posed to the witness as to the degree of certainty of identification. The question and answer must be both noted and recorded verbatim and signed by the witness. It is important to have this report on record before there is any possibility of contamination or reinforcement of the witness.

- The line-up should contain a minimum of 10 persons. The greater the number of persons in the line-up, the less likelihood there is a wrong identification.

Improprieties in line-up procedures do not necessarily destroy otherwise good evidence and damage done by the improper procedure can often be remedied by a proper caution.[40]

It is recommended that someone from counsel's office be present when possible at the line-up in order to witness the procedure and the exact words spoken by the witness who makes or fails to make an identification. At the very least police notes of the line-up procedures and what was said by the witnesses should be carefully examined.

Inquiries at trial should be made of any conversation between the police and the witness prior to the line-up similar to those alluded to above when the witness identifies the accused in a photograph. One question to a police officer by the witness that could easily arise is whether the person who did it would be there. If so, what was the officer's reply? Did he or she indicate in any fashion that they caught the culprit? The witness may have asked such a question not only to the officer at the lineup but to the officer who picked the witness up from his or her home and transported the witness to the police station. Did the officer who called the witness ask him or her to come down to view a line-up because they've got the man? Even if nothing was said by the police that might influence the witness's identification it is worthwhile asking that witness if he/she thought that the culprit would in

_____

40   *Mezzo v. R.*, *supra*.

fact be in the line-up. If so, that could have influenced the witness's identification.

Asking the suspect in a line-up to repeat memorable words heard by the victim has been frowned upon by the courts and held to be worthless for identification purposes.[41]

It should be remembered that some Canadian police departments are now videotaping line-ups and questions should be put to officers in charge of investigations, usually at a preliminary inquiry, to ascertain if this was done in the case. The presence or absence of such a tape will obviously affect how counsel wishes to approach the question of attacking the propriety of line-up procedures.

THE MINOR LEAGUE LINE-UP

The witness is taken to a public place, for example, a mall, and asked to look to see if he recognizes the suspect (who will be somewhere within his range of vision). The witness will no doubt conclude that culprit has been caught as she has to know that he is at least in custody. There will probably be a police officer (in uniform or not) who is beside him. The suspect may change directions, even more than once, because an identification has not been made, and so will stand out amongst others. He may appear nervous. There may be no one around him that has any physical similarities. He may stand out on the basis of the clothing he is wearing. There will probably be no recorded record of what the police told the witness before or after an arrest was made.

If counsel is retained in time she should object to any such process.

PRISONER DOCK IDENTIFICATION

A prisoner dock identification is of little value particularly if the identification is for the first time after the event.[42]

Some counsel have requested the Court to permit the accused, before evidence is called, to sit in the body of the courtroom rather than the prisoner's dock to determine if the eye witness can pick out the accused. The trial Judge has the discretion to permit this but don't expect a warm

---

41 *R. v. Riddle* (1993), 84 C.C.C. (3d) 430 (Ont. C.A.); *R. v. Todish* (1985), 18 C.C.C. (3d) 159 (Ont. C.A.); *R. v. Lee* (1986), 16 W.C.B. 464 (Ont. C.A.); *R. v. Winterhalt* (1986), 45 Sask. R. 303 (Sask. C.A.).

42 *R. v. Holmes* (2003), 169 C.C.C. (3d) 344 (Ont. C.A.), leave to appeal refused (2003), 313 N.R. 398 (note) (S.C.C.); *R. v. Williams* (1982), 66 C.C.C. (2d) 234 (Ont. C.A.). See also *R. v. Ranger* (2003), 14 C.R. (6th) 324 (Ont. C.A.); *R. v. Tebo* (2003), 175 C.C.C. (3d) 116 (Ont. C.A.); *R. v. Reitsma* (1998), 125 C.C.C. (3d) 1 (S.C.C.).

response if the accused is in custody, particularly for a crime of violence.[43] If you wish to take this gamble then you obviously want a sufficient number of persons in the body of the courtroom who are not significantly different than your client in appearance. It would be best to try this tactic at the preliminary inquiry stage in case it fails although the Crown may make something of it at trial. If you are successful you can bring out at trial the failure of the eye witness through the officer who was sitting with the Crown at the preliminary or perhaps through an agreed statement of fact. You will want to put on the record at the preliminary inquiry a description of the persons sitting in the courtroom, i.e., how many, male or female, ages, clothing, etc. If the eye witness identifies your client for the first time whilst he or she is sitting in the prisoner's dock you may not want to try the above-mentioned tactic given that it is a risky gamble and the law relating to prisoner dock identification greatly favours your client.

Courthouses are now providing a victim's assistance office. Part of that assistance is to make the victim, particularly a young person, feel more comfortable in the courtroom setting. The complainant is taken into a court-room before the trial and is shown where the various players sit (and told their function), including the accused who is in the prisoner's dock. This may be a significant occurrence where the identity of the perpetrator is in issue as the complainant has in effect been told where the accused will be when it comes to making her identification, particularly if the witness is a young person. Defence counsel's cross-examination should seek out from the complainant that if he/she was prepared in such a fashion that he/she knew exactly where the accused would be seated before entering the court-room to testify. If there is a concern that the witness has been forewarned as to the accused's location in the courtroom, counsel might consider asking the judge to permit the client to sit in a place of his/her choosing just before the complainant enters the courtroom.

HYPNOTICALLY INDUCED IDENTIFICATION

Hypnotically induced eyewitness identification was held to be admissible when the trial Judge was made aware by expert evidence of the difficulties with the evidence but found that it was sufficiently reliable to warrant reception.[44]

---

43 *R. v. Conrad* (1973), 12 C.C.C. (2d) 405 (N.S. T.D.); *R. v. Grant* (1973), 13 C.C.C. (2d) 495 (Ont. H.C.); *R. v. Dubois* (1975), 29 C.R.N.S. 220 (B.C. S.C.); *R. v. Vaudrin* (1982), 2 C.C.C. (3d) 214 (B.C. S.C.); *R. v. Nicholson* (1984), 11 W.C.B. 488 (Alta. C.A.).
44 *R. v. Baltovich* (2004), 191 C.C.C. (3d) 289 (Ont. C.A.).

VOICE IDENTIFICATION

Failure to testify to factors going to peculiarity or distinctiveness of an accused's voice goes to weight and there is no particular instruction that a trial Judge must give himself concerning voice identification.[45] A police officer is not allowed to give his opinion that the voice he heard on the *voir dire* is the same voice he heard on the tape recordings as a *voir dire* is another proceeding within section 13 of the *Charter*.[46]

A person familiar with the voice of an accused is permitted to give evidence of that fact. If voice identification is the only evidence of identification the jury is to be given a warning regarding its reliability.[47]

DIRECTED VERDICT OF ACQUITTAL

While a number of the aforementioned cases indicate that weak identification or improper identification procedures could lead to a submission of no evidence, the Supreme Court of Canada in *Mezzo v. R.*[48] indicates any evidence should be left to the trier-of-fact. The Court recognized that in a case involving visual identification there is a need for careful and complete direction to the jury with regard to their treatment of such evidence. Questions of credibility and weight to be given to such evidence are peculiarly the province of the jury.

JUDGE ALONE

For those who think that a trial Judge sitting without a jury should not put themselves in the position of a witness by relying on their own observations about the identification of the accused will not find comfort from *R. v. Slater, supra.* The Court held that the trial Judge could use her own observations of the accused and the photographs taken during the robbery in concluding that the accused was the person in the photographs. Identifi-

---

45 *R. v. Williams* (1995), 98 C.C.C. (3d) 160 (Ont. C.A.).

46 *R. v. Tarafa* (1989), 53 C.C.C. (3d) 472 (Que. S.C.); *R. v. Gordon* (1998), 130 C.C.C. (3d) 129 (Ont. Gen. Div.).

47 *R. v. Grabowski* (1983), 8 C.C.C. (3d) 78 (Que. C.A.), affirmed (1985), 22 C.C.C. (3d) 449 (S.C.C.); *R. v. Murray* (1916), 27 C.C.C. 247 (Alta. C.A.).

48 (1986), 27 C.C.C. (3d) 97 (S.C.C.). See also decision in *R. v. Arcuri* (2001), 157 C.C.C. (3d) 21 (S.C.C.) referred to in the Chapter, "The Preliminary Inquiry." At the preliminary hearing stage where the test for committal is so similar to the test for a directed verdict at the trial stage it was held in *R. v. Herrera*, 2008 CarswellOnt 4622 (Ont. S.C.J.) at para. 28, that on the evidence as a whole the identification evidence was "unclear, tentative and contradictory," such evidence was no evidence as it was based on assumption rather than recollection and therefore met the Sheppard test for committal.

cations by the trial Judge were made of the accused from videotapes installed in corner stores clearly capturing the faces of the accused in *R. v. Leaney*, [1989] 2 S.C.R. 393 and *R. v. Nikolovski* (1996), 111 C.C.C. (3d) 403 (S.C.C.).

JUDGE'S CHARGE

The trial Judge should warn the jury of the special need for caution before placing reliance on the correctness of the identification and convicting. The jury should be instructed as to the reasons for such warning and the Judge should make some reference to the possibility that a mistaken witness could be a convincing one and that a number of such witnesses could all be mistaken. The jury should be charged not only as to the frailties of the eyewitness identification but also be advised that there is a very weak link between the confidence level of a witness and the accuracy of that witness.[49] The Judge should point out that although identification by one witness can support that of another, even a number of honest witnesses can be mistaken. The jury should be directed to examine closely the circumstances in which the identification by each witness came to be made and, finally, the Judge should remind the jury of any specific weaknesses which had appeared in the identification evidence.[50] The trial Judge should point out that the aforementioned warning is given because of the experience of the legal system that in several cases a number of honest witnesses have mistakenly identified someone.[51]

In *R. v. Virk* (1983), 33 C.R. (3d) 378 (B.C. C.A.) it was held that jurors are to be given detailed instructions about the difficulties with eyewitness identification and told the evidence should be scrutinized with care and conflicts are to be reviewed and highlighted. Where there is a clear dissimilarity in the identification, the jury must be told there is no identification.

---

49 *R. v. Richards* (2004), 186 C.C.C. (3d) 333 (Ont. C.A.); *R. v. Hibbert* (2002), 163 C.C.C. (3d) 129 (S.C.C.); *R. v. Knox*, 80 O.R. (3d) 515 (Ont. C.A.).

50 *R. v. Baltovich* (2004), 73 O.R. (3d) 481 (C.A.).

51 *R. v. Sophonow (No. 2)* (1986), 25 C.C.C. (3d) 415 (Man. C.A.). See also *R. v. Olbey* (1971), 13 C.R.N.S. 316 (Ont. C.A.); *R. v. Turnbull* (1976), 63 Cr. App. R. 132 (C.A.); *Mezzo v. R.*, *supra*. See also article by E. Then, Q.C. and P. Stern, "Evidence and Advocacy in the Charter Era" (1987), 3 Nat. Criminal Law Program, pp. N-52 to N-64. For a slightly more restrictive approach to the judge's charge on identification evidence than the aforementioned cases. See *R. v. Edwardson* (1993), 79 C.C.C. (3d) 508 (B.C. C.A.).

CHECK LIST OF THOUGHTS IN PREPARING FOR CROSS-EXAMINATION

Having regard to the aforementioned body of law which has developed to prevent wrongful identifications, the following is a list of suggested thoughts when considering questions to be put to an identification witness.

Witness's Physical and Mental Condition

1. Does the witness have any physical defects, such as poor eyesight or other health problems which would hinder concentration or ability to observe?
2. What was the witness's emotional condition? For example, was he in a state of fear or stress so that his powers of observation would be distracted? Was the witness interested and attentive or was his mind elsewhere, such as on business or family problems?

Memory

1. How long after the event was it before the witness made her first identification to the police. Memory tends to fade with the passage of time. Was memory influenced by what the witness saw or heard after the event, for example by media reports, speaking with other witnesses?

Opportunity to Observe

1. What was the witness's opportunity to observe considering such matters as vantage point, distance, lighting, length of time and impediments such as traffic, people or other obstructions; or distractions such as concentrating on the weapon? Was the witness standing still or moving when making his observations? Were there weather conditions that interfered with the witness's observations?

Accused's Physical Characteristics

1. Has the witness ever seen the accused before the incident in question?
2. What is there about the accused that stands out in the witness's mind and allows him to identify the accused or does the witness's description fit thousands of people equally? Does the accused have any distinguishing features such as height, weight, clothing, scars, moustache, beard, facial attachments or insertions, tattoos etc., which the eye witness failed to notice?

3. What was the witness's original description of the offender given to the police and was there any material discrepancy between the original description and the accused's actual appearance? If the witness could not give a description to the police at the scene of the crime, giving a description at a later date would be suspect.
4. What was the length of time between the incident and the time the witness was first asked to make an identification? Would that length of time be such as to cause the witness's memory to fade?
5. Was the witness in receipt of any information from the police or others after the event which helped her to recall?
6. Were the words of the identification by the witness definite or was there any uncertainty expressed?
7. Does the witness acknowledge difficulty in recognizing persons of a particular racial group, such as differentiating between Japanese, Chinese and Korean persons?

Media Coverage

1. Did the witness see any descriptions of the accused in the newspapers or on television before identifying the accused from a photograph display, in any kind of line-up, on a remand date in Court or testifying in Court? If so, how long before? (There is the danger that the witness will be more influenced by what he saw in the media coverage than by what he saw at the scene.)

MOTIVE TO LIE

Was the witness interested in a monetary reward, is he an attention seeker, or an exaggerator who falsely convinces himself of the truth because he believes in the police who would not wrongly arrest the suspect?

Photographs

1. Was the witness shown a photographic display? If so, how many photographs? Were the photographs shown together?
2. Were any of the photographs mug shots? That is, did they indicate in any way that the accused had been in jail or had a criminal record?
3. Were the faces in the photographs conspicuously different? Was there face shots only, so that the witness was unable to know the weight and height of the person in the photograph?
4. What were the exact words spoken by the witness when referring to

any of the photographs, particularly the one that was identified? How certain was the identification?

5. Was the witness alone when he identified the photograph or were there other potential witnesses in the room at the same time? Did these witnesses overhear each other or talk to one another regarding the identification?

6. How long before the witness attended a line-up or appeared in Court as a witness was he shown the photographs? Were the photographs shown before or after the arrest of the accused? (The issue here is whether the witness was influenced by what he saw in the photographs more than by what he saw at the scene.)

7. What, if anything, did the police officer say to the witness before showing the photographs? If the officer did say anything, would his words have been such as to influence the witness in making an identification?

8. Did the witness ask the officer whether he was correct in his identification after picking out a photograph? If the officer told the witness he or she was correct in their identification, that may serve to confirm an incorrect identification and raise the confidence of the witness in giving his or her testimony later.

9. Did the witness feel that by being subpoenaed to testify that his identification had been correct?

10. Was the witness led to believe by the Crown attorney or police that the accused was a "bad man" or had a criminal record or that the rest of the case was a strong one thereby confirming in the witness's mind that his identification was correct?

11. Did the witness see photographs of the alleged culprit in the media before identifying anyone from the police photographs?

Police Line-up

1. Did the witness attend a line-up? If so, how many people were in the line-up? Were they conspicuously different physically or in their clothing than the accused? Was a photograph taken of the line-up?

2. Was the witness asked to identify the accused in some fashion other than a properly conducted line-up, such as in a car or restaurant or in the police cells?

3. Was the accused picked out of the line-up? What were the exact words spoken by the witness at the line-up? How certain was his identification?

4. Were any other identifying witnesses in the room at the same time so that the identifying witnesses could overhear each other?

5. How long after the event was the witness called to a line-up? Was it significantly subsequent that the witness's memory would fade?

6. Prior to going to the line-up was the witness shown photographs of the accused? If so, how long before? Did the witness see any photographs of the accused in the media?

7. Was anything said by the police to the witness prior to the line-up which might influence the witness to believe that the police had caught the person they were after and he could be in the line-up? If nothing was said, did the witness expect that the culprit would be in the line-up in any event?

8. After the witness identified the accused did he ask the officer if he was correct? If the officer told the witness he or she was correct in their identification that may serve to confirm an incorrect identification and raise the confidence of the witness in giving his or her testimony later. Did the witness feel that by being subpoenaed that the police had confirmed his identification was correct?

9. Did the witness expect to see the culprit in the line-up?

10. Was the witness led to believe by the Crown Attorney or police that the accused was a "bad man" or had a criminal record or that the rest of the case was strong thereby confirming in the witness's mind that his identification was correct?

11. Was the witness "accidentally" allowed to see the suspect in custody before the line-up?

Courtroom Identification

1. If no form of line-up was held was the accused identified in the courtroom on a remand date in the prisoner's dock or, when his name was called out did he come forward to the body of the courtroom while the witness was present?

2. If the accused was in the prisoner's dock, were there other prisoners there as well? How many? Were they similar in appearance or dressed in similar clothing? Was there police or security guards sitting on either side of the accused? (How strong was the aura of guilt surrounding the accused that could influence the identification?) How many others were in the courtroom other than the Court staff and where were they seated in relation to the accused? How different was their clothing and physical appearance?

3. How long after the event did the witness identify the accused in the courtroom? How long after the witness picked out a photograph of the accused, or saw his picture in the media, or picked out the accused in a line-up, was the courtroom identification made? Was the witness remembering the photograph when pointing to the accused in the courtroom? (If the procedure in picking out the accused from a photograph

or a form of line-up was tainted it would have an impact on the court-room identification).

4. Did the police say anything to the witness prior to coming to Court to influence his identification, as for example, that they had arrested the culprit or that he would be in the courtroom? Did they show the witness a photograph of the accused just prior to his courtroom identification? Was the young or nervous witness shown the courtroom before trial and particularly where the accused as well as the other participants would be seated?

5. Notwithstanding that the police or Crown Attorney said nothing which would have influenced the witness, did the witness still expect to see the culprit in the courtroom and in the prisoner's dock? Why else would the witness have been subpoenaed?

6. Was the courtroom identification by the witness the only identification of the accused since the event in question?

A witness should rarely be asked if he is positive about his identification because experience dictates that the witness will say that he is certain. An exception is where counsel detects through his cross-examination that the witness may be beginning to have some doubts. Counsel has nothing to lose by putting this question at the preliminary hearing and if he receives a favourable answer and the client is still committed for trial he can repeat the question at trial with the transcript of the witness's answer readily available. For the Crown to ask a Crown witness if he is certain about his identification would be oath-helping and therefore objectionable. This is particularly so in identification cases where the law has recognized that wrongful convictions arising from the evidence of identification witnesses results to a large degree from the unreliability of such evidence which witnesses wrongly feel so certain about.

See Chapter, "The Preliminary Inquiry" for approach to the identification witness at that stage.

The Crown Attorney's Perspective

The above-mentioned suggestions are from the defence counsel's perspective more so than the Crown attorney's. Steve Sherriff, a Crown attorney in Brampton, Ontario, gave the following advice to Crown attorneys in preparing an examination-in-chief of an identification witness:[52]

1. Were the witness and the accused acquainted prior to the incident? If so, this area should be thoroughly canvassed.

---

52 S. Sherriff, "An Analysis of Identification Evidence," Crown's Newsletter (Ontario), December 1976.

2. Are there any outstanding physical features of the culprit which the accused also has? E.g., deformity, unusual height, weight, scars, etc. (what will contribute to substantial weight here are the features reliably peculiar to the accused not common to many people who could easily have been at the place at the time.)
3. Ae there any unusual traits or mannerisms peculiar to the culprit and the accused? E.g., a nervous twitch.
4. How do the following aspects compare?
   a) voice
   b) height
   c) weight
   d) build or physique
   e) complexion
   f) jaws
   g) nose
   h) eyes
   i) forehead
   j) carriage
   k) colour of head
   l) colour of eyes
5. What was the opportunity to observe?
   a) duration
   b) vantage point
   c) lighting
   d) presence of visual aids
6. How interested was the witness in what he or she was observing at the time of the events?
7. Does the witness have any special training or abilities which would assist observation and/or recollection?
8. What was the method (if any) used to recall or refresh the witness's memory regarding identity? E.g., photographs or line-up.

EVIDENCE OF PAST IDENTIFICATION

A witness, for example, a police officer, may testify to a prior out-of-court identification of the accused by another even where there is no in-court identification by the latter. Such evidence is admissible as independent evidence of identity and is therefore of more evidentiary value than simply showing consistency between out-of-court and in-court identification.[53] So

---

53 *R. v. Langille* (1991), 59 C.C.C. (3d) 544 (Ont. C.A.); *R. v. Swanston* (1982), 25 C.R. (3d) 385 (B.C. C.A.); *R. v. Boyd* (1953), 16 C.R. 412 at 417-418 (Ont. C.A.); but see contrary view, *McCormick on Evidence,* 2nd ed. (1972), p. 603 which states prior identification is inadmissible as hearsay. See also R. Cross, *Cross on Evidence,* 5th ed. (London: Butterworths, 1979), pp. 488-489; *R. v. McGuire* (1975), 23 C.C.C. (2d) 385 (B.C. C.A.); *R. v. Wright,* Ont. H.C., Craig J., May 18, 1984, summarized at 12 W.C.B.

that where a witness identifies the perpetrator in a line-up the day after the offence is committed but cannot identify the accused in the courtroom months later, a police officer who witnessed the identification at the line-up may testify as to what the witness said at the line-up without offending the hearsay rule. This exception that permits prior identification as original evidence applies to an early identification shortly after the event in circumstances that make the identification reliable when compared to the frailties of a dock identification.[54]

In *R. v. Starr*[55] the Supreme Court of Canada held that out-of-court statements of identification may be admitted for the truth of their contests: (1) where the witness identifies the accused at trial and (2) where the witness is unable to identify the accused at trial but can testify that he previously gave an accurate description or made an accurate identification. When the evidence is admitted it should only be to state who the witness identified and why.

DOG TRACKING

The proper foundation for the admissibility of this kind of evidence is set out in *R. v. Holmes*.[56]

---

235. See a thorough discussion in D.F. Libling. "Evidence of Past Identification," [1977] Crim. L. Rev. 268.

54 *R. v. C. (F.)* (1996), 104 C.C.C. (3d) 461 (Ont. C.A.).

55 (2000), 147 C.C.C. (3d) 449 (S.C.C.). This case also discusses whether or not prior identification can be admissible pursuant to the principled approach to hearsay. Ryan J.A. in *R. v. Campbell* (2006), 207 C.C.C. (3d) 18 (B.C. C.A.) held that the finding in *Starr* is *obiter* and *Starr* did not intend to create such an exception to the hearsay rule.

56 (2002), 169 C.C.C. (3d) 344 (Ont. C.A.), leave to appeal refused (2003), 313 N.R. 398 (note) (S.C.C.). Adopting the criteria enunciated by Wein J. In *R. v. Klymchuk* (2000), [2000] O.J. No. 4435, 2000 CarswellOnt 5334 (Ont. S.C.J.).

21

Cross-Examination of Child Witnesses

Simple Language for the Child Witness

Court Jesters Cartoons by Peter V. MacDonald, Q.C. and David Brown. Stoddart. ©
1991 by Peter V. MacDonald and David Brown.

APPROACH TO CROSS-EXAMINATION

Everyone will instinctively sympathize with a child witness. Therefore,
counsel's manner must normally be gentle, never overbearing even when

he catches the child in a seeming untruth. A distraught child may only gain the jury's disgust for the cross-examiner. However, children and young people are impressed with the authoritarian figure of the adult. A non-aggressive yet stern approach may be useful in obtaining information from a young witness, while with other young people the friendly, perhaps even grandfatherly approach may accomplish the same results.

Your language must of course be appropriate for a young child to understand. You do not want to appear insensitive or break the rhythm of your questioning by having the child constantly pausing or asking you to explain your question in simpler terms, or attempting to answer a question he or she does not fully understand. Questions should be short and simple.

These very young children may have difficulty in answering questions relating to units of measurement such as height, weight or age.[1] What is tall or big to a child may be short or small to you and other descriptions for the child may also be much different than for the adult. It would be helpful for example to have the child show what she meant by her measurement by using as comparisons, the size of an adult in the courtroom, or in other examples to the length of the courtroom, or to the age of someone in the courtroom.

It has been observed that very young children have difficult in describing properly the time sequence of events. Time comprehension does not appear to develop until a child is about ten years of age.[2]

A child's ability to observe and recall can be very important and deserving of a close cross-examination.

The following is a fictional cross-examination from the book *The Defense*[3] by D.W. Buffa, wherein defence counsel is cross-examining a young child complainant who had alleged that her stepfather sexually abused her. It was part of the defence theory that the complainant was lying because she was angry at her stepfather for sending her back to school in circumstances where she did not want to return. Also, counsel wanted to reveal that she had complained immediately to her mother after a prior "bad thing" done to her by another man which was in contrast to the complaint of sexual abuse against her stepfather which was made several months afterwards, and that she had threatened to falsely accuse another man of sexually assaulting her if he did not do something she had wanted him to do. This cross-examination is an example of how a very soft approach is conducted by counsel in order to gain the child's trust and obtain helpful testimony regarding very sensitive fact situations:

---

1   Goodman and Helgeson, "Child Sexual Assault: Children's Memory and the Law" (1985-86), 40 U.Miami L. Rev. 181 at 190.

2   Rozell, "Are Children Competent Witnesses: A Psychological Perspective" (1985), 63 Wash. U.L.Q. 815 at 822; Myers, "The Testimonial Competence of Children" (1986-87), 25 J. Fam. L. 287 at 321.

3   Fawcett Crest Books, New York, Published by The Ballantine Publishing Group (1998).

"Before we begin", I said when it was time for my cross-examination, "would you like a drink of water?"

I smiled at her when she shook her head. "I'm going to ask you a few questions. If I ask you a question that you don't understand, just tell me, okay?"

I treated her with all the deference in the world, and I did everything I could to let her know that I only wanted to help. She could say whatever she wanted. I would listen and try to understand. I was as calm as a priest in the confessional. I approached her as softly as an assassin.

"You're thirteen?" I asked as if I was not quite sure.

"Yes. Thirteen. Last month."

"And what grade are you in school?"

She looked at me with a trace of uncertainty. It was summer vacation. "I finished the seventh grade. I'll be in the eighth grade."

"School isn't always much fun, is it?" I asked with a slight, knowing smile.

"No, not always. Sometimes," she confided, "it isn't fun at all."

"I remember," I said in the tones of a co-conspirator. "I once got into a fight at school and the principal sent me home. I'll bet nothing like that has ever happened to you, though, has it?"

She could hardly wait to tell me. "Uh-huh. They sent me home last year."

"But you didn't get into a fight, did you?" I asked, letting her know I was certain she was much too nice a girl ever to get into that kind of trouble.

She shook her head. "I was making too much noise in class."

"My parents took me back to see the principal. I didn't like that very much. Did you have to go back and see the principal?"

"Yes," she admitted contritely.

"And who made you do that? Your mother or your stepfather?"

"Johnny," she answered simply.

I moved immediately to something more serious. "Do you remember what happened three years ago, when you were only ten? A man who lived in your neighbourhood did a bad thing to you, didn't he?"

She looked at me warily, suddenly unsure how far she could trust me. "Yes," she said slowly.

I tried to reassure her. "I'm not going to ask you what happened. I just want to ask you this one question. You told your mother, didn't you?"

"Uh-huh," she replied, hesitant, still not certain what I was after.

"You told her right away, didn't you?" I asked in a tone that suggested admiration for what she had done.

Her doubts about me seemed to vanish. "Yes."

There were more questions, questions about what she liked to do, questions about her friends, questions that had no purpose except to make her feel as much at ease as possible.

"We're almost finished," I told her. "Just a few more." I paused long enough to make sure she was ready to go on.

"You remember when you were talking to Mr. Woolner earlier today? When he was asking you questions and you were answering them?"

She remembered, and she seemed please when I told her I thought she had done very well.

"I just want to see if I understood what you said when you were talking to Mr. Woolner. Will you help me do that?"

"I'll try," she agreed. For a brief, passing moment, a fragile smiled formed on the corners of her small mouth.

"You told Mr. Woolner that you hurt yourself when you landed on the bed?"

"Uh-huh. I hurt my back." Her voice was steady and she sat perfectly still.

"Did you hurt it when you landed on the mattress or on the metal frame?"

She suspected nothing, "On the frame."

It was all I needed, and I left it. "And you told Mr. Woolner," I said with a helpless grin that underscored the difficulty I seemed to have remembering anything, "that you crawled out the bathroom window after your stepfather left the bedroom, and that you went to the park. Is that what you said?"

Her eyes were fixed on mine. "Yes," she agreed.

"And you stayed in the park until you saw your mother come home?"

"Uh-huh," she replied immediately.

"Before you crawled out of the bathroom window . . . Did I hear you correctly? Did you tell Mr. Woolner that there was blood in the bathroom and that you tried to clean it up?"

"I tried, but . . ." Her voice began to falter before she could finish.

"But," I interjected before she could display the kind of emotion I did not want the jury to see, "you weren't able to clean it all up. Is that what you said to Mr. Woolner?"

Her mouth was just starting to quiver. Another moment and it would have been too late. "Yes," she managed to answer.

"Just one last question, Michelle. Just one more."

She seemed relieved, glad that it was almost over. Someone, probably Horace Woolner himself, had to have told her that I would try to confuse her, try to get her to say things she did not mean. But she was just a child; she had forgotten that she was not supposed to trust me.

"Do you remember living for a few weeks with Frank Mumford and his family at their home?"

I had promised her it was the last question. "Yes, I remember," she said. She began to melt back into the witness chair. She could relax now. The last question had been asked.

"And while you were staying there," I asked without warning, "you told Mr. Mumford that if he did not do something you asked him to do you would accuse him of sexually assaulting you, didn't you?"

She had grown used to the betrayal of adults. "No, I didn't" she cried.

I had no further questions."

INHERENT VULNERABILITIES OF CHILDREN

Young children can confuse fact and fantasy. The young child witness may still believe in gremlins, E.T. and Santa Claus.[4] Children can have

---

4   A study by Johnson and Foley, ""Differentiating Fact From Fantasy" The Reliability of

vivid imaginations, are inventive and will exaggerate. They can be unreliable without being dishonest or they can be dishonest. Their recall can be more faulty than adults.[5] Because of their immaturity, they are very receptive to suggestion and as a result testimony can be implanted in their minds by what they read or by interested parties such as parents, police and counsel who prepare the witness with questions.[6] *Quaere* the child's capacity to observe and to recollect as well as to understand questions, frame answers and moral responsibility.[7] Is the child's ability to recall detail limited? Your questions should be framed to confront these issues.

The text, *Annual Review in Psychology*[8] highlights some of the dangers attendant upon interviewing child witnesses, such as when children are "repeatedly and suggestively interviewed about false events" and many will "eventually report the false events as true." These children can "appear highly credible even to trained individuals." "They perceive their adult interviewer as truthful and they want to comply with a respected adult." Some "proven techniques to bias children's recollections include leading questions (He took your clothes off, didn't he?), emotionally threatening questions (Are you afraid to tell? You'll feel better once you've told), biased introductions (Sometimes your uncle Harry does bad things. Can you tell me what he's done to you?), and the use of anatomically detailed dolls. (Give such a doll plus a stethoscope to any young child after a routine medical exam and just watch what the child will come up with.) Other problematic techniques include specific questions (Where did he hurt you?), guided imagery (Let's close our eyes and go back to your nursery school), non-verbal clues (smiling, mmhmm, etc.) and repeated information over weekly interview sessions."

By virtue of section 659 of the *Criminal Code* a warning by the trial Judge that it is dangerous to convict an accused on the evidence of a child without corroboration is abrogated.[9] The Supreme Court of Canada in *R. v. B. (G.)*,[10] has stated that the courts should take a common sense approach

---

Children's Memory" (1980), 40 J.Soc. 33, found that children over six years of age are not more likely than adults to confuse fact and fantasy.

5 But children's memory can be better than adults. See Rozell, "Are Children Competent Witnesses: A Psychological Perspective" (1985), 63 Wash. U.L.Q. 815 at 829.

6 Cohen and Harnick, *Law and Human Behaviour*, Vol. 4, No. 3, 1980, p. 201. The authors conclude from their studies that children are really no more vulnerable to suggestion than adults.

7 *R. v. Kendall* (1962), 132 C.C.C. 216 (S.C.C.), per Judson J.; *R. v. Horsburgh* (1967), [1968] 2 C.C.C. 288 (S.C.C.).

8 By Maggie Bruck, (McGill University) and Stephen Ceci (Cornell University) reported in the National Post November 8th, 1999 by Carol Milstone, PhD.

9 Section 586 of the *Criminal Code* repealed so that the unsworn evidence of a child need not be corroborated. See *R. v. Bickford* (1989), 51 C.C.C. (3d) 181 (Ont. C.A.).

9 (1990), 56 C.C.C. (3d) 200 (S.C.C.). See also *R. v. W. (R.)* (1992), 74 C.C.C. (3d) 134 (S.C.C.). See also *R. v. C. (H.)* (2009), 241 C.C.C. (3d) 45 (Ont. C.A.), following *B. (G.)*.

when dealing with the testimony of young children and not impose on them the same exacting standards as adults, such as with a flaw that amounts to a contradiction in their evidence. However, Madam Justice Wilson stated that this does not mean that the courts should not carefully assess the credibility of child witnesses nor lowering the standard of proof when dealing with children. In *R. v. Marquard*,[11] the Supreme Court of Canada held that although negative stereotypes of children should be avoided there are cases where it could be reversible error if the trial Judge fails to instruct the jury as to the frailties of a child witness's testimony. In *R. v. S. (W.)*,[12] Finlayson J., referring to the judgments of Wilson J. in *R. v. B. (G.)*[13] and McLachlin J. in *R. v. W. (R.)*,[14] opined that the courts should assess the evidence of witnesses of tender years for what they are, children, and not adults, and that we should not expect them to perform in the same manner as adults does not mean that the evidence of children should be subjected to a lower level of scrutiny for reliability than would be done for adults.

A trier-of-fact can be persuaded by demeanour, particularly that of a child witness. It is important therefore to keep in mind what Finlayson, J.A. stated in *R. v. S. (W.)*, i.e. that the issue is not the demeanour of the witness but the reliability of the child's testimony. Demeanour alone is not sufficient to find a conviction where there are significant inconsistencies and conflicting evidence.

In *R. v. C. (H.)*[15] the Court noted that a credible witness may give unreliable evidence. Credibility has to do with a witness's truthfulness, reliability with the accuracy of the witness's testimony. Accuracy takes into consideration the witness's ability to accurately observe, recall, and recount the evidence on an issue.

Child witnesses are most common in cases where sexual impropriety against them is alleged. Children can be extremely imaginative. A young child may know much about sexual matters by, unbeknownst to anyone, reading his or her brother's Playboy magazines, he or she may have overheard other people, including children, talking about their sexual exploits, or even having secretly watched their parents' X-rated movies or adult movies on T.V. without the latter's knowledge. They are exposed to sex education films at school. Children are increasingly made aware through

---

11 (1993), 85 C.C.C. (3d) 193 (S.C.C.). In *R. v. C. (F.)* (1996), 104 C.C.C. (3d) 461 (Ont. C.A.) it was held that in some cases common sense dictates that a warning be given regarding the risks in accepting a child's evidence. See also *R. v. Kendall* (1962), 132 C.C.C. 216 (S.C.C.); *R. v. C. (F.)* (1996), 104 C.C.C. (3d) 461 (Ont. C.A.); *R. v. W. (R.)* (1992), 74 C.C.C. (3d) 134 (S.C.C.), reconsideration refused (November 18, 1992), Doc. 21820 (S.C.C.).

12 (1994), 18 O.R. (3d) 509 (Ont. C.A.).

13 (1990), 56 C.C.C. (3d) 200 at 219-220 (S.C.C.).

14 (1992), 74 C.C.C. (3d) 134 (S.C.C.).

15 *Supra*, at para. 41, following *R. v. Morrissey* (1995), 97 C.C.C. (3d) 193 (Ont. C.A.).

educational sources, including the media, that they should complain about sexual abuse. The media is paying a great deal of attention to child abuse, including sexual assault, and as a result, children are more than ever being exposed to the details of sexual offences. Knowledge without first-hand experience is therefore not unusual for young children. Another source of influence for the child witness is other children who are involved or have heard about the circumstances.

Children may lie as a result of peer pressure, fear, a motive such as vindictiveness, or pressure from a parent involved in a custody or alimony battle who wants leverage against the other spouse. As someone once said — "For those who believe that a child would not lie have not been blessed with any."

If the child does have an imagination, encourage that imagination to flower so the child's evidence will offend common sense and exaggerations or bizarre testimony will be obvious to the Court and impact on credibility.[16]

Has there been any bizarre acting-out by the child since it was alleged the child was abused? Experts point to such actions as being consistent with having been sexually assaulted. However, such acting-out may be consistent with innocent explanations. If there was no bizarre acting-out by the child, if the child's school grades remained basically the same, does this mean that there was no sexual assault perpetrated? In *R. v. N. (R.A.)*[17] it was held that expert evidence is not always necessary to explain that certain behaviour of complainants is consistent with sexual abuse. The courts have recognized evidence of poor school performance, running away, nightmares, emotional change, withdrawal and unresponsiveness strengthen the child's complaints. Of course such indicia may have been caused as a result of reasons other then sexual abuse.

Counsel should be alert to internal inconsistencies in the child's testimony and inconsistencies with other witnesses and objective evidence. You will want to see all the statements by the child to various persons regarding the incident—parents, police, social workers, medical people, school records, Children's Aid workers, etc. This may involve an application for third party records pursuant to the relevant sections of the *Criminal Code*. You will want to hear any tape-recordings of any interviews of the child as they may be revealing. Does the child keep a diary which can be revealing? Because it may be difficult for the trier-of-fact to believe that a young child would have knowledge of the sexual behaviour they have described, it is important to cross-examine on the possible sources of such knowledge, such

---

16 Some observers have noted that very young children without sexual experience are incapable of lying or fantasizing about sexual acts particularly in the detail they have described. See McGrath and Clemens, "The Child Victim as a Witness in Sexual Abuse Cases" (1985), 46 Mont. L. Rev. 229 at 240.

17 (2001), 152 C.C.C. (3d) 464 (Alta. C.A.).

as: what older brothers or sisters tell them, what others have told them, magazines or videos they may have seen belonging to older siblings or parents, or adult movies on T.V., sex education in school, etc.

A child witness may have learned by rote what he or she is going to say in examination-in-chief. This may or may not mean that the witness is untruthful. Memorizing testimony may be an indication of nervousness or of being too conscientious. If it is suspected that the child has memorized his or her testimony the child should be asked to repeat the evidence given in-chief, perhaps more than once. The use of the same words, phraseology, order and even tone will make it clear to everyone that the evidence has been learned by rote. The cross-examiner can confuse the witness by quickly asking questions out of sequence, employing the "skip-round" technique and by concentrating on areas away from the memorized zone.

Counsel should inquire as to whom the child talked to about the facts of the case, the number of times and what the child was told in order to determine exactly the extent of any coaching, no matter how subtle. Has there been any attempts at re-inforcing the child's evidence, or offers of reward by the interviewer so that the child feels he or she will have disappointed the interviewer by not answering in the way that is expected, and so answer untruthfully? Does the child have any animus or motive to lie?

R. v. Sterling,[18] is an instructive case for counsel defending and prosecuting a sexual assault case involving young children both from the perspective of examination-in-chief and particularly cross-examination. Improper interviewing techniques and the suggestibility of young children is the focus of this case where a number of children who were supposedly sexually abused had been entrusted to the care of the accused and his parents at a babysitting centre in Martensville, Saskatchewan. Several police officers were also charged with sexual assault on some of the children. *Sterling* is a microcosm of the many things that can go wrong in obtaining information from young children.

During the course of the trial a number of very qualified experts testified and evidence elicited from them (with back-up studies), is a strong warning to Crowns, defence counsel and Judges about the fallibility of the evidence of young children particularly where scrupulous care has not been taken with the proper techniques of interviewing. I therefore intend to spend a little time with this case given its educational value on a very important topic. The examinations of the experts provide a great deal of material for counsel in preparing their cross-examinations of not only experts but of young children. With one exception the following examinations are taken directly from the reported case.

Dr. Yuille, a Crown expert testified during examination-in-chief about child susceptibility and memory recall:

18   (1995), 102 C.C.C. (3d) 481 (Sask. C.A.).

Q: Dr. Yuille, if we could start with some basic statements, could you answer perhaps the following question: among the leading researchers in the area of child susceptibility and accuracy, is there any consensus with respect to child memory recall and the accuracy of information children can provide?

A: Yes, the general conclusion is that if children are carefully or properly interviewed, their testimony—and they are trying to tell the truth, their testimony will be as accurate as an adult. There are no consistent age related differences in accuracy. So a six year old will be as accurate as a ten year old who will be as accurate as an adult. Again, with the caveat, as long as they are properly interviewed.

Q: With respect to the statement you just made, is the word "questioned" synonymous with "interviewed"?

A: Yes.

Q: And are children, or can children be susceptible to suggestion?

A: Yes.

Q: Are there any variables with respect to a child's susceptibility?

A: Yes.

Q: And what would that be?

A: Well, one of them is age, that the younger the child the more susceptible the child is to the influence of suggestion. And also, the nature of the interviewer. For example, if a six year old child is interviewed by a ten year old child, the effect of suggestion is much less than if they're interviewed by an adult.

Q: Children are more susceptible to suggestion by adults than by a peer?

A: Yes. Yes.

Dr. Yuille testified about contamination of the child witness, i.e. "where someone provides information to the complainant or to the witness in the course of the interview or investigation that is not in the complainant's or witness's memory". He pointed to the main mistakes or problems of inexperienced interviewers thusly:

A: ... The main problems are not establishing rapport with the child, to help the child to relax as much as those circumstances permit. Secondly, asking leading or suggestive questions, and thirdly, not giving the chance to the child to tell his or her own version of events. Not giving a chance for enough details to come out.

Dr. Yuille testified that young people are susceptible to suggestion but this decreases with age and it is therefore important that leading or suggestive questions be avoided. Interviews should be kept at a minimum in order to avoid the danger of contamination. Parents should not become involved in interviewing because they are not trained interviewers. A child may also be distracted or inhibited by the presence of a parent. Whenever possible the interviewer should not use the suspect's name in order to avoid suggestion to the child.

The following is the cross-examination of Constable Bryden:

Q: Would you agree with me as well that in every interview that you conducted you asked the children leading questions?

A: There were questions probably in every interview that I had with children that could be in and of themselves construed as leading, yes.

Q: I'm just going to refer you to—I've just randomly picked an example from each interview and I'd ask whether you agree with me that in fact these—these are examples of the leading questions you used. In—I'm referring to the November 2nd interview with J. and the question was "What happened to you?" Do you agree with me that that question is leading or suggestive in and of itself?

. . . .

A: I—I agree with you that it is in and of itself suggesting that something happened to the child, yes, in and of itself.

Q: Now, I'm going to refer to the November 8th interview. And I'm referring to page seven of that interview.

THE COURT: Or [sic] what child?

MR. KALENITH: This is of J.L.

Q: And the question, "Did Travis ever use his fingers?" Would you agree with me that that's a leading or suggestive question?

A: Yes, it is.

Q: I'm now referring to the December 20th interview with J.L. and on page three of that transcript. And the question, "Did Linda do to you what she did to K. and D.?" Is that also leading or suggestive?

A: Yes, it is.

Q: And the January 7th interview with J.L. and I'm referring to page 14 of that transcript, "Has anyone ever touched you there?"

A: Yes, in and of itself, yes.

Q: And the January 7th interview with K.L. and on page 11 of that transcript. The question, "What else did Ron touch you with besides his penis?" Is that leading and suggestive?

A: In and of itself, yes.

. . . .

Q: Okay. On the January 27th interview with S.H. and it's page six on my copy of the transcript. You asked him, "Did Ron touch you with anything else or with any part [sic] his body besides his hands?"

A: Your question?

Q: Is that a leading or suggestive question?

A: In and of itself, yes, it is.

Q: The January 29th interview with J.L. on page one of that transcript. The question, "Did anything happen to C.?"

A: Yes, that can be considered a leading question.

Q: And on you—on your February 8th interview of S.H. on page four of that transcript. And the question, "Who else touched C. with the thing?"

A: Yes, in and of itself, a leading question.

Q: On the February 9th interview of S.H. on page six of that transcript. "Did Jim touch anyone else?" Is that leading or suggestive?

A: Yes.

Q: On the April 3rd interview of C.L. and at page ten of that transcript. And the question, "Who else touched you there?"

A: Yes, again, in and of itself it could be considered a leading question. And it was based on information that I had received through conversations through parents.

Q: And on the April the 5th interview with J.L. and page five of that transcript. And the question was, "Who else touched K. at the devil church besides Jim?"

. . . .

A: Yes, the question, "Who else touched K. at the devil church besides Jim?" can be construed in and of itself as a leading question.

Q: On the May 2nd interview with S.H. and I'm referring to page 14 of that transcript. The question, "Did anyone else ever touch you?" Is that leading or suggestive?

A: Yes.

Q: And finally the last one that we saw on the 1st of June with C.L. and this question appears on pages 41, 50 and 65 of the transcript. "What else did they touch you with?" You can just refer to the page 41 question as an example. Is that leading or suggestive?

A: Yes, it is. However, that question was based specifically on information that the child gave me initially at the interview. And if I—if I recall correctly, the child mentioned the use of tools. He mentioned during the interview that they had tools with them or they used tools. The questions—the question, "Did they ever touch you with anything else?" I was trying to have the child be specific as to what in fact he was touched with. He had mentioned tools and I wanted to find out if in fact there was a specific object that he had generally alluded to previously in the interview that he could provide an answer to.

Q: And you don't think that's more specifically covered by saying, for example, what kind of tools?

A: That's a question I could have asked him.

Q: Right. I mean, this certainly includes a number of things other than tools, this question, doesn't it?

A: Which question are you referring to now?

Q: "What else were you touched with?" It's not limited to tools is it?

A: No, it gives the child an opportunity to provide any information that he wishes to provide.

Q: Or—or potentially suggest that there are other things that you would like to hear about?

A: Precisely.

Q: And again, as you've said, you don't have any expertise as to what effect these types of leading questions would have on a child's memory?

A: No, I do not have any expertise.

The following is part of a cross-examination of Rodney Butler, a social worker:

Q: When you were interviewing both S.H. and C.L. and when you were going through the disclosure part of your communication therapy, you would at times use leading questions, wouldn't you?

A: I would try not to, but there—I know that looking back some of my questions were leading, yes.

Q: Right. For example, in the first disclosure session that you had with S.H. on February the 10th you asked him, "Who were you abused by?" as one of the first questions.

A: Yeah.

Q: You agree that you asked him that?

A: M'hmm.

Q: And that you in the same session asked S.H. whether or not Travis had told him not to tell about things that happened to him.

A: I could if it's there that I did. I don't remember that specifically but —

Q: All right. And that with C.L. in the first disclosure session on June 17th you asked C.L. to tell you the names of the people who hurt you.

A: That's correct.

Mr. Butler also admitted that he had asked S.H. repeatedly to remember details of abuse, and that under such circumstances a child might feel so pressured to satisfy the interviewer that he would embellish his story.

The Court went on to note the following weaknesses in the interviews of the children:

The defence also questioned the manner in which photo exhibits and various objects were put before witnesses, often before interviewers had elicited a description of the places or things shown and sometimes before a child even mentioned the items. For example, under cross-examination Constable Bryden conceded that J.L. had made no mention of a vibrator until shown it; nor did C.L. discuss incidents involving axe handles (transcript, vol. II, p. 573). S.H. and C.L. did not cite incidents at a place other than the Sterling home until they saw pictures of the Storey-Bishoff property (trial transcript, vol. III, p. 717). The defence's point was that the children's memories had been so contaminated that it was impossible to know where memory ended and suggestion began.

Several investigators accepted unquestioningly parents' reports of their children's disclosures, without determining whether that information was obtained in a reliable manner (trial transcript, vol. VI, p. 1387). During ensuing interviews, they prompted the children, through the use of suggestive questions, to confirm the version of events recounted by their parents. Under cross-examination, Corporal Moor conceded that knowing in advance that a child might disclose certain information affected the manner in which he conducted the interview (trial transcript, vol. VI, pp. 1311-12). He further admitted that the source of the information which underpinned leading questions asked in one interview had been the testimony of a second child (trial transcript, vol. VI, p. 1468).

Interviewers were also faulted for having offered children rewards in return for their accounts of alleged occurrences. Children were often complimented for their bravery in making a disclosure (see, *e.g.*, trial transcript, vol. II, p. 425). Children were promised colouring books (trial transcript, vol. II, p. 529), and in one case, a visit to see the police dog (trial transcript, vol. VI, pp. 1359-60) at the end of their interviews. They were also encouraged that the session would soon end and they could play as soon as they had discussed a particular subject (trial transcript, vol. II, p. 388).

Sessions were sometimes conducted by more than one person and sometimes observed by others. Corporal Moor and Constable Bryden conducted several interviews together. When interviews were conducted at a witness's home, the child's parents often remained in the room, sometimes intervening. For example, on one occasion J.L.'s father interjected to disagree that he had told his son the identity of a police officer (trial transcript, vol. II, p. 542). On another, his mother urged him to reiterate for Constable Bryden information he had already told her. Even the witness's siblings were present on a few occasions.

Other aspects of the interviews were also criticized. Interviewers often failed to establish a rapport with the child interviewees, wasting little time to begin the sessions. The interviews were recorded using a variety of media, including notes jotted in an officer's notebook, questions and answers written down verbatim, audiotapes, and videotapes. Only the last process afforded subsequent viewers an opportunity to evaluate the context in which disclosures were adduced and the full range of meaning conveyed by the subjects.

Police interviewers testified that parents were all cautioned not to discuss their children's allegations amongst each other. Despite this, S.H. mentioned in one interview that I.L. had not yet revealed anything to the police and that his sister was frightened (trial transcript, vol. VI, p. 1417).

Apart from the sexually explicit nature of his disclosures, S.H. made a number of statements during interviews unusual for someone of his age and experience. He said that the Sterlings should be put in jail, that he wanted to sue them, and that he bet his mother did too (trial transcript, vol. II, p. 461). While discussing sexual abuse, he said: "In the physical sense it made me feel good, but my brain said that it was awful" (trial transcript, vol. VI, p. 1473).

Dr. Underwager expressed his concerns about the interviews of two children:

Q: Moving on to S.H., there was an audio tape made January the 15th, 1992, by Constable Bryden, it's Exhibit D-9.
A: Yes. We had the transcript here, we did not have the tape.
Q: I see.
A: That's correct.
Q: I think that's correct.
A: Yes. This is the first one for which we have a transcript, and it is very leading, suggestive and contaminating. The child is asked, again nineteen times, nineteen different times, about where else Linda touched him. The answers again that are "I don't know" or denials, are simply not accepted. It's a very coercive interview, very leading.

Q: S.H. was interviewed again by Constable Moor on video tape on March the 18th, 1992, and this is Exhibit D-27.

A: Yes, sir. Here the child—I'm sorry, the adult tells the child that he is being told true things that he knows things have happened with the defendants. That's a very powerful application of social pressure, and if it's not true, then it's a very questionable adult behaviour. The adult says he needs the help of the child, and pleads that he needs the help of the child, because the people are getting worse, and he needs to help. But it's a—those are the ways, unusual ways, in which that interview is very coercive.

Q: And S.H. was interviewed again on April 13th, 1992—

A: Right.

Q: —by Constable Moor and Constable Bryden, and that's Exhibit D-28.

A: Yes, sir. Here again, the adults tell the child that other children are talking, they've mentioned another place. The other children are supposed to have mentioned another place. They say that the bigger children are taking care of the little children by telling about what happened. They give information to him. The dolls are used. Pictures are shown. There is a positive social approval given. They praise the child for telling, and encourage statements of revenge toward the defendants, inculcating or teaching anger and hostility towards the defends.

Q: I'm going to move on to D.C., and an audio tape was made of D.C. on March the 10th, 1992, by Jo Suddy [sic], a social worker, and that's Exhibit D-34.

A: Right.

Q: Do you have any comments on that audio tape?

A: Yes, sir. Again, it's very leading and very suggestive. Suddy is doing the questioning and asks repeated questions, just a slightly different form, but the repeat of questions, it's the same thing over and over again about things that happened when he—when this child was babysat at the defendant's. And here tries to get the child to tell what was said to the mother. That's a confusing direction that I talked about yesterday, saying to the child, "Tell me what you told your mother or somebody else at an earlier time." That is a problem in this interview as well. That's what I see there.

Q: Thank you. D.C. was interviewed again, it was recorded on audio tape by Constable Materi on March the 14th, 1992, and that's Exhibit D-35.

A: Right. The mother is present in this interview, and as I said, that introduces compliance and introduces more social pressure. The responses of the adults, are again, just very leading, very suggestive, repeated questioning. It refers back to the earlier interview.

Q: And D.C. was interviewed again on March the 19th, 1992 on video tape, and that's Exhibit D-29.

A: It's almost like a litany. This is a very leading and very suggestive interview. At the beginning the adults make clear that what they want is for the child to talk about touching by the babysitters. The child is told that Moor talks to kids who help about grown-ups that touch them. He's told that the grown-ups are sick, they need help, and so Moor needs the child's help. And then variations of this are repeated throughout the interview. In many ways I regard that as very questionable. The attitude toward defendants is really not to get help, but rather to punish.

Dr. Raskin also commented on the interviewer's techniques and like Dr. Underwager he criticized the use of inappropriate pressures and social approval in addition to other mentioned techniques to encourage disclosure by the child:

Q: Okay. Very generally, Doctor, can you provide us with some of your observations in relation to the videos that you reviewed here? and I stress very generally.

Q: Yes, I can. In general I found that the interview techniques and the questioning procedures were extremely substandard and violated basically all of the major principles for properly interviewing children. The techniques that were used were leading, suggestive and coercive, that there was an extreme amount of stereotyping of a negative sort, that individuals were suggested, acts were suggested, procedures that are suggestive in themselves were used extensively. Inappropriate pressure and inducements were used with the children. Their response were selectively reinforced and rewarded by the interviewers. The interviewers used their authority as police officers and investigators to create an atmosphere of pressure and enlisted co-operation of the children as if they were almost assisting in the investigation themselves, and in general there was an atmosphere of pressure and continual questioning of a suggestive nature that caused serious problems in the statements.

Q: The two main interviewers are Claudia Bryden and Corporal Moor. Is there a difference between the two interviewing styles?

A: Yes, there was a substantial difference.

Q: First off, did you find the pitfalls that you're telling us about in the interviews of Claudia Bryden?

A: Yes.

Q: Did you find them in the interviews of Corporal Moor?

A: Yes, to an even greater extent.

Q: Okay. Do you have a general comment on the interviewing techniques of Corporal Moor?

A: Yes. Corporal Moor's interviewing techniques I found were some of the most serious violations of proper interview procedures that I have even observed in the interviews that I have reviewed. His techniques were so inappropriate that they just destroyed the integrity of the interview process and, therefore, raise substantial questions about the obtained statements.

Q: Specially, Doctor, and I'm saying generally as relating to interview techniques, and I'm moving on now, D.C. interview with Jo Suttie, do you have any comments on that? I believe that's the March 10th interview.

A: Yes. The interview by Joe Suttie, who is a social worker as I recall, was a rather suggestive and leading interview that used repeated questioning in attempts to elicit allegations, although it did not use some of the more extreme measures that I had talked about earlier, but it was inappropriate in that sense, and the child was not given an opportunity to give the child's own descriptions.

Q: Is there anything that distinguishes that interview from the other interviews that we're talking about?

A: Well, in terms of the way it was conducted?

Q: Right.

A: Well, it didn't make the appeals to authority and use the kind of pressure and highly inappropriate techniques to the extent that the other interviews did.

Q: All right. Tom Materi, Constable Tom Materi, did an interview on March the 14th. Can you comment on his interview technique of D.C.?

A: Yes. That also was a very suggestive and leading interview, and it was somewhat more problematic than the one I just mentioned because it began with an extremely suggestive question about how the child was there to talk about an incident that had happened, as if there was no question about that, instead of asking about things that may have happened.

Q: Okay. Moving along, Doctor. You've seen in these various video photos of buildings or a building shown to these children. Comments in that regard?

A: Yes. That's a very suggestive technique that is inappropriate in the way that it was used, because it was used in a way where photos were shown and they were very suggestive procedures that would not be appropriate.

Q: Okay. When you refer to stereotyping, what do you mean, Doctor?

A: Well, meaning creating an image about a person or persons of a certain sort, which would then create an emotional reaction or negative feelings in this case about certain individuals or classes of individuals. That's very dangerous, because then it can promote statements about persons consistent with that stereotype that's been created.

Q: What do you mean, Doctor, by parental influence?

A: Well, I mean anything that parents do that could affect things that children say, and it's a very, very powerful process, because parents are the most important people in most children's lives.

Q: Okay. On these tapes that you've reviewed, Doctor, do you see any signs of parental influence?

A: Yes. The parents were sometimes in the room in the interviews, which in itself is a violation of proper procedure because it then presents the parent as a potential influence and it's difficult to assess the effects, except in some instances, and one in particular I recall that's actually on the videotape where a parent engages in interaction with the child, pressure, coercion and so on, trying to get the child to say certain things that the child had not been saying in the interview.

Q: What's the proper way in a proper interview to counteract parental influence generally, sir?

A: Well, first of all, you never have the parents present during the interview. Secondly, you ask open-ended questions and you ask questions that are designed to find out what the child, him or herself, has to say about what they remember regarding the alleged incidents. It's done in a non-suggestive, non-leading manner.

Q: What should an interviewer be familiar with in going into a forensic interview?

A: They should be familiar with all of the case facts available, all of the investigative material, all of the statements made, all of the allegations that are made—been made, their sources and so on, who has talked to the child about these issues and when, so that they can then assess the various possibilities and explore those as various hypotheses about the explained behaviour—I'm sorry—the demonstrated behaviour.

Q: Doctor, is delayed reporting a factor in this case?

A: Yes, it is.

Q: How would you instruct people to deal with delayed reporting generally.

A: Well, the one has to be concerned about when there's a long delay from the alleged incidents to the time of the report about the accuracy of the memory and where the information comes from in terms of being able to attribute the source of those reports, and so the questioning has to be very careful to avoid sources of contamination that could have occurred from the time of the alleged incident until the time of the interview to make sure that the child is reporting directly from what they remember.

Q: Generally, Doctor, what is the effect of asking a child to pretend in a forensic interview?

A: In a forensic interview, first of all, it's totally inappropriate to use "pretend". This is a serious investigative matter and it has to be done in a way that the child realizes it's important to talk about facts and not pretend in fantasy. And when you instruct a child to pretend, children naturally will engage in those acts and you can get all kinds of fantasy and material that they're producing in response to that instruction rather than in response to describing what it is they remember about what actually happened.

. . . .

Q: . . . Doctor, focusing on the interview technique and not the response to any questions, is there any one interview properly conducted?

A: Not within the guidelines that we teach investigators to use. There is the one that I mentioned earlier that has the fewest problems, comes closest to being reasonable, and that's the interview by Jo Suttie. Beyond that, they all have extremely serious violations.

Dr. Bruck explained how peer pressure could improperly influence the testimony of children:

Q: Dr. Bruck, the effects of peer pressure or interaction on children's reports, within the contest of a child interview can you tell us what you mean by peer pressure?

A: What I mean is that the child tries to give an answer that he thinks is consistent with what his peer group is saying, and that peer pressure is also another suggestive component of an interview, and it's usually brought into the interview by the interviewer who says things like, "All your friends have told. Johnny down the street just told us this. Can you tell us more about it?". This is a vehicle to put pressure on the child to become more like his peers.

Q: I see. Any particular studies that you can tell us about in that regard?

A: Well, there are three studies that I know about. I wish there were more. The earliest one was by Alfred Binet who was the founder of the I.Q. test, believe it or not, the turn of the century in Paris. He was a wonderful researcher, and very few people read his work 'cause it's written in French. I had the opportunity to do that. And he was terribly surprised. He found that when there were a group of children around a table and one child was cued to give a certain answer about something that was—could be commonly seen by other members, that the other members of that group would go along with the child.

Now this is a phenomenon that's been followed up regularly throughout the twentieth century. There are other studies. Another study is one—and some children are purposely removed from the classroom during that time but are later questioned about it, and in the one study I know about six of the seven children who were not in the classroom when all their friends saw this event in fact when later questioned said yes, they were there, and in fact gave a full elaborative account of what had happened. Obviously these were things that maybe they had heard from their friends. They had picked these things up. That's another.

The third study I think is more interesting. It's a naturalistic study. I mean it's something that actually happened where there was a sniper attack on an elementary school playground.

Q: And this is an actual event?

A: This was an actual event. The experimenter did not stage this one. And six to sixteen weeks later the children were questioned about what happened. And there were a number of children who were not in the schoolyard or around the school when this happened and, nevertheless, a number of these children who were not there gave quite elaborate accounts about what happened. For example, there was one child who said that they saw someone on the ground, that he heard the shots, and this child was away on vacation. He was nowhere near the school. And there are other cases—examples of that in that same study. So here you have this very dramatic event and children who are not there in fact then believe that they were there.

It is not uncommon for an expert in the field to testify that the child exhibited certain symptoms which indicated trauma. The following cross-examination from the *Sterling* case reflects what is perhaps the obvious, namely alternative explanations for the symptoms:

Q: ... You had mentioned a number of behaviours yesterday and Mr. Bauer had mentioned a number to you, and I just want to ask you some questions about some of the specific ones. Okay? Would you agree with me that, for example, and [sic] child's fear of medical personnel is not a behaviour that is exclusive to trauma?

A: Correct.

Q: That a child having stomach problems is not a behaviour that's exclusive to trauma.

A: Correct.

Q: Likewise with a child through its development being clingy.

A: Correct.

Q: Likewise with a child exhibiting a rocking behaviour.

A: Correct.

Q: Likewise with a child, like, having an interest in drawing.

A: Correct.

Q: And likewise with a child in talking about things at times being emotionally flat.

A: Correct.

Dr. Parker testified that children may display behaviour consistent with trauma such as bed-wetting, abdominal pain, eating disorders, sleep problems and disassociation. She was cross-examined:

Q: And would you agree that—I won't go through the list but I'll say would you agree that all of these behaviours that you've heard being referred to this morning occur, to some degree, in normal children—some more than others perhaps.

A: Some more than others, yes.

Q: Would you agree that some things that happen in a family will increase the occurrence of these behaviours and I'm thinking of conflict between spouses, conflict between the parents of the child?

A: Conflict between parents of a child may, in themselves, be a stress to the child and some of the behaviours may occur in that context, yes.

Q: And if a child had moved frequently would that be a cause of stress—

A: Yes, it would.

Q: —in all likelihood. Do you think that being repeatedly interviewed, a child being repeatedly interviewed a large number of times, could that in itself be stressful for a child?

A: That is stressful, yes.

. . . .

Q: You would agree that fabrication, a child fabricating can be stressful to them.

A: I'm not quite sure I understand the question.

Q: The child not telling the truth, that can create quite a bit of stress.

A: You mean if a child was creating a story, that would be stressful for them?

Q: Right.

A: It could be.

Dr. Celia Fisher testified there is no single behaviour or group of behaviours that are reliable clues of sexual abuse. Dr. McKenna testified about certain behaviour and physical signs which were consistent with innocent explanations.

R. v. Sterling also referred to the understanding between the therapists within a clinic the children were attending that they should not discuss their cases with each other because of the possibility that the versions from their patients of events might become corrupted. The parents of the children were advised not to discuss with each other their child's version of events nor to ask their children leading questions.

Suggestive questions by parents of their children was a concern. For example, "D.C.'s parents said, 'Some of the children baby-sat at Ronald and Linda's are saying some bad stuff happened there, some bad things, and we just want to know if anything bad happened to you guys'". Also: "J.L.'s mother told him that Travis Sterling had touched his sister K.L.'s private parts."

The case noted that suggestibility could come from other sources, such as a book called the *Secret of the Silver Horse* which was read to a child by his mother after which the child began making disclosures when earlier the child had denied to his mother he had seen bad things happening at the Sterlings.

Q: You saw the—Ms. Sullivan referred you to the book *Secret of the Silver Horse*?

A: Yes.

Q: Okay. *Secret of the Silver Horse*, I'm sorry, and you recall in that book there's a reference to a big person putting a hand inside my pants and touching me down there.

A: Yes.

Q: Okay. Would you agree that—that that book can be used in a way that is suggestive or leading to a child?

A: In what sense?

Q: Well, for example, if the child has read the book and then the subject-matter is introduced by making reference to the book—

A: Yes.

Q: —and the child has been told that bad people touch privates, and as well, if the child repeats and the child's initial disclosure is virtually identical to what's in the book, isn't there a concern that the child has followed the suggestion from the book?

A: Yes. If the child's disclosure was the same as is in the book, we wouldn't know for sure whether the child was accessing memory of an experience or memory from the book. Of course, if her or his disclosure was different in some way, and the more different it was, the less this would be in issue.

Q: And the more similar, the greater the concern?

A: The—yes.

Q: The potential concern?

A: Potential concern, yes.

The popular use of anatomical dolls to bring out disclosure as opposed to just clarifying details was criticized in *Sterling* by the experts because their usage could result in suggestive questioning.

Q: Dr. Underwager, what's your opinion of the use of dolls, anatomical—anatomical dolls in interviews of children?

A: The most recent article dealing with the dolls by Wolfner, Faust and Dawes quotes us correctly as saying that it's our opinion that any use of the dolls to get information on sexual abuse is unethical. And at the final end of that article, Wolfner, Dawes and—Faust and Dawes agree with that position. And they do so on this basis, that there's absolutely no evidence whatsoever that the dolls can produce what we call incremental validity. That is, that they give you any advantage, any advance in knowledge. They don't tell you anything more. They don't produce any information more than what you can get other ways. They're redundant. And yet, they give the illusion of being objective and of adding information. And so the Wolfner, Faust and Dawes article that summarizes all the research done with the dolls concludes there's no evidence to produce any confidence that the dolls add anything. And because they are used in the way in court, and what—people's liberties are at stake, that it's completely improper to use the dolls at all. So that's what the most recent article says, and agrees with our stand earlier.

Q: I understand that they're not helpful, but is there potential harm in their use?

A: Yes, very much so.

Dr. Bruck testified that the use of anatomical dolls can be very suggestive and lead to "quite remarkable false allegations."

Dr. Underwager testified that as a result of misinformation and suggestion children can create central events that never occurred and actually believe they happened.

Q: Could that happen unwittingly to a child by someone such as a parent or a police officer questioning a child?

A: Yes, very much so.

Q: Dr. Underwager, you've said the children are suggestible and I believe you said that children are more suggestible than adults?

A: Yes, sir.

Q: And is there research to support that, and what kind of experiments have been done to establish that?

A: Well, yes, there is research that has been done. And every time you've got an age discrimination, that is you've got different groups of ages, you get a progression. Whether it's Goodman's research, it's clear age effect on the use of the dolls. Peters at the University of North Dakota and the photo-lineups, age is one of the major factors, and it appears all over the place. But you get a difference when you show children films and then ask them to describe the films. Younger children have fewer information—fewer bits that they can add more stuff and so on. They're more suggestible. Dr. Yuille mentioned the study that's famous among us because the children all looked at the shoes, the running shoes because running shoes are important, they remembered the running shoes. But apart from that kind of thing, children are just much more suggestible.

Q: Doctor, are children suggestible just for peripheral aspects of an event, or can children—can suggestion create total memories for central events that may have happened?

A: Oh, yes. Suggestion, social influence can create memories for central events, events that never occurred. Can create very detailed events, now we know that, that's what the most recent research demonstrates. For a while, people were saying that central events would not be affected by misinformation or suggestion, well we know better than that now. And as Cesi and Brook summarize in their review article, some of the most powerful evidence for this is Gaile Goodman's research which shows that, in fact, children do come up with central events that never happened. And they, let's see, they're—out of sixteen studies that they cite, fourteen showed that children produce erroneous accounts of central events.

Q: And do children come to believe these events that are suggested to them?

A: Yes, they do, and that's what makes it so difficult. This subjective belief is there that these things actually happened. They really believe it happened. And that's what makes it so devastating if they learn to believe things happened that never happened.

Q: Now, Dr. Underwager, you're talking about experiments where these suggestions are done deliberately to a child?

A: Yes.

Dr. Bruck testified that if the interviewer has a bias it can affect the accuracy of the information received; the child is more prone to be open to suggestion the longer the period of time between the event and the interview; repeated questions create a danger of suggestion and repeated misinformation can result in this information becoming part of the child's story and that children can reconstruct new information.

Accusatory tones can lead to false information.

Q: What do you mean by an accusatory tone, Dr. Bruck?

A: Well, by saying, "Something bad happened", that there are phrases that jump out that make it clear to the person being interviewed that, "Something bad happened and you have to tell me about what that bad thing is", and that's what the atmosphere or the tone of that interview becomes. It could also have another kind of tone where, "Something really good happened and I want you to try to tell me about that really good thing."

Q: What is the potential of an air of accusatory tone?

A: Well, I think that this is a highly suggestive component of an interview where the tone does provide information to the person being questioned about what the interviewer is looking for.

Q: Why?

A: Why what?

Q: Why do you think that's very suggestive?

A: Well, there are a number of studies where these kind—these accusatory tones have been set in very scripted ways, and we find that when that happens and children are brought into the laboratory and told, "You know something terrible happened. We're really worried. If you tell us you"ll feel better about it", what you find is that children will in fact start to make up all kinds of things that never happened or they never had memories for.

Adults of high status with children such as parents, teachers, police officers can have a significant impact on what the child believes:

Q: Thank you, Dr. Bruck. What about the effects of being interviewed by adults with high status?

A: Well, adults have high status to children to begin with, so they have even higher status. You know they have higher status. We think that this is a very important reason why sometimes children fall sway to suggestion. They believe adults. They have a lot of trust in adults. They think that adults know more than they do. They don't think that adults are out of there to fool them. So in certain—in interviews when adults in fact offer suggestion or misinformation, we know that it's much more likely to be incorporated than if children offer other children misinformation. So that's one thing.

Now the other point is is that suppose there's someone who's really of high status in the eyes of the child, just not an ordinary interviewer, who comes in. The child knows nothing about—like a police officer. And Gail Goodman and her colleagues actually recently did a study that's quite interesting where children came into a laboratory and played with someone they called the babysitter, and they did a number of things. And they went home, and then the next week they came back to be interviewed about it. Half the children were met by someone who was dressed up as a police officer, and these children were told something like, "I'm very concerned that something bad may have happened last time, that someone did bad things to you, and we need to find out what happened, and my partner who is inside will ask you questions about this."

Now children who were told that gave many more inaccurate and many fewer accurate events than children who were not given that kind of information, and this was—you know it took two minutes. And the kinds of things the children said—I wrote them down 'cause I thought it was quite interesting. One child said, "I think the babysitter had a gun and was going to kill me", and another child said, "I fell down. I got lost. I got hurt on my legs and I cut my ears." So here you have this very weak manipulation, and yet you have these very dramatic effects.

Q: And in that study none of the things the children said had happened. Is that—

A: None of those things happened.

The complimenting of the child by an adult for his or her disclosure can serve to be positive re-enforcement for the child as shown in the following cross-examination (by Alan Gold and not part of *R. v. Sterling*):

Q: And do you remember that towards the end of your time with Dale, Dale said you were a real "winner" for saying these things that your granddad did?

A: Yeah.

Q: Is that right? And she said no matter what happens you just keep saying these things that your granddad did?

A: Not to everybody but to some people.

Q: And Dale said that you had a lot of "courage" for saying these things that your granddad did? Do you know that word "courage"?

A: Yeah.

Q: So L., Dale would be really disappointed now if you went to her and said "I'm not sure these things happened". Wouldn't Dale be really disappointed.

A: Yeah.

Q: Yeah.

A: No, not really, sort of.

Q: And your mom and dad would be really disappointed if you went to them and said "I'm not really sure these things happened. Maybe I do love my granddad and he loves me". That would really upset your mom and dad, wouldn't it?

A: Yes.

Sterling makes it clear that there is fertile ground for the cross-examiner to explore with child complainants and other witnesses as to how the complaints emerged and if there were any influences brought to bear on the children's testimony.[19]

The reader is referred to the Chapter, "The Expert Witness" for a discussion on the expert and the child witness in abuse cases.

What happens if the child witness becomes unresponsive to questions during cross-examination? This is what occurred in *R. v. Hart*.[20] The Court held that if the unresponsiveness could have been avoided by reasonable action, or if evidence of the same value is or could have been available in some other way and within a reasonable time, the evidence should generally be inadmissible without full cross-examination. The right to cross-examine includes at the very least the right to receive answers responsive to the questions. In *Hart* the Court made these observations: was the witness unresponsive because of something his/her conduct was contributing towards frustrating the cross-examination or did it result from the process itself? Could appropriate steps be taken to reduce the embarrassment and discomfort of testifying? Were any steps taken by counsel to diminish the discomfort of testifying, for example, asking the trial Judge to direct the witness to answer? Did the manner of questioning contribute? Such examples could lead the trial Judge to hold that the trial was not being unfair to

---

19 In *R. v. C. (F.)* (1996), 104 C.C.C. (3d) 461 (Ont. C.A.), the Court stated that where a child's statements identifying the accused as the culprit were induced or encouraged and positively re-enforced by his parents and others, a serious question arises about the reliability of the identification.

20 (1999), 135 C.C.C. (3d) 377 (N.S. C.A.), leave to appeal refused (2000), 261 N.R. 391 (note) (S.C.C.). Given the circumstances in *Hart*, the evidence was admissible.

the accused. Other considerations are: was a postponement requested on the basis there was a reasonable prospect the witness would become responsive on returning to testify; how important is the witness's testimony; was effective cross-examination merely limited but not entirely negated?

Children and The Oath

See Chapter: Competency and Compellability.

Hearsay and Children's Evidence

See Chapter: The Hearsay Horror, under the heading: The Principled Approach to Hearsay: Necessity and Reliability Preconditions.

Criminal Code Protections for Children Testifying

See Chapter: Client and Witness Interviews, under the heading: The Child Witness.

22

Demonstrative Evidence

Mark Twain's warning that one should "believe nothing you hear and only half of what you see," may be an exaggeration, but when properly used, demonstrative evidence is at the very least more interesting for the jurors than simple oral testimony. The testimony surrounding the demonstrative evidence will not only have captured the jury's attention in the courtroom but will also help the jurors remember what was said about that piece of evidence when they are in the jury room determining their verdict. "It has been psychologically proven that the amount of information retained by a person is substantially increased when spoken statements are supported with visual aids." For a simple example, if the accused claimed the police had beaten him, then enlarged colour photographs taken soon after the event highlighting the injuries would obviously have a greater impact than the accused's testimony or that of his corroborating witnesses. An accurate diagram of the scene, with all witnesses pointing to the location of people and objects as the action is described and placing marks at the appropriate spots, will enable the jury to better understand what happened than just long verbal descriptions. Each witness would make his or her markings on separate signed copies of the same sketch or diagram so as not to be influenced by what other witnesses have marked. The jurors will be able to study the photographs and diagrams in the jury room and consider the testimony of the various witnesses in relation to the exhibit.

Photographs

Photographs are perhaps the most-often employed demonstrative evidence in a criminal case. The admission of photographs depends on:

1. Whether the photographs are material and relevant to the issues at trial.[1]
2. Their accuracy in truly representing the facts.[2]

---

1 *Dilabbio v. R.* (1965), 46 C.R. 131 (Ont. CA.).
2 *R. v. Creemer*, [1968] 1 C.C.C. 14 (N.S. C.A.).

3.   Their fairness and absence of any intention to mislead.[3]
4.   Their verification on oath by a person able to speak to their accuracy and fairness.[4] Normally a photograph is proven by the person who took it, however it may be established by someone present at the time it was taken or even by a person who was not present at the time, provided that person can verify its truth and accuracy for the relevant time.[5]
5.   Whether the prejudicial effect is so great that it would exceed the probative value to the extent that, even if the photograph in question met the above-mentioned requirements, the trial judge in his discretion may still exclude the evidence if it is of little probative value and could inflame the minds of the jury.[6]

R. v. Seaboyer[7] distinguishes the probative versus prejudicial balancing test based on whether it is the Crown or the defence objecting to admissibility. When evidence is tendered by the Crown admissibility depends on the probative effect of the evidence balanced against the prejudice to the accused. When the evidence is presented by the defence, because it is fundamental to our system of justice that an innocent person should not be convicted, the prejudice must substantially outweigh the value of the evidence before it can be excluded.

The prejudicial effect of the photographs may be determined by their number, their gruesomeness, their detail, their size, whether they are in black and white or in colour, whether they are close-ups, whether the body is naked or clothed and by factors unique to each situation.[8]

Where there is sufficient testimonial evidence or alternative demonstrative evidence which is less gruesome and can illustrate the point to the jury, photographic evidence should be excluded.[9] The facts concerning the injuries and the cause of death, in many cases, can be adequately established and better explained by the pathologist.[10] It has been held in the United States that to admit gory photographs to illustrate testimony was in error when a diagram would have sufficed.[11] In most cases, diagrams with the

---

3   *Ibid.*
4   *Ibid.*
5   *R. v. Bannister* (1936), 66 C.C.C. 38 (NB. C.A.).
6   *Draper v. Jacklyn*, [1970] S.C.R. 92 (S.C.C.); *Dilabbio v. R.*, note 6 above; *R. v. Gallant* (1965), 47 C.R. 309 (P.E.I. S.C.); *R. v. Maloney (No. 2)* (1976), 29 C.C.C. (2d) 431 at 433 (Ont. Co. Ct.); *R. v. Seaboyer* (1991), 66 C.C.C. (3d) 321 (S.C.C.).
7   (1991), 66 C.C.C. (3d) 321 (S.C.C.).
8   *Burdine v. State* 719 S.W. 2d 309, 316 (Tex. 1986); *Commonwealth v. Hubbard* 372 A 2d 687, 697 (P.A. 1977); *Young v. Florida* 234 S. 2d 341, 348 (Fla. 1976); *State v. Jones* 23 S.E. 2d 387 (S.C. 1942).
9   *Archina v. People* 307 P. 2d 1083 (Colo. 1957) (en banc); *State v. Morgan* 30 S.O. 2d 434 (La. 1977); *State v. Allies* 606 P. 2d 1043 (Mont. 1966).
10 *State v. Banks* 564 S.W. 2d 947, 951 (Tenn. 1978).
11 *State v. Sergeant* 698 P. 2d 598, 604 (Wash. App. 19-).

appropriate markings can illustrate what the Crown wishes to prove, such as the number, size, shape and location of wounds. In this fashion, there would be no chance that jurors would become overwhelmed by seeing the wounds and there could be no prejudice done to the Crown's case.

As a result of the decision in *Charette v. R.*[12] the questions of accuracy, identification, continuity of possession, etc., all go to the weight to be given to the evidence rather than to admissibility. Although *Charette* relates to the admission of a tape-recording, its reasoning would seem to apply to other demonstrative evidence.

If counsel does not go through the photographs with the witness before trial and presents them for the first time to the witness on the stand, there may be some embarrassing confusion as a Crown Attorney discovered in the following exchange with the 72-year-old victim of a robbery who it was anticipated would identify himself[13] and his injuries in a photograph. The victim was inebriated at the time of the attack.

Roland Taylor: Sworn

Portion Of Examination In-Chief By Mr. Kelly:

Q. Okay. And did you suffer any other injuries?

A. Oh. Oh, he just tore my pants. He got my wallet out of there.

Q. And where were your pants torn?

A. On this side. I had a brown wallet. I thought somebody maybe found it.

Q. Do you remember any photographs that were taken of you?

A. What?

Q. Were any photographs taken of you?

A. Yeah, I think somebody took a photograph.

Q. When was that taken?

A. Oh that was the night we . . . oh no, next day.

Q. Okay. And who took that photograph?

A. I think the police.

Q. Police?

A. There was some girls and the police there.

Q. I'm going to show you a photograph—two photographs. I'm showing you two photographs. Do you recognize these photographs?

A. Holy God, what happened to this guy? Is that the same guy as over there?

Q. Do you recognize that person?

A. No, I don't recognize. It was snowing. Is that that same guy over there?

Q. Okay. Unfortunately, I have to ask you the questions. Do you recognize the person in the picture?

THE COURT: Mr. Youngson may have an objection.

MR. YOUNGSON: I'm sorry, Your Honour. I'm just anticipating an objection.

---

12 (1980), 51 C.C.C. (2d) 350 (S.C.C.). See also *R. v. Parsons* (1977), 37 C.C.C. (2d) 497 (Ont. C.A.).

13 *R. v. Clifford Langevin* before His Honour Judge W.W. Cohen, September 9, 1992, Sault Ste. Marie.

MR. TAYLOR: No, I don't recognize this guy. What happened to his eye?
MR. KELLY: I'll take the pictures back.

Witness In-Court Sketches

There are times, when there are no photographs available, and it is helpful to have a witness sketch where certain persons, structures, and objects were at relevant times when certain actions were occurring or for the purpose of simply describing a scene. These signed sketches don't have to be Rembrandts, and it is readily understood they are not to scale or accurate representations. They are usually comprised of squares, rectangles, circles, arrows, letters, etc. The sketches can help the triers-of-fact better understand the oral evidence, generally as to positioning of objects, structures and individuals at relevant times.

Videotapes and Motion Pictures

Videotapes and motion pictures rest on the same criteria for admissibility as photographs.[14]

> The law establishes that movie picture and videotape evidence has been admitted to support, explain, corroborate and impeach the evidence of witnesses and in this way has assisted the trier of fact in determining which witnesses are to be believed.[15]

In *R. v. Penny*[16] the Court held that it was a precondition for admissibility that there be evidence that the video has not been altered or changed and that it accurately represents what it portrays. Did editing distort its truth? Visual evidence had greater impact on the jury than oral testimony. Did prejudicial value outweigh its probative value?

In *R. v. Maloney (No. 2)*,[17] a case involving hockey violence, LeSage J. held that in considering what is true and accurate one must consider the issues at trial and be satisfied that the movie proffered is true and accurate in relation to those issues. Where time is a significant factor, therefore, a

---

14 A.A. Moenssens, R.E. Moses, and F.E. Inbau, *Scientific Evidence in Criminal Cases* (1973), p. 503; see also 1985-86 edition J.R. Richardson, *Modern Scientific Evidence* (M.S.E.) (2nd ed.), p. 506; *R. v. Maloney (No. 2)*, note 6 above, at 433; *R. v. Williams* (1977), 35 C.C.C. (2d) 103 (Ont. G.S.P.); *R. v. Leaney and Rawlinson* (1988), 38 C.C.C. (3d) 263 (Alta. C.A.) discusses the need for more technical evidence where there is no eyewitness testimony to verify accuracy and fairness of the videotape.

15 *Army & Navy Dept. Store (Western) Ltd. v. R.W.D.S. U., Loc. 535* (1950), 97 C.C.C. 258 (B.C. S.C.); *Nag v. McKellar*, [1968] 1 O.R. 797 (Ont. C.A.).

16 (2002), 163 C.C.C. (3d) 329 (Nfld. C.A.). See also *R. v. Macdonald* (2000), 146 C.C.C. (3d) 525 (Ont. C.A.); *R. v. Wu* (2002), 170 C.C.C. (3d) 225 (Ont. C.A.).

17 *Supra.*

slow motion movie would not be admissible as it would grossly distort the reality of time. The learned trial judge pointed out, however, that he could think of instances when slow motion videotape or film would be of assistance in determining an issue at trial. Similarly, where the entire transaction was not proven to have been videotaped because of gaps created by the camera operator turning the camera off, the Crown failed to prove the videotape fairly, truly and accurately represented the action portrayed.[18] Editing (unless under directions from the Bench to exclude prejudicial material following a *voir dire*) for the purposes of isolating events would seem to be a sufficient reason to exclude the film and tape.

One complaint that can be envisaged with the use of the camera is that the camera's positioning may create a distortion of what actually occurred. Watching the different camera angle replays in a baseball game, for example, can cause the observer to change his mind back and forth as to whether the ball beat the runner to the bag. Similar frailties will presumably attach to certain filmed material offered as evidence and counsel should be alert to raise such issues if applicable.

Reconstructed Scenes, Experiments, Tests and In-Court Demonstrations

The American courts have admitted as evidence the film reconstruction of events where there was little risk of misleading the triers-of-fact.[19] The English view seems to be against admitting the filmed reconstruction of events as it is not the best evidence.[20] In *R. v. MacDonald*[21] the Court held that video re-enactments, particularly those without the participation of the accused can unfairly influence the jury. There is an immediate visual impact which could sway the jury to give the re-enactment more weight than it deserves and to discount less compelling or less vivid evidence which may be more probative of the facts in issue. Another concern is that only the Crown has the resources to produce a video and in such a case the re-enactment will be an extra witness for the state. In each case the issue is whether the prejudicial effect of the video re-enactment outweighs its probative value, having regard to its relevancy, accuracy, whether what it portrays can be verified under oath and the necessity of the evidence. In this case the violent and highly impressionistic imagery gave the Crown an unfair advantage. The dangers increase when the video only portrays one

---

18 *R. v. Miller*, B.C. Co. Ct., Sheppard Co. Ct. J., October 29, 1986, summarized at 17 W.C.B. 382.

19 3 *Wigmore on Evidence* (Chadbourn rev. 1970), p. 266.

20 *R. v. Quinn*; *R. v. Bloom*, [1961] 3 All E.R. 88 (C.C.A.). But see *R. v. Hunter*, [1985] 2 All E.R. 173 (C.A.) and commentary; *Karamat v. R.*, [1956] 1 All E.R. 415 (P.C.) and *Tameshwar v. R.*, [1957] 2 All E.R. 683 (P.C.) where demonstrations by the witnesses were permissable when a view was taken.

21 (2000), 146 C.C.C. (3d) 525 (Ont. C.A.). Videotaped re-enactment of a police takedown.

side's version of disputed facts. Factors to be weighed in determining prejudicial as opposed to probative value are the video's relevance, accuracy, fairness and whether what it portrays can be verified under oath, as well as the need for the video in light of other evidence.

In *Dilabbio v. R.*,[22] a witness who had no personal knowledge of the occurrence was called upon by the trial judge to act out a portion of the evidence of one witness which concerned the use of a gun by the accused and to re-enact the actions of the deceased as described in the testimony of another witness. Porter C.J.O. held:

> This procedure was in our opinion, improper as not being in accordance with our traditional and long established procedure in presenting evidence to a jury. It might well be prejudicial to a fair trial in that even if the witness's oral description could be accurately portrayed by the act or this particular evidence was presented to the jury in a much more vivid and forceful manner than the evidence of other witnesses whose evidence was limited to an oral description of the events witnessed by them.[23]

Where conditions of the tests or experiments can be duplicated to match those conditions in existence at the time of the offence, then evidence of the test or experiment is admissible in Court.[24] In *R. v. Nikitin*[25] it was held that this type of evidence is governed by the general principles of evidence-reliability materiality and prejudice. As long as the experiment sufficiently replicates the conditions of the original event it would be admissible. It is impossible to replicate the original event perfectly. There is a residual discretion in the trial judge to exclude if the prejudicial value outweighs its probative value.[26] There may be a significant variable in the conditions of the experiment compared to reality if there is a human element involved—for example, human reaction to a situation cannot accurately be

---

22 *Supra*. In *R. v. Francis* (2002), 2002 CarswellOnt 3473 (Ont. C.A.) it was held that experiments involving jurors are dangerous as they won't mimic the circumstances existing at the time of the offence.

23 *Ibid.*, at 133.

24 *R. v. Laverty* (1979), 47 C.C.C. (2d) 60 (Ont. C.A.). The case law has been emerging with respect to forensic computer animation resulting in videotapes. This evidence was allowed by O'Driscoll J. in *R. v. Rajic* (1993), 80 C.C.C. (3d) 533 (Ont. C.A.), although not referred to in the judgment. See also *R. v. Korbidis* unreported (Ont. Dist. Ct., Oct. 1989, Locke J.); *R. v. Droves*, unreported (Ont. Gen. Div., Corbett J., June 1991); *R. v. Nardi and Cirillo*, unreported (Ont. Prov. Div., Foster P.C.J., August 1992), *contra R. v. Silliker* (1993), 134 N.B.R. (2d) 46, 342 A.P.R. 46 (Q.B.), the evidence being rejected on the basis of lack of accuracy. In *R. v. Collins* (2002), 160 C.C.C. (3d) 85 (Ont. C.A.) is an example of where the experiment was held to be admissible.

25 *R. v. Nikitin* (2003), 176 C.C.C. (3d) 225 (Ont. C.A.).

26 See also *R. v. Walizadah* (2007), 223 C.C.C. (3d) 28 (Ont. C.A.) at para. 47, leave to appeal refused 2008 CarswellOnt 5011, 2008 CarswellOnt 5012 (S.C.C.); *R. v. Collins* (2001), 160 C.C.C. (3d) 85 (Ont. C.A.).

recreated and this recreation would not come within the tests as cited in *R. v. Laverty*.

Physical or objective tests are more easily admitted, as for example, the reaction of gasoline thrown at someone smoking a cigarette,[27] burn patterns on a tub,[28] or whether a shower curtain would tear in a particular pattern when grabbed by a falling woman.[29] However it has been held[30] that even when there were variables involved with respect to an in-court demonstration which could not be duplicated, they would not necessarily render the end result of the experiment of little or no value. In the result Justice Moldaver permitted defence counsel's request to have a police officer duplicate the statement taking process on a voir dire to determine the admissability of the confession to show that the statement could not have taken place within the eight minutes that the officer alleged as there was a credibility issue between what the officer stated and what the accused would say.

In *R. v. Howard*,[31] the Ontario Court of Appeal approved the following statement from McCormick's *Handbook of the Law of Evidence*.[32]

> Whether demonstrations in the form of experiments in Court are to be permitted is also largely subject to the discretion of the trial Judge. Unlike experiments performed out of Court, the results of which are generally communicated testimonially, in-court experimentation may involve considerable confusion and delay, and the trial Judge is viewed as in the best position to judge whether the game is worth the candle. Simple demonstrations by a witness are usually permitted, and may be strikingly effective in adding vividness to the spoken word.[33]

Other issues are: whether the re-enactment becomes overestimated by the jury or unduly raises the emotions of the jurors; will side issues result that would consume an unwarranted amount of time.

In *R. v. Brooks*,[34] Laskin J.A. held that evidence of an experiment by the police officer in his home which refuted a position taken by the accused should not have been admitted because the officer did not have the required scientific training to give his evidence and the evidence itself was of dubious relevance, relying on *R. v. Mohan* (1994), 89 C.C.C. (3d) 402 (S.C.C.).

It is improper for the trial judge to invite the jury to embark on similar experiments in the jury room.[35]

---

27 *R. v. Campbell* (1977), 38 C.C.C. (2d) 6 (Ont. C.A.).

28 *R. v. Laverty, supra.*

29 *R. v. Ruddick* (1981), 57 C.C.C. (2d) 421 (Ont. C.A.), leave to appeal to S.C.C. refused (1981), 57 C.C.C. (2d) 421n (S.C.C.).

30 *R. v. Brooks* (1998), 81 C.C.C. (3d) 428 (Ont. Gen. Div.).

31 (1983), 3 C.C.C. (3d) 399 (Ont. C.A.).

32 2nd ed. (1972), p. 536.

33 *R. v. Howard, supra,* at 416.

34 (1998), 129 C.C.C. (3d) 227 (Ont. C.A.), reversed (2000), 30 C.R. (5th) 201 (S.C.C.).

35 *R. v. McCrea* (1970), 3 C.C.C. 77 (Sask. C.A.).

Perhaps a word of warning is appropriate. Be confident by virtue of pre-trial preparation that the experiment or demonstration you want to present will work in your client's favour and not against him as reported in the 1993 appeal, 2nd edition of the Globe and Mail as follows:

> It would never have happened to Perry Mason.
>
> Victoria lawyer Doug Christie is best known for his work on behalf of Ernst Zundel, Imre Finta, David Irving, James Keegstra and assorted Ku Klux Klan members.
>
> Last month, he acted in a more run-of-the-mill suit against the City of Victoria, for a client who alleged he had been subjected to excessive force during an arrest.
>
> One of the arresting officers testified that Mr. Christie's client, although seated and handcuffed, had kicked him in the groin.
>
> Mr. Christie argued that this was impossible and—in classic Perry Mason style—had the officer handcuffed and seated on the floor in front of the jury to demonstrate it couldn't be done.
>
> The policeman issued two warnings that this was unwise. Mr. Christie, unconvinced, continued to stand over him demanding a re-enactment.
>
> The officer then kicked the lawyer in the groin, causing him to double over and hop about the Court in considerable pain.
>
> His client lost.

One of the most famous demonstrations that backfired which occurred in front of millions on T.V. was in the infamous O.J. Simpson case in California when the famous football star, sometime movie actor, T.V. colour commentator of N.F.L. football games, and T.V. commercial actor was charged with the first degree stabbing murder of his ex-wife and her male friend in 1995. A bloodstained glove was left at the scene of the murder and a matching bloodstained glove was found on the property of Mr. Simpson. The prosecutors alleged Mr. Simpson dropped this glove from the scene of the murder to his home. For some reason, perhaps overconfidence, the prosecutor asked Mr. Simpson to try the glove on in front of the jury. The glove did not fit and was no doubt a significant reason why a seemingly overwhelming prosecution case resulted in an acquittal after hearing defence counsel submit—if it doesn't fit, you must acquit.

Replicas

The case law with respect to the admissibility of replicas seems to come mainly from the United States. When the object connected with the commission of the offence, such as a knife or gun, cannot be produced at trial because it has been lost or otherwise misplaced, an object shown to fairly represent in appearance (or operation) the object involved in the offence is admissable to illustrate and clarify the testimony relative to the lost object. In order to be admissable, the replica must be relevant and material to an issue at trial, not overly inflammatory and the original, if available, would have been admissible. The admissibility of reproductions rests on the broad discretion of the trial Judge.[36]

Models, Maps, Sketches, Diagrams

These "are by their nature generally not confusable with real evidence, and are admissible simply on the basis of testimony that they are substantially accurate representations of what the witness is endeavouring to dispute. Some discretionary control in the trial Court is generally deemed appropriate, however, since exhibits of this kind, due to inaccuracies, variations of scale, etc., may on occasion become more misleading than helpful. Nevertheless, when the trial Court has exercised its discretion to admit, it will only rarely be found in error, at least if potentially misleading inaccuracies have been pointed out by witnesses for the proponent or could have been exposed upon cross-examination."[37]

Computer Simulation Models

Computer simulations are rarely used in criminal trials but when they are their main focus is in reconstruction of car crashes as well as crime scenes.[38] In the case of *Owens v. Grandell*[39] Kozack J. set out six preconditions of admissibility. Given the cost, time and chances that your opponent might successfully argue inadmissibility on the basis of distraction, confusion, inaccuracy or prejudicial effect outbalancing probative value, counsel should be confident that the computer reconstruction, which is expensive, will have a favourable impact on the outcome of the case rather than just being a sideshow. You may be able to accomplish what you wish by videotaping the crime scene as opposed to computer animation. Professor David Paciocco has noted that "when a computer re-creation is introduced the reliability of the computer program should be assessed. The data used should be reviewed. Counsel should examine what information was included and what was left out, in other words the computer program will need to pass

---

36 *People v. Jordan* 10 Cal. Rptr. 495 (Dist. Ct. 1961); *Simmons v. State* 622 S.W. 2d 111 (Tex. Cr. App. 1981); *State v. Woods* 632 S.W. 2d 113 (Mo. App. 1982); *Fields v. The State* 307 S.E. 2d 712 (Ga. App. 1983); *The State v. Gray* 395 P.2d 490 (S.C. Wash. 1964); *United States v. Golden* 671 F. 2d 369 (10th Cir. 1932).

37 *McCormick on Evidence*, 2nd ed. (St. Paul, Minnesota: West Publishing Co., 1979), p. 530.

38 In *R. v. Suzack* (2000), 141 C.C.C. (3d) 449 (Ont. C.A.), leave to appeal refused (2001), [2000] S.C.C.A. No. 583 (S.C.C.) the computer animation was held admissible to allow the Crown to help the jury understand its position as to the location of the shooters and the victim by depicting the location, angle, sequence and direction of the bullets that entered and exited the victim. This was less prejudicial than showing autopsy photographs of the victim. The computer-generated model was created and used by an expert pathologist to illustrate the Crown's theory.

39 [1994] O.J. No. 496 (Ont. Gen. Div.).

the test for admissibility of novel science and the criteria from *Mohan* should be applied."

Graphs, Summaries, Charts, Schedules and Chronologies

With the proliferation of complicated fraud cases, forensic accountants are being employed more often by both prosecution and defence. As a result the courts are seeing more summaries and graphs presented as evidence. An R.C.M.P. officer was charged with the first degree murder of his wife and one of the number of motives alleged was that the accused needed his wife's life insurance money to support his high lifestyle.[40] The accountants, using all of the financial records of the accused, plotted a large graph using different colours to show how the accused's resources had dipped before his wife's death and then suddenly increased afterwards. This picture was worth much more than a thousand words.

In *R. v. Scheel*,[41] the Ontario Court of Appeal found that accountants summaries based on exhibits, agreed statements of facts, testimony at trial and evidence given at the preliminary hearing and read in at trial were admissible to assist the jury in understanding the entire picture represented by the numerous pieces of documentary evidence. The introduction of the summaries did not offend against the "best evidence" rule, which requires that, where possible, the original documents must be produced, since the original documents, which were the primary source of the summaries, were already admitted in evidence.

In *R. v. Steel*[42] the accused were charged with a commercial fraud involving interbank transfers and the uttering of fraudulent cheques. The trial judge held that a chart offered by the prosecution was admissible as it would enable the jury to understand the expert evidence that was given on a complicated matter which was not within the jury's province and their ordinary competency to understand and which would also be of assistance in the cross-examination in order to avoid confusion.

In the U.S. it has been held that the trial Court must scrutinize charts, summaries, schedules, etc., before they can be admitted into evidence, to

---

40   *R. v. Kelly*, tried at the Toronto Assizes Court before Mr. Justice O'Driscoll.

41   (1978), 3 C.R. (3d) 359 (Ont. C.A.). See also *R. v. Bengert (No. 3)* (1980), 48 C.C.C. (2d) 413 (B.C. S.C.), which involved a lengthy complicated jury trial and the Crown was permitted to give to the jury during its address and to take into the jury room during the jury's deliberations the Crown's chronology of events consisting of references to the evidence to which the Crown would point in support of a conviction. The defence was also permitted to submit its own chronology. In complex cases chronologies can assist the jury in better understanding and following the evidence but the jury should be instructed that the chronologies are not the evidence.

42   Ont. Co. Ct., Graburn Co. Ct. J., May 5, 1976.

see whether they fairly represent and summarize the evidence on which they are based. If they are fair representations, they are admissible.[43]

EXHIBITS

When a piece of evidence is to be used as an exhibit the questioner should remember to make sure that the jury understands the complete significance of that exhibit. It is not unusual to see inexperienced counsel question a witness about a piece of evidence, such as a photograph or weapon, without the jurors seeing that evidence close up until they are in the jury room looking at the exhibits during their deliberations. Much of what was said about the exhibit in the courtroom would have had more impact if the jurors had seen the exhibit close-up during the courtroom discussion.

After a piece of evidence has been identified by a witness, offered to the judge for his inspection and shown to opposing counsel, it should, in the absence of objection, be marked as an exhibit. Counsel should request the trial judge's permission to show the jurors the exhibit, either by holding it himself/herself and slowly passing with it along the front of the jury-box or giving the exhibit to the jurors to be passed among themselves. Better still, if photocopies of the exhibit can be made they should be given to the jurors so that they can follow the evidence more closely. In those cases when an enlarged map, photograph or other such exhibit is being utilized, copies of reductions of those exhibits should be made and given to the judge, the jurors and opposing counsel.

When an enlarged exhibit, such as a map, scale drawing or graph, is being utilized the exhibit should be located in the courtroom where it can best be seen by the jurors, the judge and the accused—and it should be placed close enough to the witness-box so that the witness can use a pointer to indicate the places he or she is referring to in the evidence. Depending on the physical set-up of the courtroom the witness may have to step out of the witness box to point to spots on the exhibit.

When exhibits are introduced they should be organized. Counsel should go through the exhibits with the witness prior to trial so that counsel knows which exhibits are relevant to prevent cluttering and obscuring the important issues, to know which particular part of the exhibit to highlight, and to know which exhibits are related so that they can be grouped together and numbered accordingly, as, for example, exhibits 10(a), 10(b) and 10(c).

---

43 *U.S. v. O'Connor*, 237 F.2d 466 at 475 (2nd Cir. 1956); *Lloyd v. U.S.*, 226 F.2d 9 (5th Cir. (Ala.) 1955); *Holland v. U.S.* 348 U.S. 121 at p. 131, 75 S. Ct. 127, 99 L. Ed. 150, 54-2 USTC P9714, 46 A.F.T.R. 943 (U.S. Colo., 1954); Wigmore (3d) p. 219.

Documents should not be allowed to speak for themselves by simply filing them. The witness should be asked to comment on such exhibits so that the significance of the documents is properly brought home to the jury.

Counsel should be alert to the witness's failure to speak for the record. Often when witnesses are referring to, for example, locations, they will point to a spot on a diagram without describing for the Court reporter where he or she is pointing, so that if a transcript of that evidence is read later, the reader will be confused and have to guess about the particular location in question. Counsel should describe exactly the location to which the witness is pointing for the record so that if the transcript is read by a higher level Court there will be no difficulty in following the evidence.

When counsel wishes to have a witness identify an object which the witness has seen on a prior occasion the witness should be asked to describe the exhibit before it is shown to him. For example, showing a gun to the witness before asking him to describe the gun, and *then* asking if that is the gun that the witness found at the scene would be, in effect, leading the witness. However, if the witness has initialled the exhibit when originally in his possession there may be no need to describe it first, but a great deal will depend upon the facts of a particular case.

There are times, because of the sequence of the evidence, when it is appropriate to introduce a potential exhibit before it can be properly identified. When this occurs the evidence cannot properly be marked as an exhibit so counsel will ask that the evidence be marked by the Court clerk for identification only, perhaps marking the evidence with a letter rather than a number. Counsel will give her undertaking that the evidence will be properly identified later, at which time it will be marked as an exhibit and the letter replaced with a number.

It may be that counsel will not wish to interrupt the flow of her examination in order to deal with the exhibit. In this situation the exhibit is best introduced at the end of the examination. In this way counsel will be highlighting the important evidence at the conclusion of the witness testimony. For example, the Crown attorney may say to the witness: "Mr. Smith, you told the Court earlier that the accused pointed a gun at you—can you describe that gun?" "I am showing you a gun, Mr. Smith. How does it compare to the gun that was pointed at you?" "May I then have this gun marked as an exhibit, Your Honour?" In a strong finish counsel will slowly show the gun to the jurors.

23

Criminal Records

Lacking Confidence In Counsel

Court Jesters Cartoons. Peter V. MacDonald, Q.C. and David Brown. Stoddart. © 1991 by Peter V. MacDonald and David Brown.

The *Canada Evidence Act*, Section 12

Section 12 of the *Canada Evidence Act*[1] reads:

(1)   A witness may be questioned as to whether the witness has been convicted of any offence, excluding any offence designated as a contravention under the *Contraventions Act*, but including such an offence where the conviction was entered after a trial on an indictment.

(1.1)   If the witness either denies the fact or refuses to answer, the opposite party may prove the conviction.

(2)   The conviction may be proved by producing
   (*a*)   a certificate containing the substance and effect only, omitting the formal part, of the indictment and conviction, if it is for an indictable offence, or a copy of the summary conviction, if it is for an offence punishable on summary conviction, purporting to be signed by the clerk of the court or other officer having the custody of the records of the court in which the conviction, if on indictment, was had, or to which the conviction, if summary, was returned; and
   (*b*)   proof of identity.

What are not convictions for purposes of section 12 of the *Canada Evidence Act*:

1.   Provincial offences[2]
2.   Discipline proceedings[3]
3.   A conditional or absolute discharge[4]
   Different considerations arise when the witness is not the accused. However when the accused puts his character in issue by calling evidence of good character, evidence of a finding of guilt is admissible.[5]
4.   Section 810 peace bond[6] (probably common law peace bond too)
5.   Convictions for which a free pardon has been granted[7] (a free pardon is distinguished from an administrative pardon as the

---

1   R.S.C. 1985, c. C-5 [as amended S.C. 1992, c. 47, s. 66].

2   *Street v. Guelph (City)* (1964), 2 O.R. 421 (Ont. C.A.). See however, *R. v. Vallis* (1989), 21 M.V.R. (2d) 236 (B.C. C.A.).

3   *R. v. Stevely* (2001), 152 C.C.C. (3d) 538 (Sask. C.A.).

4   *R. v. Danson* (1982), 35 O.R. (2d) 777 (Ont. C.A.); *R. v. Conway* (1985), 17 C.C.C. (3d) 481 (Ont. C.A.); *R. v. Corbett* (1988), 41 C.C.C. (3d) 385 (S.C.C.). See also *R. v. Symonds* (1983), 9 C.C.C. (3d) 225 (Ont. C.A.); *R. v. Dodge* (1993), 81 C.C.C. (3d) 433 (Que. C.A.).

5   *R. v. Conway, ibid.*

6   *R. v. Moeineddin,* 2004 CarswellOnt 1794 (Ont. S.C.J.) at para. 3; *Haydock v. Baker* (2001), (*sub nom. J.H. v. W.B.*) [2001] Y.J. No. 37 (Y.T. Terr. Ct.) at para. 9.

7   Section 748(2), (3) of the *Criminal Code*; *R. v. Ayles*, [2003] O.J. No. 1924 per Wein J.

offender who receives it is deemed never to have committed the crime. See *R. v. Ayles, infra.*)

6. Quasi judicial proceedings, as for example, regulatory discipline matters such as under the *Police Act*[8]

Convictions for purpose of section 12 of the *Canada Evidence Act* include:

1. Indictable offences
2. Summary conviction offences
3. Foreign convictions. However the accused may explain the circumstances surrounding the conviction and if they were so oppressive the judge could rule that the adjudication was not a conviction at all.[9]
4. Findings of delinquency under the former *Juvenile Delinquents Act*[10] and findings of guilt under the *Young Offenders Act*.[11] (Now *Youth Criminal Justice Act*)
5. Any offender under a federal statute, as for example, *The Unemployment Insurance Act*, and not merely offences under the *Criminal Code*.[12]
6. Convictions for which an administrative pardon has been granted, as opposed to a free pardon.[13]

Section 667 of the *Criminal Code* also may be employed for proof of a criminal record. It may also be proven by an admissible out-of-court statement by the accused. Section 23 of the *Canada Evidence Act* may be resorted to for proof of a foreign conviction.[14]

Where an accused is unable to recall a conviction during cross-examination, the surrounding circumstances should not to be put to him to refresh his memory as, for example, the names of the victims. The prosecution should prove the conviction in reply by filing a certificate pursuant to section 12(2) of the *Canada Evidence Act*.[15]

Normally the defence has received the criminal record of the accused as part of the Crown disclosure, but not that of the Crown witnesses because

---

8 *R. v. Stevely* (2001), 152 C.C.C. (3d) 538 (Sask. Q.B.).
9 *R. v. Stratton* (1978), 42 C.C.C. (2d) 449 (Ont. C.A.).
10 R.S.C. 1970, c. J-3 [repealed S.C. 1980-81-82-83, c. 110, s. 80.]
11 R.S.C. 1985, c. Y-1. See *R. v. Morris* (1978), 43 C.C.C. (2d) 129 (S.C.C.); *R. v. Scott* (1984), 16 C.C.C. (3d) 17 (Ont. G.S.P.).
12 *R. v. Watkins* (1992), 70 C.C.C. (3d) 341 (Ont. C.A.).
13 Section 748(3) of the *Criminal Code*; *R. v. Paterson* (1988), 122 C.C.C. (3d) 254 (B.C. C.A.), leave to appeal refused (1999), 134 C.C.C. (3d) iv (S.C.C.), holding that a Crown witness cannot be cross-examined as to convictions for which a pardon has been granted.
14 *R. v. Stratton* (1978), 42 C.C.C. (2d) 449 (Ont. C.A.).
15 *R. v. Howard* (1983), 3 C.C.C. (3d) 399 (Ont. C.A.).

such records are not usually checked out by the police and therefore should be a disclosure request.

There will be times when the Crown witness will not agree with the criminal record put to him or her, either because the witness honestly fails to remember, is lying or the record provided is inaccurate. If establishing criminal record is important to the defence, then pretrial preparation should include obtaining certified copies of the conviction pursuant to section 12(2) of the *Canada Evidence Act*. Also a criminal record may be proven by obtaining a certified copy of a transcript of the proceedings wherein the accused has been convicted.[16]

In addition it could prove helpful for cross-examination purposes to request disclosure of, or subpoena any police contacts with the witness, occurrence reports and supplementary records of arrest of the various convictions, as well as outstanding charges, if any, of the Crown witnesses as they will provide the circumstances surrounding the charges and convictions as well as the names of the police officers involved who can be subpoened to testify, if needed. See Chapter, "Crown Disclosure."

Section 666, *Criminal Code*

Section 666 of the *Criminal Code* states:

> **666.** Where, at a trial, the accused adduces evidence of his good character, the prosecutor may, in answer thereto, before a verdict is returned, adduce evidence of the previous conviction of the accused for any offences, including any previous conviction by reason of which a greater punishment may be imposed.

A significant practical effect of this section is that if the accused adduces evidence of good character through Crown witnesses or defence witnesses without intending to testify, his criminal record can still be brought to the attention of the trier-of-fact.

Limits of Cross-Examination

The limit to which the Crown can go in its cross-examination of an accused's criminal record is to inquire as to what the conviction was for, the date and place of the conviction and the sentence.[17] The accused cannot

---

16 Reasonable notice to the other side should be given pursuant to sections 23(1) and 28 of the *Canada Evidence Act*, said notice not to be less than 7 days prior to trial.

17 *R. v. Boyce* (1974), 23 C.C.C. (2d) 16 (Ont. C.A.); *R. v. Shortreed* (1990), 54 C.C.C. (3d) 292 (Ont. C.A.); *R. v. McLaughlan* (1974), 20 C.C.C. (2d) 59 (Ont. C.A.) at 60-61; *R. v. Lizotte* (1980), 61 C.C.C. (2d) 423 (Que. C.A.) at 432-34; *R. v. Howard and Trudel* (1983), 3 C.C.C. (3d) 399 (Ont. C.A.) at 417.

be cross-examined as to the conduct which led to the conviction.[18] However, the circumstances of an accused's prior conviction may be admissible as similar fact evidence.

The accused cannot be cross-examined on the finding of guilt when granted an absolute or conditional discharge.[19]

A non-accused witness may be cross-examined on the conduct leading to that conviction as well as other acts of misconduct as the answers go to the credibility of the witness.[20] The witness is permitted to explain the circumstances of the conviction if he or she wishes.[21]

When the accused is acquitted, the circumstances of the charge cannot be led against him or her.[22] Similarly, when the charge was withdrawn.[23]

Normally a co-accused can cross-examine an accused as to the latter's disposition or propensity to commit an offence even when the accused has not put his character in issue, so as to allow for full answer and defence. See Chapter, "Further Limitations and Obligations, Cut-throat Defences."

An accused's acquittal means a declaration of innocence for all purposes and it is impermissible for a co-accused to cross-examine the accused with respect to the underlying facts of charges upon which he/she was acquitted whether it be for propensity or credibility issues unless properly admitted as similar fact evidence.[24]

The Crown is not permitted to go beyond prior convictions and cross-examine an accused as to discreditable conduct or association with disreputable persons in order to attack his or her credibility.[25]

---

18 *R. v. Stratton, supra; R. v. Laurier* (1983), 1 O.A.C. 128 (Ont. C.A.); *Québec (Procureur général) c. Charron* (1984), 43 C.R. (3d) 240 (Que. S.C.); *R. v. Boyce* (1974), 23 C.C.C. (2d) 16 (Ont. C.A.); *R. v. Bricker*, 90 C.C.C. (3d) 268, 1994 CarswellOnt 921 (Ont. C.A.), leave appeal refused (1994), 92 C.C.C. (3d) vi (note) (S.C.C.).

19 *R. v. Corbett, infra,* at 404; *R. v. Danson* (1982), 66 C.C.C. (2d) 369 (Ont. C.A.); *R. v. Dodge* (1993), 81 C.C.C. (3d) 433 (Que. C.A.); *R. v. Conway* (1985), 17 C.C.C. (3d) 481 (Ont. C.A.).

20 *R. v. Miller* (1998), 131 C.C.C. (3d) 141 (Ont. C.A.); *R. v. Koufis*, [1941] S.C.R. 481 (S.C.C); *R. v. Davison, infra,* at 449, leave to appeal refused 20 C.C.C. (2d) 424n (S.C.C.), quoted with approval by Pratte J. for the majority of the S.C.C. in *R. v. Morris*; *Québec (Procureur général) c. Charron, supra.*

21 *R. v. Stratton, supra.*

22 *R. v. Cullen* (1990), 52 C.C.C. (3d) 459 (Ont. C.A.); *R. v. Grant* (1992), 67 C.C.C. (3d) 268 (S.C.C.) at 279; *Grdic v. R.* (1985), 19 C.C.C. (3d) 289 (S.C.C.) at 293.

23 *R. v. Skippen, supra; R. v. Hoilett* (1991), 3 O.R. (3d) 449 (Ont. C.A.) at paras. 17, 18. As a general rule the evidence of a witness's acquittal is not relevant to the accused's guilt or innocence except where it is admitted for the limited purpose of showing that the witness has no personal interest in the case. See *R. v. Camacho* (1998), 129 C.C.C. (3d) 94 (Ont. C.A.).

24 *R. v. Atkins* (2002), 59 O.R. (3d) 546 (Ont. C.A.). But see Cory J. in *R. v. Arp* (1998), 129 C.C.C. (3d) 321 (S.C.C.) stating that in most cases it would be unfair and inappropriate to admit similar fact evidence underlying a prior acquittal.

25 *R. v. Waite* (1980), 57 C.C.C. (2d) 34 (N.S. C.A.) at 45-46; *R. v. Davison* (1974), 20

An accused's previous conviction was held by the Supreme Court of Canada to be admissible under section 666 of the *Criminal Code*, although the conviction was under appeal. The minority judgment did not distinguish between section 666 of the *Code* and section 12 of the *Canada Evidence Act*.[26] However, if the accused at trial is cross-examined on a conviction which is later overturned on appeal and that cross-examination could have played a part in the conviction, a new trial may be ordered.[27]

The defence, for tactical reasons, such as softening the blow, can lead evidence of the witness or accused's criminal record without fear of putting the accused's character in issue.[28]

A Crown witness may also disclose his or her criminal record during examination-in-chief.[29]

A witness, other than an accused, can be cross-examined with respect to the circumstances of an offence for which a conditional discharge was received.[30] Similarly, although the accused cannot be cross-examined with respect to outstanding charges, it has been held that a witness other than the accused can be so examined for the purpose of showing a possible motivation to seek favour with the prosecution,[31] in order to impeach the witness's credibility[32] or to show that the witness is the true perpetrator.[33] This reasoning is reflected in some American cases citing examples which hold that a witness other than the accused can be cross-examined to explore any motive that might affect the truthfulness or accuracy of the witness's testimony.[34]

It has been held that given the presumption of innocence it is objectionable to cross-examine defence witnesses on the mere existence of crim-

---

C.C.C. (2d) 424 (Ont. C.A.) at 444; *R. v. MacDonald* (1939), 72 C.C.C. 182 (Ont. C.A.) at 197. See exceptions in Chapter, "Character Witnesses."

26 *Hewson v. R.*, 42 C.C.C. (2d) 507, [1978] 2 S.C.R. 111 (5:4).

27 *R. v. Verney* (1993), 87 C.C.C. (3d) 363 (Ont. C.A.); *R. v. G. (K.R.)* (1991), 68 C.C.C. (3d) 268 (Ont. C.A.).

28 *R. v. St. Pierre* (1974), 3 O.R. (2d) 642 (Ont. C.A.).

29 *R. v. Boyko* (1975), 28 C.C.C. (2d) 193 (B.C. C.A.).

30 *R. v. Cullen* (1990), 52 C.C.C. (3d) 459 (Ont. C.A.).

31 *R. v. Titus* (1983), (*sub nom. Titus v. R.*) 2 C.C.C. (3d) 321 (S.C.C.). *R. v. Gassyt* (1998), 127 C.C.C. (3d) 546 (Ont. C.A.), leave to appeal refused (1999),136 C.C.C. (3d) vi (S.C.C.).

32 *R. v. Gonzague* (1983), 4 C.C.C. (3d) 505 (Ont. C.A.). Here, the outstanding charges were fraud. *Quaere* if the outstanding charges relate to non-credibility offences, such as assault, whether the witness could be cross-examined to impeach credibility? In *R. v. Cullen*, above, where the outstanding charge was possession of burglar tools and the issue was the credibility of the complainant, cross-examination was permitted.

33 *R. v. Arcangioli* (1994), 87 C.C.C. (3d) 289 (S.C.C).

34 *People v. Austin*, 35 Crim.L.Rep. (BNA) 2215 (Ill., 1984); *Piedre v. The Commonwealth*, 478 N.E. 2d 1284 (Mass.App., 1985); *State v. Baumier*, 482 A. 2d 1199 (R.I., 1984); *State v. Hubbard*, 36 Crim.L.Rep. (BNA) 2074 (Ore., 1984); *U.S. v. Abel*, 36 Crim.L.Rep. (BNA) 3003 (E.S.S.C, 1984).

inal charges that have not resulted in a conviction as opposed to the under-lying facts of the outstanding charges.[35] In *R. v. Gassyt*[36] it was held that a witness cannot be cross-examined on the fact that she is facing an outstanding charge without a proper foundation being made to show relevance; as for example, where the charge can be shown to provide the witness with a motive to favour the prosecution. The defence can still cross-examine the witness on the underlying facts of the charge as being relevant to credibility or another issue in the trial.[37] However where the facts have some relevance to the witness's credibility but not relevant to any other issue at trial, they are clearly collateral and therefore counsel is bound by the witness's answers and could not call witnesses to contradict her.

It is improper to cross-examine a witness where charges have been withdrawn.[38]

The accused's criminal record does not become admissible if he does not testify even though he has attacked the character of a Crown witness through his criminal record.[39] However it does become admissible if he adduces evidence of his good character. See section 666 of the *Criminal Code*.

The Crown is not permitted to ask the accused whether he or she testified at the proceedings that resulted in his or her convictions. This tactic would be an attempt to convey to the jury that since the accused was not believed on prior occasions leading to convictions he or she should not be believed in the present trial. Such a question goes to the accused's character, not to his or her credibility and is not permitted.[40] Neither may a non-accused witness be so questioned.[41]

It is not the role of the trial Judge to ask the accused about his or her prior record as it casts the trial Judge in the role of an adversary or inquisi-tor.[42]

Some counsel will tactically ask the accused who has a criminal record whether they pleaded guilty to all his previous convictions in an attempt to give added significance to the client's not guilty plea this time. However, as shown in the following cross-examination such a tactic can backfire and even become embarrassing for the defence. Note the devastating conclusion

---

35 *R. v. Hoilett* (1991), 3 O.R. (3d) 449 (Ont. C.A.).
36 (1998), 127 C.C.C. (3d) 546 (Ont. C.A.), leave to appeal refused (1999), 136 C.C.C. (3d) vi (S.C.C.); *R. v. Gonzague, supra; R. v. Titus, supra.*
37 *R. v. Gassyt, ibid.*
38 *R. v. Hoilett* (1991), 3 O.R. (3d) 449 (Ont. C.A.).
39 *R. v. Corbett, infra,* at 404; *R. v. Butterwasser* (1947), [1948] 1 K.B. 4 (Eng. C.A.).
40 *R. v. Geddes* (1979), 52 C.C.C. (2d) 230 (Man. C.A.); *R. v. Corbett, infra,* per Dickson C.J.C. at 403.
41 *R. v. Ghorvei* (1999), 138 C.C.C. (3d) 340 (Ont. C.A.); *R. v. Barnes,* [1999] O.J. No. 3296 (C.A.).
42 *R. v. Stewart* (1991), 62 C.C.C. (3d) 289 at 316 (Ont. C.A.).

when David Doherty, (now Doherty J. of the Ontario Court of Appeal) formerly of the Crown Law Office in Ontario, cross-examined the accused, Howard, who was charged with murder. The accused in-chief, had understated the amount of his convictions and wrongly testified that he had pleaded guilty to all the charges against him. If it was Mr. Howard's intention to underplay his criminal record in-chief, he paid for the mistake. If counsel is going to disclose the client's criminal record for a tactical reason, it is best that it be full and frank disclosure. If it is not, then what you are trying to achieve by pre-empting the Crown is lost. If you are less than forthright, you can be sure the Crown will, with the client's criminal record make you wish you were more forthcoming.[43]

> Q. Mr. Howard, I believe you told my friend you have a criminal record?
> A. That is correct.
> Q. And I think he referred you, in my notes, to some fifteen criminal offences that you've been convicted of in your life.
> A. Yes, sir.
> Q. It's actually quite a few more than fifteen, wasn't it?

MR. KLUWAK:

> That was my fault, my lord. I was the one who did the counting.

MR. DOHERTY:

> I don't know whose fault it would be. The witness answered under oath he had about fifteen criminal convictions.
> Q. I'm suggesting it's over twenty.
> A. I answered what was on the sheet there, sir.
> Q. Well, maybe we had better go over the sheet so we're clear on this. 1964, you'd be what, seventeen years of age?
> A. Yes, sir.
> Q. Do you know when you can start having a criminal record in Canada?
> A. Sixteen, I guess.
> Q. All right. In 1964, August the 7th, St. Thomas, Ontario, break, enter and theft, is that correct?
> A. Correct.
> Q. Received a suspended sentence.
> A. Yes, sir.
> Q. That means you don't go to jail?
> A. That's correct, yes.
> Q. 1966, May the 2nd, St. Thomas, possession of stolen goods. You received a fine. Do you remember that?
> A. That's correct.
> Q. 1966, May—June the 17th, London, Ontario, break and enter with intent to steal. Do you remember that?
> A. Yes, sir.
> Q. And this time you went to jail for one month.

---

43 *R. v. Howard* (November 13, 1983), 2nd Ont. S.C. Assizes, Justice Craig.

A. That's correct, yes.

Q. 1966, July the 18th, it would be a month later, break and enter. Again, do you remember that?

A. Yes, sir.

Q. And this time you went to jail for thirty days.

A. Correct.

Q. All right. November the 4th, 1966, break and enter with intent to steal, six charges. Do you remember those six?

A. Yes, sir, I do.

Q. All right. And this time you received a suspended sentence again?

A. Yes, sir.

Q. Now, we'll move to 1967. And you were convicted in July of 1967 of breach of probation.

A. Yes, sir, that's correct.

Q. That would be the probation you got for those six break and enters?

A. That's correct, yes.

Q. Before. And this time you went to jail for six months?

A. That's right.

Q. Then we move to 1970 and we have, in November of 1970, two more convictions for break and enter?

A. Yes, sir.

Q. And this time you go to jail for four months definite and eight months indefinite?

A. That's correct.

Q. And you're placed on probation again?

A. Two years, sir.

Q. All right. Then we move to December of 1971 and we have convictions, I suggest to you, for armed robbery.

A. Yes.

Q. Do you remember that one?

A. Yes, sir.

Q. Escape jail.

A. Yes, sir.

Q. We heard about that one on the tape, didn't we?

A. Yes, sir, we did.

Q. Three attempt abduction.

A. Yes, sir.

Q. An abduction.

A. Yes, sir.

Q. And another abduction.

A. Yes, sir.

Q. So in that group in 1971, we have a total, as I count them up, of five convictions.

A. That's correct.

Q. And on that occasion you were sent to jail for two years less one day definite and two years less one day indefinite.

A. Correct.

Q. All right. And that was in December 23rd of 1971 ?

A. Yes.

Q. You went to jail for two years less a day. We then move to June 28th of 1974, London, Ontario, and you were again convicted of causing a disturbance.

A. That is correct.

Q. And went back to jail for thirty days.

A. Yes, sir.

Q. And you were also required to post a peace bond in connection with a threatening charge.

A. Yes, sir, for one year.

Q. For one year.

A. Yes, sir.

Q. And that was in 1974?

A. Right.

Q. All right. And then, in April of 1976, again in London, Ontario, you were convicted of assault causing bodily harm.

A. Correct.

Q. You were convicted of forcible confinement?

A. Yes, sir.

Q. And you were convicted of a second count of forcible confinement.

A. Yes, sir, that's correct.

Q. And this time you go to the penitentiary for five years.

A. Yes, sir.

Q. And that was the sentence you just finished, sir, being a week before Mr. McCart was killed.

A. Yes, sir, that is correct.

Q. Now, my friend also asked you whether you had pleaded guilty on all of those occasions, do you remember that?

A. Yes, sir.

Q. And you said, "I had."

A. On most of the occasions, yes.

Q. So there were some you didn't plead guilty to, is that right?

A. I guess so.

Q. But you did those as well as the ones you pleaded guilty to, I take it.

A. Well, I'm not arguing with what's on the record.

Q. I'm not talking about the record now. My friend said to you, and I thought, and he'll correct me if I am wrong, I thought you had said you pleaded guilty to every other criminal offence you've been convicted of.

A. Well, I don't understand then.

Q. What don't you understand?

A. What I'm saying to you, sir, I'm not trying to be argumentative with you. What's on the record there, I'm not arguing that.

Q. No, we're past the record. We've gone through the twenty odd convictions.

A. Right.

Q. Now, this is my next question.

A. Okay.

Q. My next question is, I understood that you told Mr. Kluwak that on all of these twenty other convictions you had always pleaded guilty.

A. I think I said that, yes.

Q. Is that true?

A. Yes, sir.

Q. And you're not suggesting to us, though, that right after you did them you walked into the police station and confessed to them, are you?

A. No, sir, I'm not, no.

Q. They caught you dead in your tracks, so you pleaded guilty, isn't that a fair description?

A. I guess you could say that, sir, yes.

Q. And in all of those other cases, I take it the victim of your crime was still alive.

A. Yes, sir.

Q. And would be there to testify against you.

A. That's correct.

Judge's Charge

The trial Judge must make it clear to the jury that just because an accused has a criminal record, that record cannot be used to conclude that the accused is more likely to have committed the offence with which he or she is charged. A criminal record only goes to the witness's testimonial trustworthiness, that is, is the witness less likely to be telling the truth because he or she has a criminal record.[44]

In *R. v. Brown*,[45] the Ontario Court of Appeal held that with respect to the issues of credibility, the trial Judge has the discretion to comment on the weight of the criminal record depending on the number of convictions, whether they were offences of dishonesty, and the length of time since the prior offences occurred. But the trial Judge cannot direct the jury that the evidence of a person with a criminal record cannot be given the same weight as a person without a criminal record.[46] The Judge can, however, make positive comment on the fact, if appropriate, that the accused stands before the Court as a person of unblemished character with no previous conviction.

Trial Judge's Discretion to Exclude Convictions

As stated earlier an accused's criminal record only goes to his credibility and not as evidence of propensity to commit the crime he is presently

---

44 *R. v. Dorland*, [1948] O.R. 913 (Ont. C.A.); *R. v. Williams*, [1969] 1 O.R. 139 (Ont. C.A.); *R. v. Skippen*, [1970] 1 O.R. 689 (Ont. C.A.); *R. v. Stratton, supra*; *R. v. Arcangioli*, [1994] 1 S.C.R. 129 (S.C.C.); *R. v. Tanner* (1994), 92 C.C.C. (3d) 68 (Ont. C.A.).

45 (1978), 38 C.C.C. (2d) 339 (Ont. C.A.).

46 *R. v. Titchner*, [1961] O.R. 606 (Ont. C.A.); *R. v. Goldhar*, [1957] O.W.N. 138 (Ont. C.A.).

charged with. In *R. v. Corbett*[47] the Supreme Court of Canada held that a trial Judge does have a discretion to exclude prejudicial evidence of previous convictions "where the mechanical application of section 12 would undermine the right to a fair trial." La Forest J., after referring to the United States and United Kingdom experience, noted some factors to be considered in the trial Judge's exercise of discretion to exclude prejudicial evidence of prior convictions. These factors were endorsed by Dickson C.J.C. in *Corbett*:

1. The nature of the previous convictions, i.e., offences of dishonesty is more probative on the issue of credibility than violence offences;
2. Remoteness or nearness to the present charge, i.e., the more remote the conviction, the less probative its value;
3. The similarity of the previous convictions to the charge at hand, i.e., the greater the similarity, the greater the prejudice;
4. The interest of not presenting a distorted picture to the jury, especially when a deliberate attack has been made upon the credibility of a Crown witness.

It may be that counsel would not call his or her client if the full criminal record were to be exposed. It is therefore advisable to seek a ruling from the trial Judge as to how far the Crown can go in cross-examining the accused as to his or her criminal record before announcing whether or not the accused will testify. The Judge's ruling would also be helpful because defence counsel normally elicits the client's criminal record before the Crown has the opportunity and does not wish to bring out more than is necessary. In *R. v. Underwood*[48] the Supreme Court held the accused has the right to make a *Corbett* application at the end of the Crown's case and before electing whether to call the client to testify. The Court stated that a *voir dire* should be held before the defence opens its case wherein the defence will disclose the evidence it intends to lead, but no *voir dire* is necessary where the defence is already fairly clear. If the accused leads evidence not disclosed on the *voir dire* the trial Judge can reconsider his or her decision if that evidence would have had a material bearing on the application.

It appears from *Corbett* and the case law that has followed that an attack on the credibility of Crown witnesses can foreclose the defence in a *Corbett* application. However, if counsel can show that the defence wishes to challenge the reliability of a witness's testimony (as for example challenging the honest witness's identification) as opposed to the witness's

---

47 (1988), 41 C.C.C. (3d) 385 (S.C.C). See also *R. v. P. (G.F.)* (1994), 89 C.C.C. (3d) 176 (Ont. C.A.) at 180.
48 (1997), 121 C.C.C. (3d) 117 (S.C.C).

credibility, a successful application may still be open.[49] A distinction may be drawn between attacking the evidence of a witness and attacking the character or credibility of a witness.[50]

A prior conviction for a serious offence of violence as opposed to one of credibility, such as attempted murder, will not be ignored by the Court as being unrelated to the issue of credibility as it is such a serious offence "that a prospect of a conviction for perjury is unlikely to keep the witness in line ... and that the witness is unlikely to have more respect for the truth than he has shown for human life.[51] In *R. v. Madrusan* (2006), 203 C.C.C. (3d) 513 (B.C. C.A.) the complainant was vigorously challenged as to the truthfulness of her testimony. Accused charged with robbery. He had a very lengthy criminal record including three robberies. The trial Judge refused to limit the cross-examination of the accused on his record. The Court of Appeal upheld the trial Judge's decision but stated the trial Judge should have edited the record to remove some of the offences similar to the one charged. The edited record would have still left the jury with the impression the accused had a continuous disregard for the law without overwhelming it with offences similar to the one charged.

---

49 In *R. v. McFadyen* (2002), 161 C.C.C. (3d) 252 (Ont. C.A.), leave to appeal refused 2002 CarswellOnt 3502, 2002 CarswellOnt 3503 (S.C.C.) where there was no attack on the complainant's credibility or character, it was held that simply challenging her version of events does not amount to an attack on credibility which could present a distorted picture to the jury. See also *R. v. Batte* (2000), 145 C.C.C. (3d) 498 (Ont. C.A.); *R. v. Bomberry* (2010), 258 C.C.C. (3d) 117 (Ont. C.A.) at paras. 46, 47.

50 Professor Delisle, *R. v. P. (G.F.)* (1994), 29 C.R. (4th) 315 (Ont. C.A.) at 318; *R. v. Charland* (1996), 110 C.C.C. (3d) 300 (Alta. C.A.) at 313, affirmed (1997), 120 C.C.C. (3d) 481 (S.C.C.). See also *R. v. Riehm* (1993), 21 W.C.B. (2d) 348 (Ont. C.A.).

51 *R. v. Saroya* (1994), 36 C.R. (4th) 253 (Ont. C.A.). Also see *R. v. Charland, supra,* where the Court stated that "Generally, previous convictions for violent offences such as sexual assault do not directly reflect on honesty and truthfulness, and depending on the circumstances of the case, have limited probative value in assessing credibility. However, particularly in the context of a lengthy criminal record, such prior convictions have probative value that is greater than trifling because a jury could reasonably conclude that the convictions reflect a disregard for the laws and rules of society, making it more likely that the person who harbours such attitudes would lie." The Court also stated that excluding the sexual assault convictions would leave the jury with the false impression that the accused appeared to have led a crime-free life since 1988 when he spent most of that time in prison. In *R. v. Gayle* (2001), 54 O.R. (3d) 36 (Ont. C.A.), leave to appeal refused (2002), 159 C.C.C. (3d) vi (note) (S.C.C.) it was held that where the accused has launched an all-out attack on a material Crown witness's credibility, that offences which don't relate directly to honesty but their nature and number and close proximity painted a picture of one who had little regard for the rules of society and in particular a person who had little respect for the administration of justice, the record should be admitted. There are cases however that point out such offences as assault, dangerous driving, impaired driving are of little probative value in assessing credibility. See *R. v. Brown* (1978), 38 C.C.C. (2d) 339 (Ont. C.A.).

In a trial by Judge alone the trial Judge will hear about the fullness of the accused's record in any application to exclude it or any part of it and so a practical approach would be to not argue the exclusion of any part of the record but argue at the appropriate time that the trial Judge should not place any reliance on it, relying on the *Corbett* factors.[52]

THE EFFECTS OF A PLEA OF GUILTY BY AN ACCOMPLICE

The fact that an accomplice has been convicted and sentenced on that plea is not evidence of guilt of the accused.[53]

PARDON

By virtue of section 748(2) of the *Criminal Code* the Governor in Council may grant a free pardon or a conditional pardon to any person who has been convicted of an offence. Subsection (3) states that where a free pardon is granted to a person that person shall be deemed thereafter never to have committed the offence in respect of which the pardon is granted. Therefore a witness may not be cross-examined on conviction for which a pardon has been granted.[54]

An application may also be made to the Solicitor General of Canada for a pardon pursuant to the *Criminal Records Act*, R.S.C. 1985, c. C-47.

---

52 Criminal Lawyers' Association 25 Year Convention and Education Program, 1996 per Mark Sandier.

53 *R. v. Caron* (1971), 9 C.C.C. (2d) 447 (Ont. C.A.); *R. v. MacDonald* (1974), 21 C.C.C. (2d) 87 at 92 (Ont. C.A.), affirmed [1977] 2 S.C.R. 832 (S.C.C.); *R. v. MacGregor* (1981), 64 C.C.C. (2d) 353 at 357 (Ont. C.A.), leave to appeal refused (1982), 42 N.R. 349 (S.C.C.).

54 *R. v. Paterson* (1998), 122 C.C.C. (3d) 254 (B.C. C.A.), leave to appeal refused (1999), 134 C.C.C. (3d) iv (S.C.C.).

24

Character Witnesses

CHARACTER OF THE ACCUSED

Defence counsel should not underestimate the value of good character evidence. While the recent case of *R. v. Clarke*[1] has taken some of the impact out of character evidence, such evidence, assuming it is good evidence, can, in my view, make a difference in the verdict if properly presented, particularly so if the verdict comes down to your client's word against someone who has a blemished character or whose credibility is vulnerable. A jury who hears about an accused who has demonstrated that over a lifetime he or she has been a law-abiding and solid citizen will do its best, even lean over backwards at times, to give your client every break it can; whether it be an acquittal, a guilty verdict to a lesser charge or perhaps even a recommendation for mercy. At the end of the day you will emphasize in your jury submissions that your client's good habits and ethics developed over a lifetime did not change overnight.

An accused person can introduce evidence of good character through his or her own testimony or through the evidence of other witnesses, including Crown witnesses when possible. Such evidence is led in support of the accused's credibility and also as a basis for an inference that the accused is unlikely to have committed the crime.[2] However, if the character evidence

---

1 (1998), 129 C.C.C. (3d) 1 (Ont. C.A.).
2 *R. v. Barbour*, [1938] S.C.R. 465 at 469 (S.C.C.); *Tarrant v. R.* (1981), 25 C.R. (3d) 157 (Ont. C.A.); *R. v. Elmosri* (1985), 23 C.C.C. (3d) 503 (Ont. C.A.); see also *R. v. Dees* (1978), 40 C.C.C. (2d) 58 (Ont. C.A.); *R. v. Boles* (1978), 43 C.C.C. (2d) 414 (Ont. C.A.). In *R. v. Profit* (1993), 15 O.R. (3d) 803n, the Supreme Court of Canada held that the propensity value of character evidence as it relates to morality is diminished in sexual assault cases involving children because such assaults are normally carried out in private so that others would not know of such propensity. However, in *R. v. Norman* (1993), 16 O.R. (3d) 295 at 311, the Ontario Court of Appeal held that this does not mean the trial Judge should ignore the character evidence entirely, particularly where the character

goes only to the accused's credibility and not to his or her propensity, for example, for violence, on a charge involving violence, then the trial judge need only charge the jury that the character evidence was capable of supporting an inference that the accused should be believed.[3]

In *R. v. Clarke* it was held that where reputation evidence as to crediblity is admitted the trial Judge should instruct the jury that whatever the witness's reputation for veracity in the community, testifying under oath in Court is a very different circumstance, the character witnesses have not heard all of the evidence and are not sworn to the heavy duty of the juror to render a true verdict. The jury may find the reputation evidence helpful in determining the credibility of the witnesses, but they should not automatically defer to that evidence."

The defence may lead the character evidence even though the accused has not testified.[4]

It would be improper for Crown counsel to ask a jury to draw an adverse inference because the accused failed to call better character evidence.[5]

The personal opinion of a witness as to the accused's character is inadmissible[6] and the witness cannot testify in-chief as to particular incidents.[7] The question must be framed so that the witness is giving his or her knowledge about the accused's general reputation in the community for the relevant character trait in issue[8]—so that if the accused is charged with theft, counsel would ask: "Do you know the accused's general reputation in the community for honesty and integrity?" If there was an aspect of violence: "Do you know the accused's general reputation in the community for peacefulness (or assaultive behaviour)?" "Do you know the defendant's reputation in the community for being sexually aggressive?" Since the defendant's credibility is also important if he or she testifies, then the character witness should also be asked about his or her reputation in the community for truthfulness. The necessity for character evidence to be evidence of general reputation applies to extrinsic evidence but this rule has no application

---

evidence went to violence in a rape case, as well as morality. In *R. v. Kootenay* (1994), 87 C.C.C. (3d) 109 (Alta. C.A.), a sexual assault case, it was held that the trial judge is not required in every case to charge the jury as to the relevance of good character. The trial Judge should decide in each case what assistance the jury requires in weighing the evidence.

3   *R. v. St. Clair* (1994), 88 C.C.C. (3d) 402 (Ont. C.A.).
4   *R. v. Rowton* (1865), 169 E.R. 1497.
5   *R. v. H. (C.W.)* (1991), 68 C.C.C. (3d) 146 at 156 (B.C. C.A.).
6   *R. v. Close* (1982), 68 C.C.C. (2d) 105 (Ont. C.A.); *R. v. Rowton, ibid; R. v. Close* at 113 adopts *R. v. Demyen* (1977), 31 C.C.C. (2d) 383 (Sask. C.A.); *R. v. Clarke* (1998), 129 C.C.C. (3d) 1 (Ont. C.A.).
7   *R. v. Clarke, supra.*
8   *R. v. Close, ibid.*

where the accused gives the evidence for "it is difficult to see how an accused could give evidence of his own reputation."[9]

Many people who know an accused well are only in a position to say that they have never heard anything bad about the accused. Is this valid character evidence? In *R. v. H. (C.W.)*,[10] it was held that this negative evidence is "the most cogent evidence of a man's good character and reputation, because a man's character is not talked about till there is some fault to be found with it. It is the best evidence of his character that he is not talked about at all" so that a question to the witness might be: "In the twenty five years that you have known Mr. X, have you ever heard anything negative about his reputation for honesty and integrity?"

The character witness must obviously be of good character and the more responsible and substantial the witness's position in the community the better. The character witness should know the accused as more than a passing acquaintance with respect to the character traits involved or he will open himself up to a damaging cross-examination. It may be that the character witness is not well placed to give the evidence sought such as in *R. v. Diu*[11] where it was held that a parent is not well placed to know of a child's reputation for violence.

In *R. v. Levasseur*,[12] the Alberta Court of Appeal held that the "neighbourhood" restriction on character evidence was no longer justifiable in modern society. No purpose was served, for example, by denying an accused the opportunity of providing witnesses who could testify as to the accused's reputation in his or her work environment rather than his residential community. This case indicates how important it is that character witnesses be carefully screened because the Court found that the character witness was not properly qualified having regard to the short period of time he had known the accused and his limited exposure to persons knowing the accused.

It is important that counsel explain to the character witness the difference between giving a personal opinion based upon specific facts, which is not admissible, as opposed to giving an opinion as to the witness's general reputation in the community in which he knows the accused. If the witness is not made aware of the difference and begins to give a personal opinion, then the witness could be stopped by the trial judge or opposing counsel

---

9 *R. v. Close, supra.* However, *R. v. Mohan* (1994), 89 C.C.C. (3d) 402 (S.C.C.) at 415, Sopinka J. noted that an accused, in his or her own testimony, may rely on specific acts of good character. See also *R. v. Morris* (1978), 43 C.C.C. (2d) 129 (S.C.C.), per Pratte J.; *R. v. McNamara (No. 1)* (1981), 56 C.C.C. (2d) 193 (Ont. C.A.), affirmed (1985), (sub nom. *Canadian Dredge & Dock Co. v. R.*) 45 C.R. (3d) 289 (S.C.C.), at 348 [C.C.C.].

10 (1991), 68 C.C.C. (3d) 146 at 156, 157; *R. v. Rowton* (1865) 169 E.R. 1497 at 1505 per Cockburn C.J.

11 (2000), 49 O.R. (3d) 40 (Ont. C.A.).

12 (1987), 56 C.R. (3d) 335 (Alta. C.A.); *R. v. Clarke, supra.*

and become confused about this distinction with the result that the impact of the evidence is significantly diminished.

Character Evidence

Court Jesters Cartoons. Peter V. MacDonald, Q.C., and David Brown. Stoddart. © 1991 by Peter V. MacDonald and David Brown.

After inquiring about the witness's background and details about how long the witness has known the accused and under what circumstances, counsel's examination of the character witness should continue along these lines:

Q. Do you know persons in the community who know Mr. Jones?
A. Yes.
Q. A few or many?
A. I would say many.
Q. Do you therefore know Mr. Jones' general reputation in the community in which he lives for honesty and integrity and morality? (where the offence relates to honesty such as theft or fraud, or a sexual offence with respect to children)
A. Yes.

Q. What is that reputation?

A. He has a very good reputation.

Q. Do you know Mr. Jones' general reputation in the community for assaultive behaviour? (where the charge is assault or robbery, etc.)

A. Yes.

Q. What is that reputation?

A. Mr. Jones is known as a very peaceful man who never becomes involved in violence.

Q. Do you know Mr. Jones' general reputation for truthfulness and if so, what is that reputation?

A. Mr. Jones has an excellent reputation for truthfulness.

It would be improper to ask the witness if the accused would lie under oath as this would be usurping the function of the jury.[13]

If the accused does lead evidence of good character, whether or not he testifies, he has put his character in issue and opens the door for the Crown to lead evidence of bad character. The accused will put his character in issue by answers which expressly or by implication indicate that he is not the type of person who would have committed the offence(s) with which he is charged.[14] See Chapter, "Criminal Records." Before deciding to lead character evidence for your client, it would be the safest course, particularly if you suspect there is counter evidence, to write the Crown to ask for any evidence by way of witnesses' names and their statements which would rebut the accused's character evidence. If the Crown fails to respond, the trial Judge should be asked to direct disclosure.[15]

The common law rule was that evidence of good character could only be given by evidence of reputation and could only be rebutted by evidence of reputation and not specific acts.[16] There appears to be three exceptions to this rule: proof of convictions under section 666 of the *Criminal Code*; psychological evidence; and proof of similar fact evidence.[17] The trial Judge must instruct the jury that the reply evidence can only be used to rebut the good character evidence but not used to support a view that the accused was likely, from his or her character, to have committed the offence.[18]

Putting forth evidence of good character through the mouth of the accused can occur in any number of ways. Some examples would include the accused testifying that he or she had never previously been arrested for,

---

13 *R. v. Clarke, supra.*

14 *R. v. McFadden* (1981), 65 C.C.C. (2d) 9 (B.C. C.A.) at 12; *R. v. P. (N.A.)* (2002), 171 C.C.C. (3d) 70 (Ont. C.A.).

15 *R. v. Hutter* (1993), 86 C.C.C. (3d) 81 (Ont. C.A.).

16 *R. v. Rowton, supra; R. v. Demyen, supra.*

17 *R. v. McNamara (No. 1)* (1981), 56 C.C.C. (2d) 193 at 348-349 (Ont. C.A.). Similar fact evidence may have probative value in its own right on the issue of guilt, such as identity, intent, design, etc.; *R. v. Manahan* (1990), 11 W.C.B. (2d) 171 (Alta C.A.). See also *R. v. Tierney* (1982), 70 C.C.C. (2d) 481 (Ont. C.A.).

18 *R. v. Morris* (1978), 43 C.C.C. (2d) 129 (S.C.C.).

or convicted of, an offence, as the accused would be "projecting the image of a law abiding citizen."[19] Similarly, good character is introduced when the accused testifies, that he or she has earned an honest living;[20] and on previous occasions had returned lost property to its owners;[21] or an assault on an infant case, the accused testified he "never abused a child in his life;"[22] or where the accused was charged with manslaughter testified "he was not the kind of person who went looking for trouble or started fights and that he was not a fighter."[23]

There are scenarios where an accused has to repudiate charges by presenting his or her version without suffering the result that one's character has been put in issue. As Doherty J. stated in *R. v. P. (N.A.)*, *supra*, at para. 34, "For example, where the Crown is allowed to lead evidence to demonstrate that an accused has a controlling and dominating spouse in order to give context to the allegations, I do not think that an accused should be said to have put his character in issue when he describes himself as a loving and caring spouse." Doherty J. went on to say in para. 35 that this does not mean that the accused has "free rein" in extolling his virtues to the point where he is saying that he is not the type of person who committed the offences charged.

Introductory questions posed as to the accused's place of residence, marital status and employment do not put the accused's character into issue.[24]

Character evidence in the form of personal opinions which comes forth from a defence or Crown witness unprompted does not necessarily put character in issue;[25] nor does it when prompted by a question from the Crown.[26]

Exclusion of defence character evidence is only permissible where the potential prejudice substantially outweighs its probative value.[27]

In cross-examining witnesses as to their character or credibility, defence counsel is not putting the accused's character into issue.[28] The Crown

---

19   *R. v. Morris* (1978), 43 C.C.C. (2d) 129 (S.C.C.), per Pratte J.

20   *R. v. Baker* (1912), 7 Cr. App. R. 252 (Eng. C.C.C.).

21   *R. v. Samuel* (1956), 40 Cr. App. R. 8 (Eng. C.A.).

22   *R. v. Brown* (1999), 137 C.C.C. (3d) 400 (Ont. C.A.) at para. 32.

23   *R. v. Nealy* (1966), 30 C.C.C. (3d) 460 (Ont. C.A.) at 364.

24   *R. v. McNamara (No. 1)*, *supra*, the opposite appears true in England. See *R. v. Baldwin* (1925), 18 Cr. App. R. 175 at 177-78 (Eng. C.A.).

25   *R. v. Redd*, [1923] 1 K.B. 104 at 107 (Eng. C.A.). See also *R. v. Bricker* (1994), 90 C.C.C. (3d) 268 (Ont. C.A.).

26   *R. v. Bricker* (1994), 90 C.C.C. (3d) 268 (Ont. C.A.) at 278, leave to appeal refused (1994), 92 C.C.C. (3d) vi (note (S.C.C.).

27   *R. v. Clarke*, *supra*.

28   *R. v. Butterwasser* (1947), [1948] 1 K.B. 4 (Eng. C.A.); *R. v. Lee* (1975), 62 Cr. App. R. 33 (U.K. C.A.); *R. v. A. (W.A.)* (1996), 112 C.C.C. (3d) 83 (Man. C.A.).

cannot put the accused's character in issue through cross-examination of the defence witnesses.[29]

When evidence of bad character is led by the Crown, it cannot be used to show that the accused was likely to have committed the offence. The evidence can only be used to impeach the credit of the accused.[30] When the Crown is permitted to legitimately cross-examine on evidence of bad character it must be careful not to go so far with it as to elevate the prejudicial effect above the initial probative value.[31]

Although character evidence on behalf of the accused is led with respect to specific traits relevant to the case, it is still an open question whether the Crown is so limited in reply. However, it seems unreasonable that an accused who testifies to his good character for honesty should lay himself open to cross-examination on every phase of his character, including his sexual morality. But on the principle that the accused's character is indivisible, the Crown may not be limited to bad character traits even though such traits may be irrelevant to the actual charge.[32]

When the accused has put his or her character in issue the trial judge does have a discretion to exclude cross-examination on previous conduct which has not resulted in a conviction, that was remote in time or is of little probative value with respect to the issue of credibility and is, at the same time gravely prejudicial.[33]

As a general rule therefore, evidence which goes to the accused's bad character is inadmissible unless the accused leads evidence of good character. However, that rule is relaxed if the evidence is admissible for another valid purpose, as for example, motive. Dickson J. (as he then was) stated: "As evidence, motive is always relevant, and hence evidence of motive is admissible."[34] Where an accused was charged with possession of a weapon for a purpose dangerous to the public peace, a document was found on the accused's premises (along with the weapon) which was proven to be a rare code of the Mafia. This was held to be admissible because it linked the accused to a criminal organization which resorted to violence in pursuit of its goals and was therefore relevant as a motive for the possession of the

---

29 *R. v. A. (W.A.), supra; R. v. Jones* (1988), 44 C.C.C. (3d) 248 (Ont. C.A.).

30 *R. v. McNamara, supra; R. v. Cameron* (1995), 22 O.R. (3d) 65 (Ont. C.A.).

31 *R. v. Walker* (1994), 18 O.R. (3d) 184 (Ont. C.A.). See also *R. v. Morris* (1983), 36 C.R. (3d) 1 (S.C.C.).

32 R. Cross, *Cross on Evidence*, 4th ed. (London: Butterworths, 1974), pp. 349-350; K.L. Chasse, "Exclusion of Certain Circumstantial Evidence: Character and Other Exclusionary Rules" (1978), 16 Osgoode Hall L.J. 445 at 453.

33 *Ibid.* See also *R. v. V.* (B.C. C.A.), Lambert, Macfarlane and Locke JJ.A., June 25, 1990, summarized at 10 W.C.B. (2d) 373. *R. v. Morris, supra.*

34 *R. v. Lewis* (1979), 47 C.C.C. (2d) 24 at 34 (S.C.C.), quoting from J.C. Smith and B. Hogan, *Criminal Law*, 4th ed. (London: 1978).

weapon, namely for a purpose dangerous to the public peace.[35] Evidence that an accused belonged to a secret Chinese criminal society known as Kung Lok and the nature of its operation with specific reference to the dissuasion of witnesses from testifying or going to the police has been held to be admissible where the accused was charged with extortion and was attempting to have a witness change his evidence in the trial of a fellow Kung Lok member.[36] A Court has, however, ruled that the fact that an accused was a Rastafarian was inadmissible on a charge of obstructing justice as, on the facts of the particular case, the impugned evidence went only to character and was not relevant to motive.[37]

Character evidence may also become admissible to show habit. "Where a person's conduct in given circumstances is in issue, evidence that a person repeatedly acted in a certain way when those circumstances arose in the past has been received as circumstantial evidence that the person acted in conformity with past practice on the occasion in question." It was therefore held to be admissible that the defence could show that the deceased habitually carried a gun when he was shot by the accused.[38]

As indicated earlier counsel should keep in mind section 666 of the *Criminal Code* which states:

> **666.** Where, at a trial, the accused adduces evidence of his good character, the prosecutor may, in answer thereto, before a verdict is returned, adduce evidence of the previous conviction of the accused for any offences, including any previous conviction by reason of which a greater punishment may be imposed.

By virtue of this section, where the accused leads evidence of good character, the Crown is permitted to lead evidence of convictions registered (even though the accused has not testified) before or after the incident which led to the charge provided that the convictions after the incident relate to offences so closely related in time to the charge that they show the accused's disposition at that time.[39] Section 666 of the *Criminal Code* provides wider scope for cross-examination than section 12 of the *Canada Evidence Act* when the accused in-chief either expressly or by implication indicates she is not the type of person who would have committed the offence charged. The accused can be cross-examined about the circumstances of the criminal

---

35   *R. v. Caccamo* (1975), 21 C.C.C. (2d) 257 (S.C.C.), affirming (1973), 11 C.C.C. (2d) 249 (Ont. C.A.).

36   *R. v. Ma* (1978), 44 C.C.C. (2d) 511 (Ont. C.A.).

37   *R. v. Spence* (1979), 47 C.C.C. (2d) 167 (Ont. C.A.); see also *R. v. Nielsen* (1984), 16 C.C.C. (3d) 39 (Man. C.A.), leave to appeal to S.C.C. refused (1985), 31 Man. R. (2d) 240 (S.C.C.).

38   *R. v. Watson* (1996), 30 O.R. (3d) 161 (Ont. C.A.).

39   *R. v. Close, supra.*

convictions given that section 666 is predicated on the accused putting his character in issue.[40]

If the accused testifies section 12 of the *Canada Evidence Act* permits the Crown to put his criminal record to him in cross-examination even when the accused has not put his character in issue but only to the extent of the name of the offence, where and when it was committed and the sentence imposed.[41]

The Crown can also lead evidence which points to the accused's bad character although the accused has not put his or her character in issue if it is necessary to the development of the Crown's case. Such an instance may occur as, for example, when the accused is overheard on an intercepted communication to refer to his parole status and that he must proceed cautiously to avoid police detection in a drug conspiracy; or where the background to a relevant scenario takes place in a prison.[42] There are different scenarios where bad character evidence becomes admissible as part of the narrative.[43]

When the Crown elicits character evidence of the accused in a cross-examination of a defence witness, it does not put an accused's character in issue to permit the Crown to introduce the accused's criminal record. Even if the character evidence is elicited in cross-examination by the defence of a Crown witness, it does not bring into play section 666 if the evidence is in the nature of a personal opinion as opposed to evidence of general reputation in the community.[44]

Where the defence puts character in issue, the Crown may call evidence of general reputation[45] in reply and cross-examine the accused on specific acts of bad conduct. However, extrinsic evidence of specific incidents may not be called unless that evidence amounts to similar fact evidence (which probably should have been called as part of the Crown's case in any event) or comes within section 666 of the *Criminal Code*.[46]

Another area where evidence of the discreditable associations of the accused is admissible as an exception to the normal prohibition is where

---

40 *R. v. P. (N.A.)* (2002), 171 C.C.C. (3d) 70 (Ont. C.A.) at para. 32; *R. v. W. (L.K.)* (1999), 138 C.C.C. (3d) 449 (Ont. C.A.) at 465, leave to appeal refused 2000 CarswellOnt 4252, 2000 CarswellOnt 4253 (S.C.C.).

41 *R. v. Tierney* (1982), 70 C.C.C. (2d) 481 (Ont. C.A.). See Chapter, "Criminal Records."

42 *R. v. Rowbotham* (1988), 63 C.R. (3d) 113 (Ont. C.A.); *R. v. Nygaard* (1987), 59 C.R. (3d) 37 (Alta. C.A.), reversed (1989), 72 C.R. (3d) 257 (S.C.C.).

43 *R. v. Nygaard, supra*; *R. v. Persaud*, [1996] O.J. No. 5345 (Ont. Gen. Div.); *R. v. B. (S.)*, 1996 CarswellOnt 1576 (Ont. Gen. Div.); *R. v. Lamirande* (2002), 164 C.C.C. (3d) 299 (Man. C.A.); *R. v. J. (J.)*, 2008 ONCA 133 (Ont. C.A.); *R. v. Cuadra* (1998), 125 C.C.C. (3d) 289 (B.C. C.A.).

44 *R. v. Demyen* (1977), 31 C.C.C. (2d) 383 (Sask. C.A.), followed in *R. v. Close, supra*.

45 *R. v. Norman* (1993), 16 O.R. (3d) 295.

46 *R. v. D. (D.)* (1991), 65 C.C.C. (3d) 511 (Ont. C.A.).

the accused has associated with drug users. In *R. v. Douglas*[47] the Ontario Court of Appeal held:

> In a number of cases it has been held that association with drug addicts is relevant and admissible where an accused is charged with a drug offence. . . .
>
> . . . The fact that people who either use drugs or are addicted to them seek out or associate with a particular person, surely, can lead to a rational inference that the subject of the visits is in some way involved in drugs.

However, in these cases police officers testified as to their own knowledge and did not offer evidence of reputation. Although the law has allowed evidence of the general reputation of a house to show that the premises is a bawdy house it is submitted that there is no valid reason for this principle to be expanded to allow evidence of reputation to be used to establish that a person is a user of drugs.[48]

In *R. v. Bengert (No. 7)*,[49] it was held that there was no rule of evidence that association with drug addicts by traffickers is always admissible in drug cases.

While it is true that a witness may be cross-examined with respect to his conduct or discreditable associations to show that by reason of his bad character his evidence ought not to be believed, an accused witness may not be so cross-examined where the misconduct of discreditable associations are unrelated to the charge for which he is being tried. But such cross-examination is not forbidden where it is relevant to prove the falsity of the accused's evidence, notwithstanding that it may incidentally impact upon the accused's character by disclosing discreditable conduct. Martin J.A., delivering the judgment of the Court in *R. v. Davison*, stated:[50]

> Thus, if an accused found in possession of goods recently stolen were to give evidence that he had purchased them from X in good faith without knowing that they were stolen, it would not seem open to doubt that he could be cross-examined for the purpose of showing, if such were the fact, that he had been associated with X in the commission of prior thefts. Such cross-examination would be permissible as being directly relevant to the veracity of the accused's explanation. Such cross-examination would also be relevant to prove guilt

---

47 (1977), 33 C.C.C. (2d) 395 at 403-404 (Ont. C.A.); see also *R. v. MacDonald* (1959), 126 C.C.C. 1 (S.C.C.); *R. v. Cook* (1978), 46 C.C.C. (2d) 318 (B.C. C.A.); and *R. v. Babiak* (1974), 21 C.C.C. (2d) 464 (Man. C.A.). See also *R. v. Lyons* (1982), 69 C.C.C. (2d) 318 at 325 (B.C. C.A.) per Hinkson J.A., where past acts of certain of the co-conspirators were admitted as evidence of the relationship between the parties and of the role of one of the conspirators as the promoter of the scheme.

48 *R. v. Douglas, ibid.*

49 (1979), 15 C.R. (3d) 33 (B.C. S.C.).

50 (1974), 20 C.C.C. (2d) 424 at 444 (Ont. C.A.), leave to appeal to S.C.C. refused (1974), 6 O.R. (2d) 424n (S.C.C.).

since the rejection of the accused's explanation would permit the normal inference to be drawn from the unexplained possession of stolen property.

If the prosecution tenders psychiatric evidence, the trial judge must first decide whether it is relevant to an issue, apart from a tendency to show propensity, and if it is relevant to another issue, such as identity, it then must be decided whether its probative value on this issue outweighs its prejudicial effect on the propensity issue. If its primary relevance is to show disposition, then the evidence must be excluded.[51] For psychiatric evidence to be relevant to identity, it must show that the accused shared a distinctive unusual behavioural trait with the culprit. The trait must be significantly distinctive so that it operates as a badge or mark identifying the culprit. It is not sufficient that the accused is a member of an abnormal group, some of which have the unusual behavioural traits possessed by the perpetrator. If it is shown, however, that all members of the group have these distinctive, unusual traits and it can be inferred that the accused has these traits, then the evidence is relevant subject to the trial judge's obligation to exclude it if its prejudicial effect outweighs its probative value. The greater the number of persons that have these traits, the less relevant the evidence is on the issue of identity and the more likely the prejudicial effect predominates over its probative value.[52] While a psychiatrist cannot answer whether or not the accused committed the crime, he could testify that if he did, the psychiatrist would have expected to find certain characteristics and did not find them in this accused. For example, if the offence is of the type committed by homosexuals, psychiatric evidence that the accused does not possess the characteristics of the abnormal group is relevant to exclude him from the special class of which the perpetrator of the crime is a member.[53] Furthermore, Martin J.A. in *R. v. McMillan* stated:[54]

> I leave open, until the question is required to be decided, whether when the crime is one assumed to be committed by normal persons, e.g., rape, psychiatric evidence is admissible to show that the accused is a member of an abnormal group, possessing characteristics which make it improbable that he committed the offence, e.g., that he is a homosexual with an aversion to heterosexual relations. I am disposed, however to think that such evidence is admissible.

---

51   *R. v. Morin* (1989), 66 C.R. (3d) 1 (S.C.C.); *R. v. B. (S.C.)* (1997), 119 C.C.C. (3d) 530 (Ont. C.A.); *R. v. Pascoe* (1997), 113 C.C.C. (3d) 126 (Ont. C.A.).
52   *Ibid.*
53   *R. v. McMillan* (1975), 29 C.R.N.S. 191 (Ont. C.A.), affirmed (1977), 73 D.L.R. (3d) 759 (S.C.C.).
54   *Ibid.*, 29 C.R.N.S. 191 at 207.

In *R. v. Mohan*,[55] the issue was whether expert opinion was admissible to show that the accused did not possess the character traits which fit the psychological profile of the offender. Sopinka J. stated:

> Before an expert's opinion is admitted as evidence, the trial judge must be satisfied as a matter of law, that either the perpetrator of the crime or the accused has distinctive behavioural characteristics such that a comparison of one with the other will be of material assistance in determining innocence or guilt. . . . The trial judge should consider . . . whether the behavioural profile which the expert is putting forward is in common use as a reliable indicator of membership in a distinctive group. Put another way: has the scientific community developed a standard profile for the offender who commits this type of crime?

A psychiatrist may be called by the defence to offer an opinion whether or not the accused had a propensity to lie and was of a psychopathic personality who confessed to acts which he or she really had not done.[56]

CHARACTER OF THE CO-ACCUSED

In *Lowery v. R.*,[57] K. and L. were charged with the sadistic murder of a young girl. K. and L. each asserted the other was the completely dominating person and each claimed to be in fear of the other. The Court allowed K. to call a psychologist to state that K. was a passive, weak person, easily led and that L. was an aggressive sadist. In that case, L. put his good character in issue and blamed K. for the killing. K. was allowed to rebut the character evidence as part of his defence in blaming L. However, what would have happened if L. had not testified? Would K. have been able to adduce the evidence he did if L. had not put his character in issue? Subject to the restrictions in *R. v. Robertson*,[58] the fact that K. was an easily led person would have been admissible. But could K. have led evidence that L. was sadistic and aggressive? The Privy Council in *Lowery* held:

---

55 *Supra*; *R. c. J. (J.-L.)* (2000), (sub nom. *R. v. J. (J-L.)*) 148 C.C.C. (3d) 487 (S.C.C.) at para. 45.

56 *R. v. Dietrich* (1970), 1 C.C.C. (2d) 49 (Ont. C.A.), leave to appeal to S.C.C. refused (1970), 1 C.C.C. (2d) 68n (S.C.C.).

57 (1973), [1974] A.C. 85 (Victoria P.C.). See also *R. v. Jackson* (1991), 68 C.C.C. (3d) 385 (Ont. C.A.), where an accused was allowed to cross-examine his co-accused who had implicated the former by bringing out various unlawful acts of the accused. It was stated that the appropriate remedy was not to curtail cross-examination but to grant severance in the proper case. See also *R. v. Suzack*, 141 C.C.C. (3d) 449, 2000 CarswellOnt 95 (Ont. C.A.), leave to appeal refused 2001 CarswellOnt 1075, 2001 CarswellOnt 1076 (S.C.C.).

58 (1975), 21 C.C.C. (2d) 385 (Ont. C.A.), leave to appeal refused (1975), 21 C.C.C. (2d) 385n (S.C.C.).

It is, however, established by the highest authorities that in criminal cases the Crown is precluded from leading evidence that does no more than show that the accused has a disposition or propensity or is the sort of person likely to commit the crime charged; . . .

It is, we think, one thing to say that such evidence is excluded when tendered by the Crown in proof of guilt, but quite another to say that it is excluded when tendered by the accused in disproof of his own guilt. We see no reason of policy or fairness which justifies or requires the exclusion of evidence relevant to prove the innocence of an accused person.[59]

The policy rule that prevents the Crown from introducing evidence for the sole purpose of proving that the accused is likely to have committed the offence is not applicable when the evidence is led by the co-accused.[60]

An accused who is relying on the defence of duress from his or her co-accused may seek to show that the co-accused has a disposition for violence and if the accused was aware of that violence, his or her belief that violence would be used against him.[61]

CHARACTER OF THE WITNESS

Impeaching the character of a Crown witness does not put the character of the accused in issue, therefore the Crown is not entitled to call evidence of the accused's bad character,[62] but can call evidence in reply to rebut the bad character evidence of the witness.[63]

The credibility of an impeached witness may be rehabilitated by evidence of a good reputation for truth and veracity and personal opinion as to credibility.[64]

---

59 *Lowery v. R., supra*, at 102. *Suzack, supra*, holds that there should be a careful instruction to the jury as to the limited use of the evidence in cut-throat defence. See also *R. v. Diu* (2000), 144 C.C.C. (3d) 481 (Ont. C.A.) at 526; *R. v. Marks* (2000), 145 C.C.C. (3d) 569 (Ont. C.A.) at paras. 17, 18.

60 *R. v. Valentini* (1999), 132 C.C.C. (3d) 262 (Ont. C.A.). *R. v. Kendall* (1987), 35 C.C.C. (3d) 105 (Ont. C.A.). See also *R. v. McMillan, infra*; *R. v. Jackson* (1991), 68 C.C.C. (3d) 385 (Ont. C.A.) at 434.

61 *R. v. Gibb* (1982), 7 A.Crim. 385 (Vic. C.C.A.); "Character as a Fact in Issue in Criminal Cases," Mewett (1984-85), 27 C.L.Q. 29 at 54. By way of analogy see *R. v. Scopelliti* (1981), 63 C.C.C. (2d) 481 (Ont. C.A.), leave to appeal refused April 17th, 1992.

62 *R. v. Butterwasser*, [1948] 1 K.B. 4 (C.C.A.).

63 *R. v. Scopellete, infra*. See also *R. v. Diu* (2000), 144 C.C.C. (3d) 481 (Ont. C.A.); *R. v. Parsons* (1993), 84 C.C.C. (3d) 226 (Ont. C.A.) at 238; *R. v. O. (D.)* (2001), 156 C.C.C. (3d) 369 (Ont. C.A.).

64 R. Cross, *Cross on Evidence*, 4th ed. (London: Butterworths, 1974), p. 239; *R. v. T., supra*.

With respect to questioning a witness with respect to outstanding charges[65] and his or her criminal record, see the chapter on Criminal Records. If the accused points the finger at a witness as the culprit, the witness's criminal record is admissible not merely as going to his or her credibility but in support of the defence position that it was the witness and not the accused who was the culprit.[66] The witness may also be cross-examined on their discreditable conduct and associations that are unrelated to their testimony,[67] and the circumstance of their prior convictions.[68]

PSYCHIATRIC EVIDENCE OF THIRD PERSONS TO SHOW CULPABILITY

Where identity is in issue, the accused can introduce psychiatric evidence to show someone else has the abnormal propensity to commit the crime, but he puts his or her own character into issue through cross-examination or reply evidence to show that he or she too has such propensities.[69] If the third person has no connection with the crime, then evidence of that person's psychiatric profile is inadmissible because it is irrelevant.[70] Where there is no psychiatric evidence but the accused alleges that a third person has committed the offence in question, he opens himself to attack.[71]

CHARACTER OF THE VICTIM

Normally, the character of the victim is considered to be irrelevant.[72] These are exceptions however. In *R. v. Jack*[73] the accused was charged with

---

65   *R. v. Titus* (1983), (*sub nom. Titus v. R.*) 2 C.C.C. (3d) 321 (S.C.C.); *R. v. Chartrand*, 170 C.C.C. (3d) 97, 2002 CarswellOnt 4261 (Ont. C.A.).

66   *R. v. Butterwasser, supra.*

67   *R. v. Davison* (1974), 20 C.C.C. (2d) 424 (S.C.C.).

68   *R. v. Cullen* (1989), 52 C.C.C. (3d) 459 (Ont. C.A.); *R. v. Miller* (1998), 131 C.C.C. (3d) 141 (Ont. C.A.).

69   *R. v. McMillan* (1975), 29 C.R.N.S. 191 (Ont. C.A.), affirmed (1977) 33 C.C.C. (2d) 360 (S.C.C.); *R. v. Williams* (1985), 44 C.R. (3d) 351 (Ont. C.A.); *R. v. Parsons* (1993), 84 C.C.C. (3d) 226 (Ont. C.A.). See also *R. v. Coombs*, 2003 ABQB 318 (Alta. Q.B.).

70   *Ibid; R. v. Arcangioli, supra,* and *R. v. Latta* (1972), 8 C.C.C. (2d) 530 (Alta. C.A.).

71   *R. v. Speid* (1985), 46 C.R. (3d) 22 (Ont. C.A.). See also *R. v. Arcangioli, supra; R. v. Scopelleti, supra.*

72   R. Cross and C. Tapper, *Cross on Evidence*, 6th ed. (London: Butterworths, 1985), p. 299. *R. v. Seaboyer* (1991), 66 C.C.C. (3d) 321 (S.C.C.) supports the trial Judge's discretion that the prejudicial effect of the evidence's admission does not substantially outweigh its probative value. *R. v. Watson* (1996), 108 C.C.C. (3d) 310 (Ont. C.A.) held the prejudice in leading bad character evidence of the victim "refers to the possibility that the jury will misuse the evidence by concluding that the deceased's bad character somehow excused the otherwise criminal conduct of the accused."

73   (1992), 70 C.C.C. (3d) 67 (Man. C.A.).

the murder of his wife. The issue was whether or not the wife was actually dead. Evidence of the wife's character was admissible to show she was not the type of person who would abandon family and friends.

In *R. c. Parent*[74] the accused police officer charged with assault was allowed to call evidence of the complainant's aggressive personality to support the officer's claim of being provoked.

Character evidence of the victim going to his habit where relevant to a defence of an accused can be admissible.[75] Evidence of habit is properly viewed as circumstantial evidence that a person acted in a certain way on the occasion in issue.[76]

Evidence of prior acts of abuse would be admissible to support a plea of self-defence based on the battered-wife syndrome.[77]

What happens when the deceased, unknown to the accused, was a violent person? In *R. v. Scopelliti*,[78] Martin J.A. held that where the accused raises the defence of self-defence, evidence of the deceased's disposition for violence is admissible to show the probability that the deceased had been the aggressor and to support the accused's evidence that he was attacked by the deceased. This disposition of the deceased may be evidenced by proof of specific acts of violence unknown to the accused at the time of the incident, by evidence of reputation and by psychiatric evidence if the disposition in question comes within the proper sphere of expert evidence.[79] The accused, having introduced evidence that the deceased had a violent disposition, would open the door for the Crown to refute this by calling evidence that the deceased was of a peaceful disposition. Martin J.A. further stated that it may be open to the Crown to adduce evidence in reply in respect of the accused's disposition for violence as by introducing evidence of the deceased's character for violence, the accused impliedly puts his own character for violence in issue. In *Yaeck*, Watt J. suggests that it is "at least arguable that the prosecution may, in reply, adduce evidence of the ac-

---

74 [1989] R.J.Q. 1461 (C.A. Qué.). See also *R. v. Varga* (2001), 159 C.C.C. (3d) 502 (Ont. C.A.) at para. 71, leave to appeal refused [2002] S.C.C.A. No. 278 (S.C.C.), where evidence of the character of the victim was allowed in support of a defence of self-defence.

75 *R. v. Watson* (1996), 108 C.C.C. (3d) 310 (Ont. C.A.). Here, it was the habit of the deceased to always carry a gun and therefore relevant to infer he was carrying a gun when he was shot.

76 *Ibid.*

77 *R. v. Lavallee* (1990), 55 C.C.C. (3d) 97 (S.C.C.).

78 (1981), 63 C.C.C. (2d) 481 (Ont. C.A.). In *R. v. Yaeck*, [1989] O.J. No. 3002 (Ont. H.C.) it was held that there must be in addition some other appreciable evidence of the deceased's aggression at the material time.

79 *R. v. Hamilton* (2003), 180 C.C.C. (3d) 80 (B.C. C.A.).

cused's disposition for violence in the matter permitted in *Scopelliti*. . ." An opposite result was reached in *R. v. Wilson*.[80]

What about prior acts of violence by the deceased of which the accused is aware, whether towards the accused or others? Clearly they are relevant as they go to the accused's state of mind and particularly his or her reasonable apprehension of death or grievous bodily harm with respect to a defence of self-defence.

If the defence does not raise a violent disposition of the victim the Crown cannot raise the peaceable disposition of the victim where its probative value would be outweighed by its prejudicial effect. It would also tend to inject into the jury's deliberation feelings of sympathy for the victim and a desire to punish the accused.[81] The deceased's propensity for violence is admissible to show the deceased was probably the aggressor but evidence of bad character cannot be led merely to put the accused in a more favourable light.[82]

The defence is not required to wait until calling its case before eliciting through cross-examination evidence of the deceased's propensity for violence. However the trial Judge should be advised beforehand that self-defence will be raised.[83]

There is no rule that prior misconduct by the deceased is limited to cases where self-defence is raised. In *R. v. Watson*[84] the accused denied he shot the deceased but that he was killed in a gun battle with a third person. The fact that the deceased always carried a gun was supportive of the accused's defence as it was relevant that he had a gun at the material time. That evidence was held admissible.

Evidence of Complainant's Sexual Activity

The law relating to evidence of the sexual activity of complainants in sexual assault cases as going to character and credibility is set out in sections 276, 276.1 and 277 which states

> **276.** (1) In proceedings in respect of an offence under sections 151, 152, 153, 153.1, 155 or 159, subsections 160(2) or (3), or section 170, 171, 172, 173, 271, 272 or 273, evidence that the complainant has engaged in sexual activity, whether with the accused or with any other person, is not admissible

80 *R. v. Wilson* (1999), 136 C.C.C. (3d) 252 (Man. C.A.), leave to appeal refused (1999), 139 C.C.C. (3d) vi (note) (S.C.C.).

81 *R. v. Dejong* (1998), 125 C.C.C. (3d) 302 (B.C. C.A.); *R. v. Edelenbos* (2004), 71 O.R. (3d) 698 (Ont. C.A.).

82 *R. v. Cameron* (1995), 22 O.R. (3d) 65 (Ont. C.A.).

83 *R. v. Ryan* (1989), 49 C.C.C. (3d) 490 (Nfld. C.A.).

84 (1996), 108 C.C.C. (3d) 310 (Ont. C.A.).

to support an inference that, by reason of the sexual nature of that activity, the complainant

    (*a*) is more likely to have consented to the sexual activity that forms the subject-matter of the charge; or

    (*b*) is less worthy of belief.

(2) In proceedings in respect of an offence referred to in subsection (1), no evidence shall be adduced by or on behalf of the accused that the complainant has engaged in sexual activity other than the sexual activity that forms the subject-matter of the charge, whether with the accused or with any other person, unless the judge, provincial court judge or justice determines, in accordance with the procedures set out in sections 276.1 and 276.2, that the evidence

    (*a*) is of specific instances of sexual activity;

    (*b*) is relevant to an issue at trial; and

    (*c*) has significant probative value that is not substantially outweighed by the danger of prejudice to the proper administration of justice.

(3) In determining whether evidence is admissible under subsection (2), the judge, provincial court judge or justice shall take into account

    (*a*) the interests of justice, including the right of the accused to make a full answer and defence;

    (*b*) society's interest in encouraging the reporting of sexual assault offences;

    (*c*) whether there is a reasonable prospect that the evidence will assist in arriving at a just determination in the case;

    (*d*) the need to remove from the fact-finding process any discriminatory belief or bias;

    (*e*) the risk that the evidence may unduly arouse sentiments of prejudice, sympathy or hostility in the jury;

    (*f*) the potential prejudice to the complainant's personal dignity and right or privacy;

    (*g*) the right of the complainant and of every individual to personal security and to the full protection and benefit of the law; and

    (*h*) any other factor that the judge, provincial court judge or justice considers relevant. R.S. 1985, c. 19 (3rd Supp.), s. 12; 1992, c. 38, s. 2; 2002, c. 13, s. 13.

276.1 (1) Application may be made to the judge, provincial court judge or justice by or on behalf of the accused for a hearing under section 276.2 to determine whether evidence is admissible under subsection 276(2).

(2) An application referred to in subsection (1) must be made in writing and set out

    (*a*) detailed particulars of the evidence that the accused seeks to adduce, and

    (*b*) the relevance of that evidence to an issue at trial, and a copy of the application must be given to the prosecutor and to the clerk of the court.

(3) The judge, provincial court judge or justice shall consider the application with the jury and the public excluded.

(4) Where the judge, provincial court judge or justice is satisfied

(*a*) that the application was made in accordance with subsection (2),

(*b*) that a copy of the application was given to the prosecutor and to the clerk of the court at least seven days previously, or such shorter interval as the judge, provincial court judge or justice may allow where the interests of justice so require, and

(*c*) that the evidence sought to be adduced is capable of being admissible under subsection 276(2),

the judge, provincial court judge or justice shall grant the application and hold a hearing under section 276.2 to determine whether the evidence is admissible under subsection 276(2). 1992, c. 38, s. 2.

277. In proceedings in respect of an offence under section 151, 152, 153, 153.1, 155 or 159, subsections 160(2) or (3), or section 170, 171, 172, 173, 271, 272 or 273, evidence of sexual reputation, whether general or specific, is not admissible for the purpose of challenging or supporting the credibility of the complainant.

In *R. v. Morden*,[85] the complainant testified that a reason for ending her relationship with the accused was because she preferred women. The Court held, following the guidelines in *R. v. Seaboyer*,[86] that evidence she had sex with a male two days earlier was admissible to rebut her testimony. In *R. v. Van Oostram*,[87] the Court considered the Seaboyer guidelines and ruled consensual sexual activity on prior occasions with the accused was admissible to show the entirety of the circumstances. In *R. v. Ecker*[88] it was held that evidence of prior sexual conduct with the complainant is capable of being admissible to support the defence of honest but mistaken belief as to consent and the trial Judge erred by not holding an inquiry to determine admissibility.

The Supreme Court of Canada in *R. v. Darrach*[89] noting that section 276 of the *Criminal Code* providing that evidence of a complainant's prior sexual activity was not admissible to support inferences that the complainant was more likely to have consented or is less worthy of belief is applicable to all prior sexual activity including non-consensual activity; and also evidence tendered to support permitted inferences are only admissible where

---

85 (1991), 69 C.C.C. (3d) 123 (B.C. C.A.).

86 (1991), 66 C.C.C. (3d) 321 (S.C.C.).

87 (1993), 21 C.R. (4th) 1 (Ont. C.A.) affirming in part (1991), 10 C.R. (4th) 137 (Ont. Gen. Div.).

88 (1995), 96 C.C.C. (3d) 161 (Sask. C.A.). *R. v. Dickson* (1993), 81 C.C.C. (3d) 224 (Y.T. C.A.), affirmed (1994), 86 C.C.C. (3d) 576 (S.C.C.); *R. v Harris* (1997), 118 C.C.C. (3d) 498 (Ont. C.A.).

89 (2000), 148 C.C.C. (3d) 97 (S.C.C.).

such evidence has significant probative value that is not substantially out-weighed by its danger of prejudice. In order to meet the significant probative value aspect of the test, the evidence can not be so trifling as to be incapable of raising a reasonable doubt having regard to all of the evidence.

In *Darrach* the Supreme Court made certain procedural pronounce-ments. The application to determine whether the complainant's prior sexual activity is admissible must describe detailed particulars of the evidence and if the evidence is capable of being admissible, the trial judge is to hold a *voir dire* to determine if the evidence is admissible. The initial application does not require an affidavit from the accused and may be made on the basis of an affidavit on information and belief, but on the *voir dire* a personal affidavit is required from the individual who is the source of the evidence and the affiant must submit to cross-examination. The complainant is not compellable on the *voir dire*.

CROSS-EXAMINATION OF THE CHARACTER WITNESS

There will be those character witnesses who will have an interest or bias in the outcome of a case which should be scrutinized. For example, an employer who speaks highly of an accused may fear his or her business will suffer if the accused is sentenced to jail because the accused was so important to the functioning of the business. Then there is the character witness who may have a close personal relationship with the accused and would be upset to see the accused incarcerated. These witnesses are obviously vulnerable on cross-examination.

A way for the Crown to approach the character witness, particularly one who is not well prepared, is to show that the witness's opinion as to the accused's general reputation in the community rests on a tenuous founda-tion. An interesting cross-examination of a character witness by Assistant Crown Attorney Michael Holme[90] occurred in *R. v. Malatesta*. Mr. Malatesta was charged with attempt murder by shooting the victim. The character witness was a neighbour of Mr. Malatesta who lived in a nice neighbour-hood. He testified that the accused did not have a reputation for violence. (Although he had a criminal record but not for violence.) The cross-exam-ination went this way:

Q. Mr. S. You are a law abiding citizen who lives in a law abiding community?
A. That's correct.
Q. The persons you know that would know Mr. Malatesta are law abiding citizens as far as you know?
A. Yes.

---

90   Mr. Holme is an Assistant Crown Attorney in Newmarket, Ontario.

> Q. They are not the kind of people who would knowingly be associated with criminals or those who commit violence?
>
> A. Correct.
>
> Q. It would not be part of your conversation with such persons to talk about mutual acquaintances who are violent?
>
> A. I guess that's right.
>
> Q. You have no interest in firearms. It is not something you would talk about with the accused or mutual acquaintances?
>
> A. No.

Here we see how the Crown was able to show there was a doubtful basis on which the character witness could provide a meaningful opinion as to the reputation of the accused.

An approach for counsel is to inquire as to the number of people with whom the witness discussed the accused's reputation. Counsel should ascertain if the witness can name these people and if he can, have the witness recall when and where the accused's reputation was discussed. Was it discussed significantly prior to the event in question so that it could be put to the witness that the accused's reputation had plenty of time to change since the witness last heard about it?

An example of how quickly a character witness's evidence can be rendered meaningless was performed by Sir Henry Curtis Bennett in *Norman Thorne's Trial*.[91] The accused was charged with murder. The deceased's body had been dismembered and buried by the accused who admitted the dismembering but took the position that the deceased had committed suicide by hanging himself in the accused's room while the accused was absent. The accused stated that he tried to remove all traces of the deceased's presence in his room. The character witness was examined-in-chief:

> Q. What sort of young man is he in your judgment? (Today, a character witness could not give her personal opinion as opposed to evidence of general reputation.)
>
> A. In my judgment he is amiable, courteous, considering others more than himself, absolutely unselfish, and a general favourite with all who knew him. A popular son of a popular father. I have never seen him in a passion. He is the last person with whom I would credit any act of violence.
>
> The short cross-examination was as follows:
>
> Q. I must ask you this: Could you have imagined, from your knowledge of the Defendant, that he would be able to dismember a body?
>
> A. Certainly not.

Obviously the character witness did not know the accused as well as he thought.

---

91 *The Trial of Norman Thorne* in "Famous Trial Series." J. Normanton (ed.) (London: Geoffrey Bles, 1929). pp. 38-39.

Crown Attorneys have their stock questions that can be put to character witnesses depending on the type of charge. If the accused is charged with domestic abuse the Crown may attempt to seek an admission from the character witness that it is difficult to really know what goes on between a man and woman behind the closed doors of a relationship, distinguishing between a public social context as opposed to a private setting, as persons tend to be more charming in the former scenario. The Crown might ask questions such as whether the witness knew prior girlfriends of the accused, did any live with the accused, were women included as persons who helped the witness form his opinion, and if so, did he receive any detailed information from those women, or was the opinion based really on what other men told the character witness? If the character witness is someone very close to the accused the Crown, to show bias, often tries to make the point that the witness would want to assist the accused in any way he can with respect to the serious charges the latter is facing. An example of such an approach would be: You love your husband (the accused), do you not Mrs. Jones? You would not wish to see him go to jail, is that not so? When a police officer is charged with an offence of violence and other police are called as character witnesses, a Crown's attempt at showing bias would include a question such as: do you know of any other police officers who have a reputation for violence; perhaps expecting the police officer to say no, an answer which the trier-of-fact may have difficulty in believing?

It should also be kept in mind, that depending on the character witness, the accused may have told that witness certain things about the offence which could be damaging to the defence and revealed through cross-examination. Counsel should make sure this is not the case before calling the witness.

It is not uncommon to hear some Crown Attorneys ask a character witness if he or she would give the same evidence if the accused had in fact committed the acts that had been alleged. This is a hypothetical question which amounted to an assumption that the accused did the acts charged and led to the reversal of a conviction.[92]

The character witness should be made aware of the allegations against the client. If the witness is unaware of the charges the trier-of-fact may wonder exactly how well the witness knows the accused and no doubt the Crown will make that point in any event.

Another approach to cross-examination of the character witness is to show that the character witness has not had much to do with the accused for a long time nor heard anything about him over that period, leaving it open for the Crown to argue that the accused's character may have changed because of circumstances.

---

92 *Hooper v. State*, 523 So.2d 469 (U.S. Ala. Cr. Ct. App., 1986).

It is important that if you are calling a character witness for your client that you interview that witness carefully. Do not leave it up to your client to bring the witness to Court on the morning of trial for a quick parlay. You do not want the witness to fall flat and your defence embarrassed.

OATH-HELPING

Dr. Denton H. Cooley was a world renowned heart surgeon. He recalled that a lawyer once asked him during a trial if he considered himself the best heart surgeon in the world.

"Yes," he replied.

"Don't you think that's being rather immodest?" the lawyer asked.

"Perhaps," Dr. Cooley responded, "But remember, I'm under oath."[93]

Normally adducing evidence solely for the purpose of enhancing a witness's credibility is oath-helping and not permissible.[94] To allow oath-helping would mean that no limit could be placed on the number of witnesses who could be called to testify about the credibility of other witnesses. This would only cause confusion for jurors deflecting their attention from the real issues and the truth would more likely remain hidden than revealed.[95]

However when a witness's good character or credibility is questioned in cross-examination, oath-helping can become admissible.[96] Evidence

---

93 The New York Times, November 27th 2007. The Feud, by Lawrence K. Altman.

94 *R. c. Béland* (1987), 36 C.C.C. (3d) 481 (S.C.C.) where one of the reasons polygraph results were held to be inadmissible was that it was oath-helping, i.e., to bolster the credibility of the accused. See also *R. v. J. (F.E.)* (1990), 53 C.C.C. (3d) 64 (Ont. C.A.).

95 *R. v. Kyselka* (1962), 133 C.C.C. 103 (Ont. C.A.), reversing the admissibility of psychiatric evidence to show that because the complainant in a rape case was of low mental age she was more likely to be truthful; *R. c. Béland* (1987), (sub nom. *R. v. Béland*) 36 C.C.C. (3d) 481 (C.S.C.), refusing admissibility of polygraph; *R. v. Burkart* (1964), [1965] 3 C.C.C. 210 (Sask. C.A.), rejecting evidence from a physician that complainant likely to be truthful because of low mental classification. *R. v. J. (F.E.)* (1990), 53 C.C.C. (3d) 64 (Ont. C.A.) recognized the general principle that expert evidence is inadmissible if its sole purpose is to bolster credibility of the witness, but that expert evidence has been admitted to show that certain psychological and physical conditions are consistent with sexual abuse. See also *R. v. Marquard* (1993), 85 C.C.C. (3d) 193 (S.C.C.). In *R. v. Sauvé* (2004), *(sub nom. R. v. Trudel)* 182 C.C.C. (3d) 321 (Ont. C.A.), leave to appeal refused (2005), 2005 CarswellOnt 19 (S.C.C.) it was held inadmissible oath-helping for a police officer to testify that the informant was the best informant he has used in 31 years and his recollection of events was uncanny. It was also inadmissible for the informant to testify that in addition to hearing the accused make inculpatory statements, other inmates had confessed to him in the past and subsequently pleaded guilty. The fact others confessed to him did not prove that the accused confessed to him and that he was truthful because others pleaded guilty.

96 *Clarke v. R.* (1981), (sub nom. *R. v. Clarke*) 63 C.C.C. (2d) 224 (Alta. C.A.), leave to

which is oath-helping may be for another legitimate purpose and in such a case the Court must weigh its probative value in relation to that purpose against its prejudicial effect. If the evidence is admissible for a legitimate purpose such as part of the narrative to explain how the complainant's allegation came to light, or for example to explain the complainant's failure to expose the abuse earlier, the jury must be specifically told that the evidence was not to be used to enhance the complainant's credibility.[97]

A classic example of an examination riddled with oath-helping, which came from the witness himself as opposed to supporting witnesses, can be seen in *Clarke v. R.*[98] when a Crown called a prison inmate and after introducing his criminal record promoted the oath-helping in questioning as follows:

Q. Are you married?
A. Yes, sir.
Q. And presently you are serving these sentences you received in Saskatchewan, is that right, sir?
A. Yes, sir.
Q. And you are serving that in an institute somewhere in Canada?
A. Yes, sir.
Q. Can you tell me when your expected date of release is?
A. I finish my sentence on January the 2nd. I have over of it in right now. I am finished on January the 2nd.
Q. Now, you are married, sir. Has your wife stuck by you?
A. Yes.
Q. And do you have children?
A. Yes I do.
Q. How many, sir?
A. One.
Q. And albeit you are in an institute somewhere in Canada, are you allowed visitation privileges with your wife?
A. Yes, sir, I am.
Q. Is that within the confines of the institution itself?
A. No sir, I have been allowed visits, also on the street.
Q. On the street?

---

appeal refused December 21, 1981; *Wigmore on Evidence* (Chadbourne Rev. 1972), Vol. 4, pp. 223-224; *R. v. Martin* (1980), 53 C.C.C. (2d) 425 at 433 (Ont. C.A.); *R. v. Turner*, [1975] 1 All E.R. 70 (Eng. Q.B.).

97 *R. v. Llorenz* (2000), 145 C.C.C. (3d) 535 (Ont. C.A.). See also *R. v. J. (F.E.)* (1990), 53 C.C.C. (3d) 64 (Ont. C.A.).

98 *Supra.* The Court in *Clarke* rejected this approach by the Crown. It acknowledged that in introductory matters counsel must be permitted "to present witnesses in the best allowable light." It accepted that the witness, pursuant to *R. v. Boyko* (1975), 28 C.C.C. (2d) 193 (B.C. C.A.) could adduce the witness's prior convictions before cross-examination. But the Alberta Court of Appeal found as oath-helping the witness's reclamation was "subordinated to the overriding and dominant object of bolstering his character, and thereby his credibility—an issue new to the case."

A. Yes.

Q. With your wife?

A. Yes.

Q. Do you have an occupation or a job within this institute that is a trusted one, sir?

A. Yes, sir, I do.

Q. What do you do?

A. I am a second cook.

Q. And are you just serving your time, sir, or are you taking some courses as well?

A. I am taking two courses.

Q. What is that, sir?

A. One is Bible Study, and the other one is Alcoholics Anonymous.

Q. Do you have an alcoholic problem?

A. Yes, sir, I do.

Q. And is that AA you are attending?

A. Yes it is.

Q. And are those meetings right within the institution?

A. Yes they are.

Q. And what is this Bible Study course that you are taking, sir?

A. It is a course where we are asked questions about the Bible, given an assignment, and in turn study it for a week and complete the answers and are tested on it. The answers in turn go to Regina and our marks come back from Regina.

Q. Is this a compulsory course or something you volunteer for?

A. Volunteer for it.

Q. Why are you taking it?

A. Because, I don't know how to really put this, but I will do the best I can. I am concerned about my violence and concerned where it could possibly lead and I want to make every effort to straighten my life out. I have come to believe that it is I who must conform to society; society will not conform to me or tolerate my previous actions. I think I have made good progress with my courses. I know now that—before I always tried to justify why I ended up in jail, it was through the courts or the police who charged me. Along them lines I have come to believe that I am an alcoholic and it is when I drink I end up in trouble, fight, weapons and what have you. When I am sober, I don't want that kind of life. I can't stand violence. I also, if I may mention, whre I am currently serving time, I see a psychiatrist and psychologist.

Q. And a psychologist did you say?

A. Yes. And they have told me that I probably never would have served a sentence in my life if I didn't have an alcohol problem.

Q. Are these counsellings that you are taking from these persons, is that mandatory or on a volunteer basis?

A. I asked the judge when I was sentenced to be sentenced so that I wouldn't just sit incarcerated and I could have as much help as needed. The judge wrote a letter to the institution stating that he wanted to see that I get some help.

Q. Do you spend sometime with the Padre as well?

A. Yes I do.

Q. Is that compulsory or strictly voluntary basis?

A. No, it is voluntary.

Q. Has your attitude towards authority, particularly the police, always been the same during your life?

A. It is not the same no more.

Q. It is not the same no more. What is it now?

A. I don't hate no more.

Q. In addition to the record that we have talked about sir, that you have, are there some other things that you may have done that would be in the nature of a crime that you have set good?

A. Yes, sir. I don't want to start quoting the Bible, but I talked it over with my psychologist and Padre and my AA counsellor and he said that if I felt that I should, I should make restitution. I had some things that I had done, 1974, and one of them was that I used an assumed name and I beat the Unemployment Insurance, Canada, for $2,100. My wife and I wrote a letter to them. I gave them the name, the full particulars, and since then I have made restitution for $2,100.

Q. You made total restitution?

A. Total restitution.

Q. Were you ever charged with that fraud?

A. I was never charged.

Q. So you brought that to the attention of the authorities yourself?

A. Yes, sir, I did.

Q. Are you testifying today, sir, because you feel that it might do well with you with respect to early parole?

A. No, sir.

Q. When you are paroled, is there a person who ordinarily sponsors you?

A. I have never been paroled in my life. I have done every day of any sentence I had.

Q. Do you have a sponsor now, sir?

A. Yes, I have an AA sponsor.

Q. Who is the sponsor?

A. A corporal in the R.C.M.P.

Q. Prior to today, sir, have you spoken to me?

A. I spoke to you once.

Q. A couple of days ago?

A. Yes.

Q. And were you offered any deals by me, sir, to testify?

A. No, sir.

Q. Did you ask for any?

A. No, sir.

Q. Do you expect any?

A. No, sir.

Q. Why are you testifying?

A. Because I don't think what the man that is accused has done is right, and I don't condone any sort of violence anymore. It makes me sick.

Q. All right, and have you ever testified in this type of a situation before, sir?

A. No, sir, I have not.

Q. Now, I understand that you were remanded to the Fort Saskatchewan Correctional Institute sometime in 1978.

A. Yes, sir, I was.

Q. And when was that approximately?

A. April 19th.

Q. And that was on what charge, sir?

A. Robbery with violence.

Q. And is that robbery that was dismissed against you in May of 1979?

A. Yes, sir.

Q. And how long were you actually in custody, sir?

A. I spent two and a half months in custody before my lawyer got me Supreme Court bail.

Q. And during that two and a half months, did you meet a person by the name of Sydney Clarke?

A. Yes, sir I did.

Q. Is that person in court today?

A. Yes, he is.

Q. Would you point him out please?

    Indicating the person sitting in the prisoner's box?

A. Yes.

Q. And where in the Fort Saskatchewan Correctional Institute did you actually meet him?

A. First time I met Mr. Clarke was I just come on to the range.

Q. On to the . . .

A. On to the range, the tier. I knew all the people there, the criminal element, and Mr. Clarke was talking to other people; I just walked into the cell and sat down.

It is irrelevant that a jury believed a witness in a prior trial.[99]

---

99 *R. v. McNeill* (2000), 144 C.C.C. (3d) 551 (Ont. C.A.). In addition to being irrelevant it was also speculative in this case.

25

Privileges

PRIVILEGE GENERALLY

The common law recognizes two types of privilege: class privilege and case-by-case privilege. Class privilege entails three kinds of relationships: solicitor-client, police-informer and spousal. A presumptive protection applies to these forms of class privilege.[1]

At common law the only profession which could claim testimonial privilege is the legal profession.[2] The courts have refused to recognize privileged communications between psychiatrist and patient,[3] between doctor and patient generally, clergy, accountants, journalists, social workers and members of provincial legislative assemblies,[4] blood donor records,[5] police complaints investigation files,[6] communications to probation offi-

---

1 See *R. v. McClure* (2001), 151 C.C.C. (3d) 321 (S.C.C.) at para. 28.

2 S. Freedman, "Medical Privilege" (1954), 32 Can. Bar Rev. 1 at 2.

3 *R. v. Potvin* (1971), 16 C.R.N.S. 233 (Que. C.A.); *R. v. Warren* (1973), 14 C.C.C. (2d) 188 (N.S. C.A.), motion for leave to appeal to S.C.C. for extension of time dismissed (1973), 14 C.C.C. (2d) 188n (S.C.C.); *Nuttall v. Nuttall* (1964), 108 Sol. Jo. 605.

4 *Report of the Federal/Provincial Task Force on Uniform Rules of Evidence* (Toronto: The Carswell Company Limited, 1982), p. 418. As to privilege between priest and penitent and guarantee of freedom of religion in the *Charter of Rights and Freedoms*, Part I of the *Constitution Act, 1982*, enacted by Sched. B. to the *Canada Act, 1982* (U.K.), c. 11; see *R. v. Church of Scientology* (1987), 31 C.C.C. (3d) 449 (Ont. C.A.), where it was held that the restrictive common law view against the priest—and—penitent privilege may have to be reassessed in light of section 2(a) of the *Charter* guaranteeing freedom of conscience and religion; but if so, on a case by case basis as the freedom is not absolute: *R. v. Fosty* (1989), 68 C.R. (3d) 382 (Man. C.A.) is an example of where the Court held that the admission of a communication to the pastor of the accused's church did not impinge on the accused's religious freedom. See P.D. Stern and E.F. Then, Q.C., "Privilege, Competency and Compellability," article delivered at the National Criminal Law Program, Evidence and Advocacy in the Charter Area, Vancouver, British Columbia, 1987.

5 *Sharpe Estate v. Northwestern General Hospital* (1991), 2 O.R. (3d) 40 (Ont. Gen. Div.).

6 *R. v. Delong* (1989), 69 C.R. (3d) 147 (Ont. C.A.).

cers.[7] However, the Supreme Court of Canada left the door open for the creation of new privileges for confidential communications, adopting Wigmore's four preconditions to a valid claim for privilege which are:

1. The allegedly privileged communication must have originated in a confidence that it would not be disclosed.
2. The asserted confidentiality must be essential to the satisfactory maintenance of the relationship between the parties.
3. This relationship must be one that, in the opinion of the community, ought to be sedulously fostered.
4. The injury that would inure to the relation by the communication must be greater than the benefit thereby gained for the correct disposal of litigation.[8]

The persuasive burden of proof is on the party asserting the privilege to show that privilege applies[9] on the balance of probabilities.[10] The burden attaches to each communication or documentation sought to be protected by the privilege.[11] When issues of privilege arise, it may best be determined in a *voir dire* so that evidence may be called on the issue and submissions made in the absence of the jury. Failure to hold a formal *voir dire* does not necessarily render the trial unfair if the trial Judge provides the defence with the opportunity to call evidence and make submissions on the issue.[12]

SOLICITOR-CLIENT PRIVILEGE

The Required Relationship

For solicitor-client privilege to exist the communication must be with the solicitor or his or her agent in a professional capacity[13] and must relate to the seeking of legal advice.[14] In *R. v. Shirose* the Supreme Court held that privilege does exist between police and Crown counsel where legal advice is sought in connection with criminal investigations, subject to the

---

7   *R. v. Walker* (1992), 74 C.C.C. (3d) 97 (B.C. C.A.).
8   *Slavutych v. Baker*, [1976] 1 S.C.R. 254 at 260 (S.C.C.). The author is paraphrasing 8 *Wigmore on Evidence*, 3rd ed. (McNaughton rev.) (Boston: Little, Brown and Company, 1961), §2285. In *R. v. Fosty* (1991), (*sub nom. R. v. Gruenke*) 67 C.C.C. (3d) 289(S.C.C.), the Court held privilege relating to religious communications is now to be determined on a case-by-case basis following the four Wigmore criteria. See also *R. v. Church of Scientology, supra.*
9   *Solosky v. R.* (1979), 50 C.C.C. (2d) 495 at 508-509 (S.C.C.).
10 Campbell J. (Ont. Ct. Gen. Div.) Oct 17, 1988, summarized at 6 W.C.B. (2d) 358.
11 *Solosky v. R., supra.*
12 *R. v. Gruenke, supra.*
13 *R. v. McClure, infra, R. v. Campbell; infra; R. v. Gruenke, ibid.*
14 *Wigmore on Evidence*, note 8 above, §2292.

usual exceptions. The mere fact that the recipient is a solicitor is not enough. The solicitor must be acting in his or her professional capacity and not as a friend or business associate.[15] In *Descôteaux, infra*, at p. 413, Lamer J. stated that privilege extended to those communications made "within the framework of the solicitor-client privilege relationship."An essential condition of the solicitor-client privilege is that the communication in question has been made with the intention of confidentiality,[16] and it is immaterial that litigation was contemplated at the time of the communication.[17] No express request for confidentiality need be made, it can be presumed from the circumstances.[18]

The solicitor-client relationship and right to confidentiality arises as soon as the potential client has his or her first dealings with the lawyer's office to obtain legal advice and not later when the retainer is established.[19] The solicitor-client relationship survives the death of the client if there is no waiver but may be lifted after death if it is in the best interests of the deceased or the administration of justice.[20]

The fees paid by the client are presumptively privileged unless the billing fell within the crime exception to solicitor-client privilege.[21]

Waiver

The privilege is that of the client and only he or she can waive it,[22] except in extraordinary circumstances, such as where the client is not available.[23] The waiver of solicitor-client privilege should be considered in light of *Charter* decisions which hold that a waiver must be clear and unequivocal

---

15 In *R. v. Shirose*, (sub nom. *R. v. Campbell*) [1999] 1 S.C.R. 565 (S.C.C.) at para. 50, Binnie J. stated: "In private practice some lawyers are valued as much (or more) for raw business sense as for legal acumen. No solicitor-client privilege attaches to advice on purely business matters even where it is provided by a lawyer."

16 *R. v. Dunbar* (1982), 68 C.C.C. (2d) 13 (Ont. C.A.); *R. v. Shirose*, (sub nom. *R. v. Campbell*) [1999] 1 S.C.R. 565 (S.C.C.) at para. 50; *R. v. McClure* (2001), 151 C.C.C. (3d) 321 (S.C.C.).

17 *Greenough v. Gaskell* (1833), 39 E.R. 618 (Ch. Div.) at 621; *Re Director of Investigation and Research and Shell Canada Ltd.* (1975), 22 C.C.C. (2d) 70 (Fed. C.A.) at 80.

18 8 *Wigmore on Evidence* (McNaughton rev.) (Boston: Little, Brown & Company, 1961), §2311 at 600.

19 *Descôteaux v. Mierzwinski* (1982), 28 C.R. (3d) 289 at 305-306 (S.C.C.).

20 *Goodman Estate v. Geffen* (1991), (sub nom. *Geffen v. Goodman Estate*) 81 D.L.R. (4th) 211 (S.C.C.) at 235; *Hubbard Magetiaux and Duncan, Law of Privilege* at pp. 11-19.

21 *Maranda v. Québec (Juge de la Cour du Québec)* (2003), (sub nom. *Maranda v. Richer*) 178 C.C.C. (3d) 321 (S.C.C.).

22 P.K. McWilliams, *Canadian Criminal Evidence*, 2nd ed. (Aurora: Canada Law Book, 1984), p. 971; *R. v. Perron*, 54 C.C.C. (3d) 108 (Que. C.A.).

23 *R. v. Jack* (1992), 70 C.C.C. (3d) 67 (Man. C.A.). But it cannot be invoked by a party whose interest in the proceedings is manifestly contrary to that of the client, as for example, a husband who is charged with the murder of the client, his wife.

and that the person waiving a right does so with full knowledge and appreciation of the protected right and the consequences of giving it up.[24] Where the client on direct examination testifies to a privileged communication in part, it constitutes a waiver as to the rest of the privileged communications on the same subject-matter, but not necessarily in cross-examination.[25]

In *Descôteaux c. Mierzwinski* Lamer J. observed that "All information which a person must provide in order to obtain legal advice and which is given in confidence for that purpose enjoys the privileges attached to confidentiality."[26] This would include counsel retaining the services of a doctor or another professional. So when a psychiatrist is retained by defence counsel, the report by the psychiatrist and statements by the accused to the psychiatrist are protected by the solicitor-client privilege, unless the privilege is waived. An undertaking by defence counsel that he would report to the Crown is not a waiver where the undertaking is made without knowledge of the accused.[27] If the defence-retained psychiatrist testifies, he will be required to disclose his communications with the accused where the psychiatrist would be basing his opinion partly on what the accused told him, thereby waiving privilege.[28] Defence counsel's opening address to the jury wherein reference was made to the anticipated evidence of the defence psychiatrist constituted a waiver of any solicitor-client privilege in the report.[29] In *Shirose*, above, the Supreme Court held that notwithstanding that a solicitor-client relationship existed between a police officer and the Crown, the privilege was waived when the officer testified that he had sought the opinion of the Crown to verify his own understanding that a proposed reverse sting operation was legal.

Presence of Third Parties

If it is intended that the communication be revealed to a third party the requirement of confidentiality is lacking and therefore the presence of third

---

24 *Korponey v. A.G. Can.* (1982), 65 C.C.C. (2d) 65 at 73-74 (S.C.C.); *Clarkson v. R.* (1986), 25 C.C.C. (3d) 207 (S.C.C.) at 217; *Mills v. R.* (1986), 26 C.C.C. (3d) 481 at 544 (S.C.C). A waiver can be implied, as for example in *R. v. Stone, supra.*

25 A. Gold, *Annual Review of Criminal Law*, 1985 (Toronto: The Carswell Company Limited, 1985), p. 209; see also *R. v. Dunbar* (1982), 28 C.R. (3d) 324 at 352 (Ont. C.A.); *Wigmore on Evidence* (McNaughton rev. 1961) 635-638; *R. v. Harris*, Borins D.C.O. (Released March 2, 1985). In *Lin v. Leung*, [1991] B.C.J. No. 641 (B.C.S.C), January 24, 1991, the Court held that if privilege is waived it is waived for all purposes relevant to the issues in dispute.

26 (1982), 70 C.C.C. (2d) 385 (S.C.C.) at 413.

27 *R. v. L. (C.K.)* (1987), 39 C.C.C. (3d) 476 (Ont. Dist. Ct.); *R. v. Perron* (1990), 75 C.R. (3d) 382 (Que. C.A.).

28 *R. v. Perron, ibid; R. v. Stone* (1997), 113 C.C.C. (3d) 158 (B.C. C.A.); *R. v. Stone* (1999), 134 C.C.C. (3d) 353 (S.C.C).

29 *R. v. Stone, supra.*

parties when the communication was made in most cases will indicate that there was no intention of confidentiality attached to the communication.[30] However, there can be exceptions to the rule that the presence of a third party has this effect. One such exception is where the third party is present to protect the interests of the client[31] as, for example, a secretary or articling student[32] or communications through an interpreter, messenger or other agent of transmission,[33] or where the client passes on information to the spouse of his solicitor at the solicitor's home with the reasonable expectation that the information would be communicated to the solicitor in his professional capacity, that he would act on it and give advice accordingly.[34]

Physical Evidence

Solicitor-client privilege is concerned with communications, not physical evidence, so that the accused in *R. v. Murray*,[35] a lawyer, who was charged with obstruct justice because he withheld audio-visual tapes depicting the commission of the offences charged against his client, could not claim solicitor-client privilege with respect to those tapes, although his conversations with respect to those tapes were protected by the privilege.

Co-Accused Falling Out

Communications by one accused to counsel for two co-accused in preparing for a joint defence are privileged. The privilege is not destroyed when the two clients have a falling out in a proceeding at the suit of a third party, for example, the Crown, but only when the once jointed represented clients become pitted against one another in litigation.[36]

---

30 *R. v. Dunbar, supra.*

31 *R. v. Dunbar, supra.*

32 8 *Wigmore on Evidence, supra,* at p. 544, §2292 *Descôteaux c. Mierzwinski, supra,* at 301-302.

33 *Supra,* at pp. 618-619, §2317.

34 *R. v. Turchiuro and Prette,* February 25, 1988, Watt J. (Ont. H.C). *General Accident Assurance Co. v. Chrusz,* 180 D.L.R. (4th) 241 (Ont. C.A.) at para. 120 and *College of Physicians & Surgeons (British Columbia) v. British Columbia (Information & Privacy Commissioner),* 2002 CarswellBC 2942 (B.C. C.A.) at para. 48, leave to appeal refused 2003 CarswellBC 1468, 2003 CarswellBC 1469 (S.C.C.).

35 (2000), 144 C.C.C. (3d) 289 (Ont. S.CJ.). Mr. Murray was acquitted for reasons unrelated to this discussion.

36 *R. v. Dunbar, supra.* See also *R. v. Reid* (1994), 86 C.C.C. (3d) 574 (B.C. C.A.); *R. v. Charbonneau* (1992), 74 C.C.C. (3d) 49 (Que. C.A.).

Client Allegation of Misconduct Against Lawyer

Solicitor-client privilege gives way when the solicitor's right to make full answer and defence is impaired as when there is an allegation of fraud by the client or allegations of professional misconduct against the lawyer.[37]

Solicitor-client privilege will not apply where the client consults the solicitor to further a criminal purpose[38] since criminal enterprise falls outside the proper scope of a solicitor-client relationship.[39] The mere allegation of a criminal purpose is not enough, the party seeking to set aside the privilege must provide *prima facie* proof of the allegation.[40] In *R. v. Bastidas*,[41] the Court indicated the onus is on the balance of probabilities. The test of knowledge is objective, i.e., whether the client knew or should have known the intended conduct was unlawful.[42] There is an important distinction between a request for advice as to the legitimacy of a proposed course of action, and an intention to use the advice in effecting a criminal purpose.[43] It is irrelevant that the lawyer is unaware of the client's purpose.[44]

In Ontario it was held in *R. v. Bencardino*[45] that it only takes the mere suggestion of criminal involvement by a lawyer and a *voir dire* should be held, thereby forcing the lawyer to reveal privileged communications. In *R. v. Racco (No. 3)*[46] only "some evidence" was required.

A *prima facie* case of criminal activity was required in *Re B. and R.*[47] In *R. v. Prousky*[48] it was held that where the Crown alleges that solicitor-client privilege should be set aside on the basis of fraud, it is incumbent on the Crown to do more than merely make such allegations – the Crown should put forth particulars which point in the direction of criminality. In Quebec it was held in *R. v. Giguere*,[49] rejecting the procedure used in *Bencardino*, that the party challenging the existence of the privilege must not only allege that the communication was made in order to facilitate a crime but must show *prima facie* evidence to support the allegation before

---

37 *R. v. Murray* (2000), 48 O.R. (3d) 437 (Ont. S.C.J.).
38 *Descôteaux c. Mierzwinski* (1982), 70 C.C.C. (2d) 385 (S.C.C.).
39 8 *Wigmore on Evidence, supra*, art 2298(b).
40 Manes and Silver, *Solicitor-Client Privilege in Canadian Law* (Toronto: Butterworths, 1993), at 85; Sopinka, Lederman and Bryant, *The Law of Evidence in Canada* (Ontario, Butterworths, 1992) at 645.
41 (1993), 20 W.C.B. (2d) 30 (Alta.Q.B.).
42 *United States of America v. Down* (2000), 149 C.C.C. (3d) 314 (B.C. S.C) at para.15.
43 *United States v. Down, supra.*
44 *Solosky v. Canada* (1979), 50 C.C.C. (2d) 495 (S.C.C).
45 (1973), 15 C.C.C. (2d) 342 (Ont. C.A.). See also *Re R. and Stupp* (1982), 2 C.C.C. (3d) 111 at 116 (Ont. H.C).
46 (1975), 23 C.C.C. (2d) 209 at 213 (Ont. Prov. Ct.).
47 (1977), 36 C.C.C. (2d) 235 at 247-248 (Ont. Prov. Ct.).
48 (1986), 30 C.C.C. (3d) 353 (Ont. Prov. Ct.).
49 (1978), 44 C.C.C (2d) 525 (Que. S.C).

a *voir dire* is held requiring the solicitor to reveal the contents of the communication so that a ruling on the existence of the privilege can be made.

It would appear that the case law that has developed supports "that the onus of establishing the future crimes and fraud exception is on the Crown to show a *prima facie* case of criminal facilitation or furtherance of a crime in relation to the communications or documents sought."[50] The party attempting to displace the privilege can rely not only on privilege communications and/or documents but extrinsic evidence.[51]

In considering whether or not the solicitor-client privilege should be set aside the authors of the *Law of Evidence in Canada* favour the two-step approach by the Supreme Court in *R. v. O'Connor* (third party records)[52] where the party applying would rely on the evidence external to the communications to satisfy they are likely relevant and if found to be so the Judge would conduct an in-camera hearing to inspect the documents to decide if they are caught by the exception.

Public Safety

The courts have recognized a public safety exception to solicitor-client privilege which appears to have its basis in doctor-patient case law.[53] There are three factors to be considered before the privilege exception applies. First, is there a clear risk to an identifiable person or group of persons? Second, is there a risk of serious bodily harm or death? Third, is the danger imminent?[54]

Involuntary Disclosure

Where the contents of the privileged communication, whether oral or in a privileged document, have become known to a third party through accident or negligence of the legal advisor it is admissible in evidence,

---

50 *R. v. Claus* (1999), 1999 CarswellOnt 3932 (Ont. S.C.J.) at para. 20; *R. v. Morra* (1991), 68 C.C.C. (3d) 273 (Ont. Gen. Div.); *Hilborn v. Canada (Attorney General)*, 1990 CarswellBC 943 (B.C. S.C.), additional reasons at 1990 CarswellBC 963 (B.C. S.C.); *K-West Estates Ltd. v. Linemayr* (1984), 54 B.C.L.R. 60 (B.C. S.C.) at paras. 11, 18; *First Island Financial Services Ltd. v. Novastar Developments (Kelowna Orchard Gardens) Ltd.*, 1994 CarswellBC 2883 (B.C. Master).
51 See *K-West Estates Ltd., ibid*; *R. v. Morra, ibid*; *R. v. Shirose, supra*, per Binnie J. at para. 63.
52 (1995), 103 C.C.C. (3d) 1 (S.C.C.).
53 *Jones v. Smith; Southam Inc., Intervenor* (1999), 132 C.C.C. (3d) 225 (S.C.C).
54 *Ibid*. A discussion of the three factors is discussed.

although the trial Judge has the discretion to exclude this information.[55] Where a note that the accused had written to his counsel was found on the floor of the courtroom during an adjournment and given to the Crown, the latter was allowed to use the note in cross-examination of the accused.[56] Wigmore states:[57]

> All *involuntary* disclosures in particular, through the loss or theft of documents from the attorney's possession are not protected by the privilege, on the principle, that, since the law has granted secrecy so far as its own process goes, it leaves to the client and attorney to take measures of caution sufficient to prevent from being overheard by third parties. The risk of insufficient precautions is upon the client. This principle applies equally to documents.

In *R. v. Bruce Power Inc.*,[58] the Crown, in an Occupational Health and Safety prosecution, came into possession of a defence document protected by solicitor-client and litigation privilege. The document was obtained as a result of a section 8 breach of the *Charter* (not through any carelessness or negligence of the privilege holder). The Court held in such circumstance that prejudice is presumed and the accused does not have to prove actual prejudice. The Crown failed to rebut the presumption. Although a stay of proceedings was appropriate, not every such breach will call for a stay, as for example, when the breach is trivial.

The person asserting the privilege has the duty of proving the solicitor-client relationship on the balance of probabilities. If this burden is satisfied, the burden then shifts to the party offering the evidence to establish a waiver or circumstances which would allow for the reception of the evidence notwithstanding its privileged character.[59]

---

55 *Cross and Tapper, supra*, p. 400; *R. v. Tompkins* (1977), 67 Cr. App. R. 181 (C.A.); *Re Girouard and R.* (1982), 68 C.C.C. (2d) 262 (B.C. S.C); *R. v. Kotapski* (1981), 66 C.C.C. (2d) 78 (Que. S.C), affirmed (1984), 13 C.C.C. (3d) 185 (Que. C.A.), leave to appeal to the S.C.C. refused November 22, 1984 (S.C.C); *R. v. Dunbar* (1982), 68 C.C.C. (2d) 113 (Ont. C.A.); *R. v. Perron* (1990), 75 C.R. (3d) 382 (Que. C.A.).

56 *R. v. Tompkins, ibid.* In *Tilley v. Hails* (1993), 12 O.R. (3d) 306 (Gen. Div.), Chapnik J., a civil case, held that the loss of physical custody of a document either through inadvertence or improper conduct does not permit opposing counsel to make use of that document in litigation.

57 *Wigmore on Evidence* (McNaughton rev.) (Boston: Little, Brown & Company, 1961), p. 633, §2325. See also Sopinka, Lederman and Bryant, *The Law of Evidence*, second edition, Butterworths 1999, 9.15-9.19 and 14.114-14.124; *Williams v. Stephenson* (2005), 2005 CarswellBC 696 (B.C. S.C. [In Chambers]); *National Bank Financial Ltd. v. Potter* (2005), 233 N.S.R. (2d) 123 (N.S. S.C.), additional reasons at (2005), 237 N.S.R. (2d) 48 (N.S. S.C.), affirmed (2006), 2006 CarswellNS 242 (N.S. C.A.).

58 (2009), 98 O.R. (3d) 272 (Ont. C.A.).

59 *R. v. Harris* (1985), W.C.B. (2d) 126 (Ont. Dist. Ct.).

Innocence at Stake

The Supreme Court of Canada in *R. v. McClure*[60] observed that solicitor-client privilege may yield to allow an accused to make full answer and defence when innocence is at stake. But before the test to be applied is considered the defence must establish that the information sought is not available elsewhere and he is unable to raise a reasonable doubt in any other way. There are two stages to the test. At the first stage the accused must present some evidence to conclude that there is a communication that could raise a reasonable doubt as to his guilt. The Judge at this stage has to decide whether to review the evidence. The Judge must ask "Is there some evidentiary basis for the claim that a solicitor-client communication exists that could raise a reasonable doubt about the guilt of the accused?" Mere speculation as to what is in the file won't suffice. If the Judge is satisfied that there is some evidentiary basis, she must, at the second stage, examine the record and ask: "Is there something in the solicitor-client communication that is likely to raise a reasonable doubt as to the accused's guilt?" If this second stage is met, then the Judge should order the production but only the relevant portion.

In *R. v. McClure*[61] the Supreme Court in considering "innocence at stake" with respect to solicitor-client privilege held that it normally does not apply to relief for constitutional violations.

It would appear from a practical perspective that the issue of innocence at stake is best assessed after the Crown's case.

Police Search of Lawyer's Office

The procedure with respect to protecting any solicitor-client privilege claim that arises as a result of police searches in lawyers' offices was codified by section 488.1 of the *Criminal Code*. This was a complete code of procedure with respect to the execution of search warrants in law offices, but has been held to be unconstitutional by the Supreme Court of Canada.[62] The Supreme Court in *R. v. Lavallee*[63] has approved the procedure to be followed in searching a lawyer's office. Part of that procedure states that the investigative authorities have to satisfy the issuing justice that there was

---

60 [2001] 1 S.C.R. 445 (S.C.C.); see also *R. v. Brown*, [2002] 2 S.C.R. 185 (S.C.C.) re protection of third parties.

61 *Supra.* See also *R. v. Brown*, [2002] 2 S.C.R. 185 (S.C.C.); *R. v. Greenbird* (2003), 2003 CarswellOnt 6402 (Ont. S.CJ.); *R. v. Cresswell* (2000), 149 C.C.C. (3d) 286 (B.C. C.A.); *R. v. Schacher* (2003), 179 C.C.C. (3d) 561 (Alta. CA.).

62 *R. v. Lavallee, Rackel & Heintz* (2002), (sub nom. *Lavallee, Rackel & Heintz v. Canada (Attorney General)* 167 C.C.C. (3d) 1 (S.C.C.). See also *Maranda v. Quebec (Juge de la Cour du Quebec)* (2003), (sub nom. *Maranda v. Richer*) 178 C.C.C. (3d) 321 (S.C.C.)

63 (2002), 167 C.C.C. (3d) 1 (S.C.C.).

no reasonable alternative to the search. All documents in possession of a lawyer had to be sealed before being examined or removed. Every effort had to be made to contact the lawyer and the client at the time the warrant was executed and if they could not be contacted a representative of the Bar should be allowed to supervise the sealing and seizure of documents. Potential privilege holders should be contacted and given the opportunity to assert the privilege.

Richard Peck, Q.C. offers some practical advice to counsel when found in the position of having to protect solicitor-client privilege at the time police comes to the lawyer's office with a search warrant:[64]

(1) When presented with a search warrant the lawyer should immediately assert solicitor-client privilege and remain in attendance for the duration of the search. The lawyer has the right to remain silent during the execution of the search warrant. A statement may be admissible in evidence. It is often preferable for someone other than the lawyer involved to deal directly with the police.

(2) The lawyer should request to see the original search warrant, copy it and make note of the specific documents being sought. The lawyer should produce only the documents as described in the warrant.

(3) The lawyer should photo-copy the documents and if not practical should make an inventory list of the documents seized. The lawyer should then place the documents in his or her own envelope, seal it and initial it. At no time should the law enforcement officials be allowed to inspect or view the documents.

(4) The lawyer should make detailed notes of what happens during the search. If possible, a third party should be present in case *viva voce* or affidavit evidence is required at future proceedings.

(5) Where the lawyer or a member of the firm is the subject of the search, the lawyer should advise any affected clients to retain independent counsel to deal with issues of privilege, as the lawyer in the circumstances may well be in a situation of a conflict.

(6) Where the lawyer or a member of the firm is not the subject of the search, the lawyer should meet with the client as soon as possible to discuss the issue of solicitor-client privilege with respect to the records that have been seized. If the client intends to maintain the claim for privilege, the lawyer should notify the Crown to consider whether there is a need for the client to retain counsel. If client cannot be notified the lawyer should review the documents to

---

64   2008, National Criminal Law Programme, Charlottetown, P.E.I., Vol. No. 1. Reference was also made to Scott C Hutchison's, "Search and Seizure Checklist Redux 2005: What to Do When the Police Arrive to Search a Law Office" (Autumn 2005) 24 Advocates' Soc. J. No. 2, 18 at para. 18.

determine whether the client's privilege should be advanced and then take the necessary steps to protect the client's interest. This may involve an application to quash the warrant.

INFORMER PRIVILEGE

The reason that the identity of police informers is privileged is described by Lord Diplock as follows:[65]

> The rationale of the rule as it applies to police informers is plain. If their identity were liable to be disclosed in a court of law, these sources of information would dry up and the police would be hindered in their duty of preventing and detecting crime. So the public interest in preserving the anonymity of police informers had to be weighed against the public interest that information which might assist a judicial tribunal to ascertain facts relevant to an issue upon which it is required to adjudicate should be withheld from that tribunal. By the uniform practice of the judges which by the time of *Marks v. Beyfus*, 25 Q.B.D. 494 had already hardened into a rule of law, the balance has fallen upon the side of non-disclosure except where upon the trial of a defendant for criminal offence disclosure of the identity of the informer could help to show that the defendant was innocent of the offence. In that case, and in that case only, the balance falls upon the side of disclosure.

In *R. v. B. (G.)*[66] the Court distinguished the informer from the police agent. The informer furnishes information to the police while the agent acts on direction of the police and goes into the field to take part in an illegal endeavour. The informer's identity is protected by privilege and cannot be disclosed except for the innocence at stake exception; the agent's identity is disclosable. The informant can be a police agent in one field without losing protection as an informer in unrelated fields.[67] It is only innocence at stake that is an exception to informer privilege; full answer and defence is not an exception.[68]

In *R. v. Scott*[69] the Supreme Court held that the identity of the informer should be disclosed where necessary to demonstrate the innocence of an accused person in the following circumstances:

---

65 *D. v. National Soc. for the Prevention of Cruelty to Children*, [1978] A.C. 171 at 218 (H.L.). See also *Re Inquiry into the Confidentiality of Health Records in Ont.* (1979), 24 O.R. (2d) 545 (Ont. C.A.), *per* Dubin J.A., reversed on other grounds (*sub nom. Solicitor-Gen. Can. v. Royal Comm. of Inquiry into Confidentiality of Health Records in Ont.*) [1981] 2 S.C.R. 494 (S.C.C.); *Bisaillon v. Keable* (1983), 7 C.C.C. (3d) 385 (S.C.C.).

66 (2000), 146 C.C.C. (3d) 465 (Ont. C.A.), leave to appeal refused (2001), 151 C.C.C. (3d) vi (S.C.C.).

67 *Ibid.*

68 *Re Application to proceed in camera* (*sub nom. Named Person v. Vancouver Sun*) (2007), 224 C.C.C. (3d) 1 (S.C.C.) at para. 28.

69 (1990), 61 C.C.C. (3d) 300 at 315 (S.C.C.).

1.   Where the informer is a material witness to the crime;
2.   Where the informer acted as agent provocateur. See *R. v. Davies*;[70]
3.   Where the accused seeks to show search was not made on reasonable grounds and section 8 of the *Charter* contravened. See *R. v. Hunter*.[71]

It is the duty of the Crown to claim the privilege in order to protect the identity of the informer[72] and the privilege cannot be waived without the consent of the informer.[73] Asking a witness if he is now or has ever been a police informer is privileged and should not be asked.[74]

It was held in *Hunter* that it would be up to the informer to decide if he wanted his name to be revealed. If he did not and his identity had not become known to the accused or he had not become notorious within the community, and the Crown still sought to adduce the evidence of the results on the basis of a warrantless search, then the trial judge would have to consider section 24(2) of the *Charter* and determine whether the admission of the evidence would bring the administration of justice into disrepute.[75] The other choice for the Crown if the Court rules there is an exception to the privilege is to stay the proceedings or proceed with the evidence available, or offer no further evidence and appeal the unfavourable ruling.

In *R. v. Leipert*,[76] the defence sought disclosure of the Crime Stoppers' document reporting the tip and the Crown refused on the ground of informer privilege. The Supreme Court held that although the privilege belongs to the Crown, the Crown could not waive the privilege without the informer's consent. The Court held that informer privilege not only prevents disclosure of the informer's name but any information which might impliedly reveal identity as, for example, observation posts,[77] a particular conversation, a meeting or location,[78] a telephone call to Crimestoppers,[79] policing tech-

---

70   (1982), 31 C.R. (3d) 88 (Ont. C.A.).
71   (1987), 57 C.R. (3d) 1 (Ont. C.A.).
72   *R. v. Hunter, supra; R. v. Scott, supra.*
73   *R. v. Hunter, supra; Basaillon v. Keable, supra; R. v. Leipert, infra.*
74   *R. v. Leipert, infra.*
75   *R. v. Hunter, supra.* See also *R. v. Ross* (1984), 15 C.C.C. (3d) 177 (B.C. Co. Ct.), the Court ruled there was an exception to the privilege and stayed the proceedings because the informant was not available due to police actions. In *R. c. Khela* (1995), 102 C.C.C. (3d) 1 (S.C.C.), summarized at 1 W.C.B. (2d) 335, the *Hunter* reasoning was applied to wiretap evidence which was excluded when the informer would not come forward.
76   (1997), 112 C.C.C. (3d) 385 (S.C.C.). See also *R. v. Parmar* (1987), 53 C.C.C. (3d) 489 (Ont. H.C.), affirmed (1989), 44 C.R.R. 278 (Ont. C.A.), per Watt J.; in *Leipert*, McLachlin J. observed that when an informer is anonymous and is the only one who knows what information might tend to identify him, the Crown should claim informer privilege over all of the information provided.
77   *R. v. Thomas* (1998), 124 C.C.C. (3d) 178 (Ont. Gen. Div.); *R. v. Lam* (2000), 148 C.C.C. (3d) 379 (B.C. C.A.); *R. v. Blair* (2000), 2000 CarswellOnt 2924 (Ont. C.A.).
78   *R. v. Parmar* (1987), 53 C.C.C. (3d) 489 (Ont. H.C.), affirmed (1989), 44 C.R.R. 278 (Ont. C.A.).
79   *R. v. Leipert, infra.*

niques or ongoing investigations that will injure individuals or the interests of the state in the effective investigation of crime.

The binding procedure for the accused to follow to establish "innocence at stake" has now been set out in *R. v. McClure* described earlier in this chapter. Once the Crown establishes that the informer privilege applies, the accused bears the burden to show on the balance of probabilities that the innocence at stake exception justifies disclosure.[80]

When the identity of the informer is known, there is obviously no need for the privilege to be applicable,[81] but where the physical identity of the informer is known but not his or her name and location, the privilege will apply.[82] When disclosure of the informer's identity is ordered the Crown must disclose the full name of the informer and his/her whereabouts before trial or produce the informer and ensure he/she will co-operate and answer all proper questions.[83]

It has been held by the Saskatchewan Court of Appeal that the privilege which protects a witness from disclosing the name of an informer can be departed from under exceptions only upon the trial of an accused, not on a preliminary hearing.[84] This decision was based on case law prior to 1900 and ignored the practical difficulties which such last-minute disclosure creates. Defence counsel requires time to do the leg work to interview the informer and to find out the details of his or her background as the informer's credibility could be vital. If the informer's name and whereabouts are not disclosed until trial, a remand would be required which could cause inconvenience and hardships, particularly for jurors. Historically, preliminary hearings have had a discovery element to them and surely this is one area in which such discovery should be permitted.[85]

MARITAL PRIVILEGE

Section 4 of the *Canada Evidence Act*[86] states as follows:

Accused and spouse

---

80 *R. v. Thomas, ibid.*

81 *Quebec (A.G.) v. Dubois* (1987), 61 L.R. (3d) 159 (Que. C.A.); *R. v. Hunter*, above.

82 *R. v. Phillips* (1991), 66 C.C.C. (3d) 140 (Gen. Div.); *R. v. Lafleur* (Ont. Gen. Div.), December 9, 1992, Doc. Nos 3976/92 *et al.*

83 *R. c. Khela* (1995), 102 C.C.C. (3d) 1 (C.S.C.).

84 *A.G. Can. v. Andrychuk*, [1980] 6 W.W.R. 231 (Sask. C.A.).

85 *Re Skogman and R.* (1984), 13 C.C.C. (3d) 161 at 171 (S.C.C.). See *R. v. Gudbranson* (1987), 61 C.R. (3d) 80 (B.C. C.A.) which does not foreclose the calling of an informer at the preliminary hearing in the proper circumstances. *Quaere* whether *R. v. Cover* (1988), 44 C.C.C. (3d) 34 (Ont. H.C.) and *Stewart v. Carter* (1987), 35 C.R.R. 326 (B.C. S.C.) can be analogized to this issue?

86 R.S.C. 1985, c. C-5.

4. (1) Every person charged with an offence, and, except as otherwise provided in this section, the wife or husband, as the case may be, of the person so charged, is a competent witness for the defence, whether the person so charged is charged solely or jointly with any other person.

Accused and spouse

(2) The wife or husband of a person charged with an offence under subsection 136(1) of the *Youth Criminal Justice Act* or with an offence under any of sections 151, 152, 153, 155 or 159, subsection 160(2) or (3), or sections 170 to 173, 179, 212, 215, 218, 271 to 273, 280 to 283, 291 to 294 or 329 of the *Criminal Code*, or an attempt to commit any such offence, is a competent and compellable witness for the prosecution without the consent of the person charged.

Communications during marriage

(3) No husband is compellable to disclose any communication made to him by his wife during their marriage, and no wife is compellable to disclose any communication made to her by her husband during their marriage.

Offences against young persons

(4) The wife or husband of a person charged with an offence against any of sections 220, 221, 235, 236, 237, 239, 240, 266, 267, 268 or 269 of the *Criminal Code* where the complainant or victim is under the age of fourteen years is a competent and compellable witness for the prosecution without the consent of the person charged.

Saving

(5) Nothing in this section affects a case where the wife or husband of a person charged with an offence may at common law be called as a witness without the consent of that person.

Failure to testify

(6) The failure of the person charged, or of the wife or husband of that person, to testify shall not be made the subject of comment by the judge or by counsel for the prosecution.

By virtue of section 4(3) a spouse called as a witness may disclose a spousal communication but also may refuse to disclose "any" communication with his or her spouse. This is a testimonial privilege in nature protecting the spouse from being compelled to disclose matrimonial communications during her testimony[87] but the communications themselves are not privileged.[88] *R. v. Couture* holds that the "spouse's out-of-court statements are inadmissible because their admission under the principled exception to hearsay would, in the circumstances of this case, undermine the spousal incompetency rule and its underlying rationales" (so that where a letter from the

---

87   *R. v. Couture*, [2007] 2 S.C.R. 517 (S.C.C.) at para. 41.
88   *Ibid.*

accused to his wife, confessing to murder, fell into the hands of the police, no privilege was attached).[89]

The privilege applies even when the spouse testifies for the accused.[90] If the former wishes to waive the privilege, he or she may do so.[91] The privilege must be claimed by the recipient of the conversation before the communication is protected and if it is not claimed the communication is admissible.[92] The privilege applies to any communication and is not limited to confidential communications.[93] The privilege should be invoked in the presence of the jury otherwise the jury would wonder why the Crown did not pursue some obvious questions. But the trial Judge should instruct the jury at a minimum that the witness is asserting a statutory privilege all legally married spouses are enabled to assert and the privilege is that of the asserting spouse and not the accused and it is the witness's decision to assert.[94]

A third party who intercepts the communication, such as a letter, between the spouses can disclose that communication as it is not privileged in that party's hands.[95] However, intercepted private communications between husband and wife are inadmissible where the wife could not be a competent and compellable witness by the Crown (except with the consent of the spouse who holds the privilege) because of the combined effect of section 189(6) of the *Criminal Code* and section 4(3) of the *Canada Evidence Act*.[96]

The privilege does not apply after death or termination of the marriage by divorce or annulment with respect to crimes committed during the marriage.[97] The marriage must be a valid legal marriage for the privilege to apply.[98] If the spouses are irreconcilably separated, they are competent to

---

89 *R. v. Kotapski* (1981), 66 C.C.C. (2d) 78 (Que. S.C.), affirmed (1984), 13 C.C.C. (3d) 18S (Que. C.A.), leave to appeal to S.C.C. refused November 22, 1984 (S.C.C.). The privilege also does not apply to observable facts such as the appearance of the spouse's clothing. See *Gosselin v. R.* (1903), (sub nom. *R. v. Gosselin*) 33 S.C.R. 255 (S.C.C.)

90 *R. v. St. Jean* (1976), 32 C.C.C. (2d) 438 (Que. C.A.) per Kaufman J.A.

91 *Lloyd v. R.*, [1981] 2 S.C.R. 645 (S.C.C.) at 654-55.

92 *R. v. Jean* (1979), 46 C.C.C. (2d) 176 (Alta. C.A.), affirmed (1980), 51 C.C.C. (2d) 192 (S.C.C.).

93 *MacDonald v. Bublitz* (1960), 31 W.W.R. 478 (B.C. S.C.).

94 *R. v. Zylstra* (1995), 41 C.R. (4th) 130 (Ont. C.A.).

95 *Rumping v. D.P.P., supra.*

96 *R. v. Lloyd, supra; R. v. Hunter* (1987), 57 C.R. (3d) 1 (Ont. C.A.); *R. v. Jean* (1979), 7 C.R. (3d) 338 (Alta C.A.), affirmed (1980), 16 C.R. (3d) 193 (S.C.C.); *R. v. Pleich* (1980), 16 C.R. (3d) 194 (Ont. C.A.).

97 *Shenton v. Tyler*, [1939] Ch. 620 (C.A.); *R. v. Kanester*, [1966] 4 C.C.C. 231 (B.C. C.A.), reversed on another grounds (1966), 49 C.R. 402 (S.C.C.); *R. v. Marchand* (1980), 55 C.C.C. (2d) 77 (N.S. C.A.).

98 *R. v. Coffin* (1954), 19 C.R. 222 (Que. Q.B.); *Ex parte Cote* (1972), 5 C.C.C. (2d) 49 (Sask. C.A.). Given the acceptance of common law marriages in today's world could not

testify against each other and the communications between them are not privileged.[99] Whether or not the spouses are irreconcilably separated is to be determined on a *voir dire*[100] and the onus is on the Crown to prove it on the balance of probabilities.[101]

There appears to be a difference of opinion as to whether or not a spouse who is compellable to give evidence against the other by virtue of section 4(2) of the *Canada Evidence Act* can claim privilege for marital communications. In *R. v. St-Jean*,[102] the Quebec Court of Appeal, per Kaufman J.A., held that "in cases where a spouse is competent and compellable, he or she may testify about *all* aspects of the case, subject only to the ordinary rules of evidence." In *R. v. Mailloux*,[103] O'Driscoll J. followed *St-Jean*. However, on appeal, Martin J.A. in a strong *obiter* makes it clear that the Ontario Court of Appeal did not wish to be taken as agreeing with the conclusion of O'Driscoll J.[104] The opposite view to *St-Jean* is found in *R. v. Jean*,[105] where it was held that the spouse need not disclose any communication made by his or her spouse during marriage even when that communication is intercepted by means of wiretap.

Even if the husband and wife are discussing their involvement in a crime, it would appear that the privilege applies.[106] But no privilege attaches to communications for the purpose of planning or carrying out a crime.[107]

See also Chapter, "Competency and Credibility."

PUBLIC INTEREST IMMUNITY (CROWN PRIVILEGE)

Section 37 *Canada Evidence Act* and the Common Law

37. (1) Subject to sections 38 to 38.16, a Minister of the Crown in right of Canada or other official may object to the disclosure of information before a Court, person or body with jurisdiction to compel the production of information by certifying orally or in writing to the Court, person or body that the information should not be disclosed on the grounds of a specified public interest.

---

a valid argument be made pursuant to the Wigmore criteria that the privilege should apply?

99 *R. v. Salituro* (1991), 68 C.C.C. (3d) 189 (S.C.C.), affirming (1990), 78 C.R. (3d) 68 (Ont. C.A.).
100 *R. v. Grewal* (1992), 78 C.C.C. (3d) 188 (Ont. Gen. Div.).
101 *R. v. Jeffrey* (1993), 84 C.C.C. (3d) 31 (Alta. C.A.).
102 (1976), 34 C.R.N.S. 378 at 385 (Que. C.A.). See also *R. v. Latimer* (1988), 6 W.C.B. (2d) 83 (B.C. Co. Ct.).
103 (1980), 55 C.C.C. (2d) 193 (Ont. H.C.), affirmed (1980), 55 C.C.C. (2d) 193 at 196 (Ont. C.A.).
104 *Ibid.*, at 196.
105 (1979), 46 C.C.C. (2d) 176 (Alta. C.A.), affirmed (1980), 51 C.C.C. (2d) 192 (S.C.C.). See also *Gosselin v. R., supra*.
106 *Lloyd v. R., supra*.
107 *Gosselin v. R., supra*.

(6.1) The Court may receive into evidence anything that, in the opinion of the Court, is reliable and appropriate, even if it would not otherwise be admissible under Canadian law, and may base its decision on that evidence.

This section goes on to relate the procedures under section 37 as well as other factors.

When this immunity is claimed by the Crown, it can be made under the common law or section 37 of the *Canada Evidence Act*, or both.[108] For section 37 to apply the claimant must specifically invoke that section. A claim for immunity in the Provincial Court during the preliminary hearing or the trial is to be made under the common law while section 37 is only available in the Superior or the Federal Court (section 37(2)). The Superior Court can hear claims under both section 37 and the common law.

If the matter is in the Provincial Court and the claimant wishes to invoke section 37 there would have to be an adjournment for the application to be filed in the Superior Court. To save interrupting the trial or preliminary hearing it is best to proceed under the common law in Provincial Court. If the Judge orders disclosure in the Provincial Court the Crown can still commence proceedings in the Superior Court to defeat the lower Court ruling. The difficulty for the Crown in obtaining any favourable ruling in the Provincial Court is a preliminary hearing Judge does not have the authority to grant rulings as such powers are reserved for the trial Judge.[109]

INVESTIGATIVE TECHNIQUES

When a public interest immunity is asserted by an objection under the common law or section 37 involving police investigation methods or techniques, the Court can decide the issue on the basis of the testimony of a police officer who is involved and submissions by Crown counsel. If a government official is involved an affidavit can be filed. The Court may review relevant documents in the absence of the parties, including counsel,[110] and may hear representations in the absence of the accused if there is a concern about the safety of witnesses.[111] In *R. v. Meuckon, infra*, it was held that with proper safeguards including editing to protect the public interest, disclosure of the privileged information was admissible.

---

108   *R. v. Richards* (1997), 115 C.C.C. (3d) 377 (Ont. C.A.) at paras. 7 & 8; *R. v. Lam* (2000), 148 C.C.C. (3d) 379 (B.C. C.A.) at para. 7; *R. v. Pilotte* (2002), 163 C.C.C. (3d) 225, 2002 CarswellOnt 704 (Ont. C.A.), leave to appeal refused (2003), 170 C.C.C. (3d) vi (note) (S.C.C.).

109   *R. v. Hynes* (2001), 159 C.C.C. (3d) 359 (S.C.C) at para. 33.

110   *R. c. Pearson* (2002), 170 C.C.C. (3d) 549 (Que. C.A.). In *R. v. Desjardins* (1990), 61 C.C.C. (3d) 376, 1990 CarswellNfld 77 (Nfld. T.D.). The Court viewed the sealed packet authorizing the wiretap.

111   *Ibid.*

Privilege Beyond The Pale

"*You are accused of something. As it affects national security, I am not at liberty to say what it is. How do you plead?*"

© CRA Newsletter.

In *R. v. Meuckon*,[112] it was held that where a privilege was claimed in a criminal trial, the judge's first duty was to decide that if the privilege was upheld might it possibly affect the outcome of the trial and deprive the accused from making full answer and defence. If the trial judge so concludes, he should give the Crown the option of withdrawing the claim of privilege or stay the proceedings. If the Crown chooses to do neither, then the trial judge may impose whatever safeguards he deems necessary. In effect, the trial judge must balance the public interest against the right of an accused to have a fair trial.

Disclosure of police techniques is subject to a qualified privilege if the public interest in effective police investigation and the protection of those involved or who assist outweighs the legitimate interests of an accused in disclosure of those techniques.

---

112   (1990), 78 C.R. (3d) 196 (B.C. C.A.).

In *R. v. Trang*[113] the Court held that public interest privilege could apply over investigative techniques, ongoing police investigations, material that would affect the safety of individuals, internal police communications and police intelligence in order not to compromise investigations or put officers or civilians at risk. Civilians and police could be put in harm's way in some cases if there is disclosure of information relating to an ongoing investigation but once the investigation was concluded it would be difficult to justify non-disclosure. The claims for privilege should be analyzed on a case-by-case basis to determine whether they qualify for immunity.[114]

In the Supreme Court of Canada decisions in *R. v. Mentuck* (2001), 158 C.C.C. (3d) 449 (S.C.C.) and *R. v. E. (O.N.)* (2001), 158 C.C.C. (3d) 478 (S.C.C.) the Court was asked to consider whether bans on publication of undercover operational methods were in breach of sections 2(b) and 11(d) of the *Charter*. In *Mentuck*, the Supreme Court had this to say, per Iacobucci J.:

> ¶43 It is my view that, on balance, the appellant does not, at this first stage of the test, make out a case that the ban as to operational methods should have issued. The serious risk at issue here is that the efficacy of present and future police operations will be reduced by publication of these details. I find it difficult to accept that the publication of information regarding the techniques employed by police will seriously compromise the efficacy of this type of operation. There are a limited number of ways in which undercover operations can be run. Criminals who are able to extrapolate from a newspaper story about one suspect that their own criminal involvement might well be a police operation are likely to able to suspect police involvement based on their common sense perceptions or on similar situations depicted in popular films and books. While I accept that operations will be compromised if suspects learn that they are targets, I do not believe that media publication will seriously increase the rate of compromise. The media have reported the details of similar operations several times in the past, including this one. In spite of this publicity, Sergeant

---

113 (2002), 168 C.C.C. (3d) 145 (Alta. Q.B.).

114 Some examples of investigative methods and techniques that have been the subject of section 37 protection have been: (1) the location of police observation posts. See *R. v. Richards* (1997), 115 C.C.C. (3d) 377 (Ont. C.A.) at paras. 7 & 8; *R. v. Lam* (2000), 148 C.C.C. (3d) 379 (B.C. C.A.) at para. 7; *R. v. Blair* (2000), 2000 CarswellOnt 2924 (Ont. C.A.); (2) the location of tracking devices. See *R. v. Guilbride* (2003), 2003 BCPC 176 (B.C. Prov. Ct.); *R. v. Gerrard* (2003), 2003 CarswellOnt 421 (Ont. S.C.J.); (3) the location of secondary vehicle identification number. See *R. v. Boomer* (2000), 182 N.S.R. (2d) 49 (N.S. S.C.); *R. v. Smith* (2009), 247 C.C.C. (3d) 533 (Alta. Prov. Ct.); (4) how the police simulate the ingestion of illegal drugs. See *R. v. Meuckon* (1990), 57 C.C.C. (3d) 193 (B.C. C.A.); (5) information as to how police conduct certain investigations. See *R. v. Kim* (2003), 2003 ABQB 1025 (Alta. Q.B.); (6) ongoing police investigations. See *R. v. Bowyer* (2009), 2009 CarswellOnt 249 (Ont. S.C.J.); (7) information with respect to aspects of witness protection programs. See *R. c. Pearson* (2002), 170 C.C.C. (3d) 549 (Que. C.A.); *R. v. Le* (2008), 2008 MBQB 96 (Man. Q.B.).

German, in his affidavit, was only able to positively identify one instance in which media reports arguably resulted in the compromise of an operation.

. . .

¶45 I do not doubt that undercover operations can be risky, and that discovery by the targets may result in the resources and efforts of the police being wasted. There is a personal risk, as well, to the *[page472]* officers involved, which we must take seriously, although this risk is much less serious in this type of targeting operation (in which many officers are engaged with a single suspect) than in lone infiltrations of existing, actual criminal organizations. But, the danger to the efficacy of the operation is not significantly increased by republication of the details of similar operations that have already been well-publicized in the past. It is the incremental effect of the proposed ban, viewed in light of what has already been published before, that must be evaluated in this appeal. That is, in terms of the framework adopted above, republication of this information does not constitute a serious risk to the efficacy of police operations, and thus to that aspect of the proper administration of justice. Accordingly, in the final analysis and looking at all the circumstances, in my view this ground by itself is sufficient to dispose of, the widest part of the ban as to operational methods.

¶46 However, I accept that the publication of the names and identities of the officers in question would create a serious risk to the efficacy of current, similar operations. Given that the officers involved appear to go by their real names in the course of this undercover work, publishing their names could very easily alert targets that their apparent criminal associates are in fact police officers. Furthermore, since the operations in question have already been commenced, it would obviously be unreasonable for officers to adopt pseudonyms now. The targets already know their real names. Accordingly, I agree with Menzies J. that a ban on the publication of officers' names is necessary and that there is no reasonable alternative.

¶47 I also agree that the ban should be restricted to a period of one year. After ongoing operations have been completed, reasonable alternative measures such as the regular use of pseudonyms, the use of different officers, and the use of different scenarios will become available to the police. Should the circumstances of a particular case change, of course, the ban may need to be shortened or extended. For this reason it will be prudent for such orders of publication bans to be made subject to further order of the court.

. . .

¶49 The ban as to operational methods would have the salutary effect on the administration of justice of protecting officers in the field and ensuring that the targets of the operation continue to provide useful information. In so far as these effects are real and substantial they will constitute a salutary effect. However, as I noted above, I do not regard the proposed ban as substantially increasing the safety of officers. Since I also found above that the requested publication ban was unlikely to have significant effects on the likelihood that suspects will realize that they are being targeted in undercover operations, I do not regard the salutary effects that would be produced by the requested publication ban as significant, compelling benefits. At most this ban would produce speculative and marginal improvements in the efficacy of undercover operations and the safety of officers in the field.

¶50 The deleterious effects, however, would be quite substantial. In the first place, the freedom of the press would be seriously curtailed in respect of an issue that may merit widespread public debate. A fundamental belief pervades our political and legal system that the police should remain under civilian control and supervision by our democratically elected officials; our country is not a police state. The tactics used by police, along with other aspects of their operations, is a matter that is presumptively of public concern. Restricting the freedom of the press to report on the details of undercover operations that utilize deception, and that encourage the suspect to confess to specific crimes with the prospect of financial and other rewards, prevents the public from being informed critics of what may be controversial police actions.

¶51 As this Court recognized in Irwin Toy Ltd. v. Quebec (Attorney General), [1989] 1 S.C.R. 927 at p. 976, 58 D.L.R. (44th) 577, "participation in social and political decision-making is to be fostered and encouraged", a principle fundamental to a free and democratic society. See Switzman v. Elbling, [1957] S.C.R. 285, 117 C.C.C. 129, 7 D.L.R. (2d) 337; 337; R. v. Keegstra, [1990] 3 S.C.R. 697, 61 C.C.C. (3d) 1; Thomson Newspapers Co. v. Canada (Attorney *[page474]* General), [1998] 1 S.C.R. 877, 159 D.L.R. (45th) 385. Such participation is an empty exercise without the information the press can provide about the practices of government, including the police. In my view, a publication ban that restricts the public's access to information about the one government body that publicly wields instruments of force and gathers evidence for the purpose of imprisoning suspected offenders would have a serious deleterious effect. There is no doubt as to how crucial the role of the police is to the maintenance of law and order and the security of Canadian society. But there has always been and will continue to be a concern about the limits of acceptable police action. The improper use of bans regarding police conduct, so as to insulate that conduct from public scrutiny, seriously deprives the Canadian public of its ability to know of and be able to respond to police practices that, left unchecked, could erode the fabric of Canadian society and democracy.

R. v. Delong,[115] following the Wigmore criteria, held that the following were conditions for this privilege to apply:

1. The communication must originate in a confidence that it will not be disclosed.
2. This element of confidentiality must be essential to the full and satisfactory maintenance of the relation between the parties.

---

115   (1989), 47 C.C.C. (3d) 402 (Ont. C.A.). See also R. v. McNeil (2009), 238 C.C.C. (3d) 353 (S.C.C.).

3. The relation must be one of which in the opinion of the community ought to be sedulously fostered.
4. The inquiry that would inure to the relation by the disclosure of the communications must be greater than the benefit thereby gained for the correct disposal of the litigation.

Section 38 of the *Canada Evidence Act*

Sections 38-38.16 of the *Canada Evidence Act* are concerned with privilege as it relates to international relations, national defence and security. It relates to "potentially injurious information," which is information that, if disclosed to the public, could injure international relations or national defence and security, and "sensitive information" as information relating to international relations or national defence or national security that is in the possession of the government of Canada and is of the type the government is taking measures to safeguard. Section 38.02 prohibits disclosure of such information subject to section 38.06.[116]

Section 39 of the *Canada Evidence Act*

Section 39 of the *Canada Evidence Act* relates to confidences of the Queen's Privy Council for Canada.

JOURNALIST-INFORMANT PRIVILIGE

In *R. v. National Post*[117] the Supreme Court has recently held that in appropriate circumstances the Court will respect a promise of confidentiality given to a secret source by a journalist or editor but the issue of privilege is to be decided on a case-by-case analysis (and may be total or partial) based on the four Wigmore criteria (detailed earlier in this chapter). The media party seeking to uphold the promise of confidentiality has the burden of proving all four criteria. In the result no journalist can give the secret source an absolute assurance of confidentiality.

---

116   *Ribic v. Canada (Attorney General)* (2003), (*sub nom. R. v. Ribic*) 185 C.C.C. (3d) 129 (F.C.A.).
117   (2010), 254 C.C.C. (3d) 469 (S.C.C.). The Supreme Court held that the warrant and assistance order in this case were properly issued and must be complied with even though the result was to disclose the identity of the secret source who the police had reasonable cause to believe altered a forged document. See also Supreme Court civil case, *Globe & Mail c. Canada (Procureur général)* (2010), 2010 SCC 41 (S.C.C.).

WORK PRODUCT (OR LITIGATION) PRIVILEGE

Work product privilege is recognized in the criminal law jurisprudence based upon the need for a protected area to facilitate investigation and preparation of a case for trial by a party.[118] Such privilege will yield only if the trial Judge determines that the information is clearly relevant and important to the ability of the accused to make full answer and defence.[119]

The work product privilege applies to communications oral or written, in the course of litigation or for the "dominant purpose of litigation actual or anticipated."[120]

The privilege does not apply to material inconsistencies or additional facts not already disclosed to the defence.[121]

Where a police officer shares information protected by solicitor-client privilege with other members of the same force or with members of another force participating in a joint investigation and prosecution, the privilege extends to those officers.[122]

The privilege extends to third parties, for example, communications between the Crown and investigators.[123]

This privilege has encompassed documents which relate to the Crown's analysis of the case, legal opinions, internal notes and memoranda, correspondence, trial strategies, a lawyer's notes, comments by one Crown counsel to another, drafts of documents such as affidavits and Informations to Obtain Search Warrants, internal police memoranda concerning classified information and techniques and intelligence reports, seeking legal opinions, and Crown counsel notes of witness interviews.[124]

---

118 *Blank v. Canada, infra.*

119 *R. v. Trang* (2002), 168 C.C.C. (3d) 145 (Alta. Q.B.). See *R. v. Brown* (1997), 1997 CarswellOnt 5996 (Ont. Gen. Div.); *R. v. Regan* (1997), 1997 CarswellNS 567 (N.S. S.C) at para. 23; *R. v. McClure, supra* under heading: Solicitor-Client Privilege.

120 *Blank v. Canada (Department of Justice),* 2006 CarswellNat 2704 (S.C.C.).

121 *R. v. O'Connor* (1995), 103 C.C.C. (3d) 1 (S.C.C).

122 *R. v. Trang, supra.*

123 *R. v. Brennan Paving & Construction Ltd.* (1998), 1998 CarswellOnt 4481 (Ont. C.A.); *R. v. Trang, supra; R. v. Card* (2002), 2002 CarswellAlta 746 (Alta. Q.B.) at paras. 17-21; *R. v. Hazelwood* (2000), 2000 CarswellOnt 4590 (Ont. S.C.J.) at paras. 47, 48.

124 *R. v. O'Connor, supra; Toronto Star Newspapers Ltd. v. Canada* (2005), 204 C.C.C. (3d) 397 (Ont. S.C.J.) at para. 19; *R. v. Armstrong* (2005), 77 O.R. (3d) 437 (Ont. S.C.J.) at para. 28; *R. v. Brown* (1997), 1997 CarswellOnt 5996 (Ont. Gen. Div.) at para. 9.; *R. v. Stewart* (1997), 1997 CarswellOnt 752 (Ont. Gen. Div.) at para. 33; *R. v. Chan* (2002), 164 C.C.C. (3d) 24 (Alta. Q.B.) at para. 96; *R. v. Mah* (2001), 2001 CarswellAlta 533 (Alta. Q.B.); *R. v. Regan, supra,* at paras. 20-40; *R. v. Johal* (1995), 1995 CarswellBC 2943 (B.C. S.C.) at para. 12; *R. v. Gateway Industries Ltd.* (2003), 174 Man. R. (2d) 159 (Man. Q.B.) at paras. 86-87; *R. v. Petersen* (1997), 155 Sask. R. 133 (Sask. Q.B.) at para. 20, leave to appeal refused (1998), 1998 CarswellSask 192 (Sask. C.A.); *R. v. Brennan Paving, supra; R. v. Hazelwood, supra; R. v. Jamieson* (2003), [2003] O.J. No.

THIRD PARTY RECORDS

With the proliferation of sexual assault and domestic abuse cases before the courts there has been a concomitant increase in requests by defence for access to the records of complainant witnesses which are in the hands of third parties such as, records from Children's Aid Societies, Sexual Assault Crisis Centres, psychiatric and other medical records, therapeutic records and school and employment records.[125] Access to these records are requested to determine if the complainant has said anything to impact on his or her credibility; such as a motive to lie, a prior inconsistent statement or providing another explanation for the complainant's condition.[126] There has been an obvious reluctance on behalf of third parties to release such records on the basis that there would be an invasion of privacy. However, a third party who destroyed such records, as for example a Sexual Assault Crisis Centre destroying relevant notes of an intake interview, obviously went too far and caused a stay of proceedings for an accused on the basis that full answer and defence had been denied.[127]

R. v. O'Connor[128] and *A. (L.L.) v. B. (A.)*[129] from the Supreme Court are the leading cases governing any defence applications for disclosure and production of third party records. In response to these decisions Parliament passed sections 278.1 to 278.9 of the *Criminal Code* regarding enumerated sexual and related offences and specified third party records where there is an expectation of privacy. As a result, *O'Connor* and *B. (A.)* now apply to accessing third party records in criminal proceedings other than those relating to sexual offences although in many respects these cases contain opinions reflected in the aforementioned legislation.[130] Sections 278.1 to 278.9 set out the procedure for the defence to obtain such records relating to sexual offences and the preconditions that have to be met. They apply to

---

5248 (Ont. S.C.J.) at para. 21; *R. v. Charron* (1996), 141 Nfld. & P.E.I.R. 170 (Nfld. T.D.) at para. 29; *R. v. Giroux* (2001), 2001 CarswellOnt 4688 (Ont. S.C.J.) at para. 7.

125 Records held by a Crown entity that is a "stranger to the prosecution" are third party in nature: See *R. v. Gringas* (1992), 71 C.C.C. (3d) 53 (Alta. C.A.).

126 Some cases where production of records have been granted are: *R. v. Mills*, 1997 CarswellAlta 341, [1997] A.J. No. 324 (Alta. Q.B.); *R. v. Maramba*, [1996] O.J. No. 4721 (Ont. Gen.Div.); *R. v. J.C.B.* (1997), [1997] P.E.I.J. No. 26, 1997 CarswellPEI 105 (P.E.I. T.D.); *R. v. Forrest*, [1996] O.J. No. 4726 (Ont. Gen.Div.); *R. v. J.C.* (1995), 134 Nfld. & P.E.I.R. 222 (Nfld. T.D.). Applications were refused in *R. v. Hart* (1995), 134 Nfld. & P.E.I.R. 199 (Nfld. T.D.); *R. v. Bane*, [1996] O.J. No. 2750 (Ont. Gen.Div.).

127 *R. v. Carosella* (1997), 112 C.C.C. (3d) 289 (S.C.C.); *M. (A.) v. Ryan*, [1997] 1 S.C.R. 157 (S.C.C.).

128 (1995), 103 C.C.C. (3d) 1 (S.C.C.).

129 (1995), 103 C.C.C. (3d) 92 (S.C.C.).

130 In *R. v. M. (B.)* 42 O.R. (3d) 1 (C.A.), the Court held that the *O'Connor* procedure applied to obtaining production of telephone records as this was private information but there is a reduced expectation of privacy compared to that of theraputic records and weighs in favour of production.

records in possession of the Crown or third parties. The constitutionality of the sections have been upheld, *R. v. Mills* (2000), 139 C.C.C. (3d) 321 (S.C.C.). A preliminary hearing Judge has no jurisdiction to order production of these records.

Section 278 refers to applications by the defence. The Crown is excluded and presumably would have to resort to the search warrant provisions of the *Criminal Code* to obtain information in the control of third parties.

An application for third party records is only about the production of documents, not their admissibility. The rules of evidence apply to this latter respect.

O'Connor holds that a complainant can waive a claim of privilege for therapeutic records provided to the Crown only if "fully informed" by the Crown of the consequences of that waiver.

O'Connor further states that the onus is on defence counsel to show the "likely relevance" of the records, namely that "there is a reasonable possibility that the information is logically probative to an issue at trial or the competence of the witness to testify." The application is commenced by issuing a subpoena to the third party custodian pursuant to section 698(1) of the *Criminal Code* together with the written application with a supporting affidavit supporting the likely relevance of the records. The records and the holder should be described as well as the likely relevance. The Supreme Court stated that when speaking of relevance to "an issue at trial," it refers to not only evidence that may be probative to material issues in the case (i.e., the unfolding of events) but also to evidence relating to the credibility of witnesses and the reliability of other evidence in the case.[131] The issue is whether the failure to produce records will amount to a denial of full answer and defence. It is not enough for defence to show that the records may be useful for the defence. Mere possibility is insufficient.[132] *O'Connor* states that the onus at this stage is "significant" but "the burden not onerous."[133]

If the defence does meet this burden, the records are produced to the trial Judge who then decides what should be produced to the accused. *O'Connor* sets out what factors should be considered in the weighing process: (1) the extent to which the record is necessary to make full answer and defence; (2) the probative value of the record in question; (3) the nature and extent of the reasonable expectation of privacy vested in that record; (4) whether the production of that record would be premised upon any discriminatory belief or bias; and (5) the potential prejudice to the complainant's

---

131 *O'Connor, supra*, at para. 22.

132 *R. v. White* (1999), 132 C.C.C. (3d) 373 (Ont. C.A.).

133 However, in the recent case of *R. v. McNeil* (2009), [2009] S.C.J. No. 3 (S.C.C.) at 29, focusing on police records the Supreme Court clarified the "likely relevance test" for third party production of records to only show "... a reasonable possibility that the record may contain information logically relevant to an issue in the case or the credibility of a witness."

dignity, privacy or security of the person that would be occasioned by production of the record in question. Conditions to protect the privacy of the witness should accompany an order to produce records such as bans on publication and excluding spectators from the Court where the information is particularly sensitive.

In *McNeil*, [2009] S.C.J. No. 3 Justice Charron stated that the notion of "time relevance" is the starting point when considering the balancing stage in the *O'Connor* assessment" with the focus on the "time relevancy of the targeted record in the case against the accused." The Court went on to say that if the accused establishes relevance then "the accused's right to make full answer and defence will, with few exceptions, tip the balance in favour of allowing the application for production" particularly in cases of criminal investigation files concerning third party accused. The Court noted that where relevance is shown "... a third party privacy interest is unlikely to defeat an application for production."

Third party record provisions do not apply when the record, such as a personal diary, is already in the hands of the accused. It is not necessary for the accused to return the diary and then make the application for production.[134]

JUDICIAL PRIVILEGE

Judicial independence requires that judges are not required to be questioned as to decisions they made or as to the composition of a Court.[135]

STATEMENTS MADE DURING MENTAL ASSESSMENT

When the Court is permitted to order a mental assessment of the accused in the circumstances described in section 672.11 of the *Criminal Code*, statements made by the accused during the course of and for the purposes of the assessment are inadmissible in evidence against the accused without his consent, save in the circumstances enumerated in section 672.21(3).

---

134 *R. v. Shearing* (2002), 165 C.C.C. (3d) 225 (S.C.C.).

135 *MacKeigan v. Hickman* (1989), 50 C.C.C. (3d) 449 (S.C.C). This case concerned the inquiry into the conviction of Donald Marshall. The case does not stand for the proposition that the privilege is absolute but leaves to be determined the issue of whether the Judge might be compellable before other bodies which have express powers to compel such testimony.

The author is thankful for the article, "Third Party Records Governed by *O'Connor*" for the 2009 National Criminal Law Program, by Hugh K. O'Connell, as he then was, with the Public Prosecution Service of Canada.

26

Competency and Compellability

CHILDREN UNDER FOURTEEN YEARS OF AGE

Swearing In The Child Witness

Court Jesters Cartoons. Peter V. MacDonald, Q.C. and David Brown. Stoddart. © 1991 by Peter V. MacDonald and David Brown.

As a result of recent amendments to section 16 of the *Canada Evidence Act*, a witness under 14 years of age is now to be treated differently than the witness whose mental capacity is challenged. Section 16.1(1) of the *Canada Evidence Act* is as follows:

> **16.1** (1) A person under fourteen years of age is presumed to have the capacity to testify.
>
> (2) A proposed witness under fourteen years of age shall not take an oath or make a solemn affirmation despite a provision of any Act that requires an oath or a solemn affirmation.
>
> (3) The evidence of a proposed witness under fourteen years of age shall be received if they are able to understand and respond to questions.
>
> (4) A party who challenges the capacity of a proposed witness under fourteen years of age has the burden of satisfying the court that there is an issue as to the capacity of the proposed witness to understand and respond to questions.
>
> (5) If the court is satisfied that there is an issue as to the capacity of a proposed witness under fourteen years of age to understand and respond to questions, it shall, before permitting them to give evidence, conduct an inquiry to determine whether they are able to understand and respond to questions.
>
> (6) The court shall, before permitting a proposed witness under fourteen years of age to give evidence, require them to promise to tell the truth.
>
> (7) No proposed witness under fourteen years of age shall be asked any questions regarding their understanding of the nature of the promise to tell the truth for the purpose of determining whether their evidence shall be received by the court.
>
> (8) For greater certainty, if the evidence of a witness under fourteen years of age is received by the court, it shall have the same effect as if it were taken under oath. 2005, c. 32, s. 27.

It would now appear that much of the case law to the predecessor section 16 is no longer applicable. A person under the age of 14 is now presumed to have the capacity to testify, which means there is no absolute requirement for an inquiry to determine capacity. If capacity to testify is challenged the challenger has the burden of satisfying the Court that there is an issue as to the capacity of the child witness to understand and respond to questions; and if the Court is so satisfied that there is such an issue, it shall first conduct an inquiry to determine if the child witness is able to understand and respond to questions.

If an inquiry is to be conducted, should there be a *voir dire*? In *R. v. Ferguson*[1] the British Columbia Court of Appeal felt there was "much to recommend conducting the inquiry in the jury's presence" as the evidence by the child could well assist the jury in weighing the child's evidence if she was found to be competent to testify. However the Court held that the inquiry need not be held before the jury and could in some circumstances

---

1 (1996), 112 C.C.C. (3d) 342 (B.C. C.A.).

be prejudicial to the accused if the child was found to be incompetent to testify.

The section 16.1 amendment to the *Canada Evidence Act* also states that a proposed witness under 14 years of age "shall not take an oath or make a solemn declaration despite any previous provision of any Act that requires an oath or affirmation."

The new provisions also provide that the evidence of proposed witnesses under 14 years of age is to be received if they are able to understand and respond to questions.

Section 16.1 provides that the Court, before permitting a proposed witness under 14 years of age to give evidence requires the witness to promise to tell the truth but shall not be asked any questions regarding their understanding of the nature of the promise to tell the truth for the purpose of determining whether their evidence shall be received by the Court. If the evidence is received by the Court, it shall have the same effect as if it were taken under oath.

MENTAL INCOMPETENCY

Unlike the amendments made with respect to the competency of children under 14 years of age, the law has remained virtually the same regarding mentally challenged persons and is governed by section 16 of the *Canada Evidence Act* as follows:

16. (1) If a proposed witness is a person of fourteen years of age or older whose mental capacity is challenged, the court shall, before permitting the person to give evidence, conduct an inquiry to determine

(*a*) whether the person understands the nature of an oath or a solemn affirmation; and

(*b*) whether the person is able to communicate the evidence.

(2) A person referred to in subsection (1) who understands the nature of an oath or a solemn affirmation and is able to communicate the evidence shall testify under oath or solemn affirmation.

(3) A person referred to in subsection (1) who does not understand the nature of an oath or a solemn affirmation but is able to communicate the evidence may, notwithstanding any provision of any Act requiring an oath or a solemn affirmation, testify on promising to tell the truth.

(4) A person referred to in subsection (1) who neither understands the nature of an oath or a solemn affirmation nor is able to communicate the evidence shall not testify.

(5) A party who challenges the mental capacity of a proposed witness of fourteen years of age or more has the burden of satisfying the court that there is an issue as to the capacity of the proposed witness to testify under an oath

or a solemn affirmation. R.S., c.E-10, s. 16; R.S.C. 1985, c. 19 (3rd Supp.), s. 18; 1994, c. 44, s. 89; 2005, c. 32, s. 26.

By virtue of section16(5) of the *Canada Evidence Act* the person who challenges the mental capacity of a proposed witness has the burden of satisfying the Court that there is an issue as to the capacity of the proposed witness to testify under oath or affirmation. The burden of proof is on the balance of probabilities.

A mentally incapacitated person may testify under oath if he or she satisfies the conditions in section 16(1)(*a*) and (*b*). If the witness does not understand the nature of an oath or solemn affirmation but is able to communicate the evidence he or she may testify on promising to tell the truth. But a mentally incapacitated person who does not understand the nature of an oath or solemn affirmation and is unable to communicate the evidence shall not be permitted to testify.

Where an objection is taken that a witness is incompetent to take an oath, the trial judge must determine the issue by examination of witnesses and such other evidence as he or she deems appropriate but the judge should not rely merely on the statement of counsel.[2] Even if a witness suffers from a mental disability severe enough to require confinement, he or she may still be a competent witness capable of answering simple questions, giving rational testimony and understanding the nature of an oath.[3]

The issue of mental capacity is to be determined on a *voir dire* in the presence of the jury.[4] On this *voir dire*, the witness may be cross-examined and witnesses may be called to prove circumstances showing that the witness is incompetent, that is, his or her derangement or defect substantially negates his or her trustworthiness upon the specific subject whether from the fact of an unsoundness of mind at the time of trial or at the time of events to be testified to, by affecting his or her capacity to observe, recollect or narrate.[5] It is doubtful whether a medical witness can be asked if the witness, in his opinion, is telling the truth.[6]

In *R. v. Hawke*,[7] it was suggested that when an objection to a witness's competency on the ground of mental incapacity is successful and thereby precludes the witness from taking the oath, he or she may affirm, provided that the trial judge is satisfied that the witness appreciates the duty of speaking the truth.

---

2 *R. v. Hawke, supra.*
3 *R. v. Hill* (1851), 20 L.J.M.C. 222; *Udy v. Stewart* (1885), 10 O.R. 519 (Ont. C.A.); *R. v. Hawke, supra.*
4 *R. v. Steinberg*, [1931] O.R. 222; affirmed [1931] S.C.R. 421 (S.C.C.); *Toohey v. Metro. Police Commr.*, [1965] 1 All E.R. 506 at 512 (H.L.).
5 *R. v. Hawke, supra.* See also *R. v. Lee*, [1988] Crim. L.R. 525.
6 *R. v. Hawke, supra.*
7 *Supra.*

In *R. v. Marguard*[8] the Supreme Court held that the inquiry into the witness's competence is not limited to capacity to communicate at the time of trial but includes whether the witness had the capacity to observe what was happening, the capacity to recollect what was observed and the capacity to communicate what he or she remembers. The inquiry is limited to capacity, not whether the witness actually perceived, recollects and communicates about the events in question.

In *R. v. Caron*[9] the Court observed that the capacity to communicate the evidence requires proof that the witness has the capacity to relate the contentious parts of her evidence with some independence and not entirely in response to suggestive questions.

Expert evidence should not be part of the analysis when it comes to assessing the ability to communicate evidence. The trial Judge should form his or her own opinion based on direct observations of the witness unless there were unusual circumstances such as evidence that the complainant would be traumatized by appearing in Court.[10]

For a person who is intellectually handicapped the promise to tell the truth assumes that the witness has the capacity to make a meaningful promise and that he or she understands the duty to speak the truth in everyday social conduct.

Understanding the duty to tell the truth involves an understanding by the witness that he or she must answer all the questions in accordance with the witness's recollection of what actually happened.[11]

AFFIRMATION

Section 14(1) [as amended S.C. 1994, c. 44, s. 87] of the *Canada Evidence Act* has been amended to state:

(1) A person may, instead of taking an oath, make the following solemn affirmation:

I solemnly affirm that the evidence to be given by me shall be the truth, the whole truth and nothing but the truth.

(2) Where a person makes a solemn affirmation in accordance with subsection (1), his evidence shall be taken and have the same effect as if taken under oath.

This amendment means that the witness may now give evidence on affirmation as a matter of choice rather than because of conscientious scruples.

8 *R. v. Marquard*, [1993] 4 S.C.R. 223 (S.C.C.).
9 (1994), 94 C.C.C. (3d) 466 (Ont. C.A.).
10 *R. v. Parrott*, [2001] 1 S.C.R. 178 (S.C.C.).
11 *R. v. Farley* (1995), 99 C.C.C. (3d) 76 (Ont. C.A.).

While a witness such as a "satanist" is incompetent to take the oath because it would not bind his or her conscience, such a witness is not incompetent to affirm. A witness's moral depravity or disposition to lie does not render him incompetent to testify.[12]

If after the witness is sworn he or she states the oath is not binding, he or she must affirm.[13]

"Incompetent to take an oath" in section 14(1) refers to incompetency to take an oath because of an absence of religious belief and not mental incompetency.[14]

In *R. v. D. (T. C.)*[15] it was held a mentally retarded adult could be affirmed even though he did not understand the oath and therefore could not be sworn under the predecessor to section16 if the trial Judge was satisfied that he was competent to testify having regard to his capacity to observe, remember and recount and felt a duty to tell the truth.

SPOUSES

The common law is altered by section 4 of the Canada Evidence Act which sets out the rule of spousal competency.

> 4.(1) Every person charged with an offence, and, except as otherwise provided in this section, the wife or husband, as the case may be, of the person so charged, is a competent witness for the defence whether the person so charged is charged solely or jointly with any other person.
>
> (2) The wife or husband of a person charged with an offence against subsection 136(1) of the *Youth Criminal Justice Act* or with an offence against any of sections 151, 152, 153, 155 or 159, subsection 160(2) or (3), or sections 170 to 173, 179, 212, 215, 218, 271 to 273, 280 to 283, 291 to 294 or 329 of the *Criminal Code*, or an attempt to commit any such offence, is a competent and compellable witness for the prosecution without the consent of the person charged.
>
> (3) No husband is compellable to disclose any communication made to him by his wife during their marriage, and no wife is compellable to disclose any communication made to her by her husband during their marriage.
>
> (4) The wife or husband of a person charged with an offence against any of sections 220, 221, 235, 237, 239, 240, 266, 267, 268 or 269 of the *Criminal Code* where the complainant or victim is under the age of fourteen years is a competent and compellable witness for the prosecution without the consent of the person charged.

---

12 *R. v. Walsh* (1978), 45 C.C.C. (2d) 199 (Ont. C.A.); *R. v. Hanna* (1993), 80 C.C.C. (3d) 289 (B.C. C.A.).

13 *Roberts v. Poitras* (1962), 133 C.C.C. 86 (B.C. S.C).

14 *R. v. Walsh, supra; R. v. Hanna, supra,* at 299.

15 (1987), 38 C.C.C. (3d) 434 (Ont. C.A.).

(5) Nothing in this section affects a case where the wife or husband of a person charged with an offence may at common law be called as a witness without the consent of that person.

(6) The failure of the person charged, or of the wife or husband of such person, to testify shall not be made the subject of comment by the judge, or by counsel for the prosecution.

It has been held that while the wife or husband is competent and compellable against his or her spouse by virtue of subsection (2), he is or she is not compellable to answer any question as to whether the spouse charged has made any disclosure to the witness about the charge.[16]

The parties must be husband and wife in the law before spousal incompetency applies.[17] However where spouses are separated without any reasonable possibility of reconciliation, there is no good policy reason for the rule to apply because marital disharmony would not be at stake.[18] Whether or not the spouses are irreconcilably separated should be dealt with on a *voir dire*.[19] There is no requirement that proof of such separation be beyond a reasonable doubt.[20]

The rule that one spouse is not a competent witness against the other applies if the parties marry after the communications take place or after the charges are laid unless there is a statutory or common law exception.[21]

In *R. v. Hawkins*,[22] it was held that when an individual marries an accused after the preliminary hearing (at which time she incriminated the accused) thereby putting herself beyond the reach of the Court as a witness against the accused, is tantamount to a refusal to testify for the purpose of section 715 of the *Criminal Code*. The Crown was therefore allowed to read in her evidence from the preliminary at trial. In the alternative, the Court held the evidence was admissible as an exception to the hearsay rule as the dangers were relatively few since the evidence was given under oath and there was full opportunity to cross-examine at the preliminary hearing. In other words, the preconditions of necessity and reliability had been met.

Section 4(1)

Section 4(1) makes the spouse competent for the defence but does not affect the common law rule of incompetency for the prosecution.

---

16 *R. v. Zylstra* (1994), 88 C.C.C. (3d) 347 (Ont. Gen. Div.), *per* Salhany J.
17 *R. v. Jackson* (1981), 61 C.C.C. (2d) 540 (N.S. C.A.).
18 *R. v. Salituro* (1990), 78 C.R. (3d) 68 (Ont. C.A.), affirmed (1991), 9 C.R. (4th) 324, 68 C.C.C. (3d) 289 (S.C.C.).
19 *R. v. Grewal* (1992), 78 C.C.C. (3d) 188 (Ont. Gen. Div.).
20 *R. v. Jeffrey* (1993), 84 C.C.C. (3d) 31 (Alta. C.A.).
21 *R. v. Heilman* (1983), 22 Man. R. (2d) 173 (Man. Co. Ct.).
22 (1995), 96 C.C.C. (3d) 503 (Ont. C.A.).

The wife of an accused is not only an incompetent witness against her husband on a charge of conspiracy, she is also an incompetent witness against the husband's co-accused who is alleged to be the co-conspirator. In a charge of conspiracy the gist is a conspiratorial agreement between the co-accused and evidence against one will as of necessity be evidence against the other, even though in some instances, it is indirect.[23]

At common law, on a joint trial of co-accused, a spouse of an accused was incompetent as a witness for a co-accused if the spouse's testimony would help or hurt the spouse's defence.[24] If the spouse's evidence did not affect the other spouse's defence or if the accused persons had separate and distinct defences, a spouse was allowed to testify for a co-accused.[25] But other judges have held that where a spouse is on trial, a co-accused could not call the other spouse.[26] While a co-accused may wish to call the spouse to testify against the other spouse it is unclear whether section 4(1) of the *Canada Evidence Act* changes the common law to make a spouse competent for a co-accused against the accused spouse. The general policy of the law is to exclude a spouse's testimony directly or indirectly against the accused, unless section 4 clearly changed the law.[27]

Common Law Exceptions: Section 4(4)

Section 4(2) lists the exceptions which render the spouse of an accused both competent and compellable by the Crown. Section 4(4) preserves the common law exceptions to the law which make the accused's spouse compellable for the Crown. These exceptions relate to offences where the victim spouse alleges offences by the accused spouse affecting the former's person, health or liberty.[28] These offences include murder,[29] attempted murder,[30] aiding and abetting rape of spouse,[31] buggery of the spouse,[32] forcible entry—spouse's dwelling,[33] forcible abduction and marriage[34] and assault.[35] Crimes which have been held not to be against the spouse's liberty, health

---

23 *R. v. Singh*, [1970] 1 C.C.C. 299 (B.C. C.A.).

24 *R. v. Thompson* (1872), 12 Cox C.C. 202; *R. v. Locker* (1804), 170 E.R. 754.

25 *R. v. Bartlett* (1844), 1 Cox C.C. 105; *R. v. Sills* (1844), 1 Car. & Kir. 494.

26 *R. v. Thompson* (1870), 13 N.B.R. 71 (N.B. C.A.).

27 *R. v. Singh, supra.*

28 *R. v. Singh, supra.*

29 *R. v. Woodcock* (1789), 1 Leach. 500, where dying declarations of spouse held admissible.

30 *R. v. Lonsdale* (1973), 15 C.C.C. (2d) 201 (Alta. C.A.); *R. v. Lord Audley* (1632), 123 E.R. 1140 (P.C.).

31 *Lord Audley's Case* (1631), St. 401, 123 E.R. 1140 (C.P.)

32 *R. v. Blanchard* (1952), 35 Cr. App. R. 183.

33 *R. v. Bowles*, [1967] 3 C.C.C. 61 (Alta. Mag. Ct.).

34 *Re Wakefield's Case* (1826), 2 Lewin 279.

35 *Ex parte Abell* (1879), 18 N.B.R. 600 (N.B. C.A.).

or person include sending a letter to the spouse which contained a threat to murder,[36] extortion of spouse by threat to kill,[37] and theft of spouse's property.[38]

It does not matter that the charge in the information alleges interference with the person, liberty or health of the other spouse. The spouse will be a competent witness at the instance of the Crown where her evidence will disclose such an interference.[39]

Section 4(6)

Section 4(6) of the *Canada Evidence Act* states that the Judge and Crown are not to comment on the accused's failure to testify.[40] There are Supreme Court cases which have held that the word "comment" in section 4(6) means a comment "prejudicial to the accused, as well as a direction that the jury must not draw an unfavourable conclusion from the accused's failure to testify."[41]

In *R. v. Prokofiew*[42] the trial Judge believed that he was prevented by section 4(6) of the *Canada Evidence Act* from telling a jury that it could not use the accused's silence at trial against him and therefore did not make a specific reference to the accused's failure to testify in his instructions to the jury when the co-accused commented in his jury address on the accused's failure to testify. However, the Ontario Court of Appeal in *Prokofiew*, employing the rules of *stare decisis*, concluded that the cases such as *R. v. Noble* and *R. v. Crawford* from the Supreme Court were non-binding *obiter dicta* and that section 4(6) did not prohibit the trial Judge from instructing the jury that it could not use the defendant's silence at trial as evidence of guilt.

Section 4 of the *Canada Evidence Act* is also discussed in Chapter, "Privileges."

---

36 *R. v. Yeo*, [1951] 1 All E.R. 864n.
37 *R. v. Comiskey* (1973), 12 C.C.C. (2d) 410 (Ont. Prov. Ct.).
38 *R. v. Brittleton* (1884), 12 Q.B.D. 266.
39 *R. v. Sillars* (1978), 45 C.C.C. (2d) 283 (B.C. C.A.); *R. v. Czipps* (1979), 48 C.C.C. (2d) 166 (Ont. C.A.).
40 In *R. v. Noble* (1997), [1997] 1 S.C.R. 874 (S.C.C.), it was held that this section does not prevent a trial Judge from telling the jury that an issue is "uncontradicted."
41 Examples being *R. v. Noble*, *ibid*; *R. v. Creighton* (1995), (*sub nom. R. v. Crawford*) 96 C.C.C. (3d) 481 (S.C.C.).
42 (2010), 100 O.R. (3d) 401 (Ont. C.A.).

WHEN THE CROWN SUBPOENAS THE CO-ACCUSED CHARGED SEPARATELY WITH THE SAME OFFENCE

Where two accused are charged separately with the same offence, neither the co-accused nor the Crown is prohibited from subpoenaing the accused not being tried and the party calling the witness is not limited in the questions put to the witness as long as they are relevant.[43] However, the predominant purpose for the Crown calling the witness must be for some legitimate public purpose and not to seek evidence against the person compelled to testify.[44] The witness is entitled to "use immunity" guaranteed by section 13 of the *Charter* in any subsequent proceedings with penal sanctions or where section 7 of the *Charter* is engaged.[45]

With respect to derivative evidence immunity, there is no automatic right of exclusion but normally the trial Judge will exercise his or her discretion to exclude when the derivative evidence could not be obtained but for the witness's testimony.[46] The issue is to be decided on a *voir dire* and the burden is borne by the Crown.[47]

CORPORATIONS AND CORPORATE EMPLOYEES

A corporation is not a witness and therefore is not entitled to claim protection against self-incrimination when an officer of the corporation is compelled to testify against it.[48]

An officer or employee of an accused corporation is a compellable witness at the instance of the Crown even though such officer or employee is determined to be the directing mind and will of the accused corporation where it is sought to make the corporation liable for a mens rea offence, or where the corporation seeks to exculpate itself on the basis of due diligence

---

43 *R. v. S. (R.J.)* (1993), 80 C.C.C. (3d) 397 (Ont. C.A.), affirmed (1995), 96 C.C.C. (3d) 1 (S.C.C.); In *R. v. Jobin* (1991), 66 C.C.C. (3d) 281 (Alta. Q.B.), affirmed (1992), 75 C.C.C. (3d) 445 (Alta. C.A.), leave to appeal allowed (1993), 78 C.C.C. (3d) vi (S.C.C.); *Perreault v. Thivierge*, [1992] R.L. 581 (C.A. Qué.); *R. v. Primeau* (1993), 85 C.C.C. (3d) 188 (Sask. C.A.).

44 *British Columbia (Securities Commission) v. Branch* (1995), 97 C.C.C. (3d) 505 (S.C.C.); *R. v. S. (R.J.)* (1995), 96 C.C.C. (3d) 1 (S.C.C.). These cases also deal with shifting burdens of proof and procedural matters. See also *R. v. Z. (L.)* (2001), 54 O.R. (3d) 97 (Ont. C.A.).

45 *Ibid.* Similar considerations should apply at the preliminary hearing stage. See *R. v. Primeau* (1995), 97 C.C.C. (3d) 1 (S.C.C.) and where the witness has not been charged but is a suspect in the same offence. See *R. v. Jobin* (1995), 97 C.C.C. (3d) 97 (S.C.C.).

46 *R. v. S. (R.J.), supra.*

47 *Ibid.*

48 *R. v. Amway of Canada Ltd./Amway du Canada Ltée*, (sub nom. *R. v. Amway Corp.*) [1989] 1 S.C.R. 21 (S.C.C.).

with respect to a strict liability offence.[49] Section 11(*c*) of the *Charter of Rights*[50] does not change the pre-existing law as laid down in *R. v. N.M. Paterson & Sons Ltd.*[51]

COMPELLABILITY OF ACCUSED BY CO-ACCUSED

"Accused persons who are proceeded against on separate informations at the same time should not be any more compellable against each other that when tried on one single information or indictment."[52]

---

49 *R. v. N.M. Paterson & Sons Ltd.* (1980), 55 C.C.C. (2d) 289 (S.C.C.).
50 Part 1 of the *Constitution Act, 1982*, enacted by Sched. B. to the *Canada Act, 1982* (U.K.), c. 11.
51 *Supra.* See *R. v. Dairy Supplies Ltd.* (June 3, 1986), Wright J. (Man. Q.B.), summarized at 17 W.C.B. 74, reversed on other grounds, [1987] 2 W.W.R. 661 (Man. C.A.); *British Columbia (Securities Commission) v. Branch, supra.*
52 *R. v. Clunas* (1992), 11 C.R. (4th) 238 (S.C.C.).

27

The Hearsay Horror

As indicated earlier, counsel must have more than a passing interest in the law relating to the issues in his or her case in order to properly prepare for trial. This is particularly so given the changes in the law relating to hearsay evidence. Prior to the decision of the Supreme Court of Canada in *R. v. Khan*[1] in 1990 there existed the traditional exceptions to hearsay evidence. A number of these exceptions are surveyed in this chapter.

However with the decision in *Khan* began the evolvement of the "principled approach" to otherwise hearsay statements which allowed for such evidence to be admissible if the Crown could satisfy the Court on the balance of probabilities that such evidence was necessary and reliable. While the issue of necessity has been a relatively easy one to solve in the cases, the reliability requirement involves a two-step determination process. The first determination is whether there are sufficient circumstantial guarantees of trustworthiness surrounding how the making of the statement came about. Extrinsic evidence as to the reliability of the statement for a number of years was not permitted to be considered in this "threshold" determination by the trial Judge. If the trial Judge determined that the Crown had met its threshold burden then the statement could be presented to the trier-of-fact to determine its ultimate reliability which would broaden the scope of evidence that the trier-of-fact could consider.

This principled approach did not do away with the traditional exceptions to the hearsay evidence.

In 2005, the Supreme Court in *R. v. Khelawon*[2] concluded that the factors to be considered for admissibility were no longer to be decided on the basis of "threshold" and "ultimate" reliability but all relevant factors should be taken into account when considering the issue of "threshold" reliability, including in appropriate cases the presence of supporting or contradictory evidence.

---

1 (1990), 79 C.R. (3d) 1 (S.C.C.).
2 [2006] 2 S.C.R. 787 (S.C.C.).

Prior to 1990, counsel's role with respect to hearsay was a relatively easy one. The various hearsay exceptions belonged to established categories, the law was well-settled and any questions to be asked by counsel could come easily to mind. Not so with the "principled approach," as this chapter will demonstrate. And counsel will recognize that the prosecution's task in obtaining a conviction has been made easier as the Supreme Court has opened a wide door to the admissibility of otherwise hearsay evidence which can determine the outcome of a case in favour of the prosecution.

The Hearsay Rule

"Evidence of a statement made to a witness by a person who is not himself called as a witness may or may not be hearsay. It is hearsay and inadmissible when the object of the evidence is to establish the truth of what is contained in the statement. It is not hearsay and is admissible when it is proposed to establish by the evidence, not the truth of the statement but the fact it was made. The fact that the statement was made, quite apart from its truth, is frequently relevant in considering the mental state and conduct thereafter of the witness or some other person in whose presence the statement was made."[3]

The phrase "hearsay is no evidence" should be "hearsay is no evidence of the truth of the thing heard."[4]

This rule not only applies to oral statements, but to writings or by conduct such as nodding of the head or pointing a finger, particularly when such conduct is explanatory.[5] With respect to conduct therefore: if X asks Y, did Z stab you? Y's nod in the affirmative is as inadmissible as Y verbally saying "yes" to prove Z did the stabbing, unless some exception to the rule applies.

The Rationale

The reasons for exclusion of hearsay are: to admit such evidence would be to accept a statement of a person not under oath[6] (and therefore not subject to the sanction of perjury); the truthfulness and accuracy of the originator's statements could not be subject to cross-examination[7] and the

---

3 *R. v. Smith*, [1992] 2 S.C.R. 915 (S.C.C.); *Subramanian v. DPP*, [1956] 1 W.L.R. 965 (P.C.) at p. 972; *R. v. O'Brien* (1977), 35 C.C.C. (2d) 209 (S.C.C.) per Dickson J.
4 *R. v. Christie*, [1914] A.C. 545.
5 *R. v. Perciballi* (2001), 154 C.C.C. (3d) 481 (Ont. C.A.) at 520-21, affirmed [2002] 2 S.C.R. 761 (S.C.C.); *R. v. Deacon* (1947), 87 C.C.C. 271 (Man. C.A.) at 321, reversed on other grounds [1947] S.C.R. 531 (S.C.C.).
6 *R. v. Christie*, *supra*.
7 *R. v. Christie*, *ibid.*

demeanour of the originator which could throw light on the evidence is lost.[8] In the last analysis such evidence is untrustworthy. And so the principled approach by the courts has been to find satisfactory substitutes in the evidence to overcome these reasons that characterize evidence as hearsay. These substitutes have been termed "circumstantial guarantees of trustworthiness." The locating of these guarantees in the evidence is what the issue of "reliability" is all about.

THE TRADITIONAL EXCEPTIONS TO HEARSAY

Statutes such as the *Canada Evidence Act* have modified and codified common law exceptions, such as section 29 (financial institution records), section 30 (business documents) and section 31 (photographic film). The following is a survey of a number of the traditionally accepted exceptions to the hearsay rule:

The Fact the Statement was Made

In *R. v. Baltzer*,[9] MacDonald J. stated:

> Essentially it is not the form of the statement that gives it its hearsay or non-hearsay characteristics but the use to which it is put. Whenever a witness testifies that someone said something, immediately one should then ask, "what is the relevance of the fact that someone said something." If, therefore, the relevance of the statement lies in the fact that it was made, it is the making of the statement that is the evidence—the truth or falsity of the statement is of no consequence: if the relevance of the statement lies in the fact that it contains an assertion which is, itself, a relevant fact, then it is the truth or falsity of the statement that is in issue. The former is not hearsay, the latter is.

State of Mind

It will be noted that in *R. v. Christie*[10] it was stated that what would otherwise be thought of as hearsay may still be admitted on some other principle. In *Subramaniam v. D.P.P.*,[11] the accused was convicted of possession of ammunition contrary to the laws of Malaya. His defence was that he had been captured by terrorists and was acting under duress. He wanted to testify as to what the terrorists told him but the trial judge excluded that testimony. The Privy Council stated:

---

8 *R. v. Christie, ibid.*
9 (1974), 27 C.C.C. (2d) 118 (N.S. C.A.) at 143.
10 *Supra.*
11 [1956] 1 W.L.R. 965 (P.C.) at 970.

Evidence of a[n oral] statement made to a witness by a person who is not himself called as a witness may or may not be hearsay. It is hearsay and inadmissible when the object of the evidence is to establish the truth of what is contained in the statement. It is not hearsay and is admissible when it is proposed to establish by the evidence not the truth of the statement but the fact that it was made. The fact that the statement was made, quite apart from its truth, is frequently relevant in considering the mental state and conduct thereafter of the witness or of some other person in whose presence the statement was made. In [this case] statements could have been made to the appellant by the terrorists which, whether true or not, if they had been believed by the appellant, might reasonably have induced in him an apprehension of instant death if he failed to conform to their wishes.

An individual's state of mind creates a wide scope for the admissibility of statements which are not offered to prove the truth of their contents.[12] The fact that the statement was made may show knowledge,[13] belief,[14] motive,[15] rationality,[16] plan or design,[17] or intention as to future conduct[18]

---

12 *McCormick's Handbook of the Law of Evidence, supra*, at pp. 589-591; VI, *Wigmore on Evidence* (Chadbourne rev. S. 1789), (Boston: Little, Brown and Co., 1974).

13 *R. v. Wildman* (1984), 14 C.C.C. (3d) 321 (S.C.C.) where the Court held that answers by the wife (not called as a witness) to the accused husband may have contributed to the accused's knowledge of his stepdaughter's death which he communicated to the police before discovery of the body. This evidence was held to be admissible as otherwise the most incriminating evidence against the accused would be left unexplained.

14 *Subramanian v. D.P.P., supra*, where statements made to the accused witness were admissible as going to the accused's mental state and conduct of the accused which resulted therefrom.

15 *R. v. Malone* (1984), 11 C.C.C. (3d) 34 (Ont. C.A.) where utterances by the accused and writings found in his possession showed a disposition would be inadmissible for that purpose but were held to be admissible as relevant to motive. They were an exception to the hearsay rule in any event because they were statements of the accused.

16 *R. v. Baltzer, supra*, held admissible evidence to show accused said peculiar things in support of the defence of insanity; VI, *Wigmore on Evidence*, (Chadbourne rev.) (Boston: Little, Brown & Co., 1974).

17 *R. v. Container Materials Ltd.* (1940), 74 C.C.C. 113 (Ont. H.C.), affirmed (1941), 76 C.C.C. 18 (Ont. C.A.) affirmed (1942), 77 C.C.C. 129 (S.C.C.) as to evidence going to state of mind, i.e., an agreement (conspiracy) existing through correspondence and reports.

18 In *R. v. P. (R.)* (1990), 58 C.C.C. (3d) 334 (Ont. H.C.) it was held that statements by the deceased as to the unsatisfactory relationship with the accused and determination to permanently end it were relevant to prove that the relationship had ended and therefore relevant to prove motive where identity of the killer was in issue, even when the accused was unaware of the deceased's statements and intention. An exception to admissibility were those statements whose potential prejudicial effect outweighed their potential probative value. See also *R. v. Mafi* (1998), 21 C.R. (5th) 139 (B.C. C.A.), leave to appeal refused (1999), 240 N.R. 259 (note) (S.C.C.). *R. v. Moghal* (1977), 65 Cr. App. R. 567, evidence of a tape recording of the accused's mistress wherein she expressed her intention to kill the deceased was held admissible as to her state of mind at the time of the murder and relevant to his defence that she and not he committed the offence; *R. v. Buckley*

(except when made in circumstances of suspicion)[19] it may show such emotion as fear, anxiety, happiness, malice or affection;[20] it may also bear on the good faith or reasonableness of the conduct of the person who acts on the statement.[21]

(1873), 13 Cox C.C. 293 where the statement by the deceased that he intended to go to a particular location to observe the accused was admissible as evidence of intention and to show the deceased had done that which he said he would; however in *R. v. Wainwright* (1875), 13 Cox C.C. 171 the statement uttered by the deceased to another that she was going to the accused's premises was rejected as a mere statement of intention which might or might not be carried out *(quaere* whether the opposite conclusions in *Buckley* and *Wainwright* are based on relevance); *Mutual Life Insurance v. Hillman*, 145 U.S. 285 (1892) where an insurance company resisted payment of a claim because the body found in Crooked Creek, Kansas, was not H, but his companion W. Letters written by H that he intended to go to Crooked Creek, Kansas, were receivable in evidence as going to intention which made it more probable that H did go there; *R. v. Maskery*, November 28, 1988 *per* Watt J. (Ont. H.C.) where remarks by the deceased as to his intention to meet certain persons later in the day, including the accused, were held admissible. in *Shepherd v. United States* (1933), 290 U.S. 96 (U.S.S.C.) it was concluded that "declarations of intention casting light upon the future have been sharply distinguished from declarations of memory, pointing backwards to the past. There would be an end, or nearly that to the rule against hearsay if the distinction were ignored." Therefore the statement by the wife that her husband had poisoned her was not admissible as going to the deceased's state of mind which the prosecution alleged was inconsistent with the defence of suicide. In *R. v. Starr, ibid*, it was held that a statement of intention is not admissible to prove the intentions of someone other than the declarant unless exception to the hearsay rule is established for each level of hearsay evidence. In *R. v. Baron von Lindberg* (1977), 66 B.C.L.R. 277 (B.C. S.C.) at 278 the Court held that the declarations of the deceased as to the state of mind and body that she was going to leave the accused is admissible to show that at the time of her declaration she intended to leave but her statements as to why she was leaving, in the nature of a narrative concerning quarrels and discussions with the accused and others were inadmissible.

19 *R. v. Starr* (2000), 147 C.C.C. (3d) 449 (S.C.C.).

20 *Ratten v. R.* (1972), A.C. 378 (P.C.) where the telephone operator's evidence as to an hysterical phone call by the deceased was admissible as being relevant to the state of mind of the deceased which would be inconsistent with the defence of accident; *R. v. Bencardino* (1973), 24 C.R.N.S. 178 (Ont. C.A.) where it was held that "the authorities are clear that evidence to show a state of mind such as hatred, malice, affection or fear is always admissible to impeach a witness" and the Crown was permitted to call a witness to show that another witness had recanted his former inculpatory testimony against the accused as a result of threats when the latter had denied any intimidation.

21 *R. v. Pisani*, [1972] 5 C.C.C. (2d) 133 (Ont. C.A.) where the accused was charged with possession of counterfeit money, the Court held admissible the evidence of the accused's solicitor that the police had told her that the accused would be subject to future searches and that she passed this information to the accused. The evidence was admissible, not as proof of the facts stated but proof that such information was passed on to the accused going to his state of mind which supported his defence that it was highly unlikely he would have put the money where it was allegedly located; *R. v. Stronguil* (1978), 4 C.R. (3d) 182 (Sask. C.A.) where evidence given to the police officer by a witness not called was held admissible as it formed the basis for reasonable and probable grounds for the officer to make the demand for a breath sample; *R. v. Willis*, [1960] 1 All E.R. 331

The statements must be of a present existing state of mind and appear to have been made in a natural manner and not under circumstances of suspicion.[22]

In *R. v. Blastland*,[23] it was held that if the statement is being introduced on the basis that it was made other than for its truth, then the state of mind evidenced by the statement must be directly in issue at the trial and "must always depend on the degree of relevance of the state of mind sought to be proved to the issue in relation to which the evidence is tendered." This would seem to indicate that the state of mind must be more than minimally relevant.

McCormick points out that:

> [I]t is now clear that out-of-court statements which tend to prove plan, design or intention of the declarant are admissible, subject to the usual limitations as to remoteness in time and apparent sincerity common to all declarations of mental state, to prove that the plan, design, or intention of the declarant was carried out by the declarant.[24]

Facts Relevant to an Issue other than State of Mind

In *Ratten v. R.*,[25] the appellant was charged with the murder of his wife. He admitted shooting her but claimed the gun went off by accident while he was cleaning it. Evidence showed the wife was alive at 1:12 p.m. and less than 10 minutes later she was shot. The trial judge allowed the prosecution to call evidence from a telephone operator as to the telephone call which she received from an hysterical sounding female who said "Get me the police, please," gave her address and hung up. The judicial committee held the evidence to be admissible on two grounds, one of which was that it rebutted the appellant's statement that the only call from his house during the relevant period of time was his call for an ambulance. It would appear, therefore, that the fact the statement was made was relevant and admissible as it could contradict the appellant without regard to the truth or falsity of its contents. Lord Wilberforce stated:

> Words spoken are facts just as much as any other action by a human being. If the speaking of the words is a relevant fact, a witness may give evidence that

---

(C.C.A.) where evidence of conversation between accused and his co-accused held admissible to explain the accused's answers to the police and his conduct when charged; *Subramanian v. D.P.P.*, *supra*, where statements made to the accused witness were admissible as relevant to the mental state and conduct of the accused.

22 VI *Wigmore on Evidence*, *supra*, p. 129, §1725; followed in *R. v. Maskery and Ditta*, Nov. 28, 1985 *per* Watt J. (Ont. H.C.).

23 [1986] A.C. 41 (H.L.) *per* Lord Bridge.

24 *McCormick's Handbook of The Law of Evidence*, 2nd ed. (St. Paul: West Publishing Co., 1972), p. 697.

25 *Supra*. The evidence was also admissible on the basis that it went to the caller's state of mind, i.e., she was hysterical, which was inconsistent with the defence of accident.

they were spoken. A question of hearsay only arises when the words spoken are relied on "testimonially," i.e., as establishing some fact narrated by the words.[26]

In *R. v. Cremascoli and Goldman*,[27] the issue was whether the evidence by the police that the co-conspirator, who did not testify, consented to wear a body pack, whether his signed consent form to the wearing of a body pack and the introduction of the intercepted communications obtained thereby were admissible. It was held that the consent was an issue of fact and could be proved like any other fact in issue and therefore such evidence was admissible. Likewise in *R. v. Dunn*,[28] where the deceased had arranged for a police officer to listen in on her phone to obscene calls from the accused, the Nova Scotia Court of Appeal held admissible the arrangement between the deceased and the officer to show an arrangement was in fact made and, therefore, that consent to the interception was given, and was not to prove the truth of the words used.

In *Green v. Charterhouse Group Canada Ltd.*,[29] an action under section 113 of the *Securities Act* concerning the use of insider information, the Ontario Court of Appeal held that a document recording information transmitted by telex was admissible to prove the fact of transmission but not the truth or accuracy of its contents.

Implied Assertions

The law with respect to implied assertions arising from unintended conduct or unintended written or oral statements can be troublesome. *Cross on Evidence*[30] describes them thusly:

> [First], statements which were not intended by the maker to be assertive of the fact that they tendered to prove, and [second] non-verbal conduct not intended to be assertive of the fact it is intended to prove. An example of the first kind of implied assertion [from a statement] would be provided by a case in which efforts are made to establish X's presence at a particular place by calling a witness to swear that he heard someone say "Hello X." at that place. An example of the second kind of implied assertions [from non-verbal conduct] would be provided by a case in which it is sought to show that X was dead at a particular time by calling a witness to swear that he saw a doctor cause X's body to be placed on a mortuary van after examining him at that time. In the first case the words "Hello X.," and in the second the conduct of the doctor, are respectfully

26 *Ibid.*, at 387.
27 (1977), 1 C.R. (3d) 257 (Ont. C.A.), affirmed (*sub nom. Goldman v. R.*) (1979), 51 C.C.C. (2d) 1 (S.C.C.).
28 (1976), 33 C.R.N.S. 299 (N.S. Co. Ct.).
29 (1976), 12 O.R. (2d) 280 (Ont. C.A.).
30 3rd ed., (London: Butterworths, 1967), p. 383.

tendered as the equivalent of the express statement "X is here" and X is dead." In each instance, the express statement would be inadmissible if narrated to someone other than its maker.

The main dangers against which the hearsay rule provides are the possible insincerity and inaccuracy of the maker of the reported statement. He may have been deliberately lying, or his powers of observation, memory or narration may have been defective. These dangers are considerably reduced by the sanctions of the oath in cross-examination to which testimony is subject but each of which is usually lacking in the case of hearsay assertions. These dangers are not nearly so marked in the case of implied as opposed to expressed assertions. People do not say "Hello X." in order to deceive passersby into thinking that X is there, and doctors do not place bodies in mortuary vans unless they have good reason to believe the bodies to be corpses.

In *Wright v. Doe D.S. Tatham*[31] the Court had to decide on the mental competency of a testator. The issue was whether three letters, found in his cupboard, which had been written by persons now deceased, to the testator obviously treating the testator as a person of normal capacity for understanding, were admissible. The letters contained no express assertions of testamentary competence but obviously implied it given the subjects that were discussed and the way they were discussed. The letters were rejected as evidence on the basis that they were being introduced as to the opinions of the writers respecting the testator's capacity and that the opinions were not under oath and the opposite party was unable to test by cross-examination the foundation on which the opinions had rested.

However, subsequent case law does not appear to follow *Tatham*. In *Lloyd v. Powell Duffryn Steam Coal Co.*,[32] the issue was whether the child was that of the deceased's. Prior to his death the deceased had made statements acknowledging an awareness that the mother of the child was pregnant and that he had promised to marry her. The deceased had made no expressed statements that he was the father of the child but his statements clearly implied such was the case. The Court found that the promise to marry the mother was a powerful piece of evidence on the issue of paternity. The case may have been founded on the basis of a strong sense of Edwardian morality because the Court felt that there was a presumption that a man of ordinary feelings would not marry a woman that he knew was pregnant if he did not believe he was the father of her child.

In *R. v. Wysochan*,[33] the Saskatchewan Court of Appeal ruled admissible implied assertions as not offending the hearsay rule. The deceased was in the presence of her husband and the accused at the time of her death. She allegedly stated to her husband—"Stanley, help me because there is a bullet

---

31   (1837), 112 E.R. 488.
32   [1914] A.C. 733 (H.L.); *Rattan v. R., supra.*
33   (1930), 54 C.C.C. 172 (Sask. C.A.).

in my body," and "Stanley, help me. I am too hot." These statements were held to be admissible, not to prove the truth of their contents but to show they were made. The jury was entitled to infer the state of mind of the victim, i.e., that she would not make these statements to her husband if he had shot her. The jury was also entitled to infer what event caused the victim's state of mind, namely that the accused was the only killer. One wonders however how the Court was so certain that the deceased ever had an opportunity to see who shot her. Surely this was a case where the opportunity to cross-examine the declarant would have been vital.

McCormick notes that although the older cases tended to favour the objection to implied assertions as being hearsay, the current trend in the U.S. is in the opposite direction.[34] He states that:

> a satisfactory resolution can be had only by making an evaluation in terms of the dangers which the hearsay rule is designed to guard against, i.e., imperfections of perception, memory and narration. It is believed that such an analysis can result only in rejecting the view that evidence of conduct, from which may be inferred a belief from which may be inferred the happening of the event which produced the belief is the equivalent of an assertion that the event happened and hence hearsay.[35]

McCormick goes on to state that it was recognized long ago that purposeful deception is less likely in the absence of intent to communicate. Although

> the threshold question whether communication was in fact intended may on occasion present difficulty, yet the probabilities against intent are so great as to justify imposing the burden of establishing it upon the party urging the hearsay objection.[36]

Dean McCormick however is alive to the argument that conduct evidence ought to be admitted "only when the actor's behaviour has an element of significant reliance as an assurance of trustworthiness," noting that conduct "may be ambiguous so that the trier of fact will draw a wrong inference."[37]

Dying Declarations

In order for a dying declaration to be admissible as an exception to the hearsay rule, the trial judge must determine that the declarant at the time of the declaration had a settled, hopeless expectation that he was to die almost

---

34 *McCormick on Evidence, supra.*
35 *McCormick on Evidence, supra*, at 598-599.
36 *McCormick on Evidence, supra*, at 599.
37 *McCormick on Evidence, supra*, at 599.

immediately.[38] It is not a matter merely of thinking, but it must be a matter of a sole conviction held by the declarant that he is soon going to die and he must have no hope whatever of recovery.[39] The Judge must then consider whether the statement would be evidence if the declarant were a witness. A declaration which is a mere accusation against the accused or an expressed opinion not based on the personal knowledge cannot be received.[40]

In *R. v. Mulligan*,[41] O'Driscoll J. held that one could look to the nature, number and gravity of the injuries that could produce an expectation of almost immediate death by the declarant. In *R. v. Presley*,[42] the trial Judge refused to infer the requisite state of mind only from the wounds in the absence of evidence that the wounds were lethal.

The theory admitting dying declarations into evidence is that the settled hopeless expectation of death acts as a substitute for the oath and that no one would lie on the way to his or her maker. Glanville Williams states that "the law of dying declarations is out of accord with present thought because it is based on a theory that now appears old fashioned."[43] Even before the turn of the century, in *Tracy v. People*,[44] Milkey J. stated that

> It was clearly the right of the accused to show . . . that the deceased in making the statement was not in that frame of mind which the law presupposes and requires in such cases . . . that the deceased . . . was in a reckless irreverent state of mind, and entertained feelings of ill-will and hostility towards the accused.

Death must be as a result of the crime committed.[45]

Res Gestae

In *Teper v. R.*,[46] Lord Normand stated that hearsay evidence is admissible as forming part of the *res gestae* because utterances may be so interwoven with human action that the significance of the action cannot be understood without the correlative words and the dissociation of the words from the action would prevent the discovery of the truth. It would be essential for the words spoken, if not absolutely contemporaneous with the

---

38 *Chapdelaine v. R.*, [1935] S.C.R. 53 (S.C.C.); In *R. v. Laurin (No. 4)* (1902), 6 C.C.C. 104 (Que. K.B.) the Court held that the time at which death takes place is immaterial provided it occurs with certain proximity.
39 *R. v. Laurin, ibid.*
40 *Chapdelaine v. R., supra.*
41 (1973), 23 C.R.N.S. 1 (Ont. S.C.), affirmed (1974), 26 C.R.N.S. 179 (Ont. C.A.), affirmed another grounds (1977), 28 C.C.C. (2d) 266 (S.C.C.).
42 [1976] 2 W.W.R. 258 (B.C. S.C.).
43 G. Williams, *The Proof of Guilt*, 3rd ed. (London: Stevens and Sons, 1963) at 201-202.
44 97 Ill. 101.1061 (1880).
45 *R. v. Laurin, supra.*
46 [1952] A.C. 480 (P.C.). See also *R. v. Bedingfield* (1879), 14 Cox C.C. 341.

action or evens, to be at least so closely associated with it that they are part of the thing being done, and so an item or part of the real evidence and not merely a reported statement. The evidence is only to be admitted where it is in close association with the crime in time, place and circumstance. The identification of the assailant by the victim shortly after he was stabbed was held not to be part of the *res gestae* because the fighting had ceased and no one was pursuing the deceased or seeking to continue the struggle.[47]

However, a more liberal approach to the issue of contemporaneity has been adopted both in England and in Canada. In *Ratten v. R.*,[48] adopted by our Supreme Court in *R. v. Clark*,[49] Lord Wilberforce, in rejecting the former approach, stated:

> . . . [T]he test should be not the uncertain one whether the making of the statement was in some sense part of the event or tranaction. This may often be difficult to establish: such external matters as the time which elapses between the events and the speaking of the words (or vice versa), and differences in location being relevant factor but not, taken by themselves, decisive criteria. As regards statements made after the event it must be for the judge, by preliminary ruling, to satisfy himself that the statement was so clearly made in circumstances of spontaneity or involvement in the event that the possibility of concoction can be disregarded. Conversely, if he considers that the statement ws made by way of narrative of a detached prior event so that the speaker was so disengaged from it as to be able to construct or adapt his account, he should exclude it. And the same must in principle be true of statements made before the event. The test should be not the uncertain one, whether the making of the statement should be regarded as part of the event or transaction. This may often be difficult to show. But if the drama, leading up to the climax, has commenced and assumed such intensity and pressure that the utterance can safely be regarded as a true reflection of what was unrolling or actually happening, it ought to be received. The expression "res gestae" may conveniently sum up these criteria, but the reality of them must always be kept in mind: it is this that lies behind the best reasoned of the judges' rulings.

The modern approach concludes that the proper test was whether the statement was clearly a spontaneous one so that the possibility of concoction or fabrication by the maker could be disregarded. However, if the statement was by way of a narrative or a detached prior event enabling the maker to construct or adapt his account, it should be excluded and the same would be true for statements made prior to the event. A response was held admissible when approximately five minutes after the deceased was attacked while trying to follow the accused, he was asked "who did it?". It was held that a

---

47 *R. v. Leland* (1951), 11 C.R.N.S. 152 (Ont. C.A.).
48 (1972), A.C. 378 (P.C.) at 389-390. See also *R. v. Dakin* 80 O.A.C. 253 (C.A.); *R. v. Andrew*, [1987] 1 All E.R. 513 (H.L.).
49 (1983), 7 C.C.C. (3d) 46 (Ont. C.A.). See also *R. v. Khan* (1988), 42 C.C.C. (3d) 197 (Ont. C.A.) at 207.

statement made by a person, since deceased, in conditions of approximate contemporaneity of involvement or pressure so as to exclude the possibility of concoction or distortion so the advantage of the maker or the disadvantage of the accused is admissible as an exception to the hearsay rule.[50]

In *R. v. Clark*,[51] Dubin J.A. speaking for the Ontario Court of Appeal held that the narrow test of exact contemporaneity should no longer be followed. The Court found that the words of the deceased, repeated by the witness in Court were such as to exclude the possibility of concoction or distortion in the circumstances. The Ontario Court of Appeal has therefore followed the more liberal approach in *Rattan v. R.*[52] and rejected its earlier decision in *R. v. Leland*.[53] It was held in *R. v. Slugoski*,[54] that while a declaration, to be admissible, does not have to be immediately contemporaneous with the act to which it relates, the statement must be made in such conditions of involvement or pressure as to exclude the possibility of concoction or distortion to the advantage of the declarant or the disadvantage of the accused.

In *Slugoski* the mother of the accused, in a visible state of excitement, pounded on the door of the next door neighbour at 2:30 a.m. claiming that her son had "lit the house on fire" and that she was "barricaded in." The mother denied this at trial and her son gave an innocent explanation. The Court held that nothing in the circumstances excluded the possibility that the declarans was responsible for the fire and chose to lay the blame elsewhere so that her state of excitement had something to do with other than the assertive wrongful acts of the accused. There was nothing in her statement to show how the fire started and there was no factual basis for her allegation that she was "barricaded in" the house. These factors would have been enough to exclude the statement but is was also shown that at the material time the declarant was under treatment for schizophrenia which could cause a distorted view of reality.

In *R. v. Page*,[55] is was underscored that to be part of the *res gestae* the complaint must be a spontaneous explanation and not a narration. Mr. Justice Ewaschuk noted that an obvious situation of spontaneous exclamation would occur when the complainant is found so distraught as to be virtually hysterical. In *R. v. A. (S.)*,[56] a statement by a child of a sexual assault after a question was put was admissible even though it lacked contemporaneity with the alleged assault. However the jury should be warned that such

---

50 *R. v. Garlow* (1976), 31 C.C.C. (2d) 163 (Ont. H.C.).
51 *Supra*. See also *R. v. Slugoksi* (1985), 43 C.R. (3d) 369 (B.C. C.A.).
52 *Supra*.
53 *Supra*.
54 *Supra*, at 379.
55 (1984), 40 C.R. (3d) 85 (Ont. H.C.). See also *O'Hara v. Central Scottish Motor Traction Co.*, [1941] S.L.T. 202 at p. 212, *per* Lord Normand.
56 (1992), 76 C.C.C. (3d) 522 (Ont. C.A.).

statements by persons who do not testify are subject to certain frailties warranting a cautious approach. The statement was not under oath and the jury did not have the opportunity to see the witness testify and the child was not subject to cross-examination. The jurors must look at the other evidence in determining whether the assult had been committed and the identity of the assailant. Other factors to consider are the age and maturity of the witness, the language used in the statement, the spontaneity of the statement, the time is took to complain and the details or absence thereof provided by the witness.

Although statements by an accused person normally can only be introduced by the Crown Attorney (except to rebut an allegation of recent fabrication by the accused) exculpatory statements by the accused can be part of the *res gestae* and admissible through the defence in cross-examination. Therefore where a co-accused was shown a key to a briefcase full of recently stolen jewellery and stated "I have never seen it before in my life," such statement was held to be admissible as it was made upon his first being found in possession and therefore part of the *res gestae*.[57] Similarly, on a charge of possession of narcotics, the officer asked the accused "what's this?" in respect to a bag containing narcotics. The accused's statement "I don't know" was held, on appeal, to be admissible.[58]

Declarations Against Pecuniary or Proprietary Interest

An oral or written declaration by a deceased person of a fact which he knows to be against his pecuniary or proprietary interest at the time it is made is admissible as evidence of that fact and of all collateral matters stated, provided the declarant has personal knowledge of the facts.[59] Therefore a receipt given by a deceased for payment of a debt would be admissible as an exception to the rule, for the release of the debtor is against the creditor's interest.

In *Higham v. Ridgway*,[60] an entry made by the deceased male midwife that he had delivered a baby on a certain day and setting out payment of his charges was received as evidence of the date of the child's birth. It was held that

> if this entry had been produced when the party was making a claim for his attendance, it would have been evidence against him that his claim was satisfied.

---

57 *R. v. Graham* (1974), 19 C.R.N.S. 117 (S.C.C.).

58 *R. v. Risby* (1976), 32 C.C.C. (2d) 242 (B.C. C.A.), affirmed (1978), 39 C.C.C. (2d) 567 (S.C.C.).

59 *Cross on Evidence*, 6th ed. (Toronto: Butterworths, 1985), p. 562.

60 (1808), 10 East 109; *MacRae on Evidence*, 3rd ed. (1976), §465. In *Coward v. Motor Insurer's Bureau*, [1962] 1 All E.R. 531 (C.A.) it was held that the acknowledgment of a moral obligation to pay money was against the pecuniary interest of its maker.

It is idle to say that the word paid only shall be admitted in evidence without the context, which explains to what it refers.[61]

Therefore the collateral statement about the child's birth was also admissible.

Declaration Against Penal Interest

In *Demeter v. R.*,[62] the Supreme Court of Canada refused to hold admissible evidence that an escaped convict confessed to an associate (the witness) that he had been the killer of the accused's wife and that the accused was blameless. The Court found that the statement did not meet the third criteria of the following conditions required for the statement to be admissible as a declaration against penal interest:

1. that the deceased should have made the declaration of some fact, the truth of which he had peculiar knowledge;
2. that such fact was to his immediate prejudice at the time he stated it;
3. that the deceased knew the fact to be against his interest when he made it; and
4. that the interest to which the statement was adverse was a penal one.

The Ontario Court of Appeal in *Demeter* held that the unavailability of the witness who made the statement against penal interest could arise by reason of "death, insanity, grave illness which prevents the giving of the testimony even from a bed, or absence in a jurisdiction to which none of the processes of the Court extends."[63] In the subsequent case of *R. v. Pelletier*,[64] it was held this exception extended to whenever the declarant is unavailable (in this case the declarant could not be found). If the witness is available the exception does not apply.[65]

The Supreme Court of Canada adopted the Ontario Court of Appeal's view in *Demeter* that the declaration must be considered in its entirety and, if on balance, it is in favour of the declarant then the declaration is not against his interest[66] and is therefore inadmissible.

A declaration against penal interest receives its guarantee of trustworthiness because it is to the deceased's immediate prejudice. There must be

---

61 *Higham v. Ridgway, ibid.*, at 117.
62 (1977), 38 C.R.N.S. 317 (S.C.C.); *Sussex Peerage Case* (1844), 11 Cl. & Fin. 85 (H.L.) no longer the law in Canada.
63 (1975), 25 C.C.C. (2d) 417 (Ont. C.A.) at 440.
64 (1978), 38 C.C.C. (2d) 515 (Ont. C.A.).
65 *R. v. Williams* (1985), 44 C.R. (3d) 351 (Ont. C.A.).
66 *Lucier v. R.* (1982), 65 C.C.C. (2d) 150 (S.C.C.).

a realization by the declarant that the statement may well be used against him.[67]

Statement of Contemporaneous Bodily and Mental Feelings

A statement made by an individual as to his or her bodily or mental feelings is admissible.[68] However, these statements are not admissible to show who caused the condition or how it was caused.[69] The statement must be made contemporaneously with the physical sensation and not be a narrative of the declarant's past symptoms.[70]

Declaration Made During Performance of Duty (Business Records)

The Task Force stated the

rationale for the exception is that the servant employee or officer is under a duty to make truthful assertions and that the likelihood of detection if errors were to be made, together with the possibility of dismissal for falsehood, provide some guarantee of the trustworthiness of this form of hearsay.[71]

The leading Canadian authority on the admissibility of business records is the decision by the Supreme Court of Canada in *Ares v. Venner*, an action for negligence against a doctor.[72] In that case the Court upheld the trial Judge's ruling admitting notes made by various nurses who attended the plaintiff in hospital. Hall J. speaking for the Court stated:[73]

Hospital records, including nurses' notes, made contemporaneously by someone having personal knowledge of the matters then being recorded and under a duty to make the entry or record should be received in evidence as prima facie proof of the facts stated therein. This should, in no way, preclude a party who wishes to challenge the accuracy of the records or entries from doing so. Had the respondent here wanted to challenge the accuracy of the nurses' notes, the nurses were present in Court and available to be called as witnesses if the respondent had so wished.

---

67 *R. v. O'Brien* (1977), 38 C.R.N.S. 325 (S.C.C.) at 327-328.
68 *R. v. Nicholas*, 175 E.R. 102; *R. v. Gloster* (1888), 16 Cox C.C.C. 471 at 473; *Youlden v. London Guarantee and Accident Co.*, (1912), 26 O.L.R. 75 (Ch. Div.) at 79, affirmed (1913), 28 O.L.R. 161 (Ont. C.A.).
69 *Ibid.*
70 *R. v. Gloster, supra.*
71 *Federal Provincial Task Force on Uniform Rules of Evidence*, (Toronto: Carswell Co., 1982), p. 155.
72 (1970), 12 C.R.N.S. 349 (S.C.C.).
73 *Ibid.* at 363.

The Supreme Court of Canada, therefore, adopted the minority view in *Myers v. D. P. P.*[74] indicating the need for the Court to reshape the hearsay rule to meet modern conditions. *Quaere*—whether the decision would have been the same if the nurses were not present in court and available to be called as witnesses by the challenging side.

Ares v. Venner, therefore, overrules the earlier decisions which held that the entry was to be made by a person since deceased.[75] However, the requirements of the earlier cases for this exception to the hearsay rule to apply still appear to remain, namely, the entry must be made contemporaneously with the event recorded, in the usual and ordinary course of business by a person who is under a duty to do the very thing and record it and has no motive to misrepresent.[76]

Ares v. Venner also makes is clear that personal knowledge of the maker is required and that the exception includes knowledge and observation rather than just the recording of an act. *Ares v. Venner* permits opinion to be included which did not seem to be the case with the common law exception.

The declarations may be oral or written but the duty must be to do a particular thing and not be a general duty.[77]

This exception to the hearsay rule is not allowed to establish collateral facts.[78]

This common law exception has lost much of its impact because of the enactment of the *Canada Evidence Act* and its statutory provisions regarding business records[79] and other documentation. It must be kept in mind however that the exception affects both written and oral statements while the *Canada Evidence Act* deals only with written documents.

Statement by Accused Persons

Accused's Own Statements

The reader is referred to the judgment in *R. v. Simpson*[80] where the Supreme Court held that an accused's statement can be admissible by the defence to show that the accused's statement was relevant to the accused's

---

74 [1965] A.C. 1001 (H.L.).

75 *Myers v. D.P.P., ibid.; Conley v. Conley*, [1968] 2 O.R. 677 (Ont. C.A.); *R. v. Laverty* (1979), 9 C.R. (3d) 288 (Out. C.A.).

76 *Ibid.; R. v. Copeman, McGee, Jones* (Ont. Co. Ct.), Honsberger Co. Ct. J. (May 22, 1979), summarized at 3 W.C.B. 344.

77 *Smith v. Blakey* (1867) L.R. 2 Q.B. 326.

78 *Chambers v. Bernasconi* (1834), 1 Cr.M. & R. 347 (Ex. Ch.).

79 Section 30 *Canada Evidence Act*, R.S.C. 1985, c. C-5.

80 (1988), 62 C.R. (3d) 137 (S.C.C.) at 151-153. See also *R. v. Graham* (1972), 19 C.R.N.S. 117 (S.C.C.) at 123-124, per Ritchie J.

state of mind at a given time or rebut the suggestion of recent fabrication of a defence. Also see previous heading in this chapter, "*Res Gestae*," where exculpatory statements by an accused can be introduced through cross-examination by the defence in unlawful possession cases if part of the *res gestae*.

Acts and Declarations of Co-Conspirators

"Statements made by a person engaged in unlawful conspiracy are receivable as admissions as against all those acting in concert if the declarations were made while the conspiracy was ongoing and were made towards the accomplishment of the common object. Following *R. v. Carter*, co-conspirators' statements will be admissible against the accused only if the trier-of-fact is satisfied beyond a reasonable doubt that a conspiracy existed and if independent evidence, directly admissible against the accused, establishes on the balance of probabilities that the accused was a member of the conspiracy."[81]

The conspiracy exception to the hearsay rule is based on the principle of agency. If X and Y have agreed to achieve a common unlawful purpose, then each has made the other his agent to achieve that purpose, so that the acts and declarations of X in furtherance of the common design are also the acts and declarations of Y, even if made or done out of the presence of Y.[82] This rule does not only apply to charges of conspiracy but is applicable to any offence which is the result of a common design.[83] However, a mere narrative of past events by one of the conspirators, even during the continuance of the conspiracy, or statements made about the conspiracy is only evidence against the narrator as it is not made in furtherance of the common design.[84] Before the hearsay exception may be applied to link an accused to a conspiracy, there must first be other evidence linking the accused to the conspiracy.

Once the conspiracy has been terminated or frustrated, such as by the arrest of a co-conspirator, or, at a time when the criminal objective has been achieved, the agency rule no longer applies and any statement or act done by one of the co-conspirators is not a statement or act done in furtherance of the conspiracy. However, acts subsequent to the achievement of the object of the common design but immediately connected to that object and nec-

---

81 *R. v. Mapara*, [2005] 1 S.C.R. 358 (S.C.C.). The Supreme Court rejected the defence argument that the co-conspirators' exception to the hearsay rule did not reflect the indicia of necessity and reliability requirements.

82 *R. v. Baron* (1976), 31 C.C.C. (2d) 525 (Ont. C.A.); *R. v. Lynch* (1978), 40 C.C.C. (2d) 7 (Ont. C.A.) at 23; *R. v. Davidovic* (1990), 51 A. Crim. R. 197 (Fed. Ct.) at 208.

83 *Koufis v. R.* (1941), 76 C.C.C. 161 (S.C.C.).

84 *R. v. Baron, supra*; *R. v. Hook* (1975), 31 C.R.N.S. 124 (Alta. C.A.).

essary for its successful completion may fall within the common design and be admissible against all co-conspirators as being in furtherance of the common design. Therefore, evidence of the disposal of the deceased's body has been held to fall within the common design on a charge of conspiracy to commit murder.[85]

Statements in the Presence of the Accused

The Ontario Court of Appeal criticized a charge which stated:

> that in addition to adoption by an accused as a requirement of admissibility, statements in his presence would also be admissible against him if he (1) were merely part of the conversation or (2) acknowledged what was said . . . [conveying] the impression that all that is necessary for a statement to be admissible against an accused is that it be made in his presence and hearing. "The rule bearing on this issue is that a statement made by another in the presence of the accused is only admissible against him in circumstances when he expressly adopts the statement or where by his words, action, conduct or demeanour may be taken to have inferentially adopted it. See *R. v. Christie* [1914] A.C. 545 (H.L.) and *R. v. Baron and Wertman* (1976), 31 C.C.C. (2d) 525 at pp. 538-9; 73 D.L.R. (3d) 213, 14 O.R. 173 (Ont. C.A.).[86]

There should first be a *voir dire* to decide if there is any evidence by conduct, word or deed wherein the defendant could be said to have adopted the allegations as true. The jury must then be instructed that before they relied on the evidence they must first conclude that the defendants adopted the statements.[87] Before the evidence is ruled admissible the trial judge must determine if its probative value outweighed its prejudicial effect.[88] The evidence may also be admissible as a *Khan* exception to the hearsay rule in that it met the conditions of necessity and reliability.[89]

THE PRINCIPLED APPROACH TO HEARSAY: NECESSITY AND RELIABILITY PRE-CONDITIONS

The principled approach to hearsay evidence began in earnest with the Supreme Court's decision in *R. v. Khan*[90] where the Court held that a statement by a three and a-half-year old child to her mother incriminating the accused with respect to a sexual assault was admissible through the

---

85 *R. v. Baron, supra.*
86 *R. v. Dubois* (1986), 27 C.C.C. (3d) 325 at 342 (Ont. C.A.).
87 *R. v. Warner* (1994), 21 O.R. (3d) 136 (Ont. C.A.).
88 *Ibid.*
89 *Ibid.*
90 (1990), 79 C.R. (3d) 1 (S.C.C.); see also *R. v. Miller* (1991), 9 C.R. (4th) 347 (Ont. C.A.).

mouth of the mother thereby creating a new exception to the hearsay rule for a child's evidence based on necessity and reliability. Madam Justice McLachlin held as follows:[91]

> The first question should be whether reception of the hearsay statement is necessary. Necessity for these purposes must be interpreted as "reasonably necessary." The inadmissibility of the child's evidence might be one basis for a finding of necessity. But sound evidence based on psychological assessments that testimony in Court might be traumatic for the child or harm the child might also serve. There may be other examples of circumstances which could establish the requirement of necessity.
>
> The next question should be whether the evidence is reliable. Many considerations such as timing, demeanour, the personality of the child, the intelligence and understanding of the child, and the absence of any reason to expect fabrication in the statement may be relevant on the issue of reliability. I would not wish to draw up a strict list of considerations for reliability, nor to suggest that certain categories of evidence (for example the evidence of young children on sexual encounters) should be always regarded as reliable. The *matters relevant to reliability will vary with the child and with the circumstances, and are best left to the trial judge.*
>
> . . .
>
> I conclude that hearsay evidence of a child's statement on crimes committed against the child should be received, provided that the guarantees of necessity and reliability are met, subject to such safeguards as the judge may consider necessary and subject always to considerations affecting the weight that should be accorded to such evidence. This does not make out-of-court statements by children generally admissible; in particular the requirement of necessity will probably mean that in most cases children will still be called to give *viva voce* evidence.
>
> I conclude that the mother's statement in the case at bar should have been received. It was necessary, the child's *viva voce* evidence having been rejected. It was also reliable. The child had no motive to falsify her story, which emerged naturally and without prompting. Moreover, the fact that she could not be expected to have knowledge of such sexual acts imbues her statement with its own peculiar stamp of reliability. Finally, her statement was corroborated by real evidence. Having said this, I note that it may not be necessary to enter the statement on a new trial, if the child's *viva voce* evidence can be received as suggested in the first part of my reasons.

In *R. v. Smith*,[92] the Supreme Court of Canada made it clear that the reasoning in *Khan* was not limited to cases of sexual assault on children.

---

91   *Ibid.* at 13-15.
92   (1992), 75 C.C.C. (3d) 257 (S.C.C.). Another example is *R. v. Edwards* (1994), 19 O.R. (3d) 239 (C.A.), where the Ontario Court of Appeal held that evidence of incoming calls from those seeking drugs from the accused which the police listened to on a seized cellular

For example, in *R. v. Kharsekin*,[93] it was held that the statement of the wounded victim two hours before his death while not admissible under the hearsay exceptions of dying declaration or *res gestae* was admissible as being necessary and reliable.

It was held in *R. v. Chahley*[94] that a careful *voir dire* should be held exploring fully "with the witnesses through whose months the declarations are offerred the circumstances under which they were made" when it is sought to admit otherwise hearsay because of its necessity and reliability.

THE NECESSITY PRECONDITION TO ADMISSIBILITY

The test of necessity states: "Under the modern principled framework, hearsay evidence will be necessary in circumstances where the declarant is unavailable to testify at the trial and where the party is unable to obtain evidence of a similar quality from another source.[95]

Whether or not the evidence is necessary has been construed to mean—is the evidence "reasonably necessary" in all the circumstances?[96] It refers to the necessity or proving a fact in issue.[97] Some obvious examples are provided by the cases: if the complainant is physically unavailable;[98] not competent to testify within the meaning of section 16 of the *Canada Evidence Act* or has a mental disability;[99] if the experience would prove

---

telephone was admissible as such calls satisfy the conditions of necessity and reliability in the circumstances of the case.

93   (1994), 88 C.C.C. (3d) 193 (Nfld. C.A.).

94   (1992), 72 C.C.C. (3d) 193 (B.C. C.A.); see also *R. v. McMaster* (1998), 37 O.R. (3d) 543 (Ont. C.A.), leave to appeal refused (1999), 125 O.A.C. 399 (note) (S.C.C.).

95   *R. v. Hawkins*, [1996] 3 S.C.R. 1043 (S.C.C.).

96   *R. v. Khan* (1990), 59 C.C.C. (3d) 92 at 104 (S.C.C.).

97   *R. v. Smith* (1992), 75 C.C.C. (3d) 257 at 271 (S.C.C.).

98   *R. v. Smith, ibid.*, (death). *R. v. Finta* (1992), 14 C.R. (4th) 1 (Ont. C.A.) (death), affirmed [1994] 1 S.C.R. 701 at 852-4 (S.C.C.); *R. v. Chahley* (1992), 72 C.C.C. (3d) 193 (B.C. C.A.) (death); *R. v. Jack* (1992), 70 C.C.C. (3d) 67 (Man. C.A.), affirmed, [1994] 2 S.C.R. 310 (death) (S.C.C.); *R. v. Menard* (1996), 108 C.C.C. (3d) 424 (Ont. C.A.) (illness); *R. v. Nesbeth*, [1996] O.J. No. 4712 (Ont. Gen. Div.) (absence from jurisdiction). In *R. v. O'Connor* (2002), 62 O.R. (3d) 263 (Ont. C.A.) it was held that it was not sufficient for the Crown to just show that the witness is outside the jurisdiction and won't come to trial. Efforts should be made such as teleconferencing or taking commission evidence before reaching a conclusion of necessity. Necessity is not to be equalled with unavailability. In *R. v. Potvin* (1989), 47 C.C.C. (3d) 289 (S.C.C.) at 307 the Supreme Court noted examples of unfairness in obtaining testimony might be where the witness was temporarily absent from Canada and the Crown was aware at the time the evidence was initially taken that the witness would not be available to testify at the trial but did not inform the accused of this so that he could make the best use of the opportunity to cross-examine the witness at the earlier proceeding.

99   *R. v. Meaney* (1996), 111 C.C.C. (3d) 55 (Nfld. C.A.); *R. v. Rockey* (1995), 99 C.C.C. (3d) 31 (Ont. C.A.); *R. v. Pearson* (1994), 95 C.C.C. (3d) 365 (B.C. C.A.) (mental and

unduly traumatic for the witness;[100] if it is unlikely the witness could give a coherent and comprehensive account of events in Court;[101] if the witness is legally incompetent to testify or non-compellable;[102] or where the witness recants or refuses to repeat out-of-court statements[103] or is unco-operative,

physical disability); *R. v. D. (G.N.)* (1993), 81 C.C.C. (3d) 65 (Ont. C.A.) (three-year-old held incompetent to testify).

100 *R. v. Khan, supra*, at 105. McLachlin J. noted that necessity could not be based upon "mere discomfort." See *R. v. Robinson* (2004), C.C.C. (3d) 152 (Ont. C.A.) where the Court held that the Crown is required to show that there would be a real possibility of psychological trauma amounting to more that discomfort or even distress to meet the requirement of necessity.

101 In *Khan v. College of Physicians and Surgeons (Ontario)* (1992), 76 C.C.C. (3d) 10 (Ont. C.A.), Doherty J.A. held at p. 26 that the following list of factors would be relevant to the issue of necessity of a child's evidence:
1) The age of the child at the time of the alleged event and at the time he or she testifies.
2) The manner in which the child gives his or her evidence, including the extent to which it is necessary to resort to leading questions to elicit answers from the child.
3) The demeanour of the child when he or she testifies.
4) The substance of the child's testimony, particularly as it reflects on the coherence and completeness of the child's description of the events in question.
5) Any professed inability by the child to recall all or part of the relevant events.
6) Any evidence of matters which occurred between the event and the time of the child's testimony which may reflect on the child's ability to provide an independent and accurate account of the events in issue.
7) Any expert evidence relevant to the child's ability at the time he or she is required to give evidence to comprehend, recall or narrate the events in issue.
See also *R. v. Aguilar* (1992), 77 C.C.C. (3d) 462 (Ont. C.A.), where the Ontario Court of Appeal, distinguishing *Khan*, held the evidence inadmissible because the complainant was eight years old at the time of the alleged event, the trial took place within two years and no evidence was adduced to explain the complainant's failure to testify beyond the evidence she gave at trial. Following *Khan v. The College, R. v. D. (G.N.), supra*, at 78, leave to appeal refused (1993), 82 C.C.C. (3d) vi (S.C.C.); *R. v. Hanna* (1993), 80 C.C.C. (3d) 289 (B.C. C.A.); *R. v. C.B.*, [1995] O.J. No. 1798 (Ont. Gen. Div.); *R. v. Caron* (1994), 19 O.R. (3d) 323 (Ont. C.A.); *R. v. Collins* (1991), 9 C.R. (4th) 377 (Ont. C.A.) which was distinguished by Doherty J.A. in *Khan* with respect to a similar fact situation holding the out-of-court statement had no testimonial value because the child testified at trial. If a child is unable, for any reason, to give new evidence in a meaningful way the trial Judge may conclude that the out-of-court statements are necessary. However, fear or disinclination, without more, do not amount to necessity. The trial Judge may have to determine the reasons for the problem and at times expert evidence may be required. Reasonable efforts should be taken to obtain the evidence, such as taking a brief break. See *R. v. F. (W.J.)* (2000), 138 C.C.C. (3d) 1 (S.C.C.).

102 *R. v. Hawkins* (1996), 111 C.C.C. (3d) 129 (S.C.C.) (spousal incompetence); *R. v. Charles* (1997), 1997 CarswellSask 91 (Sask. C.A.); *R. v. C. (B.)* (1993), 80 C.C.C. (3d) 467 (Ont. C.A.), leave to appeal refused (1993), 83 C.C.C. (3d) vi (S.C.C.) where the Crown was refused permission to tender the out-of-court statement of one accused against his co-accused on the grounds of necessity because the accused could not be called to testify. The Crown could have severed the trials for this purpose.

103 *R. v. U. (F.J.)*, [1995] 3 S.C.R. 764 (S.C.C.); *R. v. B. (K.G.)* (1993), 79 C.C.C. (3d) 257 (S.C.C.) per Lamer C.J.C.; *R. v. Conway* (1997), 121 C.C.C. (3d) 397 (Ont. C.A.). See also *R. v. Dionne* (2004), 193 C.C.C. (3d) 228 (Alta. C.A.).

had a memory lapse,[104] or is out of the country.[105] Necessity is to be given a flexible definition and be capable of encompassing diverse situations.[106]

The burden on the Crown to prove necessity is on the balance of probabilities.[107]

The rule in *Khan* does not apply in a case where no evidence is adduced to show the reason for the child's inability to recall and recount events, such as the passage of time.[108]

It must be established that the authorities made sufficient efforts, or exercised due diligence, in attempting to secure the presence of the declarant at trial.[109]

Necessity is not to be equated with unavailability, as for example when a young child is unable to give a full, frank and complete account.[110]

What happens when the declarant speaks about the alleged event on more than one occasion? Is it necessary for all of the statements to be tendered in evidence? In *R. v. D. (G.N.)*[111] it was held that the answer depends on whether the statement is reasonably necessary to ensure a frank, full and accurate account of events. Subsequent out-of-court statements which are only repetitive and add no new detail will not meet the test of necessity. It has been held that a subsequent statement was admissible to assess the reliability of earlier statements[112] and to demonstrate consistency[113] (but not for their truth) in order to meet the circumstances of that case.

THE RELIABILITY PRECONDITION TO ADMISSIBILITY

In *R. v. B. (K.G.)*[114] the Supreme Court held that the best indicia of reliability is when "There will be sufficient circumstantial guarantees of

---

104 *R. v. Assoun* (2006), 207 C.C.C. (3d) 372 (N.S. C.A.), leave to appeal refused 2006 CarswellNS 400 (S.C.C.); *R. v. Kennedy*, 2008 NSPC 73 (N.S. Prov. Ct.). For an unreliable memory see *R. v. Henderson* (2008), 2008 SKPC 153 (Sask. Prov. Ct.).

105 *R. v. Underwood*, 2008 ABCA 263 (Alta. C.A.) at para. 6.

106 *Smith, supra*, p. 271; *R. v. B. (K.G.), supra*, p. 295; *R. v. Hawkins, supra*, p. 185.

107 *Khan, supra.*

108 *R. v. Aguilar* (1992), 77 C.C.C. (3d) 462 (Ont. C.A.).

109 *R. v. Nelson*, [1988] O.J. No. 374 (Ont. C.A.); *R. v. Nesbeth*, [1996] O.J. No. 4711 (Ont. Gen. Div.), reversed (1998), 1998 CarswellOnt 1289 (Ont. C.A.); *R. v. Lee*, [1996] O.J. No. 1280 (Ont. Gen. Div.). These cases indicate that the Crown must exercise due diligence in both finding and attempting to produce the witness for trial.

110 *Khan v. The College, supra.*

111 *R. v. D. (G.N.)* (1993), 81 C.C.C. (3d) 65 (Ont. C.A.), leave to appeal refused [1993] 2 S.C.R. vii (note) (S.C.C.) 3-year-old held incompetent to testify.

112 *R. v. D. (G.N.), supra.*

113 *R. v. Rockey* (1996), 110 C.C.C. (3d) 481 at 496 (S.C.C.).

114 (1993), 79 C.C.C. (3d) 257 (S.C.C.); for oath substitutes see *R. v. Mohamed* (March 18, 1997), MacDonnell Prov. J., [1997] O.J. No. 1287 (Ont. Prov. Div.); *R. v. Sharpe* (1997), 1997 CarswellMan 153 (Man. Prov. Ct.). Where the courts looked at the surrounding

reliability to allow the jury to make substantive use of the statement: (1) if the statement is made under oath, solemn affirmation, or solemn declaration following an explicit warning to the witness as to the existence of severe criminal sanctions for the making of a false statement; (2) if the statement is videotaped in its entirety; and (3) if the opposing party, whether the Crown or the defence, has a full opportunity to cross-examine the witness at trial respecting the statement. Alternatively, other circumstantial guarantees of reliability may suffice to render such statements substantively admissible, provided that the Judge is satisfied that the circumstances provide adequate assurances of reliability in place of those which the hearsay rule traditionally requires." This test as to the circumstances under which the statement in question was made was referred to as the "threshold" test of reliability.

The function of the trial Judge is limited to determining whether the particular hearsay statement exhibits sufficient indicia of reliability so as to afford the trier-of-fact a satisfactory basis for evaluating the truth of the statement. More specifically the Judge must identify the specific hearsay dangers raised by the statement, and then determine whether the facts surrounding the utterance or statement offer sufficient circumstantial guarantees of trustworthiness to compensate for the dangers.

"The ultimate reliability and the weight to be attached to the statement remain the determination for the trier-of-fact . . ."[115] An example of the distinction between threshold reliability and ultimate reliability can be seen in *Hawkins* where the Supreme Court held that the fact the declarant had contradicted herself in statements went to an assessment of ultimate reliability, not threshold reliability. The fact that the statement is confirmed and the timing of making it is shortly after the event are not factors which enhance threshold reliability.[116]

In *R. v. Clarke*[117] it was held that the prior statement can only be eligible for admissibility on the basis of reliability if it would have been otherwise admissible from the witness's testimony, as for example, an out-of-court statement which itself contains inadmissible hearsay would not qualify.

The lack of contemporaneous cross-examination is the most important of hearsay dangers.[118] But the Supreme Court in *R. v. Smith* noted that where

---

circumstances to conclude the declarants appreciated the seriousness of their statements. A transcript can suffice. See *R. v. Hawkins* (1996), 111 C.C.C. (3d) 129 (S.C.C.) at 162-163.

115 *R. v. Hawkins, supra.*

116 *R. v. Diu* (2000), 49 O.R. (3d) 40 (Ont. C.A.).

117 (1994), 95 C.C.C. (3d) 275 (Ont. C.A.); *R. v. B. (K.G.)* (1993), 79 C.C.C. (3d) 257 at 285-86 (S.C.C.).

118 *R. v. B. (K.G.), ibid.*, at 292. The apprehensions traditionally associated with hearsay evidence are the lack of oath in Court, lack of contemporaneous cross-examination and the inability of the trier-of-fact to observe the demeanour of the witness at the time of the making of the statement.

"the circumstances are not such to give rise to the apprehensions traditionally associated with hearsay evidence, such evidence should be admissible
even if cross-examination is impossible." The trial Judge must be satisfied
that if the declarant was available for cross-examination, her evidence would
not reasonably be expected to have changed significantly, if at all.[119] If so
satisfied, the lack of cross-examination goes to weight.

In *R. v. B. (K.G.)*, Lamer C.J.C. noted that among the circumstances
to be considered in assessing the credibility of the statement are "the events
leading up to the making of the . . . statement and the nature of the interview
when the statement was made (including the use of leading questions, and
the existence of pre-statement interviews or coaching)."[120]

Reliability factors for children's statements expressly mentioned by
McLachlin J. in *R. v. Khan*[121] were "timing, demeanour, the personality of
the child, the intelligence and understanding of the child, and the absence
of any reason to expect fabrication in the statement . . ." In *Khan* the statement was held to be admissible because the child did not have any motive
to lie and her story emerged naturally without prompting or leading questions, she would not otherwise have knowledge of the sex act at her age and
there was physical confirmation, i.e. semen stain on her sleeve.[122] *Khan*
hows that the contents of a hearsay statement can be used for some purposes
to determine its admissibility as the Court found that there was an indicium
of reliability in that such as young complainant was unlikely to have knowledge of the sexual acts in question and therefore unlikely to have concocted
her story.[123]

Where the declarant or whomever reports the statement is of disreputable character, the condition of reliability may not be met.[124] Where the
person is an accomplice or co-accused who may have one of a number of
reasons to implicate the accused, reliability may not be met.[125]

---

119   *R. v. Smith* (1992), 75 C.C.C. (3d) 257 at 273 (S.C.C.); *R. v. Ali* (1998), 1998 CarswellOnt
      2948 (Ont. Gen. Div.), para 42; *R. v. Czibulka* (2004), 189 C.C.C. (3d) 199 (Ont. C.A.),
      leave to appeal refused (2005), 195 C.C.C. (3d) vi (S.C.C.).
120   *Supra*, p. 300.
121   (1990), 59 C.C.C. (3d) 92 (S.C.C.).
122   While in *Khan* the utterance by the child was made approximately one hour after the
      incident, in *R. v. Sterling* (1995), 102 C.C.C. (3d) 481 (Sask. C.A.), it was held that the
      statement only need be "reasonably contemporaneous" after the incident and therefore
      a statement made three to four days after the sexual assault was sufficiently contem-
      poraneous. See also *R. v. Olsen* (1999), 131 C.C.C. (3d) 355 (Ont. C.A.), where necessity
      and reliability preconditions were met to permit the out-of-court statement of a ten-
      year-old child. See also *R. v. M. (J.)* (2010, 251 C.C.C. (3d) 325 (Ont. C.A.) at para. 54.
123   *R. v. Czibulka, supra*, at 213.
124   *R. v. Luke* (1993), 85 C.C.C. (3d) 163 (Ont. C.A.).
125   *R. v. C. (B.)* (1993), 80 C.C.C. (3d) 467 (Ont. C.A.) at 476, leave to appeal refused
      (1993), 83 C.C.C. (3d) vi (S.C.C.). Additional assurances of reliability may be required
      by the Court.

Threshold reliability is not concerned with whether the statement is true or not, that is a question of ultimate reliability[126] and so a Court in looking at a statement does not assume the contents to be true but looks to the fact that the statement was made.[127]

Preliminary hearing testimony has been held to meet the reliability test[128] as well as out-of-court statements made on a solemn occasion like a Court proceeding[129] or on solemn affirmation.[130] The transcript of a guilty plea, although not admissible under section 23 of the *Canada Evidence Act*, was admissible at common law as a record of a judicial proceeding and fulfilled the requirements of necessity and reliability.[131]

Where the deceased had peculiar means of knowledge, there was little time to plan falsifications, there was lack of motive to lie and there was confirmation by physical evidence, reliability was made out.[132]

In *R. v. Smith*,[133] Lamer C.J. concluded that the first two phone calls from the deceased to her mother met the reliability test as mistake or untruthfulness was negated by the circumstances. He ruled the third phone call inadmissible because it was unreliable. The Chief Justice admitted to engaging in "speculation" to come up with alternative hypotheses which he stated he was not advancing as "accurate reconstructions" but concluded that the hearsay evidence of the third phone call was equally consistent with the declarant's statements and also with a number of other hypotheses. He stated he could not say that this evidence could not reasonably be expected to change significantly had the declarant been subject to cross-examination. One has to wonder if the door has not been opened for defence counsel, when circumstances warrant, to validly speculate with alternative hypotheses as the Chief Justice did in order to negate reliability.

In *R. v. Cassidy*,[134] which alluded to the Chief Justice's speculation, the Court refused to admit out-of-court statements by the declarant because in the circumstances defence counsel was powerless to deal effectively with those statements. In *Cassidy* there were four different witnesses who confirmed what the deceased had to say and the deceased was partially corroborated by the accused's statement. But the Court said because of the tumultuous emotional relationship between the accused and the deceased, it

---

126 *R. v. Starr* (2000), 147 C.C.C. (3d) 449 (S.C.C.), per Iacobucci J. at para. 215.

127 *R. v. Czibulka, supra*, at paras. 31, 32.

128 *R. v. Hawkins, supra*; *R. v. Biscette* (1995), 169 A.R. 81 (Alta. C.A.), affirmed (1996), 110 C.C.C. (3d) 285 (S.C.C.).

129 *R. v. Finta* (1992), 14 C.R. (4th) 1 (Ont. C.A.), affirmed (1994), 88 C.C.C. (3d) 417 (S.C.C.).

130 *R. v. Hanna* (1993), 80 C.C.C. (3d) 289 (B.C. C.A.).

131 *R. v. C. (W.B.)* (2000), 142 C.C.C. (3d) 490 (Ont. C.A.), affirmed (2001), 153 C.C.C. (3d) 575 (S.C.C.).

132 *R. v. Kharsekin* (1994), 30 C.R. (4th) 252 (Nfld. C.A.).

133 *Supra.*

134 (1993), 26 C.R. (4th) 252 (Ont. Gen. Div.).

was not unlikely the victim's judgment could be clouded or her statements to friends and family about the accused "exaggerated, immoderate or otherwise unreliable." Her statements were straightforward and uncomplicated.

In *R. v. R. (D.)*[135] a child's statements that her father had "touched her" and "spanked her bum" made to different people after the attack were ruled inadmissible by the majority of the Court because it was felt they were equally consistent with other hypotheses, namely that she was assaulted by her brother and "the evidence that the children tended to lie to cover up the sexual activity that took place between them."

The test for reliability is more stringent in the case of a prior inconsistent statement than for other forms of hearsay, particularly when the statement is not under oath (the witness was Vietnamese) and the witness was not advised by police who took the statement of the consequences of not telling the truth.[136]

R. v. Khelawon

The decision by the Supreme Court in *R. v. Khelawon* made a significant impact on the admissibility of otherwise hearsay statements under the principled case-by-case exception to the hearsay rules based on necessity and reliability.

The Supreme Court concluded that the factors to be considered for admissibility are no longer to be decided on the basis of threshold and ultimate reliability; rather all relevant factors should be considered, including, in appropriate cases, the presence of supporting or contradictory evidence. Whether certain factors go only to ultimate reliability will depend on context.

When reliability is dependent on inherent trustworthiness of the statement, the trial Judge is to inquire into those factors tending to show whether the statement is true or not.

The availability of the declarant for cross-examination goes a long way to satisfying the requirement for adequate substitutes.[137]

The Supreme Court made it clear that the trial Judge must be mindful of the limited role that he or she plays in determining admissibility, that it is crucial to the fact-finding process that the question of ultimate reliability not be predetermined on the admissibility *voir dire*.

---

135 (1996), 107 C.C.C. (3d) 289 (S.C.C.).
136 *R. v. Diu* (2000), 49 O.R. 40 (Ont. C.A.).
137 *R. v. Khelawon*, [2006] 2 S.C.R. 787 (S.C.C.) at paras. 2 and 19.

R. v. Blackman and Motive to Lie

In *R. v. Blackman*[138] the Ontario Court of Appeal, in considering an out-of-court statement where there was no opportunity to cross-examine the declarant held that various factors may be taken into account in determining reliability in the circumstances of that case, including:

1. the motive to lie;
2. the relationship between the declarant and the narrator of the statement;
3. the state of the mind of the declarant at the time the statement was made.

The Court noted that where reliance is based on the inherent trustworthiness of the statement, the trial Judge is to inquire into those factors tending to show whether the statement is true or not.

When *Blackman* went to the Supreme Court[139] it held that the presence or absence of motive to lie is a relevant factor in assessing whether the circumstances in which the statement came about provide sufficient comfort in its truth and accuracy to warrant admission. The Court stated further it was important to keep in mind however that motive is but one factor, albeit one which may be significant depending on the circumstances (para. 42). "The focus of the admissibility inquiry in all cases must be, not on the presence or absence of motive, but on the particular dangers coming from the hearsay nature of the evidence."

Any counsel is aware that the issue of motive to lie can be a problem for the defence because although a declarant may have such a motive it can be very difficult to discern. In this regard it is worthwhile noting Justice Rosenberg's words in *R. v. Czibulka*.[140] In that case the trial Judge concluded that the letter by the deceased was reliable because he had no apparent motive to lie. There was no evidence of the circumstances under which the letter was written and in finding that the trial Judge had no evidence that the deceased had a motive to lie, Justice Rosenberg stated "the absence of evidence of motive to fabricate is not the same as evidence of the absence of motive to fabricate." The Court in *Czibulka* held that where there was no evidence of motive to lie, motive "is in effect a neutral consideration." (para. 43)

---

138 (2006), 84 O.R. (3d) 292 (Ont. C.A.), affirmed (2008), 232 C.C.C. (3d) 233 (S.C.C.).
139 [2008] 2 S.C.R. 298 (S.C.C.).
140 *R. v. Czibulka* (2004), 189 C.C.C. (3d) 199 (Ont. C.A.), leave to appeal refused (2005), 195 C.C.C. (3d) vi (S.C.C.).

Principled Approach Does Not Trump Otherwise Inadmissible Evidence

In *R. v. Hawkins*[141] the Supreme Court held that "the new hearsay analysis should not permit the admission of statements which the declarant, if he or she had been available and competent at trial, would not have been able to offer into evidence through direct testimony because of the operation of an evidentiary rule of admissibility." An example of this statement would be if the hearsay evidence was admissible by virtue of the principled approach but contained a prior consistent statement, it would be inadmissible (perhaps not if the prior consistent statement could properly be edited out).

Hearsay Admissible as Narrative

Hearsay evidence, albeit not admissible for its truth, has been held to be admissible as narrative when it provides the trier-of-fact an understanding as to how the matter came to the attention of the authorities or when it is necessary in providing an understanding as to the unfolding of events surrounding the offence.[142]

It is important for defence counsel to be prepared to make submissions when evidence is argued by the Crowns as being admissible because it is part of the narrative. This path to admissibility seems to be the new darling of the Crowns in attempting to introduce hearsay, albeit not for the truth of its contents.

Relationship Between Traditional Exceptions to Hearsay and the Principled Approach

When a traditional hearsay exception conflicts with the principled approach, the latter prevails.[143] The Court must first look to the traditional exceptions[144] to determine if they apply.

The evidence falling within a traditional exception is presumptively admissible. No *voir dire* is required.[145]

If the hearsay evidence does not fall within the traditional exceptions it is presumptively inadmissible and its admissibility is dependent on the

---

141 [1996] 3 S.C.R. 1043 (S.C.C.). See also *R. v. Michaud* (2000), 144 C.C.C. (3d) (N.B. C.A.).
142 *R. v. C. (D.)* (2008), 238 C.C.C. (3d) 16 (N.S. C.A.); *R. v. F. (J.E.)* (1993), 85 C.C.C. (3d) 457 (Ont. C.A.); *R. v. Magloir* (2003), 178 C.C.C. (3d) 310 (N.S. C.A.).
143 *R. v. Starr*, [2000] 2 S.C.R. 144 (S.C.C.) at para. 211.
144 *R. v. Mapara*, [2005] 1 S.C.R. 358 (S.C.C.).
145 *R. v. Starr, supra* at para. 211; *R. v. Mapara, ibid.*

Crown establishing the criteria of necessity and reliability on the balance of probabilities in a *voir dire*.[146]

In the rare case evidence falling within an existing exception may be excluded because the indicia of necessity and reliability are lacking in the particular circumstances of the case.[147] The burden in arguing that either of these criteria is lacking is upon the party opposing the admission of the statement.[148]

Discretionary Exclusion of Hearsay

The trial Judge has the discretion to exclude otherwise hearsay evidence even when the conditions of necessity and reliability have been met. Charron J. in *R. v. Khelawon*[149] stated:

> However, because trial fairness may encompass factors beyond the strict inquiry into necessity and reliability, even if the two criteria are met, the trial Judge has the discretion to exclude hearsay evidence where its probative value is outweighed by its prejudicial effect.

Prejudice or unfairness can arise if the trier-of-fact relies on untrustworthy evidence, the frailties of which would not be exposed through cross-examination.[150]

Prejudice does not mean that the admission of the evidence will operate unfortunately for the accused. The question is whether it will operate unfairly and unjustly.[151] Fairness to the accused is reflected in section 11 of the *Charter* which constitutionally guarantees the accused a fair trial.

In *R. v. Potvin* the Court stressed that judicial discretion should only be exercised after weighing the competing concerns of fair treatment of the accused and society's interest in the admission of probative evidence in order to get at the truth of the matter.[152]

With respect to exclusion of defence evidence, the burden upon the prosecution is a higher standard if the Crown chooses to challenge admissibility. This evidence can only be excluded where its probative value is *substantially* outweighed by its prejudicial effect.[153]

---

146 *R. v. Mapara, supra*, at para. 33. See also *R. v. Blackman*, [2008] 2 S.C.R. 298 (S.C.C.).

147 *R. v. Mapara*, at para. 60.

148 *Ibid* at para. 60.

149 [2006] 2 S.C.R. 787 (S.C.C.).

150 Marc Rosenberg: Developments in the Hearsay Rule: The Doctrine in *R. v. Smith*, Canadian Bar Association, Ontario Annual Institute, 1995.

151 *R. v. Corbett*, [1988] 1 S.C.R. 670 (S.C.C.) at 692.

152 (1989), 47 C.C.C. (3d) 289 (S.C.C.) at 308-09. See also *R. v. M. (M.)* (2001), 156 C.C.C. (3d) 560 (Ont. C.A.).

153 *R. v. Seaboyer* (1991), [1991] 2 S.C.R. 577 (S.C.C.) at 610; *R. v. Shearing*, [2002] 3

RELAXATION OF THE HEARSAY RULE FOR THE DEFENCE

Prior to the *Charter of Rights*[154] the law seemed to be that the hearsay rules could not be relaxed in favour of the accused.[155] However, in *R. v. Rowbotham*[156] Martin J. held that the accused has the right to make full answer and defence, a right encompassed in the term "fundamental justice" which is enshrined in section 7 of the *Charter*. In *Rowbotham*, the case against Y consisted in part of an allegation that he was "B.Y." referred to in intercepted conversations. The trial Judge refused to allow Y to testify (in support of his defence that he was not the "B.Y." referred to in the intercepted conversations) with respect to a conversation he had with his co-accused S after arrest wherein S advised Y as to the identity of "B.Y." The Ontario Court of Appeal followed *R. v. Williams*[157] which held that "an accused in exercising his right to make full answer and defence must comply with the established rules of procedure and the rules respecting the admissibility of evidence" but the rule is not absolute. It was the Court's view that *R. v. Williams* recognized exceptions "when the rigid adherence will prevent or hinder a fair trial." Martin J. stated that the trial Judge in *Rowbotham* might have permitted Y to state who he believed "B.Y." was and to state his reasons for that belief, but would not go so far as to say the trial Judge erred in making the ruling that he did.

Subsequent to the decision in *Williams* our courts have given effect to Martin, J.A.'s opinion in that case wherein he states:

> . . . a Court has a residual discretion to relax in favour of the accused a strict rule of evidence where it is necessary to present a miscarriage of justice and where the danger against which an exclusionary rule aims to safeguard does not exist[158]

S.C.R. 33 (S.C.C.) at 107. See also *R. v. Humaid* (2006), 208 C.C.C. (3d) 43 (Ont. C.A.) at 57, leave to appeal refused (2006), 2006 CarswellOnt 7132 (S.C.C.).

154   *Canadian Charter of Rights and Freedoms*, Part I of the *Constitution Act, 1982*, being Schedule B of the *Canada Act 1982* (U.K.), c. 11.

155   *R. v. Thomson*, [1912] 3 K.B. 19 (C.C.A.); *Sparks v. R.*, [1964] A.C. 964 (P.D.). See analysis of *R. v. Thomson* in P.K. McWilliams, *Canadian Criminal Evidence*, 2nd ed. (Aurora: Canada Law Book Ltd., 1984), pp. 146-147.

156   (1988), 63 C.R. (3d) 113 at 164 (Ont. C.A.).

157   (1985), 44 C.R. (3d) 351 at 367 (Ont. C.A.). In *R. v. Young*, February 4, 1991, Ont. S.C. Assizes, Mr. Justice Moldaver, in following *Williams* and *Rowbotham*, allowed a material and independant Crown witness to testify that a deceased person had told her on several occasions after the murders that it was he who had killed the two victims and not the accused. Furthermore, in the circumstances of this case, Justice Moldaver held these admissions constituted original evidence going to the truth of these admissions. His Lordship found in the circumstances of this case that these utterances met the tests of necessity and trustworthiness.

158   This passage was approved by Cory J. in *R. v. Finta* (1994), 88 C.C.C. (3d) 417 (S.C.C).

In cases that have followed *Williams* and relaxed the rules of hearsay for the defence the reasons for doing so were found in such phrases as: "to protect the rights of an accused to a fair trial," "to protect an accused's right to full answer and defence" and "to prevent a miscarriage of justice."[159] In one case the trial Judge stated that "when something is being advanced on behalf of an accused person the rules in effect can be stretched to accommodate the admissibility of evidence tendered by the defence, where if it were tendered by the Crown the rules would not be stretched."[160] In *R. v. Finta* the trial Judge stated: "... It would have been unfair to have deprived the respondent of having all relevant, probative and reliable evidence before the jury. This is particularly true of evidence that could be considered helpful to his position."[161]

MISCELLANY

Hearsay on Sentencing

By virtue of section 723(5) of the *Criminal Code* hearsay evidence is admissible at sentencing proceedings, but the Court may, if the Court considers it to be in the best interests of justice, compel a person to testify where the person (a) has personal knowledge of the matter; (b) is reasonably available; and (c) is a compellable witness.

In *R. v. Gardiner* the Supreme Court noted that "It is commonplace that the strict rules that govern a trial do not apply at a sentencing hearing and it would be undesirable to have the formalities and technicalities characteristic of the normal adversary proceedings prevail. The hearsay rule does not govern the sentencing hearing. Hearsay evidence may be accepted where found to be credible and trustworthy." When it comes to sentencing however "the facts which justify the sanction are no less important than the facts which justify the conviction." Where facts are disputed as to the seriousness of the offence or disproving the mitigating factors, the Crown bears the onus beyond a reasonable doubt.[162] The accused's burden of proving his version is on a balance of probabilities.

---

159 *R. v. Kimberley* (2001), 56 O.R. (3d) 18 (Ont. C.A.) at paras. 80-81, leave to appeal refused (2002), 2002 CarswellOnt 1895 (S.C.C.); *R. v. Kanthasamy* (2006), 2006 CarswellOnt 3358 (Ont. S.C.J.); *R. v. Morrissey* (2003), 12 C.R. (6th) 337 (Ont. S.C.J.); *R. v. Rowbotham* (1988), 41 C.C.C. (3d) 1 (Ont. C.A.); *R. v. Hankey* (2008), 2008 CarswellOnt 7900 (Ont. S.C.J.); *R. v. Chretien* (2009), 2009 CarswellOnt 1043 (Ont. S.C.J.); *R. v. H. (A.J.)* (September 15, 2005), CanLII 41230 (Que. S.C.).

160 *R. v. Heyden* (1999), 1999 CarswellOnt 3968 (Ont. S.C.J.).

161 (1994), 1994 CarswellOnt 61 at para. 290, reconsideration refused (June 23, 1994), Doc. 23023, 23097 (S.C.C.).

162 [1982] 2 S.C.R. 368 (S.C.C.) at 414.

Hearsay on Bail Hearings

Section 518(1)(e) of the *Criminal Code* provides that a justice on a bail hearing may receive and base his decision with respect to bail on evidence considered credible or trustworthy by him. This means that either the Crown or the accused can lead hearsay evidence. The Crown normally does this by presenting a synopsis of the facts through a Court officer or even a more detailed story through the officer in charge of the case. The defence, if possible, should attempt to show that the evidence is subject to the frailties of hearsay testimony and not credible or trustworthy or that there are mitigating factors or that a different interpretation could be placed on the hearsay evidence. (See Chapter, "The Contested Bail Hearing.")

Hearsay Evidence on Cross-Examination

Hearsay evidence is equally inadmissible in cross-examination as it is in examination-in-chief.[163] A witness's credibility cannot be tested by cross-examination from a document when that document is inadmissible. Therefore, a witness could not be asked to comment on the conclusions reached by social workers and the opinions contained in their reports,[164] otherwise the cross-examiner could indirectly place before the Court hearsay and inadmissible opinions of the experts.[165]

Hearsay at the Preliminary Hearing

See Chapter, "The Preliminary Inquiry" and *Criminal Code* section 540(7) where a justice is permitted to accept otherwise hearsay testimony that is credible and trustworthy, including a statement in writing or that is recorded.

Hearsay and Eyewitness Identification

See Chapter, "The Identification Witness" under heading "Evidence of Past Identification."

---

163 *R. v. Graham* (1972), 7 C.C.C. (2nd) 93 (S.C.C); *Phillion v. R.* (1977), 37 CR.N.S. 361 (S.C.C); *R. v. Laverty (No. 2)* (1979), 9 C.R. (3d) 288 (Ont. C.A.); *R. v. Saunders*, [1899] 1 Q.B. 490 (C.C.R.); *Forsythe v. R.* (1943), 79 C.C.C. 129 (S.C.C); *R. v. Thomson* (1912), 3 K.B. 19.

164 *R. v. W. (R.S.)* (1990), 55 C.C.C (3d) 149 (Man. C.A.).

165 *R. v. Yousry* (1914), 11 Cr. App. R. 13.

Hearsay and The Spousal Incompetency Rule

The principled approach to hearsay does not negate well-established principles of admissibility so as to allow the Crown to do indirectly what it is unable to do directly. So even though the preconditions of necessity and reliability were established with respect to a hearsay statement, it would not be admissible if it were to undermine the spousal incompetency rule or its rationales.[166]

Hearsay and the Expert

Hearsay evidence as helping to form an expert's opinion is admissible and is discussed in the Chapter, "The Expert Witness."

Negative Results of Inquiries

Evidence of negative results of inquiries is regarded as non-hearsay.[167]

Failing to Object to Hearsay

A mistake by counsel in failing to object to hearsay does not give hearsay testimony any probative value.[168] Hearsay evidence is no evidence of the thing heard.[169]

Attempting to Disguise Hearsay

Devlin L.J. in *Glynski v. McIver*[170] refers to the impropriety of disguising what is in reality hearsay by certain means. The first:

> consists in not asking what was said in a conversation or written in a document but in asking what the conversation or document was about; it is apparently thought that what would be hearsay if fully expressed is permissible if decently

---

166 *R. v. Couture*, [2007] 2 S.C.R. 517 (S.C.C.) at para. 63.
167 *McCormick on Evidence*, 3rd ed. (St. Paul: West Publishing Co., 1984) pp. 743-744; *R. v. Garofoli* (1988), 64 C.R. (3d) 193 (Ont. C.A.) per Martin J.; *R. v. Handyside* (October 5, 1988), Magginson Prov.Ct.J., [1988] O.J. No. 2550 (Ont. Prov. Ct).
168 *R. v. Augustine* (1986), 30 C.C.C. (3d) 542 (N.B. C.A.) at 551-552; *Cowan v. R.* (1962), 37 C.R. 151 (S.C.C); *R. v. Schmidt* (1948), 6 C.R. 317 (S.C.C); *R. v. Smith* (1990), 61 C.C.C. (3d) 232 (Ont. C.A.), affirmed (1992), 75 C.C.C. (3d) 257 (S.C.C.).
169 See *R. v. Christie, supra.*
170 [1962] A.C 726 at 780. See also *Cross on Evidence*, 6th ed. (Toronto: Butterworths 1985), p. 566 and dissenting judgment of Vellerand J.A. in *R. v. Delafosse* (1989), 47 C.C.C (3d) 165 (Que. CA.) at 170.

veiled ... The other device is to ask by means of "yes" or "no" questions what was done (Just answer "Yes" or "No." Did you go to see counsel? Do not tell us what he said but as a result of it did you do something? What did you do?) This device is commonly defended on the ground that counsel is asking only about what was done and not about what was said. But in truth what was done is relevant only because from it there can be inferred something about what was said. Such evidence seems to me to be clearly objectionable. If there is nothing in it, it is irrelevant, if there is something in it, what there is in it is inadmissible.

Notwithstanding the objection by Lord Devlin to the question – Do not tell us what he said but as a result of what he said – did you do something? – such question has been a normal and an acceptable practice in Canada.

Agreement to Admit Hearsay

It is the trial Judge's duty to make sure that the rules of evidence are observed and some of the case law reflects an unwillingness by the judiciary to permit an agreement by the parties to admit hearsay testimony.[171] However, "[a]s a matter of practice, technically inadmissible evidence is often let in by agreement in criminal cases."[172]

Newspaper Articles

In *R. v. Samra*[173] it was held that negative comments in a newspaper article about a witness were inadmissible hearsay. However the witness's comments in the article were subject to cross-examination 'of the witness to determine if he in fact made such statements that reflected on his bias and credibility.

---

171 *R. v. Bezanson* (1983), 8 C.C.C (3d) 493 at 506 (N.S. C.A.); *R. v. Lee Kun* (1915), 11 Cr. App. R. 293 at 300 (C.C.A.); *R. v. Ignat* (1965), 53 W.W.R. 248 at 250 (Man. C.A.).
172 *Report of the Federal/Provincial Task Force on Uniform Rules of Evidence* (Toronto: Carswell Co., 1982), pp. 136-139.
173 (1998), 129 C.C.C. (3d) 144 (Ont. C.A.), leave to appeal refused (1999), 239 N.R 400 (note) (S.C.C).

28

Opinion Evidence By Non-Experts

Opinion evidence includes inferences, deductions, impressions or conclusions made from observed facts.[1]

Generally, only an expert may provide an opinion. However, Professor Phipson points out that witnesses can give their opinion or beliefs to prove such matters as identity, age, or speed on grounds of necessity, since more direct or positive evidence is often unobtainable.[2] Non-experts have been permitted to testify on the identification of persons, things and handwritings,[3] intoxication,[4] similarity of shoe prints,[5] apparent age;[6] the bodily plight[7] or condition of a person, including death or illness;[8] the emotional state of a person;[9] the condition of things;[10] certain questions of value.[11]

In *R. v. German*,[12] it was held that there are a number of matters in respect of which a person of ordinary intelligence may be permitted to give evidence based on his personal knowledge, such as the apparent age of a person, the speed of a vehicle and whether a person was sober or not.

---

1 *R. v. Abbey* (1982), 68 C.C.C. (2d) 394 (S.C.C.).
2 *Phipson on Evidence*, 10th ed. (London, Sweet and Maxwell, 1963), p. 495. See also *Cross on Evidence*, p. 448.
3 *Sherrard v. Jacob*, [1965] N.I. 151 (N.I. C.A.), noted in *Graat*. See also *R. v. Abdi* (1997), 116 C.C.C. (3d) 385 (Ont. C.A.) wherein it was held that section 8 of the *Canada Evidence Act* does not do away with the common law rule permitting the trier-of-fact to make handwriting comparisons without the assistance of experts.
4 *R. v. Graat* (1982), 2 C.C.C. (3d) 365 (S.C.C.).
5 *R. v. Hill* (1986), 17 O.A.C. 309 (Ont. C.A.).
6 *Sherrard v. Jacob, supra*; *R. v. Graat, supra*.
7 *Ibid.*
8 *Ibid.*
9 *Ibid.*
10 *Ibid.*
11 *Ibid.*
12 (1947), 89 C.C.C. 90 (Ont. C.A.). *German* involved the issue of whether the appellant was intoxicated and in a condition to drive.

The leading case on the issue of layman proffering opinion testimony is from the Supreme Court in *R. v. Graat*.[13] The issue was whether the police officer could give a non-expert opinion as to whether the appellant's ability to drive was impaired. Justice Dickson stated that he saw no reason why a lay person should not be permitted to testify in the form of an opinion, if by doing so, he is able to more accurately express the facts he perceived. He went on to state that "there is little virtue in any distinction resting on the tenuous, and frequently false, antithesis between fact and opinion. The line between fact and opinion is not clear." Justice Dickson was no doubt referring to the line of thinking that a witness must give the facts and not their inferences, conclusions or opinions.[14] He saw no reason why a layperson should not be permitted to give an opinion if he could more accurately express the facts he perceived. He rejected the ultimate issue doctrine, i.e. that the witness would be usurping the function of the trier of fact by giving the opinion in this case. When a layperson is giving an opinion he is making a "compendious statement of fact". . . . "rolling into a statement of opinion all their observations."

In *Smith c. Desjardins*[15] the Quebec Court of Appeal reported that "habitual usage, practices or behaviour in a line of business may be established by ordinary witnesses because these are simple facts, facts that a Judge is able to understand and weigh without the help of an expert."

An expert can be called to testify as to facts he or she has observed without providing an opinion based on those facts and therefore is not subject to the opinion evidence rule.

---

13 *Supra.*
14 *Cross on Evidence*, 5th ed. (1979), p. 442.
15 2005 QCCA 1046 at para. 34.

29

Self-Incrimination

THE RIGHT TO SILENCE BEFORE AND AFTER ARREST

Even if not detained or arrested, under the traditional common law rules, individuals have the right, absent statutory requirement otherwise, whether or not to speak to the police.[1] The right to silence which is also protected by the *Charter of Rights* exists at all times against the state, whether or not the individual asserting it is within the state's power of control.[2] There is no legal duty imposed on an individual to speak or co-operate with the police.[3] By answering some of the police questions but not others, an accused does not waive his right to silence even where his inter-action with the police was upon his own initiative.[4] Such silence is rarely probative of guilt.[5] The trial Judge is to instruct the jury that the accused has a right to silence and the jurors may not draw a negative inference from that silence.

However there are circumstances when the right to silence "must bend," such as where that right conflicts with full answer and defence.[6]

---

1 *R. v. Turcotte* (2005), 200 C.C.C. (3d) 289 (S.C.C.). A trial Judge commits reversible error by relying on the failure of the accused to provide an exculpatory version of events on arrest when assessing credibility even where the accused in examination-in-chief has provided an explanation as to why he did not explain his actions immediately to the police upon arrest. See *R. v. Palmer* (2008), 2008 ONCA 797 (Ont. C.A.) (endorsement); *R. v. Rhode* (2009), 246 C.C.C. (3d) 18 (Ont. C.A.) at para. 18.

2 *Ibid.*

3 See *R. v. K. (C.)* (2005), 36 C.R. (6th) 153 (Ont. C.J.).

4 *Ibid.* See also *R. v. Kwandahor-Mensah* (2006), 205 C.C.C. (3d) 321 (Alta. C.A.) where it was held that cross-examination by the Crown about why the accused did not tell much of his evidence in his statement to the police was improper.

5 *Ibid.*

6 *Ibid.*, paras. 48 & 49. In *R. v. Crawford* co-accused blamed each other where the charge was murder and the accused cross-examined his co-accused on the latter's failure to give a statement to the police. The Supreme Court held it was permissible cross-examination

The right against self-incrimination is a personal right protecting the individual's liberty interest and therefore a corporation is not eligible for *Charter* protection, but individual representatives of the corporation may receive the benefit of immunity protection to the extent they are implicated by their own evidence.[7]

Section 11(*c*) of the *Charter* states that any person charged with a criminal offence is not to be compelled to be a witness in proceedings against that person in respect of the offence. This provision is only protection against testimonial compulsion and arises when the person has been charged with a criminal offence.[8]

By virtue of section 4(6) of the *Canada Evidence Act*, the failure of the accused or spouse to testify shall not be subject of comment by the judge of prosecution. However, Counsel for a co-accused is not forbidden from commenting on the accused's failure to testify but that counsel does not have free rein to encourage the jury to speculate or draw unwarranted inferences.[9]

It is improper to cross-examine an accused upon his or her silence when arrested. In *R. v. Symonds*,[10] Martin J.A. of the Ontario Court of Appeal stated:

> It is fundamental that a person charged with a criminal offence has the right to remain silent and a jury is not entitled to draw any inference against an accused because he chooses to exercise that right. We think that, in the absence of some issue arising in the case which makes the statement of an accused, following

---

but on the basis of assessing credibility, not guilt, in the circumstances of the case. Other examples are where "the defence seeks to emphasize the accused's co-operation with the police. See *R. v. Lavallee*, [1980] O.J. No. 540 (Ont. C.A.); where the accused testified that he had denied the charges against him at the time of his arrest: see *R. v. O. (G.A.)* (1997), 200 A.R. 363 (Alta. C.A.); and where silence is relevant to the defence theory of mistaken identity and a flawed police investigation: see *R. v. W. (M.C.)* (2002), 165 C.C.C. (3d) 129 (B.C. C.A.); where the accused failed to disclose his alibi in a timely and adequate manner: see *R. v. Cleghorn* (1995), 100 C.C.C. (3d) 393 (S.C.C.); or might be admissible if inextricably bound up with the narrative or other evidence and cannot easily be extricated. When such is the case it is important that the jury is instructed as to the limited probative value of silence and the dangers of relying on such evidence. See Cut-Throat Defence in Chapter, " Further Limitations and Obligations in Examining Witnesses."

7 *British Columbia (Securities Commission) v. Branch* (1995), 97 C.C.C. (3d) 505 (S.C.C.); *R. v. Amway of Canada Ltd./Amway du Canada Ltée* (1989), 68 C.R. (3d) 97 (S.C.C.).

8 *R. v. Altseimer* (1982), 1 C.C.C. (3d) 7 (Ont. C.A.); *R. v. Wigglesworth*, [1987] 2 S.C.R. 541 at 561 (S.C.C.). Because section 11(c) is testimonial only it does not apply to physical evidence. See A-M Boisvert "The Role of the Accused in the Criminal Process". The *Canadian Charter of Rights and Freedoms*, 3d ed. (Toronto, Carswell, 1996).

9 *R. v. Naglik* (1991), 65 C.C.C. (3d) 272 (Ont. C.A.), reversed (1993), 83 C.C.C. (3d) 526 (S.C.C.).

10 (1983), 38 C.R. (3d) 51 at 54 (Ont. C.A.); *R. v. Gottschall* (1983), 10 C.C.C. (3d) 447 (N.S. C.A.); *R. v. Rogers* (March 22, 1989), Doc. CA 693/88 (Ont. C.A.), summarized at 7 W.C.B. (2d) 103.

the giving of a caution, that he has nothing to say relevant to that issue, such evidence is inadmissible. In the present case there was no issue with respect to which the appellant's failure to reply was relevant and the evidence should not have been tendered: see *R. v. Robertson* (1975), 29 C.R.N.S. 141, 21 C.C.C. (2d) 385 (Ont. C.A.).

It would therefore be improper for the Crown to cross-examine the accused as to why she did not give a statement to the police on her arrest and, following a caution, to suggest that the explanation given at trial is the first time she told someone in authority what happened.[11] The fact that an accused did not ask why he was arrested cannot be used as evidence of guilt. Following an arrest an accused is not obliged to make any statement.[12] The accused's silence in the face of the police accusations is inadmissible in the absence of any issue raised by the defence.[13] The Crown should not lead evidence from the arresting officer that the accused did not make a statement as the accused has the right to remain silent.[14]

In *R. v. Cones*[15] the accused was charged with certain driving offences resulting in striking a man in a parking lot. His defence was that his actions were the result of panic reacting to two youths who approached him for money and punched him when he refused. Upon arrest he did not make a statement to the police. At trial the Crown was permitted to cross-examine the accused on his failure to complain to the police about being a victim of a criminal offence on the basis that this was not the same as being asked about the accused's failure to give a statement to the police as an accused. The Ontario Court of Appeal held that the question was impermissible. The accused had no obligation to report a crime. The trial Judge's ruling turned the accused's silence after being cautioned into a trap.

In *R. v. Creighton*,[16] Sopinka J., while recognizing that the exercise by the defendant of his right to pre-trial silence cannot be evidence of guilt as it may be due to factors such as a caution or advice by counsel, held that an accused is entitled to cross-examine on a co-accused's silence "to dispel the

---

11 *R. v. Chambers* (1989), 47 C.C.C. (3d) 503 (B.C. C.A.). In *R. v. Turcotte* (2004), 184 C.C.C. (3d) 242 (B.C. C.A.), application for leave to appeal to the Supreme Court of Canada filed May 20, 2004 (Court file no. 3039), it was held that because the accused had not been detained did not detract from or deflect the argument that it was wrong in law to instruct the jury that an inference of guilt could be made as a result of the accused's failure to respond to questions by the police. The accused's right to silence was engaged and infringed by the police in the circumstances.

12 *R. v. Hunter* (2001), 155 C.C.C. (3d) 225, 54 O.R. (3d) 695 (Ont. C.A.).

13 *R. v. Robertson* (1975), 21 C.C.C. (2d) 385 (Ont. C.A.), leave to appeal refused (1975), 21 C.C.C. (2d) 385 (note) (S.C.C.); *R. v. Wojcik* (2002), 166 C.C.C. (3d) 418 (Man. C.A.).

14 *R. v. Noble*, [1997] 1 S.C.R. 874 at 918, 114 C.C.C. (3d) 385 (S.C.C.). See also *R. v. Schell* (2000), 148 C.C.C. (3d) 219 (Ont. C.A.).

15 (2000), 143 C.C.C. (3d) 355 (Ont. C.A.). In this scenario the Crown was alleging recent fabrication by the accused.

16 (Sub nom. *R. v. Crawford*), [1995] 1 S.C.R. 858, 96 C.C.C. (3d) 481 at 500 (S.C.C.).

evidence which implicates him emanating from his co-accused."[17] In *Creighton*, Sopinka J. sets out some rules for the trial Judge as follows:

1. that the co-accused, who has testified against the accused, had the right to pre-trial silence and not to have the exercise of that right used as evidence as of innocence or guilt;
2. that the accused implicated by the evidence of the co-accused has the right to make full answer and defence, including the right to attack the credibility of the co-accused;
3. that the accused, implicated by the evidence of the co-accused, had the right, therefore, to attack the credibility of the co-accused by reference to the latter's failure to disclose the evidence to the investigating authorities;
4. that this evidence is not to be used as positive evidence on the issue of innocence or guilt to draw an inference of consciousness of guilt or otherwise;
5. that the evidence could be used as one factor in determining whether the evidence of the co-accused is to be believed. The failure to make a statement prior to trial may reflect on the credibility of the accused or it may be due to other factors such as the effect of a caution or the advice of counsel. If the jury concluded that such failure was due to a factor that did not reflect on the credibility of the accused, then it must not be given any weight.

Where an accused who is detained advises police that he or she does not wish to speak to them, the police are not permitted to employ subterfuge to question the accused, as for example, by placing an undercover officer in the cell with the accused to elicit evidence.[18] However, the accused's right to remain silent is not violated if the police do not elicit the evidence.[19] An agent of the state may also violate one's right to silence.[20]

The questioning of a suspect who is not under arrest but who advises that he or she does not wish to say anything on the basis of legal advice does not violate the individual's right to silence provided there is not oppressive persistence in the questioning.[21] Voluntariness is not affected and

---

17 *Ibid.*
18 *R. v. Hebert*, [1990] 2 S.C.R. 151, 57 C.C.C. (3d) 1 (S.C.C.).
19 *Ibid.*
20 *R. v. Broyles* (1991), 68 C.C.C. (3d) 308 (S.C.C.). This case defines who is an agent of the state.
21 In *R. v. Singh*, [2007] 3 S.C.R. 405 (S.C.C.) the Supreme Court held that "it is not appropriate to impose a rigid requirement that police refrain from questioning a detainee who states that he or she does not wish to speak to the police," but the case also holds that persistent questioning when there is repeated assertions of the right to silence may lead to the conclusion that an obtained statement was not the result of a free will to speak. In *R. v. Anderson* (2009), 243 C.C.C. (3d) 134 (Alta. C.A.), leave to appeal refused (2010), 2010 CarswellAlta 2265 (S.C.C.), the Alberta Court of Appeal held that it is permissible for the police during an interview to "out manoeuvre" the accused by persuading him to speak. In *R. v. Ford*, 1994 CarswellOnt 168 (Ont. C.A.), it was held that by the police falsely telling the accused that the interview will be off the record, which was relied on by the accused, will violate the accused's right to silence.

there is no infringement of any constitutional right.[22] But where an accused asserts his right to remain silent and expresses a wish to speak to counsel and no situation of urgency exists, all questioning should cease until there is an opportunity to consult counsel.[23]

Counsel should refer to Chapter, "Client and Witness Interviews (Should Your Client Give a Statement to the Police?)" which describes in part how far police tactics are sanctioned by the Supreme Court in obtaining statements with particular reference to *R. v. Oickle* (2000), 147 C.C.C. (3d) 321 (S.C.C.); *R. v. Sinclair* (2010), 259 C.C.C. (3d) 443 (S.C.C.); *R. v. Singh* (2007), 225 C.C.C. (3d) 103 (S.C.C.).

Although the trier-of-fact is not ordinarily entitled to draw an adverse inference from an accused's refusal to make a statement,[24] the courts have sanctioned adverse comment where there has been a refusal to submit to a psychiatric examination by a Crown psychiatrist and insanity or mental disorder is raised as a defence,[25] or where there was a refusal to participate in a line-up when identification procedures are challenged.[26] But there is no legal obligation for an accused to participate in a line-up.[27] Lamer J. in *R. v. Leclair*,[28] noted that since an accused has no legal obligation to participate in a line-up but failure to do so could have prejudicial consequences respecting the evidence that could be admitted at trial, an accused should be allowed access to his or her lawyer for advice as to his or her rights which might entail not participating unless given a photograph of the line-up or not to participate if others in the line-up were obviously older. In *Marcoux v. R.*[29] it was held that because the accused made something out of the fact that the police did not hold a line-up, his refusal to participate made such refusal admissible, when otherwise it would not be.

---

22 *R. v. Hicks* (1990), 54 C.C.C. (3d) 575 (S.C.C.).

23 *R. v. Manninen* (1987), 34 C.C.C. (3d) 385 at 393 (S.C.C.), affirming *R. v. Manninen* (1983), 8 C.C.C. (3d) 193 (Ont. C.A.).

24 *R. v. McIlvride* (1986), 29 C.C.C. (3d) 348 (B.C. C.A.); *R. v. Hawke* (1975), 22 C.C.C. (2d) 19 (Ont. C.A.).

25 *R. v. Sweeney (No. 2)* (1977), 35 C.C.C. (2d) 245 (Ont. C.A.). See also *R. v. Stevenson* (1990), 58 C.C.C. (3d) 464 (Ont. C.A.); *R. v. Worth* (1995), 23 O.R. (3d) 211 (Ont. C.A.).

26 *R. v. Marcoux (No. 2)* (1975), 24 C.C.C. (2d) 1 (S.C.C.). In *R. v. Shortreed* (1990), 54 C.C.C. (3d) 292 (Ont. C.A.), it was held that where the Crown can reasonably anticipate that the defence would challenge the identification procedures or the trial judge or defence would make adverse comments on the unexplained absence of an identification parade and the danger of a courtroom identification, the Crown may explain to the jury the failure to hold an identification parade in order to prevent the jury from drawing an adverse inference against the Crown's case.

27 *R. v. Leclair* (1989), 67 C.R. (3d) 209 (S.C.C.).

28 *Ibid.*

29 (1975), 24 C.C.C. (2d) 1 (S.C.C.).

In *Leclair*, *supra*, it was held that blood taken from an accused without his consent was self-incrimination.[30]

SECTION 5 OF THE *CANADA EVIDENCE ACT*:

5. (1) No witness shall be excused from answering any question on the ground that the answer to the question may tend to criminate him, or may tend to establish his liability to a civil proceeding at the instance of the Crown or of any person.

(2) Where with respect to any question a witness objects to answer on the ground that his answer may tend to criminate him, or may tend to establish his liability to a civil proceeding at the instance of the Crown or of any person, and if but for this Act, or the Act of any provincial legislature, the witness would therefore have been excused from answering the question, then although the witness is by reason of this Act or the provincial Act compelled to answer, the answer so given shall not be used or admissible in evidence against him in any criminal trial or other criminal proceeding against him thereafter taking place, other than a prosecution for perjury in the giving of that evidence or for the giving of contradictory evidence. R.S., c. C-5, s. 5; 1997, c. 18, s. 116.

Notwithstanding the witness's invocation of section 5, she must answer the question posed. However, in return the section offers protection against the state's subsequent of the incriminating answers in criminal proceedings.[31] In asking for section 5(2) protection, no specific words are required, as long as the Court is made aware that the witness wishes to avoid incrimination and the Judge at the subsequent trial will be able to recognize the claim and identify the relevant answers.[32]

The protection in section 5 can only be requested with respect to questions thought to be truly incriminating.[33] The protection is to be requested before the witness answers, not after.[34] However this protection cannot be determined at the point in time when the evidence is given, but at the subsequent proceeding when the evidence is tendered.[35] When the prior evidence was incriminating when it was given, its subsequent use is to be totally prohibited, even if it was tendered for the limited purpose of

---

30 See *R. v. Pohoretsky* (1987), 33 C.C.C. (3d) 398 (S.C.C.) and *R. v. Dyment* (1988), 45 C.C.C. (3d) 244 (S.C.C.).

31 *R. v. S. (R.J.)*, [1995] 1 S.C.R. 451 (S.C.C.) at para. 66; *R. c. Noël* (2002), 168 C.C.C. (3d) 193 (S.C.C.) at paras. 22, 36.

32 *R. v. Kuldip* (1988), 40 C.C.C. (3d) 11 (Ont. C.A.), reversed [1990] 3 S.C.R. 618 (S.C.C.), however Justice Martin's interpretation was adopted by Arbour J. in *R. c. Noël, supra*. In *R. c. Côté* (1979), 50 C.C.C. (2d) 564 (Que. C.A.), leave to appeal refused (1979), 50 C.C.C. (2d) 564n (S.C.C.) it was found sufficient to invoke section 5(2) by merely stating: "I ask the protection of the Court."

33 *R. v. Noël* (2002), 168 C.C.C. (3d) 193 (S.C.C.).

34 *R. v. Vigeant* (1982), 3 C.C.C. (3d) 445 (Que. C.A.) at pp. 453-54, leave to appeal refused (1982), 3 C.C.C. (3d) 445n (S.C.C.). However section 13 of the *Charter* applies.

35 *Ibid.*

testing credibility, unless there is no real danger of incrimination.[36] If the prior evidence was not incriminating, it may be used to challenge credibility in another proceeding.[37]

In my experience the courts accept the practice that the witness does not have to invoke section 5 at every question that he/she feels is incriminating, but only make a blanket objection for each series of questions, i.e., I object to answering the question on the grounds that my answer may incriminate me or establish my liability in a civil proceeding.[38] The judge has no authority to grant or withhold his/her consent as it is the invocation of the Act which confers the protection.[39]

The Crown is not allowed to cross-examine the accused on his/her knowledge of the protections afforded by section 5 of the *Canada Evidence Act* as this question does not shed any light on the truthfulness of the witness's answer.[40]

The accused may be cross-examined on testimony she gave at an earlier proceeding where the purpose is to impeach credit and not to incriminate the accused.[41]

SECTION 13 OF THE *CHARTER OF RIGHTS AND FREEDOMS*

Section 13 states:

A witness who testifies in any proceedings has the right not to have any incriminating evidence so given used to incriminate that witness in any other proceedings, except in a prosecution for perjury or for the giving of contradictory evidence.

Unlike section 5(2) of the *Canada Evidence Act* section 13 does not necessitate any obligation to object to answering the question.

A *voir dire* is another proceeding and so the accused's testimony therein cannot be the subject of cross-examination by the Crown on the trial proper.[42] Section 13 is breached by a police officer testifying that he could identify the accused as a result of him testifying in another proceeding.[43]

In *R. v. Jabarianha*, [2001] 3 S.C.R. 430 (S.C.C.) the Supreme Court held that the Crown should rarely be allowed to cross-examine a witness on his knowledge of section 13 because of its prejudicial effect. Such cross-

---

36 *Ibid.*
37 *Ibid.*
38 *Ibid.*
39 *Ibid.*
40 *Ibid.*
41 *Ibid.*
42 *R. v. Tarafa* (1989), 53 C.C.C. (3d) 472 (Que. S.C.).
43 *R. v. Skinner* (1988), 42 C.C.C. (3d) 575 (Ont. C.A.). See also *R. v. Sicurella* (1997), 120 C.C.C (3d) 403 (Ont. Prov. Div.).

examination may be permitted in the rare circumstance where the Crown is able to provide some evidence of a plot to lie or to obtain favours as the probative value could outweigh its prejudicial effect.[44]

Use and Derivative Use Immunity

The Supreme Court decision in *R. v. Henry* (2005), 202 C.C.C. (3d) 449 revisited its previous decisions relating to use and derivative use immunity from a perspective of self-incrimination as a consequence of section 13 of the *Charter*. The decision in *Henry* basically upholds the *quid pro quo* that when an individual is compelled by the state to testify in a proceeding and may suffer a risk of self-incrimination, the witness will be given protection against subsequent use of that testimony by the state against the witness. The Crown would be unable to use that prior compelled statement as evidence in criminal proceedings to incriminate the witness or impeach his credibility, except in a prosecution for perjury or for giving inconsistent evidence.

The Supreme Court in *Henry* does reject its previous decision in *R. v. Mannion*, [1986] 2 S.C.R. 272 which immunized an accused who had given voluntary evidence at his trial from being cross-examined by the Crown on his evidence given in his prior trial. As the accused was not a compelled witness, the *quid pro quo* does not apply, so that if the accused testifies at a prior proceeding and later at his own trial he is liable to be cross-examined on his evidence at the prior proceeding not only to challenge his credibility (which negates the ruling in *R. v. Kuldip*, [1990] 3 S.C.R. 618) but also can be used to demonstrate the guilt of the witness.

Where the Crown compels the evidence of a co-accused separately charged that compelled testimony cannot be used for any purpose against this co-accused at his own trial.[45]

In *R. v. S. (R.J.)*[46] the Supreme Court held that "derivative evidence which could not have been obtained, or the significance of which could not have been appreciated but for the testimony of the witness, is generally to be excluded under section 7 of the *Charter* in the interest of trial fairness." The burden is on the accused to show that the proposed evidence is derivative evidence deserving of immunity protection.

S. (R.J.) also decided that an exemption from testifying could be granted to the person compelled to testify if that person could establish that the "predominant purpose" of the testimony was to incriminate the accused

---

44   See also *R. c. Noël* (2002), 168 C.C.C. (3d) 193 (S.C.C.); *Re Swick* (1997), 118 C.C.C. (3d) 33 (Ont. C.A.).

45   *R. c. Noël, supra.*

46   (1995), 96 C.C.C. (3d) 1 (S.C.C); *British Columbia (Securities Commission) v. Branch* (1995), 97 C.C.C. (3d) 505 (S.C.C.).

compelled to testify. Is the purpose in calling the witness of "slight importance" to the proceedings in which it is sought to have the witness testify, but of "great importance" to incriminate the witness being compelled to testify? The burden of proof is on the witness who claims the purpose of compelling or to testify is a legitimate one.[47]

The Supreme Court in *Henry*, accepting that a retrial on the same charge or any included offences qualified as "other proceedings" in section 13, upheld the decision in *R. v. Dubois*,[48] which held that the Crown's introduction in-chief of a transcript of the accused's evidence given at his first trial resulted in the accused being compelled at his retrial to being a witness against himself, in violation of section 13 of the *Charter*.

Statutory Compulsion

In *R. v. White*[49] the accused was required by section 61(1) of the *Motor Vehicle Act*, R.S.B.C. to provide information to the person receiving the report. It was held that the statements made under compulsion of section 61(1) are inadmissible in criminal proceedings as their admission would violate the principle against self-incrimination as guaranteed by section 7 of the *Charter*. *White* holds that section 7 does not provide absolute protection for an accused against all uses of information that has been compelled by statute. In *White* the context of the case reflected that the use of the statements would violate the principles of fundamental justice. The statements taken under section 61 are taken in the context of pronounced psychological and emotional pressure. The spontaneous utterances of a driver shortly after an accident are exactly the type of communications that the principle of self-incrimination was designed to protect and the declarant is entitled to use immunity. The test for compulsion is whether at the time the driver reported the accident she gave the report on the basis of an honest and reasonably held belief that she was required by law to report the accident to the person to whom the report was given. It is the accused who must establish on the balance of probabilities the statement was compelled.

---

47 *British Columbia (Securities Commission) v. Branch, supra.*

48 (1985), 22 C.C.C. (3d) 513 (S.C.C.).

49 (1999), 135 C.C.C. (3d) 257 (S.C.C.). See also *R. v. Fitzpatrick* (1995), 102 C.C.C. (3d) 144 (S.C.C.) where it was held that the evidence was inadmissible as the accused's action in filling out fishing logs as a condition of participating in a regulated industry were voluntary and not compelled with respect to a charge of over fishing. There was no adversarial aspect to the process which involved enforcement proceedings in a regulatory context of the fishing industry in British Columbia. The process was not criminal and one which was ultimately beneficial to the fisherman. See also *R. v. Wighton* (2003), 176 C.C.C. (3d) 550 (Ont. C.J.), Weinper J., where use of force reports by police required to be made by provincial legislation held to be inadmissible.

PROTECTED STATEMENTS

By virtue of section 672.21(1) and section 672.21(2) of the *Criminal Code* no statement or reference to a statement by an accused is admissible in evidence when it has been made during the course of and for the purposes of an assessment or treatment directed by a disposition, to the person specified in the assessment order or the disposition, or to anyone acting under that person's direction, unless with consent of the accused. There are seven exceptions listed in subsection (3), one of which is when the credibility of the accused is challenged because the testimony of the accused is inconsistent in a material particular with the protected statement the accused made previously.

BODY INCRIMINATION

Where the police do not have the statutory authority to demand a hair or blood sample, they can only be taken with the consent of the suspect.[50] The consent must be a fully informed consent which includes knowledge of the use that will be made of the sample.[51] When there has not been an attack on the police procedures regarding the failure to take blood or hair samples, evidence of the accused's failure to supply such samples was held to be inadmissible.[52]

If the accused is compelled to incriminate himself or herself by a statement or use of his or her body the evidence will be considered as conscriptive and therefore in conflict with the primary aim in considering the fairness of the trial under section 24(2) of the *Charter*.[53]

Roadside co-ordination tests for the purpose of obtaining reasonable and probable grounds to justify a demand for a breathalyzer test cannot be used at trial on a charge of impaired driving as it is compelled and self-incriminating evidence and would render the trial unfair.[54]

---

50 *R. v. Arp* (1998), 129 C.C.C. (3d) 321 (S.C.C.); *R. v. Stillman* (1997), 113 C.C.C. (3d) 321 (S.C.C.).

51 *R. v. Borden* (1994), 92 C.C.C. (3d) 404 (S.C.C.), per Iacobucci J.

52 *R. v. Fyfe* (1983), 7 C.C.C. (3d) 284 (N.W.T. C.A.). The *Criminal Code* section 254 provides for the taking of blood and breath samples in impaired driving cases. Sections 487.04 to 487.09 allow for obtaining search warrants to seize bodily substances for forensic DNA analysis in generally serious bodily injury cases.

53 *R. v. Jensen* (1997), [1997] S.C.J. No. 15, 1997 CarswellOnt 201, 1997 CarswellOnt 202 (S.C.C.).

54 *R. v. Milne* (1996), 107 C.C.C. (3d) 118 (Ont. C.A.); *R. c. Roy* (1997), 1997 CarswellQue 408, [1997] A.Q. No. 1074 (Qué. C.A.).

Observing an accused and taking photographs or videotaping accused, even if accused objects to being photographed, so long as it is done unobtrusively does not offend the principle against self-incrimination.[55]

The *Criminal Code* section 487.05 provides for when a judge may issue a warrant for taking of bodily substances for DNA analysis and sections 487.051 to 487.091 provides for the collection of bodily substances from offenders for DNA analysis. However different principles apply when young offenders are involved. The assumption that for adult offenders it would be in the best interests of the administration of justice to make a DNA order in the vast majority of cases does not apply with respect to young offenders. The Judge should consider each of the three factors in section 487.051(3) of the *Criminal Code*.[56]

---

55 *R. v. Dilling* (1993), 84 C.C.C. (3d) 325 (B.C. C.A.); *R. v. Parsons* (1993), 84 C.C.C. (3d) 226 (Ont. C.A.); *R. v. Shortreed* (1990), 54 C.C.C. (3d) 292 (Ont. C.A.).
56 *R. v. B. (K.)* (2003), 67 O.R. (3d) 391 (Ont. C.A.).

30

Similar Fact Evidence

R. v. Handy, "A New Start"

The admissibility of "similar fact" or "similar act evidence" is an exception to the general principle that prevents the prosecution from leading evidence of an accused's bad character. Where such evidence is not introduced as part of the Crown's case either because the Crown chooses not to introduce it or because it has been ruled inadmissible, it becomes admissible if the accused leads evidence of good character, and so defence counsel must be alert to this potential if it is intended to call evidence of good character on behalf of the client. See Chapter, "Character Evidence."

The admissibility of similar fact evidence is now governed by the Supreme Court decision in *R. v. Handy*.[1] *Handy* represents a new start for understanding similar fact evidence which previously found its provenance in *Makin v. A.-G for New South Wales*.[2] The acres of similar fact case law that followed *Makin* was often difficult to reconcile, which has fortunately and finally resulted in the *Handy* decision. Justice Rosenberg of the Ontario Court of Appeal has observed that *Handy* should be the last occasion where any trial or appellate Court needs to go back to *Makin* to discuss or explain similar fact evidence. "It is without doubt the most important decision on this issue."[3]

In *R. v. Handy* the accused was charged with sexual assault, the allegation being that original consensual sex escalated into non-consensual vaginal and anal intercourse accompanied by physical abuse. The accused's defence was that the sexual activities were consensual and there was no violence. The Crown led evidence of seven occurrences where the accused committed similar sexual abuse in order to demonstrate that the accused had a propensity to engage in this type of sex and would not take "no" for

---

1 (2002), 164 C.C.C. (3d) 481 (Ont. C.A.).
2 (2000), 145 C.C.C. (3d) 177 (Ont. C.A.).
3 *Ibid.*

an answer. It was part of the Crown's argument that this evidence supported the credibility of the complainant with respect to the issue of consent. The defence position was that the complainant and her ex-spouse had colluded to fabricate this evidence to obtain money from the Criminal Injuries Compensation Board. The trial Judge left the issue of collusion up to the jury. The accused was convicted of sexual assault. The Supreme Court of Canada agreed with the Ontario Court of Appeal that this similar fact evidence had been wrongly admitted.

Handy holds that: ". . .the onus is on the prosecution to satisfy the trial Judge on a balance of probabilities that in the context of the particular case the probative value of the evidence in relation to a particular issue outweighs its potential prejudice and thereby justifies its reception.[4]

The Supreme Court ruled that prior discreditable acts by the accused is "presumptively inadmissible" because it creates the danger that the trier-of-fact might become confused by the multiplicity of incidents giving the evidence more weight than it logically deserves (reasoning prejudice); and, it risks the possibility that the trier-of-fact will find the accused guilty not on the basis of what he or she did with respect to the present charge, but because the accused is a bad person (moral prejudice).[5]

The Supreme Court ruled, however, that evidence of prior similar discreditable conduct can be "so highly relevant and cogent that its probative value in the search for truth outweighs any potential misuse."[6] In other words, there are cases where it would offend common sense, absent some innocent explanation, to suggest that the similarities are the result of the improbable coincidence.[7] Where prior discreditable conduct evidence is a propensity of the accused such evidence may be admitted where the Crown can establish, on the balance of probabilities that the probative value of the evidence in relation to an issue is so high that the significant prejudice suffered is outweighed by the probative value of the evidence.[8]

The Supreme Court found that it was very important for the Crown at the outset to identify the issue that the similar fact evidence relates to. In order to be admissible similar fact evidence must relate to some controversial issue in the case, not just the disposition of the accused as being of bad character and more likely to have committed the offence, and its probative

---

4   *R. v. Handy, supra*, at para. 55.
5   *R. v. Handy, supra*, at paras. 31-36.
6   *R. v. Handy, supra*, at paras. 41-46.
7   *R. v. Handy, supra*, at paras. 76-80. See also *R. v. Trochym* (2007), 216 C.C.C. (3d) 225 (S.C.C.) at paras. 72, 78 and *R. v. Arp* (1998), 129 C.C.C. (3d) 321 (S.C.C.) at para. 48. See also *R. v. James* (2006), 213 C.C.C. (3d) 235 (Ont. C.A.) at para. 39, leave to appeal refused (2007), 2007 CarswellOnt 6162 (S.C.C.).
8   *R. v. Handy, supra*, at paras. 49-55

value must outweigh its prejudicial effect.[9] Identifying the sole issue as the credibility of the complainant will not suffice.[10] And even though the similar fact may be very probative of the issue in question it must also be capable of belief before it can be admitted. Normally, frailties in the evidence would be left to the trier-of-fact. But where admissibility is bound up with, and dependent upon, probative value, the credibility of the similar fact evidence is a factor that the trial Judge is entitled to take into consideration. And where the ultimate assessment of credibility is for the jury and not the Judge, this evidence was potentially too prejudicial to be admitted unless the Judge was of the view that it met the threshold of being reasonably capable of belief.[11] In *R. v. Fiorino*[12] the Court held that where the Crown tenders similar fact evidence for multiple purposes, the trial Judge must decide which issues "predominate" in order to "correctly weigh the probative value of the evidence against its prejudical effect."

The Court concluded that there must be a high degree of similarity where the evidence is led to prove the identity of the accused. If the evidence is to prove motive, or the commission or the *actus reus* of the offence then the standard of admissibility is "different."[13]

Some Connecting and Countervailing Factors

Binnie J., pointing to the case law, referred to some factors connecting the similar facts to the circumstances set out in the charge as follows:[14]

(1) proximity in time of the similar acts;
(2) extent to which the other acts are similar in detail to the charged conduct;

---

9 *R. v. Handy, supra,* at paras. 69-75. See also *R. v. B. (F.F.)* (1993), 79 C.C.C. (3d) 112 (S.C.C.). See also *R. v. Johnson* (2010), 2010 ONCA 646 (Ont. C.A.) at para. 92.

10 *R. v. Handy, supra,* at paras. 115-116.

11 *R. v. Handy, supra,* at para. 134.

12 (2008), 233 C.C.C. (3d) 293 (Ont. C.A.).

13 See *R. v. Arp, supra,* para. 45 where phrases such as "unique trademark or signature" and "strikingly similar" were used. In *R. v. Straffen,* [1952] 2 Q.B. 911 (Eng. Q.B.) it was stated that "although the similar fact evidence is not admissible to show a propensity to commit crimes, or even crimes of a particular class, evidence of a propensity to commit a particular crime in a particular and distinctive way was admissible and sufficient to identify [*Straffen*] as the killer of the deceased." (paras. 76, 77)

14 *R. v. Handy, supra,* at paras. 81, 82. In *R. v. Shearing, infra,* at para. 60, Binnie J. observed that it is not the task of the trial Judge to simply "add up similarities and dissimilarities and then, like an accountant, derive a net balance. The list described by Binnie J. was not meant to be exhaustive. The connecting factors depend on the circumstances of the case. In *R. v. Shearing, infra,* at para. 48, the Supreme Court held that the connection should be to a "persuasive degree."

(3) the number of occurrences of the similar acts;[15]
(4) circumstances surrounding or relating to the similar acts;
(5) any distinctive features unifying the incidents;
(6) intervening events;
(7) any other factor which would tend to support to rebut the underlying unity of the similar acts.[16]

Binnie J. noted that the cogency of similar fact evidence becomes stronger when the scenario moves from a general type of propensity towards a more "situation-specific propensity and there is repeated conduct in a highly specific type of situation."[17]

However, the Court noted certain "countervailing factors" which have been found helpful in assessing the prejudice, namely the inflammatory nature of the similar acts and whether the Crown was able to make its point with less prejudicial evidence. Binnie J. noted that the Court was required to take into account the potential distraction of the trier-of-fact from its proper focus on the facts charged, and the potential for undue time consumption.[18]

Not every dissimilarity is fatal but substantial dissimilarities may dilute probative strength and, by compounding the confusion and distraction, aggravate the prejudice.

The strength of the similar fact evidence as to probative value does not have to be so high that it conclusively points to guilt. However the weight of evidence, including credibility and the relevance of the evidence is to be assessed by the trial Judge.[19]

In *R. v. MacCormack*[20] the Ontario Court of Appeal observed that the "similarity issue that lies at the threshold of the decision about the admissibility of evidence of similar acts is to be based on an examination of the acts themselves. After all, it is the high degree of similarity between or among the acts that overcomes the improbability of coincidence . . . In general, the similarity issue is to be decided without reference to evidence linking the accused to each alleged similar act (linkage evidence). . ." "Like the similarity requirement, which indicates a common perpetrator of the similar acts, a demonstrated link between the accused and the similar acts is not sufficient. . ."

---

15 An alleged pattern of conduct may be significant because of their numbers. *R. v. Handy, supra*, para. 128. Depending on the circumstances, repetition may be more cogent than distinctiveness. *R. v. Handy*, para. 131.
16 In *R. v. Shearing* (2002), 165 C.C.C. (3d) 225 (S.C.C.).
17 *R. v. Handy, supra*, at paras. 85-93.
18 *R. v. Handy, supra*, at para. 83.
19 *R. v. Handy, supra*, at paras. 99, 102, 104-107, 134.
20 (2009), 241 C.C.C. (3d) 516 (Ont. C.A.) at paras. 57, 59.

It is insufficient for the Crown to point to some past conflict between the accused and a victim and then speculate that it established motive. This does nothing more than to inject the bad character of the accused and is inadmissible as its prejudicial value exceeds any small probative value it might have.[21]

Collusion

Binnie J. noted that he "would not agree. . .that suspected collusion would play less strongly against otherwise powerful evidence than in a borderline case. In that sense, suspected collusion is more than just another "factor." Cogency is derived from the improbability of coincidence. Collusion is a factor, yes, but more than that it is a crucial factor because the existence of collusion rebuts the premise on which admissibility depends." He noted that in *Handy* the evidence went beyond mere "opportunity," which will be a feature in many cases alleging sexual abuse with multiple complainants. "The issue is concoction or collaboration, not contact. If the evidence amounts to no more than opportunity, it will usually best be left to the jury." In *Handy* there was something more. A test for the admission of the similar fact evidence is based on probability, not reasonable doubts. Where there is some evidence of actual collusion, or at least an "air of reality" to the allegations the Crown is required to satisfy the Judge on the balance of probabilities that the evidence of similar facts is not tainted with collusion.[22] Having done that it would then be for the jury to decide on its weight. It is not sufficient that the Crown just offer "dicey evidence that it believed would have probative value." There is no onus on the defence to prove collusion. The Crown must prove that the probative value of the proffered evidence outweighs its prejudicial effect. In *Handy* it was found that the trial Judge erred in law in leaving the whole issue of collusion to the jury.[23]

---

21 *R. Johnson, supra,* at paras. 97-101, 120.

22 In *R. v. B. (C.)* (2003), 171 C.C.C. (3d) 159 (Ont. C.A.) at para. 40, the Court held that collusion "can arise both from a deliberate agreement to concoct evidence" as well as "from communication among witnesses that can have the effect whether consciously or unconsciously, of coloring and tailoring their descriptions of the impugned events." In *R. v. F. (J.)* (2003), 177 C.C.C. (3d) 1 (Ont. C.A.) at para. 77, Feldman J. noted that collusion can have the effect of tainting a witness's evidence and perception of events innocently or accidentally and unknowingly, as well as deliberately and intentionally. It can arise by the influence of hearing other people's stories which can color one's interpretation of personal events or reinforce a perception.

23 *R. v. Handy, supra,* at paras. 111-113.

Prejudice

In assessing the prejudicial impact of similar fact evidence the Court in *Handy* observed that "the poisonous potential of similar fact evidence cannot be doubted." "It is as close as a Judge comes to single-handedly deciding the outcome of a case."[24] "In the end, the verdict may be based on prejudice rather than proof, thereby undermining the presumption of innocence enshrined in sections 7 and 11(d) of the *Canadian Charter of Rights and Freedoms*.[25] In looking to the moral prejudice of the evidence, there is the risk that there will be an "unfocused trial" that will result in a "wrongful conviction" based upon "prejudice rather than proof," and based on an inference of guilt from the "discreditable tendencies" of the accused.[26] In considering reasoning prejudice the main concern is that the trier-of-fact will be confused and distracted from its proper focus aggravated by the consumption of time dealing with the allegations of multiple incidents.[27]

In *R. v. Handy* the Supreme Court found that the jury might have been more appalled by the similar fact evidence than by the charges before the Court. The evidence was highly prejudicial and the jury may have been confused in its reasoning process.[28]

Prejudice has been expressed in different ways, as for example: "The jury will misuse the evidence, and convict the person. . .for the wrong reasons . . . after hearing evidence of prior discreditable acts committed by the accused and convict because of a belief that the crimes are more likely committed by those who have committed them in the past. The jury may believe that since the accused committed crimes in the past he or she probably did so again. As stated in *Cross on Evidence*:

> In short, the principle danger is that the jury may concentrate too much upon the moral infirmities of the accused, and too little upon other factors in the case leading to the opposite conclusion. It may be swayed more by revulsion for the accused than persuasion by the rest of evidence.[29]

In addition, after learning of the accused's past and misconduct, the jury may conclude that he has probably committed other discreditable acts that have gone undetected or unpunished, and convict him because of this, whether or not they are satisfied of his guilt on the charge before the Court.

---

24 *R. v. Handy, supra,* at para. 138.

25 *R. v. Handy, supra,* at para. 139.

26 *R. v. Handy, supra,* at paras. 100, 137-143; *R. v. Shearing* (2002), 165 C.C.C. (3d) 225 (S.C.C.); *R. v. Thomas* (2004), 190 C.C.C. (3d) 31 (Ont. C.A.).

27 *R. v. Handy, supra,* at paras. 100, 137-138; 144-146; *R. v. Shearing, supra,* paras. 68-70.

28 The principles governing morally repugnant similar fact evidence are considered in *R. v. C. (M.H.)* (1991), 63 C.C.C. (3d) 385 (S.C.C.). McLachlin J. held that such acts must have a high degree of relevance in order to outweigh potential prejudice.

29 Cross on Evidence (7th ed.) at 358.

Another potential prejudice from the admission of similar fact evidence is that it may cause members of the jury to lose their focus as they try to resolve the issue of the accused's guilt with respect to the prior acts, rather than concentrating on the current charge.

Where the similar fact evidence comes from the same complainant the Court's view that the potential prejudicial impact of that evidence is much reduced while the relevance and probative value is increased.[30] Often sexual abuse crimes involve similar acts committed by the accused on the same victim over a period of years[31] and such conduct has been held to be relevant to show animus towards the victim. However such evidence will not be admissible where the prior incidents are not very similar to the charge before the Court.[32]

Where there is a multi-count indictment and the Crown seeks to have the evidence relating to each count admissible in support of the allegation in the other count, the prejudice is significantly reduced given that each count is before the trier-of-fact in any event, and particularly so when the trial is heard before a Judge knowledgeable in the law and who is expected not to be swayed improperly by any prejudicial aspects of the evidence.[33]

Evidential Link to the Accused

Before any evidence of past misconduct can be admitted, however, it must be shown that the conduct comprising the evidence is in fact conduct of the accused. In other words, there must be a connection between the similar fact evidence sought to be adduced and the accused before the Court.[34] In *R. v. Sweitzer*,[35] for example, the trial judge permitted the Crown

---

30 *R. v. S. (C.J.)* (1996), 137 Nfld. & P.E.I.R. 181 (P.E.I. C.A.) at paras. 71-73, leave to appeal refused (1996), 148 Nfld. & P.E.I.R. 270 (note) (S.C.C.); *R. v. Baptiste* (2000), 2000 CarswellOnt 1594 (Ont. S.C.J.), affirmed (2003), 2003 CarswellOnt 3623 (Ont. C.A.); *R. v. B. (S.)* (1996), 1996 CarswellOnt 1576 (Ont. S.C.J.); *R. v. T. (J.E.)* (1994), 1994 CarswellOnt 3370 (Ont. Gen. Div.).

31 *R. v. S. (H.S.)* (2009), C.C.C. (3d) 262 (Ont. C.A.), per Laskin J.A. at 1-9, 16. See also *R. v. R. (B.S.)* (2006), 212 C.C.C. (3d) 65 (Ont. C.A.) at paras. 29-46; *R. v. Chapman* (2006), 204 C.C.C. (3d) 449 (Ont. C.A.).

32 *R. v. H. (J.)* (2006), 215 C.C.C. (3d) 233 (Ont. C.A.).

33 *R. v. MacCormack* (2009), 2009 CarswellOnt 345 (Ont. C.A.) at paras 56, 68, 69; *R. v. B. (R.T.)* (2009), (*sub nom. R. v. B. (T.)*) 243 C.C.C. (3d) 158 (Ont. C.A.).

34 The standard of proof for similar fact evidence is on a balance of probabilities: *R. v. Simpson* (1977), 35 C.C.C. (2d) 337 (Ont. C.A.).

35 [1982] 5 W.W.R. 555 (S.C.C.). See also *Harris v. D.P.P.*, [1952] 1 All E.R. 1044 (H.L.), a case in which the accused was charged with eight counts of office breaking and larceny, and no connection could be made to the accused with respect to the first seven counts. The Court held that evidence of the seven counts could not be used against the accused on the eighth. See also *R. v. Arp* (1998), 129 C.C.C. (3d) 321 (S.C.C.), holding that where the similar fact evidence is adduced to prove identity a link between the accused and the

to introduce similar fact evidence during a rape trial, consisting of evidence relating to 14 previous incidents of rape, indecent assault and break and enter. A new trial was ordered by the Supreme Court of Canada, however, because although there were some similarities among all the incidents, no connection to the accused could be made with respect to 11 of the episodes. As a result, these episodes could not be relevant to the charge against the accused. McIntyre J. stated that although there may have been a link to the accused with respect to a few incidents, the rest could not be admitted upon their coattails:

> In my view, this is to cast the net too wide in a search for evidence. This line of reasoning could make evidence of any nocturnal rape committed in Calgary in a period of 4 1/2 years, where some similarity could be shown, receivable in evidence against the appellant. I would confine the admission of such evidence to cases where there is some evidentiary link, direct or circumstantial, with the accused.[36]

This point is succinctly phrased by Viscount Simon in *Harris v. D.P.P.*,[37] where he stated ". . . evidence of other occurrences which merely tend to deepen suspicion does not go to prove guilt."[38]

In assessing the strength of connecting factors it is important to look beyond "generic similarities" in the similar fact evidence.[39] In *Blake* the Court held that the similarities of the sexual acts related to non-specific conduct and lacked detail; that "generic similarities" is problematic "because the initial inference arising from the prior conduct approaches bad personhood and may mask underlying dissimilarities that could be important." The Court found there were no "distinctive unifying features" between the tendered similar fact evidence and the testimony of the complainant and the "identified similarities" failed to establish "a pervasive degree of connection."

The Controversial Issues

As indicated earlier, in order to be admissible similar fact evidence must relate to some controversial issue in the case, not just the disposition

---

alleged similar acts is required, disclosing more than a mere possibility that the alleged similar and is that of the accused. See also *R. c. Lacroix* (*sub nom. R. v. Lacroix*) (2008), 2008 CarswellQue 124 (Que. C.A.), reversed on other grounds (2008), 239 C.C.C. (3d) 185, (S.C.C.); *R. v. Anderson* (2003), 179 C.C.C. (3d) 11 (Ont. C.A.) at paras. 27-30.

36 *Ibid.* at 562.
37 *Supra.*
38 *Ibid.* at 1048. See also *R. v. Arp, supra.*
39 *R. v. Blake* (2003), 181 C.C.C. (3d) 169 (Ont. C.A.), affirmed (2004), 188 C.C.C. (3d) 428 (S.C.C.); *R. v. Candale* (2006), 205 C.C.C. (3d) 167 (Ont. C.A.).

of the accused. These controversial issues that similar fact relates to have arisen in the case law prior to *R. v. Handy* which are set out below:

1. Evidence of System or a Pattern of Behaviour

The question as to whether a crime has actually occurred often arises in cases where there is direct testimony against the accused, for example, in cases of sexual assault. In many of these cases, the only evidence that a crime occurred comes from the complainant's testimony alone. The accused in these cases may either be denying that a crime occurred by alleging fabrication, or he may take the position that if a crime did occur, he was not the perpetrator. In conjunction with direct testimony, therefore, evidence may be relevant to show a system or pattern of behaviour exhibited by the accused. It should be noted that when direct testimony is available, the probative force of the similar fact evidence will not need to be as strong to outweigh potential prejudice as in cases where there is no direct testimony,[40] although the potential for concoction or collusion among witnesses will have to be addressed.[41]

R. v. B. (C.R.),[42] is a case where the majority of the Supreme Court of Canada held that similar fact evidence was admissible to support the credibility of the complainant. The complainant, the accused's daughter, testified that the accused sexually assaulted her two or three times a week from the time she was 11 years old until she was 13, and that the acts progressed from fondling to oral sex, to sexual intercourse and buggery. Similar fact evidence was admitted at trial from the daughter of the accused's ex-girlfriend. This witness testified that after the accused lived with them for a year, he made sexual advances towards her, and again, the acts started with fondling and progressed to intercourse, oral sex and masturbation. Mc-Lachlin J. stated that although there were differences between the similar fact evidence and that of the complainant,[43] it was nonetheless sufficient to show, if not a system, at least a pattern of similar behaviour suggesting that the complainant's story was true.[44] Sopinka J. (Lamer J. concurring with

---

40 A sufficient degree of similarity will nevertheless be required to find a connection between the similar fact evidence sought to be adduced and the offence before the Court: See *R. v. Tabas*, 1994 CarswellOnt 3416 (Ont. C.A.).

41 *Cross on Evidence, supra*, at 363.

42 *Supra.* See also *R. v. Handy*, discussed in more detail later in this chapter with respect to similar fact evidence bolstering credibility.

43 For example, the ages of the girls was different, as one was sexually mature while the other was a child; one girl was the accused's natural daughter while the other was not a blood relation; there was a suggestion of urination from the testimony of the accused's daughter which was absent in the similar fact evidence; finally, there was a lengthy period of time between the two alleged incidents.

44 *Ibid.* at 27-28.

dissenting opinion) took issue with the finding that similar fact evidence was admissible because it supported the credibility of the complainant. He stated that this was the same as saying similar fact was admissible because it supported guilt, and this in turn was tantamount to saying that the accused was guilty because he engaged in similar conduct in the past—the inadmissible chain or reasoning.[45] Sopinka J. stated that common features between the similar fact evidence and the acts charged could indeed render it admissible (and thereby be supportive of the complainant), but before such evidence could be found admissible, it would have to be found to be "an affront to common sense" to suggest that, in the absence of collaboration, the similarities were due to coincidence.[46] The dissent's view was that the admission of the evidence in *R. v. B. (C.R.)* was setting the standard of "striking similarity" so low "as to be virtually nonexistent."[47]

In *R. v. Litchfield*,[48] similar fact evidence was admitted to show a distinct pattern of behaviour in connection to a physician charged with 14 counts of sexual assault involving seven of his patients. Although much of the case deals with an order for severance made prior to trial,[49] Iacobucci J. held that the evidence of one complainant was admissible on the counts relating to the other complainants as it tended to show a distinct pattern of behaviour engaged in by the accused. He found that the evidence also shed light on the context in which the alleged offences occurred. Iacobucci J. added that evidence of the same complainant about events occurring on other appointments with the accused did not raise a similar fact issue, as this was simply evidence of the events surrounding the allegations.[50]

---

45 *Ibid.* at 12-13.

46 *Ibid.* at 12-13, adopting the position of Lord Simon in *D.P.P. v. Kilbourne*, [1973] A.C. 729 at 759. See *R. v. Arp* (1998), 129 C.C.C. (3d) 321 (S.C.C.).

47 *Ibid.* at 15, using the phrasing of Lord Wilberforce with respect to the admission of the similar fact evidence in *D.P.P. v. Boardman*, [1975] AC. 421 (H.L.). In *R. v. P. (G.F.)* (1994), 18 O.R. (3d) 1, the Ontario Court of Appeal also had concerns with the admission of similar fact evidence against an accused charged with sexual assault of his daughter, where the evidence was of sexual improprieties occurring 15 years before. The Court ordered a new trial with respect to other issues, but declined to interfere with the trial judge's decision to admit the evidence.

48 (1993), 86 C.C.C. (3d) 97 (S.C.C.).

49 A judge hearing the application for severance (who was not the trial judge, an error in itself) ordered that the allegations be divided according to the body part of the complainant involved in the alleged assault—*i.e.*, one trial for counts involving genitalia, one trial for counts involving breasts and a third trial for any other matters. This had the effect of dividing individual counts, so that separate trials were held for events occurring within the same visit of one complainant. This division and severance was held to have resulted in an injustice (the accused was acquitted), and revealed a misapprehension of the nature of sexual assault on the part of the judge making the order.

50 *Ibid.* at 116-117.

2. Relevant to Intent

Often, the criminality of an act depends upon intent, and in these instances, the prosecution may adduce similar fact evidence to establish the intent required to make out the offence. This evidence may be relevant to rebut a defence offered by an accused, such as accident or belief in consent, or to show a motive, or to prove that the accused has a particular state of knowledge. Below are some examples.

(a) To Show Motive or Continuing Malice

In some cases, particularly those involving an intimate relationship between the accused and the victim or complainant, evidence can be adduced to provide "background" for the trier-of-fact. For example, in *R. v. Cullen*,[51] the accused was charged with assault with a weapon after trying to run down his ex-girlfriend with a pick up truck. The Ontario Court of Appeal held that in order to try the case "intelligibly," evidence relating to the relationship between the accused and the complainant was necessary:

> Some evidence was relevant and admissible to show continuing malice or *animus* on the part of the appellant toward the complainant after the termination of their relationship. That evidence was clearly admissible on the issue of intent.[52]

In *R. v. Albert*,[53] however, the Ontario Court of Appeal found that this type of evidence was not admissible on the facts of the case, in particular, because it was all evidence of the complainant. The complainant testified that the accused and another man sexually assaulted her, and at the trial, the Crown adduced testimony from the complainant that the accused had sexually assaulted her on two prior occasions. The Crown argued that the probative value outweighed the prejudice, as the evidence was relevant to the background relationship between the parties, and that it was also probative of motive, animus and identity of the accused. The Court of Appeal disagreed:

> We are of the view that the evidence given by the complainant of the prior sexual assaults upon her by the appellant was not admissible as "part of the narrative". To the extent that it was relevant to the relationship between them, it was only relevant to show that the appellant was the type of person likely to have committed the offence. The evidence was not admissible for that purpose as it went only to disposition. The evidence was not probative to show animus, motive or identity in the circumstances of this case. Moreover, the probative

---

51 (1989), 52 C.C.C. (3d) 459 (Ont. C.A.).
52 *Ibid.* at 461.
53 (1993), 19 C.R. (4th) 322 (Ont. C.A.).

value of the evidence was undermined by the fact that it was exclusively evidence of the complainant and, therefore, subject to the same frailties as the rest of her evidence.[54]

The Court also found that the prejudicial nature of the evidence was severe, because the facts surrounding the prior assaults were far more serious than those of the charge before the Court.

Evidence of similar facts has also been admitted to prove the accused's intent to commit murder when he advances a defence of provocation. For example, in *R. v. Cormier*,[55] the accused was charged with the murder of his girlfriend, and he relied on defences of drunkenness and provocation to reduce his culpability to manslaughter. The accused and the victim had lived together off and on, and after their relationship went sour the second time, it was agreed he would move out. Before this occurred, however, the accused went on a drinking binge for a few days, and when he returned to the residence, he and his girlfriend got in an argument. He then apparently lost control, grabbed her by the neck and strangled her. The Crown adduced evidence that one month before the killing, the accused and his girlfriend had been in a bar together and the accused had grabbed her by the shoulders and neck and slapped her. A second event introduced as similar facts was a conversation the accused had with a friend in which the accused stated, "I'll give her a good beating." The Quebec Court of Appeal held that both incidents made culpable intent for murder more probable, the first incident demonstrating violent behaviour toward the victim and the second being a threat towards the victim. In this regard, probative value outweighed the prejudice to the accused.[56]

(b)   To Rebut a Defence Advanced by the Accused

R. v. Carpenter (No. 2)[57] is a classic case in which similar fact evidence was found to be admissible to rebut the defence of accident.[58] The evidence

---

54 *Ibid.* at 326.

55 (1993), 86 C.C.C. (3d) 163 (Que. C.A.).

56 See also *R. v. Robertson* (1987), 33 C.C.C. (3d) 481 (S.C.C.), where evidence of an accused's background with the complainant's roommate was ruled admissible on a charge of sexual assault to show how the accused ended up at the complainant's apartment, how he might have known she would be alone and how he knew the roommate's name assisting him in gaining entry. In addition, the evidence was also found to be relevant to the accused's motive and intent.

57 (1982), 142 D.L.R. (3d) 237 (Ont. C.A.).

58 See discussion surrounding notes 25-26 above. See also *R. v. Arason* (1992), 78 C.C.C. (3d) 1 (B.C. C.A.), where the accused was charged with cultivation of marijuana in a unit of a commercial building, and evidence that the accused was involved in similar cultivation in another unit of the same premises was found to be admissible to show system as well as to rebut a defence of innocent explanation advanced by the accused.

in an arson case was that of previous fires occurring at premises owned by the accused, both taking place within six months of the fire before the Court. The trial Judge rejected the evidence because of the numerous differences between the previous fires to the charge in question. On appeal it was held that the evidence was admissible, despite the dissimilarities, to rebut the defence of accident. Given that the case was not one of proving identity the evidence of the similar acts did not have to be "strikingly similar." It was held that the test is less stringent where the evidence is adduced to show knowledge, intent or state of mind or to refute the defence of accident.

R. v. Marquard[59] is another example where the accused advanced the defence of accident. In Marquard, the accused was charged with aggravated assault in connection with a severe facial burn suffered by her granddaughter. The Crown alleged that the burn occurred not by accident, but by the accused who put the child's face against a hot stove door as a form of discipline. One of the expert witnesses testifying on behalf of the Crown gave evidence that the child acted maturely in dealing with her injury, and this suggested that she was a victim of long-term abuse. The Supreme Court of Canada held that this evidence was only tangentially relevant, and was therefore outweighed by the prejudice caused by the suggestion that the accused systematically abused the child.

(c) To Show State of Mind

The Manitoba Court of Appeal held in R. v. Proctor[60] that similar fact evidence may be relevant to an accused's state of mind in connection with the defence of insanity. In this decision, however, the Court cautioned that rulings as to the admissibility of similar fact evidence must be made at a point in the trial when relevance can be ascertained. The accused in Proctor was charged with murder, which was alleged to have occurred during the sexual assault of the victim. Initially, the Crown sought to lead as similar fact evidence to prove identity, evidence of two other complainants who had survived attacks by the accused and could identify him. Prior to trial, however, it became clear that the accused was going to raise a defence of insanity, and the Crown amended its position, arguing the evidence was relevant to state of mind. On this basis, the trial judge ruled the evidence admissible, and in its opening address to the jury, the Crown made extensive references to the similar fact evidence including references to the accused being identified as the killer. In ordering a new trial, the Court held that the evidence should not have been mentioned in the opening statement, and stated that in particular, the references to the accused being the killer were

---

59 (1993), 85 C.C.C. (3d) 193 (S.C.C.).
60 (1992), 69 C.C.C. (3d) 436 (Man. C.A.).

improper and highly prejudicial.[61] In addition, the Court pointed out that until some evidence with respect to insanity was given, the Judge could have no way of knowing what, if any, similar fact evidence was relevant. In this respect, the Court stated that the similar fact ruling made at the outset of the trial was premature.[62]

3. Similar Fact Evidence to Establish Identity

(a) Where the Commission of a Crime is Not Established

i) *To Rebut a Defence in the Absence of Direct Testimony*

In many cases, an accused is charged with a crime even though it has not been established that a crime has in fact been committed. This was the situation, for example, in the "brides in the bath case" discussed above, where the accused argued that his wife was not murdered, but that she died as a result of an epileptic fit.[63] In this type of case, the prosecution must establish that a crime was indeed committed and that the accused was the perpetrator. Often, particularly in murder cases, this must be proven without the assistance of any direct testimony implicating the accused.[64] In the absence of direct testimony, therefore, the similar fact evidence will have to be highly probative in order to outweigh the potential prejudice.[65]

(b) Where Commission of a Crime is Established

i) *Identity*

For many cases, the fact that a crime has occurred is indisputable, and this will be the case for most murders, robberies and sexual assaults. Usually, the main issue in these cases will be identity, and there may or there may not be direct testimony against the accused. If, however, there is no direct testimony, the similar fact evidence will have to be highly probative to outweigh prejudice:

> It is in such cases that the courts require the very strongest evidence of simi-
> larity, indeed peculiarity, or technique because the evidence must by itself be

---

61 *Ibid.* at 449.
62 *Ibid.* at 446, 448. The Court also noted that it is improper for Crown counsel to artificially keep issues alive in order to secure favourable rulings with respect to similar fact evidence.
63 *R. v. Smith*, [1914-15] All E.R. 262 (C.C.A.). See also *R. v. Ball*, [1911] AC. 47 (H.L.); *Makin v. A. -G. for New South Wales, supra.*
64 *Cross on Evidence, supra,* at 362-363.
65 *Ibid.* at 363.

so compelling as to be the equivalent of a signature, or the discovery of the accused's fingerprints in each separate connection.[66]

In *R. v. Arp*,[67] the Supreme Court of Canada held similar fact evidence admissible because of an objective improbability of coincidence. "The force of the evidence subsists in the proposition that it is unlikely that the accused would be implicated more than once in offences which are unique or markedly similar. It is the unlikelihood of coincidence that gives the evidence its probative force." The Court also added that while the issue in every case is whether the probative value of the evidence outweighs its prejudicial effect, if the trial judge is satisfied that it is likely the same person committed the similar acts and the act in question, then the probative value of the similar acts will outweigh its prejudicial effort and the evidence is admissible.

The case of *R. v. Burlingham*[68] provides an example of similar fact evidence that amounts to a fingerprint left at the scene. The accused was charged with first degree murder of a young woman, and evidence of a prior conviction for murder was found to be highly probative of identity because of the following similarities: the killings occurred in the same town, three months apart; both victims had been young women who had been found nude and had been sexually assaulted; both had been shot in the head twice, at close range, with stolen shotguns that had been sawed off.[69]

R. v. Wright[70] provides another example, but in this case, evidence of subsequent acts of the accused were admitted as similar fact evidence. The accused was charged with first degree murder, and it was alleged that he strangled his victim to death while committing acts of sexual and anal intercourse. The Ontario Court of Appeal found that evidence of a prostitute who had been with the accused was of striking similarity and was therefore

---

66 *Cross on Evidence, supra*, at p. 354 (citing *R. v. Straffen*, [1952] 2All E.R. 657 (C.C.A.)); *R. v. Arp, supra*.

67 *Supra. Arp* holds that on the issue of identity, admissibility requires a high degree of similarity between the acts. In this regard the Judge should only consider the manner in which the acts were committed and not the accused's involvement in each act. Similar fact evidence however must be linked to the accused by some evidence disclosing more than mere possibility that the accused committed the alleged similar act.

68 (1993), 85 C.C.C. (3d) 343 (B.C. C.A.).

69 See also *R. v. Naldzil* (1991), 68 C.C.C. (3d) 350 (B.C. C.A.), also a murder case, where the deceased was found naked with her hands and feet bound. The Court held admissible similar fact evidence that the accused and some others robbed a man twice (once before and once after the murder) by stripping him naked and tying him up in similar way to the deceased. It was held that the evidence supported the conclusion that the same person committed both the robberies and the murder, and probative value outweighed prejudice. Clearly, the similarities in this case are not that strong so as to indicate a particular *modus operandi* as found in *Burlingham*. However, the difference in the strength of the evidence required can possibly be explained by the fact that in *Naldzil*, a co-accused testified against the accused, providing direct evidence that the accused was the perpetrator.

70 (1990), 56 C.C.C. (3d) 503 (Ont. C.A.). (Note: this decision does not refer to *R. v. B. (C.R.)*, although probative value vs. prejudice was addressed.)

admissible with respect to identity. Her evidence was that the accused had exhibited roughness in his sexual acts, attempting to have anal intercourse with her and also began to choke her during sexual intercourse. On the other hand, the Court found that other evidence adduced as similar facts at the trial was inadmissible, and this included evidence of the accused's relationship with other prostitutes and evidence that he used phone-sex lines. It was found that the evidence was not probative as it did not show the accused's need to satisfy sexual desires through violence.

R. v. Smith[71] is also a case where similar fact evidence was rejected as not being sufficiently similar. It was alleged that the accused, charged with murder, killed a woman who refused to smuggle drugs for him. The similar fact evidence considered by the Court was the testimony of another woman who stated that the accused similarly asked her to smuggle drugs for him, which she refused to do (although she was unharmed). Lamer C.J.C. held that the only relevance this evidence had was to the accused's bad character, and it was therefore inadmissible:

> It was evidence going to character, the implication being that a person who had the "character" of a drug smuggler would be more likely to have committed the murder. Such evidence, in my view, was not admissible to establish that the respondent committed the murder.[72]

In R. v. MacCormack[73] it was held that evidence of similar acts that shows a number of significant similarities in combination rather than a "unique trademark" and common to all incidents, may be admissible to help establish the identity of the person responsible for the crime. The evidence must be properly connected to the allegations in the indictment.[74] Similarities in character, proximity in time, and frequency of occurrence are important factors.

---

71 (1992), 75 C.C.C. (3d) 257 (S.C.C.).

72 *Ibid.* at 275. Lamer C.J.C. cited with approval the decision in *Cloutier v. R.* (1979), 48 C.C.C. (2d) 1 (S.C.C.), where on a charge of importing narcotics into Canada, evidence of items seized at the accused's home, included a manuscript discussing the virtues of marijuana, a metric scale, tweezers and three pipes, were found to have no probative value. On the other hand, in *Morris v. R.* (1983), 7 C.C.C. (3d) 97 (S.C.C.), the Court (Lamer J., Dickson and Wilson JJ. concurring, dissenting) held that evidence of a two-year-old newspaper clipping discussing the heroin trade in Pakistan was admissible on a charge of conspiracy to import heroin from Hong Kong and trafficking. The majority held that the evidence was relevant as it showed preparatory steps taken by the accused to import narcotics. (*Cloutier* and *Morris* are usually cases that are discussed in relation to the rule relating to character evidence, although the admissibility of extrinsic evidence is an issue that is related to the rule relating to similar fact evidence.)

73 (2009), 241 C.C.C. (3d) 516 (Ont. C.A.) at paras. 50-51.

74 *Ibid.*, at para. 62.

ii)   *Use of Psychiatric Evidence to Establish Identity*

While psychiatric evidence is normally considered under the headings of Character Evidence and Opinion Evidence it has also been recognized under the heading of Similar Fact.

In *R. v. Morin*,[75] the Supreme Court of Canada held that the same principles that apply to evidence of past misconduct to establish identity apply to psychiatric evidence adduced for the same purpose. In *Morin*, the accused was charged with murder in connection with the brutal killing of his nine-year-old next door neighbour. During the Crown's cross-examination of a defence psychiatrist, testimony was elicited that the accused was a member of an abnormal group which would have the same propensities as the perpetrator.[76] The Court ruled that the trial judge was correct in not leaving this evidence with the jury as proof of identity, as it was lacking in distinguishing features.

iii)   *Use of Other Extrinsic Evidence to Establish Identity*

The prosecution will sometimes be permitted to adduce non-similar extrinsic evidence pursuant to the similar fact rule if the evidence is relevant to issues in the case. *Morris v. R.*,[77] discussed above, is an example of such a case. This type of evidence has also been admitted in a case where the accused was charged with possession of cocaine for the purpose of trafficking, when the cocaine was actually found in the possession of another person.[78]

---

75   (1988), 44 C.C.C. (3d) 193 (S.C.C.).

76   The accused was diagnosed as a schizophrenic, and the argument by the Crown was that since a small percentage of schizophrenics would have the capability or tendency to commit the crime, this was evidence that the accused had this tendency or capability. The Court held that this line of reasoning lacked probative value on the issue of whether the accused fell within the small percentage of schizophrenics who had such tendencies, and therefore was not relevant to identification. (On a somewhat different note, the Supreme Court of Canada has also examined the issue of an attempt by defence counsel to use psychiatric evidence to *exclude* the accused as the perpetrator. See *R. v. Mohan* (1994), 89 C.C.C. (3d) 402 (S.C.C.), reversing (1992), 71 C.C.C. (3d) 321 (Ont. C.A.)).

77   *Supra*.

78   *R. v. Pugliese* (1992), 71 C.C.C. (3d) 295 (Ont. C.A.). See also *R. v. Johnston* (1991), 64 C.C.C. (3d) 233 (Ont. C.A.), leave to appeal refused 67 C.C.C. (3d) vi (S.C.C.), however, where evidence that the accused attempted to make a silencer for a shotgun three weeks before a shotgun killing was held to be inadmissible. (Nevertheless, the Court found that its admission could not have affected the verdict.)

4.   *To Explain Actions of Complainant*

In *R. v. B. (F.F.)*[79] the Supreme Court of Canada held that similar fact evidence was admissible as it was relevant to show a system of violent control exercised by the accused, and this helped to explain the complainant's delay in pressing charges.[80]

In *R. v. R. (G.)*,[81] on a charge of sexual assault against the accused, it was held that the trial Judge properly admitted evidence of the complainant with respect to three previous allegations of sexual assaults. This evidence was found to be relevant to show the motive for the complainant's complaint, which was to put an end to abuse by the accused, thereby rebutting the accused's contention that the complaint was fabricated by the complainant for reasons including a long-standing dislike for the accused.[82]

Such evidence has been admitted to show the relationship with the accused and to explain a comment made by the accused.[83] It would be improper for the trial Judge to instruct the jury that the similar fact evidence could be used by them in assessing the credibility of the complainant as this amounted to nothing more than bad character evidence of the accused.[84]

The Nature of Similar Fact Evidence

It should be recognized that evidence capable of being received as similar fact evidence will not necessarily always be evidence of criminality.[85] Similar fact evidence may also consist of instances of discreditable acts not amounting to crimes,[86] or it may simply be seemingly innocent acts which tend to show motive or intent.[87]

---

79   *R. v. B. (F.F.)* (1993), 79 C.C.C. (3d) 112 (S.C.C).

80   The evidence was also found to be relevant to other issues, including the accused's defence of innocent association, but a new trial had to be ordered because the trial Judge did not properly instruct the jury as to the use that could be made of the evidence.

81   (1993), 80 C.C.C. (3d) 130 (Ont. C.A.), leave to appeal refused (1993), 25 C.R. (4th) 102n (S.C.C.).

82   *Ibid.* at 139-140.

83   *R. v. S. (P.)* (2000), 144 C.C.C. (3d) 120 (Ont. C.A.), leave to appeal refused (2001), 266 N.R. 400 (note) (S.C.C).

84   *R. v. K. (C.P.)* (2002), 171 C.C.C. (3d) 173 (Ont. C.A.).

85   Evidence of criminality includes both evidence of unrelated criminal acts as well as criminal acts incidental to a charge. See the paper by Marc Rosenberg, above, at 4-6, where he described the similar fact evidence of an incidental crime with the help of this example: The accused is charged with murder and the deceased was killed with a particular gun. At trial, the prosecution is permitted to lead evidence that the accused committed a break and enter the night before the murder, and stole that particular gun. The break, enter and theft is a crime that is incidental to the murder case, but it is nevertheless relevant to the issue of the possession of the murder weapon.

86   As was the case in *R. v. Ball, supra.*

87   *R. v. R.(J.D.), supra.*

Effect of an Acquittal

Normally if the accused has been acquitted with respect to previous charges, the conduct giving rise to those charges cannot be adduced as similar fact evidence.[88] As stated by the Ontario Court of Appeal per Finlayson J.A.:

> Fundamental to this ground of appeal is the concept that an acquittal is more than a finding of not guilty and is in law a declaration of innocence for all purposes. This must be so, because the verdict of not guilty restores to the accused the presumption of innocence.[89]

However, in *R. v. Arp*,[90] the Supreme Court of Canada held that while in most cases it would be unfair and inappropriate to admit as similar fact evidence the evidence underlying a previous acquittal, this principle does not apply to verdicts rendered by the same trier-of-fact in a multi-count indictment. The Court went on to describe what would comprise a proper charge to the jury where similar fact evidence is admitted to prove identity in a multi-count indictment.

WHEN AND HOW IS ADMISSIBILITY TO BE ARGUED

While it would seem that the issue admissibility of similar fact evidence would appropriately be argued on a pre-trial motion before the jury selection pursuant to section 645(5) of the *Code* and for the reasons set out and in the Chapter, "Presenting the Evidence-In-Chief," there may be instances when the trial Judge has no way of knowing what, if any, similar fact evidence

---

88   *R. v. Verney* (1993), 87 C.C.C. (3d) 363 (Ont. C.A.); *R. v. G. (K.R.)* (1991), 68 C.C.C. (3d) 268 (Ont. C.A.); *R. v. Cullen* (1989), 52 C.C.C. (3d) 459 (Ont. C.A.).

89   *R. v. Verney, supra*, at p. 371, citing with approval *R. v. Grdic* (1991), 67 C.C.C. (3d) 268 at 279 (S.C.C); *R. v. Cullen* (1989), 52 C.C.C. (3d) 459 (Ont. C.A.); *R. v. M. (R.A.)* (1994), 94 C.C.C. (3d) 459 (Man. C.A.); *R. v. Merdsoy* (1994), 91 C.C.C. (3d) 517 (Nfld. C.A.). But see *R. v. Ollis*, [1900] 2 Q.B. 758, where the accused was acquitted on a charge of obtaining money by false pretenses on the basis of the accused's evidence that when he gave the cheque that was dishonoured, he had expected to receive funds to cover it. On a subsequent similar charge, the Crown was permitted the evidence of the first complaint as relevant to intent and went to the accused's knowledge of wrongdoing. The relevance of the evidence was independent of any question of the accused's guilt or innocence on the first charge.

90   *Supra.* See also *R. v. H. (T.R.)* (2002), 164 C.C.C. (3d) 522 (Ont. C.A.), which was a multi-count indictment involving 24 sexual offences involving nine different complainants. A case for admissibility of similar fact evidence was made out where the evidence on each count showed some similarities but not "striking similarity." The trial Judge was entitled to find that the evidence of each complainant had significant probative value with respect to the reliability and credibility of the other complainants and the evidence revealed a pattern of sexual predation on children.

was relevant. A ruling at the outset of the trial could therefore be premature and would have to wait until the appropriate time in the evidence to be argued.[91] In most instances, however, Crown and defence counsel are in a position to advise the Court that the issue is alive from the outset and arguing the admissibility before the jury is selected would be appropriate.

Unfavourable comment has been made by the Ontario Court of Appeal when a *voir dire* has been held to decide the admissibility of similar fact evidence.[92] That Court has held that except in rare circumstances representations by counsel should suffice to provide an outline of the evidence upon which the Court may make a decision on admissibility, otherwise the trial is unduly prolonged and its continuity unduly disturbed, the jury is absent from the courtroom too long and the opposite side is favoured with an unfair preview of the evidence. However, expediency seems to be a poor argument in the face of such impact evidence, particularly when in most cases admissibility can now be argued before the jury is selected. Further, it is difficult to understand why a preview of the evidence for the defence can be unfair at anytime – if such were the case preliminary inquiries would have fallen into disfavour many decades ago.

It is suggested that the fairest course would be for counsel to make representations without calling *viva voce* testimony unless such testimony is considered appropriate to a proper determination of the issue, with such representations to be supplemented by reference to witness statements and transcripts of the desired evidence taken at the preliminary inquiry.

THE CHARGE TO THE JURY

The trial judge is required to instruct the jury with respect to the use which can be made of similar fact evidence. This is necessary to minimize the impact of prejudicial inferences caused by the evidence. In *R. v. D. (L.E.)*,[93] for example, Sopinka J. set out the instructions that must be included by the trial judge in his or her charge to the jury. He stated:

> The jury should be instructed that if it accepts the evidence of similar acts, that evidence is relevant for the limited purpose for which it was admitted. The jury must be specifically warned that it is not to rely on the evidence as proof that the accused is the sort of person who would commit the offence charged and on that basis infer that the accused is, in fact, guilty of the offence charged.[94]

---

91 *R. v. Proctor* (1992), 69 C.C.C. (3d) 436 (Man. C.A.).
92 *R. v. Sproule* (1976), 26 C.C.C. (2d) 92 (Ont. C.A.); *R. v. Dietrich* (1970), 1 C.C.C (2d) 49 (Ont. C.A.); *R. v. Carpenter (No. 2)* (1982), 1 C.C.C. (3d) 149 (Ont. C.A.).
93 (1989), 50 C.C.C. (3d) 142 (S.C.C.).
94 *Ibid.* at 162. In this case, the Court held that charge to the jury was inadequate because the evidence was simply treated as part of the body of evidence and no special instructions were given. See also *R. v. B. (F.F.)*, *supra*, at p. 141, where the failure to charge the jury

In *R. v. B. (C.)*[95] it was held that in the future, trial judges should warn juries not to use similar fact evidence to reason from general disposition to guilt and that similar fact evidence must not be used to punish the accused for past misconduct.

Where identity is in issue the jury should basically be instructed that, if they decide the similar fact evidence is "so similar" to the offence that is alleged before the Court that "the same person likely committed both offences," then they may use the similar fact evidence, along with all the rest of the evidence, in reaching their verdict.[96]

The trial Judge is to determine whether or not there is an air of reality to a submission of collusion. The Crown must prove, on the balance of probabilities, that there has not been collusion between the witnesses to taint the similar fact evidence.[97] The trial Judge should define for the jury the meaning of "collusion" as the possibility that the complainants shared their stories with one another and, intentionally or accidentally, changed or tailored their stories in order that their testimony would seem more similar or convincing; instruct the jury that it is for them to determine whether the evidence is reliable despite the opportunity for collaboration, or no weight should be given to the evidence which might have been influenced by the sharing of information against the complainants.[98]

In *R. v. B. (C)*, *supra*, at paras. 34-35 the Ontario Court of Appeal was adamant that the "double warning" was required. It stated:

> To date, the cautionary instruction given to juries has generally taken the form suggested by Cory J. in *R. v. Arp* ... That instruction, which essentially tells the jury that they must not use similar fact evidence to infer that the accused is a person likely, by reason of his or her general bad character, to have committed the offence or offences charged, is clearly acceptable. In our view, however, it tends to focus more on the first danger (reasoning to guilt through general disposition) than on the second danger (convicting on the offences charged to punish the accused for prior misdeeds).

> Accordingly, in the future, when cautioning the jury about the misuse of similar fact evidence, we think it would be preferable for trial judges to give the jury the double warning: (1) that they may not use the similar fact evidence to reason from general disposition or character of guilt, and (2) nor may they use it to

---

as to the limited purposes for which the similar fact evidence could be used was grounds for a new trial.

95 (2003), 171 C.C.C. (3d) 159 (Ont. C.A.).

96 *R. v. Simpson* (1977), 35 C.C.C. (2d) 337 (Ont. C.A.) at 345-346; *R. v. Arp*, *supra*.

97 *R. v. Handy*, *supra*, paras. 99, 102, 104-113; *R. v. Shearing*, *supra*, paras. 39-45.

98 *R. v. D. (C.)* (2000), 145 C.C.C. (3d) 290 (Ont. C.A.) at paras. 89-90; *R. v. Shearing*, *supra*, paras. 44-45; *R. v. B. (C.)* (2003), 171 C.C.C. (3d) 159 (Ont. C.A.) at paras. 36-45.

punish the accused for past misconduct by finding the accused guilty of the offence or offences charged.[99]

Where there are a number of single counts in an indictment the evidence in relation to one count may not be used by the trier-of-fact as evidence on the other counts of the indictment unless the evidence is admissible as similar fact.[100] The jury instructions where the evidence of one or more counts in an indictment is admissible as similar fact evidence with respect to one or more other counts of the indictment are to be found in the cases of *R. v. Thomas* (2004), 190 C.C.C. (3d) 31 (Ont. C.A.) at 38-54. See also *R. v. Arp*, *supra* at p. 36 and *R. v. Simpson* (1977), 35 C.C.C. (2d) 337(Ont. C.A.) at pp. 346- 347. In *R. v. Arp* the Supreme Court held that "though the similar fact evidence, standing alone, may fall short of proof beyond a reasonable doubt, it can be relied on to assist in proving another allegation beyond a reasonable doubt." Two separate allegations can support each other to the point of constituting proof beyond a reasonable doubt, even where a reasonable doubt may have existed in relation to each in isolation.

A more complete analysis of the appropriate jury instructions to be given with respect to similar fact evidence can be found in the lecture by Kenneth L. Campbell, Director, Crown Law Office – Criminal, Ministry of the Attorney General in Evidence, Vol. 1, 2006 National Criminal Law Program from which much of the above is taken.

Appellate Review

The appellate courts will give "substantial deference" to the trial Judge's decision as to the admissibility of similar fact evidence unless there is an error in principle.[101]

---

99   *R. v. B. (C.)*, *supra*, paras. 34-35.

100   *R. v. Nikkel* (2006), 2006 CarswellMan 120 (Man. C.A.) at paras. 5, 6.

101   *R. v. Handy*, *supra*, para. 153; *R. v. James* (2006), 213 C.C.C. (3d) 235 (Ont. C.A.), leave to appeal refused (2007), 2007 CarswellOnt 6162 (S.C.C.).

31

The Preliminary Inquiry

Pursuant to section 548 of the *Criminal Code*,[1] the Crown must prove at the Preliminary Inquiry that there is "sufficient" evidence to put the accused on trial, and if there is not, the accused should be discharged. The Supreme Court of Canada in *R. v. Arcuri*[2] held that this section meant that if there is admissible evidence that could, if it were believed, result in a conviction, then the accused must be committed to stand trial. If there is direct evidence as to each element of the offence the accused must be committed for trial. When there is circumstantial evidence then there is a limited weighing of the evidence because of the inferential gap between the evidence and what is to be established. The question becomes whether the evidence is reasonably capable of supporting the inferences that the Crown asks the trier-of-fact to draw, i.e. does the evidence, if believed, reasonably support an inference of guilt?

If the defence happens to adduce exculpatory evidence under section 541 of the Criminal Code and the Crown presents direct evidence on all the elements of the offence, the case must proceed to trial. But if the Crown's case consists of or includes circumstantial evidence, the judge will be engaged in the limited weighing of the evidence as mentioned above. The judge is not to draw inferences from the facts, nor assess credibility. The judge makes an assessment of the reasonableness of the inferences to be drawn from the circumstantial evidence. Section 548(1) requires the judge to consider the "whole of the evidence." The judge therefore can not ignore any exculpatory evidence when engaging in the limited weighing of the whole of the evidence to assess whether a reasonable jury property instructed could return a finding of guilt.[3]

For defence counsel, the preliminary inquiry is the most important preparation tool at his or her disposal and in many instances this inquiry

---

1 R.S.C. 1985, c. C-46.
2 (2001), 157 C.C.C. (3d) 21 (S.C.C.).
3 *Ibid.*

can determine the outcome of the trial if used properly. Permit me to quote the words of G.A. Martin (as he then was):

> I do wish to emphasize, however, that the preliminary hearing gives defence counsel an opportunity to test the strengths and weaknesses of the Crown's case; to form a judgment as to the mental make-up or personality of the witnesses; to discover those parts of the case that are vulnerable to attack at the trial, and also those areas where he must tread warily.[4]

An example of the vulnerable witness that Mr. Martin refers to appeared in the manslaughter trial of four Toronto police officers[5] for the death of Otto Vass. Mr. Desmond Bartley claimed to be an eyewitness to the alleged brutal beating of Mr. Vass who suddenly died just after the altercation came to an end. Mr. Vass had a history of mental illness which at times caused him to become quite violent. Mr. Bartley did not see how Mr. Vass's battle with two of the officers started, namely by a sudden and unprovoked punch by Mr. Vass to the face of one of the officers. Mr. Bartley gave devastating and at times tearful evidence against the officers at the preliminary hearing as to the beating he allegedly saw the officers inflict on Mr. Vass. The following cross-examination of Mr. Bartley shows how at the trial the use of the transcript of his testimony at the preliminary hearing is used to entrap the witness by purposely allowing him to exaggerate, even lie about what he saw. It shows the use of photographs to contradict the witness and the showing of the photograph to the jurors to emphasize Mr. Bartley's untruthfulness instead of having the jurors wait to see these photographs until they were deciding the case in the jury room at the end of the trial. It was of importance to negate Mr. Bartley's evidence in cross-examination before he left the witness box at trial because of the good impression he left during examination-in-chief including his sudden choking up when he described the alleged beating.

Q. With respect to your description at the preliminary hearing of how Mr. Vass's neck was held, you recall how you described the one arm around his neck? You remember that part?

A. Yes, yes, sir.

Q. And do you recall describing it as a choke hold. You remember at the preliminary hearing?

A. Maybe I did, yes. I would say this.

Q. Would you like me to read what you said back to you?

A. Please do, sir.

---

4 Martin G.A., "Preparation for Trial" (Special Lecture Series of the Law Society of Upper Canada, 1969). *R. v. Cover* (1998), 44 C.C.C. (3d) 34 (Ont. H.C.) at 36-37, describes the purposes of the preliminary hearing.

5 *R. v. LeMaitre, Duncan, Bevalaqua and Le*, Ontario Superior Court of Justice, September-October, 2003 before Justice Lesage.

Q. All right. At page 99 you're describing the strikes with the — at page 99, and the blows with what you recall being the baton, and then at line 27 you said that you couldn't get there because the other officer had a choke hold on him.

And you said:

ANSWER: Right you are, sir.

And going over to page 100, at page (sic) 7:

QUESTION: The shorter officer, he used his left arm to choke the man on the ground.

Yes, sir.

QUESTION: He must have been doing that pretty hard?

ANSWER: If you need my opinion I would say yes.

QUESTION: Like enough as far as you could see to actually cut off his breathing. Right?

ANSWER: Sure, sir.

Sure. And to do some harm to his neck. Would you agree?

ANSWER: I agree with, sir.

QUESTION: Because it sounds to me like he still had the choke hold on him at the end of the incident.

ANSWER: Up until we drive off, yes, sir.

QUESTION: So for the whole time you were there, the shorter officer was choking this man really hard.

ANSWER: Very much so, to my opinion.

Does that refresh your memory? Do you recall being asked those questions and giving those answers?

A. Yes.

Q. Okay. And were they true at the time?

A. Yes, sir.

Q. And you also told the members of the jury how the officer who was giving the choke hold had something in his hand which you thought was something in the nature of a piece of steel. Remember saying that?

A. Yes, sir.

Q. And he was punching him in the neck with it?

A. Yes, sir.

. . .

Q. This first picture I'm going to show you is from roll 3, photo — I'm sorry, my eyesight doesn't assist me here. Roll 3, photograph 20. This is the head of Mr. Vass (post mortem photographs).

A. M'hmm.

Q. And I want you to look. It shows the left side of his neck, is that correct, and part of his chin? Is that right?

A. The left, yes, that's the left, yes.

Q. You see any marks whatsoever on the left side of his chin or neck?

A. Not that I can see.

Q. I'm showing you roll — a picture, photograph roll 3, photograph 22, the right side of his neck. Do you see any marks whatsoever on the right side of his neck or his chin?

A. Not that I can see here, sir.

MR. LEVY: Thank you. If I may just show the members of the jury, Your Honour.

THE COURT: Yes.

MR. LEVY: Those are my questions, thank you.

A TESTING GROUND

The preliminary inquiry allows the accused to ascertain the case that has to be met and in particular to determine the reliability of the Crown's evidence. The avenues open to obtain a witness's statement were discussed earlier.[6] The witness's signed statement should be studied carefully prior to cross-examination as it may provide the basis for impeachment of the witness at trial or contain favourable statements for the accused. An unsigned statement or will-say statement of the witness presents problems for the purposes of impeachment since the witness can say that the unsigned statement or will-say statement or part thereof does not contain his or her words but is the police officer's incorrect version of what was told to him or her by the witness. In such instance, if it is important enough, the police officer who took the statement will have to be called and asked whether in fact those words were taken down correctly.

With a signed statement, the content can be important but what is omitted can be even more important. The late Sir David Napley,[7] cited as an example the instance where the issue was whether an accused was in a particular vicinity at 8:00 p.m. on the 8th day of the month. The witness is being questioned as follows:

The interrogator says (trying to be desperately fair), "Did you see this man there at any time that day?"

And the fellow says, "Oh yes I saw him there, I remember seeing him, and I'm sure it was that day."

"Which day was it?"

"Well, it was the day you asked me about; which day was that, was it the 8th or the 9th?"

"Well, I asked you about the 8th."

"Oh yes, well then it was the 8th."

---

6 See Chapter, "Crown Disclosure."

7 Sir David Napley was an English solicitor. Solicitors in England were permitted to practise in the Magistrates' Court only.

Then it goes down, "on the 8th". Does the witness's statement convey the uncertainty as to whether it was the 8th or 9th? The interviewer goes on, "What time of the day was it?"

"I think it was 8:00, but I can't remember whether it was as I was going to work or as I was coming home."

"Well, think about it."

"I can't remember."

"Joe Jones, who lives around the corner, said it was 8:00 in the evening."

"Oh, then it must have been 8:00 in the evening—on the 8th of July at 8:00 in the evening I saw the defendant."

How much use is that in preparing a case if you're going to assume that the witness remembered what he has put in his statement? Therefore, the first and essential virtue of a preliminary inquiry is to enable you to assess whether or not the evidence which is given is really reliable.

The moral of Sir David's example is that the opportunity to cross-examine the witness should not be passed up even if a signed statement has been received, because the evidence under oath may come out differently from the witness either voluntarily or through some prodding by the cross-examiner. As Jack Gemmell and Dianne Martin state:[8]

Assess the statement carefully for the logically missing information, and always try to learn who else was present or should have been present. Never assume that all the questions have been asked of a witness or that all the witnesses were located.

There are individuals who, when interviewed by the police, do not have it in mind that they may become witnesses in a trial, under oath and cross-examined about the details of their testimony. When interviewed they may be careless and at times even cavalier in what they say, perhaps being influenced by negative things that they are told or have heard about the accused and/or the events in question by the police or others. However, once in the courtroom these same witnesses can become more careful and circumspect in their testimony, influenced by the solemnity of the occasion, the trappings of the courtroom and the presence of others including the accused. It is therefore important in my view that when you know that a witness, by virtue of the disclosure you have received, can give damaging evidence against your client, that you seize the opportunity of a trial run at the preliminary hearing to hear that witness in-chief and cross-examine in an attempt to negate or mitigate his or her seemingly damaging evidence for when the witness testifies at the trial stage.

---

8 J. Gemmell and D.L. Martin, "Police Beat," Criminal Lawyers' Association Newsletter, Vol. 7, No. 5, March 1986, p. 20.

Another reason why counsel should not waive the opportunity to cross-examine an important prosecution witness is that when the witness statement is under oath and is then contradicted later at trial, he or she cannot say: "Well, what I said before wasn't under oath and perhaps I was careless. I am under oath now and I am being more careful."

The preliminary inquiry is the testing ground for questions counsel will be asking at the trial. At the preliminary hearing the cross-examiner is prepared to take more of a chance with his or her questions because, unless he or she is aiming for a discharge, no verdict will be rendered. The cross-examiner will learn which of those questions that should not be repeated at trial. Of course the answers can also educate the Crown for when the trial occurs.

An example of testing questions is where counsel will ask several witnesses to the same event the same or similar questions to learn whether there will be any contradictory answers. The questioner may even present these witnesses with a diagram of the scene and ask them to mark with a pen or coloured marker where, for example, each witness was at the material time, the relevant objects at the scene, etc. Each witness will be given a different copy of the same diagram so as not to be influenced by what was marked on other witnesses' diagrams. The markings can then be compared to determine if there were any significant differences. If the different witnesses' testimony do not significantly conflict then counsel will of course abandon this approach at trial. If the testimonies do conflict then counsel will make his or her point at trial. Make certain to have the witnesses each sign their diagram and have them marked as exhibits so that if you wish to utilize them at trial there will be no confusion as to which witness belongs to which diagram.

The preliminary hearing provides an opportunity to gain a feel for the witness. It can be used to determine if the witness is inconsistent, hostile, aggressive, overbearing, meek, malleable, sympathetic, obnoxious, inarticulate, intelligent, boastful, exaggerating or offends common sense with his or her answers. Will the witness be a good or bad witness? Such insight gained at the preliminary inquiry will dictate the approach counsel will take toward the witness at trial.

At the preliminary hearing the cross-examiner will be able to test what his client has told him against the evidence presented. A previously reluctant client may wish to plea bargain because he or she recognizes there is little chance of an acquittal after the evidence produced by the Crown has been tested. On the other hand, the cross-examiner may be able to expose, at an early stage, the weaknesses of the prosecution's case or lessen the impact of what, on the surface, appears to be a serious matter with the result that the Crown may accept a plea to a lesser charge.

DEFINING AND ISOLATING THE ISSUES

The preliminary inquiry can define more clearly the issues of the case thereby enabling counsel for the Crown and defence to make informed and intelligent decisions concerning the positions they will adopt, including admissions at trial, such as admissions relating to continuity of exhibits. The preliminary inquiry is the place to determine whether or not counsel will be contesting the admissibility of evidence. If counsel feels there is an issue surrounding the voluntariness of the statement or a Charter issue then he or she should go through a dress rehearsal at the preliminary inquiry to learn whether or not there is an issue to challenge at trial. Defence counsel should not tip his or her hand to the witnesses if possible. If there is to be a contest as to the admission of statements at trial and there is sufficient other evidence to have the client committed for trial, counsel may want to waive the necessity of a *voir dire* at the preliminary inquiry but have the right to cross-examine the police officers about the circumstances surrounding the taking of the statement during the cross-examination at large. The officers may then be less prepared for an attack on their credibility at trial with respect to the voluntariness of the statements.

While a Provincial Court Judge presiding at a preliminary hearing has no jurisdiction to grant the accused any relief under the *Charter of Rights*,[9] that does not render any evidence tending to establish the right to such relief irrelevant at the preliminary hearing. To do otherwise would be to deny the accused the right to full answer and defence at trial. So a police officer may be cross-examined as to the basis on which he obtained a search warrant which would be relevant to a section 8 *Charter* challenge at trial.[10] The accused also has the right to cross-examine a witness as to his or her credibility at a preliminary hearing even though the judge is not required to make findings of credibility at that stage.[11] And although the *Criminal Code* does not permit production of third party records at the preliminary hearing, it is permissible for the accused to lay the foundation for application for production at trial for the "likely relevant" standard under section 278.3 of the *Criminal Code*.[12]

---

9 *Charter of Rights and Freedoms*. Part I of the *Constitution Act, 1982*, being part of Sched. B of the *Canada Act, 1982* (U.K.), c. 11.

10 *R. v. Cover* (1988), 44 C.C.C. (3d) 34 (Ont. H.C.); *Stewart v. Carter* (1987), 35 C.R.R. 326 (B.C. C.A.); *R. v. George* (1991), 69 C.C.C. (3d) 148 (Ont. C.A.). In *R. v. Dawson* (1998), (sub nom. *Dawson v. R.*) 39 O.R. (3d) 436 (Ont. C.A.), it was held that a preliminary hearing judge has jurisdiction to grant leave to the defence to cross-examine police witnesses on affidavits supporting wiretaps authorizations where there was a legitimate discovery purpose and not a fishing expedition. See also *R. v. Drozney* (2004), 2004 CarswellOnt 1443, 184 C.C.C. (3d) 311 (Ont. S.C.J.), *per* Dambrot J.

11 *R. v. Al-Amoud* (1992), 10 O.R. (3d) 676 (Ont. Gen. Div.).

12 *R. v. B. (E.)* (2002), 162 C.C.C. (3d) 451 (Ont. C.A.), leave to appeal refused (2002), 307

At the very least the preliminary hearing will enable counsel to know what questions should not be asked at trial.

DISCOVERY

Once the police have ascertained whom they feel has committed a crime, their only interest tends to be to strengthen the case against that person and their investigation therefore becomes aimed towards that end. Tunnel vision by the police is not unusual. Cross-questioning at the preliminary inquiry can provide evidence or clues to other evidence unknown to the Crown or known to the Crown or police but not disclosed and which would assist the defence. Over the past decades there has become a recognized element of discovery at the preliminary inquiry.[13] The preliminary inquiry gives counsel for the accused the opportunity to examine the witness to elicit every possible fact and lead which may be helpful to the defence and prevent the defence from being taken by surprise, although the element of surprise has become less of a concern with the decision in *Stinchcombe* regarding Crown's duty to disclose.[14]

The Crown need choose only to call sufficient evidence to justify a committal of the accused to stand trial.[15] If such is the case, defence counsel should then call any witnesses to the stand who are disclosed by the pre-trial material or by other witnesses at the preliminary inquiry if such witnesses are important to any of the issues at trial in order that their evidence can be discovered or to ascertain any helpful or damaging evidence from them. The judge has no discretion to refuse to hear further evidence even though he is satisfied there is sufficient evidence to commit for trial.[16]

N.R. 195 (note) (S.C.C.). Here, the defence sought to cross-examine the complainant at the preliminary hearing on the contents of his diary. The Court declined to establish general guidelines for permissible cross-examination. In this case, the defence was allowed to ask if the complainant if any particular topic is covered in the diary but not what was written concerning the topic.

13 *Re Skogman and R.* (1984), 13 C.C.C. (3d) 161 at 171 (S.C.C.). See also statement by G.A. Martin, Q.C., "Preliminary Hearings," in *Evidence*, 1955 L.S.U.C. Lectures. p. 8, wherein he likened the preliminary inquiry to an examination for discovery as it helped to ascertain the nature and strength of the Crown's case; *R. v. Churchman* (1955), 20 C.R. 137 (Ont. H.C.); *R. v. Feener* (1960), 129 C.C.C. 314 (Ont. H.C.); *R. v. Mishko* (1945), 85 C.C.C. 410 (Ont. H.C.); *Brooks v. R.* (1964), 49 W.W.R. 638 (Alta. T.D.); *R. v. Girard* (1975), 14 N.B.R. (2d) 189 (N.B. C.A.); *R. v. Ward* (1976), 35 C.R.N.S. 117 (Ont. H.C.); leave to appeal to Ont. C.A. dismissed (1977), 31 C.C.C. (2d) 466n (Ont. C.A.).

14 *R. v. Stinchombe*, [1991] 3 S.C.R.326.

15 *R. v. Arcuri, supra.*

16 *R. v. Schreder* (1987), 36 C.C.C. (3d) 216 (N.W.T. S.C.).

Assessing The Preliminary Hearing

"*I've just about resigned myself to your getting twenty years.*"

The New Yorker Book of Lawyer Cartoons. New Yorker Magazine Eds. (Illus.). Alfred
A. Knopf, Inc., 1997. © 1993 by The New Yorker Magazine, Inc.

If the Crown does not choose to call the officer in charge of the case,
defence counsel may wish to do so. The officer in charge knows the most
about the case and may be able to provide evidence that will contradict a
Crown witness, support the defence or provide important leads, or convince
the accused he/she should plea bargain. When the client has been reluctant
to plea bargain even in the face of a strong Crown case in the disclosure
materials, hearing the evidence in a courtroom, seeing the demeanour of the

important Crown witnesses and how those witnesses hold up under cross-examination may influence the client to reconsider his or her position.

Certain types of cases dictate that counsel should be asking a number of questions of the witnesses to obtain information that will help to investigate that witness later. For example, if the witness is a child, the questioner will want to know the child's birthdate, the names of schools attended and friends to whom the child spoke about the incident or who may have witnessed the event. These friends may have a different story to tell. As a result of this questioning, counsel may wish to subpoena the child's school records which could indicate something about that young person's mental or physical health or level of intelligence which would affect the child's testimony. Experts have stated that an abused's child's school work and attitude are affected negatively. Do the school records reflect this? Has the child made any complaints to his or her teachers or guidance counsellor? Other factors which experts say can be manifestations of sexual abuse are bed wetting, nightmares, anxiety, low self-esteem, depression, truancy, sexually acting out and promiscuity. Has the complainant shown any of these traits and if so, are they consistent with causes other than sexual abuse, such as the death of a parent or other trauma? See Chapter, "Cross-Examination of Child Witnesses."[17]

In questioning an adult, counsel will want to know that person's birth date and whether he/she has been known by any other names in order to better trace the witness's history and criminal record, if required. The work history of an important witness against the client should also be traced to help ascertain the reliability of the witness. The questioner will want to learn anything about the witness's life that would affect his or her character and credibility, such as whether he/she has a criminal record or if the witness is presently charged with an offence and therefore has a motive to be co-operative with the prosecution in order to obtain a lenient sentence or at least be hoping to be treated more leniently. See Chapter, "Jailhouse Informants and Analogous Witnesses" for further motives of an informer as well as Chapter, "Criminal Records," regarding admissibility of outstanding charges. Attempt to obtain any information you can about the witness's prior convictions including dates and places. Transcripts of Court proceedings can be ordered if needed. This chore can be made easier if you obtain the name of the counsel for the witness when he/she was convicted. If needed, request police occurrence forms and supplementary records, if any, which will provide details of the prior convictions or outstanding charges. Request disclosure of any records of police contacts with the witness in addition to those pertaining to the case at bar.

---

17 Counsel may be faced by the school arguing that there are privacy issues at stake in seeking to present the production of the school records.

Where counsel is concerned about the credibility of a material witness, as for example, a complainant, ascertain if that witness has spoken to anyone else about the alleged incident, the name and whereabouts of that witness, and what was said. It may turn out that different versions have been given than the one in Court. Differing versions can be important since you can make the point the witness is unable to get her story straight because it is untrue.

Counsel, in the appropriate case will want to know the relationship between the witness and the accused to determine if there is any bias or motive potentially affecting the witness's testimony. Does the witness have a financial interest in the outcome of the case such as an intended or pending law suit or application before a Criminal Injuries Compensation Board, or a matrimonial dispute involving money or custody where the complainant is looking for leverage? Does the witness dislike or hold a grudge against your client? Is the witness a publicity seeker? Is the witness attempting to minimize his/her own role in the offence or attempting to protect another by blaming your client? These are just some of the many motives that might exist for false or exaggerated testimony. Witnesses' testimony may even be coloured by police officers who have bad-mouthed the accused or convinced the witness they have the right man. See Kaufmann Inquiry Recommendations in Chapter, "Cross-Examination of Police Officers."

Recovered memories of sexual abuse and other syndromes became part of an increasing number of sexual assault cases in our courtrooms although more lately the recovered memory syndrome has come into some disrepute. Counsel should be aware of the current literature on these topics and consult with an expert if fiscally possible to prepare for cross-examination of complainants, parents of the complainants and other relevant witness; and particularly for the cross-examination of the Crown's expert who, in all likelihood, will be called to testify about matters which will explain the behaviour of the complainant in abuse cases, in order to support his or her credibility. For example, it has been recommended that the following information be obtained when concerned with recovered memory syndrome although some of these suggestions are subject to preconditions and limitations in the *Criminal Code* and case law (it is a list which can be helpful with respect to child complainants also):[18]

1. All medical, psychiatric, and school records of the person claiming abuse from childhood to present;[19]
2. Any information concerning relationships with peers, siblings and parents, or any childhood behaviour problems of the person claiming abuse;

---

18 "Opening the Doors to the Past: Decade Delayed Disclosure of Memories Of Years Gone By," L. Daly and J. Pacifico, December 1991, Isilo the Champions 43.

19 Again, Counsel should be prepared to meet resistance based on privacy concerns.

3. Any information concerning the sexual history of the person claiming abuse including rapes, other childhood sexual abuse and abortions;
4. The nature and origin of the disclosure, in as much detail and specificity as possible;
5. Information about any current problems or stresses in the life of the person claiming abuse;
6. The nature of any current therapy, e.g. whether techniques such as hypnosis and survivors' groups were used, the training and background of the therapist, and whether he or she specializes in treating "recovered" abuse;
7. Any books, television shows, or workshops about sexual abuse or rape to which the person claiming abuse may have been exposed;
8. Any exposure to recovered memory cases through a highly publicized case in the media or through friends who may have reported that this happened to them;
9. The work history of the person claiming abuse, including any problems with supervisors or co-workers, especially any allegations of sexual harassment;
10. The psychological characteristics and social and family history of the accused adult, including any drug or alcohol use, sexual history, family relationships, and job history;
11. Any criminal record or prior behaviours in the accused adult which would support or undermine the credibility of the allegations;
12. A detailed description of the behaviours alleged to have occurred; and
13. Possible ways by which the person making the accusation might benefit from or receive reinforcement from making the accusation (e.g., a civil lawsuit, an explanation for why life has not gone well, the expression of anger for perceived childhood injustices, power over a dominant parent, attention, acceptance, or new friends in a survivors' group).

Another example where defence counsel can obtain useful information is where the witness officer has interviewed a number of people who witnessed the event but the Crown only calls one or two of those witnesses. Their full names and addresses (if allowed) should be obtained. These witnesses may or may not be helpful but it may be to defence counsel's advantage to call them himself or herself at the preliminary inquiry or at least have them interviewed later to determine their value and to be prepared for their testimony if the Crown chooses to call them at trial. Their statements may already have been provided in your disclosure materials; but if they are important witnesses you will want to hear from them under oath, particularly if they appear to be helpful as you will want to preserve their testimony in case they become unavailable for trial, or they could be mined for any useful information that is not in their statements.

It should be ascertained whether or not the witness gave statements to the police, when they were given, how many were given, whether they were oral, written, audio or videotaped and any relevant circumstances which may surround the taking of the statements. Do not be satisfied with just the disclosure you received. There may be reasons you have not received all the information.

Where you feel the admissibility of your client's statements or utterances or other evidence may be at issue at the trial stage, do not pass up the opportunity at the preliminary hearing to question the police officers regarding voluntariness and *Charter* rights even though you may be agreeing to their admissibility at the preliminary stage. Both you and the Crown may then come to know whether these statements are worth fighting over at trial. While the preliminary hearing Judge has jurisdiction to rule on the voluntariness and therefore the admissibility of an accused's statement, *Charter* admissibility issues can only be ruled on at the trial stage. However it is well-accepted that counsel are permitted to ask discovery questions regarding *Charter* issues at the preliminary hearing stage.

There are, of course, areas where the preliminary hearing Judge does not have jurisdiction to order production of records, such as records where there is an expectation of privacy as in sections 278.1 to 278.9 of the *Criminal Code*. For disclosure of records in the possession of third parties the reader is directed to the chapter on "Disclosure."

If defence counsel does call a witness at the preliminary inquiry who will in all likelihood be a Crown witness at trial, counsel would obviously want to cross-examine rather than examine the witness in-chief. Defence counsel obviously would be unable to cross-examine because he or she is calling the witness. Many Crown attorneys are co-operative in this situation by advising the Court that they have no objection to defence counsel cross-examining the witness. If there are co-accused, each with their own counsel, one counsel can have his co-counsel call the witness, ask a few questions in-chief and then turn the witness over for cross-examination by the counsel who has an interest in that particular witness's evidence.

Determine the marital status of the witness. If divorced, counsel should ask those questions which will enable him to trace the Court documents relating to the marriage break-up, as they may be revealing. Find out where the ex-wife or husband can be located as they may have no qualms in telling anything unfavourable about their former spouse.

It is recommended that many of these discovery-type questions be asked at the outset of the cross-examination because if they are asked during the latter part of a lengthy cross-examination, the Judge may become impatient and start to cut off counsel or start asking him to explain the relevance of the seemingly immaterial questions.

If there is accomplice testimony, counsel should question the accomplice and the police on statements that were given to the prosecution by the accomplice; if so, the number given; whether they were oral, written or taped in some way and under what circumstances they were made, in order to discover whether or not there is a possible motive for the accomplice to lie against the client or if there are inconsistencies in the statements. Will the accomplice be sentenced only after giving his testimony? If so, this evidence is tainted.[20] The accomplice and the police, if necessary, should be questioned closely on any deals made with the accomplice in return for his or her testimony as a motive for potentially lying. Were any agreements reached and written, and if so, request a copy (see Chapter, "Jailhouse Informants and Analogous Witnesses"), if not already provided in the disclosure.

Physical evidence can be the most damning and sometimes the most helpful to an accused.

The Crown may not always be aware of all of the evidence seized or, if aware, has not grasped the significance of that evidence at the preliminary inquiry stage. While all the physical evidence may be part of the disclosure, its relevance may not be readily understood or may give rise to questions, the answers to which are better learned at the preliminary hearing stage rather than for the first time at trial.

The witness should be drawn out as much as possible about what happened at the scene of the alleged crime and any other role he or she may have played in the case. He or she should be pinned down on as many particulars as possible so that counsel will not be surprised at trial by added facts. Ascertain to whom the witness spoke about what he or she saw and heard – friends, family, co-workers, etc. Counsel may wish to subpoena these people to test the credibility of that witness or at least obtain statements from those people who may advise that the witness said something entirely different than what he or she has testified to at the preliminary hearing.

The preliminary hearing is an important discovery tool when identification evidence is part of the prosecution's case. Defence counsel should thoroughly cross-examine identification witnesses on those matters set out in the chapter on the Identification Witness where relevant.

The Crown often does not need to call their expert(s) at the preliminary hearing to meet the test for committal and will not if it is felt there is sufficient evidence for committal without the expert's testimony. The opportunity to cross-examine the Crown's expert witnesses at the preliminary hearing should not be passed up, as a case has often turned on an expert's testimony. At the very least the cross-examiner will learn which questions should not be asked of the expert at trial. Counsel will learn the full meaning and force of the expert's testimony which otherwise cannot be fully appreciated by merely reading copies of their reports you have received from the Crown, but is expanded upon by the expert when testifying. You want to hear that

---

20   *R. v. Cruikshanks* (1990), 58 C.C.C. (3d) 26 (B.C. C.A.).

evidence before the trial so as not to be caught off guard. If counsel has not decided by the time of the preliminary hearing to retain his or her own expert he or she may well decide after hearing the prosecutor's expert that such a time has come. If the Crown does not choose to call its expert(s) at the preliminary inquiry because he or she was too helpful to the defence at the preliminary hearing you should give serious consideration to asking the Crown to make the expert available for testifying because you will want to hear from that expert. If the Crown refuses, you should subpoena the expert(s).

Counsel should inquire of the expert at the preliminary inquiry whether or not he or she has written any articles or books on the subject-matter. After perusing these writings counsel may discover that the expert has taken a contrary position to that which he or she has testified and the questioner will be better prepared to cross-examine the expert at trial. At trial the cross-examiner will be able to ask the expert if he or she is the same person who wrote the particular work and then to read the relevant part to him or her that was contrary to that to which he or she now testified. Then the witness can be asked if he or she has written a new edition correcting that which was written earlier.

At the preliminary inquiry stage the questioner should also inquire of the expert the writings that he or she feels are authoritative on the subject-matter. Prior to trial counsel should read up on those works as counsel may find some very supportive material therein. When the expert testifies at trial, and after obtaining his or her admission that the particular writings are authoritative, counsel will put that supportive material to the witness, either to contradict the witness's testimony and/or to confirm the client's position.

When the Crown expert is on the witness stand, counsel should go through the expert's file as there may be material there which is helpful. If counsel is thinking of retaining its own expert, it would be helpful to file, as exhibits, photographs or documents found in the expert's file, copies of which have not been forthcoming from the Crown. The defence-retained expert can attend at the clerk's office where the exhibits are kept to see or copy those exhibits to assist in his or her preparation. For example, a pathologist may have photographs of the deceased in his or her file which the defence pathologist will want to see before forming an opinion. For a more complete approach to the examination of the Crown expert the reader is directed to the chapter on "The Expert Witness."

At the preliminary inquiry stage, counsel should permit witnesses more freedom with their answers than would be appropriate at trial. Examples include permitting witnesses to ramble on and refraining from objecting to inadmissible evidence such as hearsay. This testimony could well point to other leads or information that could be helpful to the defence if followed-up. Counsel will have had the advantage of being forewarned, at the preliminary inquiry, about the inadmissible evidence that was forthcoming thus allowing objections to be taken before the prejudicial testimony suddenly pops out of the witness's mouth at trial. Counsel must be careful, however, because by this technique the Crown may also become informed of additional evidence which may be helpful to the prosecution. The obvious exception to adopting this tactic of allowing the witness such freedom is when counsel feels that because of a lack of evidence there is the chance that the client would not be committed for trial. In such cases counsel should treat the preliminary inquiry as he or she would the trial and seek a strict application of the rules of evidence.

The more flexible approach taken at the preliminary inquiry as opposed to the trial stage can be demonstrated in the way questions are posed. At the preliminary inquiry you are concerned with gathering information and so the potentially dangerous open-ended question at the trial stage may be useful at the preliminary inquiry stage. The following cross-examination demonstrates how answers to the open-ended question at the preliminary inquiry can be turned into leading, controlling questions at the trial:[21]

Q. Describe in as much detail as you can the appearance of your assailant?
A. I believe he was approximately 6 feet tall, about 200 lbs. and he was wearing blue jeans, a sweatshirt and a cowboy hat.
Q. What about his facial hair?
A. I believe he had a moustache and a goatee and his sideburns were kind of long so that they were down below his ears.
Q. What unusual marks or scars did he have on his face?
A. None that I noticed.

Now at trial the questions will take on a very different format—again, short and sharp, the purpose being to demonstrate that the accused could not possibly have been the assailant. The questions are not open-ended, as at the preliminary hearing, but leading, allowing defence counsel to not only control the witness but to allow the defence position to unfold during the Crown's case:

Q. You did not see any distinguishing marks or scars on the face of your assailant?
A. No.
Q. When you look at the accused today, you can see that he has an obvious brown mole on the right side of his face?
A. Yes I see it.
Q. The accused does not have a moustache?
A. No.
Q. You previously described your assailant as a person with a moustache?
A. Yes.
Q. Nor does the accused have sideburns below his ears?

---

21 Patrick J. Ducharme, "The Art and Plan of Cross-Examination," Law Society of Upper Canada, Continuing Legal Education Programme, Toronto, September 24th, 1998.

A. Yes I agree with that, but he may have shaved them off.

Q. For the accused to match the description of your assailant, he would have had to remove the mole from his face and grow both a moustache and sideburns?

A. A man can easily shave his moustache and sideburns.

The preliminary inquiry has further value for the prosecution. At the preliminary inquiry the Crown attorney should be looking for weaknesses in her case so that she can, by further investigation and preparation, strengthen her case before trial. The prosecution will also become more alert to those legal issues which will have to be met at trial. The way in which the defence cross-examines the witnesses will tell the Crown attorney what defences may be presented and how they will take shape. The preliminary inquiry will also detect any amendments to the charges that should be made and what additional counts should be considered. Tactics for the trial often begin to present themselves after the evidence has been heard at the preliminary inquiry.

"TYING DOWN" THE WITNESS

The preliminary hearing permits counsel to lay a foundation for an attack on the witness's credibility at trial. The witness should be "tied down" to his or her answers, particularly those favourable to the defence so that if the witness changes testimony at trial he or she can be challenged by referring back to the appropriate spot in the transcript of the preliminary inquiry. Even if the evidence given at the preliminary hearing is unfavourable the witness should be pinned down on the particulars. If the witness changes testimony at trial by changing the already unfavourable facts to a different unfavourable version counsel will still want to show the contradictions to argue that if the witness is unable to get his story straight it is because it is untrue.

In an effort to tie the witness down, the cross-examiner should consider asking such questions as: "Is that all that you heard of that conversation?" "Was anything else said?", "Have you told us everything you saw about the accident?", "Was there anyone else present other than those about whom you have told us?" "If something like that had been said you would have heard it?", "You are sure of that?"

Where the positioning of the witness or other individuals or objects are important, pin the witness down by having him or her mark those positions on a diagram of the scene of the incident. Have the diagram marked as an exhibit so that it can be used at trial to refresh the witness's memory or contradict the witness, if he or she marks the positions differently.

All trial counsel will experience the situation where they point out to a witness that the witness never testified to a particular fact at the preliminary inquiry or never mentioned a particular fact in his statement to the police. The witness may smartly respond with the excuse that he was never asked about that particular fact. By asking the above-mentioned questions counsel will be able to respond to this excuse by pointing out to the witness that he was given the opportunity to tell all the relevant facts that were known to him. At the end of the cross-examination at the preliminary hearing, with the view of tying the witness down even further, the witness should be asked if he has told the Court everything he saw or heard and whether there is anything else he wishes to change or add. Suggest to the witness that he/ she take time before answering.

For some reason many counsel feel that a preliminary inquiry should be conducted like a trial in that if it is possible to destroy the witness at the hearing, they will do so. It is a better tactic not to attack the witness at the preliminary hearing stage but to approach him or her in a friendly manner as if you are both together in seeking the truth. In this way the witness may be lulled into a false sense of security as you cement him into answers that will favour your client at trial. He will be unprepared for your more aggressive approach at trial thereby causing him to be off balance in giving his evidence and reveal weaknesses in his testimony.

It is trite to say that a Judge cannot assess the credibility of the witness at the preliminary hearing and must accept the Crown's evidence. If the witness's credibility is severely damaged at the preliminary hearing defence counsel will, no doubt, receive the plaudits of his client. The same client could, however, become very disappointed at trial when he hears the same witness, who has now been forewarned, skirting around her previous testimony and rehabilitating herself by saying that she was very nervous, confused or mistaken at the preliminary inquiry. It is not therefore always wise to move in for the kill at the preliminary hearing. Simply setting the witness up by tying him or her down to a position can be sufficient. For example, if the cross-examiner has documentary evidence that can impeach the witness, he or she should not do it at the preliminary hearing but should cement the witness to answers that can be contradicted at trial by the documentary evidence. The exception to this tactic is where the cross-examiner has reason to believe that the witness will be out of the country, or for any other reason may not be available for trial and his or her evidence could therefore be read in pursuant to section 715 of the *Criminal Code*. If this is the case counsel should do all he or she can to destroy the witness's testimony at the preliminary inquiry, if that is his intended approach or seek favourable evidence if that is his purpose. This is always a factor to bear in mind in respect of very elderly or very ill witnesses who may be prevented by sickness or even death from attending at the trial proper. Section 715 states:

> (1) Where, at the trial of an accused, a person whose evidence was given at a previous trial upon the same charge, or whose evidence was taken in the

investigation of the charge against the accused or on the preliminary inquiry into the charge, refuses to be sworn or to give evidence, or if facts are provided on oath from which it can be inferred reasonably that the person

    (a) is dead,

    (b) has since become and is insane,

    (c) is so ill that he is unable to travel or testify, or

    (d) is absent from Canada,

and where it is proved that the evidence was taken in the presence of the accused, it may be admitted as evidence in the proceedings without further proof, unless the accused proves that the accused did not have full opportunity to cross-examine the witness.

(2) Evidence that has been taken on the preliminary inquiry or other investigation of a charge against an accused may be admitted as evidence in the prosecution of the accused for any other offence on the same proof and in the same manner in all respects, as it might, according to law, be admitted as evidence in the prosecution of the offence with which the accused is charge when the evidence was taken.

(2.1) Despite subsections (1) and (2), evidence that has been taken at a preliminary inquiry in the absence of the accused may be admitted as evidence for the purposes referred to in those subsections if the accused was absent further to the permission of a justice granted under paragraph 537(1)(j.1).

(3) For the purposes of this section, where evidence was taken at a previous trial or preliminary hearing or other proceeding in respect of an accused in the absence of the accused, who was absent by reason of having absconded, the accused is deemed to have been present during the taking of the evidence and to have had full opportunity to cross-examine the witness.

(4) Subsections (1) to (3) do not apply in respect of evidence received under subsection 540(7).

Questions should be put to the witness whom counsel suspects will be outside Canada at the time of trial and who may not appear to testify, as for example, what are the witness's intentions about returning to Canada to testify. Usually the witness will say that he or she has all the intentions in the world of showing up for the trial. If the counsel has those good intentions on the record and witness fails to appear, and if there is no satisfactory explanation for the witness's non-appearance, counsel can include in his or her address to the jury a criticism of the missing witness's credibility based on the failure to appear.

In *R. v. Menard*,[22] the Supreme Court held that although the evidence did not meet the requirements of section 715 of the *Criminal Code* for purposes of reading in the evidence at trial, that evidence can still be ad-

---

22 (1998), 39 O.R. (3d) 416 (headnote only) (S.C.C.), affirming (1996), 29 O.R. (3d) 772 (Ont. C.A.).

missible under the principled exception to the hearsay rule if shown to be necessary and reliable.

The Court in *Potvin v. R.*[23] held that if the evidence was admitted, it would be highly desirable that the trial Judge remind the jury that it did not have the opportunity of observing the witness giving testimony and should bear this in mind when weighing the evidence. Dickson C.J.C. and La Forest J. held that the trial Judge may exclude the evidence if its prejudicial effect substantially outweighs its probative value. The trial Judge in the proper case could adjourn the trial until the crucial witness, temporarily absent from the jurisdiction, returns, or until an ill witness recovers.[24]

It is not uncommon for the defence counsel to be facing a Crown witness at the preliminary inquiry who not only has evidence which is helpful to the Crown's case but can also be even more helpful to the defence. The defence is aware of this but the Crown is not. If defence counsel tips his or her hand by mining the Crown witness for all the helpful information, Crown counsel may decide not to call that witness at the trial as the witness may do more harm than good to the Crown's case. The Crown would prefer that the accused call the witness permitting the prosecution the right of cross-examination. Defence counsel therefore must make a choice at the preliminary inquiry – either to seek the favourable answers which may ultimately mean that he or she will have to call the witness in-chief at trial, if available, or remain silent and save the important questions for the trial – hopefully during cross-examination. However, if there is any concern that the witness may not be available for trial then the witness should be fully cross-examined at the preliminary inquiry on the points that favour your client with the view of reading in the transcript of his or her testimony pursuant to section 715 of the *Criminal Code*.

CROWN REASONS FOR A PRELIMINARY HEARING

Crown Attorneys, usually faced with crowded dockets in the provincial Court are at times pleased to hear defence counsel say they are prepared to consent to a committal for trial. But there are a number of reasons why a Crown Attorney would wish a preliminary hearing.[25]

1. Testing the strengths and weaknesses of its case and determining whether additional exhibits, evidence or police investiga-

---

23 (1989), 47 C.C.C. (3d) 289 (S.C.C.). See also *R. v. Davidson* (1988), 42 C.C.C (3d) 289 (Ont. C.A.).

24 *R. v. Davidson, ibid.*

25 By Richard Saull, General Counsel, Department of Justice, Winnipeg, Manitoba, 2008 National Criminal Law Programme, Charlottetown, P.E.I., Vol. 2.

tion are required, especially if a case is particularly serious or complex.

2. Learning what likely defences will arise through cross-examinations of Crown witnesses and any statements made or evidence provided by the defence, for example, alibi.

3. Discover what *Charter* issues are likely to arise at trial based on defence questioning.

4. Record evidence of witnesses for trial pursuant to section 715 of the *Criminal Code* who may not be available for trial for a variety of reasons – moving out of the country, seriously ill, likely to be absent themselves with the assistance of others and even be killed.

5. Record evidence of reluctant witnesses who may later have to have their memory refreshed or be cross-examined under section 9(2) of the *Canada Evidence Act* or *K.G.B.*

6. To determine if the charge should be amended or a new charge laid.

7. Provide a basis to seek committal on other charges disclosed by the evidence arising from the same transaction [section 548(1)(a)].

8. Provide an evidentiary basis for motions that will avoid later delays leading up to or during trial.

9. To address the Crown's ongoing obligation to assess the reasonable prospect of conviction and whether there is a public interest in proceeding with this case.

10. Provide an opportunity to test the admissibility of evidence such as statements by the accused or qualifying an expert who the Crown is attempting to qualify for the first time.

11. To satisfy defence counsel respecting certain issues such as causation and continuity which can later be agreed to for trial purposes.

12. To allow certain witnesses (including the police) an opportunity for a "dry run."

13. To demonstrate the strength (or weakness) of the Crown's case in order to encourage an easy resolution.

14. To allow defence to re-elect for trial in Provincial Court for early resolution – this might occur where the Crown's case is relatively weak and the interests of justice dictate early resolution.

15. To elicit further disclosure from the police where, for whatever reason, the Crown has concerns that they have not been provided what is required. This is in order to avoid later delays that will count against the Crown pursuant to sections 7, 11(b) and 11(d) of the *Charter*.

16. To file and preserve exhibits with the Court. This allows for defence counsel to apply for release of exhibits for scientific testing pending trial under reasonable but strict conditions that are ordered by the Court.

Section 643 (now section 715) applies to the defence as well as the Crown.[26]

CONSENTING TO A COMMITTAL FOR TRIAL

As indicated earlier, defence counsel may have reason to believe that a damaging Crown witness, although available for the preliminary inquiry, may not be available for trial. In such a situation the defence would be well-advised to waive the hearing of the evidence and consent to a committal for trial, since, if that witness testifies at the preliminary hearing, his or her evidence is preserved for trial provided that the provisions of section 715 of the *Criminal Code* apply. However counsel will consider not waiving the preliminary hearing if the prosecution is resting a committal on the evidence of a witness the defence knows will be a hostile witness who will not incriminate his client. It should be remembered that the Crown may be able to meet the precondition of necessity where a witness recants earlier testimony and may succeed in getting a prior statement admissible under the principled approach to hearsay.

Another reason to waive the hearing of any evidence at a preliminary hearing and consenting to a committal for trial is that while the client's intent is to plead guilty she does not wish to plead before the presiding Provincial Court Judge and is prepared to take her chances before a more sympathetic Superior Court Judge after a judicial pre-trial or it is hoped that the Crown is prepared at that time to agree to a less severe sentence than when in the Provincial Court.

Counsel should also be alert to the fact that the Crown Attorney can prefer an indictment on any other charges arising on the evidence at the preliminary inquiry.[27] If there is any concern by defence counsel that evidence may be forthcoming at the preliminary inquiry which would support charges not presently on the information the client is facing, counsel may wish to waive the hearing of any evidence and consent to a committal if he or she feels that the client's defence on the present charges could be successful at trial but not so if the additional charges were preferred after the preliminary inquiry.

It should also be remembered that pursuant to section 548(1)(*a*) of the *Criminal Code* the justice at the preliminary hearing may not only commit the accused for trial for the offence charged but may also commit for trial

---

26   *R. v. Davidson, supra.* In *R. v. Syliboy* (1989), 51 C.C.C. (3d) 503 (N.B. C.A.) it was held proper for the trial Judge to permit defence counsel in the course of cross-examining the co-accused to read in the evidence of a witness who was put out of the country, even though the Crown's application to do so was denied.

27   *Re McKibbon and R.* (1984), 10 C.C.C. (3d) 193 (S.C.C.); *R. v. Copeland* (1986), 27 C.C.C. (3d) 186 (B.C. C.A.)

on any other indictable offence with respect to the same transaction where in his or her opinion there is sufficient evidence. If this is a concern for the defence it may be another reason to consent to a committal and waive the hearing of any evidence. The phrase "the same transaction" has been interpreted by the Ontario Court of Appeal to include a series of connected acts extending over a period of time which prove the commission of the offence charged. So where the accused was not shown to be a party to the overall conspiracy but there was evidence to show he was a party to smaller conspiracies to traffic in drugs, he was still involved in a component part of the same transaction and properly committed on the smaller conspiracy.[28]

ADVICE TO THE CLIENT

Many defence counsel forget that their clients do not possess counsels' knowledge of the criminal law and, as a result, fail to explain to them the nature and purpose of the preliminary inquiry. Most clients, unless it is otherwise explained to them, will think that the tactics and the procedure at a preliminary hearing are the same as those to be followed at trial. This ignorance of the law and tactics can leave an accused disenchanted with his or her counsel after there has been a committal for trial, because the client has been left wondering why counsel did not press to have the charge "thrown out." It should be carefully explained to the client that the Crown does not have to prove its case beyond a reasonable doubt at the preliminary inquiry but only has to show that there is some evidence against an accused; that the Crown does not have to call its whole case against an accused but only enough to show that there is sufficient evidence; that any doubts on the evidence are resolved in favour of the Crown; that the judge cannot weigh the evidence and must accept the evidence of the Crown witnesses even though he might not believe it and that is why the accused does not testify or call a defence; and that the defence can call potential Crown witnesses to the stand to testify if the Crown does not call them in order to hear what they have to say under oath. Defence counsel should explain that the value of the preliminary inquiry to the accused is that it is the best preparation tool available to the defence because it can determine the exact case it has to meet by hearing the witnesses and cross-examining them; it can lead to helpful evidence being unearthed; and that a transcript of the witnesses testimony will be made to be used in preparation for trial, and as a potential tool for cross-examination of the witnesses who change their evidence from the preliminary hearing.

---

28 *R. v. Goldstein; R. v. Caicedo* (1988), 42 C.C.C. (3d) 548 (Ont. C.A.).

SOME *CRIMINAL CODE* SECTIONS PARTICULAR TO THE PRELIMINARY HEARING

1. Section 536(2) notes that the wording of the accused's election has been changed to eliminate automatic preliminary inquiries. A preliminary inquiry is provided only on request of the accused or the prosecutor.

2. Section 536.2 states that an accused may elect or re-elect mode of trial by the submission of a written document without the personal attendance of the accused.

3. Section 536(4.1) states that where two or more persons are jointly charged, if one of them makes a request for a preliminary inquiry, a preliminary inquiry must be held with respect to all of them.

4. Section 536.3 provides that counsel for the party requesting a preliminary inquiry must provide the Court and other party with a statement that identifies the issues on which they "*want*" evidence to be given and the witnesses that they "*want*" to hear from at the preliminary inquiry. If Crown and Defence counsel cannot agree on witnesses or issues, a hearing may be held to assist the parties (section 536.4).

5. Section 536.4 provides that if a preliminary inquiry is required, a hearing may be conducted by a justice to narrow the issues, to assist in determining the witnesses that will be called and to encourage the parties to consider matters that would promote a fair and expeditious preliminary inquiry.

6. Section 536.5 states that the accused and the prosecutor may agree to limit the scope of the preliminary inquiry to specific issues.

7. Section 537(1)(j.1) allows for a justice to permit the accused to be out of court during the whole or any part of the preliminary inquiry on any conditions that the Justice considers appropriate.

Decisions under section 650(2)(b) of the *Criminal Code*, which allows a trial Court to permit the accused to be out of Court during the whole or any part of the trial, may be instructive in the interpretation of section 527(1)(j.1). See *R. v. Brown*, [1997] O.J. No. 6166 (Ont. Gen. Div.); *R. v. Butler* (1993), 81 C.C.C. (3d) 248 (Man. Q.B.); *R. v. Chan* (2002), 169 C.C.C. (3d) 419 (Alta. Q.B.); *R. v. Pilotte*, [2002] O.J. No. 866 (Ont. C.A.). There may be circumstances, such as where the identity of the accused is an issue, in which the attendance of the accused in the courtroom will be required.

8. By virtue of section 537(1.1), a justice is required to order the immediate cessation of any examination or cross-examination that is *"abusive, too repetitive or otherwise inappropriate."* Although the description "abusive, too repetitive or otherwise inappropriate" is not defined in the legislation, resort may be had to the case law for assistance, as for example:

- During cross-examination counsel are bound by the rules of relevancy and are not to resort to harassment, misinterpretation, repetitiousness, or putting questions whose prejudicial effect outweighs their probative value. See *R. v. Meddoui*, [1991] 3 S.C.R. 320; *R. v. Logiacco* (1984), 11 C.C.C. (3d) 374 (Ont. C.A.); *R. v. McLaughlin* (1974), 15 C.C.C. (2d) 562 (Ont. C.A.); *R. v. Osolin* (1993), 86 C.C.C. (3d) 481 (S.C.C.) at pp. 515-16. Cory J. in *Osolin* recognized that a "complainant should not be unduly harassed and pilloried to the extent of becoming a victim of an insensitive judicial system, a fair balance must be achieved so that the limitations on cross-examination of complainants in sexual assault cases do not interfere with the right of the accused to a fair trial."

- While the scope of permitted cross-examination is determined by relevancy, relevancy is not to be governed solely by the narrow test for committal as a broader approach to relevancy during a preliminary hearing is mandated by the discovery feature of the inquiry. See *R. v. B. (E.)* (2002), 162 C.C.C. (3d) 451 (Ont. C.A.) at p. 470, para. 56.

- A question in cross-examination may be put that need not be proved independently provided counsel has a good faith basis for posing the question. "It is not uncommon for counsel to believe what is in fact true, without being able to prove it otherwise than by cross-examination; nor is it uncommon for reticent witnesses to concede suggested facts in the mistaken belief that they are already known to the cross-examiner and will therefore, in an event emerge.... Information falling short of admissible evidence may be put to the witness. In fact, the information may be incomplete or uncertain, provided the cross-examiner does not put suggestions to the witness recklessly or that he or she knows to be false." See *R. v. Lyttle* (2004), 180 C.C.C. (3d) 476 (S.C.C.) at p. 489, para. 47.

- "As a general rule, the trial of an accused on a charge of sexual assault need not and should not become an occasion for putting the complainant's lifestyle and reputation on trial." See *R. v. Osolin, supra.*

- Cross-examination of a sexual assault complainant about a sexual assault complaint made against a person other than the accused is normally viewed as a collateral matter, is irrelevant and the prejudicial effect exceeds probative value. See *R. v. B. (A.R.)* (1998), 128 C.C.C. (3d) 457 (Ont. C.A.); 146 C.C.C. (3d) 191 (S.C.C.); *R. v. J.M.*, [2000] O.J. No. 2407 (Ont. C.A.) para. 1-3; *R. v. W. (B.A.)*, [1992] 3 S.C.R. 811 (S.C.C.); *R. v. Riley* (1992), 11 O.R. (3d) 151 (Ont. C.A.), [1993] S.C.C.A. No. 26. However, where counsel wishes to lay the foundation for a pattern of fabrication by the complainant with respect to allegations of sexual assault by other men, such questions may be put if the defence is in a position to establish that the complainant has recanted her earlier accusations or they are demonstrably false. See *R. v. Riley, supra* and *R. v. B. (A.R.), supra.*

• Pursuant to sections 278.1-278.91 of the *Criminal Code* questions which concern a private record which intrude upon the privacy rights of the author are impermissible. A complainant may be cross-examined upon whether or not a particular topic is covered within his or her diary but the complainant may not be questioned about what he or she recalls recording concerning the topic. Also, a wide-ranging exploration of the topics addressed in the diary is impermissible. See *R. v. B. (E.), supra.*

• It is not uncommon to hear a cross-examiner question a witness as to whether he or she had been believed on a prior occasion or about a prior judicial finding that the witness had lied under oath. In *R. v. Ghorvei*, [1999] O.J. No. 3241 (Ont. C.A.) it was held that "[i]f the prior judicial finding that Constable Neilson lied under oath had formed the basis of a conviction of perjury or of giving contradictory evidence, it is clear that he could have been subjected to cross-examination on that conviction and on its underlying facts...Constable Neilson, as an ordinary witness and unlike an accused person, would also be subject to cross-examination on relevant and discreditable conduct even if the conduct has not resulted in a charge being laid or in a conviction." It was the Court's view that it was not proper to cross-examine a witness on the fact that his or her testimony had been rejected or disbelieved in a prior case. That fact, in and of itself, does not constitute discreditable conduct. The Court did not think it would be useful to allow cross-examination of a witness on what is, in essence, no more than an opinion on the credibility of unrelated testimony given by this witness in the context of another case. The triers-of-fact who had witnessed this cross-examination would not be able to assess the value of that opinion and the effect, if any, on the witness's credibility without also being provided with the factual foundation for the opinion. See also *R. v. Malabre*, [1997] O.J. No. 1109, para. 7-9; *R. v. Barnes* (1999), 138 C.C.C. (3d) 500 (Ont. C.A.) para. 14-17; *R. v. Meddoui*, [1990] A.J. No. 455 (Alta. C.A.), (upheld) [1991] 3 S.C.R. 320.

9. Section 540(7)-(9) states that a justice may receive evidence that is otherwise inadmissable, if the evidence is "*credible or trustworthy.*" The test for "credible or trustworthy" evidence is the same as for show cause hearings under section 518(1). Pursuant to section 540(8), reasonable notice of the intent to produce the information as well as a copy of any statement must be provided to the other parties. A Justice can dispense with the notice requirement. Section 540(9) permits the accused to bring an application to require the individual responsible for the hearsay evidence to appear at the

preliminary inquiry for the purposes of examination or cross-examination. Evidence received under section 540(7) would not be able to be read in at a subsequent trial under section 715 of the *Criminal Code* as section 715(4) renders the provisions of section 715 inapplicable to section 540(7). If the Crown is faced with a need to preserve the evidence pursuant to the provisions of section 715, then he or she is best advised not to file the statement of the witness under section 540(7) but to have the witness testify at the preliminary inquiry if the witness is available.

10. Section 561(2) provides that an accused who elects to be tried by a Provincial Court Judge or who does not request a preliminary inquiry may, not later than 14 days before the first day of the trial, re-elect as of right then another mode of trial and may re-elect after that time with the written consent of the prosecutor.

11. Section 574 states that if a preliminary inquiry has not been requested, the prosecutor may prefer an indictment in respect of any charge set out in the information(s) or any included charge.

32

Judicial Interference

THE ROLE OF THE TRIAL JUDGE

> There are crabby, ill-mannered, bad tempered judges. There always has been
> . . . they are an embarrassment to everyone. But to counsel who have to deal
> with them they are more than that; they are a test of skill.[1]

But what happens when a trial judge is more than ill-mannered and
bad tempered? It is one thing for the trial judge to be critical of the conduct
of defence counsel but he or she must do so in a way which will not impact
detrimentally on the accused's defence.[2]

Notwithstanding that counsel must be prepared to take the "knocks
and misfortunes of advocacy" and "they must learn to cope with the judge
who is not being entirely fair with them" there are limits beyond which the
trial judge must not go. The role of the trial judge in the adversary system
has been described by Martin J.A., in *R. v. Valley*[3] as follows:

> The judge's role in a criminal trial is a very demanding one, sometimes
> requiring a delicate balancing of the interests that he is required to protect. The
> judge presides over the trial and is responsible for ensuring that it is conducted
> in a seemly and orderly manner according to the rules of procedure governing
> the conduct of criminal trials and that only admissible evidence is introduced.
> A criminal trial is, in the main, an adversarial process, not an investigation by

---

1 R. Reid and J.A. Holland, *Advocacy: Views from the Bench* (Toronto: Canada Law Book,
  1984), p. 88.
2 *R. v. Valley* (1986), 26 C.C.C. (3d) 207 (Ont. C.A.), leave to appeal to S.C.C. refused
  (1986), 26 C.C.C. (3d) 207n (S.C.C.).
3 *Ibid.* at 230-231. See also *R. v. Roy* (2002), 167 C.C.C. (3d) 203 (Que. C.A.), leave to
  appeal refused (2003), 308 N.R. 400 (note) (S.C.C.), an example of the trial judge's
  interventions made frequently and forcefully during the examinations and cross-examinations of defence experts and hold to be inconsistent with his role and depriving the
  accused of a fair and impartial hearing.

the judge of the charge against the accused, and, accordingly, the examination and cross-examination of witnesses are primarily the responsibility of counsel.

The judge, however, is not required to remain silent. He may question witnesses to clear up ambiguities, explore some matter which the answers of a witness have left vague or, indeed, he may put questions which should have been put to bring out some relevant matter, but which have been omitted. Generally speaking, the authorities recommend that questions by the judge should be put after counsel has completed his examination, and the witnesses should not be cross-examined by the judge during their examination-in-chief. Further, I do not doubt that the judge has a duty to intervene to clear the innocent. The judge has the duty to ensure that the accused is afforded the right to make full answer and defence, but he has the right and the duty to prevent the trial from being unnecessarily protracted by questions directed to irrelevant matters. This power must be exercised with caution so as to leave unfettered the right of an accused through his counsel to subject any witness's testimony to the test of cross-examination. The judge must not improperly curtail cross-examination that is relevant to the issues or the credibility of witnesses, but he has power to protect a witness from harassment by questions that are repetitious or are irrelevant to the issues in the case or to the credibility of the witness: see *R. v. Bradbury* (1973), 14 C.C.C. (2d) 139 at pp. 140-1, 23 C.R.N.S. 293 (Ont. C.A.); *R. v. Kalia* (1974), 60 Cr. App. R. 200 at pp.209-11.[4]

Prior to the decision in *R. v. Valley* there was a history of decisions regarding the duty of a trial judge. Lord Greene, M.R.'s words on the impartiality of the trial judge are contained in the following well-known passage in *Yuill v. Yuill*:[5]

A judge who observes the demeanour of the witnesses while they are being examined by counsel has from his detached position a much more favourable opportunity of forming a just appreciation than a judge who himself conducts the examination. If he takes the latter course he, so to speak, descends into the arena and is liable to have his vision clouded by the dust of the conflict. Unconsciously de deprives himself of the advantage of calm and dispassionate observation.

The following is a transcript from the famous Toronto trial of Suchan and Jackson who were tried for the murder of police Detective Edmund Tong and the wounding of his partner, Detective Sergeant Roy Perry in the early 1950s. Both Suchan and Jackson were members of the infamous Boyd Gang, a band of bank robbers. The following is, in my view, one of the most egregious examples of a trial judge (Chief Justice McRuer) assuming the mantle of the prosecutor (descending into the arena), which occurred

---

4   See also *R. v. Watson* (2004), 191 C.C.C. (3d) 144 (Ont. C.A.); *R. v. Palosaari* (2004), 191 C.C.C. (3d) 228 (B.C. C.A.).

5   [1945] 1 All ER. 183 at 189 (C.A.); *R. c. Gagnon* (1992), 74 C.C.C. (3d) 385 (C.A. Qué.). See also *R. v. Palosaari, supra.*

after the accused Jackson was re-examined by his counsel, Arthur Maloney, with the following questions:[6]

McRuer:	One or two questions I want to ask you. Did you go by the name of Wilson in Montreal?
Jackson:	Yes, sir.
McRuer:	When you left 190 Wright Avenue on March 6, were you carrying a brief case?
Jackson:	Yes, sir.
McRuer:	Why were you carrying a brief case?
Jackson:	For a disguise, sir.
McRuer:	Was Lesso [Suchan] carrying a brief case for a disguise too?
Jackson:	In don't know sir.
McRuer:	Had you in mind what you were going to use the briefcases for?
Jackson:	No, sir. I just carried it for disguise.
McRuer:	I want to understand a little more [about your purpose for arming yourself with a loaded revolver]. Was it a revolver or a pistol?
Jackson:	A revolver.
McRuer:	Was it a .45?
Jackson:	No sir.
McRuer:	What caliber?
Jackson:	32-20.
McRuer:	That is a revolver that will cause death?
Jackson:	Yes sir.
McRuer:	No doubt about that?
Jackson:	That is right, sir.
McRuer:	What was your purpose in arming yourself with a loaded revolver?
Jackson:	To aid me in attempting to flee if I was apprehended.
McRuer:	To aid you in attempting to flee if you were apprehended. That you would fire it to assist you in attempting to flee if you were apprehended — was that the purpose?
Jackson:	Not to kill, sir.
McRuer:	I am saying to fire it.
Jackson:	Yes, sir.
McRuer:	So it is perfectly fair and perfectly clear, is it, that as you went out and got into that car and drove to the corner of Lansdowne and College, you were armed with a loaded revolver, having in your mind that you would fire it if necessary in an effort to assist you in escaping lawful apprehension?
Jackson:	Yes, sir.

George Finlayson, a former respected judge of the Ontario Court of Appeal had this to say of the above questions by the trial judge:[7]

---

6 From the book *John J. Robinette Peerless Mentor: An Appreciation* by George D. Finlayson, published by The Osgoode Society, 2003.

7 At page 174 of his book.

"The transcript records what I still think today was a remarkable display of injudicial conduct on the part of the Chief Justice. This conduct is particularly offensive when dealing with the accused. It is difficult to overstate the impact of questions from the presiding judge at a jury trial. They are given more weight by members of the jury because they trust the impartiality of the questioner and assume that he is asking questions for the purpose of eliciting the truth and not as a combatant in a forensic duel. The mere physical presence of the trial judge gives him an advantage. He is speaking from the bench, an elevated position of authority and strength, literally hovering over the witness who is obliged to look up at him in giving his answers. He can expect no help from counsel in the form of objections to unfair questions. There is no one left to rule on the objections.

The questions of the Chief Justice and the answers to them sealed Jackson's fate. They also doomed Suchan because the admission by Jackson that he intended to use his gun in order to prevent apprehension made a mockery out of Suchan's testimony that he had acted alone and on the spur of the moment. Maloney's biographer, Charles Pullen, explains that it was Jackson who changed his mind and insisted that he wanted to testify and that Maloney did not have the experience to persuade him otherwise. However it happened, with the benefit of hindsight, Jackson's decision to testify was a mistake. Jackson could not improve on the defence Suchan had provided to him, and as it turned out he destroyed himself by trying. As Robinette put it later in his oral history, "Jackson was terrible. He virtually said that he was guilty. McRuer asked him a question and Jackson made an answer virtually saying, 'Yes, I intended to kill him.' It was just about that bad."

In *Yuill v. Yuill*, Lord Greene, M.R. went on to describe the duties of the trial Judge as follows:[8]

> The part which the judge ought to take while witnesses are giving their evidence must, of course, rest with his discretion. . . . It is, of course, always proper for a judge—and it is his duty—to put questions with a view of elucidating any obscure answer or when he thinks that the witness has misunderstood a question put to him by counsel. If there are matters which the judge considers have not been sufficiently cleared up or questions which he himself thinks ought to have been put, he can, of course, take steps to see that the deficiency is made good.

Lord Greene, M.R. continued:[9]

> [I]t is for the advocates, each in his turn, to examine the witnesses, and not for the judge to take it on himself lest by so doing he appears to favour one side or the other. . . . And it is for the advocate to state his case as fairly and strongly as he can, without undue interruption, lest the sequence of his argument be lost. . . . The judge's part in all this is to hearken to the evidence, only himself asking questions of the witnesses when it is necessary to clear up any point when it has been overlooked or left obscure; to see that the advocates behave them-

---

8 *Yuill v. Yuill, supra*, at 185.
9 *Ibid.*

selves and keep to the rules laid down by law; to exclude irrelevancies and discourage repetition; to make sure by wise intervention that he follows the points that the advocates are making and can assess their worth; and at the end to make up his mind to where the truth lies. If he goes beyond this, he drops the mantle of the judge and assumes the robe of an advocate; and the change does not become him well.

An accused person must be allowed to give her evidence without being badgered and interrupted. The trial judge is not to interrupt the examination-in-chief so as to divert the questioner from his plan or line of inquiry.[10] To repeatedly remind the witness that she is under oath is improper.[11] The trial judge should refrain from intervening during cross-examination and save his/her questions until cross-examination is concluded. Lord Greene, M.R. explained in *Yuill v. Yuill* the reason for this:[12]

> It is, I think, generally more convenient to do this when counsel has finished his questions or is passing to a new subject. It must always be borne in mind that the judge does not know what is in counsel's brief and has not the same facilities as counsel for an effective examination-in-chief or cross-examtnation. In cross-examination, for instance, experienced counsel will see just as clearly as the judge that, for example, a particular question will be a crucial one. But it is for counsel to decide at what stage he will put the question, and the whole strength of the cross-examination may be destroyed if the judge, in his desire to get to what seems to him to be the crucial point, himself intervenes and prematurely puts the question himself.

Denning L.J. in *Jones v. National Coal Board* had this insight to offer:[13]

> Nevertheless, it is obvious for more than one reason that such interventions should be as infrequent as possible when the witness is under cross-examination. It is only by cross-examination that a witness's evidence can be properly tested, and it loses much of its effectiveness in counsel's hands if the witness is given time to think out the answer to awkward questions; the very gist of cross-examination lies in the unbroken sequence of question and answer. Further to this, cross-examining counsel is at a grave disadvantage if he is prevented from following a preconceived line of inquiry which is, in his view, most likely to elicit admissions from the witness or qualifications of the evidence which he has given in chief. Excessive judicial interruption inevitably weakens the effectiveness of cross-examination in relation to both the aspects which we have mentioned, for at one and the same time it gives a witness valuable time for thought before answering a difficult question, and diverts cross-examining counsel from the course which he had intended to pursue, and to which it is by no means easy sometimes to return.

---

10 *R. v. Hulusi; R. v. Purvis* (1973), 58 Cr. App. R. 378 (C.A.).
11 *R. v. Gagnon* (1992), 74 C.C.C. (3d) 385 (Que. C.A.).
12 *Yuill v. Yuill, supra,* at 185.
13 [1957] 2 Q.B. 55 at 65 (H.L.).

Counsel has the right to present his own case in the way most advantageous to his side without undue interference by the trial judge. So where the trial judge was "insistent on haste in the conduct of the trial" an unduly restricted cross-examination caused a new trial to be ordered.[14] Schultz J.A. of the Manitoba Court of Appeal had this to say about the right of the parties to present their case and the trial judge's role:[15]

Unquestionably, dilatory tactics and unnecessary delays, frivolous and pointless questions, are time-wasting and are properly subject to comment, restriction, and control by the trial judge . . . he has the sole control of his court. He has the duty to insist that the rules of evidence be observed; to intervene to clear up points when necessary for his own information, or to discourage irrelevancies; but such interventions must be justified by the circumstances under which they are made. In the instant case, defence counsel had the right to examine witnesses and state his case as fully and fairly as he could in whatever manner he deemed most advantageous to his client and, as long as he kept within the bounds of fair advocacy, it was his right to do so without interruption, for, otherwise, the sequence, the culminating effect would be lessened or lost.

In *R. v. Bradbury*,[16] Kelly JA. of the Ontario Court of Appeal made the following comments about the trial judge's role in relation to cross-examination:

The right and indeed the responsibility of the trial Judge to control the proceedings before him to prevent conduct which may well be or become an abuse of the process of the Court is unquestioned. It must, however, be exercised with caution so as to leave unfettered the right of the defendant, through his counsel, to subject any witness's testimony to the test of cross-examination. The disallowance of questions ruled improper, as inviting the introduction of hearsay evidence, or as being irrelevant or for the protection of a witness from unwarranted harassment falls within the scope of the trial Judge's authority.

We do not consider that it is allowable, in advance, to place any restriction on the length of time to be consumed by cross-examination. The rulings of the trial Judge should be made when questions are put or about to be put and should be confined to the propriety of the question or questions in issue.

Note that section 537(1.1) of the *Criminal Code*, with respect to preliminary hearings, has been amended by adding the following after subsection (1):

---

14   *R. v. Ignat* (1965), 53 W.W.R. 248 (Man. C.A.); *Boran v. Wenger*, [1942] 2 D.L.R. 528 (Ont. C.A.); *Pilon v. R.* (1973), 23 C.R.N.S. 392 (Que. C.A.); *Phillips v. Ford Motor Co.* (1971), 18 D.L.R. (3d) 641 (Ont. C.A.); *Re R. and Roulette* (1972), 7 C.C.C. (2d) 244 (Man. Q.B.).

15   *R. v. Ignat, ibid.*, at 250 (Man. C.A.); *Boran v. Wenger, ibid.; Pilon v. R., ibid.; Phillips v. Ford Motor Co., ibid.*

16   (1973), 14 C.C.C. (2d) 139 (Ont. C.A.) at 140-141. See also *R. v. McLaughlin* (1974), 2 O.R. (2d) 514 (Ont. C.A.); *R. v. Makow* (1973), 13 C.C.C. (2d) 167 (B.C. C.A.).

(1.1) A justice acting under this Part shall order the immediate cessation of any part of an examination or cross-examination of a witness that is, in the opinion of the justice, abusive, too repetitive or otherwise inappropriate.[17]

Where counsel is inept, the courts will recognize a wider latitude for intervention in order that the facts are properly brought forth but the trial judge must not permit himself to be "drawn into the arena to an extent which at times seemed to make him a protagonist."[18]

A trial judge's intervention should not give the impression of unduly favouring one of the parties. When the judge throws his weight behind one of the parties he does so with considerable influence. The words of O'Halloran J.A. in *R. v. Pavlukoff*[19] emphasize such impact stemming from judicial intervention in a jury trial:

The Judge in Court officially and physically occupies a position of great power and prestige. His power and his control of the trial plain to see in Court, are matched by his knowledge of the law and his experience weighing and analyzing evidence. His lightest word or mannerism touching the reliability of a witness and the guilt of the accused, cannot fail to bear heavily upon the members of the jury who naturally look up to him (and in more ways than one) as the embodiment of the great traditions of the law. To the jury the presiding Judge appears as the great neutral. Anything that emanates from him, carries for them at least all the ear-marks of balanced justice.

A trial judge should not make comments during a witness's evidence; indicating disbelief in that evidence as prejudgment compromises the appearance of justice which is essential to a fair trial.[20]

The Supreme Court of Canada in *Brouillard v. R.*[21] held that when the accused is testifying even greater judicial restraint should be exercised "for at the end of the day he is the only one who may be leaving the courtroom in handcuffs." Justice must be seen to be done.

---

17 One would have thought a trial Judge would have this power without such an amendment.
18 *Magel v. Krempler* (1970), 14 D.L.R. (3d) 593 (Man. C.A.).
19 (1953), 106 C.C.C. 249 (B.C. C.A.) at 267; see also *R. v. Muggli* (1961), 131 C.C.C. 363 (B.C. C.A.); *R. v. Darlyn* (1946), 88 C.C.C. 269 (B.C. C.A.); *R. v. Augello*, [1963] 3 C.C.C. 191 (Ont. C.A.). See also *R. v. Torbiak* (1974), 18 C.C.C. (2d) 229 (Ont. C.A.) *per* Kelly J.A. who pointed out that the position of the trial judge is one of great power and prestige which gives his every word a special significance; *R. c. Gagnon, supra.*
20 *R. v. Augello*, [1963] 3 C.C.C. 191 (Ont. C.A.) at 192; to repeatedly caution an accused who was under oath was improper, *R. c. Gagnon, supra*; *R. v. Cook* (1983), 4 C.C.C. (3d) 419 (N.S. C.A.) at 425. For an example when such comments by the trial judge did not offend see *R. v. Sherry* (1996), 110 C.C.C. (3d) 160 (S.C.C.) where the Supreme Court of Canada adopted the reasons of Doherty J. dissenting (1995), 103 C.C.C. (3d) 276 (Ont. C.A.).
21 (1985), 17 C.C.C. (3d) 193 (S.C.C.). See also *R. v. Goel; R. v. Salvaggio* (1986), 27 C.C.C. (3d) 438 (Ont. Dist. Ct.).

CONVICTIONS QUASHED

Martin J.A. in *R. v. Valley*[22] reviews those instances of judicial interference which will result in a conviction being quashed. He concludes:

I Questioning of an accused or his witnesses to an extent or in a manner which conveys the impression that the Judge is placing his authority on the side of the prosecution and which conveys the impression of disbelief of the accused or defence witnesses: see *Brouillard (a.k.a. Chatel) v. The Queen* (1985), 17 C.C.C. (3d) 193, 16 D.L.R. (4th) 447, [1985] 1 S.C.R. 39; *R. v. Denis*, [1967] 1 C.C.C. 196, [1966] Que. Q.B. 404*n* (Que. C.A.). In *Brouillard v. The Queen, supra*, during the accused's testimony the Judge asked more questions than both counsel, interrupted the accused's examination-in-chief and cross-examined him. The trial Judge posed about 60 questions to a defence witness and interrupted her 10 times. Both the accused and his witness were subjected to sarcastic remarks by the trial Judge.[23]

II Where the interventions have made it really impossible for counsel for the defence to do his or her duty in presenting the defence, for example, where the interruptions of the trial Judge during cross-examination divert counsel from the line of topic of his questions or break the sequence of questions and answers and thereby prevent counsel from properly testing the evidence of the witness: see *R. v. Matthews* (1983), 78 Cr. App. R. 23 at p. 31; *Jones v. National Coal Board*, [1957] 2 Q.B. 55 at p. 65.

III Where the interventions prevent the accused from doing himself justice or telling his story in his own way: see *R. v. Matthews, supra*, at p. 31; *R. v. Perks*, [1973] Crim. L.R. 388; *R. v. Cain* (1936), 25 Cr. App. R. 204; *R. v. Hulusi* (1973), 58 Cr. App. R. 378.

IV The courts have drawn a distinction between conduct on the part of the presiding Judge, which is discourteous to counsel and indicates impatience but which does not invite the jury to disbelieve defence witnesses, and conduct which actively obstructs counsel in his work: *R. v. Hircock*, [1970] 1 Q.B. 67 (C.A.); *R. v. Ptohopoulos* (1967), 52 Cr. App. R. 47. The authorities have consistently held that mere discourtesy, even gross discourtesy, to counsel cannot by itself be a ground for quashing a conviction. Where, however, the trial Judge's comments suggest that counsel is acting in a professionally unethical manner for the purpose of misleading the jury, the integrity and good faith of the defence may be denigrated and the

---

22 (1986), 26 C.C.C. (3d) 207 (Ont. C.A.) at 231-232; leave to appeal to S.C.C. refused (1986), 26 C.C.C. (3d) 207n (S.C.C.). For a more recent example of a trial Judge's interference creating a perception of lack of fairness see *R. v. Szpala* (1998), 39 O.R. (3d) 97 (Ont. C.A.). In a more recent case following *Valley*, see *R. v. Stucky* (2009), 240 C.C.C. (3d) 141(Ont. C.A.) at para. 64, application/notice of appeal 2009 CarswellOnt 3910 (S.C.C.).

23 In *R. v. Watson*, the Ontario Court of Appeal held that unnecessary multiple interjections repeatedly disrupting the flow and undermining the dynamic cross-examination of key witnesses on critical matters creates the appearance of an unfair trial.

appearance of an unfair trial created: *R. v. Turkiewicz, Barrow and MacNamara* (1979), 50 C.C.C. (2d) 406, 103 D.L.R. (3d) 332, 26 O.R. (2d) 570 (Ont. C.A.); *R. v. Hulusi, supra.*

Interventions by the Judge creating the appearance of an unfair trial may be of more than one type and the appearance of a fair trial may be destroyed by a combination of different types of intervention. The ultimate question to be answered is not whether the accused was in fact prejudiced by the interventions but whether he might *reasonably* consider that he had not had a fair trial or whether a reasonably minded person who had been present throughout the trial would consider that the accused had not had a fair trial: see *Brouillard v. The Queen, supra; R. v. Racz,* [1961] N.Z.L.R. 227 (C.A.).

The Supreme Court in *R. v. S. (R.D.)*[24] held that the Court should construe the impugned conduct in light of the whole trial and underscored the strong presumption of impartiality that applies to trial judges, and the reviewing Court's hesitancy to make a finding of bias in the absence of convincing evidence. The Court confirmed an earlier decision that the test is what an informed person viewing the matter realistically, having thought the matter through, would conclude. Would that person think it is more likely than not the Judge would consciously or unconsciously not decide fairly?

COUNSEL'S RESPONSE TO THE INTERFERING TRIAL JUDGE

An interfering or bullying trial Judge can confuse or instil fear into young counsel and will cause the stomachs of the more experienced counsel to churn and their blood to boil. Sir David Napley[25] suggests that when the Judge interrupts so much that he is in danger of taking the cross-examination away from counsel "Gentle sarcasm might be justified: Would Your Honour feel amiss, at this point, if I put a question to the witness, be that at the risk of breaking into Your Honour's long—and wholly effective cross-examination."[26]

But all counsel do not have the stature of a Sir David Napley and may be reluctant to resort to "Gentle sarcasm." An example of what not to do occurred several years ago when a young counsel, no doubt out of a sense of frustration, addressed an Ontario High Court Judge with a reputation for Crown partisanship as "the captain of the crown's ship." Counsel was found in contempt of Court and fined $2,000 (although not by the Judge in question).

---

24 (1997), 118 C.C.C. (3d) 353 (S.C.C.) at 367.
25 D. Napley, *Technique of Persuasion* (London: Sweet & Maxwell, 1970).
26 *Ibid.*, p. 73.

I Object

"I feel that I must warn you,
counselor, that you are perilously close
to a contempt-of-court citation."

© Unknown.

There are certain rules of behaviour that can be stated with some degree
of certainty. Counsel should never cower or be obsequious before an interfering or biased judge. Such behaviour will not only earn the disrespect of
the judge, but also the disrespect of the jury and even your client. Any
temper should be controlled in order to prevent saying something that

counsel might later regret. Counsel's role is to stand firm before the Court but not to be rude. Justices Reid and Holland in their book, *Views From the Bench*,[27] note: "You cannot win a contest of rudeness with a judge. If the judge interrupts unnecessarily or unfairly, displays hostility to you or your cause, appears to have made up his mind before hearing you, browbeats you or your witnesses, you have only one course of action open: stand your ground. Do that with firmness, but also with courtesy."

The judge's remarks are recorded by the Court reporter. If the trial judge continues in the same vein his or her conduct will no doubt become a main ground of appeal. Admittedly, if the trial judge's bias results in an adverse verdict then the speculation that there is a valid ground of appeal will not bring a great deal of satisfaction to the accused who has been convicted, particularly if he or she has to stay in custody pending the appeal. However, counsel can hope that there are juries who are impressed with the reminders during counsel's final address and the judge's charge to the jury that they are the sole judges of the facts and that they do not have to follow the trial judge's expressed views.

There are jurors who will not take kindly to an interfering, overbearing trial judge and will know when an accused is not receiving a fair trial. As a result they may well bend over backwards to give the accused the fair trial that they perceive he or she has not been receiving from the trial judge. This is not to say, as many counsel have learned to their dismay, that there will not be those jurors who will always look up to the trial judge and who will take their lead from him or her even when that judge displays a bias.

The following replies to an interfering trial judge have been suggested by some lawyers and these replies, of course, depend on the particular circumstances at the time: "I was intending to ask the witness about that, Your Honour. May I, with respect develop it in my own way?"; "I know the question was asked before, Your Honour, but I have a particular reason for asking it now. Would you please bear with me for a minute?"; "I would respectfully submit that Your Lordship is being unfair."

If nothing else the following examples are entertaining responses by the remarkable and quick minded English barrister, F.E. Smith who at the same time was making a career as a politician.[28] When rising to address the jury in a case before Mr. Justice Ridley, the latter had injudiciously observed: "Well, Mr. Smith, I have read the pleadings and I do not think much of your case." Stung by this remark, Smith answered: "Indeed, My Lord. I'm sorry to hear that, but your Lordship will find that the more you hear of it, the more it will grow on you."

---

27 (Toronto: Canada Law Book Co., 1984) at 89.
28 From *The Life of F.E. Smith, First Earl of Birkenhead* by his son, Frederick, second Earl of Birkenhead, 1960. Eyre and Spottiswoode, London.

It is said Smith's worst insults were reserved for Judge Willis, supposedly a sanctimonious County Court Judge "full of kindness expressed in a patronizing manner." F.E. Smith was representing a tramway company, which had been sued for damages as a result of injuries to a boy who had been run over and claimed blindness resulted. The Judge who was deeply moved said: "poor boy, poor boy, blind. Put him on the chair so that the jury can see him." F.E. Smith said harshly: "Perhaps Your Honour would like to have the boy passed round the jury box." "That is a most improper remark," said Judge Willis angrily. "It was provoked," said Smith, "by a most improper suggestion." After a pause, the Judge responded: "Mr. Smith have you ever heard of a saying by Bacon — the great Bacon — that youth and discretion are ill-wed companions?" Smith: "Indeed I have your Honour; and has Your Honour ever heard of a saying by Bacon — the great Bacon — that a much talking Judge is like an ill-tuned cymbal?" The Judge angrily responded: "You are extremely offensive, young man" and F.E. Smith replied with a rather famous jibe: "As a matter of fact we both are; the only difference between us is that I'm trying to be and you can't help it. I have been listened to by the highest tribunal in the land, and I have not come down here to be brow-beaten." Later on the trial Judge asked the following question, no doubt regretfully: "What do you think I am on the bench for, Mr. Smith?" "It's not for me, Your Honour, to attempt to fathom the inscrutable workings of Providence."[29]

In another case, when a Judge was interrupting Smith, the latter said: "If Your Honour would only be good enough not to interrupt me." The Judge responded: "I shall interrupt you and any other counsel whenever it is necessary." Smith: "I rather gather from your demeanour that you probably will."[30]

THE UNREPRESENTED ACCUSED

Where an indigent accused is unrepresented, the trial Judge has an inherent power, in order to insure a fair trial, to appoint counsel.[31] This may require the trial Judge to recognize, depending on the circumstances of the case, that a significant degree of assistance is required. This should include explaining to the accused the course the trial is to take, beginning with his

---

29 *Ibid.*

30 *Ibid.*

31 *R. v. Rowbotham* (1988), 41 C.C.C. (3d) 1 (Ont. C.A.) at p. 69. The Court may stay the proceedings until the state agrees to pay for representation. See *R. v. Phillips* (2003), 181 C.C.C. (3d) 321 (S.C.C.) where trial Judge refused to appoint counsel because accused had hired and fired several lawyers, accused employed and unlikely eligible for legal aid and case not complex. Supreme Court of Canada states that legal representation only required when assistance essential to a fair trial and representation by a lawyer not a prerequisite to a fair trial.

arraignment, the calling of witnesses by the Crown Attorney with the accused's right to cross-examine these witnesses and to object to irrelevant evidence, his right to call witnesses and to testify, the risks inherent in testifying and not testifying and the right to make a closing argument.[32] The trial Judge should also be vigilante in assisting the accused with respect to evidentiary issues, including *Charter* rights and whether evidence should be excluded under s. 24(2).[33] The trial Judge should guide the accused through the trial in such a way that his defence is brought out in full force and effect.[34]

The following cases reflect courts' decisions as to the obligations of the trial judge to the unrepresented accused:

- the trial judge cannot force representation on the accused if he/she chooses to represent themselves[35]

- there is not a duty to appoint counsel where issues are simple and the facts not really in dispute[36]

- the trial Judge does not have to provide the unrepresented accused at each stage of the trial with the kind of advice the accused could expect from being represented by a lawyer otherwise the trial judge would be in the position of both advocate and impartial arbiter at the same time[37]

- if the accused can't effectively cross-examine, the trial judge should assist and pursue lines of defence indicated by the accused[38] but not to do so beyond what would reasonably be expected from an experienced counsel[39]

- in helping an accused prepare for cross-examination the trial Judge generally has only the obligation in explaining how the transcript of the preliminary hearing can be used[40]

- the trial Judge should point out discrepancies in testimony to the accused[41]

- the waiver to have voluntariness of a statement tested on a *voir dire* must be informed and the trial Judge must take all reasonable precau-

---

32 *R. v. Tran* (2001), 55 O.R. (3d) 161 (Ont. C.A.).

33 *Ibid.*

34 *Ibid*; *R. v. McGibbon* (1988), 45 C.C.C. (3d) 334 (Ont. C.A.) at p. 347; *R. v. Darlyn* (1946), 88 C.C.C. 269 (B.C. C.A.) at p. 272.

35 *R. v. Mian* (1998), 133 C.C.C. (3d) 573 (N.S. C.A.) at 575-576.

36 *R. v. Littlejohn* (1978), 41 C.C.C. (2d) 161 (Ont. C.A.) at 174.

37 *R. v. Taubler* (1987), 20 O.A.C. 64 (Ont. C.A.) at para. 30.

38 *R. v. Huebschwerlen* (1964), 45 C.R. 393 (Y.T. C.A.) at 397.

39 *R. v. Manhas* (1980), 17 C.R. (3d) 331 (S.C.C.) at p. 337.

40 *R. v. McGibbon* (1988), 45 C.C.C. (3d) 334 (Ont. C.A.) at p. 347.

41 *Ibid.*

tions to ensure the accused has been made sufficiently aware of his rights. A simple "yes" that he or she is satisfied as to voluntariness may not qualify as a sufficiently informed waiver[42]

- the accused must be made aware of the difference between an opening and closing statement[43]

- granting the accused a recess in order that he or she can better think what else to say to the Court may be part of the trial Judge's obligation to ensure a fair trial[44]

- in order to ensure a fair trial, the Judge may direct the Crown to have a defence witness subpoenaed[45]

- the Judge should explain to the accused the difference between evidence and submissions by the accused to the jury and that the accused may not make reference to facts not in evidence.[46]

---

42   *R. v. Dimmock* (1996), 108 C.C.C. (3d) 262 (B.C. C.A.) at paras. 21-22.
43   *R. v. Littlejohn* (1978), 41 C.C.C. (2d) 161 (Ont. C.A.) at 174.
44   *R. v. McGibbon* (1988), 45 C.C.C. (3d) 334 (Ont. C.A.) at p. 347.
45   *Ibid.*
46   *R. v. Gölinas* (1998), 1998 CarswellQue 129, 1998 CarswellQue 1262 (Que. C.A.).

33

Objections by Counsel

It is clearly counsel's duty to object to inadmissible testimony being tendered by the other side where it is damaging to his or her case. The objection should, in counsel's mind at least, be a valid one with a reasonable chance of succeeding. If the objectionable evidence really does not hurt his or her case counsel should not be so technical and should just let the evidence in. Jumping up and objecting at every opportunity and spending time arguing over minor matters which do not damage the objector's case will only irritate the Judge and the jurors who may have to keep leaving the courtroom over what they will perceive to be meaningless and time-wasting issues particularly when objecting counsel is constantly being overruled. A common example of such objections is quibbling about leading questions on unimportant matters.

It is not unusual for younger or inexperienced counsel to make objections without really having thought them out. Something tells them they should object, perhaps because they were caught unawares by the evidence being led and are not really sure whether they should object and do so out of an abundance of caution; perhaps they object just because the evidence is damaging and they hope, on the off-chance that their objection will be sustained. The result is that they fumble with the reasons for their objection and will lose objection after objection—along with the patience of the trial judge and the jury. In addition, the jury may feel that counsel is being unfair by not allowing the witness to tell the story in his or her own words.

Counsel should always be alert and should not be too late with his or her objections to prevent the damage from being done before the objection can be made. Proper preparation particularly with a sound knowledge of the statements in the disclosure and the evidence given at the preliminary hearing, will help counsel as to when objectionable questions will arise but he or she will also have to be following the testimony closely. A late objection will only emphasize any damage.

Counsel may find themselves having to make a choice in a case where they have a valid objection to the admissibility of certain evidence but know that if the evidence is admitted, it can be successfully challenged in cross-examination and thus they can damage the witness's credibility. In the final analysis the choice will probably depend on how important it is to keep the evidence out as compared to how seriously the witness can be damaged after the evidence is admitted, assuming it is important to damage the witness's credibility.

There is always the concern that, by objecting, counsel will leave the jury with the impression that counsel is trying to prevent the whole story from being told and particularly that he or she is trying to suppress evidence which is damaging to his or her side. Some of the jurors may even speculate on the objectionable evidence and become consciously or subconsciously affected by it. As well counsel does not want the jurors to feel that it is he or she who is responsible for sending them out of the courtroom during argument. To minimize any possible adverse effects of objections, counsel might say something such as: "Your Honour, I do not know what the witness [or my client's] answer will be to the question put by my friend but I would respectfully suggest that the question is improper." Or, "My Lord, before the witness answers the question I believe a question of law arises." Normally after such objections the trial judge will take the hint and ask that the jury be excused from the courtroom. Another example of how to object and perhaps win some points in certain instances is to say: "Your Honour, I have not objected to a number of earlier leading questions but I feel my friend has now gone too far. We should be hearing the witness's version of events, not counsel's."

Concerns about unfavourable jury reaction to objections, particularly ones which take up some time in the argument, can be mitigated by counsel advising the trial judge before the jury is selected that there are a number of issues of law to be decided and it would be appropriate to deal with them at the outset so that the jury is not constantly sent out of the courtroom. This procedure is permitted by virtue of section 645(5) of the Criminal Code.[1] Another approach is to set aside an appropriate time before the trial date to deal with evidentiary issues before the trial judge.

During the trial, arguments on the admissibility of evidence can be a "tip-off" to the witness who cannot help but listen and possibly be influenced in some of their ensuing answers. In such situations counsel who has this concern should ask the trial judge that the witness be excused during the argument. It would be rare for a trial judge to refuse such a request.

Some counsel employ the tactic of objecting to a question in order to assist a witness, particularly a witness who is having trouble answering and needs some breathing room. Counsel is not so much concerned that his or her objection will be sustained as that the witness be warned by the way counsel words his or her objection and can then answer accordingly. An

---

1   R.S.C. 1985, c. C-46.

example of such a tactic is when objecting counsel says something such as: "Your Honour, that question is unfair. How can a witness know the answer to such a question?" After the trial judge permits the question or a rephrasing of the question the witness would then respond by answering: "I don't know the answer." Opposing counsel should object before the jury that counsel's wording of the objection is having the effect of telegraphing to the witness about how to answer the question. The cross-examiner's next question to the witness might be something like the following: "Now that you have heard the way my friend has phrased his objection, what do you say?" If there are continued objections along this line the reason for the objections will become obvious to the Court, highlighting the witness's difficulties and incurring the displeasure of the trial Judge.

Counsel should also be aware of the wily opponent who uses objections to put improper evidence before the jury or to make speeches that are best left for the final address.

Crown attorney, John Scollin, Q.C. in an address at the Federal Prosecutors' Seminar in 1980[2] made these observations when it came to making objections:

1. Be sparing with your objections and concise with your supporting reasons; and, having accepted with grace an adverse ruling on your submission on a line of evidence, do not repeat your objection to further questions pursuing that same line.

2. When opposing counsel makes an objection when you are questioning a witness or addressing the court, immediately resume your seat at the counsel table and remain seated and silent until the Judge has heard the objection and, if necessary, has called on you to reply. If you are disciplined to address the court only when you are on your feet, resuming your seat removes the risk of the Judge—and of the court reporter and possibly a mystified jury—having to cope with an unseemly double harangue. Particularly in a jury trial it is often to your advantage that a patently ill-conceived objection by opposing counsel be left to be disposed of summarily by the Judge.

3. You will have anticipated and prepared for objections on both sides and will have read the cases and selected for use—generally—only two, the leading and the latest (whether for or against you); but if, despite your efforts, you are caught unprepared to do justice to it an objection that concerns a point of importance to your case, ask for a brief recess in order to assist the court—and your case—with a proper formulation of your position. In the event your request is refused, or course, you will fall back on reason and common sense—not generally an uncomfortable fall.

---

2 Federal Prosecutors' Seminar. "The Preparation of Witnesses and the Conduct of the Trial." Ottawa, 1980.

34

The Contested Bail Hearing[*]

INTRODUCTION

From a strategic perspective, the contested bail hearing is for practical purposes, the start of many criminal trials. Frequently, the result of the bail hearing is a harbinger of the ultimate outcome of the case. Pre-trial detention can have a devastating effect of the accused's willingness and ability to mount a defence. On the other hand, pre-trial release tilts the scales against the Crown as the *Charter* clock begins to tick, witnesses relocate, memories fade, and time heals. Defence counsel will be able to spend more time preparing with their client in the office than at the jail. Sentence can be significantly affected as well, if the released accused uses the interval wisely. If plea bargaining is the ultimate route, an accused out of custody will not be as rushed as the detained accused who might be quick to accept a sentence which could be higher than if pleaded later because he or she was antsy serving "dead time."

Pursuant to section 515(10) of the *Criminal Code*, the Crown must show cause why the detention of the accused is justified. Subsection (10) states as follows:

> **515.** (10) For the purposes of this section, the detention of an accused in custody is justified only on one or more of the following grounds:
> (a) where the detention is necessary to ensure his or her attendance in court in order to be dealt with according to law;
> (b) where the detention is necessary for the protection or safety of the public, including any victim of or witness to the offence, or any person under the age of 18 years, having regard to all the circumstances including any substantial likelihood that the accused will, if released from custody, commit a criminal offence or interfere with the administration of justice; and

---

* The author is grateful to Crown Attorney Stephen Sheriff for the significant contribution to this chapter.

(c) if the detention is necessary to maintain confidence in the administration of justice, having regard to all the circumstances, including

(i)   the apparent strength of the prosecution's case,
(ii)   the gravity of the offence,
(iii) the circumstances surrounding the commission of the offence, including whether a firearm was used, and
(iv)   the fact that the accused is liable, on conviction, for a potentially lengthy term of imprisonment or, in the case of an offence that involves, or whose subject-matter is, a firearm, a minimum punishment of imprisonment for a term of three years or more.

The show cause burden shifts to the accused where he or she is charged with an indictable offence while on bail for another indictable offence or is charged with certain offences as listed in section 515(6) or is charged with an indictable offence is not ordinarily resident in Canada.

The Court, in deciding whether or not an accused should be released on bail, must act on evidence whether it is *viva voce* or in affidavit form.[1] Hearsay evidence is admissible if the Justice finds it to be credible or trustworthy.[2] The Crown is therefore precluded from simply reading in the allegations against the accused without calling a witness or witnesses to testify unless the defence agrees otherwise.[3]

Section 518(b) states that an accused cannot be examined about the circumstances of the offence except by his/her counsel and cannot be cross-examined unless the accused has testified respecting the offence.[4] An accused who testifies at the bail hearing should think hard about disclosing his or her defence at the bail hearing while under oath during examination-in-chief since the Crown will have the opportunity to cross-examine.

EXAMINATION OF THE ACCUSED AT BAIL HEARINGS

In-Chief by Defence Counsel

It is usually desirable to call the accused as a witness, particularly since he or she cannot be questioned about the offence by virtue of section 518(b) of the *Criminal Code* by anyone except counsel for the accused.[5] In a reverse onus situation, there really isn't much choice; the accused should testify.

---

1   *R. v. Woo* (1994), 90 C.C.C. (3d) 404 (B.C. S.C.).
2   Section 518(e) *Criminal Code* of Canada. This section sets out the kinds of evidence that can be led at a Show Cause hearing.
3   *R. v. Hajdu* (1984), 14 C.C.C. (3d) 563 (Ont. H.C.); also *R. v. Woo, supra.*
4   *R. v. Deom* (1981), 64 C.C.C. (2d) 222 (B.C. S.C.).
5   If the accused does testify about the offence he or she may be cross-examined about the offence. See section 518(b) of the Criminal Code.

It is vital to a successful examination-in-chief of the accused that there be a clear release plan, no matter how modest. The more realistic the plan, the better the prospect of release. Such a plan must, if at all possible, represent an improvement over past plans which have failed. Past failures should be candidly acknowledged in chief, together with some explanation for the failure, in order to take the wind out of the Crown's sails. Such a plan should include at minimum, a fixed residence, work or school plans, a recipe to stay clear of alleged victims, and some effort to address any obvious problems such as drugs or alcohol. Even though most accused persons want to rush the bail hearing, it is foolish to do so without a sound release plan including acceptable sureties, in all but the weakest of Crown bail cases.

Wise counsel will help the accused prepare the release plan in an effort to provide the necessary "comfort level" to the Judge or Justice of the Peace through the structuring of release conditions to implement and monitor the plan. One way to design the plan is to make a list of all the factors which would trouble you, if you were being asked to release the accused. The plan will hopefully provide answers to those concerns. It will also serve as the foundation for a focused examination-in-chief of the accused, as well as a convenient checklist of the topics to be covered in that examination. This approach may succeed in creating a release mindset in the Court providing the accused acknowledges the obvious, and demonstrates insight into past problems. Progress will be visible when the Judge can be seen feverishly writing notes while the accused testifies about the plan. The goal is to get the accused to clearly articulate the plan in his or her words and call the necessary witnesses or produce letters which confirm the plan.

Since it is inevitable that the accused's criminal record will be given prominence by the Crown, an effort should be made in examination-in-chief to put the record in the best possible light within reason. It is essential that the accused face up to any prior convictions involving failure to appear in Court and breach of recognizance, with a credible explanation, even if the explanation is damaging. The focus can then be changed to those aspects of the release plan designed to prevent recurrence.

What follows are sample examinations-in-chief which endeavour to navigate through hazardous waters leaving the least wake possible while squarely facing obvious concerns, and demonstrating a measure of insight into past problems:

Alcohol or Drug Problems

> Q: What do you believe is the main reason you have had problems with the law in the past?
> A: I have got an alcohol and drug problem.
> Q: What have you done about that problem?

A: Not enough. I have attended a few A.A. meetings inside jail, but I have not yet gone to one on the outside.

Q: What's your plan if you are released from custody?

A: I am going to be attending NarcAnon meetings every Wednesday and A.A. meetings every Monday at 234 Eglinton Avenue East in Toronto.

Q: How can the court count on that?

A: I have a sponsor who has agreed to help me.

Q: Who is your sponsor?

A: His name is John Smith, he's an accountant who works in Scarborough and lives with his wife and children in Etobicoke.

Q: How is he going to be able to help you?

A: He's been through what I've been through and he's been straight for eight years. He is going to provide support for me, someone to lean on when I need help. I am going to start off by staying at his house.

Poor Work Record

Q: Have you held any steady jobs in the past?

A: No, just part time.

Q: Why is that?

A: I haven't learned a trade and until lately I've never thought about making a career out of anything.

Q: Why are you thinking about it now?

A: I've got a young boy to support and I'm getting fed up with myself for wasting my life in jail. I don't want to lose my boy to Children's Aid, he's all I've got.

Q: Do you have any plans to get back on track?

A: Yes, I've decided to train as a tractor trailer driver, that's what I'd like to do for an honest living.

Q: What steps are you going to take?

A: I've made an application to George Brown College. I got a letter back, which I have right here with me, that they've got a couple of vacancies in the next course which starts two weeks tomorrow.

Failure to Appear History

Q: The court has heard that you have a number of convictions for failing to appear in court, and failing to live up to the terms of previous release orders. What can you tell us about those problems?

A: I had no respect for the court or anyone else in those days and I acted like a fool.

Q: Why will this time be any different from the other times?

A: This is the first time my mom has been willing to put up part of her house to sign me out. If I let her down, she's made it clear she'll wash her hands of me for keeps. I sure don't want that to happen.

Strong Crown Case

Section 518(1)(b) states that the accused can only be examined by his counsel respecting the offence with which he is charged.[6] The accused may feel that because the Crown has led evidence of a strong case, that the only way to mitigate that evidence is to testify about the offence. However by virtue of section 518(1)(b) he then opens himself to cross-examination on that testimony.

Where counsel is not reluctant at an early stage to disclose aspects of the defence in order to try and neutralize or minimize the Crown's argument, an approach might be to call an articling student to testify. Since *Code* section 518(1)(*e*) provides that the justice at the bail hearing "may receive and base his decision on evidence considered credible or trustworthy by him in the circumstances of each case," this approach is workable and is without risk as long as the evidence doesn't go so far as to amount to a waiver of privilege. Another approach would be to call any available witness who is able to shed a more favourable light on the circumstances. Section 518(1)(*e*) opens the door for hearsay testimony and is most often relied upon by the Crown in presenting its case. The defence should also take advantage of this opportunity when needed but it cannot be gainsaid that unshaken admissible evidence under oath should take precedence over hearsay testimony.

History of Violence and Current Allegations of Serious Violence

There are the cases where the presiding justice is well aware that they are going out on the proverbial limb if release is ordered. The "limb" can be given a trunk with roots if a psychiatrist or psychologist sees the accused while in custody, and issues a favourable report which includes a plan for continued assessment and treatment where necessary. Such a plan can provide the comfort factor the justice consciously or subconsciously seeks regardless of which party the onus is technically upon. In this situation, the expert has provided a shield for the justice and the examination-in-chief of the accused will want to stress that the accused is compliant and is keen to continue receiving the expert's assistance. In addition, character evidence when available should be called.

---

6 *R. v. Paonessa* (1982), 66 C.C.C. (2d) 300 (Ont. C.A.) held that a statement obtained from the accused at a bail hearing in violation of this section is not admissible in subsequent proceedings, even where defence counsel is the villain.

Cross-Examination by the Crown

At a bail hearing, the Crown is not constrained by the rules of evidence at trial or concern over a potential mistrial. Banned from leading evidence of bad character at trial, many Crown counsel have difficulty adjusting to the bail hearing where character is the real issue. Once the Crown realizes that these shackles have been removed, and that for practical purposes, the only remaining constraints are relevance which has wider boundaries than at trial, and the prohibition against asking questions about the offence by virtue of section 518(1)(b) of the *Criminal Code*, fertile turf comes into view.

The accused is invariably at a real disadvantage in the witness box at the bail hearing. His or her life turned upside down, likely fatigued with confidence shaken, he or she is usually desperate to regain freedom. All of these factors lead to reckless answers. Ill-prepared, and with limited awareness of the breadth of permissible cross-examination, he or she will likely be much easier to cross-examine now, rather than later at trial with months to prepare one theme. Moreover, in a very real sense, the accused testifying at a bail hearing can be called upon to defend his or her manner of life; past, present, and future.

In their desperation to secure freedom, accused persons are notoriously reckless in their evidence about employment or the prospects of employment. Vague evidence of roofing or landscaping jobs is often a surefire sign that the evidence is false.

The following are some frequently productive themes emanating from the Crown in cross-examination of the accused at bail hearings. The supposed rule that you don't ask unless you know the answer, has no application here. Indeed, at its highest this rule should only preclude questions which may evoke damaging answers. By careful control of the line of inquiry, this risk can readily be minimized. Since the Crown should simply be seeking the truth; the accused who handles cross-examination well, with sensible, candid answers revealing insight into his or her past behaviour, may be a good candidate for bail. In this case, the cross-examination has been a success if the yardstick is justice. Accordingly, it is suggested that the Crown should not lose any sleep over asking plenty of relevant questions going to the root of the accused's character, attitude, and behaviour letting the chips fall where they may. Defence counsel will wish to alert his or her client about the following types of cross-examination:

1) Q: When you went to jail in 1989, I take it you didn't enjoy it?
   A: No Sir.
   Q: If that's so, I'm sure you vowed to never again go back to jail because it was such a terrible experience, didn't you?
   A: Yes Sir.

Q: When you went back to jail in 1990, and again in 1993, you must have realized that is because you had no self control, correct?

A: Yes Sir.

Q: If you have so little self control, such that you are unable to prevent such a terrible experience from happening again and again, how can this court take a chance on your release to-day?

A: (typically) I don't know Sir.

2) Frequently, accused persons will testify at bail hearings in an effort to minimize the impact of their criminal record that they pled guilty to certain offences for the sake of expediency. The Crown can readily make some mileage when this happens as set out below:

Q: You say you weren't guilty of that offence, but you pled guilty anyway?

A: Yes Sir.

Q: So you were prepared to deceive the court just because it suited your selfish purposes?

A: I guess so.

Q: Your attitude must have been that this whole process was just some kind of a game, was that your attitude?

A: No, I don't think so.

Q: Did you care how the judge would feel if he learned he had sentenced an innocent man?

A: I guess not.

Q: Well, if you are prepared to deceive courts on the big issue of guilt or innocence, what's there to stop you tricking the court to-day on the issue of whether or not you should be released?

A: (difficult).

3) Most accused persons testifying at bail hearings have the natural instinct to make themselves look as good as possible and have programmed themselves not to admit anything that isn't obvious. Where the accused has a substantial criminal record they are vulnerable to the following line of questioning:

Q: Have you ever committed any crimes you haven't been charged with?

A: (typically) No Sir.

Q: So you've been caught each and every time you've committed an offence?

A: (now committed to this pathway) Yes Sir.

Q: You keep on committing crimes knowing it's pretty much a sure thing you'll be caught?

A: I guess that's right.

Q: How are the courts ever going to be able to stop you if virtually certain arrest can't stop you?

A: (typically) I don't know Sir.

The accused's dilemma is just as bad, if not worse if the opposite tact is taken:

Q: Tell us about some of the crimes you've gotten away with?—
Q: What percentage of the time do you get caught?—
Q: I guess the profits make getting caught an acceptable business risk, do they?—
Q: What's the crime you're proudest of getting away with?

4) Accused persons who are seriously involved in crime for financial gain may have a very difficult time trying to explain how they support themselves legitimately. They rarely receive social assistance, and commonly fail to file Income Tax returns. Any professed legitimate income source will probably not be able to withstand much scrutiny. Fearing that the Crown is going to alert Revenue Canada, the accused will not want to reveal any unreported income. Accordingly, this is a fertile field for the Crown to explore, since the accused's lifestyle cannot be reconciled with his or her professed income. After a series of probing questions, the accused may well be left in a position similar to the one set out below:

Q: How are you able to afford to pay $1200.00 per month rent if your part-time income as a disc jockey earns you only $600.00 per month? You've got to put food on the table and buy clothes as well don't you?
A: That's right sir, but my mother makes up the difference.
Q: Can we agree that the difference, after you put gas in the car, pay insurance, buy cigarettes, and so on is at least fifteen hundred dollars per month?
A: I'd say more like a grand.
Q: You're twenty eight now. We've agreed you haven't had a full time job since you were twenty one. You must owe her a pile of money by now; looks like about $84,000.00 to me which would be seven years at your figure of $1,000.00 a month. Is that what you owe her?
A: If you say so, I guess that's right.
Q: What does your mother do for a living?
A: I don't know.
Q: Well, surely you must call her at work sometimes to get more money when you run low, what number do you call her at during working hours?
A: The only number I've got is her home number, I can get her there most of the time.
Q: Is it possible your mother doesn't work at all, and is on welfare or some other form of social assistance?
A: I don't know, you'll have to ask her.

At this stage, it is highly unlikely that the accused's mother will be able or willing to verify the accused's version of her financial support if it is false, particularly if she was not in the courtroom to hear his or her evidence. If the accused's financial affairs cannot withstand such elementary scrutiny, there is a foundation for the argument that he or she is supporting himself through crime, and hence is a secondary ground risk.

5) Drug use is relevant to the accused's reliability with respect to attending

court, and the use of costly "hard" drugs is relevant to the secondary ground if it appears that the accused has no way other than crime to support an expensive addiction. Accordingly, any previous drug conviction is an invitation to explore this area.

Such a cross-examination might be along the following lines:

Q: I see that you were convicted of possession of a narcotic in July 1992, what kind of narcotic was it?

A: Heroin

Q: I also see that you were convicted a number of times around then of crimes of dishonesty, was that because you needed to support your drug habit? (Given the choice between admitting that he is a thief at heart as opposed to being driven to steal by the pressure of addiction, the answer is quite predictable)

A: Yes, I had a bad habit.

Q: Did you receive any treatment for your heroin addiction?

A: Went to a few sessions of "NarcAnon"

Q: Was that while you were in jail?

A: Yes

Q: Have you ever taken any treatment outside of jail?

A: No, I haven't

Q: If you were serious about beating this addiction, why didn't you take treatment when you got out or at least attend "NarcAnon" meetings?

A: I didn't need to, I beat it on my own.

Q: Judging from your record, you were addicted for quite a few years, how many years would you say?

A: About five.

Q: You just quit like that after a five year addiction to heroin?

A: It wasn't easy.

Q: Well if you claim you had the willpower to give up heroin on your own, why weren't you able to give up crime? I see from your record that you were still into break and enters after you supposedly gave up heroin, why were you still doing crimes of dishonesty?

A: I don't know.

Q: Well, if you don't know why you still do them, how is the court supposed to believe you'll stop if you are released?

A: I don't know.

Q: Neither do I.

6) It is surprising how frequently accused persons are unable to reliably recite their own criminal record. For some, this may be because they experience difficulty distinguishing between crimes committed and crimes for which they have been apprehended. Withdrawn or stayed charges are also a frequent source of confusion. The Crown can endeavour to capitalize upon this uncertainty in an effort to demonstrate that the accused has little or no concern for the administration of justice

and/or that the accused has actually committed many more crimes than disclosed in the criminal record.

Such a cross-examination might proceed along the following lines:

Q: Can you please tell the court how many criminal convictions you have in total?

A: I don't know, you have my record, whatever it says.

Q: I would like to test your recollection of your record, and let the court see how seriously you take your record, so I ask you again, what can you tell us about your record?

A: Well, I have been convicted of a few B and E's, and some theft unders, that kind of thing.

Q: Anything else? Anything more serious?

A: Well I think I was convicted or a robbery one time.

Q: Who did you rob?

A: A taxi driver.

Q: Where did you rob him?

A: Some street off Spadina, near the Lakeshore.

Q: What weapon did you use to rob him?

A: I think it was a knife.

Q: Well wouldn't you remember something like that, have you done so many robberies that you can't keep them all straight?

A: It was a knife, I'm sure.

Q: How much money did you get?

A: Couple a hundred bucks.

Q: When was this robbery of the taxi driver?

A: You've got the record there, what does it say?

Q: I've got some news for you, it doesn't show any robbery conviction at all. What do you make of that?

A: Well, I remember it. I think that's the time I got a deuce less.

Q: All I see is a simple assault conviction, together with six counts of break, enter, and theft at the time you received the sentence of two years less one day in May 1990.

A: I guess that's the one then—that's right, I don't think they could find the cabby to bring him to court, that's why they let me cop out to assault.

Q: Have you been convicted of any other types of crimes we haven't talked about yet?

A: No, we've covered them all.

Q: What about this conviction for obstruct justice in Ottawa in 1991?

A: Ya, I guess that's right.

Q: What happened there?

A: I offered some guy some money if he wouldn't testify against me, and he went to the cops.

Q: Well, what do you think he should have done, taken the money?

A: Some guys I know would have.

Q: Why couldn't you remember trying to bribe this fellow, and being convicted of obstruct justice?

A: Sometimes I try to block bad things out of my mind.

Q: Court dates would qualify as bad things wouldn't they?

A: I'd just as soon not be in court if that's what you mean.

Q: Why couldn't you block a court date out of your mind, the same way you block out other bad things?

A: I don't know, maybe I could.

7) More often than one would imagine, accused persons are unable to correctly recite the terms of currently existing release orders, and their apparent lack of concern can easily be exposed. Probing questions may also unearth an as yet undetected breach of such conditions particularly if those questions are asked innocuously, before the trap is sprung.

8) There seems to be no statutory prohibition against asking the accused questions about outstanding charges which are not the subject-matter of this bail hearing. Most accused persons are not ready for such questioning and tend to flounder accordingly. As such questioning may well violate section 7 *Charter* rights, it is recommended that there be no questioning as to the merits of outstanding serious offences.

EXAMINATION-IN-CHIEF OF PROPOSED SURETIES BY THE DEFENCE

It is of fundamental importance that the proposed surety have no significant criminal history of his or her own, other than perhaps an old record followed by clear rehabilitation. A conscientious Crown Attorney can have a criminal history checked in a few minutes while a witness is on the stand. Accordingly, it is crucial that potential sureties be carefully screened, not just fired into the witness box. A tarnished surety will inevitably tend to tarnish the accused.

It is also vital that any proposed surety have a basic understanding of the nature of the charges facing the accused as well as the accused's criminal record, if any. The best sureties will have a measure of insight into the source of the accused's problems and some constructive suggestions as to how those problems can best be brought under control.

Impressive sureties will have a personal interest in the accused's welfare, not just a familial or other obligation borne of perceived duty. Although financial substance remains of importance in countering primary ground concerns, a wealthy surety is not a passport to freedom, particularly with regard to secondary ground considerations.

The surety should be made aware that he or she stands to loose the amount signed for or deposited if the client fails to make any necessary Court appearance and to testify to this knowledge at the bail hearing in order that the presiding justice is aware that the surety recognizes the seriousness of his or her obligation to the Court. A proposed surety should be asked by defence counsel to articulate his or her willingness to render the accused into custody if the surety discovers that a term of release has been or is about to be broken.

It is obviously desirable to avoid calling prospective sureties who have been signatories on previously breached recognizances, unless they can testify as to favourably changed circumstances.

Cross-Examination of the Proposed Surety by the Crown

A popular area of cross-examination by many Crown attorneys is to show that the surety has a limited knowledge of the accused's present lifestyle, limited ability to control the accused effectively, and/or a lack of awareness of the accused's problems with the result that the surety's supervisory skills will be of questionable value. There has been some controversy with respect to whether or not this is a permissible line of inquiry. Those who argue that it is not would urge that the surety's only responsibility is to ensure that the accused appears for his or her required Court appearances relying on section 764 of the *Criminal Code*, and that the surety is not required to be a policeperson over the day-to-day activities of the accused. Consistent with this argument is that when bail has been noted for estreat it is normally for the accused failing to appear for his or her trial and for no other reason. However, even on this argument the Court may still be interested in the surety's supervisory powers to the limited extent that it reflects on the surety's ability to guarantee the accused's appearance for trial beyond the money that the surety has pledged. In any event the Crown would argue that section 770 of the *Criminal Code* permits the aforesaid line of cross-examination because it addresses the estreatment of bail where there is a non compliance "with a condition of the recognizance" thereby recognizing that bail can be forfeited with respect to more than just failing to appear for Court given the fact that recognizances often contain more than one condition. In addition, when one looks at form 32 in the *Code* for a recognizance, it is stated therein that the surety acknowledges his or her debt if the accused "fails in any of the conditions hereunder written." Notwithstanding that a surety may be financially responsible for any breach of condition of the recognizance, one still has to wonder whether a surety is to be a constant supervisor of the accused which in reality is an impossible task for most, although there can be certain cases where the Court would be interested in a particular surety keeping a close watch on the accused.[7]

---

7 While the surety as "jailor" or policeman over the day-to-day activities of the accused approach in today's world may be anachronistic, "requiring the surety to provide some measure of supervision over the accused's daily activities is both realistic and desirable . . . [in order] to ensure that the specific conditions of release . . . are observed." But not "to become responsible for every aspect of the accused's life." See a discussion by Gary Trotter, in *The Law of Bail in Canada*, Second Edition, Carswell p. 283.

Most proposed sureties are sincere, well-intentioned people of good character. A direct frontal assault upon such a witness is ill-advised. Accordingly, probing as opposed to confrontational questions are to be preferred.

More than a few sureties attend bail hearings out of a sense of loyalty to someone close to the accused, but not the accused. Probing questions which explore the amount of time the surety spent with the accused prior to arrest can be revealing, since not many decent ordinary citizens spend considerable time with persons mixed up in crime. To the extent that the surety frequently associated with the accused, yet was unaware of the accused's criminal propensities, there is the inference that the surety really did not know the accused and cannot communicate with the accused in a meaningful way. By the same token, the surety who rarely saw the accused will be an ineffective supervisor. There will likely be well-intentioned protestations that more time will be spent with the accused in the future, but careful questioning of geography and working hours of the surety may reveal that these hopes are unrealistic. After all such a proposed surety did not fit the accused into the surety's life in the past. For most people something has to give way in the surety's life to open up available time. The surety witness will have generally not thought this through nor have any practical recipe as to how to supervise an adult of different lifestyle which task, can be close to impossible at the best of times.

Sureties are frequently poorly briefed as to the accused's criminal history, and the circumstances of the present allegations. Since they are usually honest witnesses, they will often acknowledge genuine surprise and sometimes shock at learning this information for the first time at the bail hearing. This may make them feel uneasy and somewhat betrayed by the person or persons who conscripted them into this assignment. Such a witness will welcome the escape hatch a lack of knowledge of the accused's criminal behaviour affords. The witness may consent to being led down the path that they really do not have a handle on the situation and wish to withdraw as a potential surety. Another subtle factor which operates in the same direction is that sureties want to present a picture of respectability to the Court and will consciously or unconsciously wish to distance themselves from the accused's crimes. For example, they will rarely have discussed the crime or crimes at issue in the bail hearing with the accused though a combination of lack of opportunity as well as lack of inclination. They will frequently acknowledge that they have never had a meaningful discussion with the accused as to why the accused commits crimes. This tends to limit their potential as supervisors. Once again the cross-examining Crown is protected by a "Catch-22" escape route. In the unlikely event the surety testifies as to serious discussions with the accused about crime in the past, the surety will feel impelled to acknowledge that the accused faithfully promised the surety that he or she would renounce his or her criminal ways. The theme can then be developed that the accused has betrayed the surety's trust in the past, and may well do so in the future.

It sometimes happens that the accused will have confessed the crime or crimes at issue in the bail hearing to the proposed surety. Where this is revealed by cross-examination, the apparent strength of the Crown's case will be considerably augmented since such evidence would be admissible without a *voir dire*. Even if this line of questioning elicits the fact that the accused denied committing the crime or crimes to the surety, rarely will the denial be sufficiently comprehensive to carry much weight so as to adversely impact upon the strength of the Crown's case. For all of these reasons, exploration of the topic of discussions between the surety and the accused concerning the crimes which are subject to the hearing, as well as past crimes, are generally fertile ground worth tilling.

It is frequently helpful for the Crown to try to put himself or herself in the surety's shoes in an effort to understand why the surety is proposing to take what may be in the eyes of an outsider a considerable risk. Once the surety's motivation is understood, questions designed to lessen the surety's confidence in the motivational factors may be beneficial from the Crown's perspective.

Since in simplistic terms the surety will be making a monetary wager on the accused's future performance it is sometimes productive to explore with the surety what their betting limit would be. It can be surprising how little the surety is prepared to wager when considered as a fraction of the surety's net worth. Caution is urged however since some sureties could exhibit extreme confidence and rashly respond that they are prepared to commit all or most of their savings to demonstrate their assessment that the bet is sure. Accordingly this technique should only be explored, if at all, with sureties who have already exhibited less than complete confidence in the accused.

The following is a sample cross-examination of a proposed surety by the Crown:

Q: Were you aware of the full extent of the accused's criminal record before I read it out in the court this morning?

A: I knew he had been convicted of break and enter and impaired driving, but not the rest of it.

Q: I take it that you were not aware of his conviction for failing to appear in court until now?

A: That's right.

Q: Before you place your hard earned money in what is really a bet that he will attend court, isn't that failure to appear conviction something you would like to know more about?

A: I guess so.

Q: Whose idea was it that you come to court today?

A: His mother's.

Q: I gather that the accused's mother is a close personal friend of yours?

A: Yes.

Q: Did she tell you that she had been a surety for him in the past when he failed to appear in court?

A: No she didn't.

Q: Is that something you'd like to discuss with her, to give you a better handle on what sort of risk you'd be running with your money?

A: Yes, I'd like to do that.

Q: Is it fair to say that you are relying on her because you know her better than the accused?

A: Yes it is.

Q: And to be fair, if it weren't for her, you wouldn't be here would you?

A: No, I wouldn't.

Q: You don't talk much with her about why her son commits crimes do you? By that, I mean it wouldn't come up in normal conversation would it?

A: No, we haven't talked about it.

Q: Do I take it that you don't have any idea what the accused's real problem is, for example you don't know whether he gets in trouble because of drugs, alcohol or peer pressure?

A: No, I guess I don't but I know he did receive treatment for alcohol a few years ago.

Q: But just because he drinks too much, that wouldn't make him dishonest would it?

A: No, I guess not.

Q: He's 23 years old and he's been in trouble with the law for over six years now. It's unfair to you to think you can turn him around overnight isn't it?

A: Yes, it is.

Q: In fact, you don't have any plans other than to offer him this job in your factory, correct?

A: Well, I think that would be a good start.

Q: No doubt, but do you know anything about his past employment?

A: Not really.

Q: If I told you that he has never before held a full time job for any longer than a few months, would that surprise you?

A: I don't know what to say.

Q: I take it you don't know why he left his other jobs?

A: No, I don't.

Q: And you don't know what kind of work he is capable of doing?

A: No, I don't.

Q: You also don't know what kind of worker he is, or what his attitude to work is?

A: No, I can't say that I do.

Q: Isn't there a good chance that this job in your factory won't work out?

A: I guess so.

Q: You're not suggesting that he be thrown back into jail if he is released and this job doesn't work out are you? That would be a form of slavery wouldn't it?

A: I don't know, I'm just trying to do the family a favour.

Q: Have you ever had a man to man to man, heart to heart, talk with the accused about his criminal problems?

A: No.

Q: Why not?

A: I would find it difficult to talk about that, it's getting pretty personal.

Q: Fair enough, but that does mean you really don't know him, doesn't it?

A: I suppose it does.

Q: What would you estimate your net worth to be sir?

A: I'm worth about two million.

Q: How much of that worth are you prepared to pledge to secure the accused's release?

A: His mother told me I'd need to put up around five thousand dollars.

Q: That's not much money to you, is it?

A: No, I guess not.

Q: To be fair to you, you would want to re-think being a surety if the stakes were fifty or a hundred thousand wouldn't you?

A: Yes, I would.

Index